LADY GUEST'S

MABINOGION

With Essays on
Medieval Welsh Myths and Arthurian Legends

First published in 1877

Published by Wine Dark Press,
an imprint of Read & Co.

The Mabinogion from the Welsh of the Llyfr Coch o Hergest
(The Red Book of Hergest) first published in 1877
This edition published by Read & Co. in 2024

A catalogue record for this book is available from the British Library.

ISBN: 9781528723473

Read & Co. is part of Read Books Ltd.
For more information visit www.readandcobooks.co.uk

My dear Children,

Infants as you yet are, I feet that I cannot dedicate more fitly than to you these venerable relics of ancient lore, and I do so in the hope of inciting you to cultivate the Literature of "Gwyllt Walia," in whose beautiful language you are being initiated, and amongst whose free mountains you were born.

May you become early imbued with the chivalric and exalted sense of honour, and the fervent patriotism for which its sons have ever been celebrated.

May you learn to emulate the noble qualities of Ivor Hael, and the firm attachment to your Native Country, which distinguished that Ivor Back, after whom the elder *of you was named.*

I am,
Your affectionate Mother,

C. E. GUEST.
Dowlais, August 29th, 1838.

NOTE ON THE TEXT

Wine Dark Press presents this new edition of Lady Charlotte Guest's 1877 translation of the *Mabinogion*.

One of the cornerstones of Britain's literary history, the *Mabinogion* is a collection of prose stories, comprising early Welsh myths, legends, and folk tales. Its title has no confirmed origin or direct translation, but is thought to be derived from the Welsh *mab*, meaning son, boy, or young person.

The modern standardised version of the *Mabinogion* was originally adapted from the text in two source manuscripts, *Llyfr Coch Hergest* and *Llyfr Gwyn Rhydderch*, believed to have been scribed from oral tradition between the years 1350 and 1410. The medieval work was translated and republished in varying editions in the subsequent centuries, but the first to publish an English translation of the *Mabinogion* in modern print format was the English aristocrat Lady Charlotte Guest (1812–1895).

A talented linguist, Guest translated numerous songs and poems from the Middle Ages before commencing work on the *Mabinogion* in 1837. Her completed translation was first published in seven volumes between 1838 and 1845, then republished in three volumes in 1849. Both these editions were bilingual publications, presenting the original text transcribed by John 'Tegid' Jones (1792–1852), a Welsh clergyman and writer, alongside Guest's translations of the tales.

In 1877, the first publication of the *Mabinogion* to feature only English translations of the tales was released, and it became the well-known standard edition. Guest included twelve tales in her version, including the Four Branches of the Mabinogi, although subsequent scholars omit 'Hanes Taliesin' from their editions due to the story's absence in the original medieval manuscripts.

This edition of the *Mabinogion* has been sourced from Guest's 1877 publication and printed here with the punctuation and spelling unchanged.

MABINOGION TIMELINE

C. 1050–1200
The *Four Branches of the Mabinogi* (*Pedair Cainc y Mabinogi*), also known as simply the *Mabinogi*, were recorded from oral tradition in the eleventh century. The branches are four episodic tales, each named after their leading protagonist. The title for the later standardised edition of the *Mabinogion* takes its name from the four branches, as each story culminates with the phrase 'thus ends this branch of the Mabinogi'.

C. 1350–1410
The *White Book of Rhydderch* (*Llyfr Gwyn Rhydderch*) and the *Red Book of Hergest* (*Llyfr Coch Hergest*), the original source manuscripts for the tales of the *Mabinogion*, were compiled from oral tradition.

1632
A leading Welsh scholar of the Renaissance, John Davies (c. 1567–1644), became the first to refer to the *Mabinogion* with this now standardised title. In an article published in 1632, he cited the fourth branch, *Math Son of Mathonwy* (*Math fab Mathonwy*), with the notation 'Mabin'.

1658
The oldest remaining complete edition of the *White Book of Rhydderch* (c. 1350) was preserved in the Hengwrt library of Welsh antiquary Robert Powell Vaughan (c. 1592–1667).

1701
The earliest complete manuscript of the *Red Book of Hergest* (c. 1382–1410) was donated to Jesus College Oxford.

1795
Welsh antiquarian William Owen Pughe (1759–1835) was the first to produce modern editions of the *Mabinogion* when he published his English translations in the *Cambrian Register* journal. The title '*Mabinogion*' is believed to have initially appeared in print in Pughe's 1795 translation of the first branch, *Pwyll Prince of Dyfed* (*Pwyll Pendefig Dyfed*), which he titled *The Mabinogion, or Juvenile Amusements, being Ancient Welsh Romances*.

1818−17
Welsh clergyman John 'Tegid' Jones (1792–1852) made a copy of the *Red Book of Hergest* for an English colonial official, Charles Bosanquet (1769–1850), while studying at the University of Oxford.

1821 AND 1829
Pughe published English translations of several more tales from the *Mabinogion* in 1821 and 1829.

1838−45
The first bilingual editions of the *Mabinogion* were published by Lady Charlotte Guest (1812–1895) in seven volumes between 1838 and 1845, then as three volumes in 1849. These publications featured the original Welsh text transcribed by Tegid Jones and they standardised the volume's title.

1859
The original *White Book of Rhydderch* manuscript was moved to the Peniarth library of Welsh antiquarian William Watkin Edward Wynne (1801–1880) after he inherited Vaughan's Hengwrt collection.

1877
The first publication of the *Mabinogion* to feature only English translations of the tales was released by Guest. It included twelve tales and became the well-known standard edition.

1904
The *White Book of Rhydderch* manuscript from the Hengwrt–Peniarth library was presented to the National Library of Wales.

1948
Gwyn Jones (1907–1999) and Thomas Jones published a new English translation of the *Mabinogion* with Golden Cockerel Press, which soon replaced Guest's edition as the most frequently used English version of the volume.

2014
Both the *White Book of Rhydderch* and the *Red Book of Hergest* featured in an exhibition at the National Library of Wales, briefly seeing the two original source manuscripts for the *Mabinogion* finally under the same roof.

LADY CHARLOTTE (BERTIE) GUEST

Daughter of the 9th Earl of Lindsey. Married in 1833 to Sir Josiah J. Guest, a wealthy ironmaster, after whose death in 1852 she managed the works.

She was an enthusiastic student of Welsh literature, and aided by native scholars translated with consummate skill the *Mabinogion*, the manuscript of which in Jesus Coll., Oxf., is known as the *Red Book of Hergest*, and which is now a recognised classic of medieval romance. She also prepared a 'Boys' *Mabinogion* containing the earliest Welsh tales of Arthur.

She was also noted as a collector of china, fans, and playing cards, on which subjects she wrote several volumes.

She entered into a second marriage in 1855 with Dr. C. Schreiber, but in literature she is always referred to under her first married name.

A biography from
A Short Biographical Dictionary of English Literature, 1910
by John William Cousin

CONTENTS

ESSAYS

ROADS

A Poem by Edward Thomas

I love roads:
The goddesses that dwell
Far along invisible
Are my favourite gods.

Roads go on
While we forget, and are
Forgotten like a star
That shoots and is gone.

On this earth 'tis sure
We men have not made
Anything that doth fade
So soon, so long endure:

The hill road wet with rain
In the sun would not gleam
Like a winding stream
If we trod it not again.

They are lonely
While we sleep, lonelier
For lack of the traveller
Who is now a dream only.

From dawn's twilight
And all the clouds like sheep
On the mountains of sleep
They wind into the night.

The next turn may reveal
Heaven: upon the crest
The close pine clump, at rest
And black, may Hell conceal.

Often footsore, never
Yet of the road I weary,
Though long and steep and dreary
As it winds on for ever.

Helen of the roads,
The mountain ways of Wales
And the Mabinogion tales
Is one of the true gods,

Abiding in the trees,
The threes and fours so wise,
The larger companies,
That by the roadside be,

And beneath the rafter
Else uninhabited
Excepting by the dead:
And it is her laughter

At morn and night I hear
When the thrush cock sings
Bright irrelevant things,
And when the chanticleer

Calls back to their own night
Troops that make loneliness
With their light footsteps' press,
As Helen's own are light.

Now all roads lead to France
And heavy is the tread
Of the living; but the dead
Returning lightly dance:

Whatever the road bring
To me or take from me,
They keep me company
With their pattering,

Crowding the solitude
Of the loops over the downs,
Hushing the roar of towns
And their brief multitude.

First published in
Six Poems 1916, under the pseudonym Edward Eastaway.

THE ENGLISH
VERSION OF THE MABINOGION

By D. Rhys Phillips

There is a story current at Oxford of three scholars who had set out to produce a perfect book, the three under taking to correct separate proofs; when the work was finally issued from the press it was discovered that even the first page was not free from errors.

The literary antiquary finds pleasure in trying to solve the problems, or to correct the mistakes, of those who have gone before him, and in turn he himself provides a fair field for the eagle eyes of his successors. There are thousands of books in circulation which bear no author's name, and there are others erroneously credited to men who never put pen to paper. Imprints there are which perpetuate the names of houses that never possessed a press or a single line of type, while others credit, say, Aberavan with what was actually printed at Neath. As in the fields of printing and authorship, so also in the arena of translation: things are not always what they seem, and, conversely, facts do not always escape being mistaken for fiction.

In the *Western Mail* of April 21, 1921, there appeared a very interesting contribution by Mr. John Ballinger, C.B.E., M.A., Chief Librarian of the National Library of Wales, on the Centenary of Thomas Stephens, author of *The Literature of the Kymry*. A few days later a correspondent signing himself 'Ap Dowlais' inquired as to the truth of 'the assertion often made, particularly in the in Merthyr and Dowlais districts, that Stephens was the actual author of the Translations from the M*abinogion,* which are up to the present officially credited with being from the pen of Lady Charlotte Guest.'

In the varied but interesting correspondence which followed, Mr. E. J. Williams of Pontypridd, Mr. R. E. Williams of Llanllawddog, Mr. E. Pryce Roberts of Sully, Mr. Ifano Jones of the Cardiff Public Library, and Mr. Ballinger took part, the latter closing his letter with the words:

'There is no evidence, so far, that she did not herself plan and carry out the scheme for presenting the *Mabinogion* to English readers: until such evidence is forth coming the reasonable course is to give Lady Guest the full credit.'

All this reminded us of inquiries we had pursued in 1916. In 1911 two beautifully illustrated volumes had appeared, entitled, *Lady Charlotte Schreiber's journals: Confidences of a Collector of Ceramics and Antiques . . . from* 1869 *to* 1885. These were edited with an excellent introduction by her third son, Mr. Montague Guest (who died suddenly when on a visit to the late King

Edward VII. at Sandringham before the work was finished). We asked the late Countess of Bessborough if her mother's *earlier* Journals contained any detailed references to the Translation of the *Mabinogion*: a work handsomely printed by W. Rees of Llandovery, in seven numbers, during 1838-1846, and afterwards bound in three sumptuous volumes.

Though at that time busily engaged as Hon. Secretary of Princess Victoria's Auxiliary Committee for the inspection of the Y.M.C.A. Recreation Huts for Soldiers at the Base Camps in France (which work she did not long survive, for she died in 1919), the Countess kindly replied on September 26, and in the course of her letter said:

'I delayed answering your letter till I was able to look out extracts from my mother, Lady Charlotte Guest's Journal. I now enclose you samples of the kind of details I could send you. I have typed copies of her unpublished Journals from 1822 to 1852, and I find that I have noted in the margin where she alludes to working at her translation of the *Mabinogion*; so that I could very easily find you a great choice of extracts for publication.'

By Oct. 17. 1916, the Countess had sent us all the details she could find, covering the period 1837-45. The war being then at its height, publication was postponed and the material lay aside in the Countess's own brown envelope till this year of grace when the *Western Mail* correspondence, refreshing an erring memory, caused it to be taken out of its resting-place and made known.

Sir William Davies, the Editor of the *Western Mail,* ever keenly interested in the elucidation of Welsh literary problems, suggested that the Extracts should be printed forthwith in the columns of that journal. There were good reasons for giving the facts to the public through the medium wherein the question of authorship had been recently raised, and therefore the Extracts appeared, with an introductory note, in the issues for May 18-20, 1921.

So far as we are aware, no scholar of note (except, perhaps, the Comte Hersart de la Villemarqué, who is exposed in these extracts, under May, 1842, in a manner which somewhat conforms with the view of his countrymen) has ever doubted Lady Charlotte's office as editing translator of the various texts and compiler of the learned and voluminous notes appended thereto. Those who are familiar with the three volumes need not be told that Lady Charlotte's position is therein openly and frequently declared. But unlettered gossips and certain village writers have always found it difficult to believe that an English lady could effectually surmount the difficulty of rendering into English a series of texts written in early Mediaeval Welsh, which none but a capable Welsh scholar could at that time read with intelligence, and which but few then living had ever actually seen.

In his letter to the *Western Mail* Mr. Ballinger showed that dates alone put Thomas Stephens's name out of court; indeed, he was little known till he won the literture prize at Abergavenny in 1848.[1] He is not mentioned in Lady Charlotte's *Journals* for 1838-45. As to the point raised in Mr. R. E. Williams's letter, had he looked at Vol. III, page 72, he would have found that Lady Charlotte acknowledged in her Notes to the *Pwyll* story that

'Nearly the whole of the Mabinogi of Pwyll Pendevig Dyved has already been printed with a translation in the *Cambrian Register,* and the story has also appeared in Jones's *Welsh Bards.'*

The *Register* had ceased publication in 1818, before the serial issue of *Pwyll* came to its end. With this version at her side, it is reasonable to conclude that Lady Charlotte's task was lightened considerably; but, as Mr. Hano Jones has pointed out, the renderings are by no means identical. Lady Charlotte is by far the better stylist.

Now the translation of *Pwyll,* which appeared in the *Cambrian Register,* was the work of Dr. Owen Pughe. His translation of *Math ab Mathonwy* was printed in the first volume of the *Cambrian Quarterly,* and the fifth volume of the same magazine (1833) contains his English version of *Hanes Taliesin,* which Lady Charlotte Guest shows was less complete than her own. At Pughe's request, the London Cymmrodorion had, in 1831, resolved to print the *Mabinogion* in Denbigh 'under his superintendence' (C.Q. iii. 253), but this would seem to involve only the Welsh text. The resolution was never carried out.

How far Dr. Pughe proceeded with his translations beyond the three stories already mentioned we cannot discover, and his biographers do not help us. He died in June, 1835, and two years later Lady Charlotte Guest entered upon her task. In compiling her notes she made considerable use, with full acknowledgment, of Dr. Pughe's printed books. As to his translations of the texts, she seems to be aware only of the three printed versions we have mentioned. We may safely conclude, therefore, that she possessed none of his MSS.

It will be noticed that a *translation* of *Kilhwch and Olwen,* by Justice Bosanquet, is mentioned in the Journal for Dec. 4, 1837; but there is no further reference to it.

In *Les Mabinogion,* a scholarly French edition published in 1913 and dedicated to the memory of Gaston Paris, Professor Loth examines Lady Charlotte Guest's version at length. He points out passages that have been suppressed and, like Sir Owen Edwards, who edited the Fisher Unwin reissue in 1902, instances an occasional departure from a literal translation. He is on correct ground when he states (pp. 8-9) that Lady Charlotte's Welsh text was a copy made by Tegid from

---

1 Stephens, who was but a chemist's apprentice, aged 16, when Lady Charlotte began translating the Mabinogion in 1837, appraises her work as follows in *The Literature of the Kymry* (for printing which in 1849 he was indebted to the generosity of Sir John and Lady Charlotte Guest): "Her version correctly mirrors forth the spirit of these antique stories, and is as much distinguished for elegance as fidelity."

the *Red Book of Hergest:*

'Le texte gallois du *Livre Rouge* communiqué à lady Charlotte Guest est une copie faite par un littérateur gallois John Jones, plus connu sous le nom de Tegid.' But when (p. 6) he declares that Lady C. had at hand a literal translation made by a Welsh scholar, he is apparently less well-informed. There is clear authority only for Dr. Pughe's three renderings, whereas Lady Charlotte translated and published twelve of the romances. These are Dr. Loth's words:

'Lady Charlotte Guest ne savait guére le gallois; elle a travaillé sur une version littérale d'un savant gallois et, à force de pénétration, de conscience et de talent, réussi à en faire une traduction d'un grand charme et qui ne dénature pas l'original dans l'ensemble.'

In his second work on the *History of Merthyr* (p. 223) Charles Wilkins states that Lady Charlotte was 'aided by Tegid, by Taliesin Williams, and by Thos. Jenkins'; but probably the latter rendered assistance only at an earlier stage, when she was picking up the strands of the ancient language. As to the others, the Journals are quite clear. They show that at the outset the Rev. John Jones (Tegid) and the Rev. Thomas Price (Carnhuanawc) had promised Lady Charlotte their assistance. In the printed notes to the *Dream of Rhonabwy* there is an acknowledgment of valuable information she had received from another Welsh scholar, the Rev. Walter Davies (Gwallter Mechain). In October, 1841, Taliesin Williams, then head of a celebrated school at Merthyr, brought her a version of *Taliesin.* The numerous footnote references to books quoted or consulted indicate that she had at her elbow a host of printed authorities, quite encyclopedic in their extension.

But Lady Charlotte's chief helper and trusted friend was the great Carnhuanawc—an older man and a more fervid Welsh scholar than the coldly critical but brilliant Thomas Stephens (to us a familiar name from childhood, for his father, Evan, was the shoemaker to our grand father's establishment at Beili Glas, Rhigos), who defeated Thomas Price in more than one important eisteddfod competition. Still, Price remained a dominating personality in Welsh literary assemblies till the end of his career.

The entry dated December 8, 1837, shows that Lady C. had purposed from the first to translate the stories herself. Under January 6, 1838, she confesses that the work was difficult for her, 'being so little conversant with the Welsh'; but in the following July she found herself able to 'understand the old Welsh words' even without a dictionary.

The Journals indicate that Carnhuanawc was usually a guest at Dowlais House for one or more days preceding the dispatch to press of each number of the *Mabinogion.* He read the Notes aloud, adding his criticisms, and together he and Lady Charlotte 'polished off' the translations (see entry for Feb. 5, 1838). That he enriched the product and did it *con amore,* there is little room for doubt.

With a dominant will and exemplary fidelity Lady C. pursued her self-imposed task for a period of eight years-working at it while touring the Continent in 1838; amid the distractions of her work as one of the heads of the Dowlais Works; even during periods of child-bed in 1838 and 1839. Is there anything like it on record?

Translation apart, the voluminous notes appended to each story bespeak a range of knowledge and a breadth of scholarship-English, Welsh, and Continental—which mark her out as one of the most remarkable women of that Victorian age.

The publication of her work inaugurated a new era of Romance study in Britain, on the Continent, and in the United States of America (now a most productive field). A bibliography, though we have no space for it, would be worth undertaking. Suffice it to say that redactions of her tales are still being issued in various forms, here and elsewhere.

What was Lady Charlotte's incentive to the study of Welsh? The seat of the Lindsey family was near Lincoln; therefore it may be assumed that, except through the possible inspiration of a Welsh or Gaelic-speaking nurse, she had no predilection for that language.

Her son, Mr. Montague Guest, explains in his Introduction to the printed Journals of 1869-85 that as a child she was thrown very much on her own resources, her mother being kind but easy going, and 'her father' (more correctly her step-father, the Rev. Peter Pegus; for her own father, General Albemarle Bertie, 9th Earl of Lindsey, was 68 years old when she was born, and he died six years later) by no means indulgent or sympathetic.

'The first thing she did was to set to work to educate herself. She was a voracious reader; she learnt, and was proficient in French, German, and Italian, and, with the aid of her brother's tutor, she studied Greek, Latin, Hebrew, and Persian, for all things Oriental appealed strongly to her. She learnt to etch on the copper plate, and her productions were far above those of the ordinary amateur. She loved her Chaucer, and to the day of her death she could repeat from memory whole pages of her favourite author.

'In 1833, when she was 21 years of age, she married my father, Sir John Guest. He was then 49, and a widower, and was the owner of one of the largest iron works in the kingdom, at Dowlais, near Merthyr Tydfil, in S. Wales.

'She had not long been married before she attacked, and proceeded to make herself proficient in the Welsh language. The result of her studies was the translation and publication of the celebrated *Mabinogion*, or Tales of King Arthur's Round Table, upon which was founded *The Idylls of the King*, by Lord Tennyson. Some years after, Lord Tennyson told one of my sisters that it was the first book he read after his marriage, and that he was so struck with it that it inspired him to write his poem. He was anxious to make my mother's acquaintance, which at a later time he accomplished. He asked her, amongst other things, what was the proper pronunciation of the vowel E in Enid. Should it be short or long? In one of the passages of his book he had written "Geraint wedded Enid," which would be all right with the long E, but was impossible, he said, with the short one. When he was told that it should be short, he at once altered the word to "Geraint married Enid." It is the custom for ladies, in the present day, who have christened their daughters Enid, to pronounce it as with the long E, but in this they are undoubtedly wrong.

'She took, as was natural with her, the keenest interest in her husband's large ironworks, and under his guidance she soon mastered all the details of them. She plunged into " double entry" and kept the most accurate accounts of the works, which she balanced at the end of the year.'

Lady Charlotte began to keep a journal in 1822, at ten years of age. Her son makes various quotations from these records to illustrate his mother's varied pursuits, the catholicity of her mind, and the strength of her aspirations—though the *Mabinogion* portions of the diaries, from which we quote at length further on, were left untouched by him. One extract depicts her discussing a contract for rails for the Midland Counties Railway; another refers to the firm's new offices in the City. Hereon she makes a statement which marks her dominant personality and genius:

'They have paid me the compliment of fitting up a room for me there, and I think it is a retreat that I shall often be tempted to resort to from the gaieties and interruptions of Grosvenor Square. I have so schooled myself into habits of business that it is more congenial to me to calculate the advantage of half per cent. commission on a cargo of iron than to go to the finest ball in the world. But whatever I undertake I must reach an eminence in. I cannot endure anything in a second grade. I am happy to see we are at the head of the iron trade. Otherwise I could not take pride in my house in the City, and my works at Dowlais, and glory (playfully) in being (in some sort) a tradeswoman . . .

If I occupy myself in writing, my book must be splendidly got up and must be as far, at least, as decoration and typography are concerned, at the head of literature, and I delight in the contrast of the musty antiquarian researches and the brilliant fetes and plodding counting house, from all of which I seem to derive almost equal amusement. And then I can sit and laugh at the gravest of them all as vanities, and moralise upon the thought of how soon the most important of them will cease to be of any avail or interest to me. Yet while they last and while there is youth and health to enjoy them, surely it cannot be wrong to take pleasure in the various blessings of this life. I trust to God that I may not be puffed up with them.

For indeed to me He has been abundantly merciful, and I fully feel my entire dependence upon His mercy, and how one breath would send the whole fabric of my pleasures and my happiness to the earth, and leave worse than a blank behind' (pp. xxiii., xxiv.).

From the same source we gather that when at Canford Manor, after her marriage to Mr. Charles Schreiber, M.P., and before the marriage of her eldest son Ivor.

'She was generally to be seen busily employed setting type, or reading over and correcting proofs at my brother's private Printing Press.'

Sir Ivor Guest (Lord Wimborne) printed at this Canford Press, and bound in one volume, his mother's prose version of Enid and the poem by Tennyson.

Lady Charlotte was well over fifty years of age when she began her famous Collection of China, subsequently presented to the nation and now housed in the Victoria and Albert Museum, South Kensington. Her son tells us that

'She threw herself into her pursuit with her characteristic energy, and it from henceforth became the passion of her life. She hunted high and low, through England and abroad: France, Holland, Germany, Spain, Italy, Turkey, all were ransacked; she left no stone unturned, no difficulty, discomfort, fatigue, or hardship of travel daunted her or turned her from her purpose.'

Later she devoted herself successively to the garnering of Fans and Playing Cards, donating both collections to the British Museum.

There are not many references to Wales in the printed Journals of 1869-85. When on a visit to Turkey in July, 1878, this entry was made: 'Enid took us out for a drive in her new landau up to the Reservoir in the forest of Belgrade; most charming scenery, something like that of the Vale of Neath.' Lady Charlotte and Mr. Chas. Schreiber visited Margam in December, 1880: 'They all shot the coverts on Tuesday and Wednesday, and C. S. nearly suffered seriously in consequence. Mr. Talbot sent part of a charge into him instead of into a woodcock. The great mercy was that it did not hit his eye.' Under March 15 of the same year she refers to the political complexions of the Guests: two of them were contesting elections as Liberals and two as Conservatives:

'The political moves in my family are becoming most perplexing . . . For myself I am different from them all. I hold on to my old Whig principles in domestic policy, but I go with the Conservatives in their Eastern and other foreign policy, and I utterly abhor Gladstone and all his works, politically speaking.'

During the last five years of her life Lady Charlotte, though practically bereft of sight, was never idle, but occupied her time with knitting comforters for the London cabmen. Her son 'Monty' writes of her: 'She was a woman with a deep sense of moral duty, very self-possessed and calm, with an extraordinary control over her feelings.' She died on the ninth of January, 1895.

Of her father's lineage Burke says (Peerage, 1875, p. 725):

'This noble family, which eventually obtained the highest degree of rank in the British peerage, springs maternally from the Willoughbys, original Barons de Eresby, and paternally from the Berties of Bersted in Kent.'

In the succession are Peregrine Bertie, 1580, 11th Baron Willoughby de Eresby; Robert, 12th Baron, who in 1626 was created Earl of Lindsey; Robert,

4th Earl, who in 1706 was advanced to the Marquisate of Lindsey and in 1715 created Duke of Ancaster and Kesteven (his first wife being Mary, daughter of Sir Richard Wynne, Bart., of Gwydir); Brownlow, 5th Duke, dying without issue male, the higher honours ceased except the Earldom of Lindsey, which passed to a kinsman, General Albemarle Bertie (a descendant from the 2nd Earl, died in 1666), who became 9th Earl. By his first marriage he had no issue. His second wife was Charlotte S. Elizabeth, daughter of the Rev. C. P. Layard, D.D., Dean of Bristol, by whom he had—

(1) George A. F. A. Bertie, 10th Earl ; (2) Montagu P.; (3) *Charlotte Elizabeth,* married first, 29 July, 1833, to Sir Josiah John Guest, Bart., M.P., of Dowlais, who died in 1852; and secondly, 10 April, 1855, to Mr. Charles Schreiber, a Fellow of Trinity College, Cambridge, and son of Col. J. A. Schreiber of Melton, Suffolk (who had served under the Duke of Wellington).

Lady Charlotte's father, the 9th Earl of Lindsey, having died in 1818, her mother married secondly on 14 April, 1821, her first cousin, Rev. Peter W. (Burke insufficiently names him 'William') Pegus, by whom she had issue one daughter, Maria Antoinetta—the 'Mary' of the 1837-45 Extracts—who later became Marchioness of Huntly.

The details reproduced from her Journals in the following pages give an absolutely trustworthy account of Lady Charlotte's labours in translating the *Mabinogion* into an epoch-making English edition. They serve the useful purpose of finally laying the ghost of an oft-recurring misconception, and are, moreover, valuable as literary memoranda. The human interest which surrounds Lady Charlotte's appraisements of certain notable contemporaries adds piquancy to the narrative.

Certain explanations have been added in square brackets. The references to services rendered by the well-known Glamorgan antiquary, Mr. G. T. Clark, and to various personal and family matters, incidents, and interests should be pleasant reading to many besides those who dwell among the hills of Glamorgan.

EXTRACTS

From the Journals of Lady Charlotte Guest, 1837-1845

First mention of her intention to translate into English the Welsh Mabinogion.

1837

Nov. 30.—Mr. Justice Bosanquet has, through Tegid, kindly lent me his copy of the *Llyfr Coch yr Hergest*—the *Mabinogion,* which I hope to publish with an English translation, notes, and pictorial illustrations. Price, of Crickhowel, and Tegid have promised their assistance, and by God's blessing I hope I may accomplish the undertaking.

Dec. 4.—I returned at dusk and read part of the Tale of *Kilhwch and Olwen* translated by Justice Bosanquet from the *Mabinogion*. It pleases me much. There is a great field for Annotation.

Dec. 8.—The [Welsh] MSS. Society want to take the *Mabinogion* into their own hands, believing that I have given it up. We have to arrange to prevent this, and also to go into some plan for translating Justice Bosanquet's copy, as I do not feel inclined to give up my scheme of publishing it myself. Mr. Jones [Tegid] came shortly after this. He has taken Justice Bosanquet's MS., and is to copy from it one story at a time in a fit manner to go to the press (viz., in modern orthography which will be more generally useful) and send them to me to translate.

1838

Jan. 6.—I worked busily at my translation, which is rather difficult for me, being so little conversant with the Welsh, and the *Mabinogion* being in such a cramped and ancient style.

Jan. 9.—A good deal of translation before luncheon, after which, in spite of intense cold, I went out.

Jan. 12.—I was very busy all day with the [a name in the *Mabinogion]* and in searching for material for notes.

Feb. 5.—To-day and Tuesday I was very busy finishing my translation of the *Mabinogi of*—(which I have worked very hard at ever since the fifth day from my confinement), preparatory to Mr. Price's coming to talk over with me the method of printing, publishing, etc. To-day (Wednesday) he arrived by the mail, and just before he came I went downstairs for the first time. We had a great deal of conversation, and after dinner we polished off my translation slightly for the Press. But being willing to keep very rigidly to the original, very little alteration could be made in my version, which will, I fear, appear rather clumsy English.

Feb. 26.—up early. Wrote to Tegid, who frightens me by talking of giving someone else a *Mabinogi* to translate.

March 3.—Tegid dined with us.

July 21.—Before I had reached Newbridge I finished reading the story of *Geraint ab Erbin,* which had amused me all the way down. It is the *Mabinogi* I have fixed upon to translate next, and it is a very interesting one. I had forgotten my Dictionary, and was quite surprised to find that I could understand the old Welsh words without one.

July 30.—I saw Longman, who is publishing my *Mabinogion.*

Aug. 1.—In the present case I was more particularly hurried, having to settle against many things about my book, which will be published during my absence.

Aug. 16.—Zurich: A fine view of the lake. Here I spent the morning in writing letters and copying some Welsh.

Aug. 22.—Lausanne: I had employed myself in the morning in copying out the translation which I made in pencil in the carriage. The story I have chosen for the next number of the *Mabinogion* is *Geraint ab Erbin.*

Aug. 31.—Milan: It was a busy but not very amusing scene. After tea I wrote *Geraint.*

Sept. 15.—Como: Again it was a regular wet day. I employed it in writing Welsh.

Sept. 30.—Florence : Feeling still much tired. We read together, and I wrote some Welsh.

Oct. 1.—I wrote a good deal of Welsh this evening.

Oct. 6.—Florence: During all this week, when not sitting or driving out, I have worked very hard at my Welsh. I have been very much annoyed at still hearing nothing of the first number of my book. It ought to be out by the 9th, which is the Cymreigyddion [day at Abergavenny], but I have not yet seen it even advertised. I read over it, and fancy that I left several inaccuracies uncorrected (which I trust, however, is not the case), and sometimes I am very anxious for the result.

Nov. 2.—Lyons: It was near nine when we got to Lyons. I read the beautiful *Mabinogi* of *Breuddwyd Ronabwy* to-day. Yesterday I read *Ludd Llevelys.*

Nov. 8.—Paris: I went to some of the booksellers to try and see my book, but I could not even make out that it is published. It is not in any of the advertising lists. Singular it is that I have never once heard it mentioned, or received the slightest intelligence respecting it, since I left England more than three months ago.

Nov. 11.—Paris: I was awake very early and got up fatigued. I wrote a little Welsh.

Nov. 17.—I went, however, to Longman's, and got a copy of my *book,* which is certainly got up most beautifully. Dec. 6.—Tegid came to see me before I proceeded on my journey to-day. Mr. Clark (his friend) also called and brought with him the *Llyfr Coch* for me to look at.

Dec. 10.—Mr. Price came to-day to pay us a visit, and in the evening we glanced over the list of notes to *Geraint*. Dec. 11.— Mr. Price drove to Crickhowel to fetch my translation, which I had sent him from abroad, and which he had immediately left there.

Dec. 12.—This translation we began reading over quietly and correcting together.

Dec. 13.—Mrs. Crawshay called. Worked hard at the translation both to-day and Friday.

Dec. 15.—To-day Mr. Price went home. The time during his visit has been much broken in upon, and consequently we had only time to read over and correct the translation of *Geraint*.

Dec. 17.—Mr. Price and Mons. de la Villemarqué came to-day. The latter is a Breton, and came over to attend the Abergavenny Cymreigyddion. He has also a commission from the French Ecole des Chartres to investigate Welsh literature and write a report upon it. He is a celebrated and agreeable young man. He it is who made me the translation of the *Chevalier au Lion,* which I have printed at the end of the first number of the *Mabinogion.* He is well versed in these matters.

Dec. 22.—Mr. Price, after talking over my notes with me, went away this morning.

1839

Jan. 20.—I finished the abstract of the French *Geraint ab Erbin, Erec and Enide.*

Jan. 23.—I wrote part of a note on Breceliande in the morning, but was far from well.

Jan. 27.—My Book is now quite at a stand. I have but little time and no energy to pursue it. The woodcuts are still uncommenced. But that is no fault of mine.

Jan. 31.—Much the same sort of day as the two preceding, with the addition of a bad face ache; still I have struggled hard against suffering, and done more to my book this week than for an age before. Note on Breceliande. Villemarqué is becoming wild in his notions and presumes on my good nature, because he corrected the press of the last part of the *Chevalier au Lion* (which it was necessary he should, as no one could correctly read his transcript, so vilely was it written): he writes to insist on Rees signing his name to the printed copy and saying it is published by him. Poor Rees is annoyed. Of course, I can consent to nothing of the sort.

Feb. 1.—Wrote much to-day.

Feb. 5.—I set to work in earnest about writing my notes for *Geraint,* but did not do much. The same occupation entirely filled the two succeeding days likewise . . . I scribbled a great deal about Enid, and gave my fancy play. I do not know yet whether I shall be able to make a pretty note on the subject of her very interesting character.

Feb. 8.—I had written hard all day.

Feb. 17.—Almost every day I have been busy writing notes for the 2nd No. of my *Mabinogion* for several hours. Feb. 22.—I went to the British Museum to make some references which I required . . . Though tired I set to work hard on my notes. 'Merthyr' [Sir John Guest] went to Brooke's in the evening, so I applied myself in right earnest, and by midnight had finished all that it was in my power to do to them at the present stage. They have taken me altogether about a fortnight. One week before I left home, and about the same time since I have been here. But while engaged upon them I have had many other things to do, so that they have not occupied my time exclusively.

Mar. 2.—A very busy day . . . I went on, however, with my notice of the German version of the *Chevalier au Lion,* by Hartmann von der Aue, for my second number. On comparison I find it coincides almost entirely with Chrestien's *Romance.*

Mar. 6.—Sent off a packet to Rees of notes to the *Chevalier au Lion.*

Mar. 8.—I tried to begin translating a new story for my third number, the *Dream of Ronabwy.* It is very tiresome and difficult Welsh, and I did not get on much with it.

Mar. 10.—Fearing to put anything off, I have been writing my notice of the Icelandic *Sir Gawaine,* and now except corrections and revisions, I consider my part of the second number quite off my hands.

Mar. 13.— . . . Worked very hard during the day. Villemarqué has got Tegid to copy for him one of the *Mabinogion (Peredur),* and he is going to publish it immediately in France. This, I consider, will be forestalling me, and it annoys me a good deal. Tegid sends me, however, the transcript as it proceeds that I may make a copy of it for my own use, and I shall bring it out next after *Geraint,* who is going rapidly through the press. Villemarqué will, I fear, get the start of me, as I must wait for some information I expect from Stockholm respecting *Geraint* before I close that subject altogether by beginning to print *Peredur,* or any other story. It is very singular that *Peredur* (as well as the two tales already done) exists in several other modern languages, Icelandic, English, French, etc. The tale is the same as that well known under the title of *Percival de Galles.* I work very hard.

Mar. 27.—I to-day finished my transcript of *Peredur* . . . in the morning arranged the subject of the two first woodcuts, which will be required for it.

Mar. 28.—To-day I worked hard at the translation of *Peredur.* I had the pleasure of giving birth to my fifth child and third boy to-day.

Mar. 30.—I was well enough in the afternoon to correct with 'Merthyr's' assistance one of the proof sheets of my book sent up by Rees.

Mar. 31.—On the sofa, wrote several letters there. Several of which were on my business, and in furtherance of my design of printing *Peredur* as soon as possible My dear husband has been extremely kind about all this.

April 1.—I had to finish correcting my proofs.

April 9.—Nethercliff came here and made me a facsimile from Sir John Bosanquet's MS. of *Peredur*, which is an ancient and curious one, and which he has been kind enough to lend me. I was employed also about other woodcuts for the work. W. Landell sent me a beautiful sketch for one. I am having another copy made from my transcript of *Peredur*, that I may have it to translate from, while Rees prints from mine. Researches are being made for me at the British Museum as to *Percival de Galles* and the *Sangrael,* so that I have much going on towards my book in different directions. Although I have twice written to beg Tegid to get me a facsimile from the *Llyfr Coch,* he has given me no answer. I returned his *Peredur* to him the 1st of the month. He has promised to copy for me all the Mabinogion in the *Llyfr Coch* which are not in the collection I printed from. It would be a great advantage if he would correct the press of *Peredur.* I hesitate asking him. I am not sure that he may be safely trusted with the secret of my proceedings. [She was bent on forestalling Villemarqué.]

April 12.—I wrote my book on retiring to my own room.

May 4.—All this time my book occupied me much, but made little progress.

May 6.—I spent this day again in the City, taking my proof sheets there to correct.

May 10.—*Peredur* had for a long time languished, but I occupied myself much with him to-day. Writing much of the translation with a pencil as I went along.

May 11.—Much of the time in the Cabin. I had a long sleep, and also wrote a good deal of my translation.

May 14.—Mr. Price, of Crickhowel, came to-day, and we looked over part of my translation in the evening.

May 15.—*Peredur* is, I may now say, quite ready for the press. Only a few pages of translation remain uncompleted. I do think it has been got up and brought through the press with great speed, considering that seven weeks ago I never dreamt of printing anything but *Geraint.* Since that time I have transcribed it, translated it, written the notes, provided the decorations, and brought it almost out of the printer's hands.

June 15.—After 'Merthyr' [Sir John Guest] went I wrote for my book till late.

July 17.—I had a visit from Tegid.

July 30.—I believe it was yesterday that Col. Vaughan called on me (who lent me his fragment MS. of *Geraint ab Erbin* to get a facsimile from it), and it was yesterday that I received the first copies of my second number of the *Mabinogion,* which contains *Peredur ab Evrawc.*

July 31.—Lord Mostyn kindly promised to lend me, at some time, his copies of the *Mabinogion.*

Aug. 5.—This was a very busy day with me, yet I found time to go to the British Museum.

Aug. 29.—In the evening I wrote some Welsh. I am now preparing *Kilhwch and*

Olwen for my fourth number, the third is in the press, and will contain *Geraint.*

Nov. 20.—I wrote a little Welsh to-day.

Dec. 12.—I worked, and did a good deal towards revising *Geraint* notes, both this day and Friday.

Dec. 18.—During Mr. Layard's absence I read over some of my notes with Mr. Price.

Dec. 19.—Gave some time to reading over the remainder of my notes with Mr. Price.

1 8 4 0

Jan. 31.—Then I took 'Merthyr' [Sir John Guest] down to the House of Commons, and I spent the rest of the evening in writing my poor neglected *Mabinogion.*

Feb. 27.—Mr. Briddle and 'Merthyr' were out much to day. Mr. Price and I read over my printed *Peredur,* comparing it with that in the Cymmrodorion MS., from which it differs but slightly.

Feb. 29.—Mr. Price went away early.

March 22.—Saw Dr. Locock, for I am very unwell indeed, and have quite lost all energy, so much so that I have left off printing No. III till after Easter. I am now quite unfit for any exertion. Martin [late tutor to her brother, the Earl of Lindsey] has sent me some notes on origin of Romantic Fiction, but they will be of no use for my book.

April 20.—On this and the three following days I was engaged in translating *Kilhwch,* and did a great deal although extremely ill, quite unable to enjoy the beautiful warm weather which we now have.

April *25.*—I did but little comparatively to my Welsh to-day, for the weather was delicious, and 'Merthyr' took me out in his gig.

May 2.—I was very ill and languid, and lay most of the day on the sofa writing but little of *Kilhwch* . . .

June 27.—A very busy morning correcting proof sheets, etc . . .

July 22.—This and the three following days were spent much alike by me. I finished *Ronabwy* on Thursday. On Friday I had a great deal to do with accounts, and on Saturday copied a great deal for the press, a considerable portion of my translation of *Kilhwch.*

July 29.—Mr. Price finished reading my *Percival* to me, and in the afternoon we looked over some other matters connected with the MS. and M. and L. No. of my book.

July 31.—Prepared notices of foreign compositions to follow *Peredur.*

Aug 1.—I was fully employed, till midnight indeed, in making a kind of abstract of the English metl. *Percival,* for the notes on *Peredur.* The MS. in parts is rather difficult to copy from. I have some thoughts of transcribing it entirely.

Aug. 2.—I have been very busy during the week, for not having any other occupation that presses more particularly, I betook myself to transcribing the MS. of the English *Percival,* and truly with such weather and with all attendant circumstances, it has been the very luxury of copying. The poem consists of 2288 lines. I began on Monday morning and on Saturday strove to finish it, as no other version exists of the romance in English (indeed the very copy I have been transcribing from is unique). I am greatly disposed to print it in notes to *Peredur,* which commences the 3rd No. of the *Mabinogion,* now so long in the press. There is much unity of design in this *Percival* and naivete, though it can boast but little poetical excellence.

Aug. 10.—To-day I pursued my transcript of the *Kilhwch* for the press.

Aug. 17.—To-day I recommenced work by beginning to translate the *Amlyn and Amyc* as I lay in bed.

Aug. 18.—Translation in the morning, which in the evening Miss Rudecour began to put on paper for me.

Aug. 20.—I am now set on studying the costume of the *Mabinogion,* with the view to determining more precisely the date in the present form.

Aug. 31.—I have been employed to-day altering copy for the notes to *Peredur.*

Sept. 11.—I always rally when I have plenty of work to do. To-day I had cheques to draw for the works and other things appertaining to business to attend to, besides correcting a proof sheet for the *Mabinogion.*

Sept. 19.—I sat alone in the library doing the *Geraint* notes.

Sept. 24.—Spent a pleasant day at home, colouring some facsimiles for the *Mabinogion* in the morning.

Oct. 6 (at the opening of the Taff Vale Railway).—My third No. of the *Mabinogion,* which I had been taking great pains to bring out of the press in time, was produced during Mr. Price's speech, and elicited some very flattering expressions on my behalf. Those from the Bishop of St. David's [Dr. Thirlwall] were most gratifying to me as coming from one whose praise is, indeed, valuable.

Nov. 11.—Mrs. Waddington [mother of Lady Llanover] brought me the essays written for the prize given at Abergavenny 'on the influence of the Welsh Traditions on the Literature of Europe.' The prize was given to Schulz. Villemarqué also wrote for it, [and so did the Rev. Thomas Price]. His essay was really very amusing to me. He [Villemarqué] made great use of my *Mabinogion* and scarcely made any acknowledgment. On the contrary he delicately insinuated that I did not write the book myself. (A degree of moral turpitude which he dare not openly accuse me of). The secret of all this is his anger at being unable to forestall me in the publication of *Peredur,* M arch, 1839.

Nov. 16.—We were quite alone to-day, and I worked away transcribing for No. 4.

Nov. 20.—Breakfast over, we went into the library. I set to work copying out my English translation of *Kilhwch.*

Nov. 21.—Again to-day I wrote *Kilhwch,* and finished my transcript late in the evening.

Nov. 24.—I wrote some Welsh, but felt idle and dispirited.

Nov. 28.—I wrote a little of *Amlyn and Amyc.*

1841

Jan. 4.—Mr. Clark and I had a tête-à-tête dinner, and in the evening he made some criticisms on my MS. Translation of *Kilhwch* . . .

Jan. 16.—Meantime I have been very busy translating Welsh. The story I am now engaged in is *Amlyn and Amyc.* It is not a very interesting one.

Jan. 18.—Wrote some Welsh very industriously.

Jan. 28.—I seldom read, and when I do so, it is for most part to cram for notes for my book. No. 4 goes on very slowly.

Feb. 12.—I sat writing Welsh till near midnight. First part of the evening was taken up by business in the schoolroom, and then I wrote Welsh.

Feb. 24.—Finished *Amlyn and Amyc,* about which I have been so long occupied.

Feb. 26.—Studied for notes to *Kilhwch,* and commenced translating *Pwyll Pendevig Dyved.*

March 23.—Went on with translation of *Branwen.*

March 26.—Very poorly all day; I wrote *Branwen.*

Aug. 3.—I was quietly at home, scarcely stirring out of the house, and worked hard at my *Kilhwch.*

Aug. 7.—The same routine of assiduous note writing on my part continued uninterruptedly.

Aug. 14.—I worked very hard . . . I sat up late this evening, and had the pleasure of entirely finishing my *Kilhwch* notes before going to bed. I need not say how glad I was to have completed this lengthy task, yet, perhaps, hardly any portion of my life has passed more agreeably than the days which I have spent working hard with them.

Sept. 27.—I wrote some Welsh after the children had gone to bed, and felt desolate beyond expression.

Sept. 30.—Welsh in the evening.

Oct. 1.—Wrote some Welsh this evening.

Oct. 4.—Finished my translation of *Branwen* this evening.

Oct. 5.—Late in the evening Mr. Price arrived; we read over some of my *Kilhwch* notes after the late dinner.

Oct. 6.—Mr. Price read aloud more of my notes, criticising them as he went on.

Oct. 8.—Read over notes until evening; the only interruption was a visit from Mr. Buckland, and after dinner I went to work again, and 'Merthyr' assisted me by copying, etc.

Oct. 18.—I have been well but sometimes rather tired, yet I have not given way and have even continued finishing up my *Kilhwch* notes in the evening when the children have gone to bed.

Oct. 26.—The first event was a visit from Taliesin Williams. He came to see me on the subject of the *Mabinogion* of *Taliesin,* which is imperfectly printed from his father's MS. of it in the *Cambrian Quarterly.* He gives me a correct translation script to appear in my series.

Oct. 27.—Translated some of the *Mabinogion* of *Manawyddan Mab Llyr,* which I have just commenced working upon.

Nov. 5.—Finished translating the *Mabinogi* of *Manawyddan Mab Llyr* this evening.

Nov. 6.—To-day I made a translation of the *Dammeg yr hanner Dyn* for the *Kilhwch* notes. I felt on going to bed to-night that I had at length got comfortably through all that had to be done for my present number.

Nov. 19.—Translation, and took up *Math ab Mathonwy* as my next story.

Nov. 21.—I got to my dressing-room about twelve or one o'clock, and wrote a certain amount of Welsh.

Dec. 2.—I was much engaged with my books.

Dec. 3.—Mr. Sheridan called before going to Cardiff. After his visit I wrote until dinner, and had just finished my translation of the *Mabinogi* of *Math ab Mathonwy* when, to my surprise, dear 'Merthyr' returned.

Dec. 28.—I sat up upstairs correcting proofs, etc. I felt weak and poorly.

Dec. 30.—Very busy correcting proof sheets in the morning.

Dec. 31.—I spent the morning in my own room and corrected proof sheets.

1842

Jan. 18.—'Merthyr,' who seems to have plenty to do everywhere, had to be in the town for the rest of the day. I spent it alone at the inn, and took the opportunity of reading over the Welsh *Mabinogi* (or, rather, romance) of *Bown*—the Sir Bevis of English celebrity. It is nearly as dull an affair as *Amlyn and Amic,* and certainly is not improved in its Welsh dress.

Jan. 19.—This morning we again embarked to go back to Wales, but we went upon the Newport Packet, Newport being more convenient to us than Cardiff for going on to Llansaintffread, where we were engaged to visit the Hutchinses that day. It was one of the most beautiful mornings I ever saw. The sky so clear, yet the air so mild for the season. We had a most agreeable passage, and were met at Newport by the carriage to take us on. It was about half-past two, I think, when we proceeded. As we had to pass through Caerlleon I could not resist the temptation of going to see the site of the old Roman Amphitheatre there, which goes by the name of Arthur's Round Table. It is in a field near the river, and is of considerable extent. There are no inequalities in the ground to mark where the seats have been, but the form of the theatre in general is very clearly defined. It would require a great stretch of imagination to suppose that the hero of the

Mabinogion had really anything to do with this interesting spot. However, the name of King Arthur is so associated with that of Caerlleon upon Usk, that I did not wish to be too critical, but tried to fancy the British monarch's court held among the mountains here. The town itself is not good, but its position is very beautiful, and the situation of the castle, which I had not time to explore, very imposing. I doubt not but the place and the scenery look much more to advantage in summer—the snow which was over part of the country was a great drawback to-day. Before leaving Caerlleon we called at the house of Mr. Jenkins, a tradesman in the town, who was said to possess some curious coins that had been found here. I was disappointed, however, in what he showed us. From Caerlleon we had a delightful drive to Llansaintffread, passing through Usk, of which the castle is apparently a beautiful ruin.

Feb. 22.—No. 4 of my *Mabinogion* is published. A copy of it came to me in town. A very great relief to me to have it out of my hands, for correcting the notes was very tedious, and required a great deal of care and precision. March 11.—Went to Williams about the woodcuts for No. 5, which is to contain *Breuddwyd Rhonabwy,* and is already in the press.

March 17.—I tried, though not very successfully, to do something towards the notes of *Rhonabwy.*

March 24.—It was fine, and 'Merthyr' went out, but I was anxious to get on with my *Rhonabwy* notes, and sat writing alone. I did most completely enjoy this day. It was all so calm., and my work prospered nicely.

May 20.—At lunch-time George Clark came. I showed him a book I had received from Villemarqué called *Contes Bretons,* which contains a translation into French of the first three parts of the *Mabinogion,* and in which he tries to make it appear that he has translated straight from the Welsh without any obligation to my version. He has followed me servilely throughout, and taken my notes, without any acknowledgment except in one unimportant instance. Altogether it is a most shabby proceeding, but the man is too contemptible to be noticed. During the morning 'Merthyr' sent me most kind notes from the House of Commons, doing all he could to soothe my ruffled feelings, but though he might calm me about what had passed in the morning before he went out, he could not prevent my feeling very ill. At night I was hardly fit to move, but I took Mary [Lady Charlotte's half-sister, Miss Pegus, afterwards Marchioness of Huntly] to Lady Powis's, and stayed there with her at a ball till daylight.

June 8.—Rio called yesterday morning. I showed him Villemarqué's book, and he expressed himself very disgusted. 'He may now,' he said, 'be called L'homme Marqué more aptly than La Villemarqué.'

June 28.—I had a visit to-day from Mr. Lockhart. I showed him Villemarqué's book, and asked if he thought anything could be done about it; he said it was difficult, but if a good review were sent to him of my book and exposing Villemarqué's dishonesty, he would put it in the *Quarterly.* George Clark has undertaken to do it. I am all anxiety to see how he will manage it. The subject is a large and interesting one. It requires to be lightly and skilfully handled.

July 22.—Lepsius to-day brought me a copy of Schulz's translation of the *Mabinogion* into German, given in a very different spirit from that of Villemarqué's. Schulz is scrupulous in all his acknowledgements. In the midst of all my private anxieties, I have forgotten all note of public sorrow. The premature death of the Duke of Orleans throws a gloom, even in England; how much more deeply it must be felt in France.

July 28.—George Clark here. Some discussion about the best course to adopt, the *Athenœum* having reviewed Villemarqué's book with great praise, and treated it as an original. We concocted a letter to Rees, my publisher [of Llandovery], to send to the Editor explaining the facts.

Aug. 1.—I worked hard at the notes of *Rhonabwy* until very late.

Aug. 2.—I was very busy all day with notes, but did not accomplish much.

Aug. 3.—Notes again... At eight I left town with Katherine by the railway, reading for my notes all the way.

Aug. 5.—I wrote notes busily all day, and did not go out.

Aug. 11.—It was a lovely day. 'Merthyr' went into Cardiff, and I sat writing notes all the morning.

Aug. 19.—I had the pleasure of finishing all my *Rhonabwy* notes to-day. They may require to be copied again, and perhaps slightly altered; but, at all events, it is a great relief to have the groundwork done.

[Here there is an interval, during which Lady Charlotte was touring in Germany.]

Nov. 14.—Notes for the *Mabinogion* occupied most of my time.

Nov. 15. and 16.—I may give a similar account.

Nov. 21.—'Merthyr' went early to Sully. It was such a lovely day I felt tempted to go with him, but gave it up and turned as cheerfully as I could to my dull *Mabinogion* notes.

Nov. 23.—To-day I wrote notes till the last moment.

Nov. 28.—I did not go out, but I worked hard and sent off a vast number of notes.

Dec. 24—At night we had a disagreeable game of whist, after which I sat up writing *Mabinogion* notes till very late.

Dec. 29.—Mary [Miss Pegus] and I amused ourselves colouring one of the *Percival* tracings *to M ab.* No. 3.

1843

Feb. 6.—All this week I remained at home (except today I took some of the children to see the soldiers manoeuvring) and never ceased working at the *Mabinogion* notes for the future numbers. I believe I have finished all now except the topographical notes, which will not take very long.

Feb. 18.—I have been reading the first number of my *Mabinogion*,

'Iarlles y . . . '[*sic*] to Ivor and Maria [Lady Charlotte's two eldest children], and I never saw anything equal to their delight. It was so great that it would alone have been sufficient to repay me for all time and trouble I have bestowed upon the book. It is astonishing the ideas they have of middle-age manners and society, without which these tales would be quite unintelligible.

March 3.—I wrote hard and finished my translation of *Maxen Wledig*, enjoying the fine weather by means of an open window.

March 6.—My day was a very busy one, yet I found time for some Welsh.

March 7.—Again very busy; a little Welsh, but not much, in the evening.

March 8.—I have to-day finished all that is in my power to do towards the *Mabinogion*. It is a vast weight off my mind. The only stories I have to print, viz., *Branwen, Manawyddan, Math ab Mathonwy, Hanes Taliesin,* and *Breuddwyd Maxen Wledig,* are now in MS. translation, and so are their notes, all except the topographical ones, which I am forced to leave until I get materials for them from those who know the localities, but which take only a very short time for me afterwards to throw together. I may have to make transcripts of some of these again for the press, but that is mere mechanical work. The *Gral* is the only other story I contemplate giving, but of that I have as yet no Welsh copy. I have written to Col. Vaughan to beg the loan of his, but though it is two months since I have received no answer. The tales of *Amlyn and Amic, Seith Doethion, Bown o Hampton,* which have generally been considered to be *Mabinogion,* I find to be mere vapid translation from some Norman original, and shall, therefore, exclude them from my series, or if I give them at all I shall do so in an appendix, printing the Welsh only untranslated and in smaller type. Perhaps the *Historia Charlamaen* and the *Historia Charlys* ought to stop? *Rhonabwy* and *Pwyll* are now nearly through the press. The only thing that now presses upon me is the introduction and a preface, which I am more or less appalled at. And now that my seven babies are growing up and require so much attention, it is quite right that I should have done with authorship. I am quite content with what will have been done when the present work is concluded, and I am sure if a woman is to do her duty as a wife and mother, the less she meddles with pen and ink the better. I shall feel very glad when the last number is out of the press; as it is, the respite is a great relief. With much to do on my hands it was near midnight before I got to bed, and soon after six I was called to prepare for the journey.

March 24.—I had letters to write this morning, and also proofs to correct.

June 1.—Maria's lessons occupied this and the next two days almost incessantly, but I have begun a transcript for the press of *Math ab Mathonwy,* for which I have managed to find some spare moments.

June 6.—I transcribed *Math ab Mathonwy* most assiduously.

June 17.—I took advantage of Maria's afternoon walk to finish entirely the notes to *Math ab Mathonwy,* a task which has been long on my mind, and which I felt the greatest satisfaction in having got through.

June 21.—These two days I have been busy translating the story of *Lludd and Llevelys,* which I finished this afternoon.

June 28.—In every interval during the day I employed myself upon my Welsh, and transcribed the *Dream of Maxen Wledig* for the press before night. I had begun it yesterday, but wrote then only about half a page.

June 29.—I have begun copying *Sir Degrenance* from Thornton MS., but do not get on very quickly with it.

July 22.—To-day our youngest baby [Enid, christened 'Mary Enid Evelyn,' who afterwards became wife of Sir Henry Layard, G.C.B., the discoverer of Nineveh] was four weeks old, and we took her to be christened . . . The baby's names are given, the first after my sister, Enid after the heroine of the *Mabinogion* (see No. 3), and the last because it was a fancy of Mary's. Enid is such a favourite character with the elder children (as well as with myself) that they begged hard that she might be called so. Besides, as being born in Wales, it is fitting she should have a Welsh name to mark her origin. All our Welsh-born children have except Augustus, whom, however, I always call Geraint, though he has no baptismal right to the appellation.

1844

Feb. 3.—The carriage went in early to-day to meet the packet in case 'Merthyr' should return by it. I was consequently in a considerable state of excitement. I took care to keep myself incessantly employed, and before four o'clock I had finished transcribing *Lludd and Llevelys* for the press . . . I have finished the story of *Pwyll* to the children this evening after tea. They delight in these *Mabinogion* readings.

Feb. 8.—I wrote letters and copied from the Thornton MS. *Sir Degrenance,* and spent a very busy happy day.

Feb. 9.—I did not go out, but occupied myself almost incessantly with my transcript of *Sir Degrenance.*

Feb. 16.—As soon as dinner was over 'Merthyr' went to the House. I made an effort, and sat up and finished copying *Sir Degrenance,* so that the Thornton MS. might be returned to Mr. Pretyman on the morrow.

1845

Oct. 21.—After this I confined myself steadily in correcting the proof sheets of the Welsh *Taliesin—the Mabinogi* I have now in press, and about which I have been very idle for some time. I finished my task before the time of starting, having spent three very quiet hours.

First published in 1921,
*Lady Charlotte Guest and the Mabinogion: Some Notes on the Work
and its Translator, with Extracts from her Journals.*

THE MABINOGION

from the Welsh of

THE LLYFR COCH O HERGEST

(The Red Book of Hergest)

PREFACE

THE Arthurian Legends have at all times furnished a congenial subject to the students of Romance; and in the eight-and-thirty years which have elapsed since the first part of this Translation appeared, my "Mabinogion" have found their way into the hands of the learned both among ourselves and on the Continent.

More recently, however, the publication of the "Idyls of the King"—and among them of "Enid," which is founded on my version of "Geraint"—has interested a much wider circle of readers in the Legends, and there has arisen a demand for a new and more popular edition of my work, which it is the object of the present issue to supply.

It will be found to differ from its predecessor in the omission of the Welsh text, of all Welsh quotations in the Notes, and of the French Metrical Romance of the "Chevalier au Lion." The notices relating to the corresponding versions of the Tales in other European languages have also been condensed.

It is, then, under these altered conditions, and in the absence of all means of comparison on their part, that I ask my new readers to believe that I have striven to preserve in Saxon English the primitive simplicity of the Welsh original.

To these remarks it only remains for me to add, that the text of the Mabinogion exists in the Llyfr Coch o Hergest (or Red Book of Hergest) preserved in the Library of Jesus College, Oxford, and that for the accurate copy which I used, I was indebted to the learned labours of the Rev. John Jones (Tegid), Fellow of that College, and to the courtesy of the late Mr. Justice Bosanquet, for whom the transcript in question was originally made.

Langham House, London,
18th January, 1877.

INTRODUCTION

Whilst engaged on the Translations contained in these volumes, and on the Notes appended to the various Tales, I have found myself led unavoidably into a much more extensive course of reading than I had originally contemplated, and one which in great measure bears directly upon the earlier Mediæval Romance.

Before commencing these labours, I was aware, generally, that there existed a connexion between the Welsh Mabinogion and the Romance of the Continent; but as I advanced, I became better acquainted with the closeness and extent of that connexion, its history, and the proofs by which it is supported.

At the same time, indeed, I became aware, and still strongly feel, that it is one thing to collect facts, and quite another to classify and draw from them their legitimate conclusions; and though I am loth that what has been collected with some pains, should be entirely thrown away, it is unwillingly, and with diffidence, that I trespass beyond the acknowledged province of a translator.

In the twelfth and thirteenth centuries there arose into general notoriety in Europe, a body of "Romance," which in various forms retained its popularity till the Reformation. In it the plot, the incidents, the characters, were almost wholly those of Chivalry, that bond which united the warriors of France, Spain, and Italy, with those of pure Teutonic descent, and embraced more or less firmly all the nations of Europe, excepting only the Slavonic races, not yet risen to power, and the Celts, who had fallen from it. It is not difficult to account for this latter omission. The Celts, driven from the plains into the mountains and islands, preserved their liberty, and hated their oppressors with fierce, and not causeless, hatred. A proud and free people, isolated both in country and language, were not likely to adopt customs which implied brotherhood with their foes.

Such being the case, it is remarkable that when the chief romances are examined, the name of many of the heroes and their scenes of action are found to be Celtic, and those of persons and places famous in the traditions of Wales and Brittany. Of this the romances of Ywaine and Gawaine, Sir Perceval de Galles, Eric and Enide, Mort d'Arthur, Sir Lancelot, Sir Tristan, the Graal, &c., may be cited as examples. In some cases a tendency to triads, and other matters of internal evidence, point in the same direction.

It may seem difficult to account for this. Although the ancient dominion of the Celts over Europe is not without enduring evidence in the names of the mountains and streams, the great features of a country, yet the loss of their prior language by the great mass of the Celtic nations in Southern Europe (if indeed their successors in territory be at all of their blood), prevents us from clearly seeing, and makes us wonder, how stories, originally embodied in the Celtic dialects of Great Britain and France, could so influence the literature of nations to whom the Celtic languages were utterly unknown. Whence then came these internal marks, and these proper names of persons and places, the features of a story usually of earliest date and least likely to change?

These romances were found in England, France, Germany, Norway, Sweden, and even Iceland, as early as the beginning of the thirteenth and end of the twelfth century. The Germans, who propagated them through the nations of the North, derived them certainly from France. Robert Wace published his Anglo-Norman Romance of the Brut d'Angleterre about 1155. Sir Tristan was written in French prose in 1170; and The Chevalier au Lion, Chevalier de l'Epee, and Sir Lancelot du Lac, in metrical French, by Chrestien de Troyes, before 1200.

From these facts it is to be argued that the further back these romances are traced, the more clearly does it appear that they spread over the Continent from the North-west of France. The older versions, it may be remarked, are far more simple than the later corruptions. In them there is less allusion to the habits and usages of Chivalry, and the Welsh names and elements stand out in stronger relief. It is a great step to be able to trace the stocks of these romances back to Wace, or to his country and age. For Wace's work was not original. He himself, a native of Jersey, appears to have derived much of it from the "Historia Britonum" of Gruffydd ab Arthur, commonly known as "Geoffrey of Monmouth," born 1128, who himself professes to have translated from a British original. It is, however, very possible that Wace may have had access, like Geoffrey, to independent sources of information.

To the claims set up on behalf of Wace and Geoffrey, to be regarded as the channels by which the Cymric tales passed into the Continental Romance, may be added those of a third almost contemporary author. Layamon, a Saxon priest, dwelling, about 1200, upon the banks of the upper Severn, acknowledges for the source of his British history, the *English* Bede, the *Latin* Albin, and the *French* Wace. The last-named however is by very much his chief, and, for Welsh matters, his only avowed authority. His book, nevertheless, contains a number of names and stories relating to Wales, of which no traces appear in Wace, or indeed in Geoffrey, but which he was certainly in a very favourable position to obtain for himself. Layamon, therefore, not only confirms Geoffrey in some points, but it is clear, that, professing to follow Wace, he had independent access to the great body of Welsh literature then current. Sir F. Madden has put this matter very clearly, in his recent edition of Layamon. The Abbé de la Rue, also, was of opinion that Gaimar, an Anglo-Norman, in the reign of Stephen, usually regarded as a translator of Geoffrey of Monmouth, had access to a Welsh independent authority.

In addition to these, is to be mentioned the English version of Sir Tristrem, which Sir Walter Scott considered to be derived from a distinct Celtic source, and not, like the later Amadis, Palmerin, and Lord Berners's Canon of

Romance, imported into English literature by translation from the French. For the Auntours of Arthur, recently published by the Camden Society, their Editor, Mr. Robson, seems to hint at a similar claim.

Here then are various known channels, by which portions of Welsh and Armoric fiction crossed the Celtic border, and gave rise to the more ornate, and widely-spread romance of the Age of Chivalry. It is not improbable that there may have existed many others. It appears then that a large portion of the stocks of Mediæval Romance proceeded from Wales. We have next to see in what condition they are still found in that country.

That Wales possessed an ancient literature, containing various lyric compositions, and certain triads, in which are arranged historical facts or moral aphorisms, has been shown by Sharon Turner, who has established the high antiquity of many of these compositions.

The more strictly Romantic Literature of Wales has been less fortunate, though not less deserving of critical attention. Small portions only of it have hitherto appeared in print, the remainder being still hidden in the obscurity of ancient Manuscripts: of these the chief is supposed to be the Red Book of Hergest, now in the Library of Jesus College, Oxford, and of the fourteenth century. This contains, besides poems, the prose romances known as Mabinogion. The Black Book of Caermarthen, preserved at Hengwrt, and considered not to be of later date than the twelfth century, is said to contain poems only. [1]

The Mabinogion, however, though thus early recorded in the Welsh tongue, are in their existing form by no means wholly Welsh. They are of two tolerably distinct classes. Of these, the older contains few allusions to Norman customs, manners, arts, arms, and luxuries. The other, and less ancient, are full of such allusions, and of ecclesiastical terms. Both classes, no doubt, are equally of Welsh root, but the former are not more overlaid or corrupted, than might have been expected, from the communication that so early took place between the Normans and the Welsh; whereas the latter probably migrated from Wales, and were brought back and re-translated after an absence of centuries, with a load of Norman additions. Kilhwch and Olwen, and the dream of Rhonabwy, may be cited as examples of the older and purer class; the Lady of the Fountain, Peredur, and Geraint ab Erbin, of the later, or decorated.

Besides these, indeed, there are a few tales, as Amlyn and Amic, Sir Bevis of Hamtoun, the Seven Wise Masters, and the story of Charlemagne, so obviously of foreign extraction, and of late introduction into Wales, not presenting even a Welsh name, or allusion, and of such very slender intrinsic merit, that although comprised in the Llyvr Coch, they have not a shadow of claim to form part

---

1 It is also stated, that there is in the Hengwrt Library, a MS. containing the Graal in Welsh, as early as the time of Henry I. I had hoped to have added this to the present collection; but the death of Col. Vaughan, to whom I applied, and other subsequent circumstances, have prevented me from obtaining access to it.

of the Canon of Welsh Romance. Therefore, although I have translated and examined them, I have given them no place in these volumes.

There is one argument in favour of the high antiquity in Wales of many of the Mabinogion, which deserves to be mentioned here. This argument is founded on the topography of the country. It is found that Saxon names of places are very frequently definitions of the nature of the locality to which they are attached, as Clifton, Deepden, Bridge-ford, Thorpe, Ham, Wick, and the like; whereas those of Wales are more frequently commemorative of some event, real or supposed, said to have happened on or near the spot, or bearing allusion to some person renowned in the story of the country or district. Such are "Llyn y Morwynion," the Lake of the Maidens; "Rhyd y Bedd," the Ford of the Grave; "Bryn Cyfergyr," the Hill of Assault; and so on. But as these names could not have preceded the events to which they refer, the events themselves must be not unfrequently as old as the early settlement in the country. And as some of these events and fictions are the subjects of, and are explained by, existing Welsh legends, it follows that the legends must be, in some shape or other, of very remote antiquity. It will be observed that this argument supports *remote* antiquity only for such legends as are connected with the greater topographical features, as mountains, lakes, rivers, seas, which must have been named at an early period in the inhabitation of the country by man. But there exist, also, legends connected with the lesser features, as pools, hills, detached rocks, caves, fords, and the like, places not necessarily named by the earlier settlers, but the names of which are, nevertheless, probably very old, since the words of which they are composed are in many cases not retained in the colloquial tongue, in which they must once have been included, and are in some instances lost from the language altogether, so much so as to be only partially explicable even by scholars. The argument applies likewise, in their degree, to camps, barrows, and other artificial earth-works.

Conclusions thus drawn, when established, rest upon a very firm basis. They depend upon the number and appositeness of the facts, and it would be very interesting to pursue this branch of evidence in detail. In following up this idea, the names to be sought for might thus be classed:—

I. Names of the great features, involving proper names and actions.

Cadair Idris and Cadair Arthur both involve more than a mere name. Idris and Arthur must have been invested with heroic qualifications to have been placed in such "seats."

II. Names of lesser features, as "Bryn y Saeth," Hill of the Dart; "Llyn Llyngclys," Lake of the Engulphed Court; "Ceven y Bedd," the Ridge of the Grave; "Rhyd y Saeson," the Saxons' Ford.

III. Names of mixed natural and artificial objects, as "Coeten Arthur," Arthur's Coit; "Cerrig y Drudion," the Crag of the Heroes; which involve actions. And such as embody proper names only, as "Cerrig Howell," the Crag of

Howell; "Caer Arianrod," the Camp of Arianrod; "Bron Goronwy," the Breast (of the Hill) of Goronwy; "Castell mab Wynion," the Castle of the son of Wynion; "Nant Gwrtheyrn," the Rill of Vortigern.

The selection of names would demand much care and discretion. The translations should be indisputable, and, where known, the connexion of a name with a legend should be noted. Such a name as "Mochdrev," Swine-town, would be valueless unless accompanied by a legend.

It is always valuable to find a place or work called after an individual, because it may help to support some tradition of his existence or his actions. But it is requisite that care be taken not to push the etymological dissection too far. Thus, "Caer Arianrod" should be taken simply as the "Camp of Arianrod," and not rendered the "Camp of the silver circle," because the latter, though it might possibly have something to do with the reason for which the name was borne by Arianrod herself, had clearly no reference to its application to her camp.

It appears to me, then, looking back upon what has been advanced:—

I. That we have throughout Europe, at an early period, a great body of literature, known as Mediæval Romance, which, amidst much that is wholly of Teutonic origin and character, includes certain well-marked traces of an older Celtic nucleus.

II. Proceeding backwards in time, we find these romances, their ornaments falling away at each step, existing towards the twelfth century, of simpler structure, and with less encumbered Celtic features, in the works of Wace, and other Bards of the Langue d'Oil.

III. We find that Geoffrey of Monmouth, Layamon, and other early British and Anglo-Saxon historians, and minstrels, on the one hand, transmitted to Europe the rudiments of its after romance, much of which, on the other hand, they drew from Wales.

IV. Crossing into Wales we find, in the Mabinogion, the evident counterpart of the Celtic portion of the continental romance, mixed up, indeed, with various reflex additions from beyond the border, but still containing ample internal evidence of a Welsh original.

V. Looking at the connexion between divers of the more ancient Mabinogion, and the topographical nomenclature of part of the country, we find evidence of the great, though indefinite, antiquity of these tales, and of an origin, which, if not indigenous, is certainly derived from no European nation.

It was with a general belief in some of these conclusions, that I commenced my labours, and I end them with my impressions strongly confirmed. The subject is one not unworthy of the talents of a Llwyd or a Prichard. It might, I think, be shown, by pursuing the inquiry, that the Cymric nation is not only, as Dr. Prichard has proved it to be, an early offshoot of the Indo-European family, and a people of unmixed descent, but that when driven out of their conquests by the later nations, the names and exploits of their heroes, and the compositions of their bards, spread far and wide among the invaders, and affected intimately their tastes and literature for many centuries, and that it has strong claims to be considered the cradle of European Romance.

Dowlais, August 29th, 1848.

THE LADY OF THE FOUNTAIN

KING ARTHUR [3a] was at Caerlleon upon Usk [3b]; and one day he sat in his chamber; and with him were Owain the son of Urien [3c], and Kynon [3d] the son of Clydno [3e], and Kai the son of Kyner [3f]; and Gwenhwyvar [3g] and her handmaidens at needlework by the window. And if it should be said that there was a porter [3h] at Arthur's palace, there was none. Glewlwyd Gavaelvawr [3i] was there, acting as porter, to welcome guests and strangers, and to receive them with honour, and to inform them of the manners and customs of the Court; and to direct those who came to the Hall or to the presence-chamber, and those who came to take up their lodging.

In the centre of the chamber King Arthur sat upon a seat of green rushes [3j], over which was spread a covering of flame-coloured satin [3k], and a cushion of red satin was under his elbow.

Then Arthur spoke, "If I thought you would not disparage me," said he, "I would sleep while I wait for my repast; and you can entertain one another with relating tales, and can obtain a flagon of mead and some meat from Kai." And the King went to sleep. And Kynon the son of Clydno asked Kai for that which Arthur had promised them. "I, too, will have the good tale which he promised to me," said Kai. "Nay," answered Kynon, "fairer will it be for thee to fulfill Arthur's behest, in the first place, and then we will tell thee the best tale that we know." So Kai went to the kitchen and to the mead-cellar, and returned bearing a flagon of mead and a golden goblet, and a handful of skewers, upon which were broiled collops of meat. Then they ate the collops and began to drink the mead. "Now," said Kai, "it is time for you to give me my story." "Kynon," said Owain, "do thou pay to Kai the tale that is his due." "Truly," said Kynon, "thou are older, and art a better teller of tales, and hast seen more marvellous things than I; do thou therefore pay Kai his tale." "Begin thyself," quoth Owain, "with the best that thou knowest." "I will do so," answered Kynon.

"I was the only son of my mother and father, and I was exceedingly aspiring, and my daring was very great. I thought there was no enterprise in the world too mighty for me, and after I had achieved all the adventures that were in my own country, I equipped myself, and set forth to journey through deserts and distant regions [4a]. And at length it chanced that I came to the fairest valley in the world, wherein were trees of equal growth [4b]; and a river ran through the valley, and a path was by the side of the river. And I followed the path until mid-day, and continued my journey along the remainder of the valley until the evening; and at the extremity of a plain I came to a large and lustrous Castle, at the foot of which was a torrent. And I approached the Castle, and there I beheld two youths with yellow curling hair, each with a frontlet of gold upon his head, and clad in a garment of yellow satin[4c], and they had gold clasps upon their insteps. In the hand of each of them was an ivory bow, strung with the sinews of the stag[5a]; and their arrows had shafts of the bone of the whale[5b], and were winged with peacock's feathers[5c]; the shafts also had golden heads[5d]. And they had daggers with blades of gold[5d], and with hilts of the bone of the whale. And they were shooting their daggers.

"And a little way from them I saw a man in the prime of life, with his beard newly shorn, clad in a robe and a mantle of yellow satin; and round the top of his mantle was a band of gold lace. On his feet were shoes of variegated leather[5e], fastened by two bosses of gold. When I saw him, I went towards him and saluted him, and such was his courtesy that he no sooner received my greeting than he returned it. And he went with me towards the Castle. Now there were no dwellers in the Castle except those who were in one hall. And there I saw four-and-twenty damsels, embroidering satin at a window. And this I tell thee, Kai, that the least fair of them was fairer than the fairest maid thou hast ever beheld in the Island of Britain, and the least lovely of them was more lovely than Gwenhwyvar[5f], the wife of Arthur, when she has appeared loveliest at the Offering, on the day of the Nativity, or at the feast of Easter. They rose up at my coming[5g], and six of them took my horse, and divested me of my armour; and six others took my arms, and washed them in a vessel until they were perfectly bright. And the third six spread cloths upon the tables and prepared meat. And the fourth six took off my soiled garments, and placed others upon me; namely, an under-vest and a doublet of fine linen, and a robe, and a surcoat, and a mantle of yellow satin with a broad gold band upon the mantle[5h]. And they placed cushions both beneath and around me, with coverings of red linen; and I sat down. Now the six maidens who had taken my horse, unharnessed him, as well as if they had been the best squires in the Island of Britain. Then, behold, they brought bowls of silver wherein was water to wash, and towels of linen, some green and some white; and I washed. And in a little while the man sat down to the table. And I sat next to him, and below me sat all the maidens, except those who waited on us. And the table was of silver, and the cloths upon the table were of linen; and no vessel was served upon the table that was not either of gold or of silver, or of buffalo-horn[6a]. And our meat was brought to us. And verily, Kai, I saw there every sort of meat and every sort of liquor that I have ever seen elsewhere; but the meat and the liquor were better served there than I have ever seen them in any other place.

"Until the repast was half over, neither the man nor any one of the damsels spoke a single word to me; but when the man perceived that it would be more agreeable to me to converse than to eat any more, he began to inquire of me who I was. I said I was glad to find that there was some one who would discourse with me, and that it was not considered so great a crime at that Court for people to hold converse together. 'Chieftain,' said the man, 'we would have talked to thee sooner, but we feared to disturb thee during thy repast; now, however, we will discourse.' Then I told the man who I was, and what was the cause of my journey; and said that I was seeking whether any one was superior to me, or whether I could gain the mastery over all. The man looked upon me, and he smiled and said, 'If I did not fear to distress thee too much, I would show thee that which thou seekest.' Upon this I became anxious and sorrowful, and when the man perceived it, he said, 'If thou wouldest rather that I should show thee thy disadvantage than thine advantage, I will do so. Sleep here to-night, and in the morning arise early, and take the road upwards through the valley until thou reachest the wood through which thou camest hither. A little way within the wood thou wilt meet with a road branching off to the right, by which thou must proceed, until thou comest to a large sheltered glade with a mound in the centre. And thou wilt see a black man of great stature on the top of the mound. He is not smaller in size than two of the men of this world. He has but one foot; and one eye in the middle of his forehead.

And he has a club of iron, and it is certain that there are no two men in the world who would not find their burden in that club. And he is not a comely man, but on the contrary he is exceedingly ill-favoured; and he is the woodward of that wood. And thou wilt see a thousand wild animals grazing around him. Inquire of him the way out of the glade, and he will reply to thee briefly, and will point out the road by which thou shalt find that which thou art in quest of.'

"And long seemed that night to me. And the next morning I arose and equipped myself, and mounted my horse, and proceeded straight through the valley to the wood; and I followed the cross-road which the man had pointed out to me, till at length I arrived at the glade. And there was I three times more astonished at the number of wild animals that I beheld, than the man had said I should be. And the black man was there, sitting upon the top of the mound. Huge of stature as the man had told me that he was, I found him to exceed by far the description he had given me of him. As for the iron club which the man had told me was a burden for two men, I am certain, Kai, that it would be a heavy weight for four warriors to lift; and this was in the black man's hand. And he only spoke to me in answer to my questions. Then I asked him what power he held over those animals. 'I will show thee, little man,' said he. And he took his club in his hand, and with it he struck a stag a great blow so that he brayed vehemently, and at his braying the animals came together, as numerous as the stars in the sky, so that it was difficult for me to find room in the glade to stand among them. There were serpents, and dragons, and divers sorts of animals. And he looked at them, and bade them go and feed; and they bowed their heads, and did him homage as vassals to their lord.

"Then the black man said to me, 'Seest thou now, little man, what power I hold over these animals?' Then I inquired of him the way, and he became very rough in his manner to me; however, he asked me whither I would go? And when I told him who I was and what I sought, he directed me. 'Take,' said he, 'that path that leads towards the head of the glade, and ascend the wooded steep until thou comest to its summit; and there thou wilt find an open space like to a large valley, and in the midst of it a tall tree, whose branches are greener than the greenest pine-trees. Under this tree is a fountain[8a], and by the side of the fountain a marble slab, and on the marble slab a silver bowl, attached by a chain of silver, so that it may not be carried away. Take the bowl and throw a bowlful of water upon the slab, and thou wilt hear a mighty peal of thunder, so that thou wilt think that heaven and earth are trembling with its fury. With the thunder there will come a shower so severe that it will be scarce possible for thee to endure it and live. And the shower will be of hailstones; and after the shower, the weather will become fair, but every leaf that was upon the tree will have been carried away by the shower. Then a flight of birds will come and alight upon the tree; and in thine own country thou didst never hear a strain so sweet as that which they will sing. And at the moment thou art most delighted with the song of the birds, thou wilt hear a murmuring and complaining coming towards thee along the valley. And thou wilt see a knight upon a coal-black horse, clothed in black velvet, and with a pennon of black linen upon his lance; and he will ride unto thee to encounter thee with the utmost speed. If thou fleest from him he will overtake thee, and if thou abidest there, as sure as thou art a mounted knight, he will leave thee on foot. And if thou dost not find trouble in that adventure, thou needest not seek it during the rest of thy life.'

"So I journeyed on, until I reached the summit of the steep, and there I found everything as the black man had described it to me. And I went up to the tree, and beneath it I saw the fountain, and by its side the marble slab, and the silver bowl fastened by the chain. Then I took the bowl, and cast a bowlful of water upon the slab; and thereupon, behold, the thunder came, much more violent than the black man had led me to expect; and after the thunder came the shower; and of a truth I tell thee, Kai, that there is neither man nor beast that can endure that shower and live. For not one of those hailstones would be stopped, either by the flesh or by the skin, until it had reached the bone. I turned my horse's flank towards the shower, and placed the beak of my shield over his head and neck, while I held the upper part of it over my own head. And thus I withstood the shower. When I looked on the tree there was not a single leaf upon it, and then the sky became clear, and with that, behold the birds lighted upon the tree, and sang. And truly, Kai, I never heard any melody equal to that, either before or since. And when I was most charmed with listening to the birds, lo, a murmuring voice was heard through the valley, approaching me and saying, 'Oh, Knight, what has brought thee hither? What evil have I done to thee, that thou shouldst act towards me and my possessions as thou hast this day? Dost thou not know that the shower to-day has left in my dominions neither man nor beast alive that was exposed to it?' And thereupon, behold, a Knight on a black horse appeared, clothed in jet-black velvet, and with a tabard of black linen about him. And we charged each other, and, as the onset was furious, it was not long before I was overthrown. Then the Knight passed the shaft of his lance through the bridle rein of my horse, and rode off with the two horses, leaving me where I was. And he did not even bestow so much notice upon me as to imprison me, nor did he despoil me of my arms. So I returned along the road by which I had come. And when I reached the glade where the black man was, I confess to thee, Kai, it is a marvel that I did not melt down into a liquid pool, through the shame that I felt at the black man's derision. And that night I came to the same castle where I had spent the night preceding. And I was more agreeably entertained that night than I had been the night before; and I was better feasted, and I conversed freely with the inmates of the castle, and none of them alluded to my expedition to the fountain, neither did I mention it to any; and I remained there that night. When I arose on the morrow, I found, ready saddled, a dark bay palfrey, with nostrils as red as scarlet; and after putting on my armour, and leaving there my blessing, I returned to my own Court. And that horse I still possess, and he is in the stable yonder. And I declare that I would not part with him for the best palfrey in the Island of Britain.

"Now of a truth, Kai, no man ever before confessed to an adventure so much to his own discredit[10a], and verily it seems strange to me, that neither before nor since have I heard of any person besides myself who knew of this adventure, and that the subject of it should exist within King Arthur's dominions, without any other person lighting upon it."

"Now," quoth Owain, "would it not be well to go and endeavour to discover that place?"

"By the hand of my friend," said Kai, "often dost thou utter that with thy tongue which thou wouldst not make good with thy deeds."

"In very truth," said Gwenhwyvar, "it were better thou wert hanged, Kai, than to use such uncourteous speech[10b] towards a man like Owain."

"By the hand of my friend, good Lady," said Kai, "thy praise of Owain is not greater than mine."

With that Arthur awoke, and asked if he had not been sleeping a little.

"Yes, Lord," answered Owain, "thou hast slept awhile."

"Is it time for us to go to meat?"

"It is, Lord," said Owain.

Then the horn for washing[10c] was sounded, and the King and all his household sat down to eat. And when the meal was ended, Owain withdrew to his lodging, and made ready his horse and his arms.

On the morrow, with the dawn of day, he put on his armour, and mounted his charger, and travelled through distant lands and over desert mountains. And at length he arrived at the valley which Kynon had described to him; and he was certain that it was the same that he sought. And journeying along the valley by the side of the river, he followed its course till he came to the plain and within sight of the Castle. When he approached the Castle, he saw the youths shooting their daggers in the place where Kynon had seen them, and the yellow man, to whom the Castle belonged, standing hard by. And no sooner had Owain saluted the yellow man than he was saluted by him in return.

And he went forward towards the Castle, and there he saw the chamber, and when he had entered the chamber he beheld the maidens working at satin embroidery, in chairs of gold. And their beauty and their comeliness seemed to Owain far greater than Kynon had represented to him. And they rose to wait upon Owain, as they had done to Kynon, and the meal which they set before him gave more satisfaction to Owain than it had done to Kynon.

About the middle of the repast, the yellow man asked Owain the object of his journey. And Owain made it known to him, and said, "I am in quest of the Knight who guards the fountain." Upon this the yellow man smiled, and said that he was as loth to point out that adventure to Owain as he had been to Kynon. However, he described the whole to Owain, and they retired to rest.

The next morning Owain found his horse made ready for him by the damsels, and he set forward and came to the glade where the black man was. And the stature of the black man seemed more wonderful to Owain than it had done to Kynon, and Owain asked of him his road, and he showed it to him. And Owain followed the road, as Kynon had done, till he came to the green tree; and he beheld the fountain, and the slab beside the fountain, with the bowl upon it. And Owain took the bowl, and threw a bowlful of water upon the slab. And, lo, the thunder was heard, and after the thunder came the shower, much more violent than Kynon had described, and after the shower the sky became bright. And when Owain looked at the tree, there was not one leaf upon it. And immediately the birds came, and settled upon the tree, and sang. And when their song was most pleasing to Owain, he beheld a Knight[12a] coming towards him through the valley, and he prepared to receive him; and encountered him violently. Having broken both their lances, they drew their swords, and fought blade to blade. Then Owain struck the Knight a blow through his helmet, head-piece and visor, and through the skin, and the flesh, and the bone, until it wounded the very brain. Then the black Knight felt that he had received a mortal wound, upon which he turned his horse's head, and fled. And Owain pursued him, and followed close upon him, although he was not near enough to strike him with his sword. Thereupon Owain descried a vast and resplendent Castle. And they came to the Castle gate. And the black Knight was allowed to enter, and the portcullis was let fall upon Owain; and it struck his horse behind the saddle, and cut him in two, and carried away the rowels of the spurs that were upon Owain's heels. And the portcullis descended to the floor. And the rowels of the spurs and part of the horse were without, and Owain with the other part of the horse remained between the two gates, and the inner gate was closed, so that Owain could not go thence; and Owain was in a perplexing situation. And while he was in this state, he could see through an aperture in the gate, a street facing him, with a row of houses on each side. And he beheld a maiden[12b], with yellow curling hair, and a frontlet of gold upon her head; and she was clad in a dress of yellow satin, and on her feet were shoes of variegated leather. And she approached the gate, and desired that it should be opened. "Heaven knows, Lady," said Owain, "it is no more possible for me to open to thee from hence, than it is for thee to set me free." "Truly," said the damsel, "it is very sad that thou canst not be released, and every woman ought to succour thee, for I never saw one more faithful in the service of ladies than thou. As a friend thou art the most sincere, and as a lover the most devoted. Therefore," quoth she, "whatever is in my power[13a] to do for thy release, I will do it. Take this ring[13b] and put it on thy finger, with the stone inside thy hand; and close thy hand upon the stone. And as long as thou concealest it, it will conceal thee. When they have consulted together, they will come forth to fetch thee, in order to put thee to death; and they will be much grieved that they cannot find thee. And I will await thee on the horseblock[13c] yonder; and thou wilt be able to see me, though I cannot see thee; therefore come and place thy hand upon my shoulder, that I may know that thou art near me. And by the way that I go hence, do thou accompany me."

Then she went away from Owain, and he did all that the maiden had told him. And the people of the Castle came to seek Owain, to put him to death, and when they found nothing but the half of his horse, they were sorely grieved.

And Owain vanished from among them, and went to the maiden, and placed his hand upon her shoulder; whereupon she set off, and Owain followed her, until they came to the door of a large and beautiful chamber, and the maiden opened it, and they went in, and closed the door. And Owain looked around the chamber, and behold there was not even a single nail in it that was not painted with gorgeous colours[13d]; and there was not a single panel that had not sundry images in gold portrayed upon it.

The maiden kindled a fire, and took water in a silver bowl, and put a towel of white linen on her shoulder, and gave Owain water to wash. Then she placed before him a silver table, inlaid with gold; upon which was a cloth of yellow linen; and she brought him food. And of a truth, Owain had never seen any kind of meat that was not there in abundance, but it was better cooked there than he had ever found it in any other place. Nor did he ever see so excellent a display of meat and drink, as there. And there was not one vessel from which he was served, that was not of gold or of silver. And Owain ate and drank, until late in the afternoon, when lo, they heard a mighty clamour in the Castle; and Owain asked the maiden what that outcry was. "They are administering extreme unction," said she, "to the Nobleman who owns the Castle." And Owain went to sleep.

The couch which the maiden had prepared for him was meet for Arthur himself; it was of scarlet, and fur, and satin, and sendall, and fine linen. In the middle of the night they heard a woful outcry. "What outcry again is this?" said Owain. "The Nobleman who owned the Castle is now dead," said the maiden. And a little after daybreak, they heard an exceeding loud clamour and wailing. And Owain asked the maiden what was the cause of it. "They are bearing to the church the body of the Nobleman who owned the Castle."

And Owain rose up, and clothed himself, and opened a window of the chamber, and looked towards the Castle; and he could see neither the bounds, nor the extent of the hosts that filled the streets. And they were fully armed; and a vast number of women were with them, both on horseback and on foot; and all the ecclesiastics in the city, singing. And it seemed to Owain that the sky resounded with the vehemence of their cries, and with the noise of the trumpets, and with the singing of the ecclesiastics. In the midst of the throng, he beheld the bier, over which was a veil of white linen; and wax tapers were burning beside and around it, and none that supported the bier was lower in rank than a powerful Baron.

Never did Owain see an assemblage so gorgeous with satin, and silk, and sendall[14a]. And following the train, he beheld a lady with yellow hair falling over her shoulders, and stained with blood; and about her a dress of yellow satin, which was torn. Upon her feet were shoes of variegated leather. And it was a marvel that the ends of her fingers were not bruised, from the violence with which she smote her hands together. Truly she would have been the fairest lady Owain ever saw, had she been in her usual guise. And her cry was louder than the shout of the men, or the clamour of the trumpets. No sooner had he beheld the lady, than he became inflamed with her love, so that it took entire possession of him.

Then he inquired of the maiden who the lady was. "Heaven knows," replied the maiden, "she may be said to be the fairest, and the most chaste, and the most liberal, and the wisest, and the most noble of women. And she is my mistress; and she is called the Countess[15a] of the Fountain, the wife of him whom thou didst slay yesterday." "Verily," said Owain, "she is the woman that I love best." "Verily," said the maiden, "she shall also love thee not a little."

And with that the maid arose, and kindled a fire, and filled a pot with water, and placed it to warm; and she brought a towel of white linen, and placed it around Owain's neck; and she took a goblet of ivory, and a silver basin, and filled them with warm water, wherewith she washed Owain's head[15b]. Then she opened a wooden casket, and drew forth a razor, whose haft was of ivory, and upon which were two rivets of gold. And she shaved his beard, and she dried his head, and his throat, with the towel. Then she rose up from before Owain, and brought him to eat. And truly Owain had never so good a meal, nor was he ever so well served.

When he had finished his repast, the maiden arranged his couch. "Come here," said she, "and sleep, and I will go and woo for thee." And Owain went to sleep, and the maiden shut the door of the chamber after her, and went towards the Castle. When she came there, she found nothing but mourning, and sorrow; and the Countess in her chamber could not bear the sight of any one through grief. Luned came and saluted her, but the Countess answered her not. And the maiden bent down towards her, and said, "What aileth thee, that thou answerest no one to-day?" "Luned," said the Countess, "what change hath befallen thee, that thou hast not come to visit me in my grief? It was wrong in thee, and I having made thee rich; it was wrong in thee that thou didst not come to see me in my distress. That was wrong in thee." "Truly," said Luned, "I thought thy good sense was greater than I find it to be. Is it well for thee to mourn after that good man, or for anything else, that thou canst not have?" "I declare to heaven," said the Countess, "that in the whole world there is not a man equal to him." "Not so," said Luned, "for an ugly man would be as good as, or better than he." "I declare to heaven," said the Countess, "that were it not repugnant to me to cause to be put to death one whom I have brought up, I would have thee executed, for making such a comparison to me. As it is, I will banish thee." "I am glad," said Luned, "that thou hast no other cause to do so, than that I would have been of service to thee where thou didst not know what was to thine advantage. And henceforth evil betide whichever of us shall make the first advance towards reconciliation to the other; whether I should seek an invitation from thee, or thou of thine own accord shouldst send to invite me."

With that Luned went forth: and the Countess arose and followed her to the door of the chamber, and began coughing loudly. And when Luned looked back, the Countess beckoned to her; and she returned to the Countess. "In truth," said the Countess, "evil is thy disposition; but if thou knowest what is to my advantage, declare it to me." "I will do so," quoth she.

"Thou knowest that except by warfare and arms it is impossible for thee to preserve thy possessions; delay not, therefore, to seek some one who can defend them." "And how can I do that?" said the Countess. "I will tell thee," said Luned. "Unless thou canst defend the fountain, thou canst not maintain thy dominions; and no one can defend the fountain, except it be a knight of Arthur's household; and I will go to Arthur's Court, and ill betide me, if I return thence without a warrior who can guard the fountain as well as, or even better than, he who defended it formerly." "That will be hard to perform," said the Countess. "Go, however, and make proof of that which thou hast promised."

Luned set out, under the pretence of going to Arthur's Court; but she went back to the chamber where she had left Owain; and she tarried there with him as long as it might have taken her to have travelled to the Court of King Arthur. And at the end of that time, she apparelled herself and went to visit the Countess. And the Countess was much rejoiced when she saw her, and inquired what news she brought from the Court. "I bring thee the best of news," said Luned, "for I have compassed the object of my mission. When wilt thou, that I should present to thee the chieftain who has come with me hither?" "Bring him here to visit me to-morrow, at mid-day," said the Countess, "and I will cause the town to be assembled by that time."

And Luned returned home. And the next day, at noon, Owain arrayed himself in a coat, and a surcoat, and a mantle of yellow satin, upon which was a broad band of gold lace; and on his feet were high shoes of variegated leather, which were fastened by golden clasps, in the form of lions. And they proceeded to the chamber of the Countess.

Right glad was the Countess of their coming, and she gazed steadfastly upon Owain, and said, "Luned, this knight has not the look of a traveller." "What harm is there in that, lady?" said Luned. "I am certain," said the Countess, "that no other man than this chased the soul from the body of my lord." "So much the better for thee, lady," said Luned, "for had he not been stronger than thy lord he could not have deprived him of life. There is no remedy for that which is past, be it as it may." "Go back to thine abode," said the Countess, "and I will take counsel."

The next day the Countess caused all her subjects to assemble, and showed them that her earldom was left defenceless, and that it could not be protected but with horse and arms, and military skill. "Therefore," said she, "this is what I offer for your choice: either let one of you take me, or give your consent for me to take a husband from elsewhere to defend my dominions."

So they came to the determination that it was better that she should have permission to marry some one from elsewhere; and, thereupon, she sent for the bishops and archbishops to celebrate her nuptials with Owain[18a]. And the men of the earldom did Owain homage.

And Owain defended the Fountain with lance and sword. And this is the manner in which he defended it: Whensoever a knight came there he overthrew him, and sold him for his full worth, and what he thus gained he divided among his barons and his knights; and no man in the whole world could be more beloved than he was by his subjects. And it was thus for the space of three years.

It befell that as Gwalchmai[18b] went forth one day with King Arthur, he perceived him to be very sad and sorrowful. And Gwalchmai was much grieved to see Arthur in this state; and he questioned him, saying, "Oh, my lord! what has befallen thee?" "In sooth, Gwalchmai," said Arthur, "I am grieved concerning Owain, whom I have lost these three years, and I shall certainly die if the fourth year passes without my seeing him. Now I am sure, that it is through the tale which Kynon the son of Clydno related, that I have lost Owain." "There is no need for thee," said Gwalchmai, "to summon to arms thy whole dominions on this account, for thou thyself and the men of thy household will be able to avenge Owain, if he be slain; or to set him free, if he be in prison;

and, if alive, to bring him back with thee." And it was settled according to what Gwalchmai had said.

Then Arthur and the men of his household prepared to go and seek Owain, and their number was three thousand, besides their attendants. And Kynon the son of Clydno acted as their guide. And Arthur came to the Castle where Kynon had been before, and when he came there the youths were shooting in the same place, and the yellow man was standing hard by. When the yellow man saw Arthur he greeted him, and invited him to the Castle; and Arthur accepted his invitation, and they entered the Castle together. And great as was the number of his retinue, their presence was scarcely observed in the Castle, so vast was its extent. And the maidens rose up to wait on them, and the service of the maidens appeared to them all to excel any attendance they had ever met with; and even the pages who had charge of the horses were no worse served, that night, than Arthur himself would have been in his own palace.

The next morning Arthur set out thence, with Kynon for his guide, and came to the place where the black man was. And the stature of the black man was more surprising to Arthur than it had been represented to him. And they came to the top of the wooded steep, and traversed the valley till they reached the green tree, where they saw the fountain, and the bowl, and the slab. And upon that, Kai came to Arthur and spoke to him. "My lord," said he, "I know the meaning of all this, and my request is, that thou wilt permit me to throw the water on the slab, and to receive the first adventure that may befall." And Arthur gave him leave.

Then Kai threw a bowlful of water upon the slab, and immediately there came the thunder, and after the thunder the shower. And such a thunderstorm they had never known before, and many of the attendants who were in Arthur's train were killed by the shower. After the shower had ceased the sky became clear; and on looking at the tree they beheld it completely leafless. Then the birds descended upon the tree, and the song of the birds was far sweeter than any strain they had ever heard before. Then they beheld a knight on a coal-black horse, clothed in black satin, coming rapidly towards them. And Kai met him and encountered him, and it was not long before Kai was overthrown. And the knight withdrew, and Arthur and his host encamped for the night.

And when they arose in the morning, they perceived the signal of combat upon the lance of the Knight. And Kai came to Arthur, and spoke to him: "My lord," said he, "though I was overthrown yesterday, if it seem good to thee, I would gladly meet the Knight again to-day." "Thou mayst do so," said Arthur. And Kai went towards the Knight. And on the spot he overthrew Kai, and struck him with the head of his lance in the forehead, so that it broke his helmet and the head-piece, and pierced the skin and the flesh, the breadth of the spear-head, even to the bone. And Kai returned to his companions.

After this, all the household of Arthur went forth, one after the other, to combat the Knight, until there was not one that was not overthrown by him, except Arthur and Gwalchmai. And Arthur armed himself to encounter the Knight. "Oh, my lord," said Gwalchmai, "permit me to fight with him first." And Arthur permitted him. And he went forth to meet the Knight, having over himself and his horse a satin robe of honour[20a] which had been sent him by the daughter of the Earl of Rhangyw[20b], and in this dress he was not known by any of the host. And they charged each other, and fought all that day until the evening, and neither of them was able to unhorse the other.

The next day they fought with strong lances[20c], and neither of them could obtain the mastery.

And the third day they fought with exceeding strong lances. And they were incensed with rage, and fought furiously, even until noon. And they gave each other such a shock that the girths of their horses were broken, so that they fell over their horses' cruppers to the ground. And they rose up speedily, and drew their swords, and resumed the combat; and the multitude that witnessed their encounter felt assured that they had never before seen two men so valiant or so powerful. And had it been midnight, it would have been light from the fire that flashed from their weapons. And the Knight gave Gwalchmai a blow that turned his helmet from off his face, so that the Knight knew that it was Gwalchmai. Then Owain said, "My lord Gwalchmai, I did not know thee for my cousin[21a], owing to the robe of honour that enveloped thee; take my sword and my arms." Said Gwalchmai, "Thou, Owain, art the victor; take thou my sword." And with that Arthur saw that they were conversing, and advanced towards them. "My lord Arthur," said Gwalchmai, "here is Owain, who has vanquished me, and will not take my arms." "My lord," said Owain, "it is he that has vanquished me, and he will not take my sword." "Give me your swords[21b]," said Arthur, "and then neither of you has vanquished the other." Then Owain put his arms around Arthur's neck, and they embraced. And all the host hurried forward to see Owain, and to embrace him; and there was nigh being a loss of life, so great was the press.

And they retired that night, and the next day Arthur prepared to depart. "My lord," said Owain, "this is not well of thee; for I have been absent from thee these three years, and during all that time, up to this very day, I have been preparing a banquet[21c] for thee, knowing that thou wouldst come to seek me. Tarry with me, therefore, until thou and thy attendants have recovered the fatigues of the journey, and have been anointed."

And they all proceeded to the Castle of the Countess of the Fountain, and the banquet which had been three years preparing was consumed in three months. Never had they a more delicious or agreeable banquet. And Arthur prepared to depart. Then he sent an embassy to the Countess, to beseech her to permit Owain to go with him for the space of three months, that he might show him to the nobles and the fair dames of the Island of Britain. And the Countess gave her consent, although it was very painful to her. So Owain came with Arthur to the Island of Britain. And when he was once more amongst his kindred and friends, he remained three years, instead of three months, with them.

And as Owain one day sat at meat, in the city of Caerlleon upon Usk, behold a damsel entered upon a bay horse[21d], with a curling mane and covered with foam, and the bridle and so much as was seen of the saddle were of gold. And the damsel was arrayed in a dress of yellow satin. And she came up to Owain, and took the ring from off his hand. "Thus," said she, "shall be treated the deceiver, the traitor, the faithless, the disgraced, and the beardless." And she turned her horse's head and departed.

Then his adventure came to Owain's remembrance, and he was sorrowful; and having finished eating he went to his own abode and made preparations that night. And the next day he arose but did not go to the Court, but wandered to the distant parts of the earth and to uncultivated mountains. And he remained there until all his apparel was worn out, and his body was wasted away, and his hair was grown long. And he went about with the wild beasts and fed with them, until they became familiar with him; but at length he grew so weak that he could no longer bear them company. Then he descended from the mountains to the valley, and came to a park that was the fairest in the world, and belonged to a widowed Countess.

One day the Countess and her maidens went forth to walk by a lake, that was in the middle of the park. And they saw the form of a man. And they were terrified. Nevertheless they went near him, and touched him, and looked at him. And they saw that there was life in him, though he was exhausted by the heat of the sun. And the Countess returned to the Castle, and took a flask full of precious ointment, and gave it to one of her maidens. "Go with this," said she, "and take with thee yonder horse and clothing, and place them near the man we saw just now. And anoint him with this balsam[22a], near his heart; and if there is life in him, he will arise through the efficacy of this balsam. Then watch what he will do."

And the maiden departed from her, and poured the whole of the balsam upon Owain, and left the horse and the garments hard by, and went a little way off, and hid herself to watch him. In a short time she saw him begin to move his arms; and he rose up, and looked at his person, and became ashamed of the unseemliness of his appearance. Then he perceived the horse and the garments that were near him. And he crept forward till he was able to draw the garments to him from off the saddle. And he clothed himself, and with difficulty mounted the horse. Then the damsel discovered herself to him, and saluted him. And he was rejoiced when he saw her, and inquired of her, what land and what territory that was. "Truly," said the maiden, "a widowed Countess owns yonder Castle; at the death of her husband, he left her two Earldoms, but at this day she has but this one dwelling that has not been wrested from her by a young Earl[23a], who is her neighbour, because she refused to become his wife." "That is pity," said Owain. And he and the maiden proceeded to the Castle; and he alighted there, and the maiden conducted him to a pleasant chamber, and kindled a fire and left him.

And the maiden came to the Countess, and gave the flask into her hand. "Ha! maiden," said the Countess, "where is all the balsam?" "Have I not used it all?" said she. "Oh, maiden," said the Countess, "I cannot easily forgive thee this; it is sad for me to have wasted seven-score pounds' worth of precious ointment upon a stranger whom I know not. However, maiden, wait thou upon him, until he is quite recovered."

And the maiden did so, and furnished him with meat and drink, and fire, and lodging, and medicaments, until he was well again. And in three months he was restored to his former guise, and became even more comely than he had ever been before.

One day Owain heard a great tumult, and a sound of arms in the Castle, and he inquired of the maiden the cause thereof. "The Earl," said she, "whom I mentioned to thee, has come before the Castle, with a numerous army, to subdue the Countess." And Owain inquired of her whether the Countess had a horse and arms in her possession. "She has the best in the world," said the maiden. "Wilt thou go and request the loan of a horse and arms for me," said Owain, "that I may go and look at this army?" "I will," said the maiden.

And she came to the Countess, and told her what Owain had said. And the Countess laughed. "Truly," said she, "I will even give him a horse and arms for ever; such a horse and such arms had he never yet, and I am glad that they should be taken by him to-day, lest my enemies should have them against my will to-morrow. Yet I know not what he would do with them."

The Countess bade them bring out a beautiful black steed[24a], upon which was a beechen saddle, and a suit of armour, for man and horse. And Owain armed himself, and mounted the horse, and went forth, attended by two pages completely equipped, with horses and arms. And when they came near to the Earl's army, they could see neither its extent nor its extremity. And Owain asked the pages in which troop the Earl was. "In yonder troop," said they, "in which are four yellow standards. Two of them are before, and two behind him." "Now," said Owain, "do you return and await me near the portal of the Castle." So they returned, and Owain pressed forward until he met the Earl. And Owain drew him completely out of his saddle, and turned his horse's head towards the Castle, and though it was with difficulty, he brought the Earl to the portal, where the pages awaited him. And in they came. And Owain presented the Earl as a gift to the Countess. And said to her, "Behold a requital to thee for thy blessed balsam."

The army encamped around the Castle. And the Earl restored to the Countess the two Earldoms he had taken from her, as a ransom for his life; and for his freedom he gave her the half of his own dominions, and all his gold, and his silver, and his jewels, besides hostages.

And Owain took his departure. And the Countess and all her subjects besought him to remain, but Owain chose rather to wander through distant lands and deserts.

And as he journeyed, he heard a loud yelling in a wood. And it was repeated a second and a third time. And Owain went towards the spot, and beheld a huge craggy mound, in the middle of the wood; on the side of which was a grey rock. And there was a cleft in the rock, and a serpent was within the cleft. And near the rock stood a black lion, and every time the lion sought to go thence, the serpent darted towards him to attack him. And Owain unsheathed his sword, and drew near to the rock; and as the serpent sprang out, he struck him with his sword, and cut him in two. And he dried his sword, and went on his way, as before[25a]. But behold the lion followed him, and played about him, as though it had been a greyhound that he had reared.

They proceeded thus throughout the day, until the evening. And when it was time for Owain to take his rest, he dismounted, and turned his horse loose in a flat and wooded meadow. And he struck fire, and when the fire was kindled, the lion brought him fuel enough to last for three nights. And the lion disappeared. And presently the lion returned, bearing a fine large roebuck. And he threw it down before Owain, who went towards the fire with it.

And Owain took the roebuck, and skinned it, and placed collops of its flesh upon skewers, around the fire. The rest of the buck he gave to the lion to devour. While he was doing this, he heard a deep sigh near him, and a second, and a third. And Owain called out to know whether the sigh he heard proceeded from a mortal; and he received answer that it did. "Who art thou?" said Owain. "Truly," said the voice, "I am Luned, the handmaiden of the Countess of the Fountain." "And what dost thou here?" said Owain. "I am imprisoned," said she, "on account of the knight who came from Arthur's Court, and married the Countess. And he stayed a short time with her, but he afterwards departed for the Court of Arthur, and has not returned since. And he was the friend I loved best in the world. And two of the pages in the Countess's chamber traduced him, and called him a deceiver. And I told them that they two were not a match for him alone. So they imprisoned me in the stone vault[25b], and said that I should be put to death, unless he came himself to deliver me, by a certain day; and that is no further off than the day after to-morrow. And I have no one to send to seek him for me. And his name is Owain the son of Urien." "And art thou certain that if that knight knew all this, he would come to thy rescue?" "I am most certain of it," said she.

When the collops were cooked, Owain divided them into two parts, between himself and the maiden; and after they had eaten, they talked together, until the day dawned. And the next morning Owain inquired of the damsel, if there was any place where he could get food and entertainment for that night. "There is,

Lord," said she; "cross over yonder, and go along the side of the river, and in a short time thou wilt see a great Castle, in which are many towers, and the Earl who owns that Castle is the most hospitable man in the world. There thou mayst spend the night."

Never did sentinel keep stricter watch over his lord, than the lion that night over Owain.

And Owain accoutred his horse, and passed across by the ford, and came in sight of the Castle. And he entered it, and was honourably received. And his horse was well cared for, and plenty of fodder was placed before him. Then the lion went and lay down in the horse's manger; so that none of the people of the Castle dared to approach him. The treatment which Owain met with there was such as he had never known elsewhere, for every one was as sorrowful as though death had been upon him. And they went to meat; and the Earl sat upon one side of Owain, and on the other side his only daughter. And Owain had never seen any more lovely than she. Then the lion came and placed himself between Owain's feet, and he fed him with every kind of food that he took himself. And he never saw anything equal to the sadness of the people.

In the middle of the repast the Earl began to bid Owain welcome. "Then," said Owain, "behold, it is time for thee to be cheerful." "Heaven knows," said the Earl, "that it is not thy coming that makes us sorrowful, but we have cause enough for sadness and care." "What is that?" said Owain. "I have two sons," replied the Earl, "and yesterday they went to the mountains to hunt. Now there is on the mountain a monster[27a] who kills men and devours them, and he seized my sons; and to-morrow is the time he has fixed to be here, and he threatens that he will then slay my sons before my eyes, unless I will deliver into his hands this my daughter. He has the form of a man, but in stature he is no less than a giant."

"Truly," said Owain, "that is lamentable. And which wilt thou do?" "Heaven knows," said the Earl, "it will be better that my sons should be slain against my will, than that I should voluntarily give up my daughter to him to ill-treat and destroy." Then they talked about other things, and Owain stayed there that night.

The next morning they heard an exceeding great clamour, which was caused by the coming of the giant with the two youths. And the Earl was anxious both to protect his Castle and to release his two sons. Then Owain put on his armour and went forth to encounter the giant, and the lion followed him. And when the giant saw that Owain was armed, he rushed towards him and attacked him. And the lion fought with the giant much more fiercely than Owain did. "Truly," said the giant, "I should find no difficulty in fighting with thee, were it not for the animal that is with thee." Upon that Owain took the lion back to the Castle and shut the gate upon him, and then he returned to fight the giant, as before. And the lion roared very loud, for he heard that it went hard with Owain. And he climbed up till he reached the top of the Earl's hall, and thence he got to the top of the Castle, and he sprang down from the walls and went and joined

Owain. And the lion gave the giant a stroke with his paw, which tore him from his shoulder to his hip, and his heart was laid bare, and the giant fell down dead. Then Owain restored the two youths to their father.

The Earl besought Owain to remain with him, and he would not, but set forward towards the meadow where Luned was. And when he came there he saw a great fire kindled, and two youths with beautiful curling auburn hair were leading the maiden to cast her into the fire. And Owain asked them what charge they had against her. And they told him of the compact that was between them, as the maiden had done the night before. "And," said they, "Owain has failed her, therefore we are taking her to be burnt." "Truly," said Owain, "he is a good knight, and if he knew that the maiden was in such peril, I marvel that he came not to her rescue; but if you will accept me in his stead, I will do battle with you." "We will," said the youths, "by him who made us."

And they attacked Owain, and he was hard beset by them. And with that the lion came to Owain's assistance, and they two got the better of the young men. And they said to him, "Chieftain, it was not agreed that we should fight save with thyself alone, and it is harder for us to contend with yonder animal than with thee." And Owain put the lion in the place where the maiden had been imprisoned, and blocked up the door with stones, and he went to fight with the young men, as before. But Owain had not his usual strength, and the two youths pressed hard upon him. And the lion roared incessantly at seeing Owain in trouble; and he burst through the wall until he found a way out, and rushed upon the young men, and instantly slew them. So Luned was saved from being burned.

Then Owain returned with Luned to the dominions of the Countess of the Fountain. And when he went thence he took the Countess with him to Arthur's Court, and she was his wife as long as she lived.

And then he took the road that led to the Court of the savage black man, and Owain fought with him, and the lion did not quit Owain until he had vanquished him. And when he reached the Court of the savage black man he entered the hall, and beheld four-and-twenty ladies, the fairest that could be seen. And the garments which they had on were not worth four-and twenty pence, and they were as sorrowful as death. And Owain asked them the cause of their sadness. And they said, "We are the daughters of Earls, and we all came here with our husbands, whom we dearly loved. And we were received with honour and rejoicing. And we were thrown into a state of stupor[29a], and while we were thus, the demon who owns this Castle slew all our husbands, and took from us our horses, and our raiment, and our gold, and our silver; and the corpses of our husbands are still in this house, and many others with them. And this, Chieftain, is the cause of our grief, and we are sorry that thou art come hither, lest harm should befall thee."

And Owain was grieved when he heard this. And he went forth from the Castle, and he beheld a knight approaching him, who saluted him in a friendly and cheerful manner, as if he had been a brother. And this was the savage black man. "In very sooth," said Owain, "it is not to seek thy friendship that I am here." "In sooth," said he, "thou shalt not find it then." And with that they charged each other, and fought furiously. And Owain overcame him, and bound his hands behind his back. Then the black savage besought Owain to spare his life, and spoke thus: "My lord Owain," said he, "it was foretold that thou shouldst come hither and vanquish me, and thou hast done so. I was a robber here, and my house was a house of spoil; but grant me my life, and I will become the keeper of an Hospice[29b], and I will maintain this house as an Hospice for weak and for strong, as long as I live, for the good of thy soul." And Owain accepted this proposal of him, and remained there that night.

And the next day he took the four-and-twenty ladies, and their horses, and their raiment, and what they possessed of goods and jewels, and proceeded with them to Arthur's Court. And if Arthur was rejoiced when he saw him, after he had lost him the first time, his joy was now much greater. And of those ladies, such as wished to remain in Arthur's Court remained there, and such as wished to depart departed.

And thenceforward Owain dwelt at Arthur's Court greatly beloved, as the head of his household, until he went away with his followers; and those were the army of three hundred ravens[30a] which Kenverchyn had left him. And wherever Owain went with these he was victorious.

And this is the tale of the Lady of the Fountain.

NOTES TO
THE LADY OF THE FOUNTAIN

3a —ARTHUR

AMONG the various characters introduced into the foregoing tale, none is more strictly and successfully maintained than that of Arthur. In him we see the dignified and noble-hearted sovereign, the stately warrior, and the accomplished knight, courteous of demeanour and dauntless in arms. And whilst the lofty bearing of the monarch himself excites our admiration, we are scarcely less struck with the devoted attachment evinced towards him by his knights, who are ever solicitous that he should be the last to encounter danger, and ever ready themselves to dare the most perilous adventures to uphold the dignity of his crown. But it is not merely the consistency observed in these several characters that arrests our attention in this and similar compositions professing to record the achievements of Arthur and his knights; we are also forcibly struck with the powerful influence which those legends exercised over society, and the ascendancy which their principal hero so decidedly maintained. Nor can we withhold our wonder at the singular destiny which has awaited this extraordinary being. Whilst by some his very existence has been called in question, his name has become celebrated throughout the civilised world; and his exploits, whether fabulous or real, have afforded the most ample and interesting materials to the poet, the antiquary, and the historian. To this very day the memory of the mighty warrior, "whose sword extended from Scandinavia to Spain," exercises a power over our imagination which we are as unable as we are unwilling to dispel. His image adorned our earliest visions of Chivalry and Romance, and though the weightier cares of maturer age must supervene, they serve but to deepen, not to efface the impression; and while in the eddying stream of life we pause to look back upon the days when Caerlleon and its Round Table formed to us an ideal world, we feel that, in our hearts at least, "King Arthur is not dead."

The real history of this chieftain is so veiled in obscurity, and has led to so much unsatisfactory discussion, that I shall in this place only consider him with reference to the position which he occupies in the regions of Fiction.

Amongst the many incidents of a highly imaginative character, in the legendary history of Arthur, we may more particularly notice his introduction upon the scene of his exploits.

During the turbulent times which followed the death of Uther Pendragon, the nobles of Britain assembled to elect a successor to him, but, after protracted debate, they were unable to come to any decision upon the subject. At length a large stone was discovered near the place of assembly, in which was a sword fastened as it were in a sheath. Around it was an inscription in gold letters, signifying that whoever should draw out that sword was rightful heir to the throne. After all those who were ambitious of this dignity had made the attempt in vain, Arthur, who was previously unknown, came forward, and drew out the sword from the stone as easily as he would have drawn it out of the scabbard. He was thereupon immediately acknowledged king.

Being thus placed at the head of the Chivalry of Britain, he proceeded in a glorious and triumphant career, until, by the treachery of his nephew, Modred, he sustained a defeat in the battle of Camlan.

After witnessing the destruction of his army in that fatal conflict, Arthur, finding himself mortally wounded, delivered his sword to Caliburn one of his knights, with a request that he would cast it into a certain lake. The knight, thus commissioned, proceeded to the appointed spot, and, standing upon the bank, flung the sword forward with all his might. As it was descending, a hand and arm came out of the lake, and seizing it by the hilt brandished it three times, and disappeared with it in the water.

Arthur was afterwards conducted by the Knight to the border of the lake, where he found a little bark moored, in which were Viviane, the Lady of the Lake, and Morgan le Fay, and other ladies, who carried him off to the Island of Avalon, in Fairy-laud, where it was affirmed that he was healed of his wounds, and continued to live in all the splendour of that luxurious country, waiting for the time when he should return once more to take possession of his ancient dominions.

In confirmation of this idea it was asserted that the place of his sepulture was not known. This tradition was current for many ages, and is found among the Welsh, in the Memorials of the Graves of the Warriors,—

> "The grave of March is this, and this the grave of Gwythyr.
> Here is the grave of Gwgawn Gleddyfrudd
> But unknown is the grave of Arthur."[1]

Our English ears are so familiarized with the name of *King* Arthur, that it seems impossible to give him the appellation of Emperor, by which he is designated in the original Welsh, and to which, according to the old Romances, he was fully entitled, since once upon a time, "at crystemas," he was crowned "Emperour with creme as it bylongeth to so hyhe astate."—Morte d'Arthur.

We find the title of Emperor bestowed upon Arthur in Llywarch Hên's Elegy upon Geraint ab Erbin.

---

1 March ap Meirchion, Gwythyr ap Greidiol, and Gwgawn Gleddyfrudd, were three of Arthur's Knights; the second of them was father to Queen Gwenhwyvar.

"At Llongborth were slain to Arthur
Valiant men, who hewed down with steel;
He was the emperor, and conductor of the toil of war."

Owen's Heroic Elegies.

3b — CAERLLEON UPON USK

THIS place derives its name from the circumstance of its being the station of the Second Legion (Legio Secunda Augusta) during the dominion of the Romans. The name by which they originally called it was Isca Silurum, evidently from its situation upon the river Usk; but by later Latin writers it is named Urbs Legionum, which probably is a translation of the Welsh Caer-lleon, and not the original of that appellation.

This place still exhibits many traces of Roman magnificence, and among others the remains of an amphitheatre. It is natural to suppose that, upon the departure of the Legions, Caerlleon would attract the attention of the native Sovereigns, who were at that time beginning to resume their power; accordingly, tradition informs us that it was the principal residence of King Arthur; and the amphitheatre is still called Arthur's Round Table. In confirmation of this traditionary evidence, Nennius asserts that one of Arthur's battles was fought at *Cairlion.*

In the old English version of this tale the opening scene is laid at Cardiff.

"He made a feste, the soth to say,
Opon the Witsononday,
At Kerdyf, that es in Wales."—line 17.

And on a subsequent occasion we find the City of Chester named—

"The kyng that time at Cester lay."—line 1567.

In the French Copy,-

"Q' li rois cort a cestre tint."

Of CHESTER it may be remarked, that it bears in Welsh the name of *Caerlleon Gawr,* which seems to indicate its having been the station of the Twentieth Legion, called *Legio Vicesima Valens Victrix,* the word *Gawr* being nearly equivalent to the Latin *Valens.*

3c — OWAIN THE SON OF URIEN

OWAIN AB URIEN RHEGED.—AMONGST all the characters of ancient British history, none is more interesting, or occupies a more conspicuous place, than the hero of this tale. Urien, his father, was prince of Rheged, a district comprising the present Cumberland and part of the adjacent country. His valour and the consideration in which he was held, are a frequent theme of Bardic song, and form the subject of several very spirited odes by Taliesin, particularly those upon the battles of Gwenystrad and Argoed Llwyfein, which are given, with English translations, in the Myvyrian Archaiology, i. 52, 3, 4. The name of Fflamddwyn, the flame-bearer, which occurs in these poems, is supposed to be that by which the Welsh designated Ida, the Anglian King of Northumberland. In the Appendix to Gale's Nennius, it is mentioned that Urien was one of the four Northern princes who opposed the progress of Deodric the Son of Ida. Urien besieged the latter in the island of Lindisfarne. The other princes were Rhydderch Hael, Gwallawc ap Llenawc, and Morcant,[1] the latter of whom being jealous of Urien's military skill, in which he is said to have excelled all the other kings, procured his assassination during the expedition.

According to Llywarch Hen's Elegy upon Urien Rheged, this event occurred in a place called Aberlleu.[2]

The Triads mention Llovan Llawdivo as the assassin. Of him little is known; but that he was a person of some note is evident from the circumstance of his grave being recorded.

> "The grave of Llovan Llawdivo
> is on the strand of Menai, where makes the wave a sullen sound."[3]

"The Genealogy of the Saints records that Urien came into South Wales, and Was instrumental with the sons of Ceredig ab Cunedda, and his nephews, in expelling the Gwyddelians, who had gained a footing there from about the time of Maxen Wledig."—Camb. Biog.

The old Romancers connect him with South Wales, and call him King Uryens of Gore, evidently intended for Gower in Glamorganshire.

---

1 In the Life of St. Kentigern, mention is made of a wicked king of Strathclyde, called Morken. Perhaps he is the Morcant, who caused the death of Urien Rheged.Probably it is through a confusion of names, by no means unusual in those days, that Urien's wife, Morgan le Fay, is by the old romancers accused of an attempt to assassinate him.

2 Myv. Arch. i. 105.

3 Myv. Arch. i. 78.

Thus it is recorded in the Morte d'Arthur, "Thenne the Kyng remeued in to Walys, and lete crye a grete feste that it shold be holdyn at Pentecost after the incoronacion of hym at the Cyte of Carlyon, vnto the feste come kyng Lott of Lowthean, and of Orkeney with fiue C knygtes with hym. Also there come to the feste kynge Uryens of gore with four C knyghtes with hym."

But to return to Owain; it appears from the manner in which he is always mentioned by contemporary Bards, that he greatly distinguished himself in his country's cause, subsequently to the death of his father, but with what ultimate success we are not acquainted.

There exists an ancient Poem, printed among those of Taliesin, called the Elegy of Owain ap Urien, and containing several very beautiful and spirited passages. It commences,

> The soul of Owain ap Urien
> May its Lord consider its exigencies,—
> Reged's chief the green turf covers."

In the course of this Elegy, the Bard bursts forth with all the energy of the Awen,

> "Could Lloegria sleep with the light upon her eyes?" [1]

Alluding to the incessant warfare with which this chieftain, during his lifetime, had harassed his Saxon foes.

In the Myvyrian Archaiology (II. 80) we have the following Triad relating to him.

"Three Knights of battle were in the Court of Arthur; Cadwr, the Earl of Cornwall; Lancelot du Lac;[2] and Owain the son of Urien Rheged. And this was their characteristic, that they would not retreat from battle, neither for Spear, nor for Arrow, nor for Sword, and Arthur never had shame in battle, the day he

---

1 This line, with the substitution of Cambria for Lloegria [England], was taken as the subject of a speech to rouse the Welsh to the due consideration of their literature, by the Rev. Thomas Price of Crickhowel, at the Meeting of the Cymreigyddion Society of Abergavenny, in the Autumn of 1835. The effect it produced was quite electric.

2 Lancelot du Lac is generally considered as an exception to the general rule, that all the heroes of the Arthurian Romances are of Welsh origin. But it has been suggested to me by a learned Antiquary, that this distinction does not really exist, the name of Lancelot being nothing more than a translation of Paladr-ddellt (splintered spear), which was the name of a knight of Arthur's Court, celebrated in the Triads.

saw their faces there, and they were called the Knights of Battle."

Owain is also mentioned with Rhun mab Maelgwn, and Rhufawn befr mab Deorath Wledig, as one of the Three blessed Kings;[1] and in the 52nd Triad, we are informed that his Mother's name was Modron, the daughter of Afallach, and that he was born a twin with his sister Merwydd, or Morvyth, to whom Cynon ap Clydno's attachment is well known.

His place of sepulture is thus mentioned in the Graves of the Warriors.

> "The grave of Owain ap Urien is of quadrangular form,
> Under the turf of Llan Morvael."

Frequent allusions are made to Owain by the Bards of the Middle Ages, especially by Lewis Glyn Cothi, who in an ode to Gruffudd ap Nicholas, a powerful chieftain of Carmarthenshire, and one of the descendants of Urien Rheged, has, among other things, the following passage:

> "Gruffudd will give three ravens of one hue,
> And a white lion to Owain, [his son]."—I. 133.

The Editor of the works of Glyn Cothi supposes that "this expression may allude to Griffith presenting his son with a shield, with his own arms emblazoned upon it, and the royal lion for a crest," The three ravens undoubtedly apply to the armorial bearings of Urien Rheged, which are still borne by his descendants of the House of Dynevor; the lion also may have been an heraldic bearing of the family, but I am inclined to think that the Bard here intended an allusion to one of the principal incidents of the Lady of the Fountain. That he was acquainted with this Tale is evident, from some lines occurring in one of his Poems, addressed to Thomas ap Philip of Picton Castle, in which Owain and Luned are mentioned together.

In the early French compositions, called Lays and Fabliaux, Owain's name frequently occurs. He is mentioned in the Lay of Lanfal, and in Court Mantel, where he is particularized for his love of dogs and hawks.

> "Li rois prit par la destre main
> L'amiz monsegnor Ivain,
> Qui au roi Urien fu filz,

---

1 The arrangement of ancient pedigrees is at all times attended with difficulty, but vain indeed would be the attempt to reconcile the genealogies of Romance with those of history. In Morte d'Arthur, Owain's Mother is Morgan le Fay, sister to King Arthur.

Et bons chevaliers et hardiz
Qui tant ama chiens et oisiaux."

(Fab. MSS. du roi, n. 7615, fol. 114 recto, col. 3.)

He acts a conspicuous part in the Romances of the Round Table; and it is on such authority that Ste. Palaye celebrates him, "pour avoir introduit l'usage des fourrures ou zibelines aux manteaux, des ceintures aux robes, et des boucles pour attacher les éperons et Den, et pour avoir encore inventé la mode des gants."

3 d —KYNON THE SON OF CLYDNO

CYNON AP CLYDNO EIDDIN.—This ancient British Warrior is celebrated in the Triads as one of the Three wisely-counselling Knights of Arthur's Court.

'Three counselling Knights were in the Court of Arthur, which were Cynon the son of Clydno Eiddin, Aron the son of Kynfarch ap Meirchion gul, and Llywarch hen the son of Elidir Lydanwyn. And these three knights were the Counsellors of Arthur, and whatever dangers threatened him in any of his wars, they counselled him, so that none was able to overcome Arthur; and thus he conquered all the nations through three things which followed him; and these were, Good hope, and the consecrated arms which had been sent him, and the virtue of his warriors; and through these he came to wear twelve crowns upon his head, and he became Emperor of Rome."

And in another place it is added,

"And he had nothing but success when he acted by the advice which he received from them, and reverses when he did not follow their counsel."

Kynon is also called one of the three ardent Lovers, on account of his passion for Morvyth, daughter of Urien Rheged, and sister of Owain, the Hero of this Tale.

"The three ardent lovers of the Island of Britain, Caswallawn the son of Beli for Flur the daughter of Mugnach Gorr, and Trystan the son of Talluch for Yseult the wife of March Meirchawn his uncle, and Kynon the son of Clydno Eiddin for Morvyth the daughter of Urien."

This warrior is mentioned by Aneurin,

"And Kynon——like rushes they fell before his hand.———
O son of Clydno, a song of lasting praise will I sing unto thee."

And it is probable that he was one of the three, who, together with the Bard himself, escaped from the disastrous battle of Cattraeth.

The Warriors who went to Cattraeth were renowned;
Wine and Mead out of golden goblets was their beverage.
That year was to them. one of exalted dignity,
Three warriors and three score and three hundred, wearing the golden
    torques— —
Of those who marched forth after the excess of revelling,
But three escaped from the conflict of gashing weapons;
The two War-dogs of Aeron and *Kynon* the dauntless,
(And I myself from the spilling of blood) worthy are they of my song."

Gray has given a poetical version of this passage in his fragments, commencing with the words, "To Cattraeth's vale in glittering row."

Also, in another poem by Aneurin, named the Gwarchan (or Incantation) of Cynvelyn, are the following lines:

"Three Warriors and three score and three hundred,
To the conflict of Cattraeth went forth.
Of those who hastened from the banquet of mead,
Three only returned,
Kynon, and Kadreith, and Katlew of Catnant,
And I myself from the shedding of blood."

Kynon is frequently mentioned by the bards of the Middle Ages, and celebrated both for his bravery and for his devotion as a lover.

It is in the latter character that be is alluded to by Gruffudd ap Meredith, in the beginning of the fourteenth Century, who compares the force of his own passion to that of Kynon for Morvyth, and that of Uther Pendragon for the fair Ygrayne.

"As the sigh of Uther for the love of Ygraine, the fair and splendid,
And the sigh of Kynon for the love of the beauteous daughter of Urien,
Such is the sigh of the bard for the lovely object of his affections.

                                      Myv. Arch.

In the Memorials of the Graves of the Warriors, the following stanza records the place of the sepulture of Kynon.

"The grave of a warrior of high renown
Is in a lofty region—but a lowly bed,
The grave of Kynon the son of Clydno Eiddin."

In another stanza, the term *lowly bed* seems to be explained, and it would appear that a little hollow among the mountains was meant:

Whose is the grave beneath the hill?
It is the grave of a warrior valiant in the conflict
The grave of Kyrion the son of Clydno Eiddin."

3e — CLYDNO

CLYDNO EIDDIN, the father of Cynon.—But little is known of the history of this Chieftain, although as late as the fourteenth Century, his name is found recorded by the Bards, in such terms as to make it evident that he still continued to occupy a place of considerable distinction among the heroes of the Principality, as may be seen in a poem by Risierdyn, a bard who flourished about the year 1300. In this poem, which records the burial of Hywel ap Gruffudd in the Church of St. Benno, that Warrior is compared in point of bravery, to Clydno.

"The red-weaponed chief, the ruler of the golden region of costly wine,
Saint Beuno's blessed choir now conceals;
The mighty high-famed leader, daring as *Clydno*.
Silent are his remains within their oaken cell."

Myv. Arch. I. 432.

3f — KAI THE SON OF KYNER

CAI AP CYNYR.—According to the Welsh pedigrees, Kai was the son of Cynyr Cainvarvawc, the son of Gwron, the son of Cunedda Wledig. In the Triads he is called one of the three diadem'd chiefs of battle, and is said to have been possessed of magical powers, by which he could transform himself into any shape he pleased.[1] Of his real history, however, nothing is known. It is supposed that Caer Gai, in North Wales, bear his name; and it was the opinion of Iolo Morganwg, that the place of his sepulture was at Cai Hir, at Aberavan, in Glamorganshire.

In the Brut he is called the *Dapifer*, or Sewer of King Arthur. And in the French Romances he is mentioned as the Seneschal, and is styled *Messire Queux*, and *Maitre Queux*, or *Keux*—the original name being evidently altered in this manner in order to adapt it to his office of Chief of the Cooks. In these productions, his general character is a compound of valour and buffoonery:

---

1 Kai's horse, according to the Welsh authorities, was called *Gwineu gwddwf hir*, the *long-necked bay*.

always ready to fight, and generally getting the worst of the battle.

There is much that is very entertaining concerning him in the Morte d'Arthur, particularly a story of his want of courtesy to Sir Gareth, Gwalchmai's (Gawain's) brother, which led him into trouble.

"Whan Arthur held his round table moost plenour, it fortuned that he commaunded that the hyhe feest of Pentecost shold be holden at a cyte and a Castel the whiche in tho dayes was called kynke kenadonne upon the sondes that marched nyghe walys." Upon this occasion, a youth who would not declare his name, presented himself before Arthur, and craved a boon, which the monarch immediately promised to grant. The boon he asked was, that he should be allowed meat and drink for the space of a twelvemonth in the King's palace. This the King considered a very unworthy petition, and counselled him to ask something more honourable, but the youth still persisted in his request. "Well sayde the kynge ye shal haue mete and drynke ynouz, I neuer deffended yt none, nother my frende ne my foo." "Thenne the kyng betook hym to sir Kay the steward and charged hym that he shold gyue hym of al manner of metes and drynkes of the best, and also that he hadde al maner of fyndynge as though he were a lordes sone. That shal lytel nede sayd syr Kay to doo suche cost upon hym. For I dare undertake he is a vylayne borne, and neuer will make man, for and he had come of gentylmen he wold haue axed of you hors and armour, but such as he is so he asketh. And sythen he hath no name, I shall yeue hym a name that shall be Beaumayns that is fayre handes, and in to the kechen I shalle brynge hym, and there he shalle haue fatte broweys euery day yt he shall be as fatte by the twelue monethes ende as a porke hog." So Sir Kai "scorned hym and mocked hym."

At the end of the twelvemonth, Beaumayns desired to be knighted, in order to achieve a certain perilous adventure;[1] and Sir Kai called him a "kechyn knave." And when the young man left the Court, to set out on his expedition, Kai armed himself and followed him, thinking to vanquish him without difficulty, and bring him to disgrace. But Beaumayns unhorsed Sir Kai, and took possession of his arms, with which he performed several gallant exploits to the great surprise of all, inasmuch as he was taken by his shield to be Sir Kai, whose prowess was by no means in high repute. Afterwards Beaumayns proved to be Sir Gareth of Orkney, the son of King Lot, and brother of Sir Gawain.

---

1 It is somewhat singular that this adventure was undertaken on behalf of Luned, who, under the title of the damoysel saueage, rode to Arthur's Court, to beseech the championship of some of the Knights of the Table rounde, for her' sister dame Lyones, of the Castel peryllous. The story is again referred to in a subsequent Note.

3g — GWENHWYVAR

ACCORDING to the Welsh Legends, Arthur had three queens, one of whom was daughter of Gwythyr ap Greidiol, another of Gwryd Gwent, and a third of Gogyrvan Gawr; and each of them bore the name of Gwenhwyvar. Concerning the latter lady,[1] the following couplet is still current in the Principality:—

"Gwenhwyvar, the daughter of Gogyrvan the Giant,
Bad when little, worse when great."

This confusion of names and persons is only what might be expected from the mass of traditionary matter that has accumulated among the Welsh. As the exploits of Arthur began to assume a fabulous character, it is evident that many of the more ancient legends of Britain became blended with those of the Round Table, and perhaps some of the mythological traditions of the Druidic age are to be found amongst them. This continual accession of fable tends to render still more obscure that which a redundancy of imagination had already sufficiently involved. The name of Gwenhwyvar, under the various forms of *Guenever*, *Genievre*, and *Geneura*, must be familiar to all who are conversant with chivalric lore. And it is to her adventures, and those of her true knight, Sir Lancelot, that Dante alludes in the beautiful episode of Francesca da Rimini.

3h — PORTER

THE absence of a Porter was formerly considered as an indication of hospitality, and as such is alluded to by Rhys Brychan, a bard who flourished at the close of the fifteenth century.

"The stately entrance is without porters,
And his mansions are open to every honest man."

Lewis Glyn Cothi also (about 1450), in an eulogium upon Owain, the son of Gruffudd ap Nicholas, says, that his establishment was complete in every respect, with the exception of a Porter:—

"Every officer there is to the great Knight
Of the South, except a Porter."—I. 139.

---

1 According to the Romances, Arthur's Queen was daughter of King Leodegrance.

3i — GLEWLWYD GAVAELVAWR

"THE dusky hero of the mighty grasp" is said to have escaped from the battle of Camdan by means of his extraordinary strength and stature. There is nothing of his real history known: indeed, from the construction of his name, he appears to be altogether a fictitious character; and it is not impossible that he may be one of those mythological personages who formed the subjects of the Welsh legendary tales, before the adventures of Arthur had assumed the character of fiction, and that when those adventures became objects of fabulous composition, this and other ancient Druidical traditions were incorporated with them.

Among the Bardic remains there is a poem, called a Dialogue betwixt Arthur and Kai, and Glewlwyd, some lines in which are considered by Davies to have reference to some Druidical mysteries. Although it may appear presumptuous to differ from so high an authority, I shall venture to give the following translation-

"Who is the Porter?
Glewlwyd Gavaelvawr.
Who is it that asks?
Arthur and the blessed Kai.
If thou shouldst bring with thee
The best wine in the world,
Into my house thou shalt not come,
Unless it be by force, &c."

3j — ON A SEAT OF GREEN RUSHES

THE use of green rushes in apartments was by no means peculiar to the Court of Caerleon upon Usk. Our ancestors had a great predilection for them, and they seem to have constituted an essential article, not only of comfort but of luxury. The custom of strewing the floor with rushes is well known to have existed in England during the Middle Ages, and that it also prevailed in the Principality we have evidence from allusions which occur in the works of native writers. Of this, one example will suffice, from a tale written apparently in the 14th Century; and as the passage contains several curious traits of ancient manners, I shall give it at some length.

In this tale Davydd ap Owain Gwynedd, Prince of North Wales, wishing to send an embassy to Rhys, Prince of South Wales, and having fixed upon Gwgan the Bard as a proper person for that mission, despatches a messenger called *y Paun Bach* (the Little Peacock) in search of him. This person, after a long and tedious journey, arrives towards the close of evening at a house in a wooded valley, where he hears the tuning of a harp. From the style of playing, and the modulation, he supposes that the performer can be no other than Gwgan himself. In order to ascertain if his surmise is correct, be addresses him in a rambling high-flown style of language. The Bard answers him in the same strain, and asks him what he requires. To which Y Paun Bach thus replies:— "I want lodging for to-night . . . And that not better than I know how to ask for . . . A lightsome hall, floored with tile, and swept, in which there has been neither flood nor rain-drop for the last hundred years, dressed with *fresh green rushes*, laid so evenly that one rush be not higher than the other the height of a gnat's eye, so that my foot should not slip either backward or forward the space of a mote in the sunshine of June. Then I would have a chair with a cushion beneath me, and a pillow under each elbow,"[1] &c. Y Paun Bach then goes on to describe the entertainment he desires to have. The fire is to be of ashen billets, without smoke or sparks; and the supper is to consist of wine, and swans,[2] and bitterns, and sundry spiced collops besides; and the servants, all dressed in one livery,[3] are to ply him continually with ale, and urge him to drink, for his own

---

1 We trace the customs of a country in what may appear accidental expressions. Thus a cushion in a chair was one of the requisites of a Welsh establishment. Three things proper for a man to have in his house,—

> A virtuous wife,
> His cushion in his chair,
> And his harp in tune.

In like manner it is particularly mentioned in the present tale, that Arthur had "a cushion of red satin under his elbow"; and that at the Castle where Kynon was received, on his way to the adventure of the Fountain, the maidens, in doing him honour, " placed cushions both beneath and around him," when he sat down to meat. In this latter instance, the cushions we find were covered with red linen.

2 Swans appear to have been a great dainty in those days. Of the luxurious Monk in the Pilgrimage to Canterbury, Chaucer tells us, "A fat swan loved he best of any rost."—line 206.

3 Uniformity of dress in those who held the same office, appears to be dwelt upon with much satisfaction by the writers of the Middle Ages. In Geoffrey of Monmouth, the thousand young noblemen, who, at Arthur's Coronation Banquet, assisted Kai in serving up the dishes, were clothed like him in robes of Ermine. The same writer proceeds to tell us, that "at that Time Britain was arrived to such a pitch of Grandeur, that whether we respect its Affluence of Riches, Luxury of Ornaments, or Politeness of Inhabitants, it far surpassed all other Kingdoms." And he adds, "The Knights in it that were famous for Feats

good and the honour of his entertainers.

In France, the practice of strewing rushes on the floor was also prevalent. We find the Seigneur Amanieu des Escas giving his instructions to the young men of his household on the Art of Love, "dans sa salle bien jonchée."—Poésies Provençales, cited by Ste. Palaye, I. 453.

3k — FLAME-COLOURED SATIN

THE literal translation of this expression is yellow-red. With regard to this mixture of colours, Ellis, in his notes to Way's Fabliaux, remarks, "The old French writers speak also of *pourpre* and *écarlate blanches* (*white crimson*); of *pourpre sanguine* (*sanguine crimson*); and, in the Fabliau de Gautier d'Aupais, mention is made of "*un vert mantel porprin*, (*a mantel of green crimson*)." Hence, M. Le Grand conjectures, "that the crimson dye being, from its costliness, used only on cloths of the finest manufacture, the term crimson came at length to signify, not the *colour*, but the *texture*, of the stuff. Were it allowable to attribute to the Weavers of the Middle Ages the art now common amongst us, of making what are usually called *shot* silks (or silks of two colours, predominating interchangeably as in the neck of the drake or pigeon), the contradictory compounds above given (*white* crimson, *green* crimson, &c.) would be easily accounted for." II. 227.

4a — DISTANT REGIONS

LITERALLY, "desert places, and the extremities of the earth." It is possible that some peculiar district of romantic geography was intended to be here alluded to, since we find that "la terre deserte" was formerly a kingdom of no inconsiderable importance, the sovereign of which, named Claudas, overran the territories of King Ban of Benoic, one of Arthur's allies in Gaul. And in the Morte d'Arthur, it is said that Arthur, being wounded in the battle of Camlan, was conveyed to the Island of Avalon "in a shyppe wherin were thre quenes,

---

of Chivalry, wore their Clothes and Arms all of the same colour and Fashion. And the Women also no less celebrated for their Wit, wore all the same Kind of Apparel."—Thompson's Translation. In the Procession to Canterbury, Chaucer relates that

"An HABERDASHER, and A CARPENTER,
A WEBBE, a DYER, and a TAPISER,
Were alle yclothed in o livere,
Of a solemne and grete fraternite."—line 363.

that one was kyng Arthurs syster quene Morgan le fay, the other was the quene of North galys, the thyrd was the quene of the waste londes. Also there was Nynyue (Viviane) the chyef lady of the lake," &c.

4b — TREES OF EQUAL GROWTH

THIS species of scenery appears to have been much admired by our ancestors.

A similar description occurs in a chivalric tale of considerable interest, by Gruffydd ab Adda, a Bard who was killed at Dolgellau, about 1370.

"In the furthermost end of this forest he saw a level green valley, and trees of equal height, &c."

Chaucer describes a bower in the same style, in his Flour and Leaf. It was composed of "sicamour and eglatere,"

> Wrethen in fere so well and cunningly
> That every branch and leafe grew by mesure
> Plaine as a bord, of *an height by and by.*"

The whole account which he gives us of the "pleasaunt herber" is very poetical, particularly the following beautiful lines, descriptive of the avenues of "okes" which led to it.

> "In which were okes great, streight as a line,
> Under the which the grasse so fresh of hew
> Was newly sprong, and an eight foot or nine
> Every tree well fro his fellow grew,
> With branches brode, laden with leves new,
> That sprongen out agen the sunne-shene,
> Some very red, and some a glad light grene."

4c — YELLOW SATIN

PALI MELYN.—The exact signification of the word Pali in the original is not quite obvious, as it sometimes seems to imply satin and sometimes velvet, according to the rank of the persons who are represented as wearing it. Nor is the question so immaterial as at first sight it may appear; for, in the best days of Chivalry, the most exact etiquette was observed by the different grades of society with regard to the materials of which their dress was composed. Ste. Palaye mentions that, on occasions where the Knights wore cloth of damask, the Squires were restricted to dresses of satin; and where the Knights were clothed in velvet, the Squires could only appear in cloth of damask. The colour of scarlet was permitted to be worn only by Knights. (I. 247, 283.)

5a — SINEWS OF THE STAG

MOSELEY, in his work upon Archery, says that "bowstrings were composed from the sinews of beasts, and on that account are termed '*Nervus*,' νευρά."

"It was customary for this purpose," says he, "to select the sinews of several of those kinds of animals remarkable for their strength or activity, such as Bulls, Lions, Stags, &c., and from those particular parts of each animal in which their respective strength was conceived to lie. From Bulls, the sinews about the back and shoulders were collected; and from Stags, they took those of the legs."

5b — BONE OF THE WHALE

A SIMILAR substance is mentioned in the ancient Romance of "The Erle of Tolous,"—

"Hur hondys whyte as whallys bonne,"—verse 355.

Upon which Ritson has the following note:—"This allusion is not to what we now call *whale-bone*, which is well known to be *black*, but to the *ivory* of the horn or tooth of the *Narwhal*, or *Sea-unicorn*, which seems to have been mistaken for the *whale*. The similé is a remarkable favourite. Thus, in *Syr Eglamour of Artoys*,

"The erle had no chylde but one,
A mayden *as white as whalës bone*."

Again, in *Syr Isembras*,

'His wyfe *as white as whalës bone*.'

Again, in 'The Squyr of low degree,'

'Lady *as white as whalës bone*.'

It even occurs in Skelton's and Surrey's Poems; and, what is still more extraordinary, in Spenser's *Faëry Quene*, and Shakespeare's *Love's Labour Lost* (if, in fact, that part of it ever received the illuminating touch of our great dramatist). Mister Steevens, in his Note on the last instance, observes that *whales* 'is the Saxon genitive case,' meaning that it requires to be pronounced as a dissyllable (thus, *whalës*, or, more properly, *whaleës*), which it certainly is, in every instance."—Rit. Met. Rom. III. 343, 344.

5c — WINGED WITH PEACOCK'S FEATHERS

THAT it was fashionable to feather arrows in this manner, we learn from the following description of the Yeman who attended upon the Knight, in the Prologue to Chaucer's Canterbury Tales.

> "A shefe of peacock arwes bright and kene
> Under his belt he bare ful thriftily,
> Wel coude he dresse his takel yemanly:
> His arwes drouped not with fetheres low,
> And in his hond he bare a mighty bowe."—line 104-8.

In a Wardrobe account, 4th of Ed. II., the following entry occurs "Pro duodecim flecchiis cum pennis de pavone emptis pro rege, de 12 den'." For twelve arrows with peacock's feathers, bought for the King, twelvepence.

There was much art and care required in the construction and feathering of arrows. That the Welsh archers paid much attention to their equipments may be seen in an interesting passage from the composition already noticed. In this Tale the messenger from the Court of North Wales, who appears to be a skilful archer, on being told by Gwgan the Bard that a robber will ride away with his horse, answers, "But what if I were opposite to him in yonder Wood, with a bow of red yew in my hand, ready bent, with a tough tight string, and a straight round shaft with a compass-rounded neck, and long slender feathers fastened on with green silk, and a steel head heavy and thick, and an inch across, of a green blue temper, that would draw blood out of a weathercock; and with my foot to a hillock, and an oak behind me, and the wind to my back, and the sun to my side, and the maid I love best on the footpath hard by looking at me, and I conscious of her being there; then would I shoot him such a shot, so strong and long-drawn, so low and sharp, that it would be no more avail to him there were between him and me a breastplate and Milan hauberk, than a tuft of fern, or a kiln mat, or a herring net."

It is well known that bows and arrows formed a subject of legislation in England, and among the Welsh Laws we find the following clause—

"Three weapons by law:—A sword, a spear, and a bow with twelve arrows in a quiver. And it is required of every master of a family to keep them in readiness against the attacks of a foreign army, and of strangers, and other depredators."

5d — GOLDEN HEADS —BLADES OF GOLD

TO Knights and to their families was exclusively confined the privilege of decorating their dress, their arms, and the accoutrements of their horses with gold; Squires being only permitted the use of silver.—Ste. Palaye, I. 247, 283. By the sumptuary laws of Ed. III. (an. 27. c. ix. x. xi. xii.) Esquires were to possess property of at least 200 marks yearly value, before they could be permitted to wear "cloth of silk and of silver, ribband, girdle, and other apparel reasonably garnished with silver." And Knights, their wives, daughters, and children, were not entitled to wear "cloth of gold, nor cloths, mantle, nor gold furred with miniver, nor of ermins, nor no apparel bordered of stone, nor otherwise," if their possessions were below the yearly value of 251 marks. But to such Knights and Ladies as possessed 400 marks annually, there was no restriction as to dress, except with respect to "ermins and letuses and apparel of pearl and stone," which they might only wear upon the head. Merchants and burgesses of 500 marks had the same privilege of dress as Esquires of 200 markland. Hence perhaps it may be inferred that the two Youths mentioned in this Tale were of knightly origin.

That the gilding of bows was customary in the 14th Century, we have the authority of Davydd ap Gwilym. In lines addressed to his fair countrywomen against gaudiness of dress, and which have been thus elegantly rendered by Arthur Johnes, Esq., in his Poetical Translation of the Works of that celebrated Bard, he says:—

"The vilest bow that e'er was framed of Yew,
That in the hand abruptly snaps in two,
When all its faults are varnished o'er with gold,
Looks strong, and fair, and faultless, and—is sold."—(p. 412.)

Lewis Glyn Cothi has the following line,

"With gold shall be adorned thy fingers, thy sword, and thy mantle."

And examples might be multiplied to almost any extent.

Where arrow-heads, and the blades of weapons are mentioned as golden, it is very evident that in many instances steel inlaid with gold is meant. Thus, the Bard above alluded to says,—

"A gold Brigandine like the casting of a Dragon's skin."

And subsequently this gold Brigandine is said to be of steel,—

Good is the band of this steel vestment.—(I. 158.)

5e — VARIEGATED LEATHER

CORDWAL.—This word occurs in another of the Mabinogion; and from the manner that it is used, it is evidently intended for the French Cordouan, or Cordovan leather, which derived its name from Cordova, where it was manufactured.

5f — DAMSELS EMBROIDERING SATIN

IN the English Romance of "Ywayne and Gawain," paraphrased from the French "Chevalier an Lyon," we find a similar picture. In a beautiful city, named in English the "Castel of the Hevy Sorrow," and in the French the "Chastel de Pesme Auenture," the hero, Ywayne or Owen, finds a number of ladies, "wirkand silk and gold wir." They are very meanly attired, and inform Owen that they were once of great estate in the country of Mayden-land, whence they were sent as hostages by their sovereign. They complain that they have to work very hard, and for a very slight remuneration; the best of them receiving only "four penys" in a week, which was scarce sufficient to maintain them, whereas they consider that they might earn "fourty shilling."

5f — MORE LOVELY THAN GWENHWYVAR

THIS was the highest compliment that Kynon could pay to the beauty of these four-and-twenty damsels, since Gwenhwyvar is celebrated in the Triads (with Enid and Tegau Euron,) as one of the three fair ladies of Arthur's Court.

Lewis Glyn Cothi, in extolling the charms of Annes, the daughter of John, of Caerlleon upon Usk, has the following allusion to this Triad:—

The beauteous and amiable Annes is where Tegau was,
Where Gwenhwyvar was, with all her charms;
Where Enid was seen, wearing azure robes,
Where the Castle of the valorous Arthur stands."

5g — THEY ROSE UP AT MY COMING

IT was very usual in the chivalric days, for the ladies to perform those courteous offices for the Knights, even where there were male attendants, to whom we may consider that they would have been more appropriately assigned. Ste. Palaye tells its, "Les jeunes demoiselles . . . prévenoient de civilité les chevaliers qui arrivoient dans les châteaux; suivant nos romanciers, elles les désarmoient au retour des tournois et des expéditions de guerre, leur donnoient de nouveaux habits et les servoient à table. Les exemples en sont trop souvent et trop uniformément répétés, pour nous permettre de révoquer en doute la réalité de cet usage." (I. 10.) I should imagine, however, it was the absence of male assistance that induced the damsels in Kynon's story to extend their cares to his horse, for I am not aware that in general their courtesy went so far.

5h — GOLD BAND UPON THE MANTLE

THE word in the original Welsh is *gorffoys*, which is evidently the same as *orfrays*, or *aurifrigia*.[1] This was a kind of fretwork, or embroidery of gold, and is mentioned thus in the playful description of the allegorical figure of Idlenesse, which occurs in the Romaunt of the Rose:

"And of fine orfrais had she eke
A chapelet, so semely on,
Ne wered never maide upon;
And faire above that chapelet
A rose garlonde had she set."—562-6.

6a — BUFFALO HORN

DRINKING-HORNS of this material are frequently mentioned by the Bards, and appear to have been made use of by the Welsh in all their banquets.

There is still extant in the Welsh language, a spirited poem by Owain Kyveiliog, Prince of Powis, called the Hirlas, a name by which his drinking-horn was known, and which he describes as

"The highly honoured buffalo-horn Hirlas, enriched with ancient silver."

In the course of this poem, one passage occurs of a highly dramatic character. The Prince having sent round the horn to several chieftains, at length orders it

---

1 See Du Cange, *in voce*.

to be filled with the choicest beverage, and borne to Tudur and Moreiddig, at the same time expatiating with gratitude and admiration upon their valour, and the eminent services they had tendered him in the arduous conflicts ill which he had been engaged. Turning round in the fulness of his heart to address them personally, he perceives their places vacant; and suddenly recollecting that they had both fallen in one of the late encounters, he bursts out in a pathetic strain of lamentation, "The wail of death has been heard, they both have departed!—O, lost Moreiddig, how greatly shall I miss thee!"

8a — FOUNTAIN

THIS description answers to that of the Fountain of Barenton, in the forest of Breceliande, to which locality it is referred in the "Chevalier au Lion."[1] Breceliande is in Brittany, and is the fabled scene of Merlin's imprisonment, by the enchantments of his Mistress Viviane, the Lady of the Lake. Within the precincts of this Forest also lay the Val sans Retour, or the Vallon des Faux Amans.

> An amerawd was the stane,
> Richer saw i never nane,
> On fowr rubyes on heght standand,
> Their light lasted over al the land."—line 364.

10a — AN ADVENTURE SO MUCH TO HIS OWN DISCREDIT

BY the laws of Chivalry, the knights were under a solemn obligation, when relating their adventures, to give a faithful account of what befell them, without concealing anything, however disadvantageous to themselves.

10b — UNCOURTEOUS SPEECH

SIR KAI's uncourteous speech was proverbial. In Ywain and Gawin, we are told,

---

1 A long note on the story of the Fountain of Barenton in printed separately. A fountain possessed of the like properties occurs in the Fabliau of "The Paradise of Love," and a similar one is mentioned in "The noble Hystory of Kyng Ponthus of Galyce."

"And than als smertly sayd Sir Kay;
He karpet to tham wordes grete."

And so rude was his manner, that at length

"The quene answered, with milde mode,
And said, Sir Kay, ertow wode?
What the devyl es the withyn,
At thi tong may never blyn
Thi felows so fowly to shende?
Sertes, sir Kay, thou ert unhende."—line 488.

10c — HORN FOR WASHING

IT was customary to prepare for dinner by washing the hands, and the summons for this preparation was given by sounding a horn, which, by the French, was termed *corner l'eau*, or *corner l'eue*. Amongst the Monks, the same notice was given by ringing a bell.

12a — BLACK KNIGHT

WE have the name of the Black Knight given us both in the English and in the French version. In the former, the appellation of *Salados the rouse* is bestowed upon him, and in the latter he is called *Elcadoc le rous*, which bears some resemblance to the Welsh Cadoc or Cattwg.

12b — MAIDEN

THIS maiden, whose name we subsequently find to be Luned, is supposed, in the Notes to Jones's Welsh Bards, to be the same person as Elined the daughter of Brychan; although from the accounts transmitted to us of that illustrious lady, she appears to have differed much in disposition and pursuits from the handmaid of the Lady of the Fountain. Mr. Rees, in his valuable Essay on the Welsh Saints, has the following notice concerning her:—

"Elined, the Almedha of Giraldus Cambrensis, who says that she suffered martyrdom upon a hill called Penginger, near Brecknock, which the Historian of that County, so often quoted, identifies with Slwch.

'Crug gorseddawl,'[1] mentioned after the name of Elined in the Myvyrian

---

1 Crug gorseddawl, "the hill of Judicature."—Dr. Pughe's Welsh Dictionary.

Archaiology, has been taken for Wyddgrug, or Mold, in Flintshire; but it may be no more than a descriptive appellation of Slwch, on which there were lately some remains of a British Camp. Cressy, speaking of St. Almedha, says, 'This devout virgin, rejecting the proposals of an earthly prince, who sought her in marriage, and espousing herself to the eternal king, consummated her life by a triumphant martyrdom. The day of her solemnity is celebrated every year on the firstday of August.'"—(149-50.)

The beauty of Luned was much celebrated amongst the Bards of the Middle Ages. Gruffudd ap Meredydd, who flourished between 1290 and 1340, thus alludes to her charms, in an Elegy on Gwenhwyvar of Anglesey:—

"Alas, for the loss of her who was equal to Luned, that gem of light!"

And Dafydd ap Gwilym mentions her in the same strain.

She is in the French Romances generally called Lunette, and in the Morte d'Arthur she acts a conspicuous part in the story of Sir Gareth of Orkney, who undertook the adventure of the "Castel peryllous" on her behalf, and whose illtreatment by Sir Kai is related. Sir Gareth took his full revenge upon Sir Kai, but his conduct under the taunts he received from Luned, who called. him a *kechen knaue*, and used towards him very discourteous language, considering that he was taking up her quarrel, is generous and high-minded in the extreme. It ended in Sir Gareth marrying Luned's sister, Dame Lyones, of the Castel peryllous; and in Luned herself, who is also called the "daymoysel saueage," becoming the wife of Sir Gaherys, who was Sir Gareth's brother. And these nuptials were solemnized with great pomp and splendour at King Arthur's Court. See Morte d'Arthur, Book VII. Compare Mr. Tennyson's poem of Gareth and Lynette in the Idylls of the King.

13a — WHATEVER IS IN MY POWER

IT appears rather extraordinary at first sight that Luned should take so lively an interest in Owain, and give herself so much trouble to forward his suit with the Countess, and also that she should express herself so well acquainted with his character. But from the English Metrical Romance, we find that they were old friends, Luned having been on an embassy to Arthur's Court some time previously.

13b — TAKE THIS RING

THE ring is enumerated among the "Thirteen Rarities of Kingly Regalia of the Island of Britain, which were formerly kept at Caerlleon, on the river Usk, in Monmouthshire. These curiosities went with Myrddin the son of Morvran, into the house of Glass, in Enlli, or Bardsey Island. It has also been recorded by others that it was Taliesin, the Chief of the Bards, who possessed them."

"The Stone of the Ring of Luned, which liberated Owen the son of Urien from between the portcullis and the wall. Whoever concealed that stone, the stone or bezel would conceal him."

The properties of this magical ring, will, doubtless, call to mind the ring of Gyges, which was most probably the prototype from which it was indirectly derived.

13c — HORSEBLOCK

ELLIS, in his Notes to Way's Fabliaux, has the following remarks upon horseblocks, which are mentioned in a vast number of the old Romances: "They were frequently placed on the roads and in the forests, and were almost numberless in the towns. Many of them still remain in Paris, where they were used by the magistrates in order to mount their mules, on which they rode to the courts of justice. On these blocks, or on the tree which was generally planted near them, were usually suspended the shields of those Knights who wished to challenge all comers to feats of arms. They were also sometimes used as a place of judgment, and a rostrum, on which the barons took their seats when they determined the differences between their vassals, and from whence the publick criers made proclamations to the people."—(II. 229.)

13d — PAINTED WITH GORGEOUS COLOURS

THIS custom of painting figures upon the panels of rooms was much practised and esteemed at the time when we may suppose that this Tale was put into its present dress. Chaucer has several instances, of which we may notice more particularly the allegorical figures on the wall, at the opening of the Romaunt of the Rose, and the far more interesting and descriptive representations in the Temples of Mars, Venus, and Diana, in the "Knightes Tale." The paintings at the Temple of Mars were executed with so much art that even sounds were emitted by them.

"First on the wall was peinted a forest
In which ther wonneth neyther man ne best
With knotty knarry barrein trees old
Of stubbes sharpe and hidous to behold,
In which ther ran a romble and a swough,
As though a storme shuld bresten every bough," &c.—(1977.)

14a — SENDALL

THIS Word is the same as that in the original Welsh, and is used by the old writers to signify a thin kind of silk like cyprus. The dress of the *"Doctour of Phisike,"* one of the pilgrims to Canterbury, was, no doubt, a handsome one, and of him we are told—

"In sanguine and in perse he clad was alle
Lined with taffata and with sendalle."—(441.)

15b — SHE WASHED OWAIN'S HEAD

HOWEVER these personal services may appear to be at variance with the manners of the present day, it is clear that they were in perfect accordance with those of our ancestors. Of this, the following passage from the Life of Merlin will afford an example:—

"When. they went to the palace and had disarmed themselves,

King Leodagan made his daughter Genievre (Gwenhwyvar) take the richest cloths which were in the house, and warm water, and fair basins of silver, and made them be placed before King Arthur, and King Ban, and King Boors; and his daughter would wait upon Arthur, and would wash his neck and his face; but he would not allow thereof, till Leodagan and Merlin requested him, and made him accept the lady's service. The damsel washed his face right humbly, and then she wiped it with a fine towel, full gently; and then she went and ministered in like manner to the other twain."

15a — COUNTESS

THE English Version gives this Countess the title of

"The riche lady Alundyne,
The dukes doghter of Landuit."—line 1255.

And it is very satisfactory to find that she was not that Penarwen, daughter of Culfynawyt Prydein, who is mentioned as Owain's wife in the Triads, though in terms which are anything but complimentary. Perhaps Penarwen may have been a subsequent wife, since we may infer that Owain survived the Lady of the Fountain, from the circumstance so naively mentioned in the text, of her continuing to be his wife as long as she lived.

In Owen's Llywarch Hên, it is stated that after the death of Penarwen, Owain, was married to Denyw, the daughter of Llewddyn Luyddawg of Edinburgh, by whom he had Kendeyrn Garthwys, the celebrated St. Kentigern, who founded the Cathedral at Glasgow.

18a — HER NUPTIALS WITH OWAIN

THIS trait of manners is very characteristic of the times in which the present Tale was written. It was very usual for widows and heiresses in the troublous days of Knight-errantry to marry those whose strength and valour rendered them best able to defend and preserve to them their possessions. Ste. Palaye, in enumerating the advantages of the order of Knighthood, does not forget to mention this easy mode of advancing to fortune.—(I. 267, 326.)

18b — GWALCHMAI

GWALCHMAI AP GWYAR.—This ancient British name, Gwalchmai, which signifies the *Hawk of Battle*, is in the French Romances changed into the not very similar form of Gawain, having first been Latinized into Walganus and Walweyn. In the Triads, he is mentioned in the following manner:—

"There were three golden-tongued Knights in the Court of Arthur: Gwalchmai the son of Gwyar; Drudwas the son of Tryffin, and Eliwlod the son of Madog ap Uthur. For there was neither King, nor Earl, nor Lord, to whom these came, but would listen to them before all others; and whatever request they made, it would be granted them, whether willingly or unwillingly; and thence were they called the *Golden Tongued*."

As a proof of the high estimation in which Gwalchmai's powers of persuasion were held, the following translation from the Myvyrian Archaiology (I. 178) may be adduced:—

HERE ARE ENGLYNS

Between Trystan the son of Tallwch, and Gwalchmai the son of Gwyar, after Trystan had been absent three years from Arthur's Court, in displeasure, and Arthur had sent eight-and-twenty warriors to seize him, and bring him to Arthur, and Trystan smote them all down, one after another, and came not for any one, but for Gwalchmai with the Golden Tongue.

GWALCHMAI.
Tumultuous is the nature of the wave,
When the sea is at its height—
Who art thou, mysterious warrior?

TRYSTAN.
Tumultuous are the waves and the thunder.
In their bursting forth let them be tumultuous.
In the day of conflict I am Trystan.

GWALCHMAI.
Trystan of the faultless speech,
Who, in the day of battle, would not retreat,
A companion of thine was Gwalchmai.

TRYSTAN.
I would do for Gwalchmai in that day,
In the which the work of slaughter is let loose,
That which one brother would not do for another.

GWALCHMAI.
Trystan, endowed with brilliant qualities,
Whose spear has oft been shivered in the toil of war,
I am Gwalchmai the nephew of Arthur.

TRYSTAN.
Gwalchmai, there swifter than Mydrin,
Shouldst thou be in danger,
I would cause blood to flow till it reached the knees.

GWALCHMAI.
Trystan, for thy sake would I strive
Until my wrist should fail me;
Also for thee I would do my utmost.

TRYSTAN.
I ask it in defiance,
I ask it not through fear,—
Who are the warriors before me?

GWALCHMAI.
Trystan, of distinguished qualities,
Are they not known to thee?
It is the household of Arthur that comes.

TRYSTAN.
Arthur will I not shun,
To nine hundred combats will I dare him,—
If I am slain, I will also slay.

GWALCHMAI.
Trystan, the friend of damsels,
Before commencing the work of strife,
The best of all things is peace.

TRYSTAN.
Let me but have my sword upon my thigh,
And my right hand to defend me,
And I myself will be more formidable than they all.

GWALCHMAI.
Trystan of brilliant qualities,
Before exciting the tumult of conflict,—
Reject not Arthur as a friend.

TRYSTAN.
Gwalchmai, for thy sake will I deliberate,
And with my mouth I utter it.
As I am loved, so will I love.

GWALCHMAI.
Trystan, of aspiring mind,
The shower wets a hundred oaks.
Come to an interview with thy kinsman.

TRYSTAN.
Gwalchmai, of persuasive answers,
The shower wets a hundred furrows.
I will go where'er thou wilt.

Then came Trystan with Gwalchmai to Arthur.

GWALCHMAI.
Arthur, of courteous replies,
The shower wets a hundred heads.
Here is Trystan, be thou joyful.

ARTHUR.
Gwalchmai, of faultless answers,
The shower wets a hundred dwellings.
A welcome to Trystan, my nephew.

Worthy Trystan, chief of the host,
Love thy race, remember the past
Am I not the Chief of the Tribe?

Trystan, leader of onsets,
Take equal with the best,
But leave the sovereignty to me.

Trystan, wise and mighty chieftain,
Love thy kindred, none shall harm thee,
Let there be no coldness between friend and friend.

TRYSTAN.
Arthur, to thee will I attend,
To thy command will I submit,
And that thou wishest will I do.

In one Triad we find Gwalchmai extolled as one of the three most courteous men towards guests and strangers; and from another we learn that be added scientific attainments to his other remarkable qualities.

"The three learned ones of the island of Britain, Gwalchmai ab Gwyar, and Llecheu ab Arthur, and Rhiwallon with the broom-bush hair; and there was nothing of which they did not know the elements and the material essence."

William of Malmsbury says, that during the reign of William the Conqueror (A.D. 1086) the tomb of Gwalchmai, or *Walwen*, as he calls him, was discovered on the sea-shore, in a certain province of Wales called Rhôs, which is understood to be that still known by the same name, in the county of Pembroke, where there is a district called in Welsh Castell Gwalchmai, and in English Walwyn's Castle.

In the Graves of the Warriors a similar locality is indicated:—

The grave of Gwalchmai is in Pyton,
Where the ninth wave flows."

The Romances make Gawain one of the four sons of King Lot of Orkney, and of Morgawse, sister to King Arthur; and in them the character for courtesy given to him in the Triads is fully maintained. So proverbial, indeed, was he for this quality, that the highest praise the Squier could bestow upon the address of the Knight who rode the "stede of bras" was,

That Gawain with his olde curtesie,
Though he were come agen out of faerie
Ne coude him not amenden with a word."—line 10410.

20a — SATIN ROBE OF HONOUR

THIS species of honourable dress could only be worn by knights; and, according to Ste. Palaye, was generally the gift of the sovereign, who accompanied it with a palfrey, or, at least, with a horse's bit, either golden or gilded. His words are,

"Le manteau long et trainant qui enveloppoit toute la personne, étoit reservé particulièrement au chevalier, comme la plus auguste et la plus noble décoration qu'il pût avoir lorsqu'il n'étoit point paré de ses armes . . . on l'appeloit le manteau d'honneur."—(I. 287.)

20b — EARL OF RHANGYW

PROBABLY this is meant for the Earl of Anjou, and was originally written *Iarll yr Angyw*, the Welsh particle yr, in its contracted form 'r, being by some error of the transcriber incorporated with Angyw, which is the Welsh name for Anjou. What renders this the more likely is, that the Earldom of Anjou, or Angyw, was according to the Brut, one of the possessions of Arthur, who bestowed it upon his seneschal Sir Kai.

20c — STRONG LANCES

IT would be vain to attempt to find English terms corresponding precisely with those used in the Welsh text, to designate the various kinds of arms which the knights fought with, in this Tale.

21a — COUSIN

THE following genealogical table will explain this consanguinity, as given in the Welsh Pedigrees.

Genealogical chart

From very remote periods down to the time of Elizabeth, the Welsh kept up their Pedigrees with much care, and many copies of them are extant both in public and private collections; and although in these occasional discrepancies may be perceived, yet, in general, their authenticity is well established. It must be allowed, that it appears somewhat extraordinary that these family records should be transmitted with such accuracy through so many generations. But when we consider the imperative obligations of the Welsh Laws upon this subject, we are no longer surprised at the existence of such ancient documents, nor at the solicitude of the Welsh to preserve them.

"It has been observed," says the Essayist on Welsh Pedigrees, in the Transactions of the Cymmrodorion Society, "that genealogies were preserved as a matter of necessity, under the ancient British constitution. A man's pedigree was to him of the first importance, as thereby be was enabled to ascertain and prove his birthright, and claim the privileges which the law attached to it. Every one was obliged to show his descent through nine generations, in order to be acknowledged a free native, by which right he claimed his portion of land in the community. He was also affected with respect to legal Process in his collateral affinities through nine degrees; for instance, every murder committed had a fine levied on the relations of the murderer, divided into nine degrees; his brother paying the greatest, and the *ninth* in relationship the least. The fine thus levied was in the same proportions distributed among the relations of the victim. A person beyond the *ninth* descent formed a new family; every family was represented by its elder, and these elders from every family were delegates to the national council."

21b — GIVE ME YOUR SWORDS

THIS modesty, in disclaiming praise, and attaching merit to others, was one of the most esteemed qualities of knighthood. Ste. Palaye quotes from Olivier de la Marche (Mém. i. 315), a contest of generosity somewhat similar to that between Owain and Gwalchmai. "Jacques de Lalain et Piétois, en 1450, ayant fait armes à pied, se renverserent lun sur l'autre; ils furent relevés par les escortes et amenés aux juges qui les firent toucher ensemble en Signe de paix. Comme Lalain, par modestie, voulut envoyer son bracelet, suivant la convention faite pour le prix, Pietois déclara qu'ayant ete aussi bien que lui porté par terre, il se croiroit également obligé de lui donner le sien. Ce nouveau combat de politesse finit par ne plus parler de bracelet, et par former une etroite liaison d'amitié entre ces genereux ennemis."—(I. 150.)

21c — BANQUET

A FEAST which took three years to prepare, and three months to consume, appears in our degenerate days as something quite enormous; but it is a trifle to what we read in another of the Mabinogion, where a party spend eighty years in listening to the songs of the birds of Rhianon, that charm away the remembrance of their sorrows.

21d — A DAMSEL ENTERED, UPON A BAY HORSE

THE custom of riding into a hall, while the Lord and his guests sat at meat, the memory of which is still preserved in the coronation ceremonials of this country, might be illustrated by innumerable passages of ancient Romance and History. But I shall content myself with a quotation from Chaucer's beautiful and half-told Tale of Cambuscan.

And so befell that after the thridde cours
While that this king sit thus in his nobley,
Herking his ministralles hir thinges pley
Beforne him at his bord deliciously,
In at the halle dore al sodenly
Ther came a knight upon a stede of bras,
And in his hond a brod mirrour of glas;
Upon his thombe he had of gold a ring,
And by his side a naked swerd hanging:
And up be rideth to the highe bord.
In all the halle ne was ther spoke a word,
For mervaille of this knight; him to behold
Ful besily they waiten yong and old."—10,390-10,401.

22a — AND ANOINT HIM WITH THIS BALSAM

THE healing art was always confined to females in chivalric times, a principal part of whose education it formed, and to the -wives and daughters of knights was confided the care of such as were sick or wounded. Of this, the instances are so numerous, that it is needless to adduce any here.

We find, from the English metrical version of this Tale, that the ointment here mentioned, was the gift of Morgant le sage, very probably the same as Morgan le fay, who was sister of King Arthur, and wife to Urien Rheged, and whose skill in magic was justly celebrated, as the adventure of the Manteau mal taillé will unfortunately prove.

23a — WRESTED FROM HER BY A YOUNG EARL

THE name of this invader is in Ywain and Gawin, "The ryche eryl, syr Alers,"—line 1871; and the "Cuens Alers," in the Chevalier au Lion.

24a — A BEAUTIFUL BLACK STEED

THE name of Owain's horse is recorded, with the epithet of "irrestrainable" (Anrheithfarch), but we cannot venture to affirm that the Carn Aflawg (or grasping-hoofed) of the Triads, was either the charger which he received from the Lady of the Castle, or that which met with so disastrous a fate at the falling of the portcullis.

25a — WENT ON HIS WAY, AS BEFORE

THE story of this adventure, as well as that of the fountain, appears to have been popular in the Principality, during the Middle Ages, as it is alluded to in an Ode addressed to Owain Glendower, by Gruffydd Llwyd ab Davydd ab Einion, one of his Bards, about the year 1400.

Of this, the following translation is given in Jones's Welsh Bards, I. 41:—

> "On sea, on land, thou still didst brave
> The dangerous cliff, and rapid wave;
> Like *Owain*, who subdued the knight,
> And the fell dragon put to flight,
>   Yon moss-grown fount beside;
> The grim, black warrior of the flood,
> The dragon, gorged with human blood,
>   The water's scaly pride."

25b — STONE VAULT

THIS part of the Tale is by no means clearly expressed, but it is evidently intended to be understood that Luned was incarcerated in a stone cell, near which Owain chanced to halt for the night. We subsequently find that he shut up the Lion in the same place, during his contest with Luned's persecutors.

27a — A MONSTER

THIS monster is in the English called "Harpyns of Mowntain," and he is, moreover, said to have been "a devil of mekil pryde."

According to this and the French version, the good knight (who, it appears, had married a sister of Sir Gawain) was, originally, the, father of "sex knyghts," two of whom Harpyns had already slain, while he threatened to put the remaining four to death, unless their sister was given "hym to wyve." The costume of the Harpyns and the four young men is very characteristic.

> "With wreched ragges war thai kled
> And fast bunden thus er thai led:
> The geant was both large and lang,
> And bar a lever of yren ful strang,
> Tharwith he bet them bitterly,
> Grete rewth it was to her tham cry,

Thai had no thing tham for to hyde.
A dwergh yode on the tother syde;
He bar a scowrge with cordes ten,
Thar-with he bet tha gentil men."

And further on, it is said of the giant,

"Al the armure he was yn
Was noght bot of a bul-skyn."

29a — STATE OF STUPOR

THE literal meaning of this passage is not advantageous to the four-and-twenty ladies, as it gives them a character for anything but sobriety. It is possible, however, that allusion is made to some act of necromancy (not by any means unusual in the old writers of romance), by which they were thrown into a state of insensibility.

29b — HOSPICE

SPYTTY.—This term is derived from the Latin word Hospitium, and is used to designate those establishments which were erected and maintained by the monks for the reception of travellers.

They bore some remote resemblance to our present inns, and were generally placed in secluded spots at a distance, from any town. Several places in Wales retain the recollection of these hospitable institutions in the name they still bear, as Spytty Ivan, Spytty Cynvyn, &c.

30a — RAVENS

AS some explanation of this strange expression, it may, be noticed, that in another of the Mabinogion, called the "Dream of Rhonabwy," Owain is represented as having an army of Ravens in his service, which are engaged in combat with some of Arthur's attendants.

But in that, as well as in the present Tale, the adventure is introduced with an abruptness that can only be accounted for by supposing that the story was well known, and that it formed a part of that great store of Romance which existed among the Welsh, and which furnished to the other nations of Europe the earliest materials of imaginative composition.

This Raven Army of the Prince of Rheged has evidently a connection with the armorial hearings of that house already alluded to.

VERSIONS IN OTHER LANGUAGES OF THE TALE OF "THE LADY OF THE FOUNTAIN"

THE story of Owain and the Lady of the Fountain was very popular in the days of Chivalry, and we meet with it in many European languages besides the Welsh.

The English version, under the title of "Ywaine and Gawin " (derived from the French work of Chrestien de Troyes), was published by Ritson in the first volume of his Metrical Romances, from a MS. in the British Museum, supposed by him to be of the reign of Richard II.

Towards the end of the 12th century, the trouvère Chrestien de Troyes made Owain's adventures the subject of his metrical Romance of the "Cheualier an Lyon," which I have printed in the first edition of this work, and of which there are several MS. copies in the Bibliothèque Nationale.

Chrestien's French poem was turned into German verse by Hartmann von der Aue, a Meister-sänger of the end of the 12th or the beginning of the 13th century. Of this production many copies exist, that in the Library of the Vatican being considered by Tieck to be the oldest German MS, preserved there. It has appeared more than once in print, and is to be found in Professor Myller's Collection of Teutonic Romances, 2 vols. 4to., Berlin, 1784. It was also published by Michaeler in four small 8vo. volumes. Vienna, 1786.

Ulrich Fürterer, a Bavarian rhymer, who flourished in the later part of the 15th century, has likewise left a poem on the subject of "Ivain," as one of an immense series of metrical compositions embracing the entire story of the Grail and the Round Table heroes.

In the Royal Library at Stockholm are preserved MS. versions of the Tale of "Ivain," both in the Danish and Swedish languages, and the British Museum, as well as the University Library of Copenhagen, possesses MSS. of the Icelandic "Ivent Saga."

NOTE ON THE
FOREST OF BRECELIANDE,
AND THE FOUNTAIN OF BARANTON

THE Forest of Brécéliande, in Brittany, the scene of the leading incident in the Chevalier au Lion, has ever been one of the most favoured haunts of Romance, and one whose marvels the Trouvères have most delighted to celebrate. Amongst those whose names have contributed to add to the renown of this remarkable spot, is the mighty Enchanter, Merlin, whose prison it became through the artifices of his Lady love. The manner of his being incarcerated there is very circumstantially detailed in the Romance which bears his name, as quoted by Mr. Southey, in the Preface to the Morte d'Arthur.

Merlin, having become enamoured of the fair Viviane,[1] was weak enough to impart to her various important secrets of his art,[2] being impelled by a fatal

---

1 This Viviane is said to be the daughter of a Vavasour of high lineage, called Dyonas, from Dyane, a goddess of the sea. He married a niece of the Duchess of Burgundy, with whom he received as a dowry half the Forest of Briogne; the other half was granted him soon after in reward for his good services. Under the title of the "Lady of the Lake" Viviane is well known.

2 Of the nature and extent of the powers with which Merlin was endowed, Spenser has left us a most marvellous account.

> "For he by wordes could call out of the sky
> Both sunne and moone, and make them him obey;
> The land to sea, and sea to maineland dry,
> And darksom night he eke could turne to day;
> Huge hostes of men he could alone dismay,
> And hostes of men of meanest thinges could frame,
> Whenso him list his enimies to fray:
> That to this day, for terror of his fame,
> The feendes do quake when any him to them does name."
> Faerie Queens, b. iii. c. 3. st. xii.

What wonder is it then that he should elsewhere characterize him as the being

> "Which whylome did excell
> All living wightes in might of magicke spell."
> Ibid. b. i. c. 7. at. xxxvi.

destiny, of which he was at the same time fully aware. The Lady, however, was not content with his devotion, unbounded as it seems to have been, but "cast about," as the Romance tells us, how she might "detain him for evermore," and with a view of learning some mode of accomplishing this object, she one day addressed him in these terms,—"Sir," said she, "I would have you teach and show me how to enclose and imprison a man without a tower, without walls, without chains, but by enchantment alone, in such manner that he may never be able to go out, except by me." Aware of her design, Merlin shook his head, and evinced great reluctance to comply with her request. But Viviane, "for her great treason," began to fawn and to flatter him, and used many subtle arguments to prove that he ought to perform her will, whatever it might be. So at last he said to her, "Certes, lady, yes, and I will do it; tell me what you would have." "Sir," said she, "I would that we should make a fair place and a suitable, so contrived by art and by cunning, that it might never be undone, and that you and I should be there in joy and in solace." "My lady," said Merlin, "I will perform all this." " Sir," said she, "I would not have you do it, but you shall teach me, and I will do it, and then it will be more to my will." "I grant you this," said Merlin. Then he began to devise, and the damsel put it all in writing. And when he had devised the whole, then had the damsel full great joy, and showed him greater semblance of loving him than she had ever before made; and they sojourned together a long while. At length it fell out that, as they were going one day hand in hand through the forest of Broceliande, they found a bush of white thorn which was laden with flowers; and they seated themselves under the shade of this white thorn upon the green grass, and they disported together and took their solace, and Merlin laid his head upon the damsel's lap, and then she began to feel if he were asleep. Then the damsel rose and made a ring with her wimple round the bush and round Merlin, and began her enchantments such as he himself had taught her; and nine times she made the ring, and nine times she made the enchantments; and then she went and sate down by him, and placed his head again upon her lap; and when he awoke, and looked round him, it seemed to him that he was enclosed in the strongest tower in the world, and laid upon a fair bed. Then said he to the dame, "My lady, you have deceived me unless you abide with me, for no one hath power to unmake this tower, save you alone." She then promised she would be often there, and we are told that in this she held her covenant to him. "And Merlin never went out of that tower where his mistress Viviane had enclosed him. But she entered and went out again when she listed; and oftentime she regretted what she had done, for she had thought that the thing which he taught her could not be true, and willingly would she have let him out if she could."—(T. 2. f. 134.)

From the same authority, it appears that after this event Merlin was never more known to hold converse with any mortal but Viviane, except on one occasion. Arthur having for some time missed him from his Court, sent several of his Knights in search of him, and among the number Sir Gawain, who met with a very unpleasant adventure while engaged in this quest. Happening to pass a damsel on his road, as he journeyed along, and neglecting to salute her, she revenged herself for his incivility, by transforming him into a hideous dwarf. He was bewailing aloud his evil fortune as he went through the Forest of Brécéliande, when "suddenly he heard the voice of one groaning on his right hand;" and "looking that way he could see nothing save a kind of smoke which seemed like air, and through which be could not pass." Merlin then addressed him from out the smoke, and told him by what misadventure be was imprisoned there. "Ah, Sir," he added, "you will never see me more, and that grieves me, but I cannot remedy it; and when you shall have departed from this place, I shall never more speak to you, nor to any other person, save only my mistress." And after this he comforted Gawain under his transformation, assuring him that he should speedily be disenchanted, and he predicted to him that he should find the King at Carduel, in Wales, on his return, and that all the other Knights who had been on the like quest, would arrive there the same day as himself. And all this came to pass as Merlin had said.—(T. 2. f, 146.)[1]

It is evident that the wonders ascribed by Chrestien de Troyes to the Fountain of Baranton, in this famous Forest, were not the creation of his own fancy, but were in his time already in no small repute; for we find his precursor Wace so much impressed with the desire to be an eye-witness of them, that he actually made a journey to the spot for that purpose. In his Roman de Rou be relates the whole affair with admirable naïveté. After adverting to the marvels of the slab, he tells us, that if what the Bretons say is true, Fairies are often to be seen sporting on the Fountain's bank; but he very frankly owns that he met with nothing but disappointment to repay the trouble of his expedition, and he reproaches himself for his folly in having ever undertaken it.

The passage is brought in by the mention of the Barons who accompanied

---

1 Preface—Morte d'Arthur, xliii—xlviii. In the "Prophecies of Merlin," though the result is the same, the circumstances attending his disappearance are differently related. There the scene is laid, not in Brécéliande, but in the Forest of Arvantes, and Merlin's living sepulchre is not a white-thorn bush, but a tomb which he had constructed for himself, and which Viviane persuaded him to lie down in, under pretence of trying whether it would be large enough for her to be buried in it with him. As soon as he had entered it, Viviane put down the lid, and closed it so effectually, by arts which he himself had taught her, that it never after could be opened.—See Morte d'Arthur, ii. 463-8. It is this version that Ariosto appears to have followed; but he places in the South of France, somewhere in the neighbourhood of the Garonne, the tomb in which

"Col corpo morto il vivo spirto alberga."

Orlando Furioso, C. iii.

William of Normandy to the conquest of England, some of whom he says were

> "de verz Brecheliant,
> Dune Bretunz vont sovent fablant,
> Une forest mult lunge è lée,
> Ki en Bretaigne est mult loée;
> La Fontaine de Berenton
> Sort d'une part lez le perron;
> Aler i solent venéor
> A Berenton par grant chalor,
> Et o lor cors l'ewe puisier
> Et li perron de suz moillier,
> Por ço soleient pluée aveir;
> Issi soleit jadis pluveir
> En la forest tut envirun,
> Maiz jo ne sai par kel raisun.
> Là solt l'en li fées véir,
> Se li Bretunz disent veir,
> Et altres merveilles plusors;
> Aigres solt avéir destors
> E de granz cers mult grant plenté,
> Maiz li vilain ont deserté.
> Là alai jo merveilles querre,
> Vis la forest è vis la terre;
> Merveilles quis, maiz nes' trovai;
> Fol m'en revins, fol i alai,
> Fol i alai, fol m'en revins,
> Folie quis, per fol me tins."—v. 11514-11539.

Roman de Rou, publié par F. Pluquet.
Rouen, 1827—ii. 143, 4.

Huon de Méry, a subsequent trouvère, set out on a similar errand, and was either more fortunate, or less ingenuous than Wace. One cannot help suspecting him of reckoning rather largely upon the credulity of his readers, in the narrative he gives of his journey however, he shall tell his story in his own words.

Being one of those who accompanied an expedition made by the "Rois Loeys en Bretaingne," he considered the opportunity thus afforded him of visiting its Forest of wonders too tempting to be overlooked.

> "Por çou que n'iert pas mult lontaingne
> La forès de Brecéliande,
> Mes cuers ki souvent me commande

Faire autre cose ke mon preu,
Me fist faire, aussi comme veu,
Ke ge en Brecéliande iroie,
Ge m'en tornai et pris ma voie
Vers la forest, sans plus atendre,
Kar la Vreté voloie aprendre
De la périlleuse fontaine,
Une espée ou ot fer d'Andainne
Dont lameure n'estoit pas double
Et un hauberc à maille double
Portai qui puis m'orent mestier,
Sans tenir voie ne sentier
Chevauchai iiij. jours entiers.
Adonc m'aparut uns sentiers
Qui par une gaste lande,
Me mena en Brecéliande,
Mult est espesse et oscure,
En la forest par aventure
Perdi le sens de mon sentier,
Car li solaus s'aloit couchier,
Qui avoit faite sa journée.
Mais la clartés est ajornée
De la lune qui lors leva."

* * * * *

"Cele nuis resambla le jour.
Sans faire alonge ne séjour,
Ce fu la quinte nuis de mai;
La fontainne mult esgardai
Ke la trouvai par aventure.
La fontaine n'iert pas oscure
Ains ert clere com fins argens,
Mult estoit li praales gens.
Qui sombroioit de desous l'arbre
Le bachin, le perron de marbre,
Et le vert pin et la caière
Trouvai en icele manière,
Comme l'a descrit *Crestiens*
En plus clère eve crestiens . . . .
Ne sambla pas que ce fust cresme.
Quant le bachin ting en ma main,
Car tout aussi le puisai plain

Com se la vousisse espuisier.
Quand ge mis la main au puisier,
Lors vi le firmament doubler.
Quant oi puisié, lors vi doubler
Le torment, quant l'eve versai,
Je qui, tous seus le sai,
Ne talent n'en ai du mentir,
Mais le chiel oï desmentir
Et eselarcir de toutes pars.
De plus de .vc. mile pars
Ert la forès enluminée;
Se tous li chiex ert queminée
Et tous li mons ardoit ensamble,
Ne fesist-il pas, ce me samble,
Tel clarté, ne si grant orage.
.C. fois maudis en mon corage
Par cui conseill ting là mon oirre,
Car à cascun cop de tonnoirre
La foudre du ciel descendoit
Qui tronçounoit et porfendoit
Parmi le bois, caines et fals.
Or escoutés com ge fui fals
Et tresperdus et entrepris,
K'encor plain bachin d'iaue pris
Et seur le perron le flasti
Mais se le ciel ot bien glati
Et envoiés foudres en terre.
Lors double la noise et la guerre
Ke j'oï mené à tout le monde,
Can del' tounoire à la réonde
Toute la terre vi tranbler
Ge cuidai bien que assambler
Fesist del' chiel et terre ensamble.
Ce fu folie, ce me samble,
De .ij. fois le bachin widier,
Mais ce fu pair mon fol cuidier,
Car le tans apaisier cuidai
Quant le secont bachin widai;
Mais lors perchui que cil qui cuide
Qu'il a de seus la teste wide.

* * * * *

Lours commencha à aprochier
Li jours dont l'aube ert ja' venue;
Joie firent de sa venue
Trestout li oiseillon menu
Ke à voleter ai véu
De par tout Berchéliande.
En broche, n'en forest, n'en lande
N'en vit mais nus tant amassés
Sus le pin en ot plus amassés.
Ke n'en vit Kalogrinans.
Et faisoient de divers cans
Une si douce mélodie
Ke à ma mort, ni à ma vie,
Ne kéisse avoir autre gloire.
Encore, quant me vient en mémoire,
En mon cuer en ai si grant joie
Qn'encore me sanlle qu'eus ge oie;
M'est-il tous vraiement avis
Que c'est terrestre paradis.

Tournoiement Ante-Crist,[1] MS. du Roi,
No. 541. S. F. (fol. 72. col. 2. v. 5)

The Fairies, who are reported to haunt the Forest of Brécéliande, appear to have patronized children in an especial manner, and to have delighted in showering down gifts upon such as were brought there soon after their birth to receive their benediction. There is extant in the Bibliothèque du Roi (MS. du Roi, n. 7989—4 Bal.) a fragment of a curious Romance, named Brun de la Montague, which is founded entirely upon this circumstance. It is printed in Le Roux de Lincy's Livre des Légendes. The outline of the story, is as follows:—

Butor de la Montague, on the birth of his infant son, is desirous that he should receive a Fairy's blessing; and after revolving in his mind the names of all the "lieux fäes"[2] with which he is acquainted, he determines on sending him

---

1 Livre des Legendes. Par le Roux de Lincy. Intro. 230, 4. Paris, 1836. Huon de Mery was a Monk of St. Germain des Prés, near Paris. He wrote the Poem above quoted about A.D. 1228. See Warton's History of English Poetry, ii. 121.

2 "a des lieux fäes ès marches de Champaigne,
    Et ausi en a il en la roche grifaigne,
    Et si croy qu'il en a aussi en Alemaigne,
    Et on bois Bersillant, par desous la montaigne;
    Et non por quant ausi en a il en Espaigne,
    Et tout cil lieu faë sont Artu de Bretaigne."

to the haunt of the Fairies in the "bois Bersillant." The little Brun is accordingly conveyed thither by a trusty Knight, and placed on the margin of the enchanted fountain. It is not long before the Fairies[1] appear, and the child is endowed with the choicest gifts which they have in their power to bestow. One of them, however, envious of the extreme brightness of his prospects, dooms him to misfortune and disappointment in love.

On his return to his parents, one of the benevolent Fairies, who had taken a particular liking to him, disguises herself, and becomes his nurse. The MS. breaks off abruptly, just as the story of his disastrous love-adventure is about to commence.[2]

I shall conclude this Note with a description of the state of the famous Forest of Brécéliande, in our own times, from an account of a visit made to it by the Vicomte de la Villemarqué, and published by him in the Revue de Paris for May, 1837.

"J'avais tant de fois, dans mon enfance, entendu parler de Merlin, et lu, dans nos romans de chevalerie bretonne, de si merveilleuses choses sur son tombeau, la forêt de Brécilien, la fontaine de Baranton, et la vallée de Concoret, que je fus pris d'un vif désir de visiter ces lieux, et qu'un beau matin je partis.

"Ploërmel est la ville la plus voisine de Concoret; de là an bourg la route est longue et difficile; toujours des chemins creux, des montagnes, des bois, on des landes sans fin."

Livre des Légendes, 264.

1 The following is the description given of these Ladies in the Romance;—

> Les dames dont je di si estoient faées
> Qui si très noblement estoient asesmées.
> Leur cors furent plus blanc que n'est noif sor gelée,
> Et si très chierement estoient atournées.
> Car de couronnes d'or furent tontes dorées
> Et de blaus dras de soie estoient aournées;
> En mi de la portrine estoient escollées.
> Se uns hom en eust erré .ij. c. mile journées
> Ne fussent point par li trois plus belles trouvées
> Et s'eust conversé en cent mile contrées."
>   Liv. des Lég. 267-8.

2 Ibid. 260, 284.

* * * * *

"La plaine qu'on appelle en breton Concoret,[1] et dans les romans da moyen-âge le *Val-des-Fées*, est un immense amphithéâtre couronné de bois sombres, jadis nommés Broc'hallean,[2] aujourd'hui par corruption Brécilien. A l'une de ses extrémités, coule une fontaine près de laquelle on voit deux pierres couvertes de mousse que domine une vieille croix de bois vermoulue; c'est la fontaine de Barandon et le tombeau de Merlin; là dort, dit-on, le vieux druide, au murmure des eaux et du vent qui gémit dans les bruyères d'alentour.

"De cette hauteur, l'œil embrasse toute la vallée, et un horizon sans bornes de bois, de champs remplis de blés on de genets aux fleurs jaunes, de paroisses et de lointains clochers.

"Brécilien était une de ces fôrets sacrées qu'habitaient les prêtresses du druidisme dans les Gaules; son nom et celui de sa vallée l'attesteraient à défaut d'autre témoignage; les noms de lieux sont les plus sûrs garans des événemens passés."

All the old traditions which give an interest to the Forest continue to be current there. The Fairies, who are kind to children, are still reported to be seen in their white apparel upon the banks of the Fountain; and the Fountain itself (whose waters are now considered salubrious) is still said to be possessed of its marvellous rain-producing properties. In seasons of drought, the inhabitants of the surrounding parishes go to it in procession, headed by their five great banners, and their priests, ringing bells and chanting Psalms. On arriving at the Fountain, the Rector of the Canton dips the foot of the Cross into its waters, and it is sure to rain before a week elapses.

The Fountain of Baranton is supplied by a mineral spring, and it bubbles up on a piece of iron or copper being thrown into it.

"Les enfans s'amusent a y jeter des épingles, et disent par commun proverbe: '*Ris donc, fontaine de Berendon, et je te donnerai une épingle.*'"[3]

---

1 "*Kun-kored*, vallée des druidesses."

2 "Le bois de la Nonne, de l'Hermite, de la Solitaire."

3 Revue de Paris. Tome 41. 7 Mai, 1837, pp. 47-58, article "*Visite ou Tombeau de Merlin*," par Théodore de la Villemarqué.

LLYN DULYN IN SNOWDON

THE extraordinary property of producing rain, when spilt upon a stone, is attributed to the waters of Llyn Dulyn, in Snowdon, according to the following account, which is translated from the Greal, a Welsh Magazine, published in London, 1805.

"There is a lake in the mountains of Snowdon, called Dulyn, in a rugged valley, encircled by high steep rocks. This lake is extremely black, and its fish are deformed and unsightly, having large heads and small bodies. No wild swans are ever seen alighting upon it (such as are on all the other lakes in Snowdon), nor ducks, nor any bird whatever. And there is a causeway of stones leading into this lake; and if any one goes along this causeway, even when it is hot sunshine, and throws water so as to wet the furthest stone, which is called the Red Altar [yr Allawr Goch], it is a chance if it do not rain before night. Witness, T. Prys, of Plas Iolyn, and Sion Davydd, of Rhiwlas, in Llan Silin."

PEREDUR THE SON OF EVRAWC

[81a]EARL EVRAWC owned the Earldom of the North. And he had seven sons. And Evrawc maintained himself not so much by his own possessions as by attending tournaments[81b], and wars, and combats[81c]. And, as it often befalls those who join in encounters and wars, he was slain, and six of his sons likewise. Now the name of his seventh son was Peredur, and he was the youngest of them. And he was not of an age to go to wars and encounters, otherwise he might have been slain as well as his father and brothers. His mother was a scheming and thoughtful woman, and she was very solicitous concerning this her only son and his possessions. So she took counsel with herself to leave the inhabited country, and to flee to the deserts and unfrequented wildernesses. And she permitted none to bear her company thither but women and boys, and spiritless men, who were both unaccustomed and unequal to war and fighting. And none dared to bring either horses or arms where her son was, lest he should set his mind upon them. And the youth went daily to divert himself in the forest, by flinging sticks and staves. And one day he saw his mother's flock of goats, and near the goats two hinds were standing. And he marvelled greatly that these two should be without horns, while the others had them. And he thought they had long run wild, and on that account they had lost their horns. And by activity and swiftness of foot, he drove the hinds and the goats together into the house which there was for the goats at the extremity of the forest. Then Peredur returned to his mother. "Ah, mother," said he, "a marvellous thing have I seen in the wood; two of thy goats have run wild, and lost their horns, through their having been so long missing in the wood. And no man had ever more trouble than I had to drive them in." Then they all arose and went to see. And when they beheld the hinds they were greatly astonished.

And one day they saw three knights coming along the horse-road on the borders of the forest. And the three knights were Gwalchmai the son of Gwyar, and Geneir Gwystyl, and Owain the son of Urien. And Owain kept on the track of the knight who had divided the apples in Arthur's Court, whom they were in pursuit of. "Mother," said Peredur, "what are those yonder?" "They are angels, my son[82a]," said she. "By my faith," said Peredur, "I will go and become an angel with them." And Peredur went to the road, and met them. "Tell me, good soul," said Owain, "sawest thou a knight pass this way, either to-day or yesterday?" "I know not," answered he, "what a knight is." "Such an one as I am," said Owain. "If thou wilt tell me what I ask thee, I will tell thee that which thou askest me." "Gladly will I do so," replied Owain. "What is this?" demanded Peredur, concerning the saddle. "It is a saddle," said Owain. Then he asked about all the accoutrements which he saw upon the men, and the horses, and the arms, and what they were for, and how they were used. And Owain shewed him all these things fully, and told him what use was made of them. "Go forward," said Peredur, "for I saw such an one as thou inquirest for, and I will follow thee."

Then Peredur returned to his mother and her company, and he said to her, "Mother, those were not angels, but honourable knights." Then his mother swooned away. And Peredur went to the place where they kept the horses that carried firewood, and that brought meat and drink from the inhabited country to the desert. And he took a bony piebald horse, which seemed to him the strongest of them. And he pressed a pack into the form of a saddle, and with twisted twigs he imitated the trappings which he had seen upon the horses. And when Peredur came again to his mother, the Countess had recovered from her swoon. "My son," said she, "desirest thou to ride forth?" "Yes, with thy leave," said he. "Wait, then, that I may counsel thee before thou goest." "Willingly," he answered; "speak quickly." "Go forward, then," she said, "to the Court of Arthur, where there are the best, and the boldest, and the most bountiful of men. And wherever thou seest a church, repeat there thy Paternoster unto it. And if thou see meat and drink, and have need of them, and none have the kindness or the courtesy to give them to thee, take them thyself. If thou hear an outcry, proceed towards it, especially if it be the outcry of a woman. If thou see a fair jewel, possess thyself of it, and give it to another[83a], for thus thou shalt obtain praise. If thou see a fair woman, pay thy court to her, whether she will or no; for thus thou wilt render thyself a better and more esteemed man than thou wast before."

After this discourse, Peredur mounted the horse, and taking a handful of sharp-pointed forks in his hand, he rode forth. And he journeyed two days and two nights in the woody wildernesses, and in desert places, without food and without drink. And then he came to a vast wild wood, and far within the wood he saw a fair even glade, and in the glade he saw a tent, and the tent seeming to him to be a church, he repeated his Paternoster to it. And he went towards it, and the door of the tent was open. And a golden chair was near the door. And on the chair sat a lovely auburn-haired maiden, with a golden frontlet on her forehead, and sparkling stones in the frontlet, and with a large gold ring on her hand. And Peredur dismounted, and entered the tent. And the maiden was glad at his coming, and bade him welcome. At the entrance of the tent he saw food, and two flasks full of wine, and two loaves of fine wheaten flour, and collops of the flesh of the wild boar. "My mother told me," said Peredur, "wheresoever I saw meat and drink, to take it." "Take the meat and welcome, chieftain," said she. So Peredur took half of the meat and of the liquor himself, and left the rest to the maiden. And when Peredur had finished eating, he bent upon his knee before the maiden. "My mother," said he, "told me, wheresoever I saw a fair jewel, to take it." "Do so, my soul," said she. So Peredur took the ring. And he mounted his horse, and proceeded on his journey.

After this, behold the knight came to whom the tent belonged; and he was the Lord of the Glade. And he saw the track of the horse, and he said to the maiden, "Tell me who has been here since I departed." "A man," said she, "of wonderful demeanour." And she described to him what Peredur's appearance and conduct had been. "Tell me," said he, "did he offer thee any wrong?" "No," answered the maiden, "by my faith, he harmed me not." "By my faith, I do not believe thee; and until I can meet with him, and revenge the insult he has done me, and wreak my vengeance upon him, thou shalt not remain two nights in the same house." And the knight arose, and set forth to seek Peredur.

Meanwhile Peredur journeyed on towards Arthur's Court. And before he reached it, another knight had been there, who gave a ring of thick gold at the door of the gate for holding his horse, and went into the Hall where Arthur and his household, and Gwenhwyvar and her maidens, were assembled. And the page of the chamber was serving Gwenhwyvar with a golden goblet. Then the knight dashed the liquor that was therein upon her face, and upon her stomacher, and gave her a violent blow on the face, and said, "If any have the boldness to dispute this goblet with me, and to revenge the insult to Gwenhwyvar, let him follow me to the meadow, and there I will await him." So the knight took his horse, and rode to the meadow. And all the household hung down their heads, lest any of them should be requested to go and avenge the insult to Gwenhwyvar. For it seemed to them, that no one would have ventured on so daring an outrage, unless he possessed such powers, through magic or charms[85a], that none could be able to take vengeance upon him. Then, behold, Peredur entered the Hall, upon the bony piebald horse, with the uncouth trappings upon it; and in this way he traversed the whole length of the Hall. In the centre of the Hall stood Kai. "Tell me, tall man," said Peredur, "is that Arthur yonder?" "What wouldest thou with Arthur?" asked Kai. "My mother told me to go to Arthur, and receive the honour of knighthood." "By my faith," said he, "thou art all too meanly equipped with horse and with arms." Thereupon he was perceived by all the household, and they threw sticks at him. Then, behold, a dwarf came forward. He had already been a year at Arthur's Court, both he and a female dwarf. They had craved harbourage of Arthur, and had obtained it; and during the whole year, neither of them had spoken a single word to any one. When the dwarf beheld Peredur, "Haha!" said he, "the welcome of Heaven be unto thee, goodly Peredur, son of Evrawc, the chief of warriors, and flower of knighthood." "Truly," said Kai, "thou art ill-taught to remain a year mute at Arthur's Court, with choice of society; and now, before the face of Arthur and all his household, to call out, and declare such a man as this the chief of warriors, and the flower of knighthood." And he gave him such a box on the ear that he fell senseless to the ground. Then exclaimed the female dwarf, "Haha! goodly Peredur, son of Evrawc; the welcome of Heaven be unto thee, flower of knights, and light of chivalry." "Of a truth, maiden," said Kai, "thou art ill-bred to remain mute for a year at the Court of Arthur, and then to speak as thou dost of such a man as this." And Kai kicked her with his foot, so that she fell to the ground senseless. "Tall man," said Peredur, "shew me which is Arthur." "Hold thy peace," said Kai, "and go after the knight who went hence to the meadow, and take from him the goblet, and overthrow him, and possess thyself of his horse and arms, and then thou shalt receive the order of knighthood." "I will do so, tall man," said Peredur. So he turned his horse's head towards the meadow. And when he came there, the knight was riding up and down, proud of his strength, and valour, and noble mien. "Tell me," said the knight, "didst thou see any one coming after me from the Court?" "The tall man that was there," said he, "desired me to come, and overthrow thee, and to take from thee the goblet, and thy horse and thy armour for myself." "Silence!" said the knight; "go back to the Court, and tell Arthur, from me, either to come himself, or to send some other to fight with me; and unless he do so quickly, I will not wait for him." "By my faith," said Peredur, "choose thou whether it shall be willingly or unwillingly, but I will have the horse, and the arms, and the goblet." And upon this the knight ran at him furiously, and struck him a violent blow with the shaft of his spear, between the neck and the shoulder[86a]. "Haha! lad," said Peredur, "my mother's servants were not used to play with me in this wise; therefore, thus will I play with thee." And thereupon he struck him with a sharp-pointed fork, and it hit him in the eye, and came out at the back of his neck, so that he instantly fell down lifeless.

"Verily," said Owain the son of Urien to Kai, "thou wert ill-advised, when thou didst send that madman after the knight. For one of two things must befall him. He must either be overthrown, or slain. If he is overthrown by the knight, he will be counted by him to be an honourable person of the Court, and an eternal disgrace will it be to Arthur and his warriors. And if he is slain, the disgrace will be the same, and moreover, his sin will be upon him; therefore will I go to see what has befallen him." So Owain went to the meadow, and he found Peredur dragging the man about. "What art thou doing thus?" said Owain. "This iron coat[86b]," said Peredur, "will never come from off him; not by my efforts, at any rate." And Owain unfastened his armour and his clothes. "Here, my good soul," said he, "is a horse and armour better than thine. Take them joyfully, and come with me to Arthur, to receive the order of knighthood, for thou dost merit it." "May I never shew my face again if I go," said Peredur; "but take thou the goblet to Gwenhwyvar, and tell Arthur, that wherever I am, I will be his vassal, and will do him what profit and service I am able. And say that I will not come to his Court until I have encountered the tall man that is there, to revenge the injury he did to the dwarf and dwarfess." And Owain went back to the Court, and related all these things to Arthur and Gwenhwyvar, and to all the household.

And Peredur rode forward. And as he proceeded, behold a knight met him. "Whence comest thou?" said the knight. "I come from Arthur's Court," said Peredur. "Art thou one of his men?" asked he. "Yes, by my faith," he answered. "A good service, truly, is that of Arthur." "Wherefore sayest thou so?" said Peredur. "I will tell thee," said he; "I have always been Arthur's enemy, and all such of his men as I have ever encountered I have slain." And without further parlance they fought, and it was not long before Peredur brought him to the ground, over his horse's crupper. Then the knight besought his mercy. "Mercy thou shalt have," said Peredur, "if thou wilt make oath to me, that thou wilt go to Arthur's Court, and tell him that it was I that overthrew thee, for the honour of his service; and say, that I will never come to the Court until I have avenged the insult offered to the dwarf and dwarfess." The knight pledged him his faith of this, and proceeded to the Court of Arthur, and said as he had promised, and conveyed the threat to Kai.

And Peredur rode forward. And within that week he encountered sixteen knights, and overthrew them all shamefully. And they all went to Arthur's Court, taking with them the same message which the first knight had conveyed from Peredur, and the same threat which he had sent to Kai. And thereupon Kai was reproved by Arthur; and Kai was greatly grieved thereat.

And Peredur rode forward. And he came to a vast and desert wood, on the confines of which was a lake. And on the other side was a fair castle. And on the border of the lake he saw a venerable, hoary-headed man, sitting upon a velvet cushion, and having a garment of velvet upon him. And his attendants were fishing in the lake. When the hoary-headed man beheld Peredur approaching, he arose and went towards the castle. And the old man was lame. Peredur rode to the palace, and the door was open, and he entered the hall. And there was the hoary-headed man sitting on a cushion, and a large blazing fire burning before him. And the household and the company arose to meet Peredur, and disarrayed him. And the man asked the youth to sit on the cushion; and they sat down, and conversed together. When it was time, the tables were laid, and they went to meat. And when they had finished their meal, the man inquired of Peredur if he knew well how to fight with the sword. "I know not," said Peredur, "but were I to be taught, doubtless I should." "Whoever can play well with the cudgel and shield, will also be able to fight with a sword." And the man had two sons; the one had yellow hair, and the other auburn. "Arise, youths," said he, "and play with the cudgel and the shield." And so did they. "Tell me, my soul," said the man, "which of the youths thinkest thou plays best." "I think," said Peredur, "that the yellow-haired youth could draw blood from the other, if he chose." "Arise thou, my life, and take the cudgel and the shield from the hand of the youth with the auburn hair, and draw blood from the yellow-haired youth if thou canst." So Peredur arose, and went to play with the yellow-haired youth; and he lifted up his arm, and struck him such a mighty blow, that his brow fell over his eye, and the blood flowed forth. "Ah, my life," said the man, "come now, and sit down, for thou wilt become the best fighter with the sword of any in this island; and I am thy uncle, thy mother's brother. And with me shalt thou remain a space, in order to learn the manners and customs of different countries, and courtesy, and gentleness, and noble bearing. Leave, then, the habits and the discourse of thy mother, and I will be thy teacher; and I will raise thee to the rank of knight from this time forward. And thus do thou. If thou seest aught to cause thee wonder, ask not the meaning of it; if no one has the courtesy to inform thee, the reproach will not fall upon thee, but upon me that am thy teacher." And they had abundance of honour and service. And when it was time they went to sleep. At the break of day, Peredur arose, and took his horse, and with his uncle's permission he rode forth. And he came to a vast desert wood, and at the further end of the wood was a meadow, and on the other side of the meadow he saw a large castle. And thitherward Peredur bent his way, and he found the gate open, and he proceeded to the hall. And he beheld a stately hoary-headed man sitting on one side of the hall, and many pages around him, who arose to receive and to honour Peredur. And they placed him by the side of the owner of the palace. Then they discoursed together; and when it was time to eat, they caused Peredur to sit beside the nobleman during the repast. And when they had eaten and drunk as much as they desired, the nobleman asked Peredur whether he could fight with a sword? "Were I to receive instruction," said Peredur, "I think I could." Now, there was on the floor of the hall a huge staple, as large as a warrior could grasp. "Take yonder sword," said the man to Peredur, "and strike the iron staple." So Peredur arose and struck the staple, so that he cut it in two; and the sword broke into two parts also. "Place the two parts together, and reunite them," and Peredur placed them together, and they became entire as they were before. And a second time he struck upon the staple, so that both it and the sword broke in two, and as before they reunited. And the third time he gave a like blow, and placed the broken parts together, and neither the staple nor the sword would unite as before. "Youth," said the nobleman, "come now, and sit down, and my blessing be upon thee. Thou fightest best with the sword of any man in the kingdom. Thou hast arrived at two-thirds of thy strength, and the other third thou hast not yet obtained; and when thou attainest to thy full power, none will be able to contend with thee. I am thy uncle, thy mother's brother, and I am brother to the man in whose house thou wast last night." Then Peredur and his uncle discoursed together, and he beheld two youths enter the hall, and proceed up to the chamber, bearing a spear of mighty size[90a], with three streams of blood flowing from the point to the ground. And when all the company saw this, they began wailing and lamenting. But for all that, the man did not break off his discourse with Peredur. And as he did not tell Peredur the meaning of what he saw, he forbore to ask him concerning it. And when the clamour had a little subsided, behold two maidens entered, with a large salver between them, in which was a man's head, surrounded by a profusion of blood. And thereupon the company of the court made so great an outcry, that it was irksome to be in the same hall with them. But at length they were silent. And when time was that they should sleep, Peredur was brought into a fair chamber.

And the next day, with his uncle's permission, he rode forth. And he came to a wood, and far within the wood he heard a loud cry, and he saw a beautiful woman with auburn hair, and a horse with a saddle upon it, standing near her, and a corpse by her side. And as she strove to place the corpse upon the horse, it fell to the ground, and thereupon she made a great lamentation. "Tell me, sister," said Peredur, "wherefore art thou bewailing?" "Oh! accursed Peredur, little pity has my ill-fortune ever met with from thee." "Wherefore," said Peredur, "am I accursed?" "Because thou wast the cause of thy mother's death; for when thou didst ride forth against her will, anguish seized upon her heart, so that she died; and therefore art thou accursed. And the dwarf and the dwarfess that thou sawest at Arthur's Court were the dwarfs of thy father and mother; and I am thy foster-sister, and this was my wedded husband, and he was slain by the knight that is in the glade in the wood; and do not thou go near him, lest thou shouldest be slain by him likewise." "My sister, thou dost reproach me wrongfully; through my having so long remained amongst you, I shall scarcely vanquish him; and had I continued longer, it would, indeed, be difficult for me to succeed. Cease, therefore, thy lamenting, for it is of no avail, and I will bury the body, and then I will go in quest of the knight, and see if I can do vengeance upon him." And when he had buried the body, they went to the place where the knight was, and found him riding proudly along the glade; and he inquired of Peredur whence he came. "I come from Arthur's Court." "And art thou one of Arthur's men?" "Yes, by my faith." "A profitable alliance, truly, is that of Arthur." And without further parlance, they encountered one another, and immediately Peredur overthrew the knight, and he besought mercy of Peredur. "Mercy shalt thou have," said he, "upon these terms, that thou take this woman in marriage, and do her all the honour and reverence in thy power, seeing thou hast, without cause, slain her wedded husband; and that thou go to Arthur's Court, and shew him that it was I that overthrew thee, to do him honour and service; and that thou tell him that I will never come to his Court again until I have met with the tall man that is there, to take vengeance upon him for his insult to the dwarf and dwarfess." And he took the knight's assurance, that he would perform all this. Then the knight provided the lady with a horse and garments that were suitable for her, and took her with him to Arthur's Court. And he told Arthur all that had occurred, and gave the defiance to Kai. And Arthur and all his household reproved Kai, for having driven such a youth as Peredur from his Court.

Said Owain the son of Urien, "This youth will never come into the Court until Kai has gone forth from it." "By my faith," said Arthur, "I will search all the deserts in the Island of Britain, until I find Peredur, and then let him and his adversary do their utmost to each other."

Then Peredur rode forward. And he came to a desert wood, where he saw not the track either of men or animals, and where there was nothing but bushes and weeds. And at the upper end of the wood he saw a vast castle, wherein were many strong towers; and when he came near the gate, he found the weeds taller than he had seen them elsewhere. And he struck the gate with the shaft of his lance, and thereupon behold a lean, auburn-haired youth came to an opening in the battlements. "Choose thou, chieftain," said he, "whether shall I open the gate unto thee, or shall I announce unto those that are chief, that thou art at the gateway?" "Say that I am here," said Peredur, "and if it is desired that I should enter, I will go in." And the youth came back, and opened the gate for Peredur. And when he went into the hall, he beheld eighteen youths, lean and red-headed, of the same height, and of the same aspect, and of the same dress, and of the same age as the one who had opened the gate for him. And they were well skilled in courtesy and in service. And they disarrayed him. Then they sat down to discourse. Thereupon, behold five maidens came from the chamber into the hall. And Peredur was certain that he had never seen another of so fair an aspect as the chief of the maidens. And she had an old garment of satin upon her, which had once been handsome, but was then so tattered, that her skin could be seen through it. And whiter was her skin than the bloom of crystal, and her hair and her two eyebrows were blacker than jet, and on her cheeks were two red spots, redder than whatever is reddest. And the maiden welcomed Peredur, and put her arms about his neck, and made him sit down beside her. Not long after this he saw two nuns enter, and a flask full of wine was borne by one, and six loaves of white bread by the other. "Lady," said they, "Heaven is witness, that there is not so much of food and liquor as this left in yonder Convent this night." Then they went to meat, and Peredur observed that the maiden wished to give more of the food and of the liquor to him than to any of the others. "My sister," said Peredur, "I will share out the food and the liquor." "Not so, my soul," said she. "By my faith but I will." So Peredur took the bread, and he gave an equal portion of it to each alike, as well as a cup full of the liquor. And when it was time for them to sleep, a chamber was prepared for Peredur, and he went to rest.

"Behold, sister," said the youths to the fairest and most exalted of the maidens, "we have counsel for thee." "What may it be?" she inquired. "Go to the youth that is in the upper chamber, and offer to become his wife, or the lady of his love, if it seem well to him." "That were indeed unfitting," said she. "Hitherto I have not been the lady-love of any knight, and to make him such an offer before I am wooed by him, that, truly, can I not do." "By our confession to Heaven, unless thou actest thus, we will leave thee here to thy enemies, to do as they will with thee." And through fear of this, the maiden went forth; and shedding tears, she proceeded to the chamber. And with the noise of the door opening, Peredur awoke; and the maiden was weeping and lamenting. "Tell me, my sister," said Peredur, "wherefore dost thou weep?" "I will tell thee, lord," said she. "My father possessed these dominions as their chief, and this palace was his, and with it he held the best earldom in the kingdom; then the son of another earl sought me of my father, and I was not willing to be given unto him, and my father would not give me against my will, either to him or any earl in the world. And my father had no child except myself. And after my father's death, these dominions came into my own hands, and then was I less willing to accept him than before. So he made war upon me, and conquered all my possessions, except this one house. And through the valour of the men whom thou hast seen, who are my foster-brothers, and the strength of the house, it can never be taken while food and drink remain. And now our provisions are exhausted; but, as thou hast seen, we have been fed by the nuns, to whom the country is free. And at length they also are without supply of food or liquor. And at no later date than to-morrow, the earl will come against this place with all his forces; and if I fall into his power, my fate will be no better than to be given over to the grooms of his horses.

Therefore, lord, I am come to offer to place myself in thy hands, that thou mayest succour me, either by taking me hence, or by defending me here, whichever may seem best unto thee." "Go, my sister," said he, "and sleep; nor will I depart from thee until I do that which thou requirest, or prove whether I can assist thee or not." The maiden went again to rest; and the next morning she came to Peredur, and saluted him. "Heaven prosper thee, my soul, and what tidings dost thou bring?" "None other, than that the earl and all his forces have alighted at the gate, and I never beheld any place so covered with tents, and thronged with knights challenging others to the combat." "Truly," said Peredur, "let my horse be made ready." So his horse was accoutred, and he arose and sallied forth to the meadow. And there was a knight riding proudly along the meadow, having raised the signal for battle. And they encountered, and Peredur threw the knight over his horse's crupper to the ground. And at the close of the day, one of the chief knights came to fight with him, and he overthrew him also, so that he besought his mercy. "Who art thou?" said Peredur. "Verily," said he, "I am Master of the Household to the earl." "And how much of the countess's possessions is there in thy power?" "The third part[94a], verily," answered he. "Then," said Peredur, "restore to her the third of her possessions in full, and all the profit thou hast made by them, and bring meat and drink for a hundred men, with their horses and arms, to her court this night. And thou shalt remain her captive, unless she wish to take thy life." And this he did forthwith. And that night the maiden was right joyful, and they fared plenteously.

And the next day Peredur rode forth to the meadow; and that day he vanquished a multitude of the host. And at the close of the day, there came a proud and stately knight, and Peredur overthrew him, and he besought his mercy. "Who art thou?" said Peredur. "I am Steward of the Palace," said he. "And how much of the maiden's possessions are under thy control?" "One-third part," answered he. "Verily," said Peredur, "thou shalt fully restore to the maiden her possessions, and, moreover, thou shalt give her meat and drink for two hundred men, and their horses and their arms. And for thyself, thou shalt be her captive."

And immediately it was so done.

And the third day Peredur rode forth to the meadow; and he vanquished more that day than on either of the preceding. And at the close of the day, an earl came to encounter him, and he overthrew him, and he besought his mercy. "Who art thou?" said Peredur. "I am the earl," said he. "I will not conceal it from thee." "Verily," said Peredur, "thou shalt restore the whole of the maiden's earldom, and shalt give her thine own earldom in addition thereto, and meat and drink for three hundred men, and their horses and arms, and thou thyself shalt remain in her power." And thus it was fulfilled. And Peredur tarried three weeks in the country, causing tribute and obedience to be paid to the maiden, and the government to be placed in her hands. "With thy leave," said Peredur, "I will go hence." "Verily, my brother, desirest thou this?" "Yes, by my faith; and had it not been for love of thee, I should not have been here thus long." "My soul," said she, "who art thou?" "I am Peredur the son of Evrawc from the North; and if ever thou art in trouble or in danger, acquaint me therewith, and if I can, I will protect thee."

So Peredur rode forth. And far thence there met him a lady, mounted on a horse that was lean, and covered with sweat; and she saluted the youth. "Whence comest thou, my sister?" Then she told him the cause of her journey. Now she was the wife of the Lord of the Glade. "Behold," said he, "I am the knight through whom thou art in trouble, and he shall repent it, who has treated thee thus." Thereupon, behold a knight rode up, and he inquired of Peredur, if he had seen a knight such as he was seeking. "Hold thy peace," said Peredur, "I am he whom thou seekest; and by my faith, thou deservest ill of thy household for thy treatment of the maiden, for she is innocent concerning me." So they encountered, and they were not long in combat ere Peredur overthrew the knight, and he besought his mercy. "Mercy thou shalt have," said Peredur, "so thou wilt return by the way thou camest, and declare that thou holdest the maiden innocent, and so that thou wilt acknowledge unto her the reverse thou hast sustained at my hands." And the knight plighted him his faith thereto.

Then Peredur rode forward. And above him he beheld a castle, and thitherward he went. And he struck upon the gate with his lance, and then, behold, a comely auburn-haired youth opened the gate, and he had the stature of a warrior, and the years of a boy. And when Peredur came into the hall, there was a tall and stately lady sitting in a chair, and many handmaidens around her; and the lady rejoiced at his coming. And when it was time, they went to meat. And after their repast was finished, "It were well for thee, chieftain," said she, "to go elsewhere to sleep." "Wherefore can I not sleep here?" said Peredur. "Nine sorceresses are here, my soul, of the sorceresses of Gloucester, and their father and their mother are with them; and unless we can make our escape before daybreak, we shall be slain; and already they have conquered and laid waste all the country, except this one dwelling." "Behold," said Peredur, "I will remain here to-night, and if you are in trouble, I will do you what service I can; but harm shall you not receive from me." So they went to rest. And with the break of day, Peredur heard a dreadful outcry. And he hastily arose, and went forth in his vest and his doublet, with his sword about his neck, and he saw a sorceress overtake one of the watch, who cried out violently. Peredur attacked the sorceress, and struck her upon the head with his sword, so that he flattened her helmet and her head-piece like a dish upon her head. "Thy mercy, goodly Peredur, son of Evrawc, and the mercy of Heaven." "How knowest thou, hag, that I am Peredur?" "By destiny, and the foreknowledge that I should suffer harm from thee. And thou shalt take a horse and armour of me; and with me thou shalt go to learn chivalry and the use of thy arms." Said Peredur, "Thou shalt have mercy, if thou pledge thy faith thou wilt never more injure the dominions of the Countess." And Peredur took surety of this, and with permission of the Countess, he set forth with the sorceress to the palace of the sorceresses. And there he remained for three weeks, and then he made choice of a horse and arms, and went his way.

And in the evening he entered a valley, and at the head of the valley he came to a hermit's cell, and the hermit welcomed him gladly, and there he spent the night. And in the morning he arose, and when he went forth, behold a shower of snow had fallen the night before, and a hawk had killed a wild fowl in front of the cell. And the noise of the horse scared the hawk away, and a raven alighted upon the bird. And Peredur stood, and compared the blackness of the raven and the whiteness of the snow, and the redness of the blood, to the hair of the lady that best he loved, which was blacker than jet, and to her skin which was whiter than the snow, and to the two red spots upon her cheeks, which were redder than the blood upon the snow appeared to be.

Now Arthur and his household were in search of Peredur. "Know ye," said Arthur, "who is the knight with the long spear that stands by the brook up yonder?" "Lord," said one of them, "I will go and learn who he is." So the youth came to the place where Peredur was, and asked him what he did thus, and who he was. And from the intensity with which he thought upon the lady whom best he loved, he gave him no answer. Then the youth thrust at Peredur with his lance, and Peredur turned upon him, and struck him over his horse's crupper to the ground. And after this, four-and-twenty youths came to him, and he did not answer one more than another, but gave the same reception to all, bringing them with one single thrust to the ground. And then came Kai, and spoke to Peredur rudely and angrily; and Peredur took him with his lance under the jaw, and cast him from him with a thrust, so that he broke his arm and his shoulder-blade, and he rode over him one-and-twenty times. And while he lay thus, stunned with the violence of the pain that he had suffered, his horse returned back at a wild and prancing pace. And when the household saw the horse come back without his rider, they rode forth in haste to the place where the encounter had been. And when they first came there, they thought that Kai was slain; but they found that if he had a skilful physician, he yet might live. And Peredur moved not from his meditation, on seeing the concourse that was around Kai. And Kai was brought to Arthur's tent, and Arthur caused skilful physicians to come to him. And Arthur was grieved that Kai had met with this reverse, for he loved him greatly.

"Then," said Gwalchmai[98a], "it is not fitting that any should disturb an honourable knight from his thought unadvisedly; for either he is pondering some damage that he has sustained, or he is thinking of the lady whom best he loves. And through such ill-advised proceeding, perchance this misadventure has befallen him who last met with him. And if it seem well to thee, lord, I will go and see if this knight hath changed from his thought; and if he has, I will ask him courteously to come and visit thee." Then Kai was wroth, and he spoke angry and spiteful words. "Gwalchmai," said he, "I know that thou wilt bring him because he is fatigued. Little praise and honour, nevertheless, wilt thou have from vanquishing a weary knight, who is tired with fighting. Yet thus hast thou gained the advantage over many. And while thy speech and thy soft words last, a coat of thin linen were armour sufficient for thee, and thou wilt not need to break either lance or sword in fighting with the knight in the state he is in." Then said Gwalchmai to Kai, "Thou mightest use more pleasant words, wert thou so minded: and it behoves thee not upon me to wreak thy wrath and thy displeasure. Methinks I shall bring the knight hither with me without breaking either my arm or my shoulder." Then said Arthur to Gwalchmai, "Thou speakest like a wise and prudent man; go, and take enough of armour about thee, and choose thy horse." And Gwalchmai accoutred himself and rode forward hastily to the place where Peredur was.

And Peredur was resting on the shaft of his spear, pondering the same thought, and Gwalchmai came to him without any signs of hostility, and said to him, "If I thought that it would be as agreeable to thee as it would be to me, I would converse with thee. I have also a message from Arthur unto thee, to pray thee to come and visit him. And two men have been before on this errand." "That is true," said Peredur, "and uncourteously they came. They attacked me, and I was annoyed thereat, for it was not pleasing to me to be drawn from the thought that I was in, for I was thinking of the lady whom best I love, and thus was she brought to my mind:—I was looking upon the snow, and upon the raven, and upon the drops of the blood of the bird that the hawk had killed upon the snow. And I bethought me that her whiteness was like that of the snow, and that the blackness of her hair and her eyebrows like that of the raven, and that the two red spots upon her cheeks were like the two drops of blood." Said Gwalchmai, "This was not an ungentle thought, and I should marvel if it were pleasant to thee to be drawn from it." "Tell me," said Peredur, "is Kai in Arthur's Court?" "He is," said he, "and behold he is the knight that fought with thee last; and it would have been better for him had he not come, for his arm and his shoulder-blade were broken with the fall which he had from thy spear." "Verily," said Peredur, "I am not sorry to have thus begun to avenge the insult to the dwarf and dwarfess." Then Gwalchmai marvelled to hear him speak of the dwarf and the dwarfess; and he approached him, and threw his arms around his neck, and asked him what was his name. "Peredur the son of Evrawc am I called," said he; "and thou, Who art thou?" "I am called Gwalchmai," he replied. "I am right glad to meet with thee," said Peredur, "for in every country where I have been I have heard of thy fame for prowess and uprightness, and I solicit thy fellowship." "Thou shalt have it, by my faith, and grant me thine," said he, "Gladly will I do so," answered Peredur.

So they rode forth together joyfully towards the place where Arthur was, and when Kai saw them coming, he said, "I knew that Gwalchmai needed not to fight the knight. And it is no wonder that he should gain fame; more can he do by his fair words than I by the strength of my arm." And Peredur went with Gwalchmai to his tent, and they took off their armour. And Peredur put on garments like those that Gwalchmai wore, and they went together unto Arthur, and saluted him. "Behold, lord," said Gwalchmai, "him whom thou hast sought so long." "Welcome unto thee, chieftain," said Arthur. "With me thou shalt remain; and had I known thy valour had been such, thou shouldst not have left me as thou didst; nevertheless, this was predicted of thee by the dwarf and the dwarfess, whom Kai ill-treated and whom thou hast avenged." And hereupon, behold there came the Queen and her handmaidens, and Peredur saluted them. And they were rejoiced to see him, and bade him welcome. And Arthur did him great honour and respect, and they returned towards Caerlleon.

And the first night Peredur came to Caerlleon to Arthur's Court, and as he walked in the city after his repast, behold, there met him Angharad Law Eurawc[100a]. "By my faith, sister," said Peredur, "thou art a beauteous and lovely maiden; and, were it pleasing to thee, I could love thee above all women." "I pledge my faith," said she, "that I do not love thee, nor will I ever do so." "I also pledge my faith," said Peredur, "that I will never speak a word to any Christian again[100b], until thou come to love me above all men."

The next day Peredur went forth by the high road, along a mountain-ridge, and he saw a valley of a circular form, the confines of which were rocky and wooded. And the flat part of the valley was in meadows, and there were fields betwixt the meadows and the wood. And in the bosom of the wood he saw large black houses of uncouth workmanship. And he dismounted, and led his horse towards the wood. And a little way within the wood he saw a rocky ledge, along which the road lay. And upon the ledge was a lion bound by a chain, and sleeping. And beneath the lion he saw a deep pit of immense size, full of the bones of men and animals. And Peredur drew his sword and struck the lion, so that he fell into the mouth of the pit and hung there by the chain; and with a second blow he struck the chain and broke it, and the lion fell into the pit; and

Peredur led his horse over the rocky ledge, until he came into the valley. And in the centre of the valley he saw a fair castle, and he went towards it. And in the meadow by the castle he beheld a huge grey man sitting, who was larger than any man he had ever before seen. And two young pages were shooting the hilts of their daggers, of the bone of the sea-horse. And one of the pages had red hair, and the other auburn. And they went before him to the place where the grey man was, and Peredur saluted him. And the grey man said, "Disgrace to the beard of my porter." Then Peredur understood that the porter was the lion.—And the grey man and the pages went together into the castle, and Peredur accompanied them; and he found it a fair and noble place. And they proceeded to the hall, and the tables were already laid, and upon them was abundance of food and liquor. And thereupon he saw an aged woman and a young woman come from the chamber; and they were the most stately women he had ever seen. Then they washed and went to meat, and the grey man sat in the upper seat at the head of the table, and the aged woman next to him. And Peredur and the maiden were placed together, and the two young pages served them. And the maiden gazed sorrowfully upon Peredur, and Peredur asked the maiden wherefore she was sad. "For thee, my soul; for, from when I first beheld thee, I have loved thee above all men. And it pains me to know that so gentle a youth as thou should have such a doom as awaits thee to-morrow. Sawest thou the numerous black houses in the bosom of the wood? All these belong to the vassals of the grey man yonder, who is my father. And they are all giants.

And to-morrow they will rise up against thee, and will slay thee. And the Round Valley is this valley called." "Listen, fair maiden, wilt thou contrive that my horse and arms be in the same lodging with me to-night?" "Gladly will I cause it so to be, by Heaven, if I can."

And when it was time for them to sleep rather than to carouse, they went to rest. And the maiden caused Peredur's horse and arms to be in the same lodging with him. And the next morning Peredur heard a great tumult of men and horses around the castle. And Peredur arose, and armed himself and his horse, and went to the meadow. Then the aged woman and the maiden came to the grey man: "Lord," said they, "take the word of the youth, that he will never disclose what he has seen in this place, and we will be his sureties that he keep it." "I will not do so, by my faith," said the grey man. So Peredur fought with the host, and towards evening he had slain the one-third of them without receiving any hurt himself. Then said the aged woman, "Behold, many of thy host have been slain by the youth; do thou, therefore, grant him mercy." "I will not grant it, by my faith," said he. And the aged woman and the fair maiden were upon the battlements of the castle, looking forth. And at that juncture, Peredur encountered the yellow-haired youth and slew him. "Lord," said the maiden, "grant the young man mercy." "That will I not do, by Heaven," he replied; and thereupon Peredur attacked the auburn-haired youth, and slew him likewise. "It were better that thou hadst accorded mercy to the youth before he had slain thy two sons; for now scarcely wilt thou thyself escape from him." "Go, maiden, and beseech the youth to grant mercy unto us, for we yield ourselves into his hands." So the maiden came to the place where Peredur was, and besought mercy for her father, and for all such of his vassals as had escaped alive. "Thou shalt have it, on condition that thy father and all that are under him go and render homage to Arthur, and tell him that it was his vassal Peredur that did him this service." "This will we do willingly, by Heaven." "And you shall also receive baptism; and I will send to Arthur, and beseech him to bestow this valley upon thee and upon thy heirs after thee for ever." Then they went in, and the grey man and the tall woman saluted Peredur. And the grey man said unto him, "Since I have possessed this valley I have not seen any Christian depart with his life, save thyself. And we will go to do homage to Arthur, and to embrace the faith and be baptized." Then said Peredur, "To Heaven I render thanks that I have not broken my vow to the lady that best I love, which was, that I would not speak one word unto any Christian."

That night they tarried there. And the next day, in the morning, the grey man, with his company, set forth to Arthur's Court; and they did homage unto Arthur, and he caused them to be baptized. And the grey man told Arthur that it was Peredur that had vanquished them. And Arthur gave the valley to the grey man and his company, to hold it of him as Peredur had besought. And with Arthur's permission, the grey man went back to the Round Valley.

Peredur rode forward next day, and he traversed a vast tract of desert, in which no dwellings were. And at length he came to a habitation, mean and small. And there he heard that there was a serpent that lay upon a gold ring, and suffered none to inhabit the country for seven miles around. And Peredur came to the place where he heard the serpent was. And angrily, furiously, and desperately fought he with the serpent; and at last he killed it, and took away the ring. And thus he was for a long time without speaking a word to any Christian. And therefrom he lost his colour and his aspect, through extreme longing after the Court of Arthur, and the society of the lady whom best he loved, and of his companions. Then he proceeded forward to Arthur's Court, and on the road there met him Arthur's household going on a particular errand, with Kai at their head. And Peredur knew them all, but none of the household recognized him. "Whence comest thou, chieftain?" said Kai. And this he asked him twice and three times, and he answered him not.

And Kai thrust him through the thigh with his lance. And lest he should be compelled to speak, and to break his vow, he went on without stopping. "Then," said Gwalchmai, "I declare to Heaven, Kai, that thou hast acted ill in committing such an outrage on a youth like this, who cannot speak."

And Gwalchmai returned back to Arthur's Court. "Lady," said he to Gwenhwyvar, "seest thou how wicked an outrage Kai has committed upon this youth who cannot speak; for Heaven's sake, and for mine, cause him to have medical care before I come back, and I will repay thee the charge."

And before the men returned from their errand, a knight came to the meadow beside Arthur's Palace, to dare some one to the encounter. And his challenge was accepted; and Peredur fought with him, and overthrew him. And for a week he overthrew one knight every day.

And one day, Arthur and his household were going to Church, and they beheld a knight who had raised the signal for combat. "Verily," said Arthur, "by the valour of men, I will not go hence until I have my horse and my arms to overthrow yonder boor." Then went the attendants to fetch Arthur's horse and arms. And Peredur met the attendants as they were going back, and he took the horse and arms from them, and proceeded to the meadow; and all those who saw him arise and go to do battle with the knight, went upon the tops of the houses, and the mounds, and the high places, to behold the combat. And Peredur beckoned with his hand to the knight to commence the fight. And the knight thrust at him, but he was not thereby moved from where he stood. And Peredur spurred his horse, and ran at him wrathfully, furiously, fiercely, desperately, and with mighty rage, and he gave him a thrust, deadly-wounding, severe, furious, adroit, and strong, under his jaw, and raised him out of his saddle, and cast him a long way from him. And Peredur went back, and left the horse and the arms with the attendant as before, and he went on foot to the Palace.

Then Peredur went by the name of the Dumb Youth. And behold, Angharad Law Eurawc met him. "I declare to Heaven, chieftain," said she, "woful is it that thou canst not speak; for couldst thou speak, I would love thee best of all men; and by my faith, although thou canst not, I do love thee above all." "Heaven reward thee, my sister," said Peredur, "by my faith I also do love thee." Thereupon it was known that he was Peredur. And then he held fellowship with Gwalchmai, and Owain the son of Urien, and all the household, and he remained in Arthur's Court.

Arthur was in Caerlleon upon Usk; and he went to hunt, and Peredur went with him. And Peredur let loose his dog upon a hart, and the dog killed the hart in a desert place. And a short space from him he saw signs of a dwelling, and towards the dwelling he went, and he beheld a hall, and at the door of the hall he found bald swarthy youths playing at chess. And when he entered, he beheld three maidens sitting on a bench, and they were all clothed alike, as became persons of high rank. And he came, and sat by them upon the bench; and one of the maidens looked steadfastly upon Peredur, and wept. And Peredur asked her wherefore she was weeping. "Through grief, that I should see so fair a youth as thou art, slain." "Who will slay me?" inquired Peredur. "If thou art so daring as to remain here to-night, I will tell thee." "How great soever my danger may be from remaining here, I will listen unto thee." "This Palace is owned by him who is my father," said the maiden, "and he slays every one who comes hither without his leave." "What sort of a man is thy father, that he is able to slay every one thus?" "A man who does violence and wrong unto his neighbours, and who renders justice unto none." And hereupon he saw the youths arise and clear the chessmen from the board. And he heard a great tumult; and after the tumult there came in a huge black one-eyed man, and the maidens arose to meet him. And they disarrayed him, and he went and sat down; and after he had rested and pondered awhile, he looked at Peredur, and asked who the knight was. "Lord," said one of the maidens, "he is the fairest and gentlest youth that ever thou didst see. And for the sake of Heaven, and of thine own dignity, have patience with him." "For thy sake I will have patience, and I will grant him his life this night." Then Peredur came towards them to the fire, and partook of food and liquor, and entered into discourse with the ladies. And being elated with the liquor, he said to the black man, "It is a marvel to me, so mighty as thou sayest thou art, who could have put out thine eye." "It is one of my habits," said the black man, "that whosoever puts to me the question which thou hast asked, shall not escape with his life, either as a free gift or for a price." "Lord," said the maiden, "whatsoever he may say to thee in jest, and through the excitement of liquor, make good that which thou saidst and didst promise me just now." "I will do so, gladly, for thy sake," said he. "Willingly will I grant him his life this night." And that night thus they remained.

And the next day the black man got up, and put on his armour, and said to Peredur, "Arise, man, and suffer death." And Peredur said unto him, "Do one of two things, black man; if thou wilt fight with me, either throw off thy own armour, or give arms to me, that I may encounter thee." "Ha, man," said he, "couldst thou fight, if thou hadst arms? Take, then, what arms thou dost choose." And thereupon the maiden came to Peredur with such arms as pleased him; and he fought with the black man, and forced him to crave his mercy. "Black man, thou shalt have mercy, provided thou tell me who thou art, and who put out thine eye." "Lord, I will tell thee; I lost it in fighting with the Black Serpent of the Carn. There is a mound, which is called the Mound of Mourning; and on the mound there is a carn, and in the carn there is a serpent, and on the tail of the serpent there is a stone, and the virtues of the stone are such, that whosoever should hold it in one hand, in the other he will have as much gold as he may desire. And in fighting with this serpent was it that I lost my eye. And the Black Oppressor am I called. And for this reason I am called the Black Oppressor, that there is not a single man around me whom I have not oppressed, and justice have I done unto none." "Tell me," said Peredur, "how far is it hence?" "The same day that thou settest forth, thou wilt come to the Palace of the Sons of the King of the Tortures." "Wherefore are they called thus?" "The Addanc[107a] of the Lake slays them once every day. When thou goest thence, thou wilt come to the Court of the Countess of the Achievements." "What achievements are there?"

asked Peredur. "Three hundred men there are in her household, and unto every stranger that comes to the Court, the achievements of her household are related. And this is the manner of it,—the three hundred men of the household sit next unto the Lady; and that not through disrespect unto the guests, but that they may relate the achievements of the household. And the day that thou goest thence, thou wilt reach the Mound of Mourning, and round about the mound there are the owners of three hundred tents guarding the serpent." "Since thou hast, indeed, been an oppressor so long," said Peredur, "I will cause that thou continue so no longer." So he slew him.

Then the maiden spoke, and began to converse with him. "If thou wast poor when thou camest here, henceforth thou wilt be rich through the treasure of the black man whom thou hast slain. Thou seest the many lovely maidens that there are in this Court; thou shalt have her whom thou best likest for the lady of thy love." "Lady, I came not hither from my country to woo; but match yourselves as it liketh you with the comely youths I see here; and none of your goods do I desire, for I need them not." Then Peredur rode forward, and he came to the Palace of the Sons of the King of the Tortures; and when he entered the Palace, he saw none but women; and they rose up, and were joyful at his coming; and as they began to discourse with him, he beheld a charger arrive, with a saddle upon it, and a corpse in the saddle. And one of the women arose, and took the corpse from the saddle, and anointed it in a vessel of warm water, which was below the door, and placed precious balsam upon it; and the man rose up alive, and came to the place where Peredur was, and greeted him, and was joyful to see him. And two other men came in upon their saddles, and the maiden treated these two in the same manner as she had done the first. Then Peredur asked the chieftain wherefore it was thus. And they told him, that there was an Addanc in a cave, which slew them once every day. And thus they remained that night.

And next morning the youths arose to sally forth, and Peredur besought them, for the sake of the ladies of their love, to permit him to go with them; but they refused him, saying, "If thou shouldst be slain there, thou hast none to bring thee back to life again." And they rode forward, and Peredur followed after them; and, after they had disappeared out of his sight, he came to a mound, whereon sat the fairest lady he had ever beheld. "I know thy quest," said she; "thou art going to encounter the Addanc, and he will slay thee, and that not by courage, but by craft. He has a cave, and at the entrance of the cave there is a stone pillar, and he sees every one that enters, and none see him; and from behind the pillar he slays every one with a poisonous dart. And if thou wouldst pledge me thy faith to love me above all women, I would give thee a stone, by which thou shouldst see him when thou goest in, and he should not see thee." "I will, by my troth," said Peredur, "for when first I beheld thee I loved thee; and where shall I seek thee?" "When thou seekest me, seek towards India." And the maiden vanished, after placing the stone in Peredur's hand.

And he came towards a valley, through which ran a river; and the borders of the valley were wooded, and on each side of the river were level meadows. And on one side of the river he saw a flock of white sheep, and on the other a flock of black sheep. And whenever one of the white sheep bleated, one of the black sheep would cross over and become white; and when one of the black sheep bleated, one of the white sheep would cross over and become black. And he saw a tall tree by the side of the river, one half of which was in flames from the root to the top, and the other half was green and in full leaf. And nigh thereto he saw a youth sitting upon a mound, and two greyhounds, white-breasted and spotted, in leashes, lying by his side. And certain was he that he had never seen a youth of so royal a bearing as he. And in the wood opposite he heard hounds raising a herd of deer. And Peredur saluted the youth, and the youth greeted him in return. And there were three roads leading from the mound; two of them were wide roads, and the third was more narrow. And Peredur inquired where the three roads went. "One of them goes to my palace," said the youth; "and one of two things I counsel thee to do; either to proceed to my palace, which is before thee, and where thou wilt find my wife, or else to remain here to see the hounds chasing the roused deer from the wood to the plain. And thou shalt see the best greyhounds thou didst ever behold, and the boldest in the chase, kill them by the water beside us; and when it is time to go to meat, my page will come with my horse to meet me, and thou shalt rest in my palace to-night." "Heaven reward thee; but I cannot tarry, for onward must I go." "The other road leads to the town, which is near here, and wherein food and liquor may be bought; and the road which is narrower than the others goes towards the cave of the Addanc." "With thy permission, young man, I will go that way."

And Peredur went towards the cave. And he took the stone in his left hand, and his lance in his right. And as he went in he perceived the Addanc, and he pierced him through with his lance, and cut off his head. And as he came from the cave, behold the three companions were at the entrance; and they saluted Peredur, and told him that there was a prediction that he should slay that monster. And Peredur gave the head to the young men, and they offered him in marriage whichever of the three sisters he might choose, and half their kingdom with her. "I came not hither to woo," said Peredur, "but if peradventure I took a wife, I should prefer your sister to all others." And Peredur rode forward, and he heard a noise behind him. And he looked back, and saw a man upon a red horse, with red armour upon him; and the man rode up by his side, and saluted him, and wished him the favour of Heaven and of man. And Peredur greeted the youth kindly. "Lord, I come to make a request unto thee." "What wouldest thou?" "That thou shouldest take me as thine attendant." "Whom then should I take as my attendant, if I did so?" "I will not conceal from thee what kindred I am of. Etlym Gleddyv Coch[110a] am I called, an Earl from the East Country." "I marvel that thou shouldest offer to become attendant to a man whose possessions are no greater than thine own; for I have but an earldom like thyself. But since thou desirest to be my attendant, I will take thee joyfully."

And they went forward to the Court of the Countess, and all they of the Court were glad at their coming; and they were told it was not through disrespect they were placed below the household, but that such was the usage of the Court. For, whoever should overthrow the three hundred men of her household, would sit next the Countess, and she would love him above all men. And Peredur having overthrown the three hundred men of her household, sat down beside her, and the Countess said, "I thank Heaven that I have a youth so fair and so valiant as thou, since I have not obtained the man whom best I love." "Who is he whom best thou lovest?" "By my faith, Etlym Gleddyv Coch is the man whom I love best, and I have never seen him." "Of a truth, Etlym is my companion; and behold here he is, and for his sake did I come to joust with thy household. And he could have done so better than I, had it pleased him. And I do give thee unto him." "Heaven reward thee, fair youth, and I will take the man whom I love above all others." And the Countess became Etlym's bride from that moment.

And the next day Peredur set forth towards the Mound of Mourning. "By thy hand, lord, but I will go with thee," said Etlym. Then they went forwards till they came in sight of the mound and the tents. "Go unto yonder men," said Peredur to Etlym, "and desire them to come and do me homage." So Etlym went unto them, and said unto them thus,—"Come and do homage to my lord." "Who is thy lord?" said they. "Peredur with the long lance is my lord," said Etlym. "Were it permitted to slay a messenger, thou shouldest not go back to thy lord alive, for making unto Kings, and Earls, and Barons so arrogant a demand as to go and do him homage." Peredur desired him to go back to them, and to give them their choice, either to do him homage, or to do battle with him. And they chose rather to do battle. And that day Peredur overthrew the owners of a hundred tents; and the next day he overthrew the owners of a hundred more; and the third day the remaining hundred took counsel to do homage to Peredur. And Peredur inquired of them, wherefore they were there. And they told him they were guarding the serpent until he should die. "For then should we fight for the stone among ourselves, and whoever should be conqueror among us would have the stone." "Await here," said Peredur, "and I will go to encounter the serpent." "Not so, lord," said they; "we will go altogether to encounter the serpent." "Verily," said Peredur, "that will I not permit; for if the serpent be slain, I shall derive no more fame therefrom than one of you." Then he went to the place where the serpent was, and slew it, and came back to them, and said, "Reckon up what you have spent since you have been here, and I will repay you to the full." And he paid to each what he said was his claim. And he required of them only that they should acknowledge themselves his vassals. And he said to Etlym, "Go back unto her whom thou lovest best, and I will go forwards, and I will reward thee for having been my attendant." And he gave Etlym the stone.

"Heaven repay thee and prosper thee," said Etlym.

And Peredur rode thence, and he came to the fairest valley he had ever seen, through which ran a river; and there he beheld many tents of various colours. And he marvelled still more at the number of water-mills and of wind-mills that he saw. And there rode up with him a tall auburn-haired man, in workman's garb, and Peredur inquired of him who he was. "I am the chief miller," said he, "of all the mills yonder." "Wilt thou give me lodging?" said Peredur. "I will, gladly," he answered. And Peredur came to the miller's house, and the miller had a fair and pleasant dwelling. And Peredur asked money as a loan from the miller, that he might buy meat and liquor for himself and for the household, and he promised that he would pay him again ere he went thence. And he inquired of the miller, wherefore such a multitude was there assembled. Said the miller to Peredur, "One thing is certain: either thou art a man from afar, or thou art beside thyself. The Empress of Cristinobyl the Great is here; and she will have no one but the man who is most valiant; for riches does she not require. And it was impossible to bring food for so many thousands as are here, therefore were all these mills constructed." And that night they took their rest.

And the next day Peredur arose, and he equipped himself and his horse for the tournament. And among the other tents he beheld one, which was the fairest he had ever seen. And he saw a beauteous maiden leaning her head out of a window of the tent, and he had never seen a maiden more lovely than she. And upon her was a garment of satin. And he gazed fixedly on the maiden, and began to love her greatly. And he remained there, gazing upon the maiden from morning until mid-day, and from mid-day until evening; and then the tournament was ended and he went to his lodging and drew off his armour. Then he asked money of the miller as a loan, and the miller's wife was wroth with Peredur; nevertheless, the miller lent him the money. And the next day he did in like manner as he had done the day before. And at night he came to his lodging, and took money as a loan from the miller. And the third day, as he was in the same place, gazing upon the maiden, he felt a hard blow between the neck and the shoulder, from the edge of an axe. And when he looked behind him, he saw that it was the miller; and the miller said to him, "Do one of two things: either turn thy head from hence, or go to the tournament." And Peredur smiled on the miller, and went to the tournament; and all that encountered him that day he overthrew. And as many as he vanquished he sent as a gift to the Empress, and their horses and arms he sent as a gift to the wife of the miller, in payment of the borrowed money. Peredur attended the tournament until all were overthrown, and he sent all the men to the prison of the Empress, and the horses and arms to the wife of the miller, in payment of the borrowed money. And the Empress sent to the Knight of the Mill, to ask him to come and visit her. And Peredur went not for the first nor for the second message. And the third time she sent a hundred knights to bring him against his will, and they went to him and told him their mission from the Empress. And Peredur fought well with them, and caused them to be bound like stags, and thrown into the mill-dyke. And the Empress sought advice of a wise man who was in her counsel; and he said to her, "With thy permission, I will go to him myself." So he came to Peredur, and saluted him, and besought him, for the sake of the lady of his love, to come and visit the Empress. And they went, together with the miller. And Peredur went and sat down in the outer chamber of the tent, and she came and placed herself by his side. And there was but little discourse between them. And Peredur took his leave, and went to his lodging.

And the next day he came to visit her, and when he came into the tent there was no one chamber less decorated than the others. And they knew not where he would sit. And Peredur went and sat beside the Empress, and discoursed with her courteously. And while they were thus, they beheld a black man enter with a goblet full of wine in his hand. And he dropped upon his knee before the Empress, and besought her to give it to no one who would not fight with him for it. And she looked upon Peredur. "Lady," said he, "bestow on me the goblet." And Peredur drank the wine, and gave the goblet to the miller's wife. And while they were thus, behold there entered a black man of larger stature than the other, with a wild beast's claw in his hand, wrought into the form of a goblet and filled with wine. And he presented it to the Empress, and besought her to give it to no one but the man who would fight with him. "Lady," said Peredur, "bestow it on me." And she gave it to him. And Peredur drank the wine, and sent the goblet to the wife of the miller. And while they were thus, behold a rough-looking, crisp-haired man, taller than either of the others, came in with a bowl in his hand full of wine; and he bent upon his knee, and gave it into the hands of the Empress, and he besought her to give it to none but him who would fight with him for it; and she gave it to Peredur, and he sent it to the miller's wife. And that night Peredur returned to his lodging; and the next day he accoutred himself and his horse, and went to the meadow and slew the three men. Then Peredur proceeded to the tent, and the Empress said to him, "Goodly Peredur, remember the faith thou didst pledge me when I gave thee the stone, and thou didst kill the Addanc." "Lady," answered he, "thou sayest truth, I do remember it." And Peredur was entertained by the Empress fourteen years, as the story relates.

Arthur was at Caerlleon upon Usk, his principal palace; and in the centre of the floor of the hall were four men sitting on a carpet of velvet, Owain the son of Urien, and Gwalchmai the son of Gwyar, and Howel the son of Emyr Llydaw[114a], and Peredur of the long lance. And thereupon they saw a black curly-headed maiden enter, riding upon a yellow mule, with jagged thongs in her hand to urge it on; and having a rough and hideous aspect. Blacker were her face and her two hands than the blackest iron covered with pitch; and her hue was not more frightful than her form. High cheeks had she, and a face lengthened downwards, and a short nose with distended nostrils. And one eye was of a piercing mottled grey, and the other was as black as jet, deep-sunk in her head. And her teeth were long and yellow, more yellow were they than the flower of the broom. And her stomach rose from the breast-bone, higher than her chin. And her back was in the shape of a crook, and her legs were large and bony. And her figure was very thin and spare, except her feet and her legs, which were of huge size. And she greeted Arthur and all his household except Peredur. And to Peredur she spoke harsh and angry words. "Peredur, I greet thee not, seeing that thou dost not merit it. Blind was fate in giving thee fame and favour. When thou wast in the Court of the Lame King, and didst see there the youth bearing the streaming spear, from the points of which were drops of blood flowing in streams, even to the hand of the youth, and many other wonders likewise, thou didst not inquire their meaning nor their cause. Hadst thou done so, the King would have been restored to health, and his dominions to peace. Whereas from henceforth, he will have to endure battles and conflicts, and his knights will perish, and wives will be widowed, and maidens will be left portionless, and all this is because of thee." Then said she unto Arthur, "May it please thee, lord, my dwelling is far hence, in the stately castle of which thou hast heard, and therein are five hundred and sixty-six knights of the order of Chivalry, and the lady whom best he loves with each; and whoever would acquire fame in arms, and encounters, and conflicts, he will gain it there, if he deserve it. And whoso would reach the summit of fame and of honour, I know where he may find it. There is a castle on a lofty mountain, and there is a maiden therein, and she is detained a prisoner there, and whoever shall set her free will attain the summit of the fame of the world." And thereupon she rode away.

Said Gwalchmai, "By my faith, I will not rest tranquilly until I have proved if I can release the maiden." And many of Arthur's household joined themselves with him. Then, likewise, said Peredur, "By my faith, I will not rest tranquilly until I know the story and the meaning of the lance whereof the black maiden spoke." And while they were equipping themselves, behold a knight came to the gate. And he had the size and the strength of a warrior, and was equipped with arms and habiliments. And he went forward, and saluted Arthur and all his household, except Gwalchmai. And the knight had upon his shoulder a shield, ingrained with gold, with a fesse of azure blue upon it, and his whole armour was of the same hue. And he said to Gwalchmai, "Thou didst slay my lord by thy treachery and deceit, and that will I prove upon thee." Then Gwalchmai rose up. "Behold," said he, "here is my gage against thee, to maintain, either in this place or wherever else thou wilt, that I am not a traitor or deceiver." "Before the King whom I obey, will I that my encounter with thee take place," said the knight. "Willingly," said Gwalchmai; "go forward, and I will follow thee." So the knight went forth, and Gwalchmai accoutred himself, and there was offered unto him abundance of armour, but he would take none but his own. And when

Gwalchmai and Peredur were equipped, they set forth to follow him, by reason of their fellowship and of the great friendship that was between them. And they did not go after him in company together, but each went his own way.

At the dawn of day Gwalchmai came to a valley, and in the valley he saw a fortress, and within the fortress a vast palace and lofty towers around it. And he beheld a knight coming out to hunt from the other side, mounted on a spirited black snorting palfrey, that advanced at a prancing pace, proudly stepping, and nimbly bounding, and sure of foot; and this was the man to whom the palace belonged. And Gwalchmai saluted him. "Heaven prosper thee, chieftain," said he, "and whence comest thou?" "I come," answered Gwalchmai, "from the Court of Arthur." "And art thou Arthur's vassal?" "Yes, by my faith," said Gwalchmai. "I will give thee good counsel," said the knight. "I see that thou art tired and weary; go unto my palace, if it may please thee, and tarry there to-night." "Willingly, lord," said he, "and Heaven reward thee." "Take this ring as a token to the porter, and go forward to yonder tower, and therein thou wilt find my sister." And Gwalchmai went to the gate, and showed the ring, and proceeded to the tower. And on entering he beheld a large blazing fire, burning without smoke and with a bright and lofty flame, and a beauteous and stately maiden was sitting on a chair by the fire. And the maiden was glad at his coming, and welcomed him, and advanced to meet him. And he went and sat beside the maiden, and they took their repast. And when their repast was over, they discoursed pleasantly together. And while they were thus, behold there entered a venerable hoary-headed man. "Ah! base girl," said he, "if thou didst think it was right for thee to entertain and to sit by yonder man, thou wouldest not do so." And he withdrew his head, and went forth. "Ah! chieftain," said the maiden, "if thou wilt do as I counsel thee, thou wilt shut the door, lest the man should have a plot against thee." Upon that Gwalchmai arose, and when he came near unto the door, the man, with sixty others, fully armed, were ascending the tower. And Gwalchmai defended the door with a chessboard, that none might enter until the man should return from the chase. And thereupon, behold the Earl arrived. "What is all this?" asked he. "It is a sad thing," said the hoary-headed man; "the young girl yonder has been sitting and eating with him who slew your father. He is Gwalchmai, the son of Gwyar." "Hold thy peace, then," said the Earl, "I will go in." And the Earl was joyful concerning Gwalchmai. "Ha! chieftain," said he, "it was wrong of thee to come to my court, when thou knewest that thou didst slay my father; and though we cannot avenge him, Heaven will avenge him upon thee." "My soul," said Gwalchmai, "thus it is: I came not here either to acknowledge or to deny having slain thy father; but I am on a message from Arthur, and therefore do I crave the space of a year until I shall return from my embassy, and then, upon my faith, I will come back unto this palace, and do one of two things, either acknowledge it, or deny it." And the time was granted him willingly; and he remained there that night. And the next morning he rode forth. And the story relates nothing further of Gwalchmai respecting this adventure.

And Peredur rode forward. And he wandered over the whole island, seeking tidings of the black maiden, and he could meet with none. And he came to an unknown land, in the centre of a valley, watered by a river. And as he traversed the valley he beheld a horseman coming towards him, and wearing the garments of a priest; and he besought his blessing. "Wretched man," said he, "thou meritest no blessing, and thou wouldest not be profited by one, seeing that thou art clad in armour on such a day as this." "And what day is to-day?" said Peredur. "To-day is Good Friday," he answered. "Chide me not that I knew not this, seeing that it is a year to-day since I journeyed forth from my country." Then he dismounted, and led his horse in his hand. And he had not proceeded far along the high road before he came to a cross road, and the cross road traversed a wood. And on the other side of the wood he saw an unfortified castle, which appeared to be inhabited. And at the gate of the castle there met him the priest whom he had seen before, and he asked his blessing. "The blessing of Heaven be unto thee," said he, "it is more fitting to travel in thy present guise than as thou wast erewhile; and this night thou shalt tarry with me." So he remained there that night.

And the next day Peredur sought to go forth. "To-day may no one journey. Thou shalt remain with me to-day and to-morrow, and the day following, and I will direct thee as best I may to the place which thou art seeking." And the fourth day Peredur sought to go forth, and he entreated the priest to tell him how he should find the Castle of Wonders. "What I know thereof I will tell thee," he replied. "Go over yonder mountain, and on the other side of the mountain thou wilt come to a river, and in the valley wherein the river runs is a King's palace, wherein the King sojourned during Easter. And if thou mayest have tidings anywhere of the Castle of Wonders, thou wilt have them there."

Then Peredur rode forward. And he came to the valley in which was the river, and there met him a number of men going to hunt, and in the midst of them was a man of exalted rank, and Peredur saluted him. "Choose, chieftain," said the man, "whether thou wilt go with me to the chase, or wilt proceed to my palace, and I will dispatch one of my household to commend thee to my daughter, who is there, and who will entertain thee with food and liquor until I return from hunting; and whatever may be thine errand, such as I can obtain for thee thou shalt gladly have." And the King sent a little yellow page with him as an attendant; and when they came to the palace the lady had arisen, and was about to wash before meat. Peredur went forward, and she saluted him joyfully, and placed him by her side. And they took their repast. And whatsoever Peredur said unto her, she laughed loudly, so that all in the palace could hear. Then spoke the yellow page to the lady. "By my faith," said he, "this youth is already thy husband; or if he be not, thy mind and thy thoughts are set upon him." And the little yellow page went unto the King, and told him that it seemed to him that the youth whom he had met with was his daughter's husband, or if he were not so already that he would shortly become so unless he were cautious. "What is thy counsel in this matter, youth?" said the King. "My counsel is," he replied, "that thou set strong men upon him, to seize him, until thou hast ascertained the truth respecting this." So he set strong men upon Peredur, who seized him and cast him into prison. And the maiden went before her father, and asked him wherefore he had caused the youth from Arthur's Court to be imprisoned. "In truth," he answered, "he shall not be free to-night, nor to-morrow, nor the day following, and he shall not come from where he is." She replied not to what the King had said, but she went to the youth. "Is it unpleasant to thee to be here?" said she. "I should not care if I were not," he replied. "Thy couch and thy treatment shall be in no wise inferior to that of the King himself, and thou shalt have the best entertainment that the palace affords. And if it were more pleasing to thee that my couch should be here, that I might discourse with thee, it should be so, cheerfully." "This can I not refuse," said Peredur. And he remained in prison that night. And the maiden provided all that she had promised him.

And the next day Peredur heard a tumult in the town. "Tell me, fair maiden, what is that tumult?" said Peredur. "All the King's hosts and his forces have come to the town to-day." "And what seek they here?" he inquired. "There is an Earl near this place who possesses two Earldoms, and is as powerful as a King; and an engagement will take place between them to-day." "I beseech thee," said Peredur, "to cause a horse and arms to be brought, that I may view the encounter, and I promise to come back to my prison again." "Gladly," said she, "will I provide thee with horse and arms." So she gave him a horse and arms, and a bright scarlet robe of honour over his armour, and a yellow shield upon his shoulder. And he went to the combat; and as many of the Earl's men as encountered him that day he overthrew; and he returned to his prison. And the maiden asked tidings of Peredur, and he answered her not a word. And she went and asked tidings of her father, and inquired who had acquitted himself best of the household. And he said that he knew not, but that it was a man with a scarlet robe of honour over his armour, and a yellow shield upon his shoulder. Then she smiled, and returned to where Peredur was, and did him great honour that night. And for three days did Peredur slay the Earl's men; and before any one could know who he was, he returned to his prison. And the fourth day Peredur slew the Earl himself. And the maiden went unto her father, and inquired of him the news. "I have good news for thee," said the King; "the Earl is slain, and I am the owner of his two Earldoms." "Knowest thou, lord, who slew him?" "I do not know," said the King. "It was the knight with the scarlet robe of honour and the yellow shield." "Lord," said she, "I know who that is." "By Heaven!" he exclaimed, "who is he?" "Lord," she replied, "he is the knight whom thou hast imprisoned." Then he went unto Peredur, and saluted him, and told him that he would reward the service he had

done him, in any way he might desire. And when they went to meat, Peredur
was placed beside the King, and the maiden on the other side of Peredur. "I will
give thee," said the King, "my daughter in marriage, and half my kingdom with
her, and the two Earldoms as a gift." "Heaven reward thee, lord," said Peredur,
"but I came not here to woo." "What seekest thou then, chieftain?" "I am seeking
tidings of the Castle of Wonders." "Thy enterprise is greater, chieftain, than thou
wilt wish to pursue," said the maiden, "nevertheless, tidings shalt thou have of
the Castle, and thou shalt have a guide through my father's dominions, and
a sufficiency of provisions for thy journey, for thou art, O chieftain, the man
whom best I love." Then she said to him, "Go over yonder mountain, and thou
wilt find a lake, and in the middle of the lake there is a Castle, and that is the
Castle that is called the Castle of Wonders; and we know not what wonders are
therein, but thus is it called."

And Peredur proceeded towards the Castle, and the gate of the Castle was
open. And when he came to the hall, the door was open, and he entered. And
he beheld a chessboard in the hall, and the chessmen were playing[121a] against
each other, by themselves. And the side that he favoured lost the game, and
thereupon the others set up a shout, as though they had been living men. And
Peredur was wroth, and took the chessmen in his lap, and cast the chessboard
into the lake. And when he had done thus, behold the black maiden came in, and
she said to him, "The welcome of Heaven be not unto thee. Thou hadst rather do
evil than good." "What complaint hast thou against me, maiden?" said Peredur.
"That thou hast occasioned unto the Empress the loss of her chessboard, which
she would not have lost for all her empire. And the way in which thou mayest
recover the chessboard is, to repair to the Castle of Ysbidinongyl, where is a
black man, who lays waste the dominions of the Empress; and if thou canst slay
him, thou wilt recover the chessboard. But if thou goest there, thou wilt not
return alive." "Wilt thou direct me thither?" said Peredur. "I will show thee the
way," she replied. So he went to the Castle of Ysbidinongyl, and he fought with
the black man. And the black man besought mercy of Peredur. "Mercy will I
grant thee," said he, "on condition that thou cause the chessboard to be restored
to the place where it was when I entered the hall." Then the maiden came to
him, and said, "The malediction of Heaven attend thee for thy work, since thou
hast left that monster alive, who lays waste all the possessions of the Empress."
"I granted him his life," said Peredur, "that he might cause the chessboard to be
restored." "The chessboard is not in the place where thou didst find it; go back,
therefore, and slay him," answered she. So Peredur went back, and slew the black
man. And when he returned to the palace, he found the black maiden there.
"Ah! maiden," said Peredur, "where is the Empress?" "I declare to Heaven that
thou wilt not see her now, unless thou dost slay the monster that is in yonder
forest." "What monster is there?" "It is a stag that is as swift as the swiftest bird;
and he has one horn in his forehead, as long as the shaft of a spear, and as sharp

as whatever is sharpest. And he destroys the branches of the best trees in the forest, and he kills every animal that he meets with therein; and those that he doth not slay perish of hunger. And what is worse than that, he comes every night, and drinks up the fish-pond, and leaves the fishes exposed, so that for the most part they die before the water returns again." "Maiden," said Peredur, "wilt thou come and show me this animal?" "Not so," said the maiden, "for he has not permitted any mortal to enter the forest for above a twelvemonth. Behold, here is a little dog belonging to the Empress, which will rouse the stag, and will chase him towards thee, and the stag will attack thee." Then the little dog went as a guide to Peredur, and roused the stag, and brought him towards the place where Peredur was. And the stag attacked Peredur, and he let him pass by him, and as he did so, he smote off his head with his sword. And while he was looking at the head of the stag, he saw a lady on horseback coming towards him. And she took the little dog in the lappet of her cap, and the head and the body of the stag lay before her. And around the stag's neck was a golden collar. "Ha! chieftain," said she, "uncourteously hast thou acted in slaying the fairest jewel that was in my dominions." "I was entreated so to do; and is there any way by which I can obtain thy friendship?" "There is," she replied. "Go thou forward unto yonder mountain, and there thou wilt find a grove; and in the grove there is a cromlech; do thou there challenge a man three times to fight, and thou shalt have my friendship."

So Peredur proceeded onward, and came to the side of the grove, and challenged any man to fight. And a black man arose from beneath the cromlech, mounted upon a bony horse, and both he and his horse were clad in huge rusty armour. And they fought. And as often as Peredur cast the black man to the earth, he would jump again into his saddle. And Peredur dismounted, and drew his sword; and thereupon the black man disappeared with Peredur's horse and his own, so that he could not gain sight of him a second time. And Peredur went along the mountain, and on the other side of the mountain he beheld a castle in the valley, wherein was a river. And he went to the castle; and as he entered it, he saw a hall, and the door of the hall was open, and he went in. And there he saw a lame grey-headed man sitting on one side of the hall, with Gwalchmai beside him. And Peredur beheld his horse, which the black man had taken, in the same stall with that of Gwalchmai. And they were glad concerning Peredur. And he went and seated himself on the other side of the hoary-headed man. Then, behold a yellow-haired youth came, and bent upon the knee before Peredur, and besought his friendship. "Lord," said the youth, "it was I that came in the form of the black maiden to Arthur's Court, and when thou didst throw down the chessboard, and when thou didst slay the black man of Ysbidinongyl, and when thou didst slay the stag, and when thou didst go to fight the black man of the cromlech. And I came with the bloody head in the salver, and with the lance that streamed with blood from the point to the hand, all along the shaft; and the head was thy cousin's, and he was killed by the sorceresses of Gloucester, who also lamed thine uncle; and I am thy cousin. And there is a prediction that thou art to avenge these things." Then Peredur and Gwalchmai took counsel, and sent to Arthur and his household, to beseech them to come against the sorceresses. And they began to fight with them; and one of the sorceresses slew one of Arthur's men before Peredur's face, and Peredur bade her forbear. And the sorceress slew a man before Peredur's face a second time, and a second time he forbad her. And the third time the sorceress slew a man before the face of Peredur; and then Peredur drew his sword, and smote the sorceress on the helmet; and all her head-armour was split in two parts. And she set up a cry, and desired the other sorceresses to flee, and told them that this was Peredur, the man who had learnt Chivalry with them, and by whom they were destined to be slain. Then Arthur and his household fell upon the sorceresses, and slew the sorceresses of Gloucester every one. And thus is it related concerning the Castle of Wonders.

NOTES TO
PEREDUR THE SON OF EVRAWC

81a — PEREDUR

OF the real history of Peredur, nothing is known. It is probable that he fell in the battle of Cattraeth, in the beginning of the 6th century, as Aneurin mentions a chieftain of this name among the slain.

> "Warriors marched forth,—unanimously they bounded forward;—
> Short-lived were they,—they had revelled over the flowing mead;
> The host of Mynyddawc renowned in battle;
> Their life was the price of their banquet.
> Caradawc, and Madawc, Pyll, and Yeuan,
> Gwgawn, and Gwiawn, Gwynn, and Kynvan,
> *Peredur of steel arms*, Gwawrdur, and Aedan.
> A defence in the tumult, a shield in the conflict;
> When they were slain they also slaughtered.
> None to his home returned."

Peredur is frequently alluded to by the Bards of the Middle Ages, in terms illustrative of the high esteem in which his deeds of prowess then were held. Gruffydd ab Meredydd, who flourished about the end of the 13th century, in his Elegy on Tudur ap Goronwy, one of the ancestors of the House of Tudor, thus mentions him:—

> "O Bountiful Creator of the radiant sun and waning moon,
> Sad is the fall of the chief of valiant deeds,
> Eagle of the battle-charge, equal to Peredur,
> Tudor, assaulter of the Angles, he who never shunned the fight."

In the old Romances, as Morte d'Arthur, &c., be is celebrated, under the name of Perceval, as one of those engaged in the quest of the Sangreal, in which character he is also spoken of in the Triads, together with Bort, the son of the King of that name, and Galath, the son of Lancelot du Lac.—Tri. lxi. Myv. Ar. II. 14.

Like Owain, his exploits were sung by Chrestiens de Troyes, and they also form the subject of romantic compositions in German, and in other languages of Northern Europe.

Our own Chaucer alludes to him in his Rime of Sire Thopas, Cant. Tales, 1384-5—

> Himself drank water of the well,
> As did the Knight, Sire Percivell,
> So worthy under wede."

81b — ATTENDING TOURNAMENTS

WE find various instances of knights, who made it a practice to resort to Tournaments as a lucrative occupation; for, on those occasions, not only the home and arms of the vanquished frequently became the property of the victor, but the prizes contested for were often of so valuable a nature as greatly to enrich those who were fortunate enough to win them. Sometimes they consisted of diamonds and precious stones, and sometimes even of the revenues of different domains.[1] In the Romance of Ipomydon, "a thousand pound" is the guerdon bestowed on the successful combatant. Our Henry the VII. proposed a ring of gold, set with a ruby, and another set with a diamond, as the reward of the knights who should be victorious at a Tournament at which he was to be present.[2] And there is a characteristic story on record of the Chevalier Bayard, who being the conqueror on one of these occasions, refused to take the prize, which was a ruby worth a hundred ducats attached to a lady's sleeve, saying that the honour of the victory was entirely due to the sleeve, for which he had contended. The ruby was accordingly presented to the knight who had acquitted himself best after Bayard, and the lady herself resumed possession of the sleeve, declaring that after what Bayard had said, she should keep it all her life for his sake.[3]

81c — WARS AND COMBATS

FROM this passage we may probably infer that Evrawc was one of those knights who, during the Middle Ages, ranked themselves under the banners of such princes as were disposed to engage their services. Many of these adventurers were held in high estimation, and Froissart, in speaking of Sir John Hawkwood, who was one of the most distinguished of them, calls him "a right valiant English knight who had performed many most gallant deeds of arms."

---

1 Mém. de Chev. I. 322.

2 Strutt's Sports and Pastimes, 134.

3 Hist. of the Chev. Bayard (Lond. 1825) I. 84.

He gives the following account of Hawkwood's progress, from which an idea may be formed of the emoluments that accrued to those mercenary bands, and of the manner in which they were employed.

"He had left France at the conclusion of the peace of Bretigny, and was at that time a poor knight, who thought it would not be of any advantage to him to return home; but when he saw, that by the treaties, all men-at-arms would be forced to leave France, he put himself at the head of those free companions called late-comers, and marched into Burgundy. Several such companions, composed of English, Gascons, Bretons, Germans, and of men from every nation, were collected there. Hawkwood was one of the principal leaders, with Bricquet and Carnelle, by whom the battle of Brignais was fought, and who aided Bernard de la Salle to take the Pont du St. Esprit.

"When they had harassed the country for some time, the marquis de Montferrat made a treaty with them to assist him in his war with the lords of Milan. This marquis led them over the Alps, after he had paid them sixty thousand francs, of which Hawkwood received, for himself and his troops, ten thousand. When they had finished the war for the marquis, the greater part of them returned to France; for sir Bertrand du Guesclin, the lords de la Marche, de Beaujeu, and sir Arnold d'Andreghen, marshal of France, wished to lead them into Spain, to don Henry de Trastamare, against don Pedro, king of Spain.

Sir John Hawkwood and his companions remained in Italy, and were employed by pope Urban as long as he lived, in his wars in the Milanese. Pope Gregory, successor to Urban, engaged him in the same manner. Sir John had also a profitable employment, under the lord de Coucy, against the count de Vertus and his barons; in which, some say, the lord de Coucy would have been slain, if sir John Hawkwood had not come to his assistance with five hundred combatants, which he was solely induced to do because the lord de Coucy had married one of the king of England's daughters. This sir John Hawkwood was a knight much inured to war, which he had long followed, and had gained great renown in Italy from his gallantry.

"The Romans, therefore, and Urban, who called himself pope, resolved, on Clement leaving Italy, to send for Hawkwood, and appoint him commander-in-chief of all their forces: they made him large offers of retaining him and his whole troop at a handsome subsidy, which he accepted, and acquitted himself loyally for it."—Johnes's Froissart, 4to. II. c. 97.

82a — THEY ARE ANGELS, MY SON

INCIDENTS similar to that in the text are of frequent occurrence in the old Romances. St. John of Damascus, a Greek writer of the 8th century, has a story of a youth brought up in utter ignorance of all worldly affairs, in order to evade a prophecy which existed against him. Here, however, the compliment paid by Peredur's mother to the knights, in calling them Angels, is far from being returned to her sex. For, in describing to him all the objects he meets on his first going out, and mixing with the world, the Greek writer makes the young man's father apply an appellation to the ladies, which is the very reverse of angelic.

There is another story to the same effect, in a Latin Collection of Materials for composing Sermons, by John Herolt, sirnamed Discipulus, a Dominican friar of Basil, who flourished about 1450.[1]

From these the idea has been adopted and worked up by the Italian novelist.

83a — POSSESS THYSELF OF IT, AND GIVE IT TO ANOTHER

THE ideas of liberality entertained in the days of Chivalry were often widely at variance with every principle of justice. That the advice given to Peredur by his mother was consistent with the feelings of the day, may be gathered from various passages in the works of contemporary writers. An amusing anecdote, illustrative of this, is thus quoted by Mr. Hallam, from Joinville's celebrated History of St. Louis.

"He is speaking of Henry count of Champagne, who acquired, says he, very deservedly, the sirname of Liberal, and adduces the following proof of it:—

A poor knight implored of him on his knees one day as much money as would serve to marry his two daughters. One Arthault de Nogent, a rich burgess, willing to rid the count, of this importunity, but rather awkward, we must own, in the turn of big argument, said to the petitioner: My lord has already given away so much that he has nothing left. Sir Villain, replied Henry, turning round to him, you do not speak truth, in saying that I have nothing left to give, when I have got yourself. Here, Sir Knight, I give you this man and warrant your possession of him. Then, says Joinville, the poor knight was not at all confounded, but seized hold of the burgess fast by the collar, and told him he should not go till he had ransomed himself. And in the end he was forced to pay a ransom of five hundred pounds. The simple-minded writer who brings this evidence of the count of Champagne's liberality is not at all struck with the facility of a virtue that is exercised at the cost of others."[2]

---

1 Hist. Eng. Poe. I. ccxxiv. cclxv.

2 Middle Ages, III. 499, 500.

85a — THROUGH MAGIC OR CHARMS

THE dread of supernatural agency has in all ages exerted a powerful influence over the human mind. Even in the present day, instances are not wanting of men of the most approved natural courage, quailing with fear at the idea of an invisible enemy. It must, therefore, not be surprising, if, in less enlightened times, we find this superstitious feeling interfering still more generally with the common affairs of life. So decidedly was it acknowledged in the Middle Ages, that a solemn oath was required to be taken by every knight previous to his engaging in wager of battle, that he did not bear about him any charm or spell, and that he was not protected by magic or enchantment.

86b — THIS IRON COAT

IN the English version, Perceval, after several vain attempts to disencumber the dead knight of his armour, betakes himself to rather a curious expedient for effecting his object:—

"He sayd my moder bad me,
When my dart solde broken be,
Owte of ye Iren bren ye tree
    Now es me fyre ynede.
Now he getis hȳ flynt,
His fyre Iren he hent,
And yen wt owtten any stynt,
    He kyndilt a glede."

86a — BETWEEN THE NECK AND THE SHOULDER

IT should seem that this was a favourite point of attack in the energetic encounters of those days; for in the Morte d'Arthur we meet with a similar expression to the above. It is stated, that when Arthur first assumed the government of Britain, several kings and knights would not acknowledge his authority, and assembled in order to oppose him. Believing their visit to have a friendly object, he sent them many valuable presents, which they refused to accept, rebuking "the messagers shamefully," and sending Arthur "word, they wold none of his yeftes. But that they were come to gyue hym yeftes with hard swerdys betwixt the neck and the sholders."—B. I. c. 8.

89a — STAPLE

THIS was, probably, a staple for fastening horses to, as it is well known that the horses were often brought into the hall among the guests. In the account of the thirteen rarities of the Island of Britain, as enumerated in an unpublished MS. in the possession of Mr. Justice Bosanquet, it is said that one chieftain had the staple for holding his horse at the foot of his bed.

"The halter of Clydno Eiddyn, which was in a staple below the feet of his bed; and whatever horse he wished for in it, he would find there."

90a — SPEAR OF MIGHTY SIZE

IN the French version of this tale, the spear here alluded to is said to have been the Holy Lance, and with it is brought in the celebrated Sangreal. The latter was the great object of research with the Knights of the Round Table, and its recovery was ultimately achieved by Perceval of Wales, the Peredur ab Evrawc of Welsh Romance.

94a — THE THIRD PART

THIS apportionment is strictly in accordance with ancient Welsh customs; for by the Laws of Howel Dda, it appears the Master of the Royal Household and the Steward (*Penteulu* and *Distein*), were each entitled to a third part of certain fines there mentioned; to express which portion the same word (*trayan*) is used as in the present tale.

98a — GWALCHMAI

GWALCHMAI's reputation for courtesy and eloquence is here admirably kept up, and we find him fully entitled to the appellation of the Golden Tongued, so poetically bestowed upon him in the Triads. No less faithfully is Kai's character for the very opposite quality of detraction sustained.

100a — ANGHARAD LAW EURAWC

THIS name literally signifies Angharad with the Golden Hand, an epithet which was most probably bestowed on her, to designate her liberality.

100b — SPEAK A WORD TO ANY CHRISTIAN AGAIN

DURING the days of Chivalry, vows for the performance of some singular or romantic feat, of a similar nature with that mentioned in the text, were greatly in vogue. In an ancient French Poem, entitled Le Vœu du Héron, printed by Ste. Palaye, an amusing instance of this occurs.

Robert of Artois presents himself at the Court of Edward the III. and incites that Monarch to the conquest of France. One day he enters the hall in which the King and his courtiers are assembled, accompanied by musicians and two noble damsels, and bearing in great pomp a Heron, which he had killed, and which be ironically offers to Edward, as a compensation for the French crown. Edward, roused by the taunt, immediately swears upon the Heron, that the year shall not elapse without his entering France with fire and sword. His nobles follow his example. Among them is the Earl of Salisbury, who is seated by the daughter of the Earl of Derby, to whom he was devotedly attached. He asks the lady to lend him one of her fingers and to place it upon his eye.

> "Si pri à la pucelle, de ceur devotement,
> Qu'elle me preste un doit de sa main seulement,
> Et methe sur mon œil destre parfaitement."

She is complaisant enough to grant him two fingers, which she puts upon his eye, so as to close it. Whereupon the Earl makes oath never more to open that eye until he shall have done battle against the army of the French King. And this he faithfully performs.

> "Les deux dois, sur l'œil destre, li mist isnelement,[1]
> Et si li a clos l'œil, et fremé[2] fermement,
> Et chix[3] a demandé moult gracieusement:
> Bele, est-il bien clos? Oyl certainement.
> A dont dist, de la bouche, du ceur le pensement;
> Et je veu, et prometh à Dieu omnipotent,
> Et a sa douche mere, que de beaute resplent,
> Qu'i n'est jamais ouvers, pour ore,[4] ne pour vent,

---

1 Promptement.

2 Fermé.

3 Celui-ci.

4 Temps, heure.

Pour mal, ne pour martire, ne pour encombrement,[1]
Si seray dedans Franche, où il a bonne gent,
Et si aray le fu[2] bouté entièrement,
Et serai combatus a grand efforchement,
Contre les gens Philype, qui taut a hardement;
Je ne sui en bataille prins, par boin ensient,[3]
Bien li ederai[4] a acomplir son talent:
Or aviegne qu'aviegne, car il n'est autrement.
Adonc osta son doit la puchelle an cors gent,
Et li iex[5] clos demeure, si ques virent le gent,
Et quand Robert l'entent, moult de joie l'enprent.
Quant li quens Salebrin ot voué son avis,[6]
Et demoura l'œil clos en la guerre toudis.
Li bers[7] Robers d'Artois ne s'est mie alentis."[8]

In the same reign, Froissart mentions a number of young bachelors who appeared with a bandage over one eye, which they had sworn to their ladies not to remove until they had distinguished themselves by come deed of prowess against the French.

105a — SITTING ON A BENCH

BENCHES were formerly much more general than chairs. Wherever the latter are spoken of by our old English writers, it appears to have been as an article of luxury, and even of magnificence; and there is very reason to believe that they were far from being common, even in the houses of the great. No

---

1 Empêchement.

2 Feu.

3 A bon escient, savoir ou certitude.

4 Edouard aiderai.

5 Œil.

6 Souhait, dessein.

7 Baron.

8 Mém Chev. II. 102 103.

mention whatever is made of chairs in the catalogue of the furniture in the chamber of the Bishop of Winchester, in 1266, where benches, or *forms*, are, however, particularly enumerated.

> "Et de i. mensa cum tressellis in camera dom. episcopi. Et v. *formis* in eadem camera."[1]

This is also the case in the inventory preserved of the goods belonging to Contarini, a rich Venetian trader, at his house in St Botolph's-lane, A.D. 1481, and in that of the furniture of Skipton Castle, the great honour of the Earls of Cumberland, and one of the most splendid mansions of the North, A.D. 1572.[2]

And the more general use of benches may be gathered from many passages in the elder poets. In the Geste of King Horne, we find,—

> "Horne sett him *abenche*."

And in Piers Plowman's Crede, the author, describing the luxury of the monks, tells us of

> "An halle for an hygh kynge an houshold to holden,
> With brode bordes abouten, *ybenched* wel clene."

Ellis remarks, that "from this usage our Court of King's *Bench* had its name."[3]

107a — ADDANC

IN the Triads mention is made of the Addanc, or Avanc of the Lake, as an aquatic monster which exercised a mysterious influence over some tremendous inundation, there alluded to and generally considered to have been the universal deluge, of which event most primitive nations have preserved a traditional recollection. The drawing of the Avanc from the Lake was an exploit performed by the horned Oxen of Hu Gadarn, or the Mighty, the hero who is recorded as having first conducted the nation of the Cymry into the Island of Britain.—See Triad 4. Myv. Arch. II. 57.

---

1 Warton's Hist. Eng. Poe. 1824. I. 43.

2 Hallam's Middle Ages. Chap. on the State of Society,. 1834. III. 427 There were, however, a *few* chairs in Mr. Fermor's house at Easton, according to the inventory printed by Strutt.

3 Notes to Way's Fabliaux, I. 222.

"The three great exploits of the Island of Britain: The ship of Nevydd Nav Neivion, which carried in it a male and female of all things living, when the Lake of floods burst forth. And the horned oxen of Hu the Mighty, which drew the Avanc of the Lake to land, so that the Lake burst forth no more. And the stones of Gwyddon Ganhebon, on which were read all the arts and sciences of the world."—T. 97. Myv. Arch. II. 71.

There are many popular traditions connected with this event still existing in different parts of the Principality.

110a — ETLYM GLEDDYV COCH

LITERALLY, Etlym. with the red sword.

114a — HOWEL THE SON OF EMYR LLYDAW

HOWEL, the Prince of Llydaw, or Armorica, distinguished himself greatly in Arthur's wars against the Romans, and was one of the most strenuous in urging his Sovereign to resist their unjust claims. When Arthur was called suddenly home, by the news of Modred's treachery, he left Howel with part of his army in Gaul, to secure his possessions in that country. [1]

He was one of the three knights of princely bearing in Arthur's Court, who were so kind and gentle, and so courteous of demeanour, that it was difficult for any one in the world to refuse or deny them anything they asked.—T. 118. Myv. Arch. II. 74.

The Cambrian Biography places Howel's tomb at Llan. Illtyd Vawr, or Lantwit, in Glamorganshire.

Emyr Llydaw, Howel's father, was nephew of the celebrated St. Germanus, or Garmon. A great number of his descendants, headed by Cadvan, emigrated to this country from Armorica, and are ranked among the most eminent of the Welsh Saints.[2]

---

1 See Gruffydd ab Arthur, Wace's Brut, Rob. of Glou., &c. The tragical story of Howel's niece Helen, the victim of Dinabuc, the Spanish Giant of St. Michael's Mount, forms a long episode in all these accounts of the expedition against Rome. The St. Michael's Mount here alluded to is that in Normandy. Arthur went there with no other escort than his two knights, Kai and Bedwer, and had the satisfaction of overcoming and slaying the Giant, who, from all the descriptions, must have been a most fierce and savage monster.

2 See Professor Rees's Essay, p. 213.

121a — CHESSMEN WERE PLAYING

A CHESSBOARD and men possessed of similar qualities with those in the tale, belonged to Gwenddolen, the celebrated beauty of Arthur's Court, and are thus described:—

"The Chessboard of Gwenddolen; when the men were placed upon it, they would play of themselves. The Chessboard was of gold, and the men of silver."— Bosanquet MS.

Something of the same kind occurs in the Romance of Sir Gaheret. That champion is entertained in the Enchanted Castle of a beautiful Fairy, who engages him in a party at Chess, in a large hall, where flags of black and white marble form the chequer, and the pieces, consisting of massive statues of gold and Silver, move at the touch of the magic rod held by the player.

A similar adventure occurs in the Romance of Lancelot du Lac.—II. P. 101.[1]

NOTICE OF VARIOUS OTHER VERSIONS

THE story of Peredur exists in the French language in two different forms: one of these is a Metrical Romance, by Chrestien de Troyes, entitled "Perceval le Galois," of which several MSS. are deposited in the Bibliothèque du Roi; the other is a Prose Composition, and has appeared in print. This last is of small folio size, bearing the date of Paris, March 20, 1529. Copies of it are extremely rare.

Of the English Metrical Romance of Perceval, only one ancient copy is known to be extant. It is contained in a very curious folio MS. on paper, belonging to the library of Lincoln Cathedral, and which from the name of its transcriber, Robert de Thornton, a monk who lived in the 15th century, is commonly known by the name of the Thornton MS. Sir Frederick Madden, in his Introduction to the Romance of Sir Gawaine, gives a particular description of the MS. and its contents.

I possess a transcript of it, which, by the kind permission of the Chapter, I made in 1840.

Amongst the various Romances of the Round Table none appears to have enjoyed a larger share of popularity in Germany than that of Perceval. It is the subject of a poem written by Wolfram von Eschenbach, about the year 1200, which he professedly derived from a French original totally distinct from that of Chrestien. The author's name is given as Kyot, or Guyot, of Provence; apparently a different person from Guyot of Provins, whose satirical poem, written at the same period, is well known in old French literature. Kyot seems to have been

---

1 Sir W. Scott's Notes to Sir Tristram (1811), p. 275.

acquainted with the wild fictions of the Arabic story-tellers in Spain, and to have blended them in his own work with the Welsh legends which, either in Latin or French form, had already made their way to Southern France, and were eagerly listened to at the court of Anjou.

Numerous MS. copies of Wolfram's poem are in existence, and a printed edition, now of extreme rarity, appeared as early as the end of the 15th century. It is also comprised in Myller's Selection of Ancient Poems, and in Karl Lachmann's edition of Wolfram von Eschenbach's Works. Berlin, 1833. 8vo. Mr. Albert Schulz (San Marte) has published a modern German translation of it. Magdeburg, 1836. 8vo.

The Romance of Peredur is found in Icelandic under the title of the Saga of Perceval, of which there are copies in the British Museum and in the Royal Library at Stockholm.

GERAINT THE SON OF ERBIN

ARTHUR was accustomed to hold his Court at Caerlleon upon Usk. And there he held it seven Easters and five Christmases[141a]. And once upon a time he held his Court there at Whitsuntide. For Caerlleon was the place most easy of access in his dominions, both by sea and by land. And there were assembled nine crowned kings, who were his tributaries, and likewise earls and barons. For they were his invited guests at all the high festivals, unless they were prevented by any great hindrance. And when he was at Caerlleon, holding his Court, thirteen churches were set apart for mass[141b]. And thus were they appointed: one church for Arthur, and his kings, and his guests; and the second for Gwenhwyvar and her ladies; and the third for the Steward of the Household[141c] and the suitors; and the fourth for the Franks and the other officers; and the other nine churches were for the nine Masters of the Household[141d] and chiefly for Gwalchmai; for he, from the eminence of his warlike fame, and from the nobleness of his birth, was the most exalted of the nine. And there was no other arrangement respecting the churches than that which we have mentioned above.

Glewlwyd Gavaelvawr was the chief porter; but he did not himself perform the office, except at one of the three high festivals, for he had seven men to serve him, and they divided the year amongst them. They were Grynn, and Pen Pighon, and Llaes Cymyn, and Gogyfwlch, and Gwrdnei with cat's eyes, who could see as well by night as by day, and Drem the son of Dremhitid, and Clust the son of Clustveinyd; and these were Arthur's guards[142a]. And on Whit-Tuesday, as the King sat at the banquet, lo! there entered a tall, fair-headed youth, clad in a coat and a surcoat of diapered satin[142b], and a golden-hilted sword about his neck, and low shoes of leather upon his feet. And he came, and stood before Arthur. "Hail to thee, Lord!" said he. "Heaven prosper thee," he answered, "and be thou welcome. Dost thou bring any new tidings?" "I do, Lord," he said. "I know thee not," said Arthur. "It is a marvel to me that thou dost not know me. I am one of thy foresters, Lord, in the Forest of Dean[142c], and my name is Madawc, the son of Twrgadarn." "Tell me thine errand," said Arthur. "I will do so, Lord," said he. "In the Forest I saw a stag, the like of which beheld I never yet." "What is there about him," asked Arthur, "that thou never yet didst see his like?" "He is of pure white, Lord, and he does not herd with any other animal through stateliness and pride, so royal is his bearing. And I come to seek thy counsel, Lord, and to know thy will concerning him." "It seems best to me," said Arthur, "to go and hunt him to-morrow at break of day; and to cause general notice thereof to be given to-night in all quarters of the Court." And Arryfuerys was Arthur's chief huntsman[142d], and Arelivri was his chief page[142e]. And all received notice; and thus it was arranged. And they sent the youth before them. Then Gwenhwyvar said to Arthur[142f], "Wilt thou permit me, Lord," said she, "to go to-morrow to see and hear the hunt of the stag of which the young man spoke?" "I will gladly," said Arthur. "Then will I go," said she. And Gwalchmai said to Arthur, "Lord, if it seem well to thee, permit that into whose hunt soever the stag shall come, that one, be he a knight, or one on foot, may cut off his head, and give it to whom he pleases[143a], whether to his own lady-love, or to the lady of his friend." "I grant it gladly," said Arthur, "and let the Steward of the Household be chastised, if all are not ready to-morrow for the chase."

And they passed the night with songs, and diversions, and discourse, and ample entertainment. And when it was time for them all to go to sleep, they went. And when the next day came, they arose; and Arthur called the attendants, who guarded his couch. And these were four pages, whose names were Cadyrnerth the son of Porthawr Gandwy[143b], and Ambreu the son of Bedwor, and Amhar the son of Arthur, and Goreu the son of Custennin[143c]. And these men came to Arthur and saluted him, and arrayed him in his garments. And Arthur wondered that Gwenhwyvar did not awake, and did not move in her bed; and the attendants wished to awaken her. "Disturb her not," said Arthur, "for she had rather sleep than go to see the hunting."

Then Arthur went forth, and he heard two horns sounding, one from near the lodging of the chief huntsman, and the other from near that of the chief page. And the whole assembly of the multitudes came to Arthur, and they took the road to the Forest.

And after Arthur had gone forth from the palace, Gwenhwyvar awoke, and called to her maidens, and apparelled herself. "Maidens," said she, "I had leave last night to go and see the hunt. Go one of you to the stable, and order hither a horse such as a woman may ride." And one of them went, and she found but two horses in the stable, and Gwenhwyvar and one of her maidens mounted them, and went through the Usk, and followed the track of the men and the horses. And as they rode thus, they heard a loud and rushing sound; and they looked behind them, and beheld a knight upon a hunter foal of mighty size; and the rider was a fair-haired youth, bare-legged, and of princely mien, and a golden-hilted sword was at his side, and a robe and a surcoat of satin were upon him, and two low shoes of leather upon his feet; and around him was a scarf of blue purple, at each corner of which was a golden apple. And his horse stepped stately, and swift, and proud; and he overtook Gwenhwyvar, and saluted her. "Heaven prosper thee, Geraint,"[144a] said she, "I knew thee when first I saw thee just now. And the welcome of Heaven be unto thee. And why didst thou not go with thy lord to hunt?" "Because I knew not when he went," said he. "I marvel, too," said she, "how he could go unknown to me." "Indeed, lady," said he. "I was asleep, and knew not when he went; but thou, O young man, art the most agreeable companion I could have in the whole kingdom; and it may be, that I shall be more amused with the hunting than they; for we shall hear the horns when they sound, and we shall hear the dogs when they are let loose, and begin to cry." So they went to the edge of the Forest, and there they stood. "From this place," said she, "we shall hear when the dogs are let loose." And thereupon, they heard a loud noise, and they looked towards the spot whence it came, and they beheld a dwarf riding upon a horse, stately, and foaming, and prancing, and strong, and spirited. And in the hand of the dwarf was a whip. And near the dwarf they saw a lady upon a beautiful white horse, of steady and stately pace; and she was clothed in a garment of gold brocade. And near her was a knight upon a warhorse of large size, with heavy and bright armour both upon himself and upon his horse. And truly they never before saw a knight, or a horse, or armour, of such remarkable size. And they were all near to each other.

"Geraint," said Gwenhwyvar, "knowest thou the name of that tall knight yonder?" "I know him not," said he, "and the strange armour that he wears prevents my either seeing his face or his features." "Go, maiden," said Gwenhwyvar, "and ask the dwarf who that knight is." Then the maiden went up to the dwarf; and the dwarf waited for the maiden, when he saw her coming towards him. And the maiden inquired of the dwarf who the knight was. "I will not tell thee," he answered. "Since thou art so churlish as not to tell me," said she, "I will ask him himself." "Thou shalt not ask him, by my faith," said he. "Wherefore?" said she. "Because thou art not of honour sufficient to befit thee to speak to my Lord." Then the maiden turned her horse's head towards the knight, upon which the dwarf struck her with the whip that was in his hand across the face and the eyes, until the blood flowed forth. And the maiden, through the hurt she received from the blow, returned to Gwenhwyvar, complaining of the pain. "Very rudely has the dwarf treated thee," said Geraint. "I will go myself to know who the knight is." "Go," said Gwenhwyvar. And Geraint went up to the dwarf. "Who is yonder knight?" said Geraint. "I will not tell thee," said the dwarf. "Then will I ask him himself," said he. "That wilt thou not, by my faith," said the dwarf, "thou art not honourable enough to speak with my Lord." Said Geraint, "I have spoken with men of equal rank with him." And he turned his horse's head towards the knight; but the dwarf overtook him, and struck him as he had done the maiden, so that the blood coloured the scarf that Geraint wore. Then Geraint put his hand upon the hilt of his sword, but he took counsel with himself, and considered that it would be no vengeance for him to slay the dwarf, and to be attacked unarmed by the armed knight, so he returned to where Gwenhwyvar was.

"Thou hast acted wisely and discreetly," said she. "Lady," said he, "I will follow him yet, with thy permission; and at last he will come to some inhabited place, where I may have arms either as a loan or for a pledge, so that I may encounter the knight." "Go," said she, "and do not attack him until thou hast good arms, and I shall be very anxious concerning thee, until I hear tidings of thee." "If I

am alive," said he, "thou shalt hear tidings of me by to-morrow afternoon;" and
with that he departed.

And the road they took was below the palace of Caerlleon, and across the
ford of the Usk; and they went along a fair, and even, and lofty ridge of ground,
until they came to a town, and at the extremity of the town they saw a Fortress
and a Castle. And they came to the extremity of the town. And as the knight
passed through it, all the people arose, and saluted him, and bade him welcome.
And when Geraint came into the town, he looked at every house, to see if he
knew any of those whom he saw. But he knew none, and none knew him to do
him the kindness to let him have arms either as a loan or for a pledge. And every
house he saw was full of men, and arms, and horses. And they were polishing
shields, and burnishing swords, and washing armour, and shoeing horses. And
the knight, and the lady, and the dwarf rode up to the Castle that was in the
town, and every one was glad in the Castle. And from the battlements and the
gates they risked their necks, through their eagerness to greet them, and to
show their joy.

Geraint stood there to see whether the knight would remain in the Castle;
and when he was certain that he would do so, he looked around him; and at a
little distance from the town he saw an old palace in ruins, wherein was a hall
that was falling to decay. And as he knew not any one in the town, he went
towards the old palace; and when he came near to the palace, he saw but one
chamber, and a bridge of marble-stone leading to it. And upon the bridge he
saw sitting a hoary-headed man, upon whom were tattered garments. And
Geraint gazed steadfastly upon him for a long time. Then the hoary-headed
man spoke to him. "Young man," he said, "wherefore art thou thoughtful?" "I
am thoughtful," said he, "because I know not where to go to-night." "Wilt thou
come forward this way, chieftain?" said he, "and thou shalt have of the best that
can be procured for thee." So Geraint went forward. And the hoary-headed man
preceded him into the hall. And in the hall he dismounted, and he left there
his horse. Then he went on to the upper chamber with the hoary-headed man.
And in the chamber he beheld an old decrepit woman, sitting on a cushion,
with old, tattered garments of satin upon her; and it seemed to him that he
had never seen a woman fairer than she must have been, when in the fulness
of youth. And beside her was a maiden, upon whom were a vest and a veil,
that were old, and beginning to be worn out. And truly, he never saw a maiden
more full of comeliness, and grace, and beauty than she. And the hoary-headed
man said to the maiden, "There is no attendant for the horse of this youth but
thyself." "I will render the best service I am able," said she, "both to him and to
his horse." And the maiden disarrayed the youth, and then she furnished his
horse with straw and with corn. And she went to the hall as before, and then she
returned to the chamber. And the hoary-headed man said to the maiden, "Go to
the town," said he, "and bring hither the best that thou canst find both of food

and of liquor." "I will, gladly, Lord," said she. And to the town went the maiden.
And they conversed together while the maiden was at the town. And, behold!
the maiden came back, and a youth with her, bearing on his back a costrel full
of good purchased mead, and a quarter of a young bullock. And in the hands of
the maiden was a quantity of white bread, and she had some manchet bread in
her veil, and she came into the chamber. "I could not obtain better than this,"
said she, "nor with better should I have been trusted." "It is good enough," said
Geraint. And they caused the meat to be boiled; and when their food was ready,
they sat down. And it was on this wise; Geraint sat between the hoary-headed
man and his wife, and the maiden served them. And they ate and drank.

And when they had finished eating, Geraint talked with the hoary-headed
man, and he asked him in the first place, to whom belonged the palace that he
was in. "Truly," said he, "it was I that built it, and to me also belonged the city
and the castle which thou sawest." "Alas!" said Geraint, "how is it that thou hast
lost them now?" "I lost a great Earldom as well as these," said he; "and this is how
I lost them. I had a nephew, the son of my brother, and I took his possessions
to myself; and when he came to his strength, he demanded of me his property,
but I withheld it from him. So he made war upon me, and wrested from me all
that I possessed." "Good Sir," said Geraint, "wilt thou tell me wherefore came
the knight, and the lady, and the dwarf, just now into the town, and what is the
preparation which I saw, and the putting of arms in order?" "I will do so," said
he. "The preparations are for the game that is to be held to-morrow by the young
Earl, which will be on this wise. In the midst of a meadow which is here, two
forks will be set up, and upon the two forks a silver rod, and upon the silver rod
a Sparrow-Hawk[148a], and for the Sparrow-Hawk there will be a tournament. And
to the tournament will go all the array thou didst see in the city, of men, and of
horses, and of arms. And with each man will go the lady he loves best; and no
man can joust for the Sparrow-Hawk, except the lady he loves best be with him.
And the knight that thou sawest has gained the Sparrow-Hawk these two years;
and if he gains it the third year, they will, from that time, send it every year to
him, and he himself will come here no more. And he will be called the Knight
of the Sparrow-Hawk from that time forth." "Sir," said Geraint, "what is thy
counsel to me concerning this knight, on account of the insult which I received
from the dwarf, and that which was received by the maiden of Gwenhwyvar,
the wife of Arthur?" And Geraint told the hoary-headed man what the insult
was that he had received. "It is not easy to counsel thee, inasmuch as thou hast
neither dame nor maiden belonging to thee, for whom thou canst joust. Yet,
I have arms here, which thou couldest have; and there is my horse also, if he
seem to thee better than thine own." "Ah! Sir," said he, "Heaven reward thee. But
my own horse, to which I am accustomed, together with thy arms, will suffice
me. And if, when the appointed time shall come to-morrow, thou wilt permit
me, Sir, to challenge for yonder maiden that is thy daughter, I will engage, if I

escape from the tournament, to love the maiden as long as I live; and if I do not escape, she will remain unsullied as before." "Gladly will I permit thee," said the hoary-headed man, "and since thou dost thus resolve, it is necessary that thy horse and arms should be ready to-morrow at break of day. For then the Knight of the Sparrow-Hawk will make proclamation, and ask the lady he loves best to take the Sparrow-Hawk. 'For,' will he say to her, 'thou art the fairest of women, and thou didst possess it last year, and the year previous; and if any deny it thee to-day, by force will I defend it for thee.' And therefore," said the hoary-headed man, "it is needful for thee to be there at daybreak; and we three will be with thee." And thus was it settled.

And at night, lo! they went to sleep; and before the dawn they arose, and arrayed themselves; and by the time that it was day, they were all four in the meadow. And there was the Knight of the Sparrow-Hawk making the proclamation, and asking his lady-love to fetch the Sparrow-Hawk. "Fetch it not," said Geraint, "for there is here a maiden, who is fairer, and more noble, and more comely, and who has a better claim to it than thou." "If thou maintainest the Sparrow-Hawk to be due to her, come forward, and do battle with me." And Geraint went forward to the top of the meadow, having upon himself and upon his horse armour which was heavy, and rusty, and worthless, and of uncouth shape. Then they encountered each other, and they broke a set of lances, and they broke a second set, and a third. And thus they did at every onset, and they broke as many lances as were brought to them. And when the Earl and his company saw the Knight of the Sparrow-Hawk gaining the mastery, there was shouting, and joy, and mirth amongst them. And the hoary-headed man, and his wife, and his daughter were sorrowful. And the hoary-headed man served Geraint lances as often as he broke them, and the dwarf served the Knight of the Sparrow-Hawk. Then the hoary-headed man came to Geraint. "Oh! chieftain," said he, "since no other will hold with thee, behold, here is the lance which was in my hand on the day when I received the honour of knighthood; and from that time to this I never broke it. And it has an excellent point." Then Geraint took the lance, thanking the hoary-headed man. And thereupon the dwarf also brought a lance to his lord. "Behold, here is a lance for thee, not less good than his," said the dwarf. "And bethink thee, that no knight ever withstood thee before so long as this one has done." "I declare to Heaven," said Geraint, "that unless death takes me quickly hence, he shall fare never the better for thy service." And Geraint pricked his horse towards him from afar, and warning him, he rushed upon him, and gave him a blow so severe, and furious, and fierce, upon the face of his shield, that he cleft it in two, and broke his armour, and burst his girths, so that both he and his saddle were borne to the ground over the horse's crupper. And Geraint dismounted quickly. And he was wroth, and he drew his sword, and rushed fiercely upon him. Then the knight also arose, and drew his sword against Geraint. And they fought on foot with their swords until their arms struck sparks of fire like stars from one another; and thus they continued fighting until the blood and sweat obscured the light from their eyes. And when Geraint prevailed, the hoary-headed man, and his wife, and his daughter were glad; and when the knight prevailed, it rejoiced the Earl and his party. Then the hoary-headed man saw Geraint receive a severe stroke, and he went up to him quickly, and said to him, "Oh, chieftain, remember the treatment which thou hadst from the dwarf; and wilt thou not seek vengeance for the insult to thyself, and for the insult to Gwenhwyvar the wife of Arthur!" And Geraint was roused by what he said to him, and he called to him all his strength, and lifted up his sword, and struck the knight upon the crown of his head, so that he broke all his head-armour, and cut through all the flesh and the skin, even to the skull, until he wounded the bone.

Then the knight fell upon his knees, and cast his sword from his hand, and besought mercy of Geraint. "Of a truth," said he, "I relinquish my overdaring and my pride in craving thy mercy; and unless I have time to commit myself to Heaven for my sins, and to talk with a priest, thy mercy will avail me little." "I will grant thee grace upon this condition," said Geraint, "that thou wilt go to Gwenhwyvar[151a] the wife of Arthur, to do her satisfaction for the insult which her maiden received from thy dwarf. As to myself, for the insult which I received from thee and thy dwarf, I am content with that which I have done unto thee. Dismount not from the time thou goest hence until thou comest into the presence of Gwenhwyvar, to make her what atonement shall be adjudged at the Court of Arthur." "This will I do gladly. And who art thou?" said he. "I am Geraint the son of Erbin. And declare thou also who thou art." "I am Edeyrn the son of Nudd[151b]." Then he threw himself upon his horse, and went forward to Arthur's Court, and the lady he loved best went before him and the dwarf, with much lamentation. And thus far this story up to that time.

Then came the little Earl and his hosts to Geraint, and saluted him, and bade him to his castle. "I may not go," said Geraint, "but where I was last night, there will I be to-night also." "Since thou wilt none of my inviting, thou shalt have abundance of all that I can command for thee, in the place thou wast last night. And I will order ointment for thee, to recover thee from thy fatigues, and from the weariness that is upon thee." "Heaven reward thee," said Geraint, "and I will go to my lodging." And thus went Geraint, and Earl Ynywl, and his wife, and his daughter. And when they reached the chamber, the household servants and attendants of the young Earl had arrived at the Court, and they arranged all the houses, dressing them with straw and with fire; and in a short time the ointment was ready, and Geraint came there, and they washed his head. Then came the young Earl, with forty honourable knights from among his attendants, and those who were bidden to the tournament. And Geraint came from the anointing. And the Earl asked him to go to the hall to eat. "Where is the Earl

Ynywl," said Geraint, "and his wife, and his daughter?" "They are in the chamber yonder," said the Earl's chamberlain, "arraying themselves in garments which the Earl has caused to be brought for them." "Let not the damsel array herself," said he, "except in her vest and her veil, until she come to the Court of Arthur, to be clad by Gwenhwyvar in such garments as she may choose." So the maiden did not array herself.

Then they all entered the hall, and they washed, and went, and sat down to meat. And thus were they seated. On one side of Geraint sat the young Earl, and Earl Ynywl beyond him; and on the other side of Geraint were the maiden and her mother. And after these all sat according to their precedence in honour[152a]. And they ate. And they were served abundantly, and they received a profusion of divers kind of gifts. Then they conversed together. And the young Earl invited Geraint to visit him next day. "I will not, by Heaven," said Geraint. "To the Court of Arthur will I go with this maiden to-morrow. And it is enough for me, as long as Earl Ynywl is in poverty and trouble; and I go chiefly to seek to add to his maintenance." "Ah, chieftain," said the young Earl, "it is not by my fault that Earl Ynywl is without his possessions." "By my faith," said Geraint, "he shall not remain without them, unless death quickly takes me hence." "Oh, chieftain," said he, "with regard to the disagreement between me and Ynywl, I will gladly abide by thy counsel, and agree to what thou mayest judge right between us." "I but ask thee," said Geraint, "to restore to him what is his, and what he should have received from the time he lost his possessions, even until this day." "That I will do gladly, for thee," answered he. "Then," said Geraint, "whosoever is here who owes homage to Ynywl, let him come forward, and perform it on the spot." And all the men did so. And by that treaty they abided. And his castle, and his town, and all his possessions were restored to Ynywl. And he received back all that he had lost, even to the smallest jewel.

Then spoke Earl Ynywl to Geraint. "Chieftain," said he, "behold the maiden for whom thou didst challenge at the tournament, I bestow her upon thee." "She shall go with me," said Geraint, "to the Court of Arthur; and Arthur and Gwenhwyvar they shall dispose of her as they will." And the next day they proceeded to Arthur's Court. So far concerning Geraint.

Now, this is how Arthur hunted the stag[153a]. The men and the dogs were divided into hunting parties, and the dogs were let loose upon the stag. And the last dog that was let loose was the favourite dog of Arthur. Cavall was his name[153b]. And he left all the other dogs behind him, and turned the stag. And at the second turn, the stag came towards the hunting party of Arthur. And Arthur set upon him. And before he could be slain by any other, Arthur cut off his head. Then they sounded the death horn for slaying[153c], and they all gathered round.

Then came Kadyrieith to Arthur, and spoke to him. "Lord," said he, "behold, yonder is Gwenhwyvar, and none with her save only one maiden." "Command

Gildas the son of Caw[153d], and all the scholars of the Court," said Arthur, "to attend Gwenhwyvar to the palace." And they did so.

Then they all set forth, holding converse together concerning the head of the stag, to whom it should be given. One wished that it should be given to the lady best beloved by him, and another to the lady whom he loved best. And all they of the household, and the knights, disputed sharply concerning the head. And with that they came to the palace. And when Arthur and Gwenhwyvar heard them disputing about the head of the stag, Gwenhwyvar said to Arthur, "My lord, this is my counsel concerning the stag's head; let it not be given away until Geraint the son of Erbin shall return from the errand he is upon." And Gwenhwyvar told Arthur what that errand was. "Right gladly shall it be so," said Arthur. And thus it was settled. And the next day Gwenhwyvar caused a watch to be set upon the ramparts for Geraint's coming. And after mid-day they beheld an unshapely little man upon a horse, and after him, as they supposed, a dame or a damsel, also on horseback, and after her a knight of large stature, bowed down, and hanging his head low and sorrowfully, and clad in broken and worthless armour.

And before they came near to the gate, one of the watch went to Gwenhwyvar, and told her what kind of people they saw, and what aspect they bore. "I know not who they are," said he. "But I know," said Gwenhwyvar; "this is the knight whom Geraint pursued, and methinks that he comes not here by his own free will. But Geraint has overtaken him, and avenged the insult to the maiden to the uttermost." And thereupon, behold a porter came to the spot where Gwenhwyvar was. "Lady," said he, "at the gate there is a knight, and I saw never a man of so pitiful an aspect to look upon as he. Miserable and broken is the armour that he wears, and the hue of blood is more conspicuous upon it than its own colour." "Knowest thou his name?" said she. "I do," said he; "he tells me that he is Edeyrn the son of Nudd." Then she replied, "I know him not."

So Gwenhwyvar went to the gate to meet him, and he entered. And Gwenhwyvar was sorry when she saw the condition he was in, even though he was accompanied by the churlish dwarf. Then Edeyrn saluted Gwenhwyvar. "Heaven protect thee," said she. "Lady," said he, "Geraint the son of Erbin, thy best and most valiant servant, greets thee." "Did he meet thee?" she asked. "Yes," said he, "and it was not to my advantage; and that was not his fault, but mine, Lady. And Geraint greets thee well; and in greeting thee he compelled me to come hither to do thy pleasure for the insult which thy maiden received from the dwarf. He forgives the insult to himself, in consideration of his having put me in peril of my life. And he imposed on me a condition, manly, and honourable, and warrior-like, which was to do thee justice, Lady." "Now, where did he overtake thee?" "At the place where we were jousting, and contending for the Sparrow-Hawk, in the town which is now called Cardiff[155a]. And there were none with him save three persons, of a mean and tattered condition. And these were an aged, hoary-headed man, and a woman advanced in years, and a fair young maiden, clad in worn-out garments. And it was for the avouchment of the love of that maiden that Geraint jousted for the Sparrow-Hawk at the tournament, for he said that that maiden was better entitled to the Sparrow-Hawk than this maiden who was with me. And thereupon we encountered each other, and he left me, Lady, as thou seest." "Sir," said she, "when thinkest thou that Geraint will be here?" "To-morrow, Lady, I think he will be here with the maiden."

Then Arthur came to him, and he saluted Arthur; and Arthur gazed a long time upon him, and was amazed to see him thus. And thinking that he knew him, he inquired of him, "Art thou Edeyrn the son of Nudd?" "I am, Lord," said he, "and I have met with much trouble, and received wounds unsupportable." Then he told Arthur all his adventure. "Well," said Arthur, "from what I hear, it behoves Gwenhwyvar to be merciful towards thee." "The mercy which thou desirest, Lord," said she, "will I grant to him, since it is as insulting to thee that an insult should be offered to me as to thyself." "Thus will it be best to do," said Arthur; "let this man have medical care until it be known whether he may live. And if he live, he shall do such satisfaction as shall be judged best by the men of the Court; and take thou sureties to that effect. And if he die, too much will be the death of such a youth as Edeyrn for an insult to a maiden." "This pleases me," said Gwenhwyvar. And Arthur became surety for Edeyrn[155b], and Caradawc the son of Llyr, Gwallawg the son of Llenawg[155c] and Owain the son of Nudd, and Gwalchmai, and many others with them. And Arthur caused Morgan Tud[155d] to be called to him. He was the chief physician155e. "Take with thee Edeyrn the son of Nudd, and cause a chamber to be prepared for him, and let him have the aid of medicine as thou wouldst do unto myself, if I were wounded, and let none into his chamber to molest him, but thyself and thy disciples, to administer to him remedies." "I will do so gladly, Lord," said Morgan Tud. Then said the steward of the household, "Whither is it right, Lord, to order the maiden?" "To Gwenhwyvar and her handmaidens," said he. And the steward of the household so ordered her. Thus far concerning them.

The next day came Geraint towards the Court; and there was a watch set on the ramparts by Gwenhwyvar, lest he should arrive unawares. And one of the watch came to the place where Gwenhwyvar was. "Lady," said he, "methinks that I see Geraint, and the maiden with him. He is on horseback, but he has his walking gear upon him, and the maiden appears to be in white, seeming to be clad in a garment of linen." "Assemble all the women," said Gwenhwyvar, "and come to meet Geraint, to welcome him, and wish him joy." And Gwenhwyvar went to meet Geraint and the maiden. And when Geraint came to the place where Gwenhwyvar was, he saluted her. "Heaven prosper thee," said she, "and welcome to thee. And thy career has been successful, and fortunate, and resistless, and glorious. And Heaven reward thee, that thou hast so proudly caused me to have retribution." "Lady," said he, "I earnestly desired to obtain thee satisfaction according to thy will; and, behold, here is the maiden through whom thou hadst thy revenge." "Verily," said Gwenhwyvar, "the welcome of Heaven be unto her; and it is fitting that we should receive her joyfully." Then they went in, and dismounted. And Geraint came to where Arthur was, and saluted him. "Heaven protect thee," said Arthur, "and the welcome of Heaven be unto thee. And since Edeyrn the son of Nudd has received his overthrow and wounds from thy hands, thou hast had a prosperous career." "Not upon me be the blame," said Geraint, "it was through the arrogance of Edeyrn the son of Nudd himself that we were not friends. I would not quit him until I knew who he was, and until the one had vanquished the other." "Now," said Arthur, "where is the maiden for whom I heard thou didst give challenge?" "She is gone with Gwenhwyvar to her chamber."

Then went Arthur to see the maiden. And Arthur, and all his companions, and his whole Court, were glad concerning the maiden. And certain were they all, that had her array been suitable to her beauty, they had never seen a maid fairer than she. And Arthur gave away the maiden to Geraint. And the usual bond made between two persons was made between Geraint and the maiden, and the choicest of all Gwenhwyvar's apparel was given to the maiden; and thus arrayed, she appeared comely and graceful to all who beheld her. And that day and that night were spent in abundance of minstrelsy, and ample gifts of liquor, and a multitude of games. And when it was time for them to go to sleep, they went. And in the chamber where the couch of Arthur and Gwenhwyvar was, the couch of Geraint and Enid was prepared. And from that time she became his bride. And the next day Arthur satisfied all the claimants upon Geraint with bountiful gifts. And the maiden took up her abode in the palace; and she had many companions, both men and women, and there was no maiden more esteemed than she in the Island of Britain.

Then spake Gwenhwyvar. "Rightly did I judge," said she, "concerning the head of the stag, that it should not be given to any until Geraint's return; and, behold, here is a fit occasion for bestowing it. Let it be given to Enid the daughter of Ynywl[157a], the most illustrious maiden. And I do not believe that any will begrudge it her, for between her and every one here there exists nothing but love and friendship." Much applauded was this by them all, and by Arthur also. And the head of the stag was given to Enid. And thereupon her fame increased, and her friends thenceforward became more in number than before. And Geraint from that time forth loved the stag, and the tournament, and hard encounters; and he came victorious from them all. And a year, and a second, and a third, he proceeded thus, until his fame had flown over the face of the kingdom.

And once upon a time Arthur was holding his Court at Caerlleon upon Usk, at Whitsuntide. And, behold, there came to him ambassadors, wise and

prudent, full of knowledge, and eloquent of speech, and they saluted Arthur.
"Heaven prosper you," said Arthur, "and the welcome of Heaven be unto you.
And whence do you come?" "We come, Lord," said they, "from Cornwall; and we
are ambassadors from Erbin the son of Custennin, thy uncle, and our mission is
unto thee. And he greets thee well, as an uncle should greet his nephew, and as a
vassal should greet his lord. And he represents unto thee that he waxes heavy and
feeble, and is advancing in years. And the neighbouring chiefs, knowing this,
grow insolent towards him, and covet his land and possessions. And he earnestly
beseeches thee, Lord, to permit Geraint his son to return to him, to protect his
possessions, and to become acquainted with his boundaries. And unto him he
represents that it were better for him to spend the flower of his youth and the
prime of his age in preserving his own boundaries, than in tournaments, which
are productive of no profit, although he obtains glory in them."

"Well," said Arthur, "go, and divest yourselves of your accoutrements, and
take food, and refresh yourselves after your fatigues; and before you go forth
hence you shall have an answer." And they went to eat. And Arthur considered
that it would go hard with him to let Geraint depart from him and from his
Court; neither did he think it fair that his cousin should be restrained from going
to protect his dominions and his boundaries, seeing that his father was unable
to do so. No less was the grief and regret of Gwenhwyvar, and all her women,
and all her damsels, through fear that the maiden would leave them. And that
day and that night were spent in abundance of feasting. And Arthur showed
Geraint the cause of the mission, and of the coming of the ambassadors to him
out of Cornwall. "Truly," said Geraint, "be it to my advantage or disadvantage,
Lord, I will do according to thy will concerning this embassy." "Behold," said
Arthur, "though it grieves me to part with thee, it is my counsel that thou go to
dwell in thine own dominions, and to defend thy boundaries, and to take with
thee to accompany thee as many as thou wilt of those thou lovest best among
my faithful ones, and among thy friends, and among thy companions in arms."
"Heaven reward thee; and this will I do," said Geraint. "What discourse," said
Gwenhwyvar, "do I hear between you? Is it of those who are to conduct Geraint
to his country?" "It is," said Arthur. "Then it is needful for me to consider," said
she, "concerning companions and a provision for the lady that is with me?"
"Thou wilt do well," said Arthur.

And that night they went to sleep. And the next day the ambassadors were
permitted to depart, and they were told that Geraint should follow them. And
on the third day Geraint set forth, and many went with him. Gwalchmai the
son of Gwyar, and Riogonedd the son of the king of Ireland, and Ondyaw the
son of the duke of Burgundy, Gwilim the son of the ruler of the Franks, Howel
the son of Emyr of Brittany, Elivry, and Nawkyrd, Gwynn the son of Tringad,
Goreu the son of Custennin, Gweir Gwrhyd Vawr[159a], Garannaw the son of
Golithmer, Peredur the son of Evrawc, Gwynnllogell, Gwyr a judge in the Court

of Arthur, Dyvyr the son of Alun of Dyved, Gwrei Gwalstawd Ieithoedd[159b], Bedwyr the son of Bedrawd[159c], Hadwry the son of Gwryon, Kai the son of Kynyr, Odyar the Frank, the Steward of Arthur's Court, and Edeyrn the son of Nudd. Said Geraint, "I think that I shall have enough of knighthood with me." "Yes," said Arthur, "but it will not be fitting for thee to take Edeyrn with thee, although he is well, until peace shall be made between him and Gwenhwyvar." "Gwenhwyvar can permit him to go with me, if he give sureties." "If she please, she can let him go without sureties, for enough of pain and affliction has he suffered for the insult which the maiden received from the dwarf." "Truly," said Gwenhwyvar, "since it seems well to thee and to Geraint, I will do this gladly, Lord." Then she permitted Edeyrn freely to depart. And many there were who accompanied Geraint, and they set forth; and never was there seen a fairer host journeying towards the Severn[160a]. And on the other side of the Severn were the nobles of Erbin the son of Custennin, and his foster-father at their head, to welcome Geraint with gladness; and many of the women of the Court, with his mother, came to receive Enid the daughter of Ynywl, his wife. And there was great rejoicing and gladness throughout the whole Court, and throughout all the country, concerning Geraint, because of the greatness of their love towards him, and of the greatness of the fame which he had gained since he went from amongst them, and because he was come to take possession of his dominions and to preserve his boundaries[160b]. And they came to the Court. And in the Court they had ample entertainment, and a multitude of gifts and abundance of liquor, and a sufficiency of service, and a variety of minstrelsy and of games[160c]. And to do honour to Geraint, all the chief men of the country were invited that night to visit him. And they passed that day and that night in the utmost enjoyment. And at dawn next day Erbin arose, and summoned to him Geraint, and the noble persons who had borne him company. And he said to Geraint, "I am a feeble and aged man, and whilst I was able to maintain the dominion for thee and for myself, I did so. But thou art young, and in the flower of thy vigour and of thy youth; henceforth do thou preserve thy possessions." "Truly," said Geraint, "with my consent thou shalt not give the power over thy dominions at this time into my hands, and thou shalt not take me from Arthur's Court." "Into thy hands will I give them," said Erbin, "and this day also shalt thou receive the homage of thy subjects."

Then said Gwalchmai, "It were better for thee to satisfy those who have boons to ask, to-day, and to-morrow thou canst receive the homage of thy dominions." So all that had boons to ask were summoned into one place. And Kadyrieith came to them, to know what were their requests. And every one asked that which he desired. And the followers of Arthur began to make gifts, and immediately the men of Cornwall came, and gave also. And they were not long in giving, so eager was every one to bestow gifts. And of those who came to ask gifts, none departed unsatisfied. And that day and that night were spent in the utmost enjoyment.

And the next day, at dawn, Erbin desired Geraint to send messengers to the men, to ask them whether it was displeasing to them that he should come to receive their homage, and whether they had anything to object to him. Then Geraint sent ambassadors to the men of Cornwall, to ask them this. And they all said that it would be the fulness of joy and honour to them for Geraint to come and receive their homage. So he received the homage of such as were there. And they remained with him till the third night. And the day after the followers of Arthur intended to go away. "It is too soon for you to go away yet," said he, "stay with me until I have finished receiving the homage of my chief men, who have agreed to come to me." And they remained with him until he had done so. Then they set forth towards the Court of Arthur; and Geraint went to bear them company, and Enid also, as far as Diganhwy[161a]: there they parted. Then Ondyaw the son of the duke of Burgundy said to Geraint, "Go first of all and visit the uppermost parts of thy dominions, and see well to the boundaries of thy territories; and if thou hast any trouble respecting them, send unto thy companions." "Heaven reward thee," said Geraint, "and this will I do." And Geraint journeyed to the uttermost part of his dominions. And experienced guides, and the chief men of his country, went with him. And the furthermost point that they showed him he kept possession of.

And, as he had been used to do when he was at Arthur's Court, he frequented tournaments. And he became acquainted with valiant and mighty men, until he had gained as much fame there as he had formerly done elsewhere. And he enriched his Court, and his companions, and his nobles, with the best horses and the best arms, and with the best and most valuable jewels, and he ceased not until his fame had flown over the face of the whole kingdom. And when he knew that it was thus, he began to love ease and pleasure, for there was no one who was worth his opposing. And he loved his wife, and liked to continue in the palace, with minstrelsy and diversions. And for a long time he abode at home. And after that he began to shut himself up in the chamber of his wife, and he took no delight in anything besides, insomuch that he gave up the friendship of his nobles, together with his hunting and his amusements, and lost the hearts of all the host in his Court; and there was murmuring and scoffing concerning him among the inhabitants of the palace, on account of his relinquishing so completely their companionship for the love of his wife. And these tidings came to Erbin. And when Erbin had heard these things, he spoke unto Enid, and inquired of her whether it was she that had caused Geraint to act thus, and to forsake his people and his hosts. "Not I, by my confession unto Heaven," said she, "there is nothing more hateful to me than this." And she knew not what she should do, for, although it was hard for her to own this to Geraint, yet was it not more easy for her to listen to what she heard, without warning Geraint concerning it. And she was very sorrowful.

And one morning in the summer time, they were upon their couch, and Geraint lay upon the edge of it. And Enid was without sleep in the apartment, which had windows of glass[162a]. And the sun shone upon the couch. And the clothes had slipped from off his arms and his breast, and he was asleep. Then she gazed upon the marvellous beauty of his appearance, and she said, "Alas, and am I the cause that these arms and this breast have lost their glory and the warlike fame which they once so richly enjoyed!" And as she said this, the tears dropped from her eyes, and they fell upon his breast. And the tears she shed, and the words she had spoken, awoke him; and another thing contributed to awaken him, and that was the idea that it was not in thinking of him that she spoke thus, but that it was because she loved some other man more than him, and that she wished for other society, and thereupon Geraint was troubled in his mind, and he called his squire; and when he came to him, "Go quickly," said he, "and prepare my horse and my arms, and make them ready. And do thou arise," said he to Enid, "and apparel thyself; and cause thy horse to be accoutred, and clothe thee in the worst riding-dress that thou hast in thy possession. And evil betide me," said he, "if thou returnest here until thou knowest whether I have lost my strength so completely as thou didst say. And if it be so, it will then be easy for thee to seek the society thou didst wish for of him of whom thou wast thinking." So she arose, and clothed herself in her meanest garments. "I know nothing, Lord," said she, "of thy meaning." "Neither wilt thou know at this time," said he.

Then Geraint went to see Erbin. "Sir," said he, "I am going upon a quest, and I am not certain when I may come back. Take heed, therefore, unto thy possessions, until my return." "I will do so," said he, "but it is strange to me that thou shouldest go so suddenly. And who will proceed with thee, since thou art not strong enough to traverse the land of Lloegyr[163a] alone?" "But one person only will go with me." "Heaven counsel thee, my son," said Erbin, "and may many attach themselves to thee in Lloegyr." Then went Geraint to the place where his horse was, and it was equipped with foreign armour, heavy and shining. And he desired Enid to mount her horse, and to ride forward, and to keep a long way before him. "And whatever thou mayest see, and whatever thou mayest hear concerning me," said he, "do thou not turn back. And unless I speak unto thee, say not thou one word either." And they set forward. And he did not choose the pleasantest and most frequented road, but that which was the wildest and most beset by thieves, and robbers, and venomous animals. And they came to a high road, which they followed till they saw a vast forest, and they went towards it, and they saw four armed horsemen come forth from the forest. When the horsemen had beheld them, one of them said to the others, "Behold, here is a good occasion for us to capture two horses and armour, and a lady likewise; for this we shall have no difficulty in doing against yonder single knight, who hangs his head so pensively and heavily." And Enid heard this discourse, and she knew not what she should do through fear of Geraint, who had told her to be silent. "The vengeance of Heaven be upon me," she said, "if I would not rather receive my death from his hand than from the hand of any other; and though he should slay me yet will I speak to him, lest I should have the misery to witness his death." So she waited for Geraint until he came near to her. "Lord," said she, "didst thou hear the words of those men concerning thee?" Then he lifted up his eyes, and looked at her angrily. "Thou hadst only," said he, "to hold thy peace as I bade thee. I wish but for silence, and not for warning. And though thou shouldest desire to see my defeat and my death by the hands of those men, yet do I feel no dread." Then the foremost of them couched his lance, and rushed upon Geraint. And he received him, and that not feebly. But he let the thrust go by him, while he struck the horseman upon the centre of his shield in such a manner that his shield was split, and his armour broken, and so that a cubit's length of the shaft of Geraint's lance passed through his body, and sent him to the earth, the length of the lance over his horse's crupper. Then the second horseman attacked him furiously, being wroth at the death of his companion. But with one thrust Geraint overthrew him also, and killed him as he had done the other. Then the third set upon him, and he killed him in like manner. And thus also he slew the fourth. Sad and sorrowful was the maiden as she saw all this. Geraint dismounted from his horse, and took the arms of the men he had slain, and placed them upon their saddles, and tied together the reins of their horses, and he mounted his horse again. "Behold what thou must do," said he; "take the four horses, and drive them before thee, and proceed forward, as I bade thee just now. And say not one word unto me, unless I speak first unto thee. And I declare unto Heaven," said he, "if thou doest not thus, it will be to thy cost." "I will do, as far as I can, Lord," said she, "according to thy desire." Then they went forward through the forest; and when they left the forest, they came to a vast plain, in the centre of which was a group of thickly tangled copsewood; and from out thereof they beheld three horsemen coming towards them, well equipped with armour, both they and their horses. Then the maiden looked steadfastly upon them; and when they had come near, she heard them say one to another, "Behold, here is a good arrival for us; here are coming for us four horses and four suits of armour. We shall easily obtain them spite of yonder dolorous knight, and the maiden also will fall into our power." "This is but too true," said she to herself, "for my husband is tired with his former combat. The vengeance of Heaven will be upon me, unless I warn him of this." So the maiden waited until Geraint came up to her. "Lord," said she, "dust thou not hear the discourse of yonder men concerning thee?" "What was it?" asked he. "They say to one another, that they will easily obtain all this spoil." "I declare to Heaven," he answered, "that their words are less grievous to me than that thou wilt not be silent, and abide by my counsel." "My Lord," said she, "I feared lest they should surprise thee unawares." "Hold thy peace, then," said he, "do not I desire silence?"

And thereupon one of the horsemen couched his lance, and attacked Geraint. And he made a thrust at him, which he thought would be very effective; but Geraint received it carelessly, and struck it aside, and then he rushed upon him, and aimed at the centre of his person, and from the shock of man and horse, the quantity of his armour did not avail him, and the head of the lance and part of the shaft passed through him, so that he was carried to the ground an arm and a spear's length over the crupper of his horse. And both the other horsemen came forward in their turn, but their onset was not more successful than that of their companion. And the maiden stood by, looking at all this; and on the one hand she was in trouble lest Geraint should be wounded in his encounter with the men, and on the other hand she was joyful to see him victorious. Then Geraint dismounted, and bound the three suits of armour upon the three saddles, and he fastened the reins of all the horses together, so that he had seven horses with him. And he mounted his own horse, and commanded the maiden to drive forward the others. "It is no more use for me to speak to thee than to refrain, for thou wilt not attend to my advice." "I will do so, as far as I am able, Lord," said she; "but I cannot conceal from thee the fierce and threatening words which I may hear against thee, Lord, from such strange people as those that haunt this wilderness." "I declare to Heaven," said he, "that I desire nought but silence; therefore, hold thy peace." "I will, Lord, while I can." And the maiden went on with the horses before her, and she pursued her way straight onwards. And from the copse-wood already mentioned, they journeyed over a vast and dreary open plain. And at a great distance from them they beheld a wood, and they could see neither end nor boundary to the wood, except on that side that was nearest to them, and they went towards it. Then there came from out the wood five horsemen, eager, and bold, and mighty, and strong, mounted upon chargers that were powerful, and large of bone, and high-mettled, and proudly snorting, and both the men and the horses were well equipped with arms. And when they drew near to them, Enid heard them say, "Behold, here is a fine booty coming to us, which we shall obtain easily and without labour, for we shall have no trouble in taking all those horses and arms, and the lady also, from yonder single knight, so doleful and sad."

Sorely grieved was the maiden upon hearing this discourse, so that she knew not in the world what she should do. At last, however, she determined to warn Geraint; so she turned her horse's head towards him. "Lord," said she, "if thou hadst heard as I did what yonder horsemen said concerning thee, thy heaviness would be greater than it is." Angrily and bitterly did Geraint smile upon her, and he said, "Thee do I hear doing everything that I forbade thee; but it may be that thou will repent this yet." And immediately, behold, the men met them, and victoriously and gallantly did Geraint overcome them all five. And he placed the five suits of armour upon the five saddles, and tied together the reins of the twelve horses, and gave them in charge to Enid. "I know not," said he, "what

good it is for me to order thee; but this time I charge thee in an especial manner."
So the maiden went forward towards the wood, keeping in advance of Geraint,
as he had desired her; and it grieved him as much as his wrath would permit,
to see a maiden so illustrious as she having so much trouble with the care of
the horses. Then they reached the wood, and it was both deep and vast; and
in the wood night overtook them. "Ah, maiden," said he, "it is vain to attempt
proceeding forward!" "Well, Lord," said she, "whatsoever thou wishest, we will
do." "It will be best for us," he answered, "to turn out of the wood, and to rest,
and wait for the day, in order to pursue our journey." "That will we, gladly," said
she. And they did so. Having dismounted himself, he took her down from her
horse. "I cannot, by any means, refrain from sleep, through weariness," said
he. "Do thou, therefore, watch the horses, and sleep not." "I will, Lord," said
she. Then he went to sleep in his armour, and thus passed the night, which was
not long at that season. And when she saw the dawn of day appear, she looked
around her, to see if he were waking, and thereupon he woke. "My Lord," she
said, "I have desired to awake thee for some time." But he spake nothing to her
about fatigue, as he had desired her to be silent. Then he arose, and said unto
her, "Take the horses, and ride on; and keep straight on before thee as thou didst
yesterday." And early in the day they left the wood, and they came to an open
country, with meadows on one hand, and mowers mowing the meadows. And
there was a river before them, and the horses bent down, and drank the water.
And they went up out of the river by a lofty steep; and there they met a slender
stripling, with a satchel about his neck, and they saw that there was something
in the satchel, but they knew not what it was. And he had a small blue pitcher
in his hand, and a bowl on the mouth of the pitcher. And the youth saluted
Geraint. "Heaven prosper thee," said Geraint, "and whence dost thou come?" "I
come," said he, "from the city that lies before thee. My Lord," he added, "will it be
displeasing to thee if I ask whence thou comest also?" "By no means—through
yonder wood did I come." "Thou camest not through the wood to-day." "No," he
replied, "we were in the wood last night." "I warrant," said the youth, "that thy
condition there last night was not the most pleasant, and that thou hadst neither
meat nor drink." "No, by my faith," said he. "Wilt thou follow my counsel," said
the youth, "and take thy meal from me?" "What sort of meal?" he inquired. "The
breakfast which is sent for yonder mowers, nothing less than bread and meat
and wine; and if thou wilt, Sir, they shall have none of it." "I will," said he, "and
Heaven reward thee for it."

So Geraint alighted, and the youth took the maiden from off her horse. Then
they washed, and took their repast. And the youth cut the bread in slices, and
gave them drink, and served them withal. And when they had finished, the
youth arose, and said to Geraint, "My Lord, with thy permission, I will now
go and fetch some food for the mowers." "Go, first, to the town," said Geraint,
"and take a lodging for me in the best place that thou knowest, and the most

commodious one for the horses, and take thou whichever horse and arms thou choosest in payment for thy service and thy gift." "Heaven reward thee, Lord," said the youth, "and this would be ample to repay services much greater than those I have rendered unto thee." And to the town went the youth, and he took the best and the most pleasant lodgings that he knew; and after that he went to the palace, having the horse and armour with him, and proceeded to the place where the Earl was, and told him all his adventure. "I go now, Lord," said he, "to meet the young man, and to conduct him to his lodging." "Go, gladly," said the Earl, "and right joyfully shall he be received here, if he so come." And the youth went to meet Geraint, and told him that he would be received gladly by the Earl in his own palace; but he would go only to his lodgings. And he had a goodly chamber, in which was plenty of straw, and drapery, and a spacious and commodious place he had for the horses; and the youth prepared for them plenty of provender. And after they had disarrayed themselves, Geraint spoke thus to Enid: "Go," said he, "to the other side of the chamber, and come not to this side of the house; and thou mayest call to thee the woman of the house, if thou wilt." "I will do, Lord," said she, "as thou sayest." And thereupon the man of the house came to Geraint, and welcomed him. "Oh, chieftain," he said, "hast thou taken thy meal?" "I have," said he. Then the youth spoke to him, and inquired if he would not drink something before he met the Earl. "Truly I will," said he. So the youth went into the town, and brought them drink. And they drank. "I must needs sleep," said Geraint. "Well," said the youth; "and whilst thou sleepest, I will go to see the Earl." "Go, gladly," he said, "and come here again when I require thee." And Geraint went to sleep; and so did Enid also.

And the youth came to the place where the Earl was, and the Earl asked him where the lodgings of the knight were, and he told him. "I must go," said the youth, "to wait on him in the evening." "Go," answered the Earl, "and greet him well from me, and tell him that in the evening I will go to see him." "This will I do," said the youth. So he came when it was time for them to awake. And they arose, and went forth. And when it was time for them to take their food, they took it. And the youth served them. And Geraint inquired of the man of the house, whether there were any of his companions that he wished to invite to him, and he said that there were. "Bring them hither, and entertain them at my cost with the best thou canst buy in the town."

And the man of the house brought there those whom he chose, and feasted them at Geraint's expense. Thereupon, behold, the Earl came to visit Geraint, and his twelve honourable knights with him. And Geraint rose up, and welcomed him. "Heaven preserve thee," said the Earl. Then they all sat down according to their precedence in honour. And the Earl conversed with Geraint, and inquired of him the object of his journey. "I have none," he replied, "but to seek adventures, and to follow my own inclination." Then the Earl cast his eye upon Enid, and he looked at her steadfastly. And he thought he had never seen a maiden fairer or more comely than she. And he set all his thoughts and his affections upon her. Then he asked of Geraint, "Have I thy permission to go and converse with yonder maiden, for I see that she is apart from thee?" "Thou hast it gladly," said he. So the Earl went to the place where the maiden was, and spake with her. "Ah, maiden," said he, "it cannot be pleasant to thee to journey thus with yonder man!" "It is not unpleasant to me," said she, "to journey the same road that he journeys." "Thou hast neither youths nor maidens to serve thee," said he. "Truly," she replied, "it is more pleasant for me to follow yonder man, than to be served by youths and maidens." "I will give thee good counsel," said he. "All my Earldom will I place in thy possession, if thou wilt dwell with me." "That will I not, by Heaven," she said; "yonder man was the first to whom my faith was ever pledged; and shall I prove inconstant to him!" "Thou art in the wrong," said the Earl; "if I slay the man yonder, I can keep thee with me as long as I choose; and when thou no longer pleasest me I can turn thee away. But if thou goest with me by thine own good will, I protest that our union shall continue eternal and undivided as long as I remain alive." Then she pondered these words of his, and she considered that it was advisable to encourage him in his request. "Behold, then, chieftain, this is most expedient for thee to do to save me any needless imputation; come here to-morrow, and take me away as though I knew nothing thereof." "I will do so," said he. So he arose, and took his leave, and went forth with his attendants. And she told not then to Geraint any of the conversation which she had had with the Earl, lest it should rouse his anger, and cause him uneasiness and care.

And at the usual hour they went to sleep. And at the beginning of the night Enid slept a little; and at midnight she arose, and placed all Geraint's armour together, so that it might be ready to put on. And although fearful of her errand, she came to the side of Geraint's bed; and she spoke to him softly and gently, saying, "My Lord, arise, and clothe thyself, for these were the words of the Earl to me, and his intention concerning me." So she told Geraint all that had passed. And although he was wroth with her, he took warning, and clothed himself. And she lighted a candle, that he might have light to do so. "Leave there the candle," said he, "and desire the man of the house to come here." Then she went, and the man of the house came to him. "Dost thou know how much I owe thee?" asked Geraint. "I think thou owest but little." "Take the eleven horses and the eleven suits of armour." "Heaven reward thee, lord," said he, "but I spent not the value of one suit of armour upon thee." "For that reason," said he, "thou wilt be the richer. And now, wilt thou come to guide me out of the town?" "I will, gladly," said he, "and in which direction dost thou intend to go?" "I wish to leave the town by a different way from that by which I entered it." So the man of the lodgings accompanied him as far as he desired. Then he bade the maiden to go on before him; and she did so, and went straight forward, and his host returned home. And he had only just reached his house, when, behold, the greatest tumult approached that was ever heard. And when he looked out, he saw fourscore knights in complete armour around the house, with the Earl Dwrm at their head. "Where is the knight that was here?" said the Earl. "By thy hand," said he, "he went hence some time ago." "Wherefore, villain," said he, "didst thou let him go without informing me?" "My Lord, thou didst not command me to do so, else would I not have allowed him to depart." "What way dost thou think that he took?" "I know not, except that he went along the high road." And they turned their horses' heads that way, and seeing the tracks of the horses upon the high road, they followed. And when the maiden beheld the dawning of the day, she looked behind her, and saw vast clouds of dust coming nearer and nearer to her. And thereupon she became uneasy, and she thought that it was the Earl and his host coming after them. And thereupon she beheld a knight appearing through the mist. "By my faith," said she, "though he should slay me, it were better for me to receive my death at his hands, than to see him killed without warning him. My Lord," she said to him, "seest thou yonder man hastening after thee, and many others with him?" "I do see him," said he; "and in despite of all my orders, I see that thou wilt never keep silence." Then he turned upon the knight, and with the first thrust he threw him down under his horse's feet. And as long as there remained one of the fourscore knights, he overthrew every one of them at the first onset. And from the weakest to the strongest, they all attacked him one after the other, except the Earl: and last of all the Earl came against him also. And he broke his lance, and then he broke a second. But Geraint turned upon him, and struck him with his lance upon the centre of his shield, so that by that single thrust the shield was split, and all his armour broken, and he himself was brought over his horse's crupper to the ground, and was in peril of his life. And Geraint drew near to him; and at the noise of the trampling of his horse the Earl revived. "Mercy, Lord," said he to Geraint. And Geraint granted him mercy. But through the hardness of the ground where they had fallen, and the violence of the stroke which they had received, there was not a single knight amongst them that escaped without receiving a fall, mortally severe, and grievously painful, and desperately wounding, from the hand of Geraint.

And Geraint journeyed along the high road that was before him, and the maiden went on first; and near them they beheld a valley which was the fairest ever seen, and which had a large river running through it; and there was a bridge over the river, and the high road led to the bridge. And above the bridge upon the opposite side of the river, they beheld a fortified town, the fairest ever seen. And as they approached the bridge, Geraint saw coming towards him from a thick copse a man mounted upon a large and lofty steed, even of pace and spirited though tractable. "Ah, knight," said Geraint, "whence comest thou?" "I come," said he, "from the valley below us." "Canst thou tell me," said Geraint, "who is the owner of this fair valley and yonder walled town?" "I will tell thee, willingly," said he. "Gwiffert Petit he is called by the Franks, but the Cymry call him the Little King." "Can I go by yonder bridge," said Geraint, "and by the lower highway that is beneath the town?" Said the knight, "Thou canst not go by his tower on the other side of the bridge, unless thou dost intend to combat him; because it is his custom to encounter every knight that comes upon his lands." "I declare to Heaven," said Geraint, "that I will, nevertheless, pursue my journey that way." "If thou dost so," said the knight, "thou wilt probably meet with shame and disgrace in reward for thy daring." Then Geraint proceeded along the road that led to the town, and the road brought him to a ground that was hard, and rugged, and high, and ridgy. And as he journeyed thus, he beheld a knight following him upon a warhorse, strong, and large, and proudly-stepping, and wide-hoofed, and broad-chested. And he never saw a man of smaller stature than he who was upon the horse. And both he and his horse were completely armed. When he had overtaken Geraint, he said to him, "Tell me, chieftain, whether it is through ignorance or through presumption that thou seekest to insult my dignity, and to infringe my rules." "Nay," answered Geraint, "I knew not this road was forbid to any." "Thou didst know it," said the other; "come with me to my Court, to give me satisfaction." "That will I not, by my faith," said Geraint; "I would not go even to thy Lord's Court, excepting Arthur were thy Lord." "By the hand of Arthur himself," said the knight, "I will have satisfaction of thee, or receive my overthrow at thy hands." And immediately they charged one another. And a squire of his came to serve him with lances as he broke them. And they gave each other such hard and severe strokes that their shields lost all their colour[174a]. But it was very difficult for Geraint to fight with him on account of his small size, for he was hardly able to get a full aim at him with all the efforts he could make. And they fought thus until their horses were brought down upon their knees; and at length Geraint threw the knight headlong to the ground; and then they fought on foot, and they gave one another blows so boldly fierce, so frequent, and so severely powerful, that their helmets were pierced, and their skullcaps were broken, and their arms were shattered, and the light of their eyes was darkened by sweat and blood. At the last Geraint became enraged, and he called to him all his strength; and boldly angry, and swiftly resolute, and furiously determined, he lifted up his sword, and struck him on the crown of his head a blow so mortally painful, so violent, so fierce, and so penetrating, that it cut through all his head armour, and his skin, and his flesh, until it wounded the very bone, and the sword flew out of the hand of the Little King to the furthest end of the plain, and he besought Geraint that he would have mercy and compassion upon him. "Though thou hast been neither courteous nor just," said Geraint, "thou shalt have mercy, upon condition that thou wilt become my ally, and engage never to fight against me again, but to come to my assistance whenever thou hearest of my being in trouble." "This will I do, gladly, Lord," said he. So he pledged him his faith thereof. "And now, Lord, come with me," said he, "to my Court yonder, to recover from thy weariness and fatigue." "That will I not, by Heaven," said he.

Then Gwiffert Petit beheld Enid where she stood, and it grieved him to see one of her noble mien appear so deeply afflicted. And he said to Geraint, "My Lord, thou doest wrong not to take repose, and refresh thyself awhile; for, if thou meetest with any difficulty in thy present condition, it will not be easy for thee to surmount it." But Geraint would do no other than proceed on his journey, and he mounted his horse in pain, and all covered with blood. And the maiden went on first, and they proceeded towards the wood which they saw before them.

And the heat of the sun was very great, and through the blood and sweat, Geraint's armour cleaved to his flesh; and when they came into the wood, he stood under a tree, to avoid the sun's heat; and his wounds pained him more than they had done at the time when he received them. And the maiden stood under another tree. And lo! they heard the sound of horns, and a tumultuous noise; and the occasion of it was, that Arthur and his company had come down to the wood. And while Geraint was considering which way he should go to avoid them, behold, he was espied by a foot-page, who was an attendant on the Steward of the Household; and he went to the Steward, and told him what kind of man he had seen in the wood. Then the Steward caused his horse to be saddled, and he took his lance and his shield, and went to the place where Geraint was. "Ah, knight!" said he, "what dost thou here?" "I am standing under a shady tree, to avoid the heat and the rays of the sun." "Wherefore is thy journey, and who art thou?" "I seek adventures, and go where I list." "Indeed," said Kai; "then come with me to see Arthur, who is here hard by." "That will I not, by Heaven," said Geraint. "Thou must needs come," said Kai. Then Geraint knew who he was, but Kai did not know Geraint. And Kai attacked Geraint as best he could. And Geraint became wroth, and he struck him with the shaft of his lance, so that he rolled headlong to the ground. But chastisement worse than this would he not inflict on him.

Scared and wildly Kai arose, and he mounted his horse, and went back to his lodging. And thence he proceeded to Gwalchmai's tent. "Oh, Sir," said he to Gwalchmai, "I was told by one of the attendants, that he saw in the wood above a wounded knight, having on battered armour; and if thou dost right, thou wilt go and see if this be true." "I care not if I do so," said Gwalchmai. "Take, then, thy horse, and some of thy armour," said Kai; "for I hear that he is not over courteous to those who approach him." So Gwalchmai took his spear and his shield, and mounted his horse, and came to the spot where Geraint was. "Sir Knight," said he, "wherefore is thy journey?" "I journey for my own pleasure, and to seek the adventures of the world." "Wilt thou tell me who thou art; or wilt thou come and visit Arthur, who is near at hand?" "I will make no alliance with thee, nor will I go and visit Arthur," said he. And he knew that it was Gwalchmai, but Gwalchmai knew him not. "I purpose not to leave thee," said Gwalchmai, "till I know who thou art." And he charged him with his lance, and struck him on his shield, so that the shaft was shivered into splinters, and their horses were front to front. Then Gwalchmai gazed fixedly upon him, and he knew him. "Ah, Geraint," said he, "is it thou that art here?" "I am not Geraint," said he. "Geraint thou art, by Heaven," he replied, "and a wretched and insane expedition is this." Then he looked around, and beheld Enid, and he welcomed her gladly. "Geraint," said Gwalchmai, "come thou and see Arthur; he is thy lord and thy cousin." "I will not," said he, "for I am not in a fit state to go and see any one." Thereupon, behold, one of the pages came after Gwalchmai to speak to him. So he sent him to apprise Arthur that Geraint was there wounded, and that he would not go to visit him, and that it was pitiable to see the plight that he was in. And this he did without Geraint's knowledge, inasmuch as he spoke in a whisper to the page. "Entreat Arthur," said he, "to have his tent brought near to the road, for he will not meet him willingly, and it is not easy to compel him in the mood he is in." So the page came to Arthur, and told him this. And he caused his tent to be removed unto the side of the road. And the maiden rejoiced in her heart. And Gwalchmai led Geraint onwards along the road, till they came to the place where Arthur was encamped, and the pages were pitching his tent by the roadside. "Lord," said Geraint, "all hail unto thee." "Heaven prosper thee; and who art thou?" said Arthur. "It is Geraint," said Gwalchmai, "and of his own free will would he not come to meet thee." "Verily," said Arthur, "he is bereft of his reason." Then came Enid, and saluted Arthur. "Heaven protect thee," said he. And thereupon he caused one of the pages to take her from her horse. "Alas! Enid," said Arthur, "what expedition is this?" "I know not, Lord," said she, "save that it behoves me to journey by the same road that he journeys." "My Lord," said Geraint, "with thy permission we will depart." "Whither wilt thou go?" said Arthur. "Thou canst not proceed now, unless it be unto thy death." "He will not suffer himself to be invited by me," said Gwalchmai. "But by me he will," said Arthur; "and, moreover, he does not go from here until he is healed." "I had rather, Lord," said Geraint, "that thou wouldest let me go forth." "That will I not, I declare to Heaven," said he. Then he caused a maiden to be sent for to conduct Enid to the tent where Gwenhwyvar's chamber was. And Gwenhwyvar and all her women were joyful at her coming; and they took off her riding-dress, and placed other garments upon her. Arthur also called Kadyrieith, and ordered him to pitch a tent for Geraint and the physicians; and he enjoined him to provide him with abundance of all that might be requisite for him. And Kadyrieith did as he had commanded him. And Morgan Tud and his disciples were brought to Geraint.

And Arthur and his hosts remained there nearly a month, whilst Geraint was being healed. And when he was fully recovered, Geraint came to Arthur, and asked his permission to depart. "I know not if thou art quite well." "In truth I am, Lord," said Geraint. "I shall not believe thee concerning that, but the physicians that were with thee." So Arthur caused the physicians to be summoned to him, and asked them if it were true. "It is true, Lord," said Morgan Tud. So the next day Arthur permitted him to go forth, and he pursued his journey. And on the same day Arthur removed thence. And Geraint desired Enid to go on, and to keep before him, as she had formerly done. And she went forward along the high road. And as they journeyed thus, they heard an exceeding loud wailing near to them. "Stay thou here," said he, "and I will go and see what is the cause of this wailing." "I will," said she. Then he went forward unto an open glade that was near the road. And in the glade he saw two horses, one having a man's saddle, and the other a woman's saddle[178a] upon it. And, behold, there was a knight lying dead in his armour, and a young damsel in a riding-dress standing over him, lamenting. "Ah! Lady," said Geraint, "what hath befallen thee?" "Behold," she answered, "I journeyed here with my beloved husband, when, lo! three giants came upon us, and without any cause in the world, they slew him." "Which way went they hence?" said Geraint. "Yonder by the high road," she replied. So he returned to Enid. "Go," said he, "to the lady that is below yonder, and await me there till I come." She was sad when he ordered her to do thus, but nevertheless she went to the damsel, whom it was ruth to hear, and she felt certain that Geraint would never return. Meanwhile Geraint followed the giants, and overtook them. And each of them was greater of stature than three other men, and a huge club was on the shoulder of each. Then he rushed upon one of them, and thrust his lance through his body. And having drawn it forth again, he pierced another of them through likewise. But the third turned upon him, and struck him with his club, so that he split his shield, and crushed his shoulder, and opened his wounds anew, and all his blood began to flow from him. But Geraint drew his sword, and attacked the giant, and gave him a blow on the crown of his head so severe, and fierce, and violent, that his head and his neck were split down to his shoulders, and he fell dead. So Geraint left him thus, and returned to Enid. And when he saw her, he fell down lifeless from his horse. Piercing, and loud, and thrilling was the cry that Enid uttered. And she came and stood over him where he had fallen. And at the sound of her cries came the Earl of Limours, and the host that journeyed with him, whom her lamentations brought out of their road. And the Earl said to Enid, "Alas, Lady, what hath befallen thee?" "Ah! good Sir," said she, "the only man I have loved, or ever shall love, is slain." Then he said to the other, "And what is the cause of thy grief?" "They have slain my beloved husband also," said she. "And who was it that slew them?" "Some giants," she answered, "slew my best-beloved, and the other knight went in pursuit of them, and came back in the state thou seest, his blood flowing excessively; but it appears to me that he did not leave the giants without killing some of them, if not all." The Earl caused the knight that was dead to be buried, but he thought that there still remained some life in Geraint; and to see if he yet would live, he had him carried with him in the hollow of his shield, and upon a bier. And the two damsels went to the Court; and when they arrived there, Geraint was placed upon a litter-couch in front of the table that was in the hall. Then they all took off their travelling gear, and the Earl besought Enid to do the same, and to clothe herself in other garments. "I will not, by Heaven," said she. "Ah! Lady," said he, "be not so sorrowful for this matter." "It were hard to persuade me to be otherwise," said she. "I will act towards thee in such wise, that thou needest not be sorrowful, whether yonder knight live or die. Behold, a good Earldom, together with myself, will I bestow on thee; be, therefore, happy and joyful." "I declare to Heaven," said she, "that henceforth I shall never be joyful while I live." "Come, then," said he, "and eat." "No, by Heaven, I will not," she answered. "But, by Heaven, thou shalt," said he. So he took her with him to the table against her will, and many times desired her to eat. "I call Heaven to witness," said she, "that I will not eat until the man that is upon yonder bier shall eat likewise." "Thou canst not fulfil that," said the Earl, "yonder man is dead already." "I will prove that I can," said she. Then he offered her a goblet of liquor. "Drink this goblet," he said, "and it will cause thee to change thy mind." "Evil betide me," she answered, "if I drink aught until he drink also." "Truly," said the Earl, "it is of no more avail for me to be gentle with thee than ungentle." And he gave her a box on the ear. Thereupon she raised a loud and piercing shriek, and her lamentations were much greater than they had been before, for she considered in her mind that had Geraint been alive, he durst not have struck her thus. But, behold, at the sound of her cry, Geraint revived from his swoon, and he sat up on the bier, and finding his sword in the hollow of his shield, he rushed to the place where the Earl was, and struck him a fiercely-wounding, severely-venomous, and sternly-smiting blow upon the crown of his head, so that he clove him in twain, until his sword was stayed by the table. Then all left the board, and fled away. And this was not so much through fear of the living as through the dread they felt at seeing the dead man rise up to slay them. And Geraint looked upon Enid, and he was grieved for two causes; one was, to see that Enid had lost her colour and her wonted aspect, and the other, to know that she was in the right. "Lady," said he, "knowest thou where our horses are?" "I know, Lord, where thy horse is," she replied, "but I know not where is the other. Thy horse is in the house yonder." So he went to the house, and brought forth his horse, and mounted him, and took up Enid from the ground, and placed her upon the horse with him. And he rode forward. And their road lay between two hedges. And the night was gaining on the day. And lo! they saw behind them the shafts of spears betwixt them and the sky, and they heard the trampling of horses, and the noise of a host approaching. "I hear something following us," said he, "and I will put thee on the other side of the hedge." And thus he did. And thereupon, behold, a knight pricked towards him, and couched his lance. When Enid saw this, she cried out, saying, "Oh! chieftain, whoever thou art, what renown wilt thou gain by slaying a dead man?" "Oh! Heaven," said he, "is it Geraint?" "Yes, in truth," said she. "And who art thou?" "I am the Little King," he answered, "coming to thy assistance, for I heard that thou wast in trouble. And if thou hadst followed my advice, none of these hardships would have befallen thee." "Nothing can happen," said Geraint, "without the will of Heaven, though much good results from counsel." "Yes," said the Little King, "and I know good counsel for thee now. Come with me to the court of a son-in-law of my sister, which is near here, and thou shalt have the best medical assistance in the kingdom." "I will do so gladly," said Geraint. And Enid was placed upon the horse of one of the Little King's squires, and they went forward to the Baron's palace. And they were received there with gladness, and they met with hospitality and attention. And the next morning they went to seek physicians; and it was not long before they came, and they attended Geraint until he was perfectly well. And while Geraint was under medical care, the Little King caused his armour to be repaired, until it was as good as it had ever been. And they remained there a fortnight and a month.

Then the Little King said to Geraint, "Now will we go towards my own Court, to take rest, and amuse ourselves." "Not so," said Geraint, "we will first journey for one day more, and return again." "With all my heart," said the Little King, "do thou go then." And early in the day they set forth. And more gladly and more joyfully did Enid journey with them that day than she had ever done. And they came to the main road. And when they reached a place where the road divided in two, they beheld a man on foot coming towards them along one of these roads, and Gwiffert asked the man whence he came. "I come," said he, "from an errand in the country." "Tell me," said Geraint, "which is the best for me to follow of these two roads?" "That is the best for thee to follow," answered he, "for if thou goest by this one, thou wilt never return. Below us," said he, "there is a hedge of mist, and within it are enchanted games[181a], and no one who has gone there has ever returned. And the Court of the Earl Owain is there, and he permits no one to go to lodge in the town, except he will go to his Court." "I declare to Heaven," said Geraint, "that we will take the lower road." And they went along it until they came to the town. And they took the fairest and pleasantest place in the town for their lodging. And while they were thus, behold, a young man came to them, and greeted them. "Heaven be propitious to thee," said they. "Good Sirs," said he, "what preparations are you making here?" "We are taking up our lodging," said they, "to pass the night." "It is not the custom with him who owns the town," he answered, "to permit any of gentle birth, unless they come to stay in his Court, to abide here; therefore, come ye to the Court." "We will come, gladly," said Geraint. And they went with the page, and they were joyfully received. And the Earl came to the hall to meet them, and he commanded the tables to be laid. And they washed, and sat down. And this is the order in which they sat: Geraint on one side of the Earl, and Enid on the other side, and next to Enid the Little

King, and then the Countess next to Geraint; and all after that as became their rank. Then Geraint recollected the games, and thought that he should not go to them; and on that account he did not eat. Then the Earl looked upon Geraint, and considered, and he bethought him that his not eating was because of the games, and it grieved him that he had ever established those games, were it only on account of losing such a youth as Geraint. And if Geraint had asked him to abolish the games, he would gladly have done so. Then the Earl said to Geraint, "What thought occupies thy mind, that thou dost not eat? If thou hesitatest about going to the games, thou shalt not go, and no other of thy rank shall ever go either." "Heaven reward thee," said Geraint, "but I wish nothing better than to go to the games, and to be shown the way thither." "If that is what thou dost prefer, thou shalt obtain it willingly." "I do prefer it, indeed," said he. Then they ate, and they were amply served, and they had a variety of gifts, and abundance of liquor. And when they had finished eating they arose. And Geraint called for his horse and his armour, and he accoutred both himself and his horse. And all the hosts went forth until they came to the side of the hedge, and the hedge was so lofty, that it reached as high as they could see in the air, and upon every stake in the hedge, except two, there was the head of a man, and the number of stakes throughout the hedge was very great. Then said the Little King, "May no one go in with the chieftain?" "No one may," said Earl Owain. "Which way can I enter?" inquired Geraint. "I know not," said Owain, "but enter by the way that thou wilt, and that seemeth easiest to thee."

Then fearlessly and unhesitatingly Geraint dashed forward into the mist. And on leaving the mist, he came to a large orchard; and in the orchard he saw an open space, wherein was a tent of red satin; and the door of the tent was open, and an apple-tree stood in front of the door of the tent; and on a branch of the apple-tree hung a huge hunting-horn. Then he dismounted, and went into the tent; and there was no one in the tent save one maiden sitting in a golden chair, and another chair was opposite to her, empty. And Geraint went to the empty chair, and sat down therein. "Ah! chieftain," said the maiden, "I would not counsel thee to sit in that chair." "Wherefore?" said Geraint. "The man to whom that chair belongs has never suffered another to sit in it." "I care not," said Geraint, "though it displease him that I sit in the chair." And thereupon they heard a mighty tumult around the tent. And Geraint looked to see what was the cause of the tumult. And he beheld without a knight mounted upon a warhorse, proudly snorting, high-mettled, and large of bone; and a robe of honour in two parts was upon him and upon his horse, and beneath it was plenty of armour. "Tell me, chieftain," said he to Geraint, "who it was that bade thee sit there?" "Myself," answered he. "It was wrong of thee to do me this shame and disgrace. Arise, and do me satisfaction for thine insolence." Then Geraint arose; and they encountered immediately; and they broke a set of lances, and a second set, and a third; and they gave each other fierce and frequent strokes; and at last Geraint became enraged, and he urged on his horse, and rushed upon him, and gave him a thrust on the centre of his shield, so that it was split, and so that the head of his lance went through his armour, and his girths were broken, and he himself was borne headlong to the ground the length of Geraint's lance and arm, over his horse's crupper. "Oh, my Lord!" said he, "thy mercy, and thou shalt have what thou wilt." "I only desire," said Geraint, "that this game shall no longer exist here, nor the hedge of mist, nor magic, nor enchantment." "Thou shalt have this gladly, Lord," he replied. "Cause, then, the mist to disappear from this place," said Geraint. "Sound yonder horn," said he, "and when thou soundest it, the mist will vanish; but it will not go hence unless the horn be blown by the knight by whom I am vanquished." And sad and sorrowful was Enid where she remained, through anxiety concerning Geraint. Then Geraint went and sounded the horn. And at the first blast he gave, the mist vanished. And all the hosts came together, and they all became reconciled to each other. And the Earl invited Geraint and the Little King to stay with him that night. And the next morning they separated. And Geraint went towards his own dominions; and thenceforth he reigned prosperously, and his warlike fame and splendour lasted with renown and honour both to him and to Enid from that time forth.

NOTES TO
GERAINT THE SON OF ERBIN

141a — EASTER—CHRISTMAS—WHITSUNTIDE

RITSON, in a note to his "Metrical Romancëes," mentions, that our early historians, as Roger Hoveden, Matthew Paris, &c., often advert to the custom of the ancient monarchs of France and England, of holding a cour plénière, or plenary court, at the three principal feasts of Easter, Whitsuntide, and Christmas. On those occasions "they were attended by the earls and barons of the kingdom, their ladys and children; who dine'd at the royal table with great pomp and eclat; minstrels flocking thither from all parts; justs and tournaments being perform'd, and various other kinds of divertisements, which lasted several days."—III. 235.

These three principal festivals, or *prif wyl*, "Pasc, Nadolic, a Sulgwyn," are commemorated as such in one of the Triads, lvii.

141b — CHURCHES WERE SET APART FOR MASS

IN another part of this work, the word Offeren is rendered *offering*; but here it has been thought advisable to use the more general term *Mass*, although the former seems to correspond best with the language of the day.

Thus Chaucer, in his description of the Wif of Bathe, tells us, that

In all the parish wif ne was ther non,
That to the *offring* before hire shulde gon,
And if ther did, certain so wroth was She,
That she was out of alle charitee."

Pro. v. 451-4.

141c — STEWARD OF THE HOUSEHOLD

HE was the chief of all the officers of the Court, who had each to pay him a fee of twenty-four pence upon their installation. On him devolved the important care of providing food for the kitchen, and liquor for the mead-cellar; and he had the charge of the king's share of booty, until the king desired to dispose of it, when he was allowed to choose from it a steer, as his own share. It was his particular duty, "to swear for the king." Besides his clothes, and four horse-shoes, and various perquisites of the skins of beasts, he was entitled to a "male hawk, from the master of the hawks, every feast of St. Michael."—Welsh Laws.

141d — MASTER OF THE HOUSEHOLD

THE post of Master of the Household was one of much honour and distinction; and in the Laws of Howel Dda it is ordained that it should be filled by the king's son or nephew, or one of dignity sufficient for so high a situation. Gwalchmai was therefore peculiarly eligible to it from the relation in which he stood to King Arthur.

The privileges attached to this office were important, while its duties do not appear to have been of a very arduous nature; one of them consisted in giving the harp into the hands of the domestic bard at the three great festivals.

The Master of the Household had the largest and most central house in the town for his lodging. He was entitled to the second most honourable dish in the Court, and to be served first after the king; and his allowance was three dishes and three hornfuls of the best liquor in the Court. Besides other perquisites, some of which were in money, he claimed his clothes at the three great festivals, and also his horses, his dogs, his hawks, and his arms, from the king; and from the smith of the Court he had four horse-shoes once a year, with their complement of nails.

142a — GRYNN, AND PEN PIGEON, &c.

THESE personages appear to have received their names altogether from the office which they held; and we cannot expect to find any very authentic records concerning "Sight the son of Seer," and "Ear the son of Hearer," which is the interpretation of Drem vab Dremhitid, and Clust vab Clustveinyd.

To these two worthies, however, the following allusion is made in a composition attributed to Iolo Goch, 1400.

"When will that be?

"When Bleuddyn Rabi Rhol is as quick-sighted as Tremydd ap Tremhidydd, the man who could discern a mote in the sunbeam, in the four corners of the world.

"When the ears of deaf Deicin Fongam of Machynlleth are as good as those of Clustfain ap Clustfeinydd, the man who could hear the sound of the dewdrop, in June falling from the grass stalk, in the four corners of the world."

It may be well to remark in this place, that several of the characters which are incidentally introduced in Geraint ab Erbin, appear again in others of the

Mabinogion, where they will be more particularly noticed.

142b — DIAPERED SATIN

HAVE ventured thus to translate the words Pali caerawg," though the strict meaning of "caerawg" is "mural"; and Dr. Owen Pughe, in his Dictionary, gives it the signification of "kersey-woven," as applied to a particular kind of cloth, and says that the epithet is derived "from the similitude of its texture to the work in stone walls."

In speaking of satin, it seemed, however, more appropriate to use the term diapered, which Wharton, who has a long note upon the subject (Eng. Poe. II. 9, 1824), believes, properly, to signify "embroidering on a rich ground, as tissue, cloth of gold, &c." Thus, in the Squire of Low Degree, the King of Hungary promises his daughter "clothes of fyne golds" for her head.

> With damaske Whyte and asure blewe,
> Well dyaperd with lyllyes newe."

And Chaucer talks of

> * * "a stede bay, trapped in stele,
> Covered with cloth of gold diapred wele."

Cant. T. v. 2159.

142c — FOREST OF DEAN

THE history of the Forest of Dean is much too interesting and important to be compressed within the limits of a note; the very derivation of its name having alone afforded materials for very lengthened discussion. Many suppose that it was so called in consequence of the Danes having taken up their residence there; and Giraldus Cambrensis appears to have inclined to this opinion, at least if we may judge from the name by which he designates it, Danubiæ Sylva, which is similar to that used by Asser Menevensis, in speaking of Denmark.[1] It argues, however, greatly against this etymology, that Dean was a common name in forests among the Celts, both of Britain and Gaul. Besides Ardennes in France, and Arden in Warwickshire, many forest towns still bear the appellation, as Dean in Rockingham Forest, Dean in the New Forest, &c. From this circumstance, it has occurred to me that the name was very probably derived from the Welsh or

---

1 Asser Menevensis speaks of a great fleet of Pagans Corning to Britain, "de Danubio."—Annales de rebus gestis Ælfredi.

Celtic word DIN, which signifies "a fortified mount, or fort." For Sharon Turner informs us, on the authority of Cæsar, Strabo, and Diodorus Siculus, that the Britons "cleared a space in the *wood*, on which they built their huts and folded their cattle; and they fenced the avenues by ditches and barriers of trees. *Such a collection of houses formed one of their towns.*"—Ang.-Sax. B. I. c. v. Din is the root of Dinas, the Welsh word in actual use for a city.

The Rev. T. Price, in his History of Wales, gives it as his opinion, that the Forest of Dean was the original Feryllwg, or land betwixt the Wye and the Severn, which at one time formed a part of one of the five divisions of Wales. The name of Feryllwg, corrupted into Ferleg and Ferreg, he supposes to have been given to this district from the iron-works with which it abounded, the word Feryll signifying "a worker in metal." It appears also to have been considered as one of the three Gwents, and to have borne the appellation of "Gwent Coch yn y Dena," or the *Red* Gwent in the Deans, for which epithet it is most likely indebted to the colour of its ferruginous soil.

In the time of Giraldus Cambrensis, this district "amply supplied Gloucester with iron and venison." The renowned Spanish Armada was strictly charged to destroy its noble oaks, which were then considered of the highest importance to our naval pre-eminence.

I will not here enter into detail upon the mining history of the Forest of Dean, as I shall probably have occasion again to allude to it. it is said that the peculiar and extensive mining privileges of its inhabitants were confirmed to them by the grant of one of our sovereigns, in acknowledgment for the good service done him by its archers against the Scots; for, like most foresters, they were skilful bowmen. The yew-tree, sacred to archers, which is still seen to mark the site of almost every ancient mine in the forest, might seem to have a fanciful allusion to the nature of the grant, and a lingering desire to perpetuate the recollection of its origin.

142d — CHIEF HUNTSMAN

IN the Laws of Howel Dda, this important personage ranks as the tenth officer of the Court, and his duties and immunities are very clearly defined. From Christmas to February he was to be with the king when required, and took the seat appointed for him in the palace, which was "about the recess with the domestic chaplain." After the 8th of February he was to go with his dogs, his horns, and his greyhounds to hunt the young stags until the feast of St. John, which is in the middle of summer; and during that time he was not bound to make compensation (that is, in a Court of Law) to any one who had a claim upon him, except it were one of his fellow-officers. He was to hunt deer from the feast of St. John till the ninth day of winter; and unless he could be taken before he had risen from his bed, and put on his boots, he was not obliged to render compensation to any who had a claim upon him during all that period. From the ninth day of winter to the 1st of December he went to hunt badgers, and was not accountable for his conduct to any except his fellow-officers; and after that he was employed in sharing the skins of the beasts that had been slain, to a portion of which he had himself a right. His lodging was in the kilnhouse, and his allowance was three hornfuls of liquor and a dish of meat. The value of his horn was one pound, and it was to be of buffalo-horn (buelin).

142e — CHIEF PAGE

THE Chief Page, or Penn Mackwy, appears to have been the officer designated in the Welsh Laws as the Gwas Ystavell, and, as that name implies, he was required to attend to the arrangements of the king's chamber. It was his business to seek the burden of straw for the king to lie on, to make his bed, and to spread the clothes upon it; and in his keeping were the king's treasures, "his cups, his horns, and his rings," for the losing of which he was punished. He lodged in the royal chamber, and, except during the three great festivals, acted as cupbearer to the king.

142f — GWENHWYVAR SAID TO ARTHUR, "WILT THOU PERMIT ME, LORD TO GO TO-MORROW TO SEE AND HEAR THE HUNT OF THE STAG?"

IT was formerly very customary for ladies to join in the pleasures of the chase; and Strutt informs us that when they did so it was usual to draw the game into a small compass by means of inclosures; and temporary stands were erected for them, from which, when not contented with being merely spectators of the sport, they shot at the game with arrows as it passed by. This appears to be the manner in which the hunting party was to be conducted, which was promised by the king of Hungary to his daughter in the old romance of the Squire of Low Degree, where he tells her,

> "A lese of grehound with you to stryke,
> And hert and hynde and other lyke,
> Ye shal be set at such a tryst,
> That herte and hynde shall come to your fyst."—765-8.

Strutt is of opinion that the ladies had even separate hunting parties of their own.—Sports and Pastimes, p. 12.

143a — GIVE IT TO WHOM HE PLEASES

GAWAIN (Gwalchmai) gives a different counsel in the French Romance of Eric and Enide, and endeavours to dissuade the King from the hunting of the White Stag.

"Monsignor Gauvain ne plot mie
Quant il ot la parole oïe.
Sire, fet-il, de ceste cace
N'aurois vous ja ne gré, ne grâce,
Nous savons bien trestot pieça
Quel costume le blanc cerf a;
Qui le blanc cerf ocire puet,
Par raison baisier li estuet
Le plus bele à quanqu'il cort,
Des puceles de vostre cort;
Mais en porroit venir molt grant
Error, A il çaians cinq cens
Damoiselles de halt paraiges
Filles à Roi gentis et saiges
Ne n'i a nul qui n'ait ami
Chevalier vaillant et hardi
Qui tost desrainer la voldroit
Ou fust à tort, ou fust à droit
Que cele qui li atalente
Ert la plus bele et la plus gente.
Li Rois respont ce sai ge bien
Mais porce nel lairrai jo rien;
Mais ne puest estre contredite
Parole, puisque Rois l'a dite."

This recalls the words which Chaucer puts into the mouth of "Pluto, that is the King of Faerie," when urged by his Queen to deviate from a resolution once declared:

"I am a king, it sit me not to lie."

Cant. Tales, 1. 10189.

143b — CADYRNERTH THE
SON OF PORTHAWR GANDWY

CADYRNERTH the son of Porthawr Gandwy appears to have been a very courtly personage, and a man of most polished manners; as in one Triad we find him ranked with the courteous Gwalchmai for his urbanity towards guests and strangers;[1] and in another he is said to have preferred residing with King Arthur to exercising the sovereignty over his own dominions, which was, doubtless, in some measure because the refined habits of the Court were more congenial to a person of his cultivation and taste.

"The three sovereigns of the Court of Arthur, Goronwy the son of Echel Vorddwytwll, and Cadreith the son of Porthfawr Gadw, and Ffleidwr Fflam the son of Godo;[2] because they were princes possessing territory and dominion, and in preference to which they remained as knights in the Court of Arthur, as that was considered the chief of honour and gentility in the opinion of the Three Just Knights."[3]

Nor is this characteristic lost sight of in the present Tale, for, a little further on, while every one else is engrossed by the pleasures of the chase, we find all Cadyrnerth's ideas of propriety violated by Gwenhwyvar's riding up with no other retinue than a single handmaiden; and he hastens to Arthur, to make him acquainted with so flagrant a breach of etiquette, who instantly rectifies it by commanding Gildas and the scholars of the Court to attend her.

143c — GOREU THE SON OF CUSTENNIN

HE is recorded as the deliverer of Arthur from the three imprisonments assigned to him in the Triads.

"The three supreme prisoners of the Island of Britain, Llyr Liediaith, in the prison of Euroswydd Wledig,[4] and Madoc, or Mabon,[5] son of Modron, and Geyr the son of Geyrybed, or Geiryoed; and one more exalted than the three, and that was Arthur, who was for three nights in the Castle of Oeth and Anoeth,

---

1 T. xc. The other was Gadwy the son of Geraint.

2 T. xv.

3 T. 114.

4 Probably Ostorius, the Roman commander.

5 In the Triads contained in the Llyfr Coch, these names are written Mabon, and Geiryoed (Myv. Arch. II. 6); and in the Mabinogion it is Mabon vab Modron.

and three nights in the prison of Wen Pendragon, and three nights in the dark prison under the stone ——— And one youth released him from these three prisons; that youth was Goreu the son of Custennin, his cousin."—Tr. L.

The Castle of Oeth and Anoeth is spoken of in the Mabinogion and in another series of the Triads it is named as the prison of the above-mentioned Geyr. In this version, Arthur is not alluded to, but all the members of the families of the other prisoners are said to have shared their captivity, which is designated as the most complete ever known to have taken place.—Tr. 61.

144a — HEAVEN PROSPER THEE, GERAINT

THE name of Geraint ab Erbin is familiar to all lovers of ancient Welsh literature, through the beautiful Elegy composed on him by his fellow warrior, the venerable bard Llywarch Hên. He was a Prince of Dyvnaint (Devon), and fell fighting valiantly against the Saxons, under Arthur's banner, in the battle of Llongborth.

> Before Geraint, the terror of the foe,
> I saw steeds fatigued with the toil of battle,
> And after the shout was given, bow dreadful was the onset.
>
> * * * * *
>
> At Llongborth I saw the tumult,
> And the slain drenched in gore,
> And red-stained warriors from the assault of the foe.
>
> Before Geraint, the scourge of the enemy,
> I saw steeds white with foam,
> And after the shout of battle, a fearful torrent.
>
> At Llongborth I saw the raging of slaughter,
> And an excessive carnage,
> And warriors blood-stained from the assault of Geraint.
>
> * * * * *
>
> At Llongborth was Geraint slain,
> A valiant warrior from the woodlands of Devon,
> Slaughtering his foes as he fell."[1]

---

1 See the remainder of the Elegy in Llywarch Hên's Poems, edited by Dr.
   Owen Pughe.

Llongborth, where this fatal conflict took place, is by some believed to have been Portsmouth, and the name literally signifies the Haven of Ships. But the Rev. T. Price supposes it to be Langport, in Somersetshire. This opinion he founds on the similarity of the names, and the locality; Langport being situated on the river Parret, the Peryddon of the Welsh bards, and the Pedridan of the Saxon Chronicle.

From the Triads we learn that Geraint was also a naval commander. Gwenwynwyn the son of Nav, and March the son of Meirchion, are ranked with him as such; and we are told that with each of them were six score ships, having six score men in each.—Tr. 68.

In the Gododin of Aneurin he is Spoken of in terms of high eulogium.— Myv. Arch. I. 13.

Geraint ab Erbin has had the honour of being canonized. It is said that a church was dedicated to him at Caerffawydd, or Hereford. Four of his sons, Selyf, Cyngan, Iestin, and Cado, or Cataw, are also included in the list of Saints, and were members of the college of St. Garmon. Garwy, another of his sons, appears in a very different character from his brothers, in the Triads, where he is celebrated as one of the three amorous and courteous knights of the Court of Arthur.—Tr. 119.

We can hardly identify Geraint ab Erbin with the Geraint Carnwys or Garwys of Gruffydd ab Arthur, who, in the Brut, is called Gerin de Chartres; and in Robert of Gloucester, "Gerÿn erl of Carcoÿs." This hero figures in Arthur's very latest battles, whereas Geraint ab Erbin, as we have already seen, fell at Llongborth, in an encounter with the Saxons, which must have taken place at an earlier period of that monarch's reign;—according to Dr. O. Pughe, about the year 530.[1]

In the Life of Saint Teiliaw, the second bishop of Llandaff, mention occurs of a person named Gerennius, and an account is given of his death, which is described as having taken place very differently from that of the subject of Llywarch Hên's Elegy. It is probable, however, that the same person is alluded to; but the whole narrative is of too legendary a character to be received as history, especially in opposition to the testimony of an eye-witness. In this composition, it is stated that Saint Teiliaw, when retiring to Armorica with a number of his countrymen, in order to escape from a pestilence, called Pestis Flava,[2] which was then desolating Britain, was, on his way, hospitably entertained by Gerennius, or Geraint, King of Cornwall, to whom, on his departure, the Saint confidently promised that he should not die until he had received the Holy Communion at his hands. Accordingly when the King approached his death, Teiliaw was miraculously informed of his situation, and immediately made preparations

---

1 Poems of Llywarch Hên. p. 3.

2 Called in Welsh "Y Fâd Felen."

to fulfil his promise, and at the same time to return to his own country, the pestilence having then subsided. As they were going to embark, Teiliaw desired his followers to take with them a huge sarcophagus, which he had destined for the reception of Gerennius's body; and on their declaring their inability to comply, on account of its great magnitude, inasmuch as ten yoke of oxen could scarcely move it from its place, the Saint instructed them that it should, by Divine assistance, he conveyed across the sea before the prow of the ship; which was accordingly done, and the sarcophagus reached the shore without the intervention of human aid. Having landed at the port called Dingerein,[1] Teiliaw proceeded forthwith to visit the King, whom be found still alive, but who, after the ministration of the Holy Ordinance, immediately expired; and his remains were placed by the Saint in the above-mentioned sarcophagus.[2]

148a — SPARROW-HAWK

A SIMILAR prize was contended for at the nuptials of Maximilian and Mary of Burgundy, when there were great jousts and rejoicing. In the very interesting Chronicle of the events of the reign of these two illustrious persons, translated from the Flemish by M. Octave Delepierre, and published at Brussels, it is recorded that upon that joyful occasion, "Le Margrave de Brandebourg remporta un des prix, qui consistait en un faucon d'or."

151a — THAT THOU WILT GO TO GWENHWYVAR

THIS custom of sending a conquered foe as a present to the victorious knight's lady-love forms a frequent incident in chivalric Romances. It is admirably ridiculed by Don Quixote, when he desires the released criminals to go and offer themselves to his Dulcinea. In the old French poem, entitled the Combat des Trente, which celebrates the encounter which took place in Brittany between thirty English and thirty French knights, during the reign of Edward III, Pembroke calls to Beaumanoir to surrender, telling him that he will not kill him, but will send him as a present to the lady of his affections.

---

1 Perhaps Gerrans, near Falmouth, which, as Hale suggests, was probably named after Geraint.—(Davies Gilbert's Hist. of Cornwall, II. 50.) The Welsh Chronicle mentions the Castle of Dingeraint (Cilgerran), on the river Teivy, in Pembrokeshire, as fortified in the 12th century; but it is more likely that the former is the place referred to here.

2 The Life of Saint Teiliaw forms part of the Liber Landavensis, published by the Welsh Manuscript Society.

"Rent toi tost Biaumanoir je ne tochiray mie,
Mais je feray de toy un present a ma mie."

151b — EDEYRN THE SON OF NUDD

OF Edeyrn ap Nudd but little is known, except that he was one of the most valiant knights of Arthur's Court, and that in the celebrated expedition against the Emperor of Rome he was sent by his royal master, with five thousand men under his command, to the aid of Gawain and the other ambassadors to the Roman camp, who were treacherously assailed in returning from their mission. Gruffydd ab Arthur. Myv. Arch. II. 339. In Wace's Brut, l. 12,336 (as in the romance of Eric and Enide), he is called Yder le fils Nut, or Nu.

In the account of the antiquities of Glastonbury, attributed to William of Malmesbury, the author says, "It is written in the Acts of the illustrious King Arthur, that at a certain festival of the Nativity, at Caerleon, that monarch having conferred military distinction upon a valiant youth of the name of Ider the son of King Nuth, in order to prove him, conducted him to the hill of Brentenol, for the purpose of fighting three most atrocious giants. And Ider going before the rest of the company, attacked the giants valorously, and slew them. And when Arthur came up he found him apparently dead, having fainted with the immense toil he had undergone, whereupon he reproached himself with having been the cause of his death, through his tardiness in coming to his aid; and arriving at Glastonbury, he appointed there four-and-twenty monks to say mass for his soul, and endowed them most amply with lands, and with gold and silver, chalices, and other ecclesiastical ornaments."

The name of Edeyrn ab Nudd occurs in the Catalogue of Welsh Saints, where he is noticed as a bard, who embraced a life of sanctity, and to whom the Chapel of Bodedeyrn, under Holyhead, is dedicated.[1]

152a — SAT ACCORDING TO
THEIR PRECEDENCE IN HONOUR

PRECEDENCE at table was formerly considered a point of great importance, and was even a subject of legislation with the Welsh. In the Laws of Howel Dda, all the officers of the palace have their places in the hall very particularly allotted to them; some having their seats above, and some below the partition.[2] This partition may be supposed to answer to the raised platform called the

---

1 Rees's Welsh Saints, p. 298.

2 Myv. Arch. III. 363.

dais, still seen at the upper end of all ancient baronial halls, and where the table was placed, at which the lord and his guests, and the most distinguished of his retainers, sat at meat. The honour of being admitted to it was greatly esteemed, of which innumerable instances might be adduced from passages in the older writers. Chaucer, to give a favourable idea of the consideration in which some of the characters in his Prologue were held, says,

"Wel semed eche of hem a fayre burgeis,
To sitten in a gild halle, on the *deis.*"—v. 372.

153a — THIS IS HOW ARTHUR HUNTED THE STAG

STRUTT gives a description of the various preparations formerly made or a royal hunting party, from a treatise, entitled, "The Maister of the Game," written for the use of Prince Henry, by the Master of the Game to Henry IV. It exists in the Harleian MSS., and is an enlargement of one previously composed in French, by William Twici, or Twety, grand huntsman to Edward II. The name of John Gyfford is coupled with that of Twety in an English version, of nearly the same date. It was from these two that the treatise upon hunting, contained in the Book of St. Alban's, was compiled.

As the passage is very curious, I shall make no apology for giving it at length.

"When the king shall think proper to hunt the hart in the parks or forests, either with bows or greyhounds, the master of the game, and the park-keeper, or the forester, being made acquainted with his pleasure, shall see that everything be provided necessary for the purpose. It is the duty of the sheriff of the county, wherein the hunting was to be performed, to furnish fit stabling for the king's horses, and carts to take away the dead game. The hunters and officers under the forester, with their assistants, were commanded to erect a sufficient number of temporary buildings for the reception of the royal family and their train; and, if I understand my author clearly, these buildings are directed to be covered with green boughs, to answer the double purpose of shading the company and the hounds from the heat of the sun, and to protect them from any inconveniency in case of foul weather. Early in the morning, upon the day appointed for the sport, the master of the game, with the officers deputed by him, ought to see that the greyhounds were properly placed, and the persons nominated to blow the horn, whose office was to watch what kind of game was turned out, and, by the manner of winding his horn, signify the same to the company, that they might, be prepared for its reception upon its quitting the cover. Proper persons were then to be appointed, at different parts of the inclosure, to keep the populace at due distance. The yeomen of the king's bow, and the grooms of his tutored greyhounds, had in charge to secure the king's standing, and prevent any noise being made to disturb the game before the arrival of his majesty. When the royal family and the nobility were conducted to the places appointed for their reception, the master of the game, or his lieutenant, sounded three long mootes, for the uncoupling of the hart hounds. The game was then driven from the cover, and tamed by the huntsmen and the hounds so as to pass by the stands belonging to the king and queen, and such of the nobility as were permitted to have a share in the pastime; who might either shoot at them with their bows, or pursue them with the greyhounds, at their pleasure. We are then informed that the game which the king, the queen, or the princes or princesses, slew with their own bows, or particularly commanded to be let run, was not liable to any claim by the huntsmen or their attendants; but of all the rest that was killed they had certain parts assigned to them by the master of the game, according to the ancient custom."—Sports and Pastimes, 18, 19.

153b — CAVALL WAS HIS NAME.

THE dog Cavall is mentioned in another of the Mabinogion—that of Kilhwch and Olwen.

153c — HORN FOR SLAYING

THE several incidents of the chase were wont to be announced by the different ways in which the horn was sounded. A list of these various modes of winding the horn is given in the Book of Sir Tristram, where we find,—

"14. The death of the bucke eyther with bowe hounds or grehoundes,—One longe note.

15. Knowledge of the same,—Two short and one longe.

16. The death of the bucke with houndes,—Two longe notes and the rechace."[1]

153d — GILDAS THE SON OF CAW

GILDAS was one of the numerous Sons of Caw, who sought refuge with Arthur, and were hospitably received by him, when their father, who was a prince of Strath Clyde, was expelled from his possessions by the inroads of the Saxons. It is said that Gildas was a member of the congregation of Cattwg, and also that he established a school, or college, at Caer Badon, or Bath. He is well

---

1 Reprint of the Book of St. Alban's, p. 83, the original edition of which by Wynkn de Worde, bl. let. 1486, was the first treatise upon hunting that ever issued from the press.

known as the author of an "Epistle" on the vices and miseries of his country, and of the Lamentations over the Destruction of Britain, which procured for him the title of the British Jeremiah. Some identify him with the poet Aneurin, but his history has been a subject of much controversy.

155a — CARDIFF

WHETHER regarded as the scene of Roman[1] and Norman enterprise, or of British patriotism and valour,[2] Cardiff is a spot to which much historical interest must ever attach. Its annals, however, do not always refer to deeds of open and honourable warfare; and some of the events which have taken place within its precincts are of a nature to excite feelings of pity and regret.

Among the early recollections that its name revives, is that of the unfortunate Robert, Duke of Normandy, who suffered there his six-and-twenty years of hopeless captivity. The tower which tradition has assigned as the dungeon he occupied, is pointed out at the Castle to this day, and is a most venerable ruin;[3] and there is still extant a spirited poem in the Welsh language, which he is said to have composed to beguile the tedious hours of his imprisonment. It is addressed to a solitary oak on the summit of Pennarth Point, which was visible from the scene of his sufferings, and is as follows, together with the explanatory heading.

"When Robert, Prince of Normandy, was imprisoned in Cardiff Castle, by Robert, son of Amon, he acquired the Welsh language, and seeing the Welsh bards there at the festivals, he admired them, and became a bard; and these are verses which he composed,—

---

1 It is asserted by some that Cardiff was known to the Romans by the name of Tibia Amnis.

2 Besides the contests upon record, the situation of Cardiff makes it probable that it was the scene of many others of which no notice remains. From the expression,

"And an armed band
Around Cogawn Penardd,"

it is possible that it is the neighbourhood of Cardiff that is alluded to in the poem called Armes Brydain (Myv. Arch. I. 49), and attributed to Taliesin, as there is a place called Cogan Penarth in the vicinity of this town.

3 A representation of this tower is introduced in the first vignette to the tale of Geraint ab Erbin, while the last vignette presents a view of the Keep as it appeared in 1840 and 1841. Unhappily the hand of restoration has since defaced the beauty of those interesting ruins.

'Oak that grew on battle mound,
Where crimson torrents drench'd the ground;——
Woe waits the maddening broils where sparkling wine goes round!

Oak that grew on verdant plain,
Where gush'd the blood of warriors slain;——
The wretch in hatred's grasp may well of woes complain!

Oak that grew in verdure strong,
After bloodshed's direful wrong;——
Woe waits the wretch who sits the sons of strife among!

Oak that grew on greensward bourn,
Its once fair branches tempest-torn;——
Whom envy's hate pursues shall long in anguish mourn

Oak that grew on woodcliff high,
Where Severn's waves to winds reply;——
Woe waits the wretch whose years tell not that death is nigh!

Oak that grew through year of woes,
Mid battle broil's unequall'd throes;——
Forlorn is he who prays that death his life may close!'"[1]

About the year 1091, the Normans were called into Glamorganshire by the native princes, who were in a state of enmity and warfare, and unwisely sought for foreign aid against each other. The Normans took advantage of their weakness and dissensions, and remained to conquer the province for themselves. Their leader, Robert Fitz-Hammon, while he divided the principal lordships among the twelve knights who had accompanied him in the expedition, retained that of Cardiff, as the most important, for his own portion of the spoil. His family did not, however, enjoy his newly-acquired possessions in uninterrupted tranquillity; for his descendant, William, Earl of Gloucester, having endeavoured to wrest a large tract of mountainous and woody country from a native chieftain, named Ivor Bach, or Ivor the little; "a man," as Giraldus describes him, "of small stature, but of immense courage,"[2] provoked the

---

1 The original poem is printed in the "Gentleman's Magazine" for 1794. The
translation given in the text is due to Mr. Taliesin Williams (ab Iolo), and first
appeared in the notes to his poem of "Cardiff Castle."

2 Giraldus Cambrensis, from whom this account is taken.

resolute Welshman to hostilities. One of Ivor's strongholds is said to have been the fortress of Castell Coch, whose beautiful ruin is one of the most picturesque ornaments of the lovely valley of the Taff; another was the rugged mountain-keep of Morlais, whose mound still forms a striking feature in the outline of the rising ground behind Merthyr and Dowlais, and in the vicinity of which is a spot[1] which local tradition yet points out as the scene of one of his battles.

The Castle of Cardiff was at that time surrounded with high walls, guarded by one hundred and twenty soldiers, a numerous body of archers, and a strong watch; the city also contained many stipendiary troops. Notwithstanding all these precautions, however, the daring chief, descending from his fastnesses, scaled the castle walls in the dead of night, and carried off the Earl and Countess, together with their only son, into the woods; nor did he set them free until he not only recovered all of which he had been unjustly deprived, but also had ceded to him a large additional extent of territory.

In a curious old composition, printed in 1825, by Sir Thomas Phillipps, and entitled, "A Book of Glamorganshire Antiquities, by Rice Merrick, Esq., 1578," it is mentioned that "the Earle gave him of his owne Landes a Meadow near Romney, of whose name it is at this day called Morva Yvor. And unto Griffith, Sonne to Yvor Petit, another Medowe of his name, called Morva Ryffidd, which at this day retayne those names."—29, 30. The same authority goes on to state that Sir Gilbert de Clare, successor to the Earl of Gloucester, gave his daughter in marriage to Griffith the son of Ivor, "by whome hee had diverse Sonnes, whose Grandchildren were starved in Cardiff Castle, having their eyes put out (Griffith ab Rys ab Gre ab Ifor Petit being the heire) by Sir Richard de Clare their ffather's Cousen-German, saving Ho: Velg̱. then being with his Nurse; of whom God multiplied a great people."—59.

There is a curious story in Giraldus Cambrensis, of a mysterious warning which King Henry II. received at Cardiff, where he passed the night on his return from Ireland, the first Sunday after Easter. It was accompanied by a prophecy, the due fulfilment of which the worthy historian has not neglected to note.

The great name of Owain Glendower is also connected with the history of Cardiff. Leland tells us, that "In the year 1404, and in the fourth year of the reign of King Henry, Owen Glendwr burnt the southern parts of Wales, and besieged the town and castle of Caerdyf. The besieged sent to the king for succour; but he neither came in person or sent them any assistance. Owen, therefore, took the town, and burnt it all except one street, in which the friars minors dwelled; which, together with their convent, he left standing for the love he bore them. He afterwards made himself master of the castle, and destroyed it, carrying away a rich booty which he found deposited there. But when the friars petitioned to him for their books and chalices, which they had lodged in the castle, he replied,

---

1 Pant Cad Ivor, which is, according to the tradition of the place, the Valley of the Battle of Ivor.

why did you put your goods in the castle? If you had kept them in your convent, they would have been secure."—Collect. I. 313.

155b — SURETY FOR EDEYRN

THE knights of old were very good-natured in coming forward as surety for one another; and of this we have an instance in the interesting Lai de Lanval, ("Poemes de Marie de France," I. 232). Ellis, in a note upon Mr. Way's English version of this tale, gives a curious anecdote on the subject of pledges or securities, out of the Life of St. Louis.

"On his return from Egypt to France, being in danger of shipwreck, his queen vowed to St. Nicholas a vessel of silver, and, as a further security to the saint, insisted that Joinville should become her pledge for the execution of the promise."—Fab. II. 225.

The Welsh legislator of the 10th century seems to have given the subject of bail or surety his particular attention, and his celebrated code contains a long series of enactments relating to it. The following is a specimen of their character:

"If a surety and debtor meet upon a bridge formed of a single tree, the debtor must not refuse to do one of these three things: either to pay, to give a pledge, or to go to law; and he must not move the toe of one foot towards the heel of the other," (that is to say, he must not stir from the spot,) "until he does one of these three things."

155c — GWALLAWG THE SON OF LLENAWG

IN the Triads, we find him celebrated with Dunawd Fur and Cynvelyn Drwsgl, as one of the pillars of battle of the Island of Britain, which is explained to mean that these chieftains were skilled in the disposition of the order of battle, and were battle leaders, superior to all others that ever existed.[1]—Tr. 71. Myv. Arch. II. 69.

And in a subsequent Triad, he is called one of the "Grave-slaughtering ones," from his having avenged his wrongs from his grave.—Tr. 76. Myv. Arch. II. 69.

Amongst the compositions of the early bards in the Myvyrian Archæology, there are several pieces expressly in honour of Gwallawg. In some of these the scenes of his battles are named, and one of then, signifies that his fame extended from Caer Clud to Caer Caradawc, that is, from Dumbarton to Salisbury.

His name occurs in Llywarch Hên's Elegy upon Urien Rheged; and he

---

1 In another series of the Triads, Urien ap Cynvarch's name is substituted for that of Gwallawg, as one of the pillars of battle.—(Tr xxxi Myv Arch. II. 14.)

has been already spoken of as one of the three northern kings, who united themselves with that prince for the purpose of opposing the progress of Ida's successors.—See also Turner's "Anglo-Saxons," B. III. c. iv.

In Gruffydd ab Arthur,[1] he is mentioned as one of the knights who were present at Arthur's coronation; and his death is recorded to have taken place in the last conflict between that Sovereign and the Romans. The "Englynion y Beddau" place his tomb in Carrawc.

155d — MORGAN TUD

THIS sapient personage is very probably the same as that Morgan the Wise who prepared the ointment which restored Owain to a state of health and sanity, in the romance of Ywaine and Gawin, and whom Ritson,[2] on what grounds, I know not, considered to be the same as the celebrated schismatic Pelagius. His reputation appears to have extended to Brittany, where the inhabitants still call by the name of Morgan Tut an herb, to which they ascribe the most universal healing properties. Morgant was the name of the Bishop of Caer Vudei, (Silchester,) in Arthur's reign.[3] But the appellation is a very common one in Wales.

155e — CHIEF PHYSICIAN

THE chief physician, from the nature of his office, was necessarily in very constant attendance upon the royal person; and this was carried so far, that not only was he unable to leave the palace without the king's permission, but it was ordained by the law of the land, that his seat in the hall should be near to that occupied by the monarch. His lodging was appointed him with the Pennteulu, or the master of the household, and he received his linen clothes from the queen, and his woollen clothes from the king. He was obliged to

---

1 Myv. Arch. II. 320, 347. He is there mentioned in the different versions of the Brut under the designation of Gwallawc of Amwythic (Shrewsbury), and also under that of the Earl of Salisbury. Robert of Gloucester also calls him "Galluc, erl of Salesbury," from the Gallucus Salesberiensis of Geoffrey of Monmouth. In the Cambrian Biography, Dr. Pughe says that he was a chieftain of the Vale of Shrewsbury; and Camden confounds him with the celebrated Galgacus, though he lived some centuries later.

2 Met. Rom. III. 239.

3 Gruff. ab Ar. Myv. Arch. II. 325.

supply medicine gratis to all the four-and-twenty officers of the Court, except in the case of one of the three dangerous wounds, which are explained to be a blow on the head penetrating the brain, a thrust in the body penetrating the intestines, and the breaking of one of the limbs. And for every one of these three dangerous wounds he was entitled to one hundred and eighty pence and his meat. He was to take security of the family of the wounded man (that he should not be prosecuted), in case he should die of the medicines administered to him; and if he neglected this precaution, he had to answer for the consequence. The price of some of his medicaments was established by law. For a plaster of red ointment, he was allowed to charge twelve pence, and eight pence for one of medicinal herbs.

157a — ENID THE DAUGHTER OF YNYWL

THROUGHOUT the broad and varied region of romance, it would be difficult to find a character of greater simplicity and truth than that of Enid the daughter of Earl Ynywl. Conspicuous for her beauty and noble bearing, we are at a loss whether most to admire the untiring patience with which she bore all the hardships she was destined to undergo, or the unshaken constancy and devoted affection which finally achieved the triumph she so richly deserved.

The character of Enid is admirably sustained throughout the whole tale; and as it is more natural, because less overstrained, so, perhaps, it is even more touching than that of Griselda, over which, however, Chaucer has thrown a charm that leads us to forget the improbability of her story.

There is a Triad, in which Enid's name is preserved as one of the fairest and most illustrious ladies of the Court of Arthur.—Tr. 108.

The bards of the Middle Ages have frequent allusions to her in their poems; and Davydd ap Gwilym could pay no higher compliment to his lady-love than to call her a second Enid.

Mr. Tennyson has turned the tale of Geraint and Enid into noble blank verse, heightening the picture with some additional touches of his own.

159a — GWEIR GWRHYD VAWR

WE find him noticed in the Triads as one of the three stubborn ones of the island of Britain, whom no one could turn from their purpose. Tr. 78.

159b — GWREI GWALSTAWD IEITHOEDD

THIS singular personage acts a somewhat conspicuous part in another of the Mabinogion, Kilhwch and Olwen, in which he is described knowing all languages, and being able to interpret even those of the birds and the beasts. In an old Welsh composition, attributed to Iolo Goch, and printed in the "Cydymaith Diddan," before quoted, he is alluded to under the corrupted appellation of Uriel Wastadiaith, and is spoken of as having had so wonderful an aptitude for acquiring languages, that he never heard one with his ears, that he would not utter it with his tongue as fast as he heard it.

159c — BEDWYR THE SON OF BEDRAWD

BEDWYR was one of the most valiant of Arthur's knights, and rendered him valuable service in the different wars in which be was engaged. In the king's household too he filled a very important office, that of chief butler, and there is no doubt, from the estimation in which he was ever held by his sovereign, that he acquitted himself equally well of the duties which devolved upon him in that capacity.

His name is often coupled with that of the seneschal, Sir Kai, and their fortunes in many respects appear to have been very similar. They were the two knights whom Arthur selected as his sole companions in his expedition to St. Michael's Mount, to avenge the death of Helen, the niece of Howel ab, Emyr Llydaw (already adverted to). And he took the same means of recompensing the valour and fidelity of both, by bestowing upon each of them the sovereignty of a valuable French province, which Robert of Gloucester quaintly records in these words,—

"He ȝef þat lond of Normandẏe Bedwer ẏs boteler,
And þat lond of Aungeo Kaxe ẏs panter."—I. 187.

Finally, they both shared the same fate, being slain side by side, while fighting against the Romans in the last engagement of that war, in which they had so greatly distinguished themselves. Arthur, whose supremacy was established by the event of that glorious encounter, was careful to pay every tribute to the memory of the faithful knights who had fallen in his service. He caused Bedwyr to be interred at Bayeux, which he had founded himself, as the capital of his Norman dominions, and Kai to be buried at Chinon, which town, as Wace[1]

---

1 Brut. l. 13,404.

informs us, derived its name from that circumstance.[1] The etymology, it must be confessed, is not very apparent.

The names of these two heroes occur together in the Triads, where Kai is styled one of the Three Diademed Chiefs of battle, superior to both of whom was the subject of this note, Bedwyr the son of Pedrawc. T. 69.

The place of Bedwyr's sepulture is thus recorded in the "Graves of the Warriors," together with that of another chieftain, whose name is not given.

> The grave of the son of Ossvran is in Camlan,
> After many a conflict.
> The grave of Bedwyr is in the woody steep of Tryvan.

There is a lofty mountain bearing the name of *Trivaen*, at the head of the valley of Nant-ffrancon, in Snowdon. Dunraven Castle, in Glamorganshire, is also, in ancient writings, called Dindryvan, but whether either of these is the place mentioned in the above stanza, it is not easy to determine.

160a — THE SEVERN

THE derivation of the name of this majestic river involves a very pretty though tragical story.

King; Locryn, the son of the Trojan Brutus, and sovereign of these realms, fell in love with Astrild, the King of Germany's beautiful daughter, who came over to this island in the retinue of Homber,[2] King of Hungary, when that monarch undertook his disastrous expedition to endeavour to dispossess Albanak, Locryn's brother, of his dominions in the North. Locryn, as soon as he beheld the damsel, determined to wed her, but unfortunately he had before become betrothed to Gwendolen, the daughter of Corineus, Duke of Cornwall, the conqueror of Gog and Magog; and this stern slayer of giants, on hearing of the change in his intention, declared that he would not brook so great an insult to his family. This declaration of Corineus was not to be disregarded, particularly as he made it more impressive by taking his great axe in his hand, which, in the king's presence,

> "So grisliche he schok & faste,
> þat þe kyng quakede & ys men, so sore heo were a gaste."

---

1 The Welsh Brut names Diarnum as the place of Kai's sepulture (Myv. Arch. II. 352), and in the Latin of Geoffrey of Monmouth it is said he was buried at Caen.

2 He ended his days in the Humber, which took its name from that circumstance.

So Locryn deemed it expedient to marry Gwendolen, but he could not wean his affections from the beautiful Astrild, and he had a secret subterraneous habitation contrived, where he concealed her during Corineus's lifetime, giving out, when he visited her, that he went to sacrifice to his gods. On the death of Corineus he did not consider it necessary to keep up this deception any longer, but dismissed Gwendolen, and elevated Astrild to the rank of Queen. Gwendolen, however, was far from submitting tamely to this indignity; and summoning her father's Cornish vassals to her aid she brought them into the field against her faithless husband, who was slain in the first encounter. Astrild and her daughter Averne then fell into the power of Gwendolen, who, according to old Robert of Gloucester, was a "sturne wommon," and caused them both to be drowned in the Severn.

> "And for yt was hire lorde's doȝter þat mayde Auerne,
> And for honour of hire lord, and for heo was of hys kynde,
> Heo wolde þat hire name euer more in mynde,
> And lette clepe[1] þat watur after Auerne,
> And seþþe þorȝ diuerse tonge me clepede hit Seuerne,
> And deþ a letre per to, and no more y wys,
> In þis manner þike water Seuerne y cleped is".—I. 27.

Havren, the Welsh name for this river, bears a very near affinity to that of Gwelldolen's innocent and unfortunate victim, Averne.

160b — BOUNDARIES

IN Wales, the penalties for disturbing boundaries were severe. Howel Dda enacted, that whoever should destroy a boundary between two villages, by ploughing it up, should forfeit to the king the oxen with which he ploughed, together with the wood and iron of the plough, and the value of the ploughman's right foot,[2] and the driver's left hand; and that he should pay fourpence to the owner of the land, and also restore the boundary to its original state.

Parochial perambulations were formerly performed with much solemnity in the principality, the procession being headed by the clergyman and the ceremony begun and ended with a form of prayer, the surplice and Prayer Book being carried by an attendant, to be used when required. Remains of this custom are still observable in some districts. Upon an appointed day, the inhabitants of

---

1 Clepe, to call.

2 The value of a foot was fixed by law, to be six cows and one hundred and twenty pence.

the adjoining parishes meet at a certain spot, and proceed along the boundary line, which in the cultivated land is generally a brook or a hedge-row, until they come to some particular object, which, where no natural line of demarcation exists, serves as a mark of division. This is frequently a stone or mound of earth, or perhaps an ancient carn or tumulus, especially in the mountainous part of the country. Here the procession halts, and the clergyman asks if they are all agreed upon the boundary, and being answered in the affirmative, the parties then range themselves around, each on his proper side of the earn, at the same time baring their heads, while the clergyman ascends to the top with the book in his hand, and with a loud voice pronounces the words "Cursed is he that removeth his neighbour's landmark," upon which all the people answer "Amen." He then descends, and they proceed to some similar object, where the same proceedings are repeated.

A person who has witnessed this ceremony assures me that its effect is exceedingly striking, especially when occurring upon some lonely part of the mountain. The sudden halt round the carn, the clergyman ascending with the book in his hand,—the baring of the head,—the imprecation,—and the simultaneous response, altogether form a rite so extremely impressive, that it cannot fail to contribute greatly towards preserving a recollection of the spot, and affording to landmarks in lonely situations a protection against removal, to which by design or accident, they might otherwise be liable.

160c — VARIETY OF MINSTRELSY AND OF GAMES

CHAUCER has a pretty passage illustrative of what were the diversions admitted in a baronial hall on similar occasions of state, and one which is highly descriptive of the manners of the age in which it was written.

> "This Theseus, this duk, this worthy knight,
> When he had brought hem into his citee,
> And inned hem, everich at his degree,
> He festeth hem, and doth so gret labour
> To esen hem, and don hem all honour,
> That yet men wenen that no mannes wit
> Of non estat ne coud amenden it.
> The minstralcie, the service at the feste,
> The grete yeftes to the most and leste,
> The riche array of Theseus paleis,
> Ne who sate first ne last upon the deis,
> What ladies fayrest ben or best dancing
> Or which of hem can carole best or sing,

Ne who most felingly speketh of love;
What haukes sitten on the perche above,
What houndes liggen on the floor adoun
Of all this now make I no mentioun."

Knightes Tale, v. 2192-2208.

161a — DIGANHWY

CONFUSED as the geography of Romance is known to be, yet we can hardly suppose that this is Diganwy on the Conway, in North Wales. May it not have been an error of the scribe's for Trefynwy, the Welsh name for Monmouth?

162a — WINDOWS OF GLASS

THE terms of admiration in which the older writers invariably speak of glass windows would be sufficient proof, if other evidence were wanting, how rare an article of luxury they were in the houses of our ancestors. They were first introduced in ecclesiastical architecture,[1] to which they were for a long time confined. Mr. Hallam remarks that French artificers were brought to England to furnish the windows in some new churches in the seventh century.[2] "It is said," he continues, "that in the reign of Henry III. a few ecclesiastical buildings had glazed windows.[3] Suger, however, a century before, had adorned his great work, the Abbey of St. Denis, with windows not only glazed, but painted;[4] and I presume that other churches of the same class, both in France and England, especially after the lancet-shaped window had yielded to one of ampler dimensions, were generally decorated in a similar manner. Yet glass is said not to have been employed in the domestic architecture of France before the

---

1 Paulus Silentiarius, a poet and historian of the 6th century, (about A.D. 534), speaks of the brightness of the sun's rays passing through the eastern windows of the Church of St. Sophia, at Constantinople, which windows were covered with glass. St. Jerome, about the beginning of the fifth century, also mentions glass windows. I suppose the question as to whether the ancients were acquainted with this mode of applying glass, is set at rest by the discoveries made of late years at Pompeii.

2 "Du Cauge, v. Vitreæ. Bentham's History of Ely, p. 22."

3 "Matt. Paris, Vitæ Abbatum St. Alb. 122."

4 "Recueil des Hist. t. xii. p. 101."

fourteenth century;[1] and its introduction into England was, very likely, by no means earlier. Nor, indeed, did it come into general use during the period of the Middle Ages. Glazed windows were considered as movable furniture, and probably bore a high price. When the earls of Northumberland, as late as the reign of Elizabeth, left Alnwick Castle, the windows were taken out of their frames, and carefully laid by."[2]—Middle Ages. 1834. III. 425-6[3]

A monastery having a hall

"With wyndowes of glass, wrought as a chirche,"

is spoken of in Pierce Plowman's Crede as an instance of the extreme luxury of the monks;[4] and they occur in some of the descriptions of very great regal splendour given by the old romancers. In Candace's Chamber, described in the Geste of Alexander,

"Theo wyndowes weoren of riche glas:
Theo pinnes weore of ivorye."[5]

And they were sometimes even painted. The King of Hungary's daughter, in the "Squyer of Lowe Degre," is represented

"In her oryall there she was,
Closyd well with royall glas,
Fulfylled yt was with ymagery.
Every windowe by and by,
On eche syde had ther a gynne,
Sperde with manie a dyvers pynne.

---

1 "Paulmy, t, iii. p. 132. Villaret, t. xi. p. 141. Macpherson, p. 679."

2 Northumberland Household Book, preface, p. 16. Bishop Percy says, on the authority of Harrison, that glass was not commonly used in the reign of Henry VIII."

3 Æneas Silvius, afterwards Pope Pius II., in his Treatise, De Moribus Germanorum, written in the 15th century, records that there were then glass windows in all the houses of Vienna.

4 Warton's Hist. Eng. Poetry, II. 140.

5 Ibid. III. 409.

Anone that ladie fayre and fre,
Undyd a pynne of yvere."[1]

From both these quotations, their very fastenings appear to have been of the most costly materials.

163a — LLOEGYR

LLOEGYR is the term used by the Welsh to designate England. The writers of the Middle Ages derive the name from the son of the Trojan Brutus, Locryn (already alluded to), and whose brother, Camber, bequeathed his name to the Principality.

But, from another authority, that of the Triads, we collect that the name was given to the country by an ancient British tribe, called the Lloegrwys.

174a — THEIR SHIELDS LOST ALL THEIR COLOUR

THE custom of painting and decorating shields is one which might be illustrated by innumerable instances. Sharon Turner says that they were ornamented with gold and brilliant colours, and that some knights placed on them the portrait of their favourite lady. Among these he particularizes the Count of Poitou; and he quotes a German poet, who describes a knight "with a shield fulgens auro, and a helmet vermiculated with amber."—Middle Ages, c. xiv.

Notices of arms ornamented with gold are frequently met with in the works of the Welsh Bards. Gwalchmai the son of Meilir, who flourished in the twelfth century, speaking of himself, says,—

"Bright is my sword, gleaming in battle,
Glittering and bright is the gold on my buckler."

And that he does not allude to the temporary decorations of the tournament is evident, from his immediately mentioning several of the battles of Owain Gwynedd, in which he was himself engaged.

---

1 Ibid. II. 8.

178a — WOMAN'S SADDLE

THE saddles used by the ladies of former days were often very richly decorated, and frequent descriptions of their costliness occur in the old Romances. The Lady Triamour, in that of Sir Launfal is represented to have ridden on a saddle of the most magnificent kind when she visited Arthur's Court.

> "Here sadelle was semyly sett,
> The sambus[1] were grene felvet,
>   Ipaynted with ymagerye,
> The bordure was of belles,[2]
> Of ryche gold and nothyng elles,
>   That any man myte aspye.

> In the arsouns, before and behynde,
> Were twey stones of Ynde,
>   Gay for the maystrye;
> The paytrelle[3] of her palfraye
> Was worth an erldome, stoute and gay,
>   The best yn Lumbardye."—v. 949-60.

---

1 The sambus or sambuca, was a kind of saddle-cloth, and its ornaments were usually very splendid. To such an excess were they at one time carried, that Frederick, King of Sicily, in a sumptuary law, Const. c. 92 (quoted by Warton, Hist. Poet. I. ccxiii.), forbad women, even of the highest rank, to use sambuca, or saddle-cloth, on which were gold, silver, or pearls.

2 Of the well-known custom of decking the harness and trappings of horses with bells, many instances might be mentioned. Chaucer says of the monk,—

> "And when he rode, men mighte his bridel here
> Gingeling in a whistling wind as clere,
> And eke as loude, as doth the chapell belle."—Pro. v. 169-71.

Which our "hoste of the Tabard" humorously alludes to at a subsequent stage of the Pilgrimage, v. 14,800. A traditional recollection of this custom is still preserved amongst the Welsh, who say that the Fairies may sometimes be seen riding over the mountains, on horses decorated with small silver bells, of a very shrill and musical sound.

3 Breastplate.

Strutt accuses the ladies of former times of not having adopted a very feminine mode of riding on horseback, particularly when they joined in hunting expeditions; and he quotes the authority of certain illuminations in ancient MSS.[1] which is, I fear, rather conclusive evidence. But the mention of the Lady's saddle and riding-dress in Geraint ab Erbin, will, I trust, rescue the ladies of the present Tale from the imputation of so unbecoming a practice, and show that they wore a peculiar and appropriate costume whenever they rode out. Catherine de Medicis is said to have been the first who rode like the ladies of the present age, with a high crutch to her saddle.—Mém. de Chev. II. 336.

181a — ENCHANTED GAMES

THE extent to which the belief in magic was carried, even by the most enlightened, during the Middle Ages, is really wonderful, and we cannot be surprised at its being frequently employed in the machinery of Romance, when an historian like Froissart gravely tells us of castles that were lost and won by means of optical deceptions. In the case he cites they were produced by an enchanter, "a conning man in nigromancy," who was with the army of the Duke of Anjou and the Earl of Savoy, then lying before the city of Naples. This magician proposed, by his art, to put into the power of these two princes the castle which they were besieging, and which he boasted having already delivered to Sir Charles de la Paye, who was then in possession of it. Shocked, however, at his treachery towards his former employer, they assured him that he should "never do more enchauntments to deceyve hym, nor yet any other," and repaid his offers of service by causing him to be beheaded on the spot.

The Welsh have preserved some curious Triads on the subject of magic, stating the names of their principal enchanters (who are styled, "Men of Illusion and Phantasy") to have been "Math ab Mathonwy, who declared his illusion to Gwdion the son of Don; Menyw the son of Teirgwaedd, who taught his illusion to Uthyr Pendragon; and Rhuddlwm the Giant, who learnt his illusion from Eiddilig the Dwarf, and Coll the son of Collfrewi."—T. 90.

The same names occur in other Triads relating to this subject, with the addition of that of Drych ail Cibddar.

May it not be fairly presumed, that it is to the Coll mab Collfrewi above mentioned, whose fame had descended to his times, that Chaucer alludes in the following lines?—

---

1 MS. in Royal Lib. marked 2 B. vii. Sports and Pastimes, p. 12.

"There saw I Coll Tragetour,[1]
Upon a table of sicamour,
Play an uncouth thing to tell,
I saw him carry a wind-mell,
Under a walnote shale."

House of Fame, B. III.

The Welsh Chronicle, entitled Brut y Tywysogion, states, that in the year 1135, Gruffudd ab Rhys, Prince of South Wales, after recovering his dominions, made a great feast in Ystrad Towi, to which he invited all that chose to come from the neighbouring provinces, and entertained them with minstrelsy and manly games, and with exhibitions of magic and illusions (hud a lledrith).— Myv. Arch. II. 558.

NOTICE OF VARIOUS OTHER VERSIONS

IT is to Chrestien de Troyes, the author of the "Chevalier au Lyon" and "Perceval le Galois," that we are also indebted for the French metrical version of Geraint ab Erbin, entitled "Erec et Enide." Several copies of his Romance are preserved in the Bibliothèque Nationale.

In like manner, we find that the German version of the Tale, under the title of Erec and Enite, is the production of Hartmann von der Aue, to whom the poem of "Iwein" is to be attributed.

Hartmann's "Erec" was edited in 1839 by Herr Moriz Haupt, from a MS. in the Imperial Ambraser Collection at Vienna.

The Royal Library at Stockholm possesses an Icelandic composition, called "Erik Saga," on the subject of this Tale.

In our own language I know of no other version of the Mabinogi of Geraint except that so beautifully rendered by Mr. Tennyson in his Idyll of Enid.

---

1 Treggetour, a juggler.

KILHWCH AND OLWEN
OR THE TWRCH TRWYTH

[217a]KILYDD the son of Prince Kelyddon desired a wife as a helpmate, and the wife that he chose was Goleuddydd, the daughter of Prince Anlawdd[217b]. And after their union, the people put up prayers that they might have an heir. And they had a son through the prayers of the people. From the time of her pregnancy Goleuddydd became wild, and wandered about, without habitation; but when her delivery was at hand, her reason came back to her. Then she went to a mountain where there was a swineherd, keeping a herd of swine. And through fear of the swine the queen was delivered. And the swineherd took the boy, and brought him to the palace; and he was christened, and they called him Kilhwch, because he had been found in a swine's burrow. Nevertheless the boy was of gentle lineage, and cousin unto Arthur; and they put him out to nurse.

After this the boy's mother, Goleuddydd, the daughter of Prince Anlawdd, fell sick. Then she called her husband unto her, and said to him, "Of this sickness I shall die, and thou wilt take another wife. Now wives are the gift of the Lord, but it would be wrong for thee to harm thy son. Therefore I charge thee that thou take not a wife until thou see a briar with two blossoms upon my grave." And this he promised her. Then she besought him to dress her grave every year, that nothing might grow thereon. So the queen died. Now the king sent an attendant every morning to see if anything were growing upon the grave. And at the end of the seventh year the master neglected that which he had promised to the queen.

One day the king went to hunt, and he rode to the place of burial to see the grave, and to know if it were time that he should take a wife; and the king saw the briar. And when he saw it, the king took counsel where he should find a wife. Said one of his counsellors, "I know a wife that will suit thee well, and she is the wife of King Doged[218a]." And they resolved to go to seek her; and they slew the king, and brought away his wife and one daughter that she had along with her. And they conquered the king's lands.

On a certain day, as the lady walked abroad, she came to the house of an old crone that dwelt in the town, and that had no tooth in her head. And the queen said to her, "Old woman, tell me that which I shall ask thee, for the love of Heaven. Where are the children of the man who has carried me away by violence?" Said the crone, "He has not children." Said the queen, "Woe is me, that I should have come to one who is childless!" Then said the hag, "Thou needest not lament on account of that, for there is a prediction he shall have an heir by thee, and by none other. Moreover, be not sorrowful, for he has one son."

The lady returned home with joy; and she asked her consort, "Wherefore hast thou concealed thy children from me?" The king said, "I will do so no longer." And he sent messengers for his son, and he was brought to the Court. His stepmother said unto him, "It were well for thee to have a wife, and I have a daughter who is sought of every man of renown in the world." "I am not yet of an age to wed," answered the youth. Then said she unto him, "I declare to thee, that it is thy destiny not to be suited with a wife until thou obtain Olwen[219a], the daughter of Yspaddaden Penkawr." And the youth blushed, and the love of the maiden diffused itself through all his frame, although he had never seen her. And his father inquired of him, "What has come over thee, my son, and what aileth thee?" "My stepmother has declared to me that I shall never have a wife until I obtain Olwen, the daughter of Yspaddaden Penkawr." "That will be easy for thee," answered his father. "Arthur is thy cousin. Go, therefore, unto Arthur, to cut thy hair[219b], and ask this of him as a boon."

And the youth pricked forth upon a steed with head dappled grey, of four winters old, firm of limb, with shell-formed hoofs, having a bridle of linked gold on his head, and upon him a saddle of costly gold. And in the youth's hand were two spears of silver, sharp, well-tempered, headed with steel, three ells in length, of an edge to wound the wind, and cause blood to flow, and swifter than the fall of the dewdrop from the blade of reed-grass upon the earth when the dew of June is at the heaviest. A gold-hilted sword was upon his thigh, the blade of which was of gold, bearing a cross of inlaid gold of the hue of the lightning of heaven: his war-horn was of ivory. Before him were two brindled white-breasted greyhounds, having strong collars of rubies about their necks, reaching from the shoulder to the ear. And the one that was on the left side bounded across to the right side, and the one on the right to the left, and like two sea-swallows sported around him. And his courser cast up four sods with his four hoofs, like four swallows in the air, about his head, now above, now below. About him was a four-cornered cloth of purple, and an apple of gold was at each corner, and every one of the apples was of the value of an hundred kine[219c]. And there was precious gold of the value of three hundred kine upon his shoes, and upon his stirrups, from his knee to the tip of his toe. And the blade of grass bent not beneath him, so light was his courser's tread as he journeyed towards the gate of Arthur's Palace.

Spoke the youth, "Is there a porter?" "There is; and if thou holdest not thy peace, small will be thy welcome. I am Arthur's porter every first day of January. And during every other part of the year but this, the office is filled by Huandaw, and Gogigwc, and Llaeskenym, and Pennpingyon, who goes upon his head to save his feet, neither towards the sky nor towards the earth, but like a rolling stone upon the floor of the court." "Open the portal." "I will not open it." "Wherefore not?" "The knife is in the meat, and the drink is in the horn, and there is revelry in Arthur's Hall, and none may enter therein but the son of a king of a privileged country, or a craftsman bringing his craft. But there will be refreshment for thy dogs, and for thy horses; and for thee there will be collops cooked and peppered, and luscious wine and mirthful songs, and food for fifty men shall be brought unto thee in the guest chamber, where the stranger and the sons of other countries eat, who come not unto the precincts of the Palace of Arthur. Thou wilt fare no worse there than thou wouldest with Arthur in the Court. A lady shall smooth thy couch, and shall lull thee with songs; and early to-morrow morning, when the gate is open for the multitude that come hither to-day, for thee shall it be opened first, and thou mayest sit in the place that thou shalt choose in Arthur's Hall, from the upper end to the lower." Said the youth, "That will I not do. If thou openest the gate, it is well. If thou dost not open it, I will bring disgrace upon thy Lord, and evil report upon thee. And I will set up three shouts at this very gate, than which none were ever more deadly, from the top of Pengwaed in Cornwall[220a] to the bottom of Dinsol, in the North, and to Esgair Oervel, in Ireland. And all the women in this Palace that are pregnant shall lose their offspring; and such as are not pregnant, their hearts shall be turned by illness, so that they shall never bear children from this day forward." "What clamour soever thou mayest make," said Glewlwyd Gavaelvawr, "against the laws of Arthur's Palace shalt thou not enter therein, until I first go and speak with Arthur."

Then Glewlwyd went into the Hall. And Arthur said to him, "Hast thou news from the gate?"—"Half of my life is past, and half of thine. I was heretofore in Kaer Se and Asse, in Sach and Salach, in Lotor and Fotor; and I have been heretofore in India the Great and India the Lesser; and I was in the battle of Dau Ynyr, when the twelve hostages were brought from Llychlyn. And I have also been in Europe, and in Africa, and in the islands of Corsica, and in Caer Brythwch, and Brythach, and Verthach; and I was present when formerly thou didst slay the family of Clis the son of Merin, and when thou didst slay Mil Du the son of Ducum, and when thou didst conquer Greece in the East. And I have been in Caer Oeth and Annoeth, and in Caer Nevenhyr; nine supreme sovereigns, handsome men, saw we there, but never did I behold a man of equal dignity with him who is now at the door of the portal." Then said Arthur, "If walking thou didst enter in here, return thou running. And every one that beholds the light, and every one that opens and shuts the eye, let them shew him respect, and serve him, some with gold-mounted drinking-horns, others with collops cooked and peppered, until food and drink can be prepared for him. It is unbecoming to keep such a man as thou sayest he is, in the wind and the rain." Said Kai, "By the hand of my friend, if thou wouldest follow my counsel, thou wouldest not break through the laws of the Court because of him." "Not so, blessed Kai. It is an honour to us to be resorted to, and the greater our courtesy the greater will be our renown, and our fame, and our glory."

And Glewlwyd came to the gate, and opened the gate before him; and although all dismounted upon the horseblock at the gate, yet did he not dismount, but rode in upon his charger. Then said Kilhwch, "Greeting be unto thee, Sovereign Ruler of this Island; and be this greeting no less unto the lowest than unto the highest, and be it equally unto thy guests, and thy warriors, and thy chieftains— let all partake of it as completely as thyself. And complete be thy favour, and thy fame, and thy glory, throughout all this Island." "Greeting unto thee also," said Arthur; "sit thou between two of my warriors, and thou shalt have minstrels before thee, and thou shalt enjoy the privileges of a king born to a throne, as long as thou remainest here. And when I dispense my presents to the visitors and strangers in this Court, they shall be in thy hand at my commencing." Said the youth, "I came not here to consume meat and drink; but if I obtain the boon that I seek, I will requite it thee, and extol thee; and if I have it not, I will bear forth thy dispraise to the four quarters of the world, as far as thy renown has extended." Then said Arthur, "Since thou wilt not remain here, chieftain, thou shalt receive the boon whatsoever thy tongue may name, as far as the wind dries, and the rain moistens, and the sun revolves, and the sea encircles, and the earth extends; save only my ship; and my mantle[222a]; and Caledvwlch, my sword; and Rhongomyant, my lance; and Wynebgwrthucher, my shield; and Carnwenhau, my dagger; and Gwenhwyvar, my wife. By the truth of Heaven, thou shalt have it cheerfully, name what thou wilt." "I would that thou bless my hair." "That shall be granted thee."

And Arthur took a golden comb, and scissors, whereof the loops were of silver, and he combed his hair. And Arthur inquired of him who he was. "For my heart warms unto thee, and I know that thou art come of my blood. Tell me, therefore, who thou art." "I will tell thee," said the youth. "I am Kilhwch, the son of Kilydd, the son of Prince Kelyddon, by Goleuddydd, my mother, the daughter of Prince Anlawdd." "That is true," said Arthur; "thou art my cousin. Whatsoever boon thou mayest ask, thou shalt receive, be it what it may that thy tongue shall name." "Pledge the truth of Heaven and the faith of thy kingdom thereof." "I pledge it thee, gladly." "I crave of thee then, that thou obtain for me Olwen, the daughter of Yspaddaden Penkawr; and this boon I likewise seek at the hands of thy warriors. I seek it from Kai, and Bedwyr, and Greidawl Galldonyd[223a], and Gwythyr the son of Greidawl[223b], and Greid the son of Eri, and Kynddelig Kyvarwydd, and Tathal Twyll Goleu, and Maelwys the son of Baeddan, and Crychwr the son of Nes, and Cubert the son of Daere, and Percos the son of Poch, and Lluber Beuthach, and Corvil Bervach, and Gwynn the son of Nudd[223c], and Edeyrn the son of Nudd[223d], and Gadwy the son of Geraint[223e], and Prince Fflewddur Fflam[223f], and Ruawn Pebyr[223g] the son of Dorath, and Bradwen the son of Moren Mynawc, and Moren Mynawc himself, and Dalldav the son of Kimin Côv[223h], and the son of Alun Dyved, and the son of Saidi, and the son of Gwryon, and Uchtryd Ardywad Kad, and Kynwas Curvagyl, and Gwrhyr Gwarthegvras, and Isperyr Ewingath[223i], and Gallcoyt Govynynat, and

Duach, and Grathach, and Nerthach, the sons of Gwawrddur Kyrvach (these men came forth from the confines of hell), and Kilydd Canhastyr, and Canastyr Kanllaw, and Cors Cant-Ewin, and Esgeir Gulhwch Govynkawn, and Drustwrn Hayarn, and Glewlwyd Gavaelvawr, and Lloch Llawwynnyawc[223j], and Aunwas Adeiniawc[223k], and Sinnoch the son of Seithved, and Gwennwynwyn the son of Naw[223l], and Bedyw the son of Seithved, and Gobrwy the son of Echel Vorddwyttwll, and Echel Vorddwyttwll[223m] himself, and Mael the son of Roycol, and Dadweir Dallpenn[223n], and Garwyli the son of Gwythawc Gwyr, and Gwythawc Gwyr himself, and Gormant the son of Ricca, and Menw the son of Teirgwaedd[223o], and Digon the son of Alar, and Selyf the son of Smoit, and Gusg the son of Atheu, and Nerth the son of Kedarn, and Drudwas the son of Tryffin[223p], and Twrch the son of Perif, and Twrch the son of Annwas, and Iona king of France, and Sel the son of Selgi, and Teregud the son of Iaen, and Sulyen the son of Iaen, and Bradwen the son of Iaen, and Moren the son of Iaen, and Siawn the son of Iaen, and Cradawc the son of Iaen.

(They were men of Caerdathal[224a], of Arthur's kindred on his father's side.) Dirmyg the son of Kaw[224b], and Justic the son of Kaw, and Etmic the son of Kaw, and Anghawd the son of Kaw, and Ovan the son of Kaw, and Kelin the son of Kaw, and Connyn the son of Kaw, and Mabsant the son of Kaw, and Gwyngad the son of Kaw, and Llwybyr the son of Kaw, and Coth the son of Kaw, and Meilic the son of Kaw, and Kynwas the son of Kaw, and Ardwyad the son of Kaw, and Ergyryad the son of Kaw, and Neb the son of Kaw, and Gilda the son of Kaw, and Calcas the son of Kaw, and Hueil the son of Kaw (he never yet made a request at the hand of any Lord). And Samson Vinsych, and Taliesin the chief of the bards[224c], and Manawyddan the son of Llyr[224d], and Llary the son of Prince Kasnar, and Ysperni the son of Fflergant king of Armorica, and Saranhon, the son of Glythwyr, and Llawr Eilerw, and Annyanniawc the son of Menw the son of Teirgwaedd, and Gwynn the son of Nwyvre, and Fflam the son of Nwyvre, and Geraint the son of Erbin[224e], and Ermid the son of Erbin, and Dyvel the son of Erbin[224f], and Gwynn the son of Ermid, and Kyndrwyn the son of Ermid, and Hyveidd Unllenn, and Eiddon Vawr Vrydic, and Reidwn Arwy, and Gormant the son of Ricca (Arthur's brother by his mother's side; the Penhynev of Cornwall was his father), and Llawnrodded Varvawc[224g], and Nodawl Varyf Twrch, and Berth the son of Kado, and Rheidwn the son of Beli, and Iscovan Hael, and Iscawin the son of Panon, and Morvran the son of Tegid[224h] (no one struck him in the battle of Camlan by reason of his ugliness; all thought he was an auxiliary devil. Hair had he upon him like the hair of a stag). And Sandde Bryd Angel (no one touched him with a spear in the battle of Camlan because of his beauty; all thought he was a ministering angel). And Kynwyl Sant (the third man that escaped from the battle of Camlan, and he was the last who parted from Arthur on Hengroen his horse). And Uchtryd the son of Erim, and Eus the son of Erim, and Henwas Adeinawg the son of Erim, and Henbedestyr the son of Erim, and Sgilti Yscawndroed the son of Erim. (Unto these three men belonged these three qualities,—With Henbedestyr there was not any one who could keep pace, either on horseback or on foot; with Henwas Adeinawg, no four-footed beast could run the distance of an acre, much less could it go beyond it; and as to Sgilti Yscawndroed, when he intended to go upon a message for his Lord, he never sought to find a path, but knowing whither he was to go, if his way lay through a wood he went along the tops of the trees. During his whole life, a blade of reed grass bent not beneath his feet, much less did one ever break, so lightly did he tread.) Teithi Hên the son of Gwynhan (his dominions were swallowed up by the sea, and he himself hardly escaped, and he came to Arthur; and his knife had this peculiarity, that from the time that he came there no haft would ever remain upon it, and owing to this a sickness came over him, and he pined away during the remainder of his life, and of this he died). And Carneddyr the son of Govynyon Hên, and Gwenwynwyn the son of Nav Gyssevin, Arthur's champion, and Llysgadrudd Emys, and Gwrbothu Hên (uncles unto Arthur were they, his mother's brothers). Kulvanawyd the son of Goryon, and Llenlleawg Wyddel[225a] from the headland of Ganion, and Dyvynwal Moel[225b], and Dunard king of the North, Teirnon Twryf Bliant, and Tegvan Gloff, and Tegyr Talgellawg, Gwrdinal the son of Ebrei, and Morgant Hael, Gwystyl the son of Rhun the son of Nwython[225c], and Llwyddeu the son of Nwython, and Gwydre the son of Llwyddeu (Gwenabwy the daughter of [Kaw] was his mother, Hueil his uncle stabbed him, and hatred was between Hueil and Arthur because of the wound). Drem the son of Dremidyd[225d] (when the gnat arose in the morning with the sun, he could see it from Gelli Wic[225e] in Cornwall, as far off as Pen Blathaon in North Britain[225f]). And Eidyol the son of Ner, and Glwyddyn Saer (who constructed Ehangwen, Arthur's Hall). Kynyr Keinvarvawc (when he was told he had a son born he said to his wife, 'Damsel, if thy son be mine, his heart will be always cold, and there will be no warmth in his hands; and he will have another peculiarity, if he is my son he will always be stubborn; and he will have another peculiarity, when he carries a burden, whether it be large or small, no one will be able to see it, either before him or at his back; and he will have another peculiarity, no one will be able to resist fire and water so well as he will; and he will have another peculiarity, there will never be a servant or an officer equal to him'). Henwas, and Henwyneb (an old companion to Arthur). Gwallgoyc (another; when he came to a town, though there were three hundred houses in it, if he wanted anything, he would not let sleep come to the eyes of any one whilst he remained there). Berwyn the son of Gerenhir, and Paris king of France, and Osla Gyllellvawr (who bore a short broad dagger. When Arthur and his hosts came before a torrent, they would seek for a narrow place where they might pass the water, and would lay the sheathed dagger across the torrent, and it would form a bridge sufficient for the armies of the three Islands of Britain, and of the three islands adjacent[226a],

with their spoil). Gwyddawg the son of Menestyr (who slew Kai, and whom
Arthur slew, together with his brothers, to revenge Kai). Garanwyn the son of
Kai, and Amren the son of Bedwyr, and Ely Amyr, and Rheu Rhwyd Dyrys,
and Rhun Rhudwern, and Eli, and Trachmyr (Arthur's chief huntsmen). And
Llwyddeu the son of Kelcoed, and Hunabwy the son of Gwryon, and Gwynn
Godyvron[226b], and Gweir Datharwenniddawg, and Gweir the son of Cadell the
son of Talaryant, and Gweir Gwrhyd Ennwir, and Gweir Paladyr Hir (the uncles
of Arthur, the brothers of his mother). The sons of Llwch Llawwynnyawg (from
beyond the raging sea). Llenlleawg Wyddel, and Ardderchawg Prydain. Cas
the son of Saidi, Gwrvan Gwallt Avwyn, and Gwyllennhin the king of France,
and Gwittart the son of Oedd king of Ireland, Garselit Wyddel[226c], Panawr
Pen Bagad, and Ffleudor the son of Nav, Gwynnhyvar mayor of Cornwall and
Devon (the ninth man that rallied the battle of Camlan[226d]). Keli and Kueli, and
Gilla Coes Hydd (he would clear three hundred acres at one bound: the chief
leaper of Ireland was he). Sol, and Gwadyn Ossol, and Gwadyn Odyeith. (Sol
could stand all day upon one foot.

Gwadyn Ossol, if he stood upon the top of the highest mountain in the
world, it would become a level plain under his feet. Gwadyn Odyeith, the soles
of his feet emitted sparks of fire when they struck upon things hard, like the
heated mass when drawn out of the forge. He cleared the way for Arthur when
he came to any stoppage.) Hirerwm and Hiratrwm. (The day they went on a
visit three Cantrevs provided for their entertainment, and they feasted until
noon and drank until night, when they went to sleep. And then they devoured
the heads of the vermin through hunger, as if they had never eaten anything.
When they made a visit they left neither the fat nor the lean, neither the hot nor
the cold, the sour nor the sweet, the fresh nor the salt, the boiled nor the raw.)
Huarwar the son of Aflawn (who asked Arthur such a boon as would satisfy
him. It was the third great plague of Cornwall when he received it. None could
get a smile from him but when he was satisfied). Gware Gwallt Euryn[227a]. The
two cubs of Gast Rhymi, Gwyddrud and Gwyddneu Astrus. Sugyn the son of
Sugnedydd (who would suck up the sea on which were three hundred ships so
as to leave nothing but a dry strand. He was broad-chested). Rhacymwri, the
attendant of Arthur (whatever barn he was shown, were there the produce of
thirty ploughs within it, he would strike it with an iron flail until the rafters,
the beams, and the boards were no better than the small oats in the mow
upon the floor of the barn). Dygyflwng and Anoeth Veidawg. And Hir Eiddyl,
and Hir Amreu (they were two attendants of Arthur). And Gwevyl the son of
Gwestad (on the day that he was sad, he would let one of his lips drop below his
waist, while he turned up the other like a cap upon his head). Uchtryd Varyf
Draws (who spread his red untrimmed beard over the eight-and-forty rafters
which were in Arthur's Hall). Elidyr Gyvarwydd. Yskyrdav and Yscudydd (two
attendants of Gwenhwyvar were they. Their feet were swift as their thoughts

when bearing a message). Brys the son of Bryssethach (from the Hill of the Black Fernbrake in North Britain). And Grudlwyn Gorr. Bwlch, and Kyfwlch, and Sefwlch, the sons of Cleddyf Kyfwlch, the grandsons of Cleddyf Difwlch. (Their three shields were three gleaming glitterers; their three spears were three pointed piercers; their three swords were three grinding gashers; Glas, Glessic, and Gleisad. Their three dogs, Call, Cuall, and Cavall. Their three horses, Hwyrdyddwd, and Drwgdyddwd, and Llwyrdyddwg. Their three wives, Och, and Garym, and Diaspad. Their three grandchildren, Lluched, and Neved, and Eissiwed. Their three daughters, Drwg, and Gwaeth, and Gwaethav Oll. Their three hand-maids, Eheubryd the daughter of Kyfwlch, Gorascwrn the daughter of Nerth, Ewaedan the daughter of Kynvelyn Keudawd Pwyll the half-man[228a].) Dwnn Diessic Unbenn, Eiladyr the son of Pen Llarcau, Kynedyr Wyllt the son of Hettwn Talaryant, Sawyl Ben Uchel[228b], Gwalchmai the son of Gwyar, Gwalhaved the son of Gwyar, Gwrhyr Gwastawd Ieithoedd[228c] (to whom all tongues were known), and Kethcrwm the Priest. Clust the son of Clustveinad (though he were buried seven cubits beneath the earth, he would hear the ant fifty miles off rise from her nest in the morning). Medyr the son of Methredydd (from Gelli Wic he could, in a twinkling, shoot the wren through the two legs upon Esgeir Oervel in Ireland). Gwiawn Llygad Cath (who could cut a haw from the eye of the gnat without hurting him). Ol the son of Olwydd (seven years before he was born his father's swine were carried off, and when he grew up a man he tracked the swine, and brought them back in seven herds). Bedwini the Bishop[228d] (who blessed Arthur's meat and drink). For the sake of the golden-chained daughters of this island. For the sake of Gwenhwyvar its chief lady, and Gwennhwyach her sister, and Rathtyeu the only daughter of Clemenhill, and Rhelemon the daughter of Kai, and Tannwen the daughter of Gweir Datharwenîddawg. Gwenn Alarch the daughter of Kynwyl Canbwch. Eurneid the daughter of Clydno Eiddin. Eneuawc the daughter of Bedwyr. Enrydreg the daughter of Tudvathar. Gwennwledyr the daughter of Gwaledyr Kyrvach. Erddudnid the daughter of Tryffin. Eurolwen the daughter of Gwdolwyn Gorr. Teleri the daughter of Peul. Indeg[229a] the daughter of Garwy Hir. Morvudd the daughter of Urien Rheged. Gwenllian Deg the majestic maiden. Creiddylad the daughter of Lludd Llaw Ereint. (She was the most splendid maiden in the three Islands of the mighty, and in the three Islands adjacent, and for her Gwythyr the son of Greidawl and Gwynn the son of Nudd fight every first of May until the day of doom.) Ellylw the daughter of Neol Kynn-Crog (she lived three ages). Essyllt Vinwen and Essyllt Vingul." And all these did Kilhwch the son of Kilydd adjure to obtain his boon.

Then said Arthur, "Oh! chieftain, I have never heard of the maiden of whom thou speakest, nor of her kindred, but I will gladly send messengers in search of her. Give me time to seek her." And the youth said, "I will willingly grant from this night to that at the end of the year to do so." Then Arthur sent messengers to every land within his dominions to seek for the maiden; and at the end of the year Arthur's messengers returned without having gained any knowledge or intelligence concerning Olwen more than on the first day. Then said Kilhwch, "Every one has received his boon, and I yet lack mine. I will depart and bear away thy honour with me." Then said Kai, "Rash chieftain! dost thou reproach Arthur? Go with us, and we will not part until thou dost either confess that the maiden exists not in the world, or until we obtain her." Thereupon Kai rose up. Kai had this peculiarity, that his breath lasted nine nights and nine days under water, and he could exist nine nights and nine days without sleep. A wound from Kai's sword no physician could heal. Very subtle was Kai. When it pleased him he could render himself as tall as the highest tree in the forest. And he had another peculiarity,—so great was the heat of his nature, that, when it rained hardest, whatever he carried remained dry for a handbreadth above and a handbreadth below his hand; and when his companions were coldest, it was to them as fuel with which to light their fire.

And Arthur called Bedwyr, who never shrank from any enterprise upon which Kai was bound. None was equal to him in swiftness throughout this island except Arthur and Drych Ail Kibddar[230a]. And although he was one-handed, three warriors could not shed blood faster than he on the field of battle. Another property he had; his lance would produce a wound equal to those of nine opposing lances.

And Arthur called to Kynddelig the Guide, "Go thou upon this expedition with the chieftain." For as good a guide was he in a land which he had never seen as he was in his own.

He called Gwrhyr Gwalstawt Ieithoedd, because he knew all tongues.

He called Gwalchmai the son of Gwyar, because he never returned home without achieving the adventure of which he went in quest. He was the best of footmen and the best of knights. He was nephew to Arthur, the son of his sister, and his cousin.

And Arthur called Menw the son of Teirgwaedd, in order that if they went into a savage country, he might cast a charm and an illusion over them, so that none might see them whilst they could see every one.

They journeyed until they came to a vast open plain, wherein they saw a great castle, which was the fairest of the castles of the world. And they journeyed that day until the evening, and when they thought they were nigh to the castle, they were no nearer to it than they had been in the morning. And the second and the third day they journeyed, and even then scarcely could they reach so far. And when they came before the castle, they beheld a vast flock of sheep, which was boundless and without an end. And upon the top of a mound there was a herdsman, keeping the sheep. And a rug made of skins was upon him; and by his side was a shaggy mastiff, larger than a steed nine winters old. Never had he lost even a lamb from his flock, much less a large sheep. He let no occasion ever pass without doing some hurt and harm. All the dead trees and bushes in the plain he burnt with his breath down to the very ground.

Then said Kai, "Gwrhyr Gwalstawt Ieithoedd, go thou and salute yonder man." "Kai," said he, "I engaged not to go further than thou thyself." "Let us go then together," answered Kai. Said Menw the son of Teirgwaedd, "Fear not to go thither, for I will cast a spell upon the dog, so that he shall injure no one." And they went up to the mound whereon the herdsman was, and they said to him, "How dost thou fare, O herdsman?" "No less fair be it to you than to me." "Truly, art thou the chief?" "There is no hurt to injure me but my own."[1] "Whose are the sheep that thou dost keep, and to whom does yonder castle belong?" "Stupid are ye, truly! Through the whole world is it known that this is the castle of Yspaddaden Penkawr." "And who art thou?" "I am called Custennin the son of Dyfnedig, and my brother Yspaddaden Penkawr oppressed me because of my possessions. And ye also, who are ye?" "We are an embassy from Arthur, come to seek Olwen the daughter of Yspaddaden Penkawr." "Oh men! the mercy of Heaven be upon you, do not that for all the world. None who ever came hither on this quest has returned alive." And the herdsman rose up. And as he arose, Kilhwch gave unto him a ring of gold. And he sought to put on the ring, but it was too small for him, so he placed it in the finger of his glove. And he went home, and gave the glove to his spouse to keep. And she took the ring from the glove when it was given her, and she said, "Whence came this ring, for thou art not wont to have good fortune?" "I went," said he, "to the sea to seek for fish, and lo, I saw a corpse borne by the waves. And a fairer corpse than it did I never behold. And from its finger did I take this ring." "O man! does the sea permit its dead to wear jewels? Show me then this body." "Oh wife, him to whom this ring belonged thou shalt see here in the evening." "And who is he?" asked the woman, "Kilhwch the son of Kilydd, the son of Prince Kelyddon, by Goleuddydd the daughter of Prince Anlawdd, his mother, who is come to seek Olwen as his wife." And when she heard that, her feelings were divided between the joy that she had that her nephew, the son of her sister, was coming to her, and sorrow because she had never known any one depart alive who had come on that quest.

And they went forward to the gate of Custennin the herdsman's dwelling. And when she heard their footsteps approaching, she ran out with joy to meet them. And Kai snatched a billet out of the pile. And when she met them she sought to throw her arms about their necks. And Kai placed the log between her two hands, and she squeezed it so that it became a twisted coil. "Oh woman," said Kai, "if thou hadst squeezed me thus, none could ever again have set their affections on me. Evil love were this." They entered into the house, and were served; and soon after they all went forth to amuse themselves. Then the woman opened a stone chest that was before the chimney-corner, and out of it arose a

---

1 This dialogue consists of a series of repartees with a play upon words which it is
   impossible to follow without the translation.

youth with yellow curling hair. Said Gwrhyr, "It is a pity to hide this youth. I know that it is not his own crime that is thus visited upon him." "This is but a remnant," said the woman. "Three-and-twenty of my sons has Yspaddaden Penkawr slain, and I have no more hope of this one than of the others." Then said Kai, "Let him come and be a companion with me, and he shall not be slain unless I also am slain with him." And they ate. And the woman asked them, "Upon what errand come you here?" "We come to seek Olwen for this youth." Then said the woman, "In the name of Heaven, since no one from the castle hath yet seen you, return again whence you came." "Heaven is our witness, that we will not return until we have seen the maiden." Said Kai, "Does she ever come hither, so that she may be seen?" "She comes here every Saturday to wash her head, and in the vessel where she washes, she leaves all her rings, and she never either comes herself or sends any messengers to fetch them." "Will she come here if she is sent to?" "Heaven knows that I will not destroy my soul, nor will I betray those that trust me; unless you will pledge me your faith that you will not harm her, I will not send to her." "We pledge it," said they. So a message was sent, and she came.

The maiden was clothed in a robe of flame-coloured silk, and about her neck was a collar of ruddy gold, on which were precious emeralds and rubies. More yellow was her head than the flower of the broom, and her skin was whiter than the foam of the wave, and fairer were her hands and her fingers than the blossoms of the wood anemone amidst the spray of the meadow fountain. The eye of the trained hawk, the glance of the three-mewed falcon was not brighter than hers. Her bosom was more snowy than the breast of the white swan, her cheek was redder than the reddest roses. Whoso beheld her was filled with her love. Four white trefoils sprung up wherever she trod. And therefore was she called Olwen.

She entered the house, and sat beside Kilhwch upon the foremost bench; and as soon as he saw her he knew her. And Kilhwch said unto her, "Ah! maiden, thou art she whom I have loved; come away with me, lest they speak evil of thee and of me. Many a day have I loved thee." "I cannot do this, for I have pledged my faith to my father not to go without his counsel, for his life will last only until the time of my espousals. Whatever is, must be. But I will give thee advice if thou wilt take it. Go, ask me of my father, and that which he shall require of thee, grant it, and thou wilt obtain me; but if thou deny him anything, thou wilt not obtain me, and it will be well for thee if thou escape with thy life." "I promise all this, if occasion offer," said he.

She returned to her chamber, and they all rose up and followed her to the castle. And they slew the nine porters that were at the nine gates in silence. And they slew the nine watch-dogs without one of them barking. And they went forward to the hall.

"The greeting of Heaven and of man be unto thee, Yspaddaden Penkawr," said they. "And you, wherefore come you?" "We come to ask thy daughter Olwen, for Kilhwch the son of Kilydd, the son of Prince Kelyddon." "Where are my pages and my servants? Raise up the forks beneath my two eyebrows which have fallen over my eyes, that I may see the fashion of my son-in-law." And they did so. "Come hither to-morrow, and you shall have an answer."

They rose to go forth, and Yspaddaden Penkawr seized one of the three poisoned darts that lay beside him, and threw it after them. And Bedwyr caught it, and flung it, and pierced Yspaddaden Penkawr grievously with it through the knee. Then he said, "A cursed ungentle son-in-law, truly. I shall ever walk the worse for his rudeness, and shall ever be without a cure. This poisoned iron pains me like the bite of a gadfly. Cursed be the smith who forged it, and the anvil whereon it was wrought! So sharp is it!"

That night also they took up their abode in the house of Custennin the herdsman. The next day with the dawn they arrayed themselves in haste and proceeded to the castle, and entered the hall, and they said, "Yspaddaden Penkawr, give us thy daughter in consideration of her dower and her maiden fee, which we will pay to thee and to her two kinswomen likewise. And unless thou wilt do so, thou shalt meet with thy death on her account." Then he said, "Her four great-grandmothers, and her four great-grandsires are yet alive, it is needful that I take counsel of them." "Be it so," answered they, "we will go to meat." As they rose up, he took the second dart that was beside him, and cast it after them. And Menw the son of Gwaedd caught it, and flung it back at him, and wounded him in the centre of the breast, so that it came out at the small of his back. "A cursed ungentle son-in-law, truly," said he, "the hard iron pains me like the bite of a horse-leech. Cursed be the hearth whereon it was heated, and the smith who formed it! So sharp is it! Henceforth, whenever I go up a hill, I shall have a scant in my breath, and a pain in my chest, and I shall often loathe my food." And they went to meat.

And the third day they returned to the palace. And Yspaddaden Penkawr said to them, "Shoot not at me again unless you desire death. Where are my attendants? Lift up the forks of my eyebrows which have fallen over my eyeballs, that I may see the fashion of my son-in-law." Then they arose, and, as they did so, Yspaddaden Penkawr took the third poisoned dart and cast it at them. And Kilhwch caught it and threw it vigorously, and wounded him through the eyeball, so that the dart came out at the back of his head. "A cursed ungentle son-in-law, truly! As long as I remain alive, my eyesight will be the worse. Whenever I go against the wind, my eyes will water; and peradventure my head will burn, and I shall have a giddiness every new moon. Cursed be the fire in which it was forged. Like the bite of a mad dog is the stroke of this poisoned iron." And they went to meat.

And the next day they came again to the palace, and they said, "Shoot not at us any more, unless thou desirest such hurt, and harm, and torture as thou now hast, and even more." "Give me thy daughter, and if thou wilt not give her, thou shalt receive thy death because of her." "Where is he that seeks my daughter? Come hither where I may see thee." And they placed him a chair face to face with him.

Said Yspaddaden Penkawr, "Is it thou that seekest my daughter?" "It is I," answered Kilhwch. "I must have thy pledge that thou wilt not do towards me otherwise than is just, and when I have gotten that which I shall name, my daughter thou shalt have." "I promise thee that willingly," said Kilhwch, "name what thou wilt." "I will do so," said he.

"Seest thou yonder vast hill?" "I see it." "I require that it be rooted up, and that the grubbings be burned for manure on the face of the land, and that it be ploughed and sown in one day, and in one day that the grain ripen. And of that wheat I intend to make food and liquor fit for the wedding of thee and my daughter. And all this I require done in one day."

"It will be easy for me to compass this, although thou mayest think that it will not be easy."

"Though this be easy for thee, there is yet that which will not be so. No husbandman can till or prepare this land, so wild is it, except Amaethon the son of Don[236a], and he will not come with thee by his own free will, and thou wilt not be able to compel him."

"It will be easy for me to compass this, although thou mayest think that it will not be easy."

"Though thou get this, there is yet that which thou wilt not get. Govannon the son of Don to come to the headland to rid the iron, he will do no work of his own good will except for a lawful king, and thou wilt not be able to compel him."

"It will be easy for me to compass this."

"Though thou get this, there is yet that which thou wilt not get; the two dun oxen of Gwlwlyd[236b], both yoked together, to plough the wild land yonder stoutly. He will not give them of his own free will, and thou wilt not be able to compel him."

"It will be easy for me to compass this."

"Though thou get this, there is yet that which thou wilt not get; the yellow and the brindled bull yoked together do I require."

"It will be easy for me to compass this."

"Though thou get this, there is yet that which thou wilt not get; the two horned oxen, one of which is beyond, and the other this side of the peaked mountain, yoked together in the same plough. And these are Nynniaw and Peibaw[236c] whom God turned into oxen on account of their sins."

"It will be easy for me to compass this."

"Though thou get this, there is yet that which thou wilt not get. Seest thou yonder red tilled ground?"

"I see it."

"When first I met the mother of this maiden, nine bushels of flax were sown therein, and none has yet sprung up, neither white nor black; and I have the measure by me still. I require to have the flax to sow in the new land yonder, that when it grows up it may make a white wimple for my daughter's head, on the day of thy wedding."

"It will be easy for me to compass this, although thou mayest think that it will not be easy."

"Though thou get this, there is yet that which thou wilt not get. Honey that is nine times sweeter than the honey of the virgin swarm, without scum and bees, do I require to make bragget for the feast."

"It will be easy for me to compass this, although thou mayest think that it will not be easy."

"The vessel of Llwyr the son of Llwyryon, which is of the utmost value. There is no other vessel in the world that can hold this drink. Of his free will thou wilt not get it, and thou canst not compel him."

"It will be easy for me to compass this, although thou mayest think that it will not be easy."

"Though thou get this, there is yet that which thou wilt not get. The basket of Gwyddneu Garanhir[237a], if the whole world should come together, thrice nine men at a time, the meat that each of them desired would be found within it. I require to eat therefrom on the night that my daughter becomes thy bride. He will give it to no one of his own free will, and thou canst not compel him."

"It will be easy for me to compass this, although thou mayest think that it will not be easy."

"Though thou get this, there is yet that which thou wilt not get. The horn of Gwlgawd Gododin to serve us with liquor that night. He will not give it of his own free will, and thou wilt not be able to compel him."

"It will be easy for me to compass this, although thou mayest think that it will not be easy."

"Though thou get this, there is yet that which thou wilt not get. The harp of Teirtu[237b] to play to us that night. When a man desires that it should play, it does so of itself, and when he desires that it should cease, it ceases. And this he will not give of his own free will, and thou wilt not be able to compel him."

"It will be easy for me to compass this, although thou mayest think that it will not be easy."

"Though thou get this, there is yet that which thou wilt not get. The cauldron of Diwrnach Wyddel, the steward of Odgar the son of Aedd, king of Ireland, to boil the meat for thy marriage feast."

"It will be easy for me to compass this, although thou mayest think that it will not be easy."

"Though thou get this, there is yet that which thou wilt not get. It is needful for me to wash my head, and shave my beard, and I require the tusk of

Yskithyrwyn Penbaedd to shave myself withal, neither shall I profit by its use if it be not plucked alive out of his head."

"It will be easy for me to compass this, although thou mayest think that it will not be easy."

"Though thou get this, there is yet that which thou wilt not get. There is no one in the world that can pluck it out of his head except Odgar the son of Aedd, king of Ireland."

"It will be easy for me to compass this."

"Though thou get this, there is yet that which thou wilt not get. I will not trust any one to keep the tusk except Gado of North Britain. Now the threescore Cantrevs of North Britain are under his sway, and of his own free will he will not come out of his kingdom, and thou wilt not be able to compel him."

"It will be easy for me to compass this, although thou mayest think that it will not be easy."

"Though thou get this, there is yet that which thou wilt not get. I must spread out my hair in order to shave it, and it will never be spread out unless I have the blood of the jet-black sorceress, the daughter of the pure white sorceress, from Pen Nant Govid, on the confines of Hell."

"It will be easy for me to compass this, although thou mayest think that it will not be easy."

"Though thou get this, there is yet that which thou wilt not get. I will not have the blood unless I have it warm, and no vessels will keep warm the liquid that is put therein except the bottles of Gwyddolwyd Gorr, which preserve the heat of the liquor that is put into them in the east, until they arrive at the west. And he will not give them of his own free will, and thou wilt not be able to compel him."

"It will be easy for me to compass this, although thou mayest think that it will not be easy."

"Though thou get this, there is yet that which thou wilt not get. Some will desire fresh milk, and it will not be possible to have fresh milk for all, unless we have the bottles of Rhinnon Rhin Barnawd, wherein no liquor ever turns sour. And he will not give them of his own free will, and thou wilt not be able to compel him."

"It will be easy for me to compass this, although thou mayest think that it will not be easy."

"Though thou get this, there is yet that which thou wilt not get. Throughout the world there is not a comb or scissors with which I can arrange my hair, on account of its rankness, except the comb and scissors that are between the two ears of Twrch Trwyth[239a], the son of Prince Tared. He will not give them of his own free will, and thou wilt not be able to compel him."

"It will be easy for me to compass this, although thou mayest think that it will not be easy."

"Though thou get this, there is yet that which thou wilt not get. It will not be possible to hunt Twrch Trwyth without Drudwyn the whelp of Greid, the son of Eri."

"It will be easy for me to compass this, although thou mayest think that it will not be easy."

"Though thou get this, there is yet that which thou wilt not get. Throughout the world there is not a leash that can hold him, except the leash of Cwrs Cant Ewin."

"It will be easy for me to compass this, although thou mayest think that it will not be easy."

"Though thou get this, there is yet that which thou wilt not get. Throughout the world there is no collar that will hold the leash except the collar of Canhastyr Canllaw."

"It will be easy for me to compass this, although thou mayest think that it will not be easy."

"Though thou get this, there is yet that which thou wilt not get. The chain of Kilydd Canhastyr to fasten the collar to the leash."

"It will be easy for me to compass this, although thou mayest think that it will not be easy."

"Though thou get this, there is yet that which thou wilt not get. Throughout the world there is not a huntsman who can hunt with this dog, except Mabon the son of Modron[240a]. He was taken from his mother when three nights old, and it is not known where he now is, nor whether he is living or dead."

"It will be easy for me to compass this, although thou mayest think that it will not be easy."

"Though thou get this, there is yet that which thou wilt not get. Gwynn Mygdwn, the horse of Gweddw, that is as swift as the wave, to carry Mabon the son of Modron to hunt the boar Trwyth. He will not give him of his own free will, and thou wilt not be able to compel him."

"It will be easy for me to compass this, although thou mayest think that it will not be easy."

"Though thou get this, there is yet that which thou wilt not get. Thou wilt not get Mabon, for it is not known where he is, unless thou find Eidoel, his kinsman in blood, the son of Aer. For it would be useless to seek for him. He is his cousin."

"It will be easy for me to compass this, although thou mayest think that it will not be easy."

"Though thou get this, there is yet that which thou wilt not get. Garselit the Gwyddelian is the chief huntsman of Ireland; the Twrch Trwyth can never be hunted without him."

"It will be easy for me to compass this, although thou mayest think that it will not be easy."

"Though thou get this, there is yet that which thou wilt not get. A leash made from the beard of Dissull Varvawc, for that is the only one that can hold those two cubs. And the leash will be of no avail unless it be plucked from his beard while he is alive, and twitched out with wooden tweezers. While he lives he will not suffer this to be done to him, and the leash will be of no use should he be dead, because it will be brittle."

"It will be easy for me to compass this, although thou mayest think that it will not be easy."

"Though thou get this, there is yet that which thou wilt not get. Throughout the world there is no huntsman that can hold those two whelps except Kynedyr Wyllt, the son of Hettwn Glafyrawc; he is nine times more wild than the wildest beast upon the mountains. Him wilt thou never get, neither wilt thou ever get my daughter."

"It will be easy for me to compass this, although thou mayest think that it will not be easy."

"Though thou get this, there is yet that which thou wilt not get. It is not possible to hunt the boar Trwyth without Gwynn the son of Nudd, whom God has placed over the brood of devils in Annwn, lest they should destroy the present race. He will never be spared thence."

"It will be easy for me to compass this, although thou mayest think that it will not be easy."

"Though thou get this, there is yet that which thou wilt not get. There is not a horse in the world that can carry Gwynn to hunt the Twrch Trwyth, except Du, the horse of Mor of Oerveddawg."

"It will be easy for me to compass this, although thou mayest think that it will not be easy."

"Though thou get this, there is yet that which thou wilt not get. Until Gilennhin the king of France shall come, the Twrch Trwyth cannot be hunted. It will be unseemly for him to leave his kingdom for thy sake, and he will never come hither."

"It will be easy for me to compass this, although thou mayest think that it will not be easy."

"Though thou get this, there is yet that which thou wilt not get. The Twrch Trwyth can never be hunted without the son of Alun Dyved; he is well skilled in letting loose the dogs."

"It will be easy for me to compass this, although thou mayest think that it will not be easy."

"Though thou get this, there is yet that which thou wilt not get. The Twrch Trwyth cannot be hunted unless thou get Aned and Aethlem. They are as swift as the gale of wind, and they were never let loose upon a beast that they did not kill him."

"It will be easy for me to compass this, although thou mayest think that it will not be easy."

"Though thou get this, there is yet that which thou wilt not get; Arthur and his companions to hunt the Twrch Trwyth. He is a mighty man, and he will not come for thee, neither wilt thou be able to compel him."

"It will be easy for me to compass this, although thou mayest think that it will not be easy."

"Though thou get this, there is yet that which thou wilt not get. The Twrch Trwyth cannot be hunted unless thou get Bwlch, and Kyfwlch [and Sefwlch], the grandsons of Cleddyf Difwlch. Their three shields are three gleaming glitterers. Their three spears are three pointed piercers. Their three swords are three griding gashers, Glas, Glessic, and Clersag. Their three dogs, Call, Cuall, and Cavall. Their three horses, Hwyrdydwg, and Drwgdydwg, and Llwyrdydwg. Their three wives, Och, and Garam, and Diaspad. Their three grandchildren, Lluched, and Vyned, and Eissiwed. Their three daughters, Drwg, and Gwaeth, and Gwaethav Oll. Their three hand-maids [Eheubryd, the daughter of Kyfwlch; Gorasgwrn, the daughter of Nerth; and Gwaedan, the daughter of Kynvelyn]. These three men shall sound the horn, and all the others shall shout, so that all will think that the sky is falling to the earth."

"It will be easy for me to compass this, although thou mayest think that it will not be easy."

"Though thou get this, there is yet that which thou wilt not get. The sword of Gwrnach the Giant; he will never be slain except therewith. Of his own free will he will not give it, either for a price or as a gift, and thou wilt never be able to compel him."

"It will be easy for me to compass this, although thou mayest think that it will not be easy."

"Though thou get this, there is yet that which thou wilt not get. Difficulties shalt thou meet with, and nights without sleep, in seeking this, and if thou obtain it not, neither shalt thou obtain my daughter."

"Horses shall I have, and chivalry; and my lord and kinsman Arthur will obtain for me all these things. And I shall gain thy daughter, and thou shalt lose thy life."

"Go forward. And thou shalt not be chargeable for food or raiment for my daughter while thou art seeking these things; and when thou hast compassed all these marvels, thou shalt have my daughter for thy wife."

All that day they journeyed until the evening, and then they beheld a vast castle, which was the largest in the world. And lo, a black man, huger than three of the men of this world, came out from the castle. And they spoke unto him, "Whence comest thou, O man?" "From the castle which you see yonder." "Whose castle is that?" asked they. "Stupid are ye truly, O men. There is no one in the world that does not know to whom this castle belongs. It is the castle of Gwrnach the Giant." "What treatment is there for guests and strangers that alight in that castle?" "Oh! Chieftain, Heaven protect thee. No guest ever returned thence alive, and no one may enter therein unless he brings with him his craft."

Then they proceeded towards the gate. Said Gwrhyr Gwalstawt Ieithoedd, "Is there a porter?" "There is. And thou, if thy tongue be not mute in thy head, wherefore dost thou call?" "Open the gate." "I will not open it." "Wherefore wilt thou not?" "The knife is in the meat, and the drink is in the horn, and there is revelry in the hall of Gwrnach the Giant, and except for a craftsman who brings his craft, the gate will not be opened to-night." "Verily, porter," then said Kai, "my craft bring I with me." "What is thy craft?" "The best burnisher of swords am I in the world." "I will go and tell this unto Gwrnach the Giant, and I will bring thee an answer."

So the porter went in, and Gwrnach said to him, "Hast thou any news from the gate?" "I have. There is a party at the door of the gate who desire to come in." "Didst thou inquire of them if they possessed any art?" "I did inquire," said he, "and one told me that he was well skilled in the burnishing of swords." "We have need of him then. For some time have I sought for some one to polish my sword, and could find no one. Let this man enter, since he brings with him his craft." The porter thereupon returned and opened the gate. And Kai went in by himself, and he saluted Gwrnach the Giant. And a chair was placed for him opposite to Gwrnach. And Gwrnach said to him, "Oh man! is it true that is reported of thee, that thou knowest how to burnish swords?" "I know full well how to do so," answered Kai. Then was the sword of Gwrnach brought to him. And Kai took a blue whetstone from under his arm, and asked him whether he would have it burnished white or blue. "Do with it as it seems good to thee, and as thou wouldest if it were thine own." Then Kai polished one half of the blade and put it in his hand. "Will this please thee?" asked he. "I would rather than all that is in my dominions that the whole of it were like unto this. It is a marvel to me that such a man as thou should be without a companion." "Oh! noble sir, I have a companion, albeit he is not skilled in this art." "Who may he be?" "Let the porter go forth, and I will tell him whereby he may know him. The head of his lance will leave its shaft, and draw blood from the wind, and will descend upon its shaft again." Then the gate was opened, and Bedwyr entered. And Kai said, "Bedwyr is very skilful, although he knows not this art."

And there was much discourse among those who were without, because that Kai and Bedwyr had gone in. And a young man who was with them, the only son of Custennin the herdsman, got in also. And he caused all his companions to keep close to him as he passed the three wards, and until he came into the midst of the castle. And his companions said unto the son of Custennin, "Thou hast done this! Thou art the best of all men." And thenceforth he was called Goreu, the son of Custennin. Then they dispersed to their lodgings, that they might slay those who lodged therein, unknown to the Giant.

The sword was now polished, and Kai gave it unto the hand of Gwrnach the

Giant, to see if he were pleased with his work. And the Giant said, "The work is good, I am content therewith." Said Kai, "It is thy scabbard that hath rusted thy sword, give it to me that I may take out the wooden sides of it and put in new ones." And he took the scabbard from him, and the sword in the other hand. And he came and stood over against the Giant, as if he would have put the sword into the scabbard; and with it he struck at the head of the Giant, and cut off his head at one blow. Then they despoiled the castle, and took from it what goods and jewels they would. And again on the same day, at the beginning of the year, they came to Arthur's Court, bearing with them the sword of Gwrnach the Giant.

Now, when they told Arthur how they had sped, Arthur said, "Which of these marvels will it be best for us to seek first?" "It will be best," said they, "to seek Mabon the son of Modron; and he will not be found unless we first find Eidoel the son of Aer, his kinsman." Then Arthur rose up, and the warriors of the Islands of Britain with him, to seek for Eidoel; and they proceeded until they came before the Castle of Glivi, where Eidoel was imprisoned. Glivi stood on the summit of his castle, and he said, "Arthur, what requirest thou of me, since nothing remains to me in this fortress, and I have neither joy nor pleasure in it; neither wheat nor oats? Seek not therefore to do me harm." Said Arthur, "Not to injure thee came I hither, but to seek for the prisoner that is with thee." "I will give thee my prisoner, though I had not thought to give him up to any one; and therewith shalt thou have my support and my aid."

His followers said unto Arthur, "Lord, go thou home, thou canst not proceed with thy host in quest of such small adventures as these." Then said Arthur, "It were well for thee, Gwrhyr Gwalstawt Ieithoedd, to go upon this quest, for thou knowest all languages, and art familiar with those of the birds and the beasts. Thou, Eidoel, oughtest likewise to go with my men in search of thy cousin. And as for you, Kai and Bedwyr, I have hope of whatever adventure ye are in quest of, that ye will achieve it. Achieve ye this adventure for me."

They went forward until they came to the Ousel of Cilgwri[246a]. And Gwrhyr adjured her for the sake of Heaven, saying, "Tell me if thou knowest aught of Mabon the son of Modron, who was taken when three nights old from between his mother and the wall." And the Ousel answered, "When I first came here, there was a smith's anvil in this place, and I was then a young bird; and from that time no work has been done upon it, save the pecking of my beak every evening, and now there is not so much as the size of a nut remaining thereof; yet the vengeance of Heaven be upon me, if during all that time I have ever heard of the man for whom you inquire. Nevertheless I will do that which is right, and that which it is fitting that I should do for an embassy from Arthur. There is a race of animals who were formed before me, and I will be your guide to them."

So they proceeded to the place where was the Stag of Redynvre. "Stag of Redynvre, behold we are come to thee, an embassy from Arthur, for we have not heard of any animal older than thou. Say, knowest thou aught of Mabon the son of Modron, who was taken from his mother when three nights old?" The Stag said, "When first I came hither, there was a plain all around me, without any trees save one oak sapling, which grew up to be an oak with an hundred branches. And that oak has since perished, so that now nothing remains of it but the withered stump; and from that day to this I have been here, yet have I never heard of the man for whom you inquire. Nevertheless, being an embassy from Arthur, I will be your guide to the place where there is an animal which was formed before I was."

So they proceeded to the place where was the Owl of Cwm Cawlwyd. "Owl of Cwm Cawlwyd, here is an embassy from Arthur; knowest thou aught of Mabon the son of Modron, who was taken after three nights from his mother?" "If I knew I would tell you. When first I came hither, the wide valley you see was a wooded glen. And a race of men came and rooted it up. And there grew there a second wood; and this wood is the third. My wings, are they not withered stumps? Yet all this time, even until to-day, I have never heard of the man for whom you inquire. Nevertheless, I will be the guide of Arthur's embassy until you come to the place where is the oldest animal in this world, and the one that has travelled most, the Eagle of Gwern Abwy."

Gwrhyr said, "Eagle of Gwern Abwy, we have come to thee an embassy from Arthur, to ask thee if thou knowest aught of Mabon the son of Modron, who was taken from his mother when he was three nights old." The Eagle said, "I have been here for a great space of time, and when I first came hither there was a rock here, from the top of which I pecked at the stars every evening; and now it is not so much as a span high. From that day to this I have been here, and I have never heard of the man for whom you inquire, except once when I went in search of food as far as Llyn Llyw. And when I came there, I struck my talons into a salmon, thinking he would serve me as food for a long time. But he drew me into the deep, and I was scarcely able to escape from him. After that I went with my whole kindred to attack him, and to try to destroy him, but he sent messengers, and made peace with me; and came and besought me to take fifty fish spears out of his back. Unless he know something of him whom you seek, I cannot tell who may. However, I will guide you to the place where he is."

So they went thither; and the Eagle said, "Salmon of Llyn Llyw, I have come to thee with an embassy from Arthur, to ask thee if thou knowest aught concerning Mabon the son of Modron, who was taken away at three nights old from his mother." "As much as I know I will tell thee. With every tide I go along the river upwards, until I come near to the walls of Gloucester, and there have I found such wrong as I never found elsewhere; and to the end that ye may give credence thereto, let one of you go thither upon each of my two shoulders." So Kai and Gwrhyr Gwalstawt Ieithoedd went upon the two shoulders of the salmon, and they proceeded until they came unto the wall of the prison, and they heard a great wailing and lamenting from the dungeon. Said Gwrhyr, "Who is it that laments in this house of stone?" "Alas, there is reason enough for whoever is here to lament. It is Mabon the son of Modron who is here imprisoned; and no imprisonment was ever so grievous as mine, neither that of Lludd Llaw Ereint [248a], nor that of Greid the son of Eri." "Hast thou hope of being released for gold or for silver, or for any gifts of wealth, or through battle and fighting?" "By fighting will whatever I may gain be obtained."

Then they went thence, and returned to Arthur, and they told him where Mabon the son of Modron was imprisoned. And Arthur summoned the warriors of the Island, and they journeyed as far as Gloucester, to the place where Mabon was in prison. Kai and Bedwyr went upon the shoulders of the fish, whilst the warriors of Arthur attacked the castle. And Kai broke through the wall into the dungeon, and brought away the prisoner upon his back, whilst the fight was going on between the warriors. And Arthur returned home, and Mabon with him at liberty.

Said Arthur, "Which of the marvels will it be best for us now to seek first?" "It will be best to seek for the two cubs of Gast Rhymhi." "Is it known," asked Arthur, "where she is?" "She is in Aber Deu Cleddyf," said one. Then Arthur went to the house of Tringad, in Aber Cleddyf, and he inquired of him whether he had heard of her there. "In what form may she be?" "She is in the form of a she-wolf," said he; "and with her there are two cubs." "She has often slain my herds, and she is there below in a cave in Aber Cleddyf."

So Arthur went in his ship Prydwen by sea, and the others went by land, to hunt her. And they surrounded her and her two cubs, and God did change them again for Arthur into their own form. And the host of Arthur dispersed themselves into parties of one and two.

On a certain day, as Gwythyr the son of Greidawl was walking over a mountain, he heard a wailing and a grievous cry. And when he heard it, he sprang forward, and went towards it. And when he came there, he drew his sword, and smote off an ant-hill close to the earth, whereby it escaped being burned in the fire. And the ants said to him, "Receive from us the blessing of Heaven, and that which no man can give we will give thee." Then they fetched the nine bushels of flax-seed which Yspaddaden Penkawr had required of Kilhwch, and they brought the full measure without lacking any, except one flax-seed, and that the lame pismire brought in before night.

As Kai and Bedwyr sat on a beacon carn on the summit of Plinlimmon, in the highest wind that ever was in the world, they looked around them, and saw a great smoke towards the south, afar off, which did not bend with the wind. Then said Kai, "By the hand of my friend, behold, yonder is the fire of a robber!" Then they hastened towards the smoke, and they came so near to it, that they could see Dillus Varvawc scorching a wild boar. "Behold, yonder is the greatest robber that ever fled from Arthur," said Bedwyr unto Kai. "Dost thou know him?" "I do know him," answered Kai, "he is Dillus Varvawc, and no leash in the world will be able to hold Drudwyn, the cub of Greid the son of Eri, save a leash made from the beard of him thou seest yonder. And even that will be useless, unless his beard be plucked alive with wooden tweezers; for if dead, it will be brittle." "What thinkest thou that we should do concerning this?" said Bedwyr. "Let us suffer him," said Kai, "to eat as much as he will of the meat, and after that he will fall asleep." And during that time they employed themselves in making the wooden tweezers. And when Kai knew certainly that he was asleep, he made a pit under his feet, the largest in the world, and he struck him a violent blow, and squeezed him into the pit. And there they twitched out his beard completely with the wooden tweezers; and after that they slew him altogether.

And from thence they both went to Gelli Wic, in Cornwall, and took the leash made of Dillus Varvawc's beard with them, and they gave it into Arthur's hand. Then Arthur composed this Englyn—

> Kai made a leash
> Of Dillus son of Eurei's beard.
> Were he alive, thy death he'd be.

And thereupon Kai was wroth, so that the warriors of the Island could scarcely make peace between Kai and Arthur. And thenceforth, neither in Arthur's troubles, nor for the slaying of his men, would Kai come forward to his aid for ever after.

Said Arthur, "Which of the marvels is it best for us now to seek?" "It is best for us to seek Drudwyn, the cub of Greid the son of Eri."

A little while before this, Creiddylad the daughter of Lludd Llaw Ereint, and Gwythyr the son of Greidawl, were betrothed. And before she had become his bride, Gwyn ap Nudd came and carried her away by force; and Gwythyr the son of Greidawl gathered his host together, and went to fight with Gwyn ap Nudd. But Gwyn overcame him, and captured Greid the son of Eri, and Glinneu the son of Taran, and Gwrgwst Ledlwm, and Dynvarth his son. And he captured Penn the son of Nethawg, and Nwython, and Kyledyr Wyllt his son. And they slew Nwython, and took out his heart, and constrained Kyledyr to eat the heart of his father. And therefrom Kyledyr became mad. When Arthur heard of this, he went to the North, and summoned Gwyn ap Nudd before him, and set free the nobles whom he had put in prison, and made peace between Gwyn ap Nudd and Gwythyr the son of Griedawl. And this was the peace that was made:—that the maiden should remain in her father's house, without advantage to either of them, and that Gwyn ap Nudd and Gwythyr the son of Greidawl should fight for her every first of May, from thenceforth until the day of doom, and that whichever of them should then be conqueror should have the maiden.

And when Arthur had thus reconciled these chieftains, he obtained Mygdwn, Gweddw's horse, and the leash of Cwrs Cant Ewin.

And after that Arthur went into Armorica, and with him Mabon the son of Mellt, and Gware Gwallt Euryn, to seek the two dogs of Glythmyr Ledewic. And when he had got them, he went to the West of Ireland, in search of Gwrgi Severi; and Odgar the son of Aedd king of Ireland went with him. And thence went Arthur into the North, and captured Kyledyr Wyllt; and he went after Yskithyrwyn Penbaedd. And Mabon the son of Mellt came with the two dogs of Glythmyr Ledewic in his hand, and Drudwyn, the cub of Greid the son of Eri. And Arthur went himself to the chase, leading his own dog Cavall. And Kaw, of North Britain, mounted Arthur's mare Llamrei[251a], and was first in the attack. Then Kaw, of North Britain, wielded a mighty axe, and absolutely daring he came valiantly up to the boar, and clave his head in twain. And Kaw took away the tusk. Now the boar was not slain by the dogs that Yspaddaden had mentioned, but by Cavall, Arthur's own dog.

And after Yskithyrwyn Penbaedd was killed, Arthur and his host departed to Gelli Wic in Cornwall. And thence he sent Menw the son of Teirgwaedd to see if the precious things were between the two ears of Twrch Trwyth, since it were useless to encounter him if they were not there. Albeit it was certain where he was, for he had laid waste the third part of Ireland. And Menw went to seek for him, and he met with him in Ireland, in Esgeir Oervel. And Menw took the form of a bird; and he descended upon the top of his lair, and strove to snatch away one of the precious things from him, but he carried away nothing but one of his bristles. And the boar rose up angrily and shook himself so that some of his venom fell upon Menw, and he was never well from that day forward.

After this Arthur sent an embassy to Odgar, the son of Aedd king of Ireland, to ask for the cauldron of Diwrnach Wyddel, his purveyor. And Odgar commanded him to give it. But Diwrnach said, "Heaven is my witness, if it would avail him anything even to look at it, he should not do so." And the embassy of Arthur returned from Ireland with this denial. And Arthur set forward with a small retinue, and entered into Prydwen, his ship, and went over to Ireland. And they proceeded into the house of Diwrnach Wyddel. And the hosts of Odgar saw their strength. When they had eaten and drunk as much as they desired, Arthur demanded to have the cauldron. And he answered, "If I would have given it to any one, I would have given it at the word of Odgar king of Ireland."

When he had given them this denial, Bedwyr arose and seized hold of the cauldron, and placed it upon the back of Hygwyd, Arthur's servant, who was brother, by the mother's side, to Arthur's servant, Cachamwri. His office was always to carry Arthur's cauldron, and to place fire under it. And Llenlleawg

Wyddel seized Caledvwlch, and brandished it. And they slew Diwrnach Wyddel and his company. Then came the Irish and fought with them. And when he had put them to flight, Arthur with his men went forward to the ship, carrying away the cauldron full of Irish money. And he disembarked at the house of Llwydden the son of Kelcoed, at Porth Kerddin[253a] in Dyved. And there is the measure of the cauldron.

Then Arthur summoned unto him all the warriors that were in the three Islands of Britain, and in the three Islands adjacent, and all that were in France and in Armorica, in Normandy and in the Summer Country[253b], and all that were chosen footmen and valiant horsemen. And with all these he went into Ireland. And in Ireland there was great fear and terror concerning him. And when Arthur had landed in the country, there came unto him the saints of Ireland and besought his protection. And he granted his protection unto them, and they gave him their blessing. Then the men of Ireland came unto Arthur, and brought him provisions. And Arthur went as far as Esgeir Oervel in Ireland, to the place where the Boar Trwyth was with his seven young pigs. And the dogs were let loose upon him from all sides. That day until evening the Irish fought with him, nevertheless he laid waste the fifth part of Ireland. And on the day following the household of Arthur fought with him, and they were worsted by him, and got no advantage. And the third day Arthur himself encountered him, and he fought with him nine nights and nine days without so much as killing even one little pig. The warriors inquired of Arthur what was the origin of that swine; and he told them that he was once a king, and that God had transformed him into a swine for his sins.

Then Arthur sent Gwrhyr Gwalstawt Ieithoedd, to endeavour to speak with him. And Gwrhyr assumed the form of a bird, and alighted upon the top of the lair, where he was with the seven young pigs. And Gwrhyr Gwalstawt Ieithoedd asked him, "By him who turned you into this form, if you can speak, let some one of you, I beseech you, come and talk with Arthur." Grugyn Gwrych Ereint made answer to him. (Now his bristles were like silver wire, and whether he went through the wood or through the plain, he was to be traced by the glittering of his bristles.) And this was the answer that Grugyn made: "By him who turned us into this form, we will not do so, and we will not speak with Arthur. That we have been transformed thus is enough for us to suffer, without your coming here to fight with us." "I will tell you. Arthur comes but to fight for the comb, and the razor, and the scissors which are between the two ears of Twrch Trwyth." Said Grugyn, "Except he first take his life, he will never have those precious things. And to-morrow morning we will rise up hence, and we will go into Arthur's country, and there will we do all the mischief that we can."

So they set forth through the sea towards Wales. And Arthur and his hosts, and his horses and his dogs, entered Prydwen, that they might encounter them without delay. Twrch Trwyth landed in Porth Cleis[254a] in Dyved, and Arthur came to Mynyw. The next day it was told to Arthur that they had gone by, and he overtook them as they were killing the cattle of Kynnwas Kwrr y Vagyl, having slain all that were at Aber Gleddyf, of man and beast, before the coming of Arthur.

Now when Arthur approached, Twrch Trwyth went on as far as Preseleu, and Arthur and his hosts followed him thither, and Arthur sent men to hunt him; Eli and Trachmyr, leading Drudwyn the whelp of Greid the son of Eri, and Gwarthegyd the son of Kaw, in another quarter, with the two dogs of Glythmyr Ledewic, and Bedwyr leading Cavall, Arthur's own dog. And all the warriors ranged themselves around the Nyver. And there came there the three sons of Cleddyf Divwlch, men who had gained much fame at the slaying of Yskithyrwyn Penbaedd; and they went on from Glyn Nyver, and came to Cwm Kerwyn.

And there Twrch Trwyth made a stand, and slew four of Arthur's champions, Gwarthegyd the son of Kaw, and Tarawc of Allt Clwyd, and Rheidwn the son of Eli Atver, and Iscovan Hael. And after he had slain these men, he made a second stand in the same place. And there he slew Gwydre the son of Arthur, and Garselit Wyddel, and Glew the son of Ysgawd, and Iscawyn the son of Panon; and there he himself was wounded.

And the next morning before it was day, some of the men came up with him. And he slew Huandaw, and Gogigwr, and Penpingon, three attendants upon Glewlwyd Gavaelvawr, so that Heaven knows he had not an attendant remaining, excepting only Llaesgevyn, a man from whom no one ever derived any good. And together with these he slew many of the men of that country, and Gwlydyn Saer, Arthur's chief Architect.

Then Arthur overtook him at Pelumyawc, and there he slew Madawc the son of Teithyon, and Gwyn the son of Tringad, the son of Neved, and Eiryawn Penllorau. Thence he went to Aberteivi, where he made another stand, and where he slew Kyflas the son of Kynan, and Gwilenhin king of France. Then he went as far as Glyn Ystu, and there the men and the dogs lost him.

Then Arthur summoned unto him Gwyn ab Nudd, and he asked him if he knew aught of Twrch Trwyth. And he said that he did not.

And all the huntsmen went to hunt the swine as far as Dyffryn Llychwr. And Grugyn Gwallt Ereint and Llwydawg Govynnyad closed with them and killed all the huntsmen, so that there escaped but one man only. And Arthur and his hosts came to the place where Grugyn and Llwydawg were. And there he let loose the whole of the dogs upon them, and with the shout and barking that was set up, Twrch Trwyth came to their assistance.

And from the time that they came across the Irish sea, Arthur had never got sight of him until then. So he set men and dogs upon him, and thereupon he started off and went to Mynydd Amanw. And there one of his young pigs was killed. Then they set upon him life for life, and Twrch Llawin was slain, and then there was slain another of the swine, Gwys was his name. After that he went on to Dyffryn Amanw, and there Banw and Bennwig were killed. Of all his pigs there went with him alive from that place none save Grugyn Gwallt Ereint and Llwydawg Govynnyad.

Thence he went on to Llwch Ewin, and Arthur overtook him there, and he made a stand. And there he slew Echel Forddwytwll, and Garwyli the son of Gwyddawg Gwyr, and many men and dogs likewise. And thence they went to Llwch Tawy. Grugyn Gwrych Ereint parted from them there, and went to Din Tywi. And thence he proceeded to Ceredigiawn, and Eli and Trachmyr with him, and a multitude likewise. Then he came to Garth Gregyn, and there Llwydawg Govynnyad fought in the midst of them, and slew Rhudvyw Rhys and many others with him. Then Llwydawg went thence to Ystrad Yw, and there the men of Armorica met him, and there he slew Hirpeissawg the king of Armorica, and Llygatrudd Emys, and Gwrbothu, Arthur's uncles, his mother's brothers, and there was he himself slain.

Twrch Trwyth went from there to between Tawy and Euyas, and Arthur summoned all Cornwall and Devon unto him, to the estuary of the Severn, and he said to the warriors of this Island, "Twrch Trwyth has slain many of my men, but, by the valour of warriors, while I live he shall not go into Cornwall. And I will not follow him any longer, but I will oppose him life to life. Do ye as ye will." And he resolved that he would send a body of knights, with the dogs of the Island, as far as Euyas, who should return thence to the Severn, and that tried warriors should traverse the Island, and force him into the Severn. And Mabon the son of Modron came up with him at the Severn, upon Gwynn Mygdwn, the horse of Gweddw, and Goreu the son of Custennin, and Menw the son of Teirgwaedd; this was betwixt Llyn Lliwan[256a] and Aber Gwy. And Arthur fell upon him together with the champions of Britain. And Osla Kyllellvawr drew near, and Manawyddan the son of Llyr, and Kacmwri the servant of Arthur, and Gwyngelli, and they seized hold of him, catching him first by his feet, and plunged him in the Severn, so that it overwhelmed him. On the one side, Mabon the son of Modron spurred his steed and snatched his razor from him, and Kyledyr Wyllt came up with him on the other side, upon another steed, in the Severn, and took from him the scissors. But before they could obtain the comb, he had regained the ground with his feet, and from the moment that he reached the shore, neither dog, nor man, nor horse could overtake him until he came to Cornwall. If they had had trouble in getting the jewels from him, much more had they in seeking to save the two men from being drowned. Kacmwri, as they drew him forth, was dragged by two millstones into the deep. And as Osla Kyllellvawr was running after the boar, his knife had dropped out of the sheath, and he had lost it, and after that, the sheath became full of water, and its weight drew him down into the deep, as they were drawing him forth.

Then Arthur and his hosts proceeded until they overtook the boar in Cornwall, and the trouble which they had met with before was mere play to what they encountered in seeking the comb. But from one difficulty to another, the comb was at length obtained. And then he was hunted from Cornwall, and driven straight forward into the deep sea. And thenceforth it was never known whither he went; and Aned and Aethlem with him. Then went Arthur to Gelli Wic, in Cornwall, to anoint himself, and to rest from his fatigues.

Said Arthur, "Is there any one of the marvels yet unobtained?" Said one of his men, "There is—the blood of the witch Orddu, the daughter of the witch Orwen, of Pen Nant Govid, on the confines of Hell." Arthur set forth towards the North, and came to the place where was the witch's cave. And Gwyn ab Nudd, and Gwythyr the son of Greidawl, counselled him to send Kacmwri, and Hygwyd his brother, to fight with the witch. And as they entered the cave, the witch seized upon them, and she caught Hygwyd by the hair of his head, and threw him on the floor beneath her. And Kacmwri caught her by the hair of her head, and dragged her to the earth from off Hygwyd, but she turned again upon them both, and drove them both out with kicks and with cuffs.

And Arthur was wroth at seeing his two attendants almost slain, and he sought to enter the cave; but Gwyn and Gwythyr said unto him, "It would not be fitting or seemly for us to see thee squabbling with a hag. Let Hiramreu and Hireidil go to the cave." So they went. But if great was the trouble of the first two that went, much greater was that of these two. And Heaven knows that not one of the four could move from the spot, until they placed them all upon Llamrei, Arthur's mare. And then Arthur rushed to the door of the cave, and at the door he struck at the witch, with Carnwennan his dagger, and clove her in twain, so that she fell in two parts. And Kaw, of North Britain, took the blood of the witch and kept it.

Then Kilhwch set forward, and Goreu the son of Custennin with him, and as many as wished ill to Yspaddaden Penkawr. And they took the marvels with them to his court. And Kaw of North Britain came and shaved his beard, skin, and flesh clean off to the very bone from ear to ear. "Art thou shaved, man?" said Kilhwch. "I am shaved," answered he. "Is thy daughter mine now?" "She is thine," said he, "but therefore needest thou not thank me, but Arthur who hath accomplished this for thee. By my free will thou shouldest never have had her, for with her I lose my life." Then Goreu the son of Custennin seized him by the hair of his head, and dragged him after him to the keep, and cut off his head and placed it on a stake on the citadel. Then they took possession of his castle, and of his treasures.

And that night Olwen became Kilhwch's bride, and she continued to be his wife as long as she lived. And the hosts of Arthur dispersed themselves, each man to his own country. And thus did Kilhwch obtain Olwen, the daughter of Yspaddaden Penkawr.

NOTES TO KILHWCH AND OLWEN

217a — KILHWCH AND OLWEN

THE curious tale of Kilhwch and Olwen appears to be purely British. The characters and events which it celebrates are altogether of native origin, nor has any parallel or counterpart been discovered in any other language.

It abounds in allusions to traditions of personages and incidents belonging to a remote period, and, though it is true that some few of these have now become obscure or unintelligible, yet many are, even to the present day, current in the principality. Of a much greater number, though all distinct recollection has ceased to exist, yet the frequent references made to them in Bardic and other remains, prove that, to our ancestors at least, they were well known; and so numerous are the instances we meet with of this class, that we may safely infer that all the allusions this Mabinogi contains were generally familiar to those for whom it was designed.

Beyond the adventures here ascribed to him, no particulars of the hero Kilhwch mab Kilydd mab Kelyddon have come down to us.

217b — ANLAWDD WLEDIG

THE name of this prince occurs in the Pedigrees as being father of Tywynwedd the mother of Tyvrydog mab Arwystli Gloff. Tyvrydog was a saint who flourished in the sixth century. (Rees's Welsh Saints, p. 276.) In the Pedigrees, Tywynwedd is mentioned as the mother of Caradawc Vreichvras, of Gwyn ab Nudd, and Gwallawc ab Lleenawg.

Eigr, the fair Ygraine of romance and mother of King Arthur, is likewise said to have been the daughter of Anlawdd, by Gwen, the daughter of Cunedda Wledig. This explains the relationship between Kilhwch and Arthur.

218a — KING DOGGED

THE name of this most unfortunate king is enrolled among the number of the Saints of Wales, and he is recorded as the founder or the church of Llauddogged in Denbighshire. King Dogged was the son of Cedig ab Ceredig[1] ab Cunedda. Wledig, and brother of Avan Buallt, a bishop, whose tomb still remains at the

---

1 From him the county of Cardigan (Ceredigion) received its name.

church of Llanavan Fawr, in Breconshire, which he founded. The date assigned to these brothers is from 500 to 542.—Rees's Welsh Saints, p. 209.

219a — OLWEN

OF Olwen, the daughter of Yspaddaden Penkawr, but little is now known beyond what is related concerning her in the present tale; but with the bards of old her beauty had passed into a proverb. Amongst those who made frequent allusion to her charms, we may instance Davydd ap Gwilym, the Petrarch of Wales; and Sion Brwynog, a poet who flourished in the sixteenth century, commences some complimentary verses addressed to a young damsel, by comparing her to

"Olwen of slender eyebrow, pure of heart."

219b — CUT THY HAIR

IN the eighth century, it was the custom of people of consideration to have their children's hair cut the first time by persons for whom they had a particular honour and esteem, who in virtue of this ceremony were reputed a sort of spiritual parents, or godfathers to them. This practice appears, however, to have been still more ancient, inasmuch as we read that Constantine sent the Pope the hair of his son Heraclius, as a token that he desired him to be his adoptive father.—See Rees's Cyclopædia.

219c — A HUNDRED KINE

IT appears that in early times cows formed the standard of currency among the Welsh; for in the laws of Howel Dda, after a certain enactment concerning the payment of fines, the following remark is added, "For with cows all payments were made formerly." And the price of a cow is stated to be forty pence.

The Liber Landavensis furnishes numerous examples of the custom of resorting to this method of valuation. Amongst others may be instanced the case of Brychan, the son of Gwyngon, who bought three uncias of land, on which three villages were situated, "for seven horses of the value of twenty-eight cows, and the whole apparel of one man of the value of fourteen cows, and a sword of the value of twelve cows, and a hawk of the value of six cows, with four dogs of the value of fourteen cows," p. 456.

This property, consisting of about 324 acres, was purchased by him to present to the Church of Llandaff, in the time of Bishop Trychan, who is supposed to have lived about the early part of the seventh century.

220a — PENGWAED IN CORNWALL

PENGWAED is the Land's End. In the Triad on the three divisions of Britain, it is named as the extreme point to the south of the island, which was distant nine hundred miles from Penrhyn Blathaon, supposed to be Caithness in North Britain.—Triad ii.

222a — SAVE ONLY MY SHIP AND MY MANTLE

ARTHUR's ship is mentioned several times in the course of the present tale. Its name was Prydwen, and under that appellation it is alluded to by Taliesin in his Preidden Annwn,[1] the Spoils of Hell. In that mystical poem, which appears to be full of allusions to traditions now no longer intelligible, various expeditions, consisting of as many warriors as would have thrice filled Prydwen, are represented as setting forth on different enterprises, from each of which only seven returned.

The ancient chroniclers speak of these treasures of Arthur's with due reverence. Sometimes, however, they bestow the name of Prydwen on his shield instead of his ship. Thus old Robert of Gloucester, in the following quaint description,

> Þe kynn, was aboue yarmed wyþ haubert noble & rўche,
> wỳþ helm of gold on ys heued, (nas nour hўm ўlўche)
> Þe fourme of a dragon þeron was ycast.
> Hys sseld, þat het Prydwen, was þanne ўhonge wast
> Aboute ys ssoldren, and þeron ўpeynt was and ўwort
> Þe ўmage of our Lady, inwan was al ys þoʒt.
> Mўd ўs suerd he was ўgurd, þat so strong was & kene,
> Calўbourne yt was ўcluped, nas nour no such ye wene.
> In ys rўʒt hond ўs lance he nom, pat ycluped was Ron,
> Long & gret & strong ynow, hym ne mўʒt atsytte non.

I. 174.

---

1 Myvyrian Archaiology, I. p. 45.

Gruffydd ab Arthur's account of King Arthur's arms agrees with this; but respecting his sword Caledvwlch, or Caleburn, he adds the information that it was formed in the Isle of Avallon.[1] It has already been detailed in a previous portion of this work, how Arthur finding himself mortally wounded at the battle of Camlan, confided his sword to one of his knights, charging him to cast it into the lake, and how when the knight proceeded to fulfil his behest, a hand and arm arose from the water, and seizing the precious weapon, brandished it three times, and disappeared with it in the lake. This circumstance must have been unknown to Richard the First, or he would hardly have sent to Tancred, King of Sicily, as a valuable present, a sword which was supposed to have been the, sword of Arthur.[2]

The Llenn, here rendered, the Mantle, but which appears to have served sometimes as a covering, and sometimes as a carpet, was celebrated as one of the thirteen precious things of the Island of Britain. Its property was to render invisible any one who was either under or upon it, while everything around was visible to him. In another Mabinogi it is said to have been called Gwenn.

223a — GREIDAWL GALLDONYD, OR GALLDOVYDD

ONE of the three architects of the island of Britain, whose privilege it was to go wheresoever they would, so that they did not go unlawfully.—Triad 32.

223b — GWYTHYR THE SON OF GREIDAWL

THIS warrior, whose grave is noticed in the Englynion Beddau, was father to one of the three wives of Arthur, who all bore the name of Gwenhwyvar.[3]

It is he that fights with Gwyn ab Nudd, for the fair Cordelia, every first of May.

223c — GWYN THE SON OF NUDD

IN Gwyn ab Nudd, we become acquainted with one of the most poetical characters of Welsh romance. He is no less a personage than the King of Faerie, a realm, the extent and importance of which is nowhere better appreciated, or held in greater reverence, than in Wales. Very numerous indeed are the subjects

---

1 Myvyrian Archaiology, II. p. 306.

2 Lord Lyttelton's History of Henry II.

3 Myvyrian Archaiology, II. p. 14.

of Gwyn ab Nudd, and very various are they in their natures. He is the sovereign of those beneficent and joyous beings, the Tylwyth Teg, or Family of Beauty (sometimes also called Bendith i Mammau, or Blessing of Mothers), who dance in the moonlight on the velvet sward, in their airy and flowing robes of blue or green, or white or scarlet, and who delight in showering benefits on the more favoured of the human race; and equally does his authority extend over the fantastic, though no less picturesque class of Elves, who in Welsh bear the name of Ellyllon, and who, on the other hand, enjoy nothing so much as to mislead and torment the inhabitants of earth. Indeed, if Davydd ap Gwylim may be believed, Gwyn ab Nudd himself is not averse to indulging in a little mischievous amusement of this kind; for one dark night the bard, having ridden into a turf bog on the mountain, calls it the "Fishpond of Gwyn ab Nudd, a palace for goblins and their tribe," to whom he evidently gives credit for having decoyed him into its mire. Perhaps he may have been tempted to exclaim like Shakespeare,

"Heavens defend me from that Welsh fairy."

According to the same testimony, the Owl was more particularly considered as the bird of Gwyn ab Nudd.

There is, in the Myvyrian Archaiology, a dialogue between Gwyn ab Nudd, and Gwyddno Garanhir,[1] in which he is represented as a victorious warrior. Gwyddno apostrophizes him thus, "Gwyn, son of Nudd, the hope of armies, legions fall before thy conquering arm, swifter than broken rushes to the ground."

In the same composition, Gwyn ab Nudd styles himself the lover of Cordelia the daughter of Ludd, or Lear, for whom his contest with Gwythyr mab Greidawl, on every first of May till the day of doom, is recorded in the text; he also mentions that Karngrwn was the name of his horse.

The Triads commemorate Gwyn ab Nudd, as one of the three distinguished astronomers of the Island of Britain, who by their knowledge of the nature and qualities of the stars, could predict whatever was wished to be known to the end of the world.[2]

A very curious legend, in which Gwynn ab Nudd bears a conspicuous part, is contained in the Life of St. Collen (Buchedd Collen), which is printed in a collection of Welsh remains, entitled the Greal.[3] This Saint was the son of Gwynawc, ab Caledawc, ab Cawrdav, ab Caradawc Vreichvras, and having

---

1 Myv. Arch. I. p. 165.

2 Myv. Arch. II. p. 71.

3 Greal, p. 337, 8vo. London, 1805.

distinguished himself greatly in foreign countries[1] by his zeal and piety, be returned to Britain and became Abbot of Glastonbury; after a time Collen desired to lead a life of greater austerity than his high office at Glastonbury permitted; so he departed thence, and went forth to preach to the people. The impiety, however, which he met with distressed him so much, that at length he withdrew to a mountain, "where he made himself a cell under the shelter of a rock, in a remote and secluded spot.

"And as he was one day in his cell, he heard two men conversing about Gwyn ab Nudd, and saying that he was king of Annwn and of the Fairies. And Collen put his head out of his cell, and said to them, 'Hold your tongues quickly, those are but Devils.'—Hold thou thy tongue,' said they, I thou shalt receive a reproof from him.' And Collen shut his cell as before.

"And, soon after, he heard a knocking at the door of his cell, and some one inquired if he were within. Then said Collen, 'I am; who is it that asks?' 'It is I, a messenger from Gwyn ab Nudd, the king of Annwn, to command thee to come and speak with him on the top of the hill at noon.'[2]

"But Collen did not go. And the next day behold the same messenger came, ordering Collen to go and speak with the king on the top of the hill at noon.

"But Collen did not go. And the third day behold the same messenger came, ordering Collen to go and speak with the king on the top of the hill at noon. 'And if thou dost not go, Collen, thou wilt be the worse for it.'

"Then Collen, being afraid, arose, and prepared some holy water, and put it in a flask at his side, and went to the top of the hill. And when he came there, he saw the fairest castle he had ever beheld, and around it the best appointed troops, and numbers of minstrels, and every kind of music of voice and string, and steeds with youths upon them the comeliest in the world, and maidens of elegant aspect, sprightly, light of foot, of graceful apparel, and in the bloom of youth; and every magnificence becoming the court of a puissant sovereign. And he beheld a courteous man on the top of the castle, who bade him enter, saying that the king was waiting for him to come to meat. And Collen went into the castle, and when he came there, the king was sitting in a golden chair. And he welcomed Collen honourably and desired him to eat, assuring him that, besides what he saw, he should have the most luxurious of every dainty and delicacy that the mind could desire, and should be supplied with every drink and liquor that

---

1 St. Collen, having rendered essential services against the Pagans in Greece, the Pope bestowed upon him, on his return into Britain, a precious relic, which was the lily that had suddenly blossomed before the glory on some one's saying, "It is no more true that the Virgin has a son, than that the withered lily in yonder vessel bears blossoms." "And that lily did St. Collen bring to this Island, and it is said that it is in Worcester to this day."

2 We are told that Gwyn ab Nudd greatly affects the tops of mountains.

his heart could wish; and that there should be in readiness for him every luxury of courtesy and service, of banquet and of honourable entertainment, of rank and of presents: and every respect and welcome due to a man of his wisdom.

"'I will not eat the leaves of the trees,' said Collen. 'Didst thou ever see men of better equipment than those in red and blue?' asked the king.

"'Their equipment is good enough,' said Collen, 'for such equipment as it is.'

"'What kind of equipment is that?' said the king.

"Then said Collen, 'The red on the one part signifies burning, and the blue on the other signifies coldness.' And with that Collen drew out his flask, and threw the holy water on their heads, whereupon they vanished from his sight, so that there was neither castle, nor troops, nor men, nor maidens, nor music, nor song, nor steeds, nor youth, nor banquet, nor the appearance of any thing whatever, but the green hillocks."

223d — EDEYRN THE SON OF NUDD

SEE 151b in notes for Geraint the Son of Erbin.

223e — GADWY THE SON OF GERAINT

GADWY MAB GERAINT was noticed for his courtesy to guests and strangers, as we learn from Triad xc.

223f — FFLEWDDUR FFLAM

A NOTICE concerning Flewddur Flam, occurs in Triad 114, where under the appellation of Fleidur Flam mab Godo he is ranked as one of the three sovereigns of Arthur's Court who preferred remaining with him as knights, although they had territories and dominion, of their own.—For this Triad, see the note on Cadyrnerth mab Porthawr Gandwy.

223g — RHUAWN PEBYR

RHUAWN or Rhuvawn Pebyr stands conspicuous amongst those who distinguished themselves in the battle of Cattraeth. Aneurin says,—

"The warriors went to Caltraeth with marshalled array and shout of war,
With powerful steeds and dark blue harness, and with shields.
The spears were mustered—the piercing lances,
The glittering breastplates, and the swords.
The chieftain would penetrate through the host
Five battalions fell before his blade.
Rhuvawn Hir—he gave gold to the altar,
And gifts and precious jewels to the minstrel."

Gododin, Myv. Arch. I. p. 6.

His name occurs again in the same poem, as having approved himself an intrepid warrior, standing firm in the hour of battle.—Myv. Arch. I. p. 12.

It is said that he fell in battle, and that it is owing to the circumstance of his body having been redeemed for its weight in gold that he became recorded as one of the three golden corpses of the Island of Britain.[1]

He is also spoken of with Rhun ab Maelgwn, and Owain ab Urien, as one of the Three blessed Kings;[2] and another Triad ranks him with the three imperious ones.[3] Other versions, however, of the same triad, read Rhun mab Einiawn, in the place of Rhuvawn Pebyr.

There is extant a poem composed by Hywel, the son of Owain Gwynedd, about 1160, and printed in the Myvyrian Archaiology, I. p. 277, which commences with these lines,—

The white wave mantled with foam, bedews the grave,
The resting place of Rhuvawn Pebyr, chief of kings."

Upwards of a century after this, we find the grave of Rhuvawn mentioned by the bard, Gwilym Ddu, in a manner that makes it evident that its locality was then well known.—Myv. Arch. I. p. 411.

223h — DALLDAV THE SON OF KIMIN COV

HE was one of the three compeers of the Court of Arthur with Trystan mab March, and Rhyhawd mab Morgant ab Adras. The name of his horse was Fferlas.—Triad 113, and Trioedd y Meirch, v.

---

1 Triad 77. In this triad, he is styled the son of Gwyddno Garanhir, and not of Dewrath (or Dorath) Wledig, as in Triad 25, and in the text.

2 Triad 25.

3 Triad xxxiv. Myv. Arch. II. p. 15.

223i — ISPERYR EWINGATH

THERE is an Esperir mentioned in the Englynion y Clyweid.

> Hast thou heard what Esperir said,
> When he discoursed with Meni Hir?—
> In adversity is the true friend known.
>
> Myv. Arch. I. p. 173.

It is uncertain whether he is identical with the Isperyr Ewingath of the Twrch Trwyth.

223j — LLOCH LLAWWYNNYAWC

LLOCH LLAWWYNNAWC is named, with several of the other warriors adjured by Kilhwch, in the curious dialogue between Arthur, and Kai, and Glewlwyd, of which mention has been made.

223k — AUNWAS ADEINIAWC

THE preceding note applies as well to Aunwas as to Lloch Llawwynnawc.

It is doubtful whether he may be considered as the Aedenawc of the Triads, celebrated with his brothers, Gruduei, and Henbrien, as the three brave ones of the Island of Britain, who returned from battle on their biers. The parents of these three brothers were Gleissiar Gogled and Haernwed Vradawc.—Triad xxxiii. Myv. Arch. II. p. 15.

223l — GWENNWYNWYN THE SON OF NAW

HE has been already noticed with Geraint ab Erbin, and March ab Meirchion, ai one of the three who had the command of the fleets of the Island of Britain. Each of them had six score vessels with Six score men in each.

223m — ECHEL VORDDWYTTWLL

HIS son Goronwy has already been cited as one of the Sovereigns who preferred residing at Arthur's Court, to remaining in their own dominions.

223n — DADWEIR DALLPENN

A VERY curious story concerning the sow of Dadweir (or, as he is there called, Dallweir) Dallpenn, is contained in the Triads. It is there related that Coll ab Collfrewi was one of the three powerful swineherds of the Island of Britain, and that he kept the swine of Dallweir Dallben, in the valley of Dallwyr in Cornwall. And one of these swine, named Henwen, was with young, and it was prophesied that this circumstance would bring evil to the Island of Britain. So Arthur assembled his host and sought to destroy the swine; but she went burrowing along till she came to Penhyn Austin, where she plunged into the sea, and she landed again at Aberdarogi, in Gwent Iscoed. And all the way she went Coll ab Collfrewi held by her bristles, both by sea and by land, and at Maes Gwenith (Wheatfield) in Gwent, she left three grains of wheat and three bees, since which time the best wheat and the best honey have been in Gwent. And thence she went into Dyved, and there, at Llonnio Llonnwen, she left a grain of barley and a little pig; and Dyved has produced the best pigs and barley from that time to this. And from Dyved she went into Arvon, and she left a grain of rye at Lleyn in Arvon, and thenceforth the best rye has been found at Lleyn, and at Eivionydd. And by the side of Rhiwgyverthwch, she left a wolf cub and a young eaglet, and the wolf was given to Brynach Wyddel, of Dinas Affaraon, and the eagle to Benwaedd, the lord of Arllechwedd, and there was much talk concerning the wolf of Brynach, and the eagle of Benwaedd. And when she came to Maen Du in Arvon she left there a kitten, and Coll ab Collfrew, took it, and threw it into the Menai. But the sons of Palug in Mona (Anglesey), reared this kitten, to their cost; for it became the Palug Cat, which, we are told, was one of the three plagues of the Isle of Mona which were reared therein, the second being Daronwy, and the third, Edwin king of England.

These particulars are collected from the three series of Triads, printed in the Myvyrian Archaiology. The version given in the second series is the fullest of them.—Triad lvi.

This story is supposed to have a figurative meaning, and, under the appellation of Henwen, the sow of Dallweir Dallpen, to allude to some vessel that brought to this island various sorts of grain and animals not previously known here. Indeed, there is another triad, which attributes to Coll ab Collfrewi the introduction of wheat and barley into Britain, where only oats and rye were cultivated before his time.—Triad 56.

Coll ab Collfrewi, the keeper of this marvellous sow, was one of the chief enchanters of this island, and his magical arts were taught him by Rhuddlwm Gawr. It has already been suggested as probable that it is to him that Chaucer refers in his House of Fame, under the title of Coll Tragetour, or Coll the Juggler.

223o — MENW THE SON OF TEIRGWAEDD

THE part assigned to Menw ab Teirgwaedd in the present tale, is in precise accordance with the character in which he appears in the Triads, and other legendary remains of the Welsh. He is there commemorated as one of the three men of Phantasy and Illusion in the Island of Britain, and it is said that be taught his enchantments to Uthyr Pendragon, the father of King Arthur.

In the Abergavenny Prize Essay,[1] on the Genuineness of the Coelbren y Beirdd, or Bardic Alphabet, by Mr. Taliesin Williams (Ab Iolo), there is a curious allegorical tale, which connects Menw with the discovery of that alphabet. The substance of the tale is as follows.—Einigan Gawr saw three rays of light, on which were inscribed all knowledge and science. And he took three rods of mountain ash, and inscribed all the sciences upon them, as it should seem in imitation of the three rays of light. And those who saw them, deified the rods, which so grieved Einigan, that he broke the rods and died. And after the space of a year and a day, Menw ab Teirgwaedd saw three rods growing out of the mouth of Einigan, and upon them was every kind of knowledge and science written. Then Menw took the three rods, and learned all the sciences, and taught them all, except the name of God, which has originated the Bardic secret, and blessed is he who possesses it. It may be remarked that the Bardic symbol is formed of three radiating lines / | \ which, it is said, are intended to represent the three diverging rays of light, which Einigan Gawr saw descending towards the earth; and it is somewhat curious that these three lines contain all the elements of the Bardic alphabet, as there is not a single letter in it that is not formed from them. No less singular is it, that this alphabet, which is alleged to have been only used upon wood (perhaps also implied by the three rods), is so constructed as altogether to avoid horizontal or circular lines, which could not be cut on wooden rods without splintering or running, on account of the grain of the wood.

For the proofs of the genuineness of this alphabet the reader is referred to the Essay itself.

223p — DRUDWAS THE SON OF TRYFFIN

CONCERNING Drudwas mab Tryffin, a curious tradition is presented in an interesting letter from the celebrated antiquary, Robert Vaughan, to Mr. Meredydd Lloyd, dated July 24th, 1655. It is printed in the Cambrian Register (III. p. 311). In the following extract we have that portion of it which relates to Drudwas.

"The story (or rather fable) of *Adar Llwch guin*, I have, but cannot finde it. The

---

1 Published at Llandovery 1840.

birds were two griffins, which were *Drudwas ab Tryffin's* birds, whoe had taught them to seise upon the first man that should enter into a certain fielde, and to kill him. It chanced, that having appointed a day to meete with King Arthur to fight a duell in the same fielde, he himselfe protracting the tyme of his coming soe long that he thought surely Arthur had come there long before, came first to the place, whereupon the birds presently fell upon him, and killed him; and they perceiving that he, whom they had killed was theire master, much lamented his death with fearfull screechings and mournfull cryings a long tyme; in memory whereof there is a lesson to be played upon the *crowde*, the which I have often heard played, which was made then, called *Caniad Adar llwchgwin*; and, to confirm this history in some parte, there's a British epigram extant, which I cannot remember, but, if you have the story and it, I pray you send it me."

According to the Triads, Drudwas mab Tryffin was one of the three Golden-tongued Knights, whom no one could refuse whatsoever they might ask; Gwalchmai, and Eliwlod ab Madawc ab Uthur were the other two.—Triad 115.

224a — CAERDATHAL

CAERDATHAL, which the Mabinogion assign as a residence to Math ab Mathonwy, is in Caernarvonshire, and crowns the summit of all eminence near Llanrwst. It is peculiar for having large stones set upright to guard its entrance.

The name of this place occurs in Cynddelw Brydydd Mawr's Elegy on the death of his patron Owain Gwynedd, circa 1160. The passage in the Myvyrian Archaiology, I. p. 206, is imperfect, but the Cambro-Briton, II. p. 3, gives it in the following manner:—

> "Around the region of Caer Dathal
> Lay those whom the vultures had mangled,
> Reddening the hill and the headland and the dale."

224b — KAW

CONSIDERABLE variations exist in the different catalogues which axe extant of the numerous sons of Kaw. In that, however, given by Jones, in his Welsh Bards, II. p. 22, the names exactly correspond with those in the text. Some of these personages are enumerated amongst the Saints of Wales, but of the individual history of the greater number little is known. Some account has already been given of one of the most eminent of them, Gildas mab Kaw, p. 1913. Huail, another of the brothers, obtained a less honourable notoriety for his vices which eventually cost him his life. Jones details the circumstances of his ignominious death, from the authority of Edward Llwyd, who derived them from a Welsh MS. in the handwriting of John Jones, of Gelli Lyfdy, dated June the 27th, 1611.

From this account, it appears that Huail was imprudent enough to court a lady of whom Arthur was enamoured. The monarch's suspicions being aroused, and his jealousy excited, he armed himself secretly, and determined to observe the movements of his rival. Having watched him going to the lady's house, some angry words passed between them, and they fought. After a sharp combat, Huail got the better of Arthur, and wounded him severely in the thigh, whereupon the contest ceased, and reconciliation was made upon condition that Huail, under the penalty of losing his head, should never reproach Arthur with the advantage he had obtained over him. Arthur retired to his palace, which was then at Caerwys, in Flintshire, to be cured of his wound. He recovered, but it caused him to limp a little ever after.

A short time after his recovery, Arthur fell in love with a lady at Rhuthyn, in Denbighshire, and, in order the more frequently to enjoy the pleasure of her society, he disguised himself in female attire. One day he was dancing with this lady, and her companions, when Huail happened to see him. He recognized him on account of his lameness, and said, "This dancing might do very well, but for the thigh." It chanced that Arthur overheard his remark; he withdrew from the dance, and summoning Huail before him, upbraided him angrily for the breach of his promise and oath, and commanded him to be beheaded upon a stone, which lay in the street of the town, and which, from this event, acquired the appellation of Maen Huail.[1] This stone is still to be seen in the town of Rhuthyn.

In the Triads, Huail the son of Kaw of North Britain, Lord of Cwm Cawlwyd, is represented as one of the three Diademed Chiefs of Battle (Triad 69) and the Englynion y Clyweid appropriate a stanza to one of his Sayings—

> Hast thou, heard what was Sung by Huail
> The son of Kaw, whose saying was just?
> Often will a curse fall from the bosom."—
>
> Myv. Arch. I. p. 173.

224c — TALIESIN, THE CHIEF OF THE BARDS

THE history of Taliesin, which is exceedingly wild and interesting, forms the subject of a separate Mabinogi, and as such will be given in its proper place.

---

1 Welsh Bards, II. p. 22.

224d — MANAWYDDAN THE SON OF LLYR

THIS chieftain, who figures in the Triads, will be alluded to hereafter in the notes to one of the Mabinogion more particularly relating to him.

224e — GERAINT THE SON, OF ERBIN

OF this chieftain a full account has been given in the notes to the Mabinogi bearing his name.—It may be added that a saying of his is preserved in the Englynion y Clyweid: it is as follows:—

"Hast thou heard what Geraint sang,
The son of Erbin just and Skilful?
Short-lived is the hater of the saints."—

Myv. Arch. 1. p 172.

Geraint's own designation of "the friend of the saints" (Câr i Saint) appears to be alluded to in this Englyn.—See Llyw. Hên's Elegies.

224f — DYVEL THE SON OF ERBIN

THE death of Dyvel mab Erbin is mentioned in the dialogue between Myrddin Wyllt and Taliesin, where the former says:—

"Through and through with rush and bound they came,
Yonder and still beyond, were Bran and Melgan seen approaching,
And by them, at the battle's close,
Dyvel ab Erbin and his hosts were slain."—

Myv. Arch. I. p. 48.

His grave was in the plains of Gwesledin.—*Ib.* I. p. 80.

224g — LLAWNRODDED VARVAWC

IN days when, as we have already seen, the value of articles, even of luxury and ornament, was estimated by the number of cows they were worth, we cannot be surprised that the herdsmen were sometimes men of rank and distinction, and considered worthy to occupy a place in the Triads. Accordingly we find that the subject of the present note figured in those curious records, as one of the three Tribe Herdsmen of the Island of Britain. He tended the kine of Nudd Hael, the son of Senyllt, in whose herd were twenty-one thousand milch cows. The other two herdsmen (and they had each a like number of cows under their care) were Bennren, who kept the herd of Caradawc the son of Brân and big tribe, in Gorwenydd in Glamorganshire; and Gwdion the son of Don, the celebrated enchanter, who kept the herd of the tribe of Gwynedd, above the Conwy.—Triad 85.

His own cow went by the name of Cornillo, and was one of the three chief cows of the Island.—Trioedd y Meirch, xi.

Of the no less remarkable personages, who tended the swine of the Island of Britain, an account has already been given.

Llawnrodded's knife was one of the thirteen precious things possessing marvellous properties. It would serve four-and-twenty men at once with meat.

224h — MORVRAN THE SON OF TEGID

THIS circumstance of the three warriors escaping from the battle of Camlan is related in the Triads, in words very nearly corresponding With those in the text. The two accounts differ only as regards the name of the third man, whom the Triad-, instead of Kynwyl Sant, represent to have been Glewlwyd Gavaelvawr, to whom, as King Arthur's Porter, we have already been introduced.—Triad 83.

From the Hanes Taliesin, we learn that Morvran was the son of Tegid Voel and Ceridwen.

225a — LLENLLEAWG WYDDEL

THIS name occurs in the Englynion y Clyweid.—

Hast thou heard what Llenlleawg Gwyddel sang,
The noble chief wearing the golden torques?
The grave is better than a life of want."—

Myv. Arch. I. p. 174.

225b — DYVYNWAL MOEL

DYVYNWAL MOELMUD, King of Britain, and the first lawgiver whom the nation boasts, is supposed to have lived about 400 years before the Christian era. There are four Triads relating to him, in all of which he is represented as a great benefactor to his people.[1] In one of these he is styled one of the three National Pillars of the Island: in another, one of the three Primary Inventors: and in a third, one of the beneficent Sovereigns of the Cymry, because he had first reduced to a system, and improved, and extended their laws, institutions, customs, and privileges, "so that right and justice might be obtained by every one in Britain, under the protection of God and His peace, and under the protection of the country, and the nation." Again we find him designated as one of three chief System-formers of Royalty, by reason of the excellency of his mode of government.

Howel Dda, the Welsh Legislator, in compiling his celebrated Welsh Code, in the tenth century, made great use of the laws of Dyvynwal Moelmud, some of the Triads and institutes ascribed to whom are to be found in the third volume of the Myvyrian Archaiology, and are very curious and interesting remains.

225c — GWYSTYL THE SON OF RHUN THE SON OF NWYTHON

RHUN the father of Gwystyl, was one of the chieftains mentioned by Gruffydd ab Arthur,[2] as being present at King Arthur's Coronation, at Caerlleon upon Usk.—Both he and Nwython are named in Taliesin's poem addressed to Gwallawg.[3]

225d — DREM THE SON OF DREMIDYD

IN addition to the notice already given, of this fantastic personage, who was so sharp-sighted, that he could descry a mote in the sunbeam in the four corners of the world, we may remark that in the Englynion y Clyweid, he is represented to have pronounced the very sensible opinion recorded in the following lines:—

"Hast thou heard what Dremhidydd sang,
An ancient watchman on the castle walls!
A refusal is better than a promise unperformed."—

Myv. Arch. I. p. 174.

---

1 Triads, 4, 57, 59, 36.

2 Myv. Arch. II. p. 321.

3 Myv. Arch. I. p. 58.

225e — GELLI WIC

OF Gelli Wic (or, as it is generally written, Gelliwig), in Cornwall, frequent mention is made in the Triads, where it is named as one of the three national thrones of the Island of Britain,[1] and one of King Arthur's chief seats of empire, in which he was used to celebrate the high festivals of Christmas, Easter, and Whitsuntide. At the time of Arthur's sovereignty, when he was Supreme Ruler (Penrhaith as it is called in Welsh), Bedwin was the chief Bishop, and Caradawc Vreichvras was the chief Elder, of Gelliwig. It was one of the three Archbishoprics of Britain.[2] When Medrawd, Arthur's wicked nephew, usurped the government of the island during his uncle's absence, he went to Gelliwig, and dragged Gwenhwyvar from her throne with contumely, and left neither meat nor drink in the court, "not even so much as would feed a fly," but consumed and wasted all.[3] The fatal battle of Camlan was fought to avenge this insult.

The site of Gelliwig is now a matter of some doubt. Hals places it at Callington (Kellington or Killiwick), as we learn from the following extract from his MS. quoted by Polwhele:—

"I take this to be the same place mentioned by the Welsh poets or bards, and called by them Kellywick, and Kinge Arthur's palace or court, viz., his court-leet or baylywick. Such in his time vndoubtedly it was, as Duke of Cornwall or Kinge of Britaine; for this manor of land with its appurtenances was, by act of Parliament, given to Edward the Black Prince as parcell of the lands of the ancient kinges or earles of Cornwall, then translated into a dutchy or dukedom."[4]

It may be taken as some confirmation of this opinion with regard to the locality of Gelliwig, that there is a place in the vicinity of Callington still bearing the appellation of Arthur's Hall. It is on a rocky tor in the parish of North-hill, which is in the same hundred as Callington, and within a short distance of it. Norden gives the following description of the spot:—"It is a square Plott, about 60 foote long and about 3.5 foote broade situate in a playne Mountayne, wrowghte some 3 foote in the grounds and by reason of the depression of the place there standeth a otarige or poole of water, the place (being) sett round about with flat stones." Near to the Hall are many rocky basins, called by the common people Arthur's Troughs, and in which, according to tradition, that monarch used to feed his dogs; for (says Gilbert, from whom this account is

---

1 The other two cities which ranked with Gelliwig, were Caerlleon upon Usk, and Penrhyn Rhionydd, in the North.

2 Triads 62, 64, 111.

3 Triad 52.

4 Powhele's Hist. of Cornwall, 4to. II. p. 50.

taken) it is "the custom in Cornwall to ascribe everything that is great and whose use is unknown to that immortal hero."[1]

225f — PEN BLATHAON IN NORTH BRITAIN

PEN or Penrhyn Blathaon (supposed to be Caithness in Scotland) has already been noticed as the extreme point from Penwaeth or Pengwaed, in Cornwall, from which it was distant nine hundred miles.[2] The distance between these two places was determined by the British Legislator, Dyvynwal Moelmud. In the Welsh Laws is given the following passage, relating to the admeasurement of the island made by him:—

"Before the Saxons seized the crown of London and the sceptre, Dyvynwal Moelmud was King of this Island; and he was the Earl of Cornwall, by the daughter of the King of Lloegr. And after the male line of inheritance became extinct, he came into the possession of the kingdom, by the distaff (that is by the female line), as being the grandson of the King. Now he was a man of great wisdom, and he first made laws for this Island, and those laws continued to the time of Rowel Dda, the son of Cadell. And afterwards Rowel Dda made new laws, and changed some of the laws of Dyvynwal. But Howel did not alter the measurements of the lands of this Island, but left them as Dyvynwal framed them; for he was an excellent measurer. He measured this Island from the Promontory of Blathaon, in North Britain, to the Promontory of Pengwaed, in Cornwall, which is nine hundred miles, and that is the length of the Island, and from Crugyll, in Anglesey, to Sorram (Shoreham) on the shore of the sea of Udd (the Channel), that is the breadth of the island. And the reason of his measuring it was to know the number of miles in his journeys.

"And this measurement Dyvynwal made by a grain of barley. Three lengths of a barley corn in an inch, three inches in a handbreadth, three handbreadths in a foot, three feet in a step, three steps in a jump, three jumps in a land, which is in later Welsh a ridge, and a thousand lands or ridges make a mile, and this measure is used here till now."

226a — THE THREE ISLANDS ADJACENT

ORKNEY, the Isle of Wight, and the Isle of Man, are the three primary islands lying adjacent to Britain, according to the authority of the Triads, which proceed to mention, that subsequently Anglesey was separated from the main land, and

---

1 C. S. Gilbert's Historical Survey of Cornwall, I. p. 170.

2 Triad ii.

became an island, and that in like manner the Island of Orkney was divided, and became a multitude of islands, and that other parts of Wales and Scotland became islands likewise.—Triad 67.

This coincides with Nennius's account of the three islands adjacent to Britain, which is given in these words:—

"Tres magnas insulas habet [Britannia], quarum, una vergit contra Armoricas, et vocatur Inisgueith; secunda sita est in umbilico maris inter Hiberniam et Brittanniam, et vocatur nomen ejus Eubonia, id est, Manau, alia sita est in extremo limits orbis Brittanniæ ultra Pictos, et vocatur Orc. Sic in proverbio, antiquo dicitar, quando de judicibus vel regibus sermo fuit, 'Judicavit Brittanniam cum tribus insulis.'"—P. 7, ed. 1838.

226b — GWYNN GODYVRON

MENTIONED in the dialogue between Arthur, Kai, and Glewlwyd.

226c — GARSELIT WYDDEL

"HAST thou heard what Garselit sang,
The Irishman whom it is safe to follow?
Sin is bad when long pursued."—

Englynion y Clyweid.[1]

226d — THE NINTH MAN THAT RALLIED THE BATTLE OF CAMLAN

THIS is very probably an allusion to the disposition made by Arthur of his forces, previous to the battle of Camlan. Geoffrey of Monmonth states that he arranged his army in nine divisions, with a commander over each, of whom Gwynnhyvar was possibly one.

227a — GWARE GWALLT EURYN

GWARE GWALLT EURYN was the son of Pwyll and Rhianon. The mysterious circumstances connected with his birth are detailed in another Mabinogi.

---

1 Myv. Arch. I. p. 174.

228a — KYNVELYN KEUDAWD PWYLL,
THE HALF MAN

THE Welsh have a fable on the subject of the Hanner Dyn or Half Man, taken to be illustrative of the force of habit. In this allegory Arthur is supposed to be met by a sprite, who appears at first in a small and indistinct form, but who on approaching nearer increases in size, and, assuming the semblance of half a man, endeavours to provoke the king to wrestle. Despising his weakness, and considering that he should gain no credit by the encounter, Arthur refuses to do so, and delays the contest, until at length the Half Man (Habit) becomes so strong that it requires his utmost efforts to overcome him.

228b — SAWYL BEN UCHEL

SAWYL BEN UCHEL is accused of being one of those whose arrogance produced anarchy in the Island of Britain; and the lawless party united with the Saxons, and themselves became Saxons at last.—Triad 74.

228c — GWRHYR GWASTAWD IETTHOEDD

IOLO GOCH'S allusion to Gwrhyr's extraordinary aptitude for acquiring languages has already been noticed, in the notes to Geraint ab Erbin. The Englynion y Clyweid refer in like manner to the singular talent by which he was characterised:—

> Hast thou heard what Gwrhyr Gwalstawt sang,
> He who was perfect in all languages?
> Who practises deceit will be deceived."—

Myv. Arch. I. p. 172.

228d — BEDWINI THE BISHOP

BEDWINI was Bishop of Gelliwig in Cornwall, and as such is spoken of in the Triads,[1] and in the British Chronicles. One of his sayings is preserved in the Englynion y Clyweid:—

---

1 Triad 64.

Hast thou heard what Bedwini sung,
A gifted Bishop of exalted rank?
Consider thy word before it is given."[1]

229a — INDEG

SOME of the ladies here adjured are celebrated in the Triads, and others figure in the writings of the Romancers of the Middle Ages.

Indeg, the daughter of Garwy or Afarwy hir, of Maelienydd, was one of the three ladies best beloved by Arthur.[2] Her beauty is often the theme of the bards.

Morvudd was the daughter of Urien Rheged, the twin sister of Owain, and the beloved of Cynon the son of Clydno Eiddyn. Her mother's name was Modron, the daughter of Avallach.[3]

Creiddylad is no other than Shakespeare's Cordelia, whose father, King Lear, is, by the Welsh authorities, called indiscriminately Llyr and Lludd Law Ereint. All the old chroniclers, from the Brut to Milton, give the story of her devotion to her aged parent, but none of them seem to have been aware that she is destined to remain with him until the day of doom, whilst Gwyn ab Nudd, the King of the Fairies, and Gwythyr mab Greidiawl, fight for her every first of May; and whichever of them may be fortunate enough to be the conqueror at that time, will obtain her as his bride. She is quoted in the Englynion y Clyweid:—

Hast thou heard what Creiddylad sang,
The daughter of Lludd, the constant maiden?
Much will the faithful messenger effect."—

Myv. Arch. I. p. 174.

Essyllt Vinwen or Fyngwen, the daughter of Culvanawyd Prydain, and sister of Owain's faithless wife Penarwen, is mentioned very disparagingly in the Triads.[4] She was married to March ab Meirchion, and acquired a very undesirable celebrity for her attachment to her husband's nephew Tristan ab Tallwch, the renowned Sir Tristan of the Romancers, who bestow upon Essyllt the appellation of Yseult La Belle.

Essyllt Vingul, we may presume to be the Yseullt aux Blanche Mains of

---

1 Myv. Arch. I. p. 173.

2 Triad 110.

3 Tr. lii. liii.

4 Triad 105.

romantic fiction, whom Sir Tristan, although at the same time deeply enamoured of her fairer namesake, married out of gratitude for her having effected his cure, when wounded by a poisoned arrow.

230a — DRYCH AIL KIBDDAR

ONLY the first series of the Triads, printed in the Myvyrian Archaiology, takes notice of Drych ail Kibddar, and there be is classed among the dealers in phantasy or enchantment.—Triad xxxiii.

236a — AMAETHON THE SON OF DON

AMAETHON, the signification of whose name is "husbandman," would seem to have been a very proper person to send for to perform the office. required by Yspaddaden Penkawr. He was brother to the celebrated illusionist or enchanter, Gwydion ab Don, and he appears to have had himself some dealings with the powers of darkness; for it is fabled that he brought from Annwn (the Lower Regions), a white roebuck, and a whelp, which were the occasion of the Cad Goddeu, or Battle of the Trees. Taliesin has a long mystical poem on the subject of this battle; and some curious lines relative to it are given in the Myvyrian Archaiology.[1] These, with the prose heading that accompanies them, are as follows:—

These are the Englyns that were sung at the Câd Goddeu (the Battle of the Trees), or, as others call it, the Battle of Achren, which was on account of a white roebuck, and a whelp; and they came from Hell, and Amathaon ab Don brought them. And therefore Amathaon ab Don, and Arawn, King of Annwn (Hell), fought. And there was a man in that battle, unless his name were known he could not be overcome; and there was on the other side a woman called Achren, and unless her name were known her party could not be overcome. And Gwydion ab Don guessed the name of the man, and sang the two Englyns following:—

> 'Sure-hoofed is my steed impelled by the spur;
> The high sprigs of alder are on thy shield:
> Brân art thou called, of the glittering branches.'

---

1 Myv. Arch. I. p. 167.

And thus,

'Sure-hoofed is my steed in the day of battle
The high sprigs of alder are on thy hand:
Brân . . . . .by the branch thou bearest
Has Amathaon the good prevailed.'"

These lines have the appearance of being transcribed from a very ancient and probably mutilated manuscript. Some of the words are scarcely intelligible; but perhaps the foregoing will be found not very remote from the meaning of the original.

This battle, in the Triads, is styled one of the three frivolous battles (ofergad) of the Island of Britain, and is said to have been on account of a bitch, a hind, and a lapwing; and it is added that it cost the lives of seventy-one thousand men.—Triad 50.

The brothers, Gwydion and Amaethon, are mentioned as being efficient of counsel, in Taliesin's Elegy on Aeddon of Mon.[1]

236b — OXEN OF GWLWLYD

THESE animals, to which some fabulous story probably attached, are spoken of in the Triads, together with those required by Yspaddaden in the subsequent paragraph.—Tr. y Meirch x.

One of these is alluded to in Taliesin's mystical poem, entitled Preiddeu Annwn, the spoils of Hell.[2]

"They know not the brindled ox with the broad headband;
Seven score handbreadths are in his yoke."

236c — NYNNIAW AND PEBIAW

ON turning to the ancient records, we meet with kings bearing the names of those who were turned into oxen for their crimes.

Nynniaw was a prince of Glamorgan, and his descendants appear to have profited by the lesson which his disastrous fate afforded; for we find that Marchell, his great grand-daughter, was the mother of the celebrated and

---

1 Myv. Arch. I. p. 70.

2 Myv. Arch. I. p. 45.

canonized Brychan Brycheiniog,[1] who had himself the happiness of being father to no less than forty-eight saints, twenty-three of whom were sons, and five-and-twenty daughters.

According to the Liber Landavensis, King Pebiaw, who was the son of Erb, was equally fortunate in the character of his descendants, one of whom was Saint Dubricius himself, the particulars of whose miraculous birth are there given in the following words.

"There was a certain king of the region of Ergyng[2] (Archenfield) of the name of Pebiau, called, in the British language, Claforawg, and in Latin, Spumosus, who undertook an expedition against his enemies, and returning from thence be ordered his daughter Eurddil to wash his head." The legend then goes on to state that circumstances led him to suspect that Eurddil was pregnant, and that "the King, therefore, being angry, ordered her to be put into a sack, and cast headlong into the river, that she might suffer whatever might befall; which, however, happened contrary to what was expected, for as often as she was placed in the river, so often was she, through the guidance of God, impelled to the bank. Her father, then, being indignant because he could not drown her in the river, resolved to destroy her with fire. A funeral pile was therefore prepared, into which his daughter was thrown alive. In the following morning, the messengers who had been sent by her father to ascertain whether any of the bones of his daughter remained, found her holding her son in her lap, at a spot where a stone is placed in testimony of the wonderful nativity of the boy; and the place is called Madle,[3] because therein was born the holy man. The father, bearing this, ordered his daughter with her son to be brought to him; and when they came he embraced the infant with paternal affection, as is usual, and kissing him, from the restlessness of infancy, he touched with his hands the face and mouth of his grandfather, and that not without divine appointment; for by the contact of the hands of the infant, he was healed of the incurable disease wherewith be was afflicted, for he incessantly emitted foam from his mouth which two persons who constantly attended him could scarcely wipe off with handkerchiefs.

"Who, when he knew that he had been healed by the touch of the infant, rejoiced greatly, like one who had come to a harbour after having suffered shipwreck. And he, who at first was as a roaring lion, was now turned to a lamb, and he began to love the infant above all his sons and grandsons; and of that place, Madle (that is, *Mad*, good, *Ile*, place, and whence *Madle*, a good

---

1 Jones's Hist. of Breconshire, I. p. 42.

2 Ergyng, or Archenfield, comprehended the portion of Herefordshire, S.W. of the river Wye, of which the present Ecclesiastical Deanery of Archfield, or Irchenfield, constitutes a part.

3 "Madley is a parish in Herefordshire, on the S. of the river Wye."

place), he made him heir, and also of the whole island, which took its name from his mother Eurddil, that is, *Ynys Eurddyl*, which by others is called *Maes Mail Lecheu*."[1]

Whether these events took place before or after King Pebiaw's distressing transformation does not appear. All the further information concerning him, in the Liber Landavensis, consists of the due. recital of sundry grants of land which be made to the Church, "being penitent, with an humble heart, and mindful of his evil deeds."

Lewis, in his "History of Great Britain," printed in 1729, mentions Pebiaw as King of Erchenfield, and states that in a parish church in Herefordshire is a picture of a king, with a man on each side of him, wiping his face with napkins, "which king the country people call King Dravellor."

The insane arrogance of these wicked kings is recorded in a curious Welsh legend, a translation of which is printed by Mr. Taliesin Williams, in the notes to his poem of Colyn Dolphyn. It is as follows:—

"There were two Kings, formerly in Britain, named Nynniaw and Peibiaw. As these two ranged the fields one starlight night, 'See,' said Nynniaw, 'what a beautiful and extensive field I possess!' 'Where is it?' said Peibiaw; 'the whole Firmament,' said Nynniaw, 'far as vision can extend.' 'And do thou see,' said Peibiaw, 'what countless herds and flocks of cattle and sheep I have depasturing thy field.' 'Where are they?' said Nynniaw; 'why the whole host of stars which thou seest,' said Peibiaw, 'and each of golden effulgence, with the Moon for their shepherdess, to superintend their wanderings.' 'They shall *not* graze in MY pasture,' said Nynniaw; 'They *shall*,' said Peibiaw; 'They shall *not*,' said one: 'They *shall*.' said the other, repeatedly, in bandied contradiction, until at last it arose to wild contention between them, and from contention it came to furious war; until the armies and subjects of both were nearly annihilated in the desolation. RHITTA, the Giant, King of Wales, hearing of the carnage committed by these two maniac kings, determined on hostility against them; and, having previously consulted the laws and his people, he arose and marched against them because they had, as stated, followed the courses of depopulation and devastation, under the suggestions of phrenzy. He vanquished them, and then cut off their beards. But, when the other Sovereigns included in the twenty-eight kings of the island of Britain, heard these things, they combined all their legions to revenge the degradation committed on the two disbearded kings, and made a fierce onset on Rhitta the Giant, and his forces; and furiously bold was the engagement, But Rhitta the Giant won the day. 'This is *my* extensive field,' said he, then, and immediately disbearded the other kings. When the kings of the surrounding countries heard of the disgrace inflicted on all these disbearded kings, they armed themselves against Rhitta. the Giant and his men; and tremendous was the conflict; but Rhitta the Giant achieved a most decisive victory, and then

---

1 Liber Landavensis, p. 323, 4.

exclaimed: 'This is MY immense field!' and at once the kings were disbearded by him and his men. Then pointing to the irrational monarchs, 'These,' said he, 'are the animals that grazed *my* field, but I have driven them out: they shall no longer depasture there.' After that he took up all the beards, and made out of them a mantle for himself that extended from head to heel; and Rhitta was twice as large as any other person ever seen."

This Rhitta Gawr is none other than King Ryons of North Wales, who appears to have been almost as presumptuous as the unfortunate monarchs whom he so deservedly chastised. The Morte d'Arthur represents him as sending to demand the beard of Arthur himself, which it need hardly be added that he failed to obtain.[1]

We are told that Nynniaw and Pebiaw were the names of the horned oxen (Ychain Banawg) employed by Hu Gadarn[2] to draw the Avanc out of the Lake of Floods, so that the lake burst no more. This bursting of the lake is considered to bear reference to the universal Deluge, as it is said in the same Triad, that when that occurrence took place, the male and the female of every living thing were preserved in the ship of Nevydd Nav Neivion. It would be useless to follow all the theories which have been founded on the name of Hu Gadarn, and his connexion with that important event. For these, reference may be made to Davies's Mythology of the Druids, and Celtic Researches, Dr. Owen Pughe, in his Dictionary, and Cambrian Biography, &c. &c. Suffice it to say, that Hu Gadarn or the Mighty is looked upon as a patriarch, and that there are

---

1 "This meane wbyle came a messager from kynge Ryons of Northwalys. And kynge he was of all Ireland and of many Iles. And this was his message gretynge wel kynge Arthur in this manere wyse sayenge, that kynge Ryons had discomfyte and ouercome xi kynges, and everyche of hem did hym homage, and that was this, they gaf hym their berdys clene flayne of, as moche as ther was, wherfor the messager came for kyng Arthurs berd. For kyng Ryons had purfyled a mantel with kynges berdes, and there lacked one place of the mantel, wherfor he sent for his berd or els he wold entre in to his landes, and brenne and slee, & neuer leas tyl he haue the hede and the berd. Wel sayd Arthur thow hast said thy message, the whiche is the most vylaynous and lewdest message that euer man herde sente vnto a kynge. Also thow mayst see, my berd is ful yong yet to make a purfyl of hit. But telle thow thy kynge this, I owe hym none homage, ne none of myn elders, but or it be longe to, he shall do me hommage on bothe his kneys, or els he shall lose his hede by the feith of my body, for this is the most shamefullest message that euer I herd spoke of. I have aspyed, thy kyng met neuer yet with worshipful man, but telle hym, I wyll haue his hede withoute he doo me homage, thenne the messager departed."—Morte Arthur, I, c. xxvii.

2 Cambro-Briton, I. p. 129-11. p. 61. Cambrian Register, III. p. 165.

seven[1] Triads commemorative of the benefits which he is said to have conferred upon "the Cymry," whom he is recorded to have instructed in the useful arts of agriculture, before their arrival in Britain, and while they remained in the Summer country, which an ancient commentator has described to be that part of the East now called Constantinople. The next benefit that he conferred on the people, of whom he thus appears to have been the head, was the dividing of them into various tribes, and directing them at the same time to unity of action, for which he is represented as one of the three primary System-formers of the nation of the Cymry. In addition to this, he is further commemorated as having been the first who devised the application of song to the preservation of record and invention, and as having contributed thereby to the institution of Bardism. The occurrence, last in succession, appears to have been his arrival in the Isle of Britain, with the nation of the Cymry, whom he is stated, in two Triads, to have conducted from the Summer country already noticed, here called Deffrobani, and a colony of whom he is also said to have fixed at the same time in Armorica, on the coast of Gaul. And his landing in this country, as we find from another of these ancient documents, was not marked by any characteristics of violence; for he is described as not desirous of obtaining dominion by war and bloodshed, but by justice and peace, for which reason his followers are ranked among the three gentle tribes of the Isle of Britain.[2]

237a — THE BASKET OF GWYDDNEU GARANHIR

THIS marvellous basket is reckoned amongst the thirteen precious things of the Island of Britain. In the following catalogue of these treasures, which is copied from an old MS. in the collection of Mr. Justice Bosanquet, its properties are, however, made to differ slightly from those assigned to it by Yspaddaden:—

1. Dyrnwyn the sword of Rhydderch Hael; if any man drew it except himself, it burst into a flame from the cross to the point, and all who asked it received it; but because of this property all shunned it: and therefore was he called Rhydderch Hael.

2. The basket of Gwyddno Garanhir; if food for one man were put into it, when opened it would be found to contain food for one hundred.

3. The horn of Bran Galed; what liquor soever was desired was found therein.

4. The chariot of Morgan Mwynvawr; whoever sat in it would be immediately wheresoever he wished.

5. The halter of Clydno Eiddyn, which was in a staple below the feet of his

---

1 Triads 4, 5, 54, 56, 57, 92, 97.

2 Cambro Briton II. p. 61, where will be found a summary of the opinions concerning Hu Gadarn.

bed; and whatever horse he wished for in it, he would find it there.

6. The knife of Llawfrodded Farchawg; which would serve four-and-twenty men at meat all at once.

7. The cauldron of Tyrnog; if meat were put in it to boil for a coward it would never be boiled, but if meat were put in it for a brave man it would be boiled forthwith.

8. The whetstone of Tudwal Tudclud; if the sword of a brave man were sharpened thereon, and any one were wounded therewith, he would be sure to die, but if it were that of a coward that was sharpened on it, he would be none the worse.

9. The garment of Padarn Beisrudd; if a man of gentle birth put it on, it suited him well, but if a churl it would not fit him.

10, 11. The pan and the platter of Rhegynydd Ysgolhaig; whatever food was required was found therein.

12. The chessboard of Gwenddolen; when the men were placed upon it, they would play of themselves. The chessboard was of gold, and the men of silver.

13. The mantle of Arthur; whosoever was beneath it could see everything, while no one could see him.

This version is rather different from that given by Jones, in his Welsh Bards,[1] which omits the halter of Clydno Eiddyn, but adds the mantle of Tegau Eurvron, which would only fit such ladies as were perfectly correct in their conduct, and the ring of Luned, by which she effected the release of Owain the son of Urien, as bas already been seen in the story of the Lady of the Fountain; whoever concealed the stone of this ring became invisible.

Gwyddno Garanhir, the possessor of the basket, was the Prince of Cantref y Gwaelod, which was overflowed by the sea. This event will be detailed hereafter in the notes to another Mabinogi, where it is more particularly referred to.

237b — THE HARP OF TEIRTU

THE harp of Teirtu appears to be alluded to by Davydd ab Edmwnt, a bard who flourished about the middle of the fifteenth century. In an elegy which he composed on a celebrated harper, named Sion Eôs, or John the Nightingale (who suffered death for manslaughter, although his weight in gold was offered to redeem his life), the bard, addressing Reinallt, a once rival harper, says:—

"His companion has become silent,
The turtle-dove of the Harp of Teirtud."[2]

---

1 Jones's Welsh Bards, II. p. 47.

2 Jones's Welsh Bards, I. p. 44.

This passage has generally been considered to refer to the Triple Harp; and it is likely that Teirtu, who was probably the inventor as well as the possessor of this harp, may have derived his name or cognomen from the instrument's triple row of strings.

St. Dunstan's harp is said to have been endued with the same miraculous powers as that of Teirtu; when suspended against the walls of his cell, it was wont to pour forth the most harmonious sounds, without the intervention of any visible hand.

I have heard that a Welsh nursery tale is still current, of a harp possessing equally wonderful properties. This harp belonged to a giant; and a dwarf, named Dewryn Fychan, endeavoured to purloin it; but as he carried it off the harp, commenced playing, and aroused the giant, who immediately set off in pursuit of the offender. A similar tale exists in English.

There is a place called Castell Teirtud, mentioned in the Liber Landavensis, as being in Breconshire, in the hundred of Builth.—P. 374.

239a — TWRCH TRWYTH

IT may be a matter of controversy, which in the present imperfect state of Welsh MSS. might be difficult to determine, whether certain lines of Aneurin's Gorchan Cynvelyn (Incantation of Cynvelyn) were intended to refer to the very ancient tradition of the Twrch Trwyth.—Myv. Arch. I. p. 60.

Davies, in his "Mythology of the Druids,"[1] and Jones, in his "Relics of the Welsh Bards,"[2] appear to have no doubt upon the subject, and in that spirit quote the passage, which the learned Dr. Owen Pughe has also thus translated.[3]

"Were I to compose the strain—were I to sing—magic spell, would spring, like those produced by the circle and wand of Twrch Trwyth."

Such authority is of great weight, when we consider the mass of information possessed by Dr. O. Pughe, on matters of this kind, and his facilities for consulting the various readings of different MSS. between which important variations sometimes exist.

Davies states that he considers that a passage in a very old and curious MS. of Aneurin, now in the possession of the Rev. Thomas Price, of Crickhowel, alludes to objects represented on the ancient British coins; and when the description contained in his translation is compared with the figures referred to, it must be acknowledged that the coincidence appears very striking. The Gorchegin,

---

1 Myth. of the Druids, p. 42.

2 Jones's Welsh Bards, II. p. 13.

3 Gentleman's Magazine, Nov. 1790.

high shoots, appear on several coins, but more particularly do we remark the Trychetin Trychinffwrch, or monstrous horse cut off from the haunches; the Carn Caffan, or hoof with the capped stick; the Esgyrnvyr, short bones, of the legs separated from the body; yr vach varchogion, the diminutive riders (beads or circles on the mane and the back); the ysfach, bird's beak, instead of the horse's head: and when we add to this the Incantation of Cynvelyn, corresponding with the name of Cunobeline on the coin, we can hardly suppose that the whole is the effect of accident; if the connexion is so far established, we may perhaps be allowed to suggest that the figure of the boar on some of the coins is referred to in the words Trychdrwyt in the third line of the poem.

Some have supposed that the distorted figure of the horse is merely the result of want of skill in the artist, but it is evidently a mistake, as the other parts of the coins are finished in such a manner as totally to preclude any such idea. Even the bird's beak, and the small object which it holds, are executed with considerable attention, and no small care seems to have been taken to preserve the separation between the bones of the legs and the body of the animal. All this occurring on coins of different dies, clearly Shows an uniformity of design, and tends greatly to corroborate Davies's hypothesis.

Besides the specimens in the British Museum, there is a beautiful gold coin of this class in the possession of the Rev. John Jones (Tegid), found near Oxford, which shows the above characteristics very distinctly.

During the middle ages, the story of the Twrch Trwyth was current amongst the Welsh, and Lewis Glyn Cothi alludes to him in these words, "He would destroy the towns with wrath, wounds, and violence he would tear down all the towers like the Twrch Trwyth."[1]

We find a direct reference to the hunt of the Twrch Trwyth in the catalogue of the marvels of the Island of Britain, which in some copies is appended to the "Historia Britonum" of Nennius. The MS. from which the passage is copied into this place is preserved in the British Museum (Harleian MSS. 3859), and is pronounced by the learned editor of "Nennius" to be of the tenth century.[2]

"Est aliud mirabile in regione quæ dicitur Buelt. Est ibi cumulus lapidum, et unus lapis superpositus super congestum, cum vestigio canis in eo. Quando venatus est porcum Troynt, impressit Cabal, qui erat canis Arthuri militis, vestigium in lapide, et Arthur postea congregavit congestum lapidum sub lapide in quo erat vestigium canis sui, et vocatur Carn Cabal. Et veniunt homines et tollunt lapidem in manibus suis per spacium diei et noctis, et in crastino die invenitur super congestum suum."—P. 60.

—There is another wonder in the region called Buelt. There is a heap of stones,

---

1 See Dr. Owen Pughe's Dictionary, II. p, 206. 8vo. 1832.

2 See Mr. Stevenson's Preface to the Edition of Nennius, published by the English Historical Society. London, 1838, p. xxi.

and one stone laid on the heap having upon it the footmark of a dog. When he hunted the swine Troynt,[1] Cabal, which was a dog of the warrior Arthur, impressed the stone with the print of his foot, and Arthur afterwards collected a heap of stones beneath the stone in which was the print of his dog's foot, and it is called Carn Cabal. And people come and take away the stone in their hands for the space of a day and a night, and on the next day it is found on its heap.—

The fact of this story of the Twrch Trwyth being found in a MS. of so early a date, appeared at once so interesting and important that a facsimile of the whole passage relating to the event was taken from the venerable document, and inserted in my edition of the Mabinogion, II. 1840. But if we are surprised to find this singular hunt thus recorded, and even the name of Arthur's dog Cavall preserved in connection with it, much more may we be astonished to learn that Carn Cavall is no fabulous mound, the creation of the poet or romancer's fancy, but is actually a mountain in the district of Builth, to the south of Rhayader Gwy, and within sight of that town. Such was the interest excited in my mind by the discovery of the existence of such a remarkable piece of evidence, corroborative of the great antiquity of the traditions contained in the Mabinogi of Kilhwch, that I prevailed upon a gentleman to undertake a pilgrimage for me to the summit of Cefn Carn Cavall. The following is the account he wrote me of his expedition; whether he has succeeded in finding the stone itself, bearing the imprint of Cavall's footstep, I must leave to others to determine.

"Carn Cavall, or, as it is generally pronounced, Corn Cavall, is a lofty and rugged mountain, in the upper part of the district anciently called Buellt, now written Builth, in Breconshire. Scattered over this mountain are several carns of various dimensions, some of which are of very considerable magnitude, being at least a hundred and fifty feet in circumference. On one of these carns may still be seen a stone, so nearly corresponding with the description in Nennius, as to furnish strong presumption that it is the identical object referred to. It is near two feet in length, and not quite a foot wide, and such as a man might without any great exertion, carry away in his hands. On the one side is an oval indentation, rounded at the bottom, nearly four inches long by three wide, about two inches deep, and altogether presenting such an appearance as might, without any great strain of imagination, be thought to resemble the print of a dog's foot; on a more minute inspection it will be found that although there is towards the middle part a slight mark corresponding with the ball of the foot, yet the divisions of the toes and marks of the nails are wanting; but when we make allowance for the effect of a thousand winters in this high and stormy region, it is not too much to suppose that at one time the resemblance was still more striking.

"As the stone is a species of conglomerate, it is possible that some unimaginative geologist may persist in maintaining that this footprint is nothing more than

---

1 Another MS. has Troit, which is still nearer to the Welsh Trwyth.

the cavity, left by the removal of a rounded pebble, which was once imbedded in the stone; such all opinion scarcely requires a remark. The following sketch will give an idea of the stone."

240a — MABON THE SON OF MODRON

BOTH the Triads relating to Mabon's mysterious captivity having already been cited in this volume, it is considered unnecessary to repeat them in this place. One of them (Triad 61), places his prison among the Gwyddyl Ffichti in Alban, and represents his whole kindred as having shared it with him. In the Graves of the Warriors we find,

> The grave in the upland of Nanllau;
> His story no one knows,
> Mabon the son of Modron the sincere."—Myv. Arch. I. p. 78.

He would seem to be alluded to, as Mab a Mydron, the servant of Uthir Pendragon, in the dialogue between Arthur, Kai, and Glewlwyd, where Mabon ab Mellt is also mentioned.

246a — OUSEL OF CILGWRI

DAVYDD AP GWILYM was acquainted with the tradition of these ancient animals, as is proved by his poem entitled "Yr Oed." He has, however, altered their localities. His mistress having disappointed him in keeping an engagement, he complains that the delay was so tedious to him that he might be compared to the inhabitant of Gwernabwy; for though it was true he was no Eagle, still, having waited for three generations, he had, through long tarrying, come to resemble that venerable bird; and he adds that for love he had grown as infirm as the stag of Cilgwri, and as grey as the owl of Cwm Cawlwyd.

The Cwm Cawlwyd is probably the territory which belonged to Caw and his descendants, who are always styled Lords of Cwm Cawlywd, in North Britain. There is a place of this name in Caernarvonshire, and another in Carmarthenshire. Cilgwri is in Flintsbire.

248a — LLUDD LLAW EREINT

LLUDD LLAW EREINT, an ancient king of Britain, will be better known to the English reader by the name of King Lear, or Llyr, as it is written by the Welsh, who celebrate him under the appellation of Lludd and Llyr, indiscriminately.

251a — LLAMREI

THIS Mare of Arthur's was very celebrated. Her name implies bounding or curvetting. Taliesin speaks of her in his Cân y Meirch, as "Llamrei full of vigour."—Myv. Arch. I. p. 44.

253a — PORTH KERDDIN

THE precise position of this harbour is not easily ascertained. The proximity of places called Pen Arthyr and Trelethin (probably, Tre Lwydden ap Kelcoed), would induce a conjecture of Porthmawr, near St. David's Head, Pembrokeshire, being the site of Porth Kerddin. The words in the text, however, "And there is the measure of the cauldron," would favour the supposition of Porth Kerddin being another place in the same county, now called Pwll Crochan (the pool of the cauldron), about five miles westward from the town of Fishguard. It may not be irrelevant to remark that the whole surrounding district abounds with Druidical and other ancient remains. Not far from it is a small village alleged to have been the birthplace of the celebrated Asser Menevensis, whose name it bears; and about two miles from Tre Asser is a place where an ancient British town is said to have been founded by the hero of the present tale, and after him called Tref Kilhwch, the only remains of which are some foundations of houses occasionally met with in ploughing.

253b — THE SUMMER COUNTRY (GWLAD YR HAF)

THIS name stands translated in the text as the Summer Country, which is its literal meaning. This is the way in which it is usually rendered with reference to Triad 4, where it is said that Hu Gadarn came over with the race of the Cymry from the Gwlad yr Hâv, considered to be somewhere near Constantinople. In the present instance, however, it may have been intended to allude to Somersetshire, of which Gwlad yr Hâv is the Welsh appellation, and with which the etymology of the Havren (Severn) is probably connected.

254a — PORTH CLEIS

THIS place, at which the Twrch Trwyth landed, and commenced his devastating expedition through the Principality, is a small but well-known harbour in Pembrokeshire, at the estuary of the river Alun: Although it is only capable of affording accommodation to what are now termed small craft, it was, in times past, a much frequented port, and was the landing-place in several marauding excursions of the Gwyddyl Ffichti, one of whom, named Boia, is recorded in the Liber Landavensis as having been the source of great annoyance to St. David and St. Telliaw. The former of these saints is traditionally reputed to have been a native of Porth Cleis, and to have been baptized at a holy well in its immediate vicinity.

Mynyw, or St. David's, is the next place mentioned in the progress of the Twrch Trwyth, and we thence trace him to Aber deu Gleddyf, or Milford Haven, On leaving Aber deu Gleddyf, we find him overtaken by Arthur while destroying the herds of Kynwas Kwrr y Vagyl, and this we may conjecture to have occurred at a place still called Kynwaston or Canaston, not far from Narberth. Blaengwaith Noe ab Arthur, near Lampeter Velfrey, and Buarth Arthur, and the Cromlech of Gwal y Filast, or Bwrdd Arthur (Arthur's Table), in the parish of Llanboipy, probably mark the course of this singular hunt to the Preselly Mountains, the highest range in Pembrokeshire. At the eastern extremity of these mountains rises the river Nyver, or Nevern, on the banks of which the British warriors drew themselves up in array, and close to the highest peak of the range, named Preselly Top, is the dingle of Cwm Kerwyn, where the Twrch Trwyth is said to have committed such dreadful havoc among Arthur's champions. Within a distance of two miles, Arthur's name is again perpetuated in the rugged summit of Carn Arthur, whence the imagination may easily trace some remembrance of the Twrch Trwyth and his progeny, in the names of the opposite eminence, Moel Dyrch; and of Tre Dyrch, the adjacent farm.

Leaving the Preselly Mountains, and passing through Aberteivi or Cardigan town, the Twrch Trwyth again appears in Dyffryn Llychwr, or Loughor, on the confines of Carmarthenshire and Glamorgan. The Dyffryn Amanw of the tale is identical with the valley of the river Amman, which falls into the Llychwr some few miles from the sea. In the Mynydd Amanw we recognize the lofty heights, which form a natural boundary between the counties of Brecon and Carmarthen, called Mynydd Du, and Bannau Sîr Gaer, or the Black Mountain and Carmarthenshire Vans. On this range tradition has assigned to Arthur a resting-place of the most ample dimensions, called Gwely Arthur, or Arthur's Bed, and near to the spot where the river Amman rises is an elevated knoll, called Twyn y Moch, at the foot of which is Llwyn y Moch, both of which names may bear some allusion to the adventures detailed in the text. The same remark may be said to apply to the adjacent river Twrch, which rises on the Van, and runs into the Tawy, below Ystradgynlais. Another singular coincidence may be traced between the name of 'a brook in this neighbourhood, called Echel, and the Echel Forddwyttwl, who is recorded in the tale as having been slain at this period of the chase. On the Llangadock side of the Black Mountain we meet with fresh reminiscences of the British monarch in Pen Arthur, and Coiten Arthur. The latter is one of two large rocks in the bed of the Sawdde river, said to have been the hero's quoit, which be flung from the summit of Pen Arthur to its present position; a distance of about a mile. The rock beside the Coiten was thrown into the stream from the same eminence by a lady of those days, being a pebble in her shoe which gave her some annoyance. As there are several localities on the Tywi bearing the appellation of Dinas, it would be difficult to determine to which of them Din Tywi is intended to refer.

At Ystrad Yw, we find ourselves once more on well-known ground, and hence we may conjecture that the course of the Twrch Trwyth lay across Carn Cavall and the Brecon Mountains[1] to Abergwy, where the Wye falls into the Severn below Chepstow, and where the princely monster also dashes into the flood, to appear again but for a moment in Cornwall, before he vanishes entirely from our view.

256a — LLYN LLIWAN

WHETHER the immersion of the boar Trwyth into the Severn near Llyn Lliwan, or Llinlivan, as it is generally called, has any reference to the wonders that characterise that remarkable spot, does not appear, but it would seem reasonable to suppose that something more than a natural cause must have led to the marvellous results thus related in the tract De Mirabilibus Britanniæ, attached to some of the copies of Nennius.

"There is another wonder, which is Oper Linn Liuan,[2] the mouth of which river opens into the Severn; and when the tide flows into the Severn, the sea in the like manner flows into the mouth of the above-named river, and is received into a pool at its mouth, as into a gulf, and does not proceed higher up. And there is a beach near the river, and when the tide is in the Severn, that beach is not covered; and when the sea and the Severn recede, then the pool Liuan disgorges all that it had swallowed from the sea, and that beach is covered therewith, and it discharges and pours it out in one wave, in size like to a mountain. And if there should be the whole army of all that country there, and they should turn their faces towards the wave, it would draw the army to it by force, their clothes

---

1 The summit of which still retains the name of Cadair Arthur. There is also in Breconshire a valley bearing the name of one of the pigs; Cwm Banw.

2 Probably a corrupted form of the Welsh "Aber Llyn Llivan."

being full of moisture, and their horses would be drawn in like manner. But should the army turn their backs towards the wave, it will not injure them. And when the sea has receded, then the whole beach which the wave had covered is left bare again, and the sea retires from it.[1]

In an expedition of Arthur's to the North, the Scots fled before him, and betook themselves to the Lake Llumonyw (probably Loch Lomond), in which were sixty islands and sixty rocks, and on each an eagle's nest. Every first of May these came together, and from the sound of their voices the men of that country knew what should befall during the coming year. And sixty rivers fell into this remarkable lake, but only one river ran from the lake to the sea.

Arthur soon dislodged his opponents from their stronghold, the singular nature of which excited great surprise in the mind of Howel the son of Emyr Llydaw, who accompanied him. But when Howel expressed his wonder at it, Arthur told him that there was a still more marvellous lake not far thence, which was twenty feet long and twenty feet broad, and consequently square; and it contained four different races of fishes, and a fish was never found in a part of the lake occupied by a race to which it did not belong.[2] And he told him also that there was another lake in Wales near the Severn, which the men of that country called Llyn Llivan; and that lake, when the sea flowed, received water into it, and swallowed it as though it had been a mountain, until it overflowed its banks; and if it chanced that any stood with their faces towards the lake, and any of the spray of the water touched their clothes, it was hard for them to avoid being drawn into the lake; but if their backs were towards it, how near soever they might stand to its edge, it would have no effect upon them. Brut Gruffudd ab Arthur.—Myv. Arch. II. p. 310.

---

1 Nennius. Published by the English Historical Society. London, 1838, p. 57.

2 This appears to be the same as the marvel described in the Catalogue appended to Nennius, where it is styled Finnaun Guur Helic, and is placed in the region of Cinlipluc.

THE DREAM OF RHONABWY

MADAWC the son of Maredudd[299a] possessed Powys within its boundaries[299b], from Porfoed to Gwauan in the uplands of Arwystli. And at that time he had a brother, Iorwerth the son of Maredudd[299c], in rank not equal to himself. And Iorwerth had great sorrow and heaviness because of the honour and power that his brother enjoyed, which he shared not. And he sought his fellows and his foster-brothers, and took counsel with them what he should do in this matter. And they resolved to dispatch some of their number to go and seek a maintenance for him. Then Madawc offered him to become Master of the Household and to have horses, and arms, and honour, and to fare like as himself. But Iorwerth refused this.

And Iorwerth made an inroad into Loegria, slaying the inhabitants, and burning houses, and carrying away prisoners. And Madawc took counsel with the men of Powys, and they determined to place an hundred men in each of the three Commots of Powys to seek for him. And thus did they in the plains of Powys from Aber Ceirawc, and in Allictwn Ver, and in Rhyd Wilure[300a], on the Vyrnwy, the three best Commots of Powys. So he was none the better, he nor his household, in Powys, nor in the plains thereof. And they spread these men over the plains as far as Nillystwn Trevan.

Now one of the men who was upon this quest was called Rhonabwy. And Rhonabwy and Kynwrig Vrychgoch, a man of Mawddwy[300b], and Cadwgan Vras, a man of Moelvre in Kynlleith[300c], came together to the house of Heilyn Goch the son of Cadwgan the son of Iddon. And when they came near to the house, they saw an old hall, very black and having an upright gable, whence issued a great smoke; and on entering, they found the floor full of puddles and mounds; and it was difficult to stand thereon, so slippery was it with the mire of cattle. And where the puddles were, a man might go up to his ankles in water and dirt. And there were boughs of holly spread over the floor, whereof the cattle had browsed the sprigs. When they came to the hall of the house, they beheld cells full of dust, and very gloomy, and on one side an old hag making a fire. And whenever she felt cold, she cast a lapful of chaff upon the fire, and raised such a smoke, that it was scarcely to be borne, as it rose up the nostrils. And on the other side was a yellow calf-skin on the floor; a main privilege was it to any one who should get upon that hide.

And when they had sat down, they asked the hag where were the people of the house. And the hag spoke not, but muttered. Thereupon behold the people of the house entered; a ruddy, clownish, curly-headed man, with a burthen of faggots on his back, and a pale slender woman, also carrying a bundle under her arm. And they barely welcomed the men, and kindled a fire with the boughs. And the woman cooked something, and gave them to eat, barley bread, and cheese, and milk and water.

And there arose a storm of wind and rain, so that it was hardly possible to go forth with safety. And being weary with their journey, they laid themselves down and sought to sleep. And when they looked at the couch, it seemed to be made but of a little coarse straw full of dust and vermin, with the stems of boughs sticking up there-through, for the cattle had eaten all the straw that was placed at the head and the foot. And upon it was stretched an old russet-coloured rug, threadbare and ragged; and a coarse sheet, full of slits, was upon the rug, and an ill-stuffed pillow, and a worn-out cover upon the sheet. And after much suffering from the vermin, and from the discomfort of their couch, a heavy sleep fell on Rhonabwy's companions. But Rhonabwy, not being able either to sleep or to rest, thought he should suffer less if he went to lie upon the yellow calf-skin that was stretched out on the floor. And there he slept.

As soon as sleep had come upon his eyes, it seemed to him that he was journeying with his companions across the plain of Argyngroeg[301a], and he thought that he went towards Rhyd y Groes on the Severn. As he journeyed, he heard a mighty noise, the like whereof heard he never before; and looking behind him, he beheld a youth with yellow curling hair, and with his beard newly trimmed, mounted on a chestnut horse, whereof the legs were grey from the top of the forelegs, and from the bend of the hindlegs downwards. And the rider wore a coat of yellow satin sewn with green silk, and on his thigh was a gold-hilted sword, with a scabbard of new leather of Cordova, belted with the skin of the deer, and clasped with gold. And over this was a scarf of yellow satin wrought with green silk, the borders whereof were likewise green. And the green of the caparison of the horse, and of his rider, was as green as the leaves of the fir-tree, and the yellow was as yellow as the blossom of the broom. So fierce was the aspect of the knight, that fear seized upon them, and they began to flee. And the knight pursued them. And when the horse breathed forth, the men became distant from him, and when he drew in his breath, they were drawn near to him, even to the horse's chest. And when he had overtaken them, they besought his mercy. "You have it gladly," said he, "fear nought." "Ha, chieftain, since thou hast mercy upon me, tell me also who thou art," said Rhonabwy. "I will not conceal my lineage from thee, I am Iddawc the son of Mynyo, yet not by my name, but by my nickname am I best known." "And wilt thou tell us what thy nickname is?" "I will tell you; it is Iddawc Cordd Prydain[302a]." "Ha, chieftain," said Rhonabwy, "why art thou called thus?" "I will tell thee. I was one of the messengers between Arthur and Medrawd his nephew, at the battle of Camlan[302b]; and I was then a reckless youth, and through my desire for battle, I kindled strife between them, and stirred up wrath, when I was sent by Arthur the Emperor to reason with Medrawd, and to show him, that he was his

foster-father and his uncle, and to seek for peace, lest the sons of the Kings of
the Island of Britain, and of the nobles, should be slain. And whereas Arthur
charged me with the fairest sayings he could think of, I uttered unto Medrawd
the harshest I could devise. And therefore am I called Iddawc Cordd Prydain,
for from this did the battle of Camlan ensue. And three nights before the end
of the battle of Camlan I left them, and went to the Llech Las in North Britain
to do penance. And there I remained doing penance seven years, and after that
I gained pardon."

Then lo! they heard a mighty sound which was much louder than that which
they had heard before, and when they looked round towards the sound, they
beheld a ruddy youth, without beard or whiskers, noble of mien, and mounted on
a stately courser. And from the shoulders and the front of the knees downwards
the horse was bay. And upon the man was a dress of red satin wrought with
yellow silk, and yellow were the borders of his scarf. And such parts of his
apparel and of the trappings of his horse as were yellow, as yellow were they as
the blossom of the broom, and such as were red, were as ruddy as the ruddiest
blood in the world.

Then, behold the horseman overtook them, and he asked of Iddawc a share
of the little men that were with him. "That which is fitting for me to grant I
will grant, and thou shalt be a companion to them as I have been." And the
horseman went away. "Iddawc," inquired Rhonabwy, "who was that horseman?"
"Rhuvawn Pebyr the son of Prince Deorthach."

And they journeyed over the plain of Argyngroeg as far as the ford of Rhyd
y Groes on the Severn. And for a mile around the ford on both sides of the road,
they saw tents and encampments, and there was the clamour of a mighty host.
And they came to the edge of the ford, and there they beheld Arthur sitting on
a flat island below the ford, having Bedwini the Bishop on one side of him, and
Gwarthegyd the son of Kaw on the other. And a tall, auburn-haired youth stood
before him, with his sheathed sword in his hand, and clad in a coat and cap of
jet-black satin. And his face was white as ivory, and his eyebrows black as jet,
and such part of his wrist as could be seen between his glove and his sleeve, was
whiter than the lily, and thicker than a warrior's ankle.

Then came Iddawc and they that were with him, and stood before Arthur
and saluted him. "Heaven grant thee good," said Arthur. "And where, Iddawc,
didst thou find these little men?" "I found them, lord, up yonder on the road."
Then the Emperor smiled. "Lord," said Iddawc, "wherefore dost thou laugh?"
"Iddawc," replied Arthur, "I laugh not; but it pitieth me that men of such stature
as these should have this island in their keeping, after the men that guarded
it of yore." Then said Iddawc, "Rhonabwy, dost thou see the ring with a stone
set in it, that is upon the Emperor's hand?" "I see it," he answered. "It is one of
the properties of that stone to enable thee to remember that thou seest here to-
night, and hadst thou not seen the stone, thou wouldest never have been able to

remember aught thereof."

After this they saw a troop coming towards the ford. "Iddawc," inquired Rhonabwy, "to whom does yonder troop belong?" "They are the fellows of Rhuvawn Pebyr the son of Prince Deorthach. And these men are honourably served with mead and bragget, and are freely beloved by the daughters of the kings of the Island of Britain. And this they merit, for they were ever in the front and the rear in every peril." And he saw but one hue upon the men and the horses of this troop, for they were all as red as blood. And when one of the knights rode forth from the troop, he looked like a pillar of fire glancing athwart the sky. And this troop encamped above the ford.

Then they beheld another troop coming towards the ford, and these from their horses' chests upwards were whiter than the lily, and below blacker than jet. And they saw one of these knights go before the rest, and spur his horse into the ford in such a manner that the water dashed over Arthur and the Bishop, and those holding counsel with them, so that they were as wet as if they had been drenched in the river. And as he turned the head of his horse, the youth who stood before Arthur struck the horse over the nostrils with his sheathed sword, so that, had it been with the bare blade, it would have been a marvel if the bone had not been wounded as well as the flesh. And the knight drew his sword half out of the scabbard, and asked of him, "Wherefore didst thou strike my horse? Whether was it in insult or in counsel unto me?" "Thou dost indeed lack counsel. What madness caused thee to ride so furiously as to dash the water of the ford over Arthur, and the consecrated Bishop, and their counsellors, so that they were as wet as if they had been dragged out of the river?" "As counsel then will I take it." So he turned his horse's head round towards his army.

"Iddawc," said Rhonabwy, "who was yonder knight?" "The most eloquent and the wisest youth that is in this island; Adaon, the son of Taliesin[304a]." "Who was the man that struck his horse?" "A youth of froward nature; Elphin[304b], the son of Gwyddno."

Then spake a tall and stately man, of noble and flowing speech, saying that it was a marvel that so vast a host should be assembled in so narrow a space, and that it was a still greater marvel that those should be there at that time who had promised to be by mid-day in the battle of Badon[304c], fighting with Osla Gyllellvawr [304d]. "Whether thou mayest choose to proceed or not, I will proceed." "Thou sayest well," said Arthur, "and we will go altogether." "Iddawc," said Rhonabwy, "who was the man who spoke so marvellously unto Arthur erewhile?" "A man who may speak as boldly as he listeth, Caradawc Vreichvras[305a], the son of Llyr Marini, his chief counsellor and his cousin."

Then Iddawc took Rhonabwy behind him on his horse, and that mighty host moved forward, each troop in its order, towards Cevndigoll[305b]. And when they came to the middle of the ford of the Severn, Iddawc turned his horse's head, and Rhonabwy looked along the valley of the Severn. And he beheld two fair troops coming towards the ford. One troop there came of brilliant white, whereof every one of the men had a scarf of white satin with jet-black borders. And the knees and the tops of the shoulders of their horses were jet-black, though they were of a pure white in every other part. And their banners were pure white, with black points to them all.

"Iddawc," said Rhonabwy, "who are yonder pure white troop?" "They are the men of Norway, and March the son of Meirchion[305c] is their prince. And he is cousin unto Arthur." And further on he saw a troop, whereof each man wore garments of jet-black, with borders of pure white to every scarf; and the tops of the shoulders and the knees of their horses were pure white. And their banners were jet-black with pure white at the point of each.

"Iddawc," said Rhonabwy, "who are the jet-black troop yonder?" "They are the men of Denmark, and Edeyrn the son of Nudd is their prince."

And when they had overtaken the host, Arthur and his army of mighty ones dismounted below Caer Badou, and he perceived that he and Iddawc journeyed the same road as Arthur. And after they had dismounted he heard a great tumult and confusion amongst the host, and such as were then at the flanks turned to the centre, and such as had been in the centre moved to the flanks. And then, behold, he saw a knight coming, clad, both he and his horse, in mail, of which the rings were whiter than the whitest lily, and the rivets redder than the ruddiest blood. And he rode amongst the host.

"Iddawc," said Rhonabwy, "will yonder host flee?" "King Arthur never fled, and if this discourse of thine were heard, thou wert a lost man. But as to the knight whom thou seest yonder, it is Kai. The fairest horseman is Kai in all Arthur's Court; and the men who are at the front of the army hasten to the rear to see Kai ride, and the men who are in the centre flee to the side, from the shock of his horse. And this is the cause of the confusion of the host."

Thereupon they heard a call made for Kadwr, Earl of Cornwall[306a], and behold he arose with the sword of Arthur in his hand. And the similitude of two serpents was upon the sword in gold. And when the sword was drawn from its scabbard, it seemed as if two flames of fire burst forth from the jaws of the serpents, and then, so wonderful was the sword, that it was hard for any one to look upon it. And the host became still, and the tumult ceased, and the Earl returned to the tent.

"Iddawc," said Rhonabwy, "who is the man who bore the sword of Arthur?" "Kadwr, the Earl of Cornwall, whose duty it is to arm the King on the days of battle and warfare."

And they heard a call made for Eirynwych Amheibyn, Arthur's servant, a red, rough, ill-favoured man, having red whiskers with bristly hairs. And behold he came upon a tall red horse with the mane parted on each side, and he brought with him a large and beautiful sumpter pack. And the huge red youth dismounted before Arthur, and he drew a golden chair out of the pack, and a carpet of diapered satin. And he spread the carpet before Arthur, and there was an apple of ruddy gold at each corner thereof, and he placed the chair upon the carpet. And so large was the chair that three armed warriors might have sat therein. Gwenn was the name of the carpet, and it was one of its properties that whoever was upon it no one could see him, and he could see every one. And it would retain no colour but its own.

And Arthur sat within the carpet, and Owain the son of Urien was standing before him. "Owain," said Arthur, "wilt thou play chess?" "I will, Lord," said Owain. And the red youth brought the chess for Arthur and Owain; golden pieces and a board of silver. And they began to play.

And while they were thus, and when they were best amused with their game, behold they saw a white tent with a red canopy, and the figure of a jet-black serpent on the top of the tent, and red glaring venomous eyes in the head of the serpent, and a red flaming tongue. And there came a young page with yellow curling hair, and blue eyes, and a newly-springing beard, wearing a coat and a surcoat of yellow satin, and hose of thin greenish-yellow cloth upon his feet, and over his hose shoes of parti-coloured leather, fastened at the insteps with golden clasps. And he bore a heavy three-edged sword with a golden hilt, in a scabbard of black leather tipped with fine gold. And he came to the place where the Emperor and Owain were playing at chess.

And the youth saluted Owain. And Owain marvelled that the youth should salute him and should not have saluted the Emperor Arthur. And Arthur knew what was in Owain's thought. And he said to Owain, "Marvel not that the youth salutes thee now, for he saluted me erewhile; and it is unto thee that his errand is." Then said the youth unto Owain, "Lord, is it with thy leave that the young pages and attendants of the Emperor harass and torment and worry thy Ravens? And if it be not with thy leave, cause the Emperor to forbid them." "Lord," said Owain, "thou hearest what the youth says; if it seem good to thee, forbid them from my Ravens." "Play thy game," said he. Then the youth returned to the tent.

That game did they finish, and another they began, and when they were in the midst of the game, behold, a ruddy young man with auburn curling hair and large eyes, well-grown, and having his beard new-shorn, came forth from a bright yellow tent, upon the summit of which was the figure of a bright red lion. And he was clad in a coat of yellow satin, falling as low as the small of his leg, and embroidered with threads of red silk. And on his feet were hose of fine white buckram, and buskins of black leather were over his hose, whereon were golden clasps. And in his hand a huge, heavy, three-edged sword, with a scabbard of red deer-hide, tipped with gold. And he came to the place where Arthur and Owain were playing at chess. And he saluted him. And Owain was troubled at his salutation, but Arthur minded it no more than before. And the youth said unto Owain, "Is it not against thy will that the attendants of the Emperor harass thy Ravens, killing some and worrying others? If against thy will it be, beseech him to forbid them." "Lord," said Owain, "forbid thy men, if it seem good to thee." "Play thy game," said the Emperor. And the youth returned to the tent.

And that game was ended and another begun. And as they were beginning the first move of the game, they beheld at a small distance from them a tent speckled yellow, the largest ever seen, and the figure of an eagle of gold upon it, and a precious stone on the eagle's head. And coming out of the tent, they saw a youth with thick yellow hair upon his head, fair and comely, and a scarf of blue satin upon him, and a brooch of gold in the scarf upon his right shoulder as large as a warrior's middle finger. And upon his feet were hose of fine Totness, and shoes of parti-coloured leather, clasped with gold, and the youth was of noble bearing, fair of face, with ruddy cheeks and large hawk's eyes. In the hand of the youth was a mighty lance, speckled yellow, with a newly-sharpened head; and upon the lance a banner displayed.

Fiercely angry, and with rapid pace, came the youth to the place where Arthur was playing at chess with Owain. And they perceived that he was wroth. And thereupon he saluted Owain, and told him that his Ravens had been killed, the chief part of them, and that such of them as were not slain were so wounded and bruised that not one of them could raise its wings a single fathom above the earth. "Lord," said Owain, "forbid thy men." "Play," said he, "if it please thee." Then said Owain to the youth, "Go back, and wherever thou findest the strife at the thickest, there lift up the banner, and let come what pleases Heaven."

So the youth returned back to the place where the strife bore hardest upon the Ravens, and he lifted up the banner; and as he did so they all rose up in the air, wrathful and fierce and high of spirit, clapping their wings in the wind, and shaking off the weariness that was upon them. And recovering their energy and courage, furiously and with exultation did they, with one sweep, descend upon the heads of the men, who had erewhile caused them anger and pain and damage, and they seized some by the heads and others by the eyes, and some by the ears, and others by the arms, and carried them up into the air; and in the air there was a mighty tumult with the flapping of the wings of the triumphant Ravens, and with their croaking; and there was another mighty tumult with the groaning of the men, that were being torn and wounded, and some of whom were slain.

And Arthur and Owain marvelled at the tumult as they played at chess; and, looking, they perceived a knight upon a dun-coloured horse coming towards them. And marvellous was the hue of the dun horse. Bright red was his right shoulder, and from the top of his legs to the centre of his hoof was bright yellow. Both the knight and his horse were fully equipped with heavy foreign armour. The clothing of the horse from the front opening upwards was of bright red sendal, and from thence opening downwards was of bright yellow sendal. A large gold-hilted one-edged sword had the youth upon his thigh, in a scabbard of light blue, and tipped with Spanish laton. The belt of the sword was of dark green leather with golden slides and a clasp of ivory upon it, and a buckle of jet-black upon the clasp. A helmet of gold was on the head of the knight, set with precious stones of great virtue, and at the top of the helmet was the image of a flame-coloured leopard with two ruby-red stones in its head, so that it was astounding for a warrior, however stout his heart, to look at the face of the leopard, much more at the face of the knight. He had in his hand a blue-shafted lance, but from the haft to the point it was stained crimson-red with the blood of the Ravens and their plumage.

The knight came to the place where Arthur and Owain were seated at chess. And they perceived that he was harassed and vexed and weary as he came towards them. And the youth saluted Arthur, and told him that the Ravens of Owain were slaying his young men and attendants. And Arthur looked at Owain and said, "Forbid thy Ravens." "Lord," answered Owain, "play thy game." And they played. And the knight returned back towards the strife, and the Ravens were not forbidden any more than before.

And when they had played awhile, they heard a mighty tumult, and a wailing of men, and a croaking of Ravens, as they carried the men in their strength into the air, and, tearing them betwixt them, let them fall piecemeal to the earth. And during the tumult they saw a knight coming towards them, on a light grey horse, and the left foreleg of the horse was jet-black to the centre of his hoof. And the knight and the horse were fully accoutred with huge heavy blue armour. And a robe of honour of yellow diapered satin was upon the knight, and the borders of the robe were blue. And the housings of the horse were jet-black, with borders of bright yellow. And on the thigh of the youth was a sword, long, and three-edged, and heavy. And the scabbard was of red cut leather, and the belt of new red deer-skin, having upon it many golden slides and a buckle of the bone of the sea-horse, the tongue of which was jet-black. A golden helmet was upon the head of the knight, wherein were set sapphire-stones of great virtue. And at the top of the helmet was the figure of a flame-coloured lion, with a fiery-red tongue, issuing above a foot from his mouth, and with venomous eyes, crimson-red, in his head. And the knight came, bearing in his hand a thick ashen lance, the head whereof, which had been newly steeped in blood, was overlaid with silver[311a].

And the youth saluted the Emperor: "Lord," said he, "carest thou not for the slaying of thy pages, and thy young men, and the sons of the nobles of the Island of Britain, whereby it will be difficult to defend this island from henceforward for ever?" "Owain," said Arthur, "forbid thy Ravens[311b]." "Play this game, Lord," said Owain.

So they finished the game and began another; and as they were finishing that game, lo, they heard a great tumult and a clamour of armed men, and a croaking of Ravens, and a flapping of wings in the air, as they flung down the armour entire to the ground, and the men and the horses piecemeal. Then they saw coming a knight on a lofty-headed piebald horse. And the left shoulder of the horse was of bright red, and its right leg from the chest to the hollow of the hoof was pure white. And the knight and horse were equipped with arms of speckled yellow, variegated with Spanish laton. And there was a robe of honour upon him, and upon his horse, divided in two parts, white and black, and the borders of the robe of honour were of golden purple. And above the robe he wore a sword three-edged and bright, with a golden hilt. And the belt of the sword was of yellow goldwork, having a clasp upon it of the eyelid of a black sea-horse, and a tongue of yellow gold to the clasp. Upon the head of the knight was a bright helmet of yellow laton, with sparkling stones of crystal in it, and at the crest of the helmet was the figure of a griffin, with a stone of many virtues in its head. And he had an ashen spear in his hand, with a round shaft, coloured with azure blue. And the head of the spear was newly stained with blood, and was overlaid with fine silver.

Wrathfully came the knight to the place where Arthur was, and he told him that the Ravens had slain his household and the sons of the chief men of this island, and he besought him to cause Owain to forbid his Ravens. And Arthur besought Owain to forbid them. Then Arthur took the golden chessmen that were upon the board, and crushed them until they became as dust. Then Owain ordered Gwres the son of Rheged to lower his banner. So it was lowered, and all was peace.

Then Rhonabwy inquired of Iddawc who were the first three men that came to Owain, to tell him his Ravens were being slain. Said Iddawc, "They were men who grieved that Owain should suffer loss, his fellow-chieftains and companions, Selyv the son of Kynan Garwyn[312a] of Powys, and Gwgawn Gleddyvrudd[312b], and Gwres the son of Rheged, he who bears the banner in the day of battle and strife." "Who," said Rhonabwy, "were the last three men who came to Arthur, and told him that the Ravens were slaughtering his men?" "The best of men," said Iddawc, "and the bravest, and who would grieve exceedingly that Arthur should have damage in aught; Blathaon the son of Mawrheth, and Rhuvawn Pebyr the son of Prince Deorthach, and Hyveidd Unllenn."

And with that behold four-and-twenty knights came from Osla Gyllellvawr, to crave a truce of Arthur for a fortnight and a month. And Arthur rose and went to take counsel. And he came to where a tall, auburn, curly-headed man was a little way off, and there he assembled his counsellors. Bedwini, the Bishop, and Gwarthegyd the son of Kaw, and March the son of Meirchawn, and Caradawc Vreichvras, and Gwalchmai the son of Gwyar, and Edeyrn the son of Nudd, and Rhuvawn Pebyr the son of Prince Deorthach, and Rhiogan[312c] the son of the King of Ireland, and Gwenwynwyn the son of Nav, Howel the son of Emyr Llydaw, Gwilym the son of Rhwyf Freinc, and Daned the son of Ath, and Goreu Custennin, and Mabon the son of Modron, and Peredur Paladyr Hir, and

Hyveidd Unllenn, and Twrch the son of Perif, and Nerth the son of Kadarn, and
Gobrwy the son of Echel Vorddwyttwll, Gwair the son of Gwestyl, and Gadwy
the son of Geraint, Trystan the son of Tallwch[312e], Moryen[312f] Manawc, Granwen
the son of Llyr, and Llacheu the son of Arthur312g, and Llawvrodedd Varvawc,
and Kadwr Earl of Cornwall, Morvran the son of Tegid, and Rhyawd the son of
Morgant312h, and Dyvyr the son of Alun Dyved, Gwrhyr Gwalstawd Ieithoedd,
Adaon the son of Taliesin, Llary the son of Kasnar Wledig, and Fflewddur Fflam,
and Greidawl Galldovydd, Gilbert the son of Kadgyffro[313a], Menw the son of
Teirgwaedd, Gwrthmwl Wledig[313b], Cawrdav the son of Caradawc Vreichvras,
Gildas the son of Kaw, Kadyriaith the son of Saidi, and many of the men of
Norway and Denmark, and many of the men of Greece, and a crowd of the men
of the host came to that council.

"Iddawc," said Rhonabwy, "who was the auburn haired man to whom they
came just now?" "Rhun the son of Maelgwn Gwynedd, a man whose prerogative
it is, that he may join in counsel with all." "And wherefore did they admit
into counsel with men of such dignity as are yonder a stripling so young as
Kadyriaith the son of Saidi?" "Because there is not throughout Britain a man
better skilled in counsel than he."

Thereupon, behold, bards came and recited verses before Arthur, and
no man understood those verses but Kadyriaith only, save that they were in
Arthur's praise.

And lo, there came four-and-twenty asses with their burdens of gold and of
silver, and a tired way-worn man with each of them, bringing tribute to Arthur
from the Islands of Greece. Then Kadyriaith the son of Saidi besought that a
truce might be granted to Osla Gyllellvawr for the space of a fortnight and a
month, and that the asses and the burdens they carried might be given to the
bards, to be to them as the reward for their stay and that their verse might be
recompensed during the time of the truce. And thus it was settled.

"Rhonabwy," said Iddawc, "would it not be wrong to forbid a youth who can
give counsel so liberal as this from coming to the councils of his Lord?"

Then Kai arose, and he said, "Whosoever will follow Arthur, let him be with
him to-night in Cornwall, and whosoever will not, let him be opposed to Arthur
even during the truce." And through the greatness of the tumult that ensued,
Rhonabwy awoke. And when he awoke he was upon the yellow calf-skin, having
slept three nights and three days.

And this tale is called the Dream of Rhonabwy. And this is the reason that
no one knows the dream without a book, neither bard nor gifted seer; because of
the various colours that were upon the horses, and the many wondrous colours
of the arms and of the panoply, and of the precious scarfs, and of the virtue-
bearing stones.

NOTES TO
THE DREAM OF RHONABWY

299a — MADAWC THE SON OF MAREDUDD

MAREDUDD AP BLEDDYN, the father of Madawc, after much contest acquired possession of the sovereignty of the whole principality of Powys. He married Hunydd the daughter of Eunydd, chief of one of the fifteen tribes of North Wales, and Lord of Dyffryn Clwyd and Allington, and died in 1129; his son Madawc succeeded him in one-half of his possessions, which thence acquired the name of Powys Fadawc. Maredudd had been one of the most strenuous and successful opponents of the Normans, celebrated by the national records. It was he who checked the progress of Henry I., who, in one of his invasions of Wales, narrowly escaped being slain by a body of archers that Maredudd had dispatched to meet him; an arrow shot by one of their number actually glanced from the breast-plate of the royal invader. But the son of Maredudd was not distinguished for equal ardour in his country's cause; on the contrary, Madawc combined with Henry II. in the attacks he made upon Wales in 1158, and during that monarch's first and unsuccessful campaign, took the command of the English ships, and ravaged the shores of Anglesey. In this expedition, however, Madawc was defeated with much loss. Powell says of him, that he was "euer the king of Englands freend, and was one that feared God, and releeued the poore."

He was a prince of more than common talent, and was highly extolled by contemporary bards and historians. Amongst others, Gwalchmai composed several poems in his praise.[1]

Madawc's wonted prudence appears to have forsaken him in the decline of life. There is an anecdote relating to him which, as it exists only in MS., is probably not generally known.[2] It is to the effect that in his later years he took for his second wife an English lady, Matilda Verdun by name, upon whom, and upon any children he might have by her, he settled the Lordship of Oswestry. This lady inveigled the prince to Winchester, where her party was powerful. There, upon some excuse, he was put in durance, and while in that state was prevailed upon to execute another deed, whereby he settled the said Lordship of

---

1 Myvyrian Archaiology, I. p. 200.

2 For this anecdote, as well as for much of the topographical information contained in the notes to the Tale of Rhonabwy, I am indebted to the kindness of the Rev. Walter Davies (Gwallter Mechain).

Oswestry upon Matilda, and any children she might have after his decease. The prince died soon after the execution of this deed, and his body was conveyed from Winchester to Meivod, in Montgomeryshire, the burying-place of his family, where it was deposited in the church of St. Mary, which he himself had built some years before. His widow, Matilda, scarce took time to dry her tears before she married John Fitzalan, who thereby became Lord of "Oswaldstree."[1]

By his first wife, Susanna, daughter of Gruffydd ab Conan, Prince of North Wales, Madawc left several children.

He built the Castle of Oswestry, and a castle at Caer Einion, near Welshpool. Several places in their neighbourhood, and in that of Meivod still bear his name.

299b — POWYS WITHIN ITS BOUNDARIES, &c.

THAT part of the ancient principality of Powys, which belonged to Madawc ab Maredudd, extended from the vicinity of Chester to the uplands of Arwystli, now known as the Plinlimmon range of mountains. This is expressly stated by Gwalchmai, in his Elegy upon that Prince, in which he boasts that the sovereignty of his patron reached from the summit of Plinlimmon to the gates of Caerlleon, or Chester.—Myv. Arch. I. 202.

In more remote times Powys was of much greater extent. Powell tells us, in his History of Wales, that "Powys before king Offas time reached Eastward to the riuers of Dee and Seauerne, with a right line from the end of Broxen hilles to Salop, with all the countrie betweene Wye and Seauerne, whereof Brochwel yscithroc was possessed: but after the making of Offas ditch the plaine countrie toward Salop, being inhabited by Saxons and Normans, Powys was in length from Pulford bridge Northeast, to the confines of Caerdigan shire, in the parish of Lhanguric in the Southwest; and in bredth from the furthest part of Cyuelioc Westward, to Elsmere on the Eastside. This countrie or principalitie of Powys was appointed by Roderike the Great for the portion of his third sonne Anarawd, and so continued intierlie vntill the death of Blethyn ap Convyn. After whom, although the dominion was diminished by limiting parts in seueraltie amongst his sonnes Meredyth and Cadogan, yet at length it came wholie to the possession of Meredyth ap Blethyn, who had issue two sonnes Madoc and Gruffyth, betweene whom the said dominion was diuided." Madawc's share was further divided amongst his three children, from whose immediate

---

1 John's grandson, Richard Fitzalan, was the first Earl of Arundel of that name. In the time of Edward III. another Richard Fitzalan, fourth in descent from the above-mentioned Matilda Verdun, was at the same time Earl of Arundel, and in right of his mother, Earl Warren and Surrey. He was also Lord of Clun and Oswaldstree, in Shropshire, and Lord of Bromfield, Yale, Chirkland, and Dinus Bran, in North Wales.

descendants it was gained, by fraud or violence, by their Norman neighbours. Gruffydd's descendants, the first of whom was the celebrated Owain Cyveiliog, succeeded for three generations, to an unbroken inheritance, but in the fourth it was distributed among six sons, and finally passed away to several remote heirs. One, and apparently the most considerable of them, was represented by the Cheretons, afterwards Gray, Barons of Powys, from whom are the Vernons of Hodnet and other illustrious Norman families.

This passage would lead us to consider the Porfoed mentioned in the Tale, as identical with Pulford, and the locality of this place, added to the similarity of names, favours the supposition. The situation, however, of Merford, a lordship in the parish of Gresford, Midway between Wrexham and Chester, and of which the name bears at least an equal resemblance to that of Porfoed, renders it doubtful which of the two is alluded to in the text. Merford contains some interesting remains of a British camp, called the Roft, commanding a most extensive view of the counties of Chester and Salop.

The Gwauan, in Arwystli, spoken of as being at the other extremity of Powys, may possibly be one of the several spots now bearing the name of Waun in the Plinlimmon range.

The Cambrian Quarterly gives some ancient lines on the confines of Powys.

"From Cevn yr Ais, and from Chester to Eisteddva Gurig, and from Garn Gynnull on the river Conwy to Rhyd Helyg on the river Wye."[1]

299c — IORWERTH THE SON OF MAREDUDD

IORWERTH was the son of Maredudd ap Bleddyn, by his second wife Eva, daughter of Bledrws ab Ednowain Bendew, chief of one of the fifteen noble tribes. His father bestowed upon him the Lordship of Mochnant, near Oswestry, and be went by the name of Iorwerth Goch of Mochnant. Like most princes of his age, Iorwerth was a warrior, and in 1156 he sided with Henry II. against his neighbour Owain Gwynedd, Prince of North Wales, and during the contest that ensued between the English and the Welsh, he took and razed to the ground the castle of Ial or Yale, which Owain had built only ten years previously. The site of this fortress is still to be seen on a tumulus called Tomen Rhodwydd, by the roadside about halfway between Llangollen and Rhuthin. The partiality evinced by Iorwerth to the English interest, caused his nephews, Owain Cyveiliog and Owain Vychan, to unite their forces against him, and they, succeeded in expelling him from his patrimony of Mochnant, which they divided between them, the former taking possession of Uwch Rhaiadr, and the latter of Is Rhaiadr. Iorwerth married Maude, the daughter of Roger de Manley of Cheshire.

---

1 Cambr. Quarterly, III. 403.

It is supposed by some, that the tribe (Gwelygordd) of Iorwerth is celebrated by Cynddelw, in his poem called Gwelygorddeu Powys, under the title of Yorwerthyawn.—Myv. Arch. I. 256.

It is also thought that Iorwerth, after his expulsion from Mochnant, settled on the English side of Offa's dyke, for we find his grandson (some say his son), Sir Gruffydd Vychan,[1] called by the Welsh "Y Marchog Gwyllt o Gaer Howel," the Wild Knight of Caerhowel, living at a mansion still known by that name at Edgerly, in the county of Salop, near the ford on the Vyrnwy, which in this Mabinogi is designated Rhyd y Wilure. His descendants continued in the same county; and among their number we find another "Wild Knight," Humphrey Kynaston the Wild, who during his outlawry, in the reign of Henry VII. was the inhabitant of the cave, in the bold sandstone rock at Ness Cliff, called after him Kynaston's Cave, and concerning whose feats many an old wife's tale is still current in Shropshire.

300a — FROM ABER CEIRAWC IN ALLICTWN VER, TO RHYD Y WILURE

Aberceirawc, as the name implies, is the point of the confluence of the river Ceiriog with the Dee, which is not far below the town of Chirk, and opposite to Wynnstay Park. Allictwn is doubtless to be fixed at Allington in the immediate vicinity of Pulford, which, as we have already seen, was the extreme boundary of Madawc's possessions to the north-east; and Rhyd y Wilure is Rhyd y Vorle, in English Melverley, a ford upon the Vyrnwy, not far from the spot where that river falls into the Severn. We find accordingly that, taking Aberceirawc as the centre of operations, Madawc caused the search for his brother to be made a considerable way to the south, and as far to the north as his dominion extended. It is said also that some of the men that were on this quest, went as far as Nillystan Trevan, which may possibly be Halistan Trevan, now called Halston, near Whittington, the "Tre wen (or white town) ym mron y coed" of Llywarch Hên. Haliston was a sanctuary from time immemorial; if Iorwerth was a fugitive, be might have sought it as a place of refuge.

The river Vyrnwy, "the forkt Vurnway" of Drayton, is too well known to need description; but as its name occurs in the text, it May be permitted to remark, that whenever the bards have occasion to mention it, they do so in a spirit of affection which its beauty could not fail to inspire.

---

1 Sir Gruffydd Vychan was one of the earliest knights of the military order of St. John of Jerusalem.

300b — KYNWRIG VRYCHGOCH,
A MAN OF MAWDDWY

MAWDDWY was one of the western districts of ancient Powys; it now forms, in conjunction with Talybont, one of the hundreds of Merionethshire. This district includes the wild range of mountains of which Aran Fawddwy is the chief, and was in former times notorious for the wild and lawless character of its inhabitants, too well known by the appellation of the Gwylliaid Cochion Mawddwy, the red-headed robbers of Mawddwy. The desperate deeds of these men were the terror of all the surrounding country, on which they levied a species of black-mail; and to such an extent did they carry their violence at last, that it was found necessary in 1554 to issue a commission against them, under which about a hundred of their number were hanged. Some of their kinsmen soon after revenged them by the murder of Baron Owen, of Hengwrt, the chief of the commission, whom they waylaid at Llidiart y Barwn, on his journey to the assizes at Welshpool. After this, vigorous means were taken for their extirpation, and they gradually disappeared.—See Cambro. Briton, I. 184.

Iorwerth Goch, the Iorwerth of the present Mabinogi, had a son named Madawc Goch of Mawddwy, of whom the following notice occurs in a MS. Book of Pedigrees, collected by J. G., Esq., in 1697. "One Llywarch ab Cadfan, an opponent of Prince Llywelyn ab Iorwerth, was slain by this Madog Goch of Mawddwy; and in reward the Prince gave him the lands of Llywarch and his Arms, which were, Argent, a Chevron party per pale Gules and Or, inter 3 Eagles sable, their heads and one leg grey, trippant, standing on the sable leg: 3 trefoils argent over each head." A singular piece of heraldry.

It is not impossible that Kynwrig's designation of Vrychgoch may have been given in allusion to the characteristic complexion of the men of Mawddwy.

300c — MOELVRE IN KYNLLEITH

KYNLLEITH is a division of the hundred of Chirk in Denbighshire, and takes its name from the river Kynlleith. One of the most remarkable natural features of this district is the isolated mountain Moelvre, the summit of which, called Cyrn y Moelvre, is more than seventeen hundred feet above the level of the sea, and rises precipitously from Llyn Moelvre, a lake about a mile in circumference, situate on the western side of the mountain. One of the descendants of Madawc ab Maredudd erected a residence at a place called Moeliwrch, at a considerable elevation on the southern side of Moelvre; it continued for many centuries in the possession of his family.

Kynlleith is noticed in Cynddelw's Marwnad Fadawg fab Maredudd. —Myv. Arc. I. 213.

301a — ARGYNGROEG

IN following Rhonabwy on his visionary journey, it may be allowable to suppose him crossing the Vyrnwy at Rhyd y Vorle (Melverley), and then pursuing his course through the Deuddwr between that river and the Severn, till we come to the plains of Argyngroeg. The district traversed is remarkably fertile. The Cambrian pedestrian, David Thomas, in his metrical description of the Thirteen Counties of Wales, sang its praise about the year 1720. After naming two places excelling in luxuriance, he exclaims "Dau le hyfryd," but above all, the "Dolydd Hafren." Upon the Dolydd Havren it was that Gwalchmai composed his "Gorhoffet," in the twelfth century, while he and his troop of North-Wallians were guarding the opposite fords of the Severn against the progress of the English invaders.—Myv. Arch. I. 193.

That portion of the vale that bears the name of Argyngroeg, modernized into Cyngrog, and to which this narrative more particularly relates, consists of two townships, distinguished as Cyngrog vawr, and Cyngrog vach, the former in the parish of Pool, the latter in that of Guilsfield, and both side by side stretching to the Severn. When the Irish and other freebooters were expelled in the fourth century by the family of Cunedda Wledig, his son Rhuvon had a great part of Denbighshire awarded him as his portion, which from him was called Rhuvoniog, a name it retains to the present day. In like manner, it is not improbable that Cyngar one of Cunedda's descendants had a portion allotted to him at this place, which by adding the usual termination og to his name would be called Cyngarog, and abbreviated into Cyngrog. The names of Morganwg and Brycheiniog, from Morgan and Brychan, are of similar origin. In Cyngrog vawr, lies the site of the Cistercian Abbey of Ystrad Marchell (Strata Marcella), Alba Domus de Marcella, or Street Marshall Abbey, as it is vulgarly called. Having probably been built of wood, no traces of it now remain. The house and farm bearing the name of "The Abbey" belong to the Earl of Powis. The Abbey was founded and well endowed by Owain Cyveiliog, Prince of Powys Upper, who, besides much of the upland and sheep pastures of Cyveiliog, and even of Arwystli, granted to its inmates half the fish caught in the river Dyvi. The monks of Marcella were reduced by decimation under Edward I. and finally expelled by Henry VIII.

From Cyngrog, following the Vale of the Severn, we arrive at the tributary stream of the Rhiw, whose Aber, or confluence with the main stream, gives name by an ordinary abbreviation to the church and village of Berriew; and a little lower down occur, "Rhyd-y-Groes ar Havren," "The Cross, or Ford upon the Severn."

The Ford still remains, but has been from time immemorial converted into a ferry. At this point was carried on the chief communication between western Montgomeryshire, and the adjacent district of Merioneth towards Shrewsbury.

Here also are traces of a second way leading westward towards the Gaer, an evident Roman encampment. The intersection of these two roads appears to have occurred at no great distance from the ford, which doubtless derived its distinctive appellation of Y Groes, either from this circumstance, or from the Rood or Cross often set up both in crossways and upon the margins of fords.

The name Rhyd y Groes, no longer borne by the ford or ferry, is now preserved in that of a farm about two miles and a half distant, in the parish of Fordun near Montgomery, the property of Mr. Price, of Gunley.

Upon the farm itself no remains have been discovered, but several tumuli are found in its neighbourhood, the principal of which, "Hên Domen" (formerly Tre' Baldwyn), is of considerable size. There are also British encampments in the adjacent parishes of Churchstoke and Cherbury.[1]

Rhyd y Groes is mentioned in the Welsh Chronicles, as the scene of several conflicts between the Welsh and the Saxons; in allusion to which are those lines of Drayton.

> "Here could I else recount the slaughter'd Saxon's gore,
> Our swords at Crossford spilt on Severn's wand'ring shore."
>
> Song ix.

Lines in which Drayton may probably have had in mind the victory won over the Saxons, in the early part of the eleventh century, by Gruffydd ab Llewelyn, called by way of eminence, "Y tywysog dewr."

The Ford near Montgomery, was named as the place of meeting between Prince Llewelyn ab Gruffydd, and the commissioners of Edward I.

302a — IDDAWC CORDD PRYDAIN

THE treachery of Iddawc or Eiddilig Cordd Prydain,[2] is the subject of more than one of the Triads,[3] where he is said to have betrayed Arthur by divulging his plans. The meeting between him and Medrawd, with their men at Nanhwynain before the battle of Camlan, is spoken of as one of the three traitorous meetings of the Island, for there they plotted the betrayal of Arthur, which occasioned the strength of the Saxons. In another place their ascendancy is attributed to Iddawc's magical arts, which there were not warriors in the Island capable of

---

1 Acknowledgment should again be made in this place to the Rev. Walter Davies, for the curious local information contained in this note.

2 Possibly Gordd Prydain, the hammer of Britain.

3 Triads 22, 20, 50, 90, 78.

withstanding, so that the Saxons prevailed. This magic, for which he is also greatly celebrated, was taught him by Rhuddlwm Gawr.

The Triad which ranks Iddawc Cordd Prydain amongst the enchanters is prettily versified by Davydd ap Gwilym,[1] who speaks of him as an Irishman.

Iddawc was also, with Trystan and Gweirwerydd Vawr, one of the three stubborn ones, whom none could divert from their purpose; he is supposed to have afterwards embraced a religious life, probably when he did penance at Llechlas (possibly Glasgow), in North Britain, as mentioned in the Tale. His name is found in the Catalogue of the Welsh Saints. Professor Rees, however, considers this an error for Iddew ab Cawrda ab Caradawc Vreichvras, arising from the similarity of their names.[2]

302b — CAMLAN

THE battle of Camlan was the last of Arthur's battles, and that in which he lost his life. His opponents were headed by Medrawd, his nephew, the son of his sister Anna and Llew ap Cynvarch.

The Triads assign two different causes for this battle. The one, the blow given by Gwenhwyvar, Arthur's wife, to Gwenhwyvach; the other, the blow given to Medrawd by Arthur himself. The events immediately preceding it, together with the account of the battle itself as related in the Triads, and by Gruffydd ab Arthur, are briefly as follows, Lles, emperor of Rome, demanded from Arthur the tribute that his ancestors had paid, from the time of Caswallawn the son of Beli to that of Cystennin, Arthur's grandsire. The Roman Ambassador, proceeded to Caerlleon upon Usk, when Arthur not only denied their claim, but on the ground of the British origin of Brân and Constantine, both Roman emperors, determined by a counterclaim to retaliate, Medrawd was appointed Regent of the kingdom, whilst Arthur and his Britons crossed the sea, and fought a battle in the Cisalpine territory, in which the Roman emperor was slain, and both parties sustained severe loss. The result of this encounter encouraged Medrawd to attempt his uncle's throne. He seized upon the royal residence of Gelliwig, dragged the queen Gwenhwyvar from her throne (or, according to some versions, appropriated her as his wife), and strengthening himself by making treaties with the Saxons, Scots, and Picts, collected a force of eighty thousand men to oppose his uncle's landing. Arthur, however, disembarked at Porth Hamwnt, and put his rebellious nephew to flight after a hard fought engagement. Medrawd retreated to Winchester, whither Arthur, after remaining three days on the field of battle to bury the dead, followed him, and gained

---

1 Davydd ab Gwilym's Poems, 207. Cyffelybiad rhwng Morfudd a'r Delyn.

2 Welsh Saints, p. 280.

a second victory; upon this Medrawd fled into Cornwall, but was overtaken on the banks of the Camlan, supposed to be the river Camel, in that county. The celebrated battle of Camlan ensued. Arthur there gained the victory, but received a mortal wound at the hand of Medrawd, whom, however, he slew upon the field; he did not himself die on the spot, but was conveyed to Avallach or Avalon, and the crown descended to Cystennin the son of Kadwr, his kinsman. A mystery hangs over the final fate of Arthur.

One of the Triads[1] admits that Arthur died, and was buried at Avalon, now Glastonbury, in Somersetshire, where we learn from other authorities that Henry the II. many years afterwards discovered what were said to be his remains, with the inscription,[2]

"Hic jacet Arthurus, rex quondam rexque futurus."[3]

They were also visited, and a second time disinterred, by Edward I. and his queen.

Medrawd, notwithstanding the treachery with which his career ended, had always been considered a valiant warrior, and in the Triads[4] he is styled one of the three kingly knights of Arthur's Court, to whom no one could deny any thing by reason of their courtliness. The peculiar qualities to which his persuasive powers were due, were calmness, mildness, and purity.

---

1 Myv. Arch. II. p. 4.

2 Giraldus Cambrensis, who says he saw the inscription, gives it thug: "Hic jacet sepultus inclytus Rex Arthurus in insula Avallonia."

3 It may be here permitted to quote old Lydgate's verges upon Arthur's disappearance and expected return:—

"He is a King crouned in Fairie,
    With scepter and sword and with his regally
Shall resort as Lord and Soveraigne
    Out of Fairie and reigne in Britaine;
And repaire again the Round Table.
    By prophesy Merlin set the date,
Among Princes King incomparable,
    His seate againe to Caerlion to translate,
The Parchas sustren sponne so his fate,
    His Epitaph recordeth so certaine
Here lieth K. Arthur that shall raigne againe."

4 Triad 118.

304a — ADAON THE SON OF TALIESIN

ADAON or Avaon, son of the chief of the bards, and a bard himself, was also celebrated for his valour. He was one of those three dauntless chieftains who feared nothing in the day of the battle and strife, but rushed onwards regardless of death.—Tr. 73.

This courage and daring supported him through all the dangers of war. He fell at length by the hand of an assassin Llawgad Trwm Bargawd or Llawgad Trwm Bargawd Eiddyn, whose name is preserved only as the perpetrator of this crime.—Tr. 47.

The bold and determined character of Avaon appears to have continued even after death, for there is a Triad (quoted,) in which Avaon is spoken of as one of the grave-slaughtering ones, so called from their having avenged their wrongs from their graves.

None of his poetry is known to be preserved, except the following which is given in the Englynion y Clyweid.—Myv. Arch. I. 173.

"Hast thou heard what Avaon sang,
The son of Taliesin, of the recording verse?
The cheek will not conceal the anguish of the heart."

304b — ELPHIN

ELPHIN was the son of Gwyddno Garanhir, the unfortunate king whose possessions were submerged through the intemperance of Seithenin, the person employed to attend to the sea-banks. Some further particulars concerning him will be mentioned in a subsequent Mabinogi.

304c — BATTLE OF BADON

THE battle of Badon or Badon Mount, was one of the later,—Nennius says the twelfth,—and most successful of the battles fought by Arthur and the British elders, against the Saxons under Cerdic. The Britons not only gained the victory, but were by it enabled for some time to hold the Saxons in check.

The date of the battle has been the subject of dispute. From the persons engaged in it, it must be placed in the sixth century. A passage in the Red Book of Hergest, fixes its chronology 128 years after the age of Vortigern. The later Gildas, named Badonicus, from his birth having taken place in the year of the battle, has left a passage on the subject, which Bede appears to have misinterpreted, and from which Mr. Stevenson, the last editor of Gildas, places the birth of his author, and therefore the date of the battle, in the year 520.

The site of this conflict is also doubtful. Usher, following Camden, fixes it at Bath, and Camden, led probably by the similarity of names, gives his opinion in favour of Banner Down, near that city, upon which, in common, however, with most of the neighbouring heights, are remains of entrenchments more or less perfect. Carte prefers what he calls Mount Badon, in Berkshire. It is remarkable that the latter Gildas speaks of the battle as "obsessio," a siege. He also places "Mons Badonicus" near to the mouth of the Severn "prope Sabrinæ ostium"; but this latter passage has been considered an interpolation. Mr. Freeman, whose historical and antiquarian learning entitles his opinion to respect, suggests that Badon way be identical with Badbury Rings, near Wimborne in Dorsetshire.

To quote more poetical authority, the feats performed by the hero Arthur, at the battle of Badon Mount, are thus prettily celebrated in Drayton's verse.

> They sung how he himself at Badon bore that day,
> When at the glorious gole his British scepter lay;
> Two daies together how the battel stronglie stood:
> Pendragon's worthie son, who waded there in blood,
> Three hundred Saxons slew with his owne valiant hand."
>
> Song iv.

Cynddelw, and others of the Welsh Bards, speak of this fight with becoming admiration.

304d — OSLA GYLLELLVAWR

Ossa, or Osla, Gyllellvawr has already appeared in the Mabinogi of Kilhwch, where his prowess in the hunt of the Twrch Trwyth, occasioned the loss of his marvellous knife. From his name, and from the part assigned to him in this Tale, he was probably a Saxon; the Ossa, it may be, of Nennius's genealogies. This conjecture is strengthened by the epithet "Cyllellvawr"; the great or long knife, being in some measure associated with the Saxon name, owing to the massacre of Stonehenge, commonly called the "Treachery of the Long Knives," "Brad y Cyllyll hirion."[1] Hengist on that occasion is said to have invited the British Chieftains to a banquet and conference at Ambresbury, when beside each was placed a Saxon, who, at a signal agreed upon, drew forth his long knife, and suddenly fell upon his neighbour. This scheme was so effectually executed that four hundred and sixty of the British nobles are supposed to have been slaughtered. They did not, indeed, fall wholly unavenged; some defended themselves valiantly, and killed many of the Saxons with the stones

---

1 Triad 20.—Gruffydd ab Arthur. Myv. Arch. II. 254.

that lay around. Eidiol,[1] earl of Gloucester, who was fortunate enough to escape the general carnage, slew seventy Saxons with his own hand; the Triads say six hundred and sixty. The circle of Stonehenge is said, though with small semblance of probability, to have been erected by the Britons as a monument of this massacre upon the spot on which it occurred.

305a — CARADAWC VREICHVRAS

CARADAWC, like Trystan, and many other heroes whose names occur in the Mabinogion, was celebrated both in Welsh and Norman story. He was a son of Llyr Merini, a prince of Cornwall, and himself chief elder of Gelliwig;[2] the royal residence in that part of the Island. His mother was Gwen, grand-daughter of Brychan, through whose right he is supposed to have become ruler of the district of Brycheiniog.[3] According to the Triads, he was one of the battle knights of Britain,[4] and in an Englyn attributed to Arthur himself, he is styled "Caradawc pillar of the Cymry."

His prowess at the battle of Cattraeth, is also sting in the verse of his contemporary Aneurin,[5] who calls several of his fellow-warriors in evidence of his assertion.

> "When Caradawc rushed into battle,
> It was like the tearing onset of the woodland boar,
> The bull of combat in the field of slaughter,
> He attracted the wild dogs by the action of his hand.
> My witnesses are Owain the son of Eulat,
> And Gwrien, and Gwynn, and Gwriat.

---

1 Eidiol is associated for his strength with Gwrnerth Ergydlym, who slow the largest bear that ever was seen, with an arrow of straw; and Gwgan Lawgadarn, who rolled the stone of Maenarch from the valley to the top of the hill, which not less than thirty oxen could have drawn.—Tr. 60.

2 Triad 64.

3 Jones's History of Brecknockshire, I. p. 53.

4 Triad 29.

5 Myv. Arch. 1. p. 5.

From Cattraeth and its carnage,
From the hostile encounter,
After the clear bright mead was served,
He saw no more the dwelling of his father."

From the latter part of this passage, it appears that Caradawc fell in this battle, and the same is again repeated a few lines further on in the passage already quoted in the notes to Peredur ab Evrawc. Several Welsh families trace their pedigree to Caradawc.

Caradawc's horse Lluagor is recorded as one of the three battle horses of the Island.[1]

Tegau Eurvron, the beautiful wife of Caradawc, was no less renowned for her virtue than for her charms. In the Triads she is spoken of as one of the three fair ladies, and one of the three chaste damsels of Arthur's Court.[2] She possessed three precious things of which she alone was worthy; her mantle, her goblet of gold, and her knife. She is frequently alluded to by the bards.

In Anglo-Norman Romance, Caradawc's cognomen of Vreichvras "with the brawny arm," becomes "Brise Bras" and he himself takes his place as a principal hero of the Round Table. His wife preserves her British character and attributes under a Norman garb, and is well known as "faithful among the faithless" of Arthur's Court, the heroine of the mantle, "over her decent shoulders drawn." Sir Caradawc's well-founded confidence in his wife's virtue, enabled him to empty the marvellous Horn, and carve the tough Boar's head, adventures in which his compeers failed. In token of the latter of them, the Boar's head, in some form or other, appears as the armorial bearing of all of his name.

The Trouvères have a pretty story[3] in reference to the appellation of Brise Bras which they rendered the "wasted arm." They tell of an enchanter who fixed a serpent upon Caradawc's arm, from whose wasting tooth he could never be relieved, until she whom he loved best should consent to undergo the torture in his stead. His betrothed on learning this, was not to be deterred from giving him this proof of her devotion. As, however, the serpent was in the act of springing from the wasted arm of the knight to the fair neck of the lady, her brother, Kadwr, earl of Cornwall, struck off its head with his sword, and thus dispelled the enchantment. Caradawc's arm, however, never recovered its pristine strength and size, and hence, according to some authorities, the name of Brise Bras.

In the life of St. Collen, two persons of the name are mentioned, one of whom

---

1 Trioedd y Meirch, Myv. Arch. II. p. 20.

2 Triads 103, 108.

3 See Metrical and Prose versions of Perceval le Gallois.

was the ancestor of St, Collen himself, and was called Vreichvras, because he broke his arm in the battle of Hiraddig, from which injury that arm became larger than the other. He is expressly distinguished from the other Caradawc Vreichvras the son of Llyr Merini.—See Greal, 337.

305b — CEVN DIGOLL

ON the eastern boundary of Montgomeryshire, we find situated Cevn Digoll, called also "Hir Vynydd," or the Long Mountain. From its natural position, it seems to have been considered as a military post of some importance, and is celebrated as the scene of several remarkable events. There is a Triad relating to the conflicts that took place between Cadwallawn, and Edwin, king of Northumbria, on Cevn Digoll, in the early part of the seventh century, and which is said to have occasioned one of the three discolourings of the Severn, when that river was discoloured from its source to its estuary.[1]

These engagements are thus alluded to in an Elegy upon Cadwallawn ab Cadvan.—Myv. Arch. I. 121.

"It was on Cevn Digoll that the Welsh maintained their last struggle against Edward I. when Madawc, the son of Llywellyn ab Gruffydd was defeated and taken prisoner by the Lords Marchers. It was also said that Henry VII. encamped on this mountain, on his March from Wales to Bosworth field. On the summit of Cevn Digoll is a circular encampment, called the Beacon Ring. It is several acres in extent, but there is no water within its limits."

305c — MARCH THE SON OF MEIRCHION

THIS prince, whose territory is said to have been in Cornwall, was particularly unfortunate in having such a nephew as Trystan, and such a wife as Essyllt, the Yseult La Belle of the Trouvères.

As a possessor of ships he has been already noticed, the Triad which represents him as such having been cited. His grave is mentioned by the Englynion y Beddau, Myv. Arch. II. p. 81.

306a — KADWR, EARL OF CORNWALL

IN the wars of Arthur, as recounted by Gruffydd ab Arthur, Kadwr bore a conspicuous part. He shared the dangers of the expedition against the Romans, and was present at the battle in which the emperor of Rome was slain. He assisted

---

1 Triad lxxv.

at the coronation of his sovereign at Caerlleon upon Usk. Kadwr is mentioned in the Triads as one of the three battle knights, who fled neither for spear, nor arrow, nor sword, and who never shamed their leader in the day of conflict.[1]

His son Cystennin succeeded Arthur in his kingdom. Tegau Eurvron, the virtuous wife of Caradawc Vreichvras, and the heroine of the Mantel mal taillé, appears to have been the sister of Kadwr.

Taliesin alludes to him in his poem entitled the Glaswawd—

> He will spare no kindred,
> Neither cousin nor brother;
> At the sound of Kadwr's horn
> Nine hundred are stunned."

Myv. Arch. I. p. 64.

311a — OVERLAID WITH FINE SILVER

THE words in the original are "Gwedy latteinu ac aryant coeth," being lattened over with refined silver. Latten, or laton, was a mixed metal of the colour of brass, and was much employed in the fourteenth century for monumental effigies. For this and many other purposes it was prepared in the form of plate, and hence its name seems occasionally to have been used to express a plate or coating of metal generally, as in this particular instance of silver.

It may be remarked, that the term "latten" is still technically applied to the thinnest manufactured iron plate.

311b — RAVENS

THE Ravens of Owain have already appeared in the Mabinogi of Iarlles y Ffynawn, where they are said to have been three hundred in number, and to have descended to their master from Cynvarch, his paternal grandsire. It seems from passages in the writings of various bards, that the tradition of this singular army was familiarly current in the middle ages. It is alluded to by Bleddynt Vardd, in an Elegy on Davydd, the son of Gruffydd (and brother to Llewelyn, the last of the Welsh Princes), who was imprisoned and put to death by Edward I. about 1283.

> A man he was with a battered shield and a daring lance, in the field
>   of battle;
> A man proud to seek the furious trampling;

---

1 Myv. Arch. II. p. 80

A man whose warriors were proud of their stately array;
A man of the cleaving stroke and broken spear, loving the fight;
A man who caused the birds to fly upon the hosts [of slain]
Like the ravens of Owain eager for prey."

Myv. Arch. I. p. 365.

Lewis Glyn Cothi even mentions the particular staff or shaft, by the uplifting of which the Ravens were inspirited to destroy Arthur's pages and attendants, as related in the text.

"Owain son of Urien overthrew
The three towers of Cattraeth of old,
Arthur dreaded, as the flames,
Owain, his ravens, and his parti-coloured staff."—Works, I. 140.

Another poem of his has also an allusion to the "Vran a'r vaner Vraith."—I. 72.

312a — SELYV THE SON OF KYNAN GARWYN

HE has been already noticed as one of the "grave-slaughtering" warriors of the Island of Britain, who avenged their wrongs from their Sepulchres. A satire upon his father, Kynan Garwyn, is printed in the Myvyrian Archaiology, I. p. 168, among the Poems of Taliesin, to whom it is assigned.

312b — GWGAWN GLEDDYVRUDD

WE find the name of this chieftain twice occurring in the Triads. He is first noticed as one of the three stayers of slaughter[1] (ysgymmydd aereu), and afterwards, as one of the sentinels in the battle of Bangor Orchard.—Tr. lxvi.

His grave is alluded to in the Englynion y Beddau. The passage has been already quoted.

The name of his horse, which was Buchestom, is preserved in the Trioedd y Meirch.

---

1 The others were Morvran eil Tegid, and Gilbert mab Cadgyffro.—Tr. xxix.

312c — RHIOGAN

THIS prince is mentioned in the graves of the warriors.

"Whose is the grave on the banks of the Rhydnant?
Rhun was his name, of the steady progress,
He was a king; Rhiogan slew him."—Myv. Arch. I. p. 82.

312d — GWAIR THE SON OF GWESTYL

IT would seem that this personage was distinguished as being of a peculiarly dismal disposition, for we find him referred to as such by Llywarch ap Llewelyn,[1] in an Elegy on Hywel ap Gruffydd, (who died in 1216,) where he tells us, that through grief for his loss, his friends are become like Gwair ah Gwestyl.—Myv. Arch. I. p. 294.

And Einion Wan, in his Elegy on Madawc ab Gruffydd Maelor, a few years later, has the same expression in allusion to Madawc.

"The man who has become like Gwair ab Gwestyl."

Myv. Arch. I. p. 333.

It is not impossible that he is the same person as the Gwevyl mab Gwestad, of Kilhwch and Olwen, whose melancholy was such that "on the day that he was sad, he would let one of his lips drop below his waist, while he turned up the other like a cap upon his head".

The variation in the names is perhaps not greater than may be accounted for by the errors into which the transcribers of the olden time are well known to have but too frequently fallen.

In one version of the Triads, he is mentioned m one of the three diademed chiefs of the Island, together with Kai, and Trystan mab Tallwch.[2] But others substitute for his name that of Huail, the son of Kaw of Cwm Cawlwyd.

---

1 Commonly called Prydydd y Moch.

2 Tr. xxiii. Myv. Arch. II., p. 12.

312e — TRYSTAN THE SON OF TALLWCH

THIS personage is better known as the Tristan of Chivalric, and the Sir Tristrem of Metrical Romance, than in his proper character as a chieftain of the sixth century. In the Triads,[1] he is mentioned as one of the three compeers of Arthur's Court, as one of the diademed Princes, as one of the three Heralds, and as one of the three stubborn ones, whom no one could deter from their purpose. His chief celebrity, however, is derived from his unfortunate attachment to Essyllt, the wife of his uncle, March ab Meirchion, which gained him the appellation of one of the three ardent lovers of Britain. It was owing to the circumstance of his having tended his uncle's swine, whilst he despatched their usual keeper with a message to this lady, that he became classed as one of the three swineherds of the Island. There is a further Triad concerning Trystan, in which he is represented as able to transform himself into any shape he pleased.— Myv. Arch. II. p. 80.

312f — MORYEN

A WARRIOR whose name repeatedly occurs in the Gododin.

312g — LLACHEU THE SON OF ARTHUR

LLACHEU has already been mentioned with Gwalchmai, and Rhiwallon of the broom blossom hair, as one of the learned ones of the Island of Britain, to whom the elements and material essence of every thing were known. He was no less renowned for warlike prowess than for his deep knowledge, and is said to have fallen fighting bravely for his country, in the battle of Llongborth, so celebrated in the verse of Llywarch Hên. The death of Llacheu is thus alluded to, in a curious Dialogue between Gwyn ab Nudd and Gwyddno Garanhir.[2]

> "I know where Llacheu the son of Arthur
> Renowned in song was slain,
> When the ravens rushed upon blood."

---

1 Triads 113, 32, 69, 18, 102. See also the dialogue between him and Gwalchmai.

2 Myv. Arch. I. p. 166.

312h — RHYAWD THE SON OF MORGANT

THE Triads celebrate him as one of the three irregular Bards of the Island of Britain, the other two being Arthur himself, and Cadwallawn the son of Cadvan. He also ranked with Trystan, and Dalldav mab Kynin Côv, as one of the three compeers of Arthur's court. Rhuddfrych was the name of his horse.[1]

313a — GILBERT THE SON OF KADGYFFRO

GILBERT the son of Kadgyffro, has already been cited with Gwgan Gleddyvrudd and Morvran Eil Tegid, as one of the three stayers of slaughter. His name occurs again in the Trioedd y Meirch 3, where his horse is said to have been one of the chief steeds of the Island of Britain, and to have been known by the designation of Rhuddfreon Tuthfleidd.

313b — GWRTHMWL WLEDIG

GWRTHMWL, a prince of North Britain, was the chief elder of Penrhyn Rhionydd, one of the three tribe-thrones or royal cities of the Island. The celebrated St. Kentigern was chief Bishop of Penrhyn Rhionydd, during Gwrthmwl's eldership.—Tr. vii.

Gwrthmwl's history is brief. It may be inferred that be was slain by Maelwr of Rhiw or Allt Faelwr, in Cardiganshire, since there are notices in the triads of his sons, Gwair and Clais, and Arthaual,[2] riding against Maelwr, upon Erch their horse, to avenge their father's fate. It was one of Maelwr's customs never to close his gates against a single horse-load, and thus they gained entrance, and slew him. This was one of the three great horse-loads of the Island of Britain. The first of the three was a burthen of seven persons and a half, borne by Du y Moroedd, the horse of Elidyr Mwynvawr, from Llech Elidyr in the North, to Llech Elidyr in Anglesey. The seven were Elidyr himself, and Eurgain the daughter of Maelgwn Gwynedd, his wife, and Gwynda Gyned, and Gwynda Rheimad, and Mynach Nawmon the counsellor, and Petryleu Venestyr the butler, and Arianvagyl his servant, and Gellfeinesin his jester, who held on with his two hands at the horse's crupper and so was the half person. It does not appear what was the reason of their travelling in so singular a manner.

Gwrthmwl Wledig, was also the possessor of one of the spectre bulls of the

1 Triads lxxxix. 113, and Trioedd y Meirch, 5.

2 Myv. Arch. II. 8, 10, 20, 80. In some accounts only two of his sons are said to have been on this expedition, and one of them is called Achlen.

Island of Britain, or as another version has it, one of the spectre stags; Carw and Tarw, having been evidently confounded by the copyists.[1] What these sprites were is not explained. According to Beddau y Milwyr, his grave was in the wood of Briavael.[2]

---

1 Myv. Arch. II. p. 16, 17, 71

2 Ib. I. p. 81.

PWYLL PRINCE OF DYVED

PWYLL[339a] Prince of Dyved[339b] was lord of the seven Cantrevs of Dyved; and once upon a time he was at Narberth his chief palace, and he was minded to go and hunt, and the part of his dominions in which it pleased him to hunt was Glyn Cuch[339c]. So he set forth from Narbeth that night, and went as far as Llwyn Diarwyd. And that night he tarried there, and early on the morrow he rose and came to Glyn Cuch, when he let loose the dogs in the wood, and sounded the horn, and began the chase. And as he followed the dogs, he lost his companions; and whilst he listened to the hounds, he heard the cry of other hounds, a cry different from his own, and coming in the opposite direction.

And he beheld a glade in the wood forming a level plain, and as his dogs came to the edge of the glade, he saw a stag before the other dogs. And lo, as it reached the middle of the glade, the dogs that followed the stag overtook it and brought it down. Then looked he at the colour of the dogs, staying not to look at the stag, and of all the hounds that he had seen in the world, he had never seen any that were like unto these. For their hair was of a brilliant shining white, and their ears were red; and as the whiteness of their bodies shone, so did the redness of their ears glisten. And he came towards the dogs, and drove away those that had brought down the stag, and set his own dogs upon it.

And as he was setting on his dogs he saw a horseman coming towards him upon a large light-grey steed, with a hunting horn round his neck, and clad in garments of grey woollen in the fashion of a hunting garb. And the horseman drew near and spoke unto him thus. "Chieftain," said he, "I know who thou art, and I greet thee not." "Peradventure," said Pwyll, "thou art of such dignity that thou shouldest not do so." "Verily," answered he, "it is not my dignity that prevents me." "What is it then, O Chieftain?" asked he. "By Heaven, it is by reason of thine own ignorance and want of courtesy." "What discourtesy, Chieftain, hast thou seen in me?" "Greater discourtesy saw I never in man," said he, "than to drive away the dogs that were killing the stag and to set upon it thine own. This was discourteous, and though I may not be revenged upon thee, yet I declare to Heaven that I will do thee more dishonour than the value of an hundred stags." "O Chieftain," he replied, "if I have done ill I will redeem thy friendship." "How wilt thou redeem it?" "According as thy dignity may be, but I know not who thou art?" "A crowned king am I in the land whence I come." "Lord," said he, "may the day prosper with thee, and from what land comest thou?" "From Annwvyn," answered he; "Arawn, a King of Annwvyn[340a340b], am I." "Lord," said he, "how may I gain thy friendship?" "After this manner mayest thou," he said. "There is a man whose dominions are opposite to mine, who is ever warring against me, and he is Havgan, a King of Annwvyn, and by ridding me of this oppression, which thou canst easily do, shalt thou gain my friendship." "Gladly will I do this," said he. "Show me how I may." "I will show thee. Behold thus it is thou mayest. I will make firm friendship with thee; and this will I do. I will send thee to Annwvyn in my stead, and I will give thee the fairest lady thou didst ever behold to be thy companion, and I will put my form and semblance upon thee, so that not a page of the chamber, nor an officer, nor any other man that has always followed me shall know that it is not I. And this shall be for the space of a year from to-morrow, and then we will meet in this place." "Yes," said he; "but when I shall have been there for the space of a year, by what means shall I discover him of whom thou speakest?" "One year from this night," he answered, "is the time fixed between him and me that we should meet at the Ford; be thou there in my likeness, and with one stroke that thou givest him, he shall no longer live. And if he ask thee to give him another, give it not, how much soever he may entreat thee, for when I did so, he fought with me next day as well as ever before." "Verily," said Pwyll, "what shall I do concerning my kingdom?" Said Arawn, "I will cause that no one in all thy dominions, neither man nor woman, shall know that I am not thou, and I will go there in thy stead." "Gladly then," said Pwyll, "will I set forward." "Clear shall be thy path, and nothing shall detain thee, until thou come into my dominions, and I myself will be thy guide!"

So he conducted him until he came in sight of the palace and its dwellings. "Behold," said he, "the Court and the kingdom in thy power. Enter the Court, there is no one there who will know thee, and when thou seest what service is done there, thou wilt know the customs of the Court."

So he went forward to the Court, and when he came there, he beheld sleeping-rooms, and halls, and chambers, and the most beautiful buildings ever seen. And he went into the hall to disarray, and there came youths and pages and disarrayed him, and all as they entered saluted him. And two knights came and drew his hunting-dress from about him, and clothed him in a vesture of silk and gold. And the hall was prepared, and behold he saw the household and the host enter in, and the host was the most comely and the best equipped that he had ever seen. And with them came in likewise the Queen, who was the fairest woman that he had ever yet beheld. And she had on a yellow robe of shining satin; and they washed and went to the table, and sat, the Queen upon one side of him, and one who seemed to be an Earl on the other side.

And he began to speak with the Queen, and he thought, from her speech, that she was the seemliest and most noble lady of converse and of cheer that ever was. And they partook of meat, and drink, with songs and with feasting; and of all the Courts upon the earth, behold this was the best supplied with food and drink, and vessels of gold and royal jewels.

And the year he spent in hunting, and minstrelsy, and feasting, and diversions, and discourse with his companions until the night that was fixed for the conflict. And when that night came, it was remembered even by those who lived in the furthest part of his dominions, and he went to the meeting, and the nobles of the kingdom with him. And when he came to the Ford, a knight arose and spake thus. "Lords," said he, "listen well. It is between two kings that this meeting is, and between them only. Each claimeth of the other his land and territory, and do all of you stand aside and leave the fight to be between them."

Thereupon the two kings approached each other in the middle of the Ford, and encountered, and at the first thrust, the man who was in the stead of Arawn struck Havgan on the centre of the boss of his shield, so that it was cloven in twain, and his armour was broken, and Havgan himself was borne to the ground an arm's and a spear's length over the crupper of his horse, and he received a deadly blow. "O Chieftain," said Havgan, "what right hast thou to cause my death? I was not injuring thee in anything, and I know not wherefore thou wouldest slay me. But, for the love of Heaven, since thou hast begun to slay me, complete thy work." "Ah, Chieftain," he replied, "I may yet repent doing that unto thee, slay thee who may, I will not do so." "My trusty Lords," said Havgan, "bear me hence. My death has come. I shall be no more able to uphold you." "My Nobles," also said he who was in the semblance of Arawn, "take counsel and know who ought to be my subjects." "Lord," said the Nobles, "all should be, for there is no king over the whole of Annwvyn but thee." "Yes," he replied, "it is right that he who comes humbly should be received graciously, but he that doth not come with obedience, shall be compelled by the force of swords." And thereupon he received the homage of the men, and he began to conquer the country; and the next day by noon the two kingdoms were in his power. And thereupon he went to keep his tryst, and came to Glyn Cuch.

And when he came there, the King of Annwvyn was there to meet him, and each of them was rejoiced to see the other. "Verily," said Arawn, "may Heaven reward thee for thy friendship towards me. I have heard of it. When thou comest thyself to thy dominions," said he, "thou wilt see that which I have done for thee." "Whatever thou hast done for me, may Heaven repay it thee."

Then Arawn gave to Pwyll Prince of Dyved his proper form and semblance, and he himself took his own; and Arawn set forth towards the Court of Annwvyn; and he was rejoiced when he beheld his hosts, and his household, whom he had not seen so long; but they had not known of his absence, and wondered no more at his coming than usual. And that day was spent in joy and merriment; and he sat and conversed with his wife and his nobles. And when it was time for them rather to sleep than to carouse, they went to rest.

Pwyll Prince of Dyved came likewise to his country and dominions, and began to inquire of the nobles of the land, how his rule had been during the past year, compared with what it had been before. "Lord," said they, "thy wisdom was never so great, and thou wast never so kind or so free in bestowing thy gifts, and thy justice was never more worthily seen than in this year." "By Heaven," said he, "for all the good you have enjoyed, you should thank him who hath been with you; for behold, thus hath this matter been." And thereupon Pwyll related the whole unto them. "Verily, Lord," said they, "render thanks unto Heaven that thou hast such a fellowship, and withhold not from us the rule which we have enjoyed for this year past." "I take Heaven to witness that I will not withhold it," answered Pwyll.

And thenceforth they made strong the friendship that was between them, and each sent unto the other horses, and greyhounds, and hawks, and all such jewels as they thought would be pleasing to each other. And by reason of his having dwelt that year in Annwvyn, and having ruled there so prosperously, and united the two kingdoms in one day by his valour and prowess, he lost the name of Pwyll Prince of Dyved, and was called Pwyll Chief of Annwvyn from that time forward.

Once upon a time, Pwyll was at Narberth his chief palace, where a feast had been prepared for him, and with him was a great host of men. And after the first meal, Pwyll arose to walk, and he went to the top of a mound[344a] that was above the palace, and was called Gorsedd Arberth. "Lord," said one of the Court, "it is peculiar to the mound that whosoever sits upon it cannot go thence, without either receiving wounds or blows, or else seeing a wonder." "I fear not to receive wounds and blows in the midst of such a host as this, but as to the wonder, gladly would I see it. I will go therefore and sit upon the mound."

And upon the mound he sat. And while he sat there, they saw a lady, on a pure white horse of large size, with a garment of shining gold around her, coming along the highway that led from the mound; and the horse seemed to move at a slow and even pace, and to be coming up towards the mound. "My men," said Pwyll, "is there any among you who knows yonder lady?" "There is not, Lord," said they. "Go one of you and meet her, that we may know who she is." And one of them arose, and as he came upon the road to meet her, she passed by, and he followed as fast as he could, being on foot; and the greater was his speed, the further was she from him. And when he saw that it profited him nothing to follow her, he returned to Pwyll, and said unto him, "Lord, it is idle for any one in the world to follow her on foot." "Verily," said Pwyll, "go unto the palace, and take the fleetest horse that thou seest, and go after her."

And he took a horse and went forward. And he came to an open level plain, and put spurs to his horse; and the more he urged his horse, the further was she from him. Yet she held the same pace as at first. And his horse began to fail; and when his horse's feet failed him, he returned to the place where Pwyll was. "Lord," said he, "it will avail nothing for any one to follow yonder lady. I know of

no horse in these realms swifter than this, and it availed me not to pursue her."
"Of a truth," said Pwyll, "there must be some illusion here. Let us go towards the
palace." So to the palace they went, and they spent that day. And the next day
they arose, and that also they spent until it was time to go to meat. And after the
first meal, "Verily," said Pwyll, "we will go the same party as yesterday to the top
of the mound. And do thou," said he to one of his young men, "take the swiftest
horse that thou knowest in the field." And thus did the young man. And they
went towards the mound, taking the horse with them. And as they were sitting
down they beheld the lady on the same horse, and in the same apparel, coming
along the same road. "Behold," said Pwyll, "here is the lady of yesterday. Make
ready, youth, to learn who she is." "My lord," said he, "that will I gladly do." And
thereupon the lady came opposite to them. So the youth mounted his horse;
and before he had settled himself in his saddle, she passed by, and there was a
clear space between them. But her speed was no greater than it had been the day
before. Then he put his horse into an amble, and thought that notwithstanding
the gentle pace at which his horse went, he should soon overtake her. But this
availed him not; so he gave his horse the reins. And still he came no nearer to
her than when he went at a foot's pace. And the more he urged his horse, the
further was she from him. Yet she rode not faster than before. When he saw that
it availed not to follow her, he returned to the place where Pwyll was. "Lord,"
said he, "the horse can no more than thou hast seen." "I see indeed that it avails
not that any one should follow her. And by Heaven," said he, "she must needs
have an errand to some one in this plain, if her haste would allow her to declare
it. Let us go back to the palace." And to the palace they went, and they spent that
night in songs and feasting, as it pleased them.

And the next day they amused themselves until it was time to go to meat.
And when meat was ended, Pwyll said, "Where are the hosts that went yesterday
and the day before to the top of the mound?" "Behold, Lord, we are here," said
they. "Let us go," said he, "to the mound, to sit there. And do thou," said he to
the page who tended his horse, "saddle my horse well, and hasten with him to
the road, and bring also my spurs with thee." And the youth did thus. And they
went and sat upon the mound; and ere they had been there but a short time, they
beheld the lady coming by the same road, and in the same manner, and at the
same pace. "Young man," said Pwyll, "I see the lady coming; give me my horse."
And no sooner had he mounted his horse than she passed him. And he turned
after her and followed her. And he let his horse go bounding playfully, and
thought that at the second step or the third he should come up with her. But he
came no nearer to her than at first. Then he urged his horse to his utmost speed,
yet he found that it availed nothing to follow her. Then said Pwyll, "O maiden,
for the sake of him whom thou best lovest, stay for me." "I will stay gladly," said
she, "and it were better for thy horse hadst thou asked it long since." So the
maiden stopped, and she threw back that part of her headdress which covered

her face. And she fixed her eyes upon him, and began to talk with him. "Lady,"
asked he, "whence comest thou, and whereunto dost thou journey?" "I journey
on mine own errand," said she, "and right glad am I to see thee." "My greeting be
unto thee," said he. Then he thought that the beauty of all the maidens, and all
the ladies that he had ever seen, was as nothing compared to her beauty. "Lady,"
he said, "wilt thou tell me aught concerning thy purpose?" "I will tell thee," said
she. "My chief quest was to seek thee." "Behold," said Pwyll, "this is to me the
most pleasing quest on which thou couldst have come; and wilt thou tell me
who thou art?" "I will tell thee, Lord," said she. "I am Rhiannon[347a], the daughter
of Heveydd Hên[347b], and they sought to give me to a husband against my will.
But no husband would I have, and that because of my love for thee, neither will
I yet have one unless thou reject me. And hither have I come to hear thy answer."
"By Heaven," said Pwyll, "behold this is my answer. If I might choose among
all the ladies and damsels in the world, thee would I choose." "Verily," said she,
"if thou art thus minded, make a pledge to meet me ere I am given to another."
"The sooner I may do so, the more pleasing will it be unto me," said Pwyll, "and
wheresoever thou wilt, there will I meet with thee." "I will that thou meet me
this day twelvemonth at the palace of Heveydd. And I will cause a feast to be
prepared, so that it be ready against thou come." "Gladly," said he, "will I keep
this tryst." "Lord," said she, "remain in health, and be mindful that thou keep
thy promise; and now I will go hence." So they parted, and he went back to his
hosts and to them of his household. And whatsoever questions they asked him
respecting the damsel, he always turned the discourse upon other matters. And
when a year from that time was gone, he caused a hundred knights to equip
themselves and to go with him to the palace of Heveydd Hên. And he came to
the palace, and there was great joy concerning him, with much concourse of
people and great rejoicing, and vast preparations for his coming. And the whole
Court was placed under his orders.

And the hall was garnished and they went to meat, and thus did they sit;
Heveydd Hên was on one side of Pwyll, and Rhiannon on the other. And all
the rest according to their rank. And they ate and feasted and talked one with
another, and at the beginning of the carousal after the meat, there entered a
tall auburn-haired youth, of royal bearing, clothed in a garment of satin. And
when he came into the hall, he saluted Pwyll and his companions. "The greeting
of Heaven be unto thee, my soul," said Pwyll, "come thou and sit down." "Nay,"
said he, "a suitor am I, and I will do mine errand." "Do so willingly," said Pwyll.
"Lord," said he, "my errand is unto thee, and it is to crave a boon of thee that I
come." "What boon soever thou mayest ask of me, as far as I am able, thou shalt
have." "Ah," said Rhiannon, "wherefore didst thou give that answer?" "Has he
not given it before the presence of these nobles?" asked the youth. "My soul,"
said Pwyll, "what is the boon thou askest?" "The lady whom best I love is to be
thy bride this night; I come to ask her of thee, with the feast and the banquet

that are in this place." And Pwyll was silent because of the answer which he had given. "Be silent as long as thou wilt," said Rhiannon. "Never did man make worse use of his wits than thou hast done." "Lady," said he, "I knew not who he was." "Behold this is the man to whom they would have given me against my will," said she. "And he is Gwawl the son of Clud, a man of great power and wealth, and because of the word thou hast spoken, bestow me upon him lest shame befall thee." "Lady," said he, "I understand not thine answer. Never can I do as thou sayest." "Bestow me upon him," said she, "and I will cause that I shall never be his." "By what means will that be?" asked Pwyll. "In thy hand will I give thee a small bag," said she. "See that thou keep it well, and he will ask of thee the banquet, and the feast, and the preparations which are not in thy power. Unto the hosts and the household will I give the feast. And such will be thy answer respecting this. And as concerns myself, I will engage to become his bride this night twelvemonth. And at the end of the year be thou here," said she, "and bring this bag with thee, and let thy hundred knights be in the orchard up yonder. And when he is in the midst of joy and feasting, come thou in by thyself, clad in ragged garments, and holding thy bag in thy hand, and ask nothing but a bagful of food, and I will cause that if all the meat and liquor that are in these seven Cantrevs were put into it, it would be no fuller than before. And after a great deal has been put therein, he will ask thee whether thy bag will ever be full. Say thou then that it never will, until a man of noble birth and of great wealth arise and press the food in the bag with both his feet, saying, 'Enough has been put therein;' and I will cause him to go and tread down the food in the bag, and when he does so, turn thou the bag, so that he shall be up over his head in it, and then slip a knot upon the thongs of the bag. Let there be also a good bugle horn about thy neck, and as soon as thou hast bound him in the bag, wind thy horn, and let it be a signal between thee and thy knights. And when they hear the sound of the horn, let them come down upon the palace." "Lord," said Gwawl, "it is meet that I have an answer to my request." "As much of that thou hast asked as it is in my power to give, thou shalt have," replied Pwyll. "My soul," said Rhiannon unto him, "as for the feast and the banquet that are here, I have bestowed them upon the men of Dyved, and the household, and the warriors that are with us. These can I not suffer to be given to any. In a year from to-night a banquet shall be prepared for thee in this palace, that I may become thy bride."

So Gwawl went forth to his possessions, and Pwyll went also back to Dyved. And they both spent that year until it was the time for the feast at the palace of Heveydd Hên. Then Gwawl the son of Clud set out to the feast that was prepared for him, and he came to the palace, and was received there with rejoicing. Pwyll, also, the Chief of Annwvyn, came to the orchard with his hundred knights, as Rhiannon had commanded him, having the bag with him. And Pwyll was clad in coarse and ragged garments, and wore large clumsy old shoes upon his feet. And when he knew that the carousal after the meat had begun, he went towards the hall, and when he came into the hall, he saluted Gwawl the son of Clud, and his company, both men and women. "Heaven prosper thee," said Gwawl, "and the greeting of Heaven be unto thee." "Lord," said he, "may Heaven reward thee, I have an errand unto thee." "Welcome be thine errand, and if thou ask of me that which is just, thou shalt have it gladly." "It is fitting," answered he. "I crave but from want, and the boon that I ask is to have this small bag that thou seest filled with meat." "A request within reason is this," said he, "and gladly shalt thou have it. Bring him food." A great number of attendants arose and began to fill the bag, but for all that they put into it, it was no fuller than at first. "My soul," said Gwawl, "will thy bag be ever full?" "It will not, I declare to Heaven," said he, "for all that may be put into it, unless one possessed of lands, and domains, and treasure, shall arise and tread down with both his feet the food that is within the bag, and shall say, 'Enough has been put therein.'" Then said Rhiannon unto Gwawl the son of Clud, "Rise up quickly." "I will willingly arise," said he. So he rose up, and put his two feet into the bag. And Pwyll turned up the sides of the bag, so that Gwawl was over his head in it. And he shut it up quickly and slipped a knot upon the thongs, and blew his horn. And thereupon behold his household came down upon the palace. And they seized all the host that had come with Gwawl, and cast them into his own prison. And Pwyll threw off his rags, and his old shoes, and his tattered array; and as they came in, every one of Pwyll's knights struck a blow upon the bag, and asked, "What is here?" "A Badger," said they. And in this manner they played, each of them striking the bag, either with his foot or with a staff. And thus played they with the bag. Every one as he came in asked, "What game are you playing at thus?" "The game of Badger in the Bag," said they. And then was the game of Badger in the Bag first played.

"Lord," said the man in the bag, "if thou wouldest but hear me, I merit not to be slain in a bag." Said Heveydd Hên, "Lord, he speaks truth. It were fitting that thou listen to him, for he deserves not this." "Verily," said Pwyll, "I will do thy counsel concerning him." "Behold this is my counsel then," said Rhiannon; "thou art now in a position in which it behoves thee to satisfy suitors and minstrels; let him give unto them in thy stead, and take a pledge from him that he will never seek to revenge that which has been done to him. And this will be punishment enough." "I will do this gladly," said the man in the bag. "And gladly will I accept it," said Pwyll, "since it is the counsel of Heveydd and Rhiannon." "Such then is our counsel," answered they. "I accept it," said Pwyll. "Seek thyself sureties." "We will be for him," said Heveydd, "until his men be free to answer for him." And upon this he was let out of the bag, and his liegemen were liberated. "Demand now of Gwawl his sureties," said Heveydd, "we know which should be taken for him." And Heveydd numbered the sureties. Said Gwawl, "Do thou thyself draw up the covenant." "It will suffice me that it be as Rhiannon said," answered Pwyll. So unto that covenant were the sureties pledged. "Verily, Lord," said Gwawl, "I am greatly hurt, and I have many bruises. I have need to be anointed; with thy leave I will go forth. I will leave nobles in my stead, to answer for me in all that thou shalt require." "Willingly," said Pwyll, "mayest thou do thus." So Gwawl went towards his own possessions.

And the hall was set in order for Pwyll and the men of his host, and for them also of the palace, and they went to the tables and sat down. And as they had sat that time twelvemonth, so sat they that night. And they ate, and feasted, and spent the night in mirth and tranquillity. And the time came that they should sleep, and Pwyll and Rhiannon went to their chamber.

And next morning at the break of day, "My Lord," said Rhiannon, "arise and begin to give thy gifts unto the minstrels. Refuse no one to-day that may claim thy bounty." "Thus shall it be gladly," said Pwyll, "both to-day and every day while the feast shall last." So Pwyll arose, and he caused silence to be proclaimed, and desired all the suitors and the minstrels to show and to point out what gifts were to their wish and desire. And this being done, the feast went on, and he denied no one while it lasted. And when the feast was ended, Pwyll said unto Heveydd, "My Lord, with thy permission I will set out for Dyved to-morrow." "Certainly," said Heveydd, "may Heaven prosper thee. Fix also a time when Rhiannon may follow thee." "By Heaven," said Pwyll, "we will go hence together." "Willest thou this, Lord?" said Heveydd. "Yes, by Heaven," answered Pwyll.

And the next day, they set forward towards Dyved, and journeyed to the palace of Narberth, where a feast was made ready for them. And there came to them great numbers of the chief men and the most noble ladies of the land, and of these there was none to whom Rhiannon did not give some rich gift, either a bracelet, or a ring, or a precious stone. And they ruled the land prosperously both that year and the next.

And in the third year the nobles of the land began to be sorrowful at seeing a man whom they loved so much, and who was moreover their lord and their foster-brother, without an heir. And they came to him. And the place where they met was Preseleu, in Dyved. "Lord," said they, "we know that thou art not so young as some of the men of this country, and we fear that thou mayest not have an heir of the wife whom thou hast taken. Take therefore another wife of whom thou mayest have heirs. Thou canst not always continue with us, and though thou desire to remain as thou art, we will not suffer thee." "Truly," said Pwyll, "we have not long been joined together, and many things may yet befall. Grant me a year from this time, and for the space of a year we will abide together, and after that I will do according to your wishes. So they granted it. And before the end of a year a son was born unto him. And in Narberth was he born; and on the night that he was born, women were brought to watch the mother and the boy. And the women slept, as did also Rhiannon, the mother of the boy. And the number of the women that were brought into the chamber was six. And they watched for a good portion of the night, and before midnight every one of them fell asleep, and towards break of day they awoke; and when they awoke, they looked where they had put the boy, and behold he was not there. "Oh," said one of the women, "the boy is lost?" "Yes," said another, "and it will be small vengeance if we are burnt or put to death because of the child." Said one of the women, "Is there any counsel for us in the world in this matter?" "There is," answered another, "I offer you good counsel." "What is that?" asked they. "There is here a stag-hound bitch, and she has a litter of whelps. Let us kill some of the cubs, and rub the blood on the face and hands of Rhiannon, and lay the bones before her, and assert that she herself hath devoured her son, and she alone will not be able to gainsay us six." And according to this counsel it was settled. And towards morning Rhiannon awoke, and she said, "Women, where is my son?" "Lady," said they, "ask us not concerning thy son, we have nought but the blows and the bruises we got by struggling with thee, and of a truth we never saw any woman so violent as thou, for it was of no avail to contend with thee. Hast thou not thyself devoured thy son? Claim him not therefore of us." "For pity's sake," said Rhiannon; "the Lord God knows all things. Charge me not falsely. If you tell me this from fear, I assert before Heaven that I will defend you." "Truly," said they, "we would not bring evil on ourselves for any one in the world." "For pity's sake," said Rhiannon, "you will receive no evil by telling the truth." But for all her words, whether fair or harsh, she received but the same answer from the women.

And Pwyll the chief of Annwvyn arose, and his household, and his hosts. And this occurrence could not be concealed, but the story went forth throughout the land, and all the nobles heard it. Then the nobles came to Pwyll, and besought him to put away his wife, because of the great crime which she had done. But Pwyll answered them, that they had no cause wherefore they might ask him to put away his wife, save for her having no children. "But children has she now had, therefore will I not put her away; if she has done wrong, let her do penance for it."

So Rhiannon sent for the teachers and the wise men, and as she preferred doing penance to contending with the women, she took upon her a penance. And the penance that was imposed upon her was, that she should remain in that palace of Narberth until the end of seven years, and that she should sit every day near unto a horseblock that was without the gate. And that she should relate the story to all who should come there, whom she might suppose not to know it already; and that she should offer the guests and strangers, if they would permit her, to carry them upon her back into the palace. But it rarely happened that any would permit. And thus did she spend part of the year.

Now at that time Teirnyon Twryv Vliant was Lord of Gwent Is Coed[354a], and he was the best man in the world. And unto his house there belonged a mare, than which neither mare nor horse in the kingdom was more beautiful. And on the night of every first of May she foaled, and no one ever knew what became of the colt. And one night Teirnyon talked with his wife: "Wife," said he, "it is very simple of us that our mare should foal every year, and that we should have none of her colts." "What can be done in the matter?" said she. "This is the night of the first of May," said he. "The vengeance of Heaven be upon me, if I learn not what it is that takes away the colts." So he caused the mare to be brought into a house, and he armed himself, and began to watch that night. And in the beginning of the night, the mare foaled a large and beautiful colt. And it was standing up in the place. And Teirnyon rose up and looked at the size of the colt, and as he did so he heard a great tumult, and after the tumult behold a claw came through the window into the house, and it seized the colt by the mane. Then Teirnyon drew his sword, and struck off the arm at the elbow, so that portion of the arm together with the colt was in the house with him. And then did he hear a tumult and wailing, both at once. And he opened the door, and rushed out in the direction of the noise, and he could not see the cause of the tumult because of the darkness of the night, but he rushed after it and followed it. Then he remembered that he had left the door open, and he returned. And at the door behold there was an infant boy in swaddling-clothes, wrapped around in a mantle of satin. And he took up the boy, and behold he was very strong for the age that he was of.

Then he shut the door, and went into the chamber where his wife was. "Lady," said he, "art thou sleeping?" "No, lord," said she, "I was asleep, but as thou camest in I did awake." "Behold, here is a boy for thee if thou wilt," said he, "since thou hast never had one." "My lord," said she, "what adventure is this?" "It was thus," said Teirnyon; and he told her how it all befell. "Verily, lord," said she, "what sort of garments are there upon the boy?" "A mantle of satin," said he. "He is then a boy of gentle lineage," she replied. "My lord," she said, "if thou wilt, I shall have great diversion and mirth. I will call my women unto me, and tell them that I have been pregnant." "I will readily grant thee to do this," he answered. And thus did they, and they caused the boy to be baptized, and the ceremony was performed there; and the name which they gave unto him was Gwri Wallt Euryn[355a], because what hair was upon his head was as yellow as gold. And they had the boy nursed in the Court until he was a year old. And before the year was over he could walk stoutly. And he was larger than a boy of three years old, even one of great growth and size. And the boy was nursed the second year, and then he was as large as a child six years old. And before the end of the fourth year, he would bribe the grooms to allow him to take the horses to water. "My lord," said his wife unto Teirnyon, "where is the colt which thou didst save on the night that thou didst find the boy?" "I have commanded the grooms of the horses," said he, "that they take care of him." "Would it not be well, lord," said she, "if thou wert to cause him to be broken in, and given to the boy, seeing that on the same night that thou didst find the boy, the colt was foaled and thou didst save him?" "I will not oppose thee in this matter," said Teirnyon. "I will allow thee to give him the colt." "Lord," said she, "may Heaven reward thee; I will give it him." So the horse was given to the boy. Then she went to the grooms and those who tended the horses, and commanded them to be careful of the horse, so that he might be broken in by the time that the boy could ride him.

And while these things were going forward, they heard tidings of Rhiannon and her punishment. And Teirnyon Twryv Vliant, by reason of the pity that he felt on hearing this story of Rhiannon and her punishment, inquired closely concerning it, until he had heard from many of those who came to his court. Then did Teirnyon, often lamenting the sad history, ponder within himself, and he looked steadfastly on the boy, and as he looked upon him, it seemed to him that he had never beheld so great a likeness between father and son, as between the boy and Pwyll the Chief of Annwvyn. Now the semblance of Pwyll was well known to him, for he had of yore been one of his followers. And thereupon he became grieved for the wrong that he did, in keeping with him a boy whom he knew to be the son of another man. And the first time that he was alone with his wife, he told her that it was not right that they should keep the boy with them, and suffer so excellent a lady as Rhiannon to be punished so greatly on his account, whereas the boy was the son of Pwyll the Chief of Annwvyn. And Teirnyon's wife agreed with him, that they should send the boy to Pwyll. "And three things, lord," said she, "shall we gain thereby. Thanks and gifts for releasing Rhiannon from her punishment; and thanks from Pwyll for nursing his son and restoring him unto him; and thirdly, if the boy is of gentle nature, he will be our foster-son, and he will do for us all the good in his power." So it was settled according to this counsel.

And no later than the next day was Teirnyon equipped, and two other knights with him. And the boy, as a fourth in their company, went with them upon the horse which Teirnyon had given him. And they journeyed towards Narberth, and it was not long before they reached that place. And as they drew near to the palace, they beheld Rhiannon sitting beside the horseblock. And when they were opposite to her, "Chieftain," said she, "go not further thus, I will bear every one of you into the palace, and this is my penance for slaying my own son and devouring him." "Oh, fair lady," said Teirnyon, "think not that I will be one to be carried upon thy back." "Neither will I," said the boy. "Truly, my soul," said Teirnyon, "we will not go." So they went forward to the palace, and there was great joy at their coming. And at the palace a feast was prepared, because Pwyll was come back from the confines of Dyved. And they went into the hall and washed, and Pwyll rejoiced to see Teirnyon. And in this order they sat. Teirnyon between Pwyll and Rhiannon, and Teirnyon's two companions on the other side of Pwyll, with the boy between them. And after meat they began to carouse and to discourse. And Teirnyon's discourse was concerning the adventure of the mare and the boy, and how he and his wife had nursed and reared the child as their own. "And behold here is thy son, lady," said Teirnyon. "And whosoever told that lie concerning thee, has done wrong. And when I heard of thy sorrow, I was troubled and grieved. And I believe that there is none of this host who will not perceive that the boy is the son of Pwyll," said Teirnyon. "There is none," said they all, "who is not certain thereof." "I declare to Heaven," said Rhiannon, "that if this be true, there is indeed an end to my trouble." "Lady," said Pendaran Dyved[357a], "well hast thou named thy son Pryderi,[1] and well becomes him the name of Pryderi son of Pwyll Chief of Annwvyn." "Look you," said Rhiannon, "will not his own name become him better?" "What name has he?" asked Pendaran Dyved. "Gwri Wallt Euryn is the name that we gave him." "Pryderi," said Pendaran, "shall his name be." "It were more proper," said Pwyll, "that the boy should take his name from the word his mother spoke when she received the joyful tidings of him." And thus was it arranged.

"Teirnyon," said Pwyll, "Heaven reward thee that thou hast reared the boy up to this time, and, being of gentle lineage, it were fitting that he repay thee for it." "My lord," said Teirnyon, "it was my wife who nursed him, and there is no one in the world so afflicted as she at parting with him. It were well that he should bear in mind what I and my wife have done for him." "I call Heaven to witness," said Pwyll, "that while I live I will support thee and thy possessions, as long as I am able to preserve my own. And when he shall have power, he will more fitly maintain them than I. And if this counsel be pleasing unto thee, and to my nobles, it shall be that, as thou hast reared him up to the present time, I will give him to be brought up by Pendaran Dyved, from henceforth. And you shall be companions, and shall both be foster-fathers unto him." "This is good counsel," said they all. So the boy was given to Pendaran Dyved, and the nobles of the land were sent with him. And Teirnyon Twryv Vliant, and his companions, set out for his country, and his possessions, with love and gladness. And he went not without being offered the fairest jewels and the fairest horses, and the choicest dogs; but he would take none of them.

Thereupon they all remained in their own dominions. And Pryderi, the son of Pwyll the Chief of Annwvyn, was brought up carefully as was fit, so that he became the fairest youth, and the most comely, and the best skilled in all good games, of any in the kingdom. And thus passed years and years, until the end of Pwyll the Chief of Annwvyn's life came, and he died.

And Pryderi ruled the seven Cantrevs of Dyved prosperously, and he was beloved by his people, and by all around him. And at length he added unto them the three Cantrevs of Ystrad Tywi, and the four Cantrevs of Cardigan; and these were called the Seven Cantrevs of Seissyllwch. And when he made this addition, Pryderi the son of Pwyll the Chief of Annwvyn desired to take a wife. And the wife he chose was Kicva, the daughter of Gwynn Gohoyw, the son of Gloyw Wallt Lydan, the son of Prince Casnar, one of the nobles of this Island.

And thus ends this portion of the Mabinogion.

---

1 The word "Pryder" or "Pryderi" means anxiety.

NOTES TO
PWYLL PRINCE OF DYVED

339a — PWYLL

NEARLY the whole of the Mabinogi of Pwyll Pendevig Dyved, has already been printed with a translation in the Cambrian Register, and the story has also appeared in Jones's Welsh Bards.

Who Pwyll (whose name literally signifies Prudence) really was, appears to be a matter of uncertainty, but in some of the pedigrees of Gwynvardd Dyved, Prince of Dyved, he is said to be the son of Argoel, or Aircol Law Hir,[1] son of Pyr y Dwyrain. Mr. Davies, in the "Rites and Mythology of the Druids," states that he was the son of Meirig, son of Aircol, son of Pyr, which is rather confirmed by some other MS. pedigrees. In Taliesin's Preiddeu Annwn, he is mentioned, with big son Pryderi, in such a manner as to lead to the inference that he flourished not later than the age of Arthur. The opening lines of that remarkable composition are given in the Myvyrian Archaiology, I. p. 45. It must be allowed that their exact interpretation is by no means easy to discover, but the following version is from the pen of a distinguished Welsh scholar. The allusions, it should be observed, are very old and very obscure.

> "Adorable potentate, sovereign ruler!
> Who hast extended thy dominion over the boundaries of the world!
> Arranged was the prison of Gwair in Caer Sidi
> By the ministration of Pwyll and Pryderi.
> None before him ever entered it.
> The heavy blue chain the faithful one keeps.—
> And on account of the herds of Annwn I am afflicted;
> And till doom shall my bardic prayer continue.
> Three times the loading of Prydwen we went there,
> Besides seven none returned from Caer Sidi."

In subsequent parts of the poem Arthur is spoken of as having himself taken a share in the various expeditions which it records. The ship Prydwen is well known as one of his treasures. Gwair's captivity, which one of the Triads places in the Castle of Oeth and Annoeth, has been already adverted to.

---

1 Aircol Law Hir is recorded, in the Liber Landavensis, to have been the son of Tryfun and contemporary with St. Teiliaw, who flourished in the Sixth century. We find the grave of Aircol spoken of as being in Dyved.—Myv. Arch. I. p. 82.

339b — DYVED

IT often happens, and is a cause of great confusion in comparing ancient story with modern topography, that the old names are retained while the boundaries of the territory which they indicated are changed. Not unfrequently the names of petty Celtic kingdoms were applied to modern counties. This is the case with the name now before us. Dyved, the country inhabited by the Dimetæ of the Romans, is now generally considered to apply only to the county of Pembroke. It once included also the counties of Carmarthen and Cardigan, forming, in fact, the western, while Gwent formed the eastern division of South Wales.

There appears, however, to have been an exception to this general division, a portion of Cardigan having been once exclusively termed Ceredigiawn, and one-third part of Carmarthenshire having been included in the District of Rheged, called subsequently "Cantrev Bychan and Kidwelly." Lewis Dwnn,[1] in the reign of Elizabeth, thus describes the ancient boundaries of Dyved, as he understood them to have been:—

"The kingdom of Dyved formerly extended between the rivers Teivy and Towy, from Llyn Teivy and the source of the Towy to St. David's, and the centre of this kingdom was the Dark-Gate, in Carmarthen, and there is at this day a record of these boundaries in an old parchment book of the Bishop of St. David's."

According to this Dyved would appear to have comprehended about a sixth part of Cardiganshire, two-thirds of the county of Carmarthen, and the whole county of Pembroke.

It is evident, however, that at the time the Mabinogi of Pwyll was committed to writing, Dyved was restricted to the Cantrevs (or Hundreds) of Arberth (or Narberth), Dan Gleddyv, y Coed, Penvro, Rhos, Pebidiog, and Cenmaes, to which we are told that Pryderi added the three Cantrevs of Ystrad Tywi, or Carmarthenshire, Cantrev Bychan, Cantrev Mawr, and Cantrev Eginawg, together with the four Cantrevs of Ceredigiawn, Cantrev Emlyn, Cantrev Caer Wedws, Cantrev Mabwyniawn, and Cantrev Gwarthav, which seven Cantrevs were classed together under the appellation of Seissyllwch.[2] The addition

---

1 "Heraldic Visitation of Wales," published by the Welsh MSS. Society, under the care of Sir Samuel Rush Meyrick.

2 Seissyllwch was one of the ancient kingdoms of South Wales, and must not be confounded with Essyllwg (the Welsh word for the country of the Silures), as it has sometimes been. In the life of St. Paternus (preserved among the Cotton MSS.) it is said that the whole of South Wales was divided into three kingdoms, the same forming three bishoprics. Of these, the kingdom of Seissyl received its consecration from St. Paternus, Bishop of Llanbadarn Vawr, as the other two, those of Rein and Morgant, did from St. David and St. Eliu [Teiliaw]. The

made by Pryderi probably restored Dyved to its original extent at the time of the Romans.

339c — GLYN CUCH

CUCH, or, as it is generally written, Cych, is the boundary stream between the counties of Pembroke and Carmarthen, and falls into the Teivy between Cenarth and Llechryd. In the upper part of Glyn Cuch (the valley of the Cuch) was the residence of Cadivor Vawr, a regulus or petty king of Dyved, who died in 1088, and was called lord of Blaen Cuch and Cilsant. From him many of the principal families of Pembrokeshire trace their descent.

340a — ARAWN, KING OF ANNWVYN

THIS personage is the King of Annwn, already noticed as having fought against Amaethon mab Don, in the battle of Cad Goddeu. But it is doubtful whether he can be identified either with the Arawn ab Cynvarch, whom the Triads celebrate as one of the three Knights of Counsel,[1] or with the Aron mab Dewinvin, whose grave is alluded to in the Englynion y Beddau.—Myv. Arch. I. p. 82.

340b — ANNWVYN

ANNWVYN, or Annwn, is frequently rendered "Hell," though, perhaps, "The Lower Regions" would more aptly express the meaning which the name conveys.

The Dogs of Annwn are the subject of an ancient Welsh superstition, which was once universally believed in throughout the Principality, and which it would seem is not yet quite extinct. It is said that they are sometimes heard at night passing through the air overhead, as if in full cry in pursuit of some object.

---

latter kingdom, Glamorgan, having derived its appellation from Morgan, a sovereign of the tenth century, it is probable that the name of Seissyllwch is of the same date, and also that it may be derived from Seissyll, or Sitsyllt, the father of Llewelyn ab Sitsyllt, Prince of North Wales. The name of Seissyllwch occurs in the Triads, where we are told that Cynan Meriadawc led the warriors of that district to the assistance of Maxen Wledig.—Triad 14.

1 Triad lxxxvi.

344a — MOUND

THE word in the original is Gorsedd, which signifies a tumulus or mound, used as a seat of judicature, to which in its derivative sense it is commonly applied.

The mound called the Tyn-wald, still remaining in the Isle of Man, was long the place upon which the Deemsters of that Island held their judicial assemblies.

347a — RHIANNON

AFTER the death of Pwyll, Rhiannon was, by her son Pryderi, bestowed in marriage upon Manawyddan, the son of Llyr, and her subsequent history is detailed in the Mabinogi that bears his name. Her marvellous birds, whose notes were so sweet that warriors remained spell-bound for eighty years together listening to them, are a frequent theme with the poets.

"Three things that are not often heard; the song of the birds of Rhiannon, a song of wisdom from the mouth of a Saxon, and an invitation to a feast from a miser."[1]

347b — HEVEYDD HÊN

ACCORDING to the Triads, Heveydd Hên (probably the same as Hyvaidd Hir) was the son of Bleiddan Sant[2] of Glamorgan, and was one of the three stranger kings upon whom dominion was conferred for their mighty deeds, and for their praiseworthy and gracious qualities. But in some of the pedigrees he is called the son of Caradawc Vreichvras.—See Professor Rees's Welsh Saints, p. 103.

354a — GWENT IS COED

ONE of the divisions of Gwent; the other two being Gwent Uch Coed, and Gwent Coch yn y Dena, or the Forest of Dean. Gwent was the name formerly applied to the eastern division of South Wales. In its present restricted sense it is applied only to the county of Monmouth.

---

1 Trioedd y Cybydd, The Miser's Triads. Myv. Arch. III. p. 245.

2 Written in other versions of the Triads, Bleiddig in Deheubarth.

355a — GWRI GWALLT EURYN

GWRI GWALLT EURYN, styled at the close of the present tale Pryderi (care or anxiety), is frequently alluded to by the Bards, who speak of him under either name indiscriminately. In the Mabinogi of Kilhwch and Olwen he appears under his earlier appellation, perhaps, however, Pryderi is that by which he is best known. He was one of the chief swineherds of the island, and was so called because he kept the swine of Pendaran Dyved, in the Vale of Cuch in Emlyn. One of the Triads says that the swine he tended were those of Pwyll himself, and that he had the care of them during his father's absence in Annwn. This version, however, does not correspond with the circumstances as given in the text, which imply that Pryderi's birth must have taken place long after Pwyll's mysterious expedition.

We find the adventures of Pryderi's maturer years detailed in the Mabinogi of Manawyddan, with whom his name is coupled in a passage of the Kerdd am Veib Llyr, attributed to Taliesin.

In the tale of Math ab Mathonwy it is related that Pryderi was deprived of life by Gwydion ab Don, who was enabled by magical arts to overcome him in single combat, after having by similar means defrauded him of some swine which had been sent him from Annwn, and which he and his people highly prized.

The encounter took place near Melenryd, a ford on the Cynvael, a river of Merionethshire. The same authority places his grave at Maen Tyriawg, near Ffestiniog, but a different locality is assigned to it in the Enelynion Beddau.

> "In Abergenoli is the grave of Pryderi,
> Where the waves beat against the shore."

Dyved was called by Lewis Glyn Cothi "Gwlad Pryderi," and by Davydd ab Gwilym "Pryderi dir," and sometimes "Gwlad yr Hud," or the Land of Enchantment.

357a — PENDARAN DYVED

WE learn from the Triads, that the foster-father of Pryderi was the chief of one of the principal Welsh tribes; that which extended over Dyved, Gower (in Glamorgan), and Cardigan.[1]

Beyond this, and the fact of his possessing an immense herd of swine, which his foster-son Pryderi kept for him in the Vale of Ouch, but few particulars of Pendaran Dyved are extant.

---

1 Triad 16.

BRANWEN THE DAUGHTER OF LLYR

Here is the Second Portion of the Mabinogi

BENDIGEID VRAN[369a], the son of Llyr, was the crowned king of this island, and he was exalted from the crown of London. And one afternoon he was at Harlech[369b] in Ardudwy, at his Court, and he sat upon the rock of Harlech, looking over the sea. And with him were his brother Manawyddan the son of Llyr, and his brothers by the mother's side, Nissyen and Evnissyen, and many nobles likewise, as was fitting to see around a king. His two brothers by the mother's side were the sons of Eurosswydd[369c], by his mother, Penardun, the daughter of Beli son of Manogan[369d]. And one of these youths was a good youth and of gentle nature, and would make peace between his kindred, and cause his family to be friends when their wrath was at the highest; and this one was Nissyen; but the other would cause strife between his two brothers when they were most at peace. And as they sat thus, they beheld thirteen ships coming from the south of Ireland, and making towards them, and they came with a swift motion, the wind being behind them, and they neared them rapidly. "I see ships afar," said the king, "coming swiftly towards the land. Command the men of the Court that they equip themselves, and go and learn their intent." So the men equipped themselves and went down towards them. And when they saw the ships near, certain were they that they had never seen ships better furnished. Beautiful flags of satin were upon them. And behold one of the ships outstripped the others, and they saw a shield lifted up above the side of the ship, and the point of the shield was upwards, in token of peace. And the men drew near that they might hold converse. Then they put out boats and came towards the land. And they saluted the king. Now the king could hear them from the place where he was, upon the rock above their heads. "Heaven prosper you," said he, "and be ye welcome. To whom do these ships belong, and who is the chief amongst you?" "Lord," said they, "Matholwch, king of Ireland, is here, and these ships belong to him." "Wherefore comes he?' asked the king, "and will he come to the land?" "He is a suitor unto thee, lord," said they, "and he will not land unless he have his boon." "And what may that be?" inquired the king. "He desires to ally himself with thee, lord," said they, "and he comes to ask Branwen[370a] the daughter of Llyr, that, if it seem well to thee, the Island of the Mighty[370b] may be leagued with Ireland, and both become more powerful." "Verily," said he, "let him come to land, and we will take counsel thereupon." And this answer was brought to Matholwch. "I will go willingly," said he. So he landed, and they received him joyfully; and great was the throng in the palace that night, between his hosts and those of the Court; and next day they took counsel, and they resolved to bestow Branwen upon Matholwch. Now she was one of the three chief ladies of this island, and she was the fairest damsel in the world.

And they fixed upon Aberffraw as the place where she should become his bride. And they went thence, and towards Aberffraw the hosts proceeded; Matholwch and his host in their ships; Bendigeid Vran and his host by land, until they came to Aberffraw. And at Aberffraw they began the feast and sat down. And thus sat they. The King of the Island of the Mighty and Manawyddan the son of Llyr on one side, and Matholwch on the other side, and Branwen the daughter of Llyr beside him. And they were not within a house, but under tents. No house could ever contain Bendigeid Vran. And they began the banquet and caroused and discoursed. And when it was more pleasing to them to sleep than to carouse, they went to rest, and that night Branwen became Matholwch's bride.

And next day they arose, and all they of the Court, and the officers began to equip and to range the horses and the attendants, and they ranged them in order as far as the sea.

And behold one day, Evnissyen, the quarrelsome man of whom it is spoken above, came by chance into the place, where the horses of Matholwch were, and asked whose horses they might be. "They are the horses of Matholwch king of Ireland, who is married to Branwen, thy sister; his horses are they." "And is it thus they have done with a maiden such as she, and moreover my sister, bestowing her without my consent? They could have offered no greater insult to me than this," said he. And thereupon he rushed under the horses and cut off their lips at the teeth, and their ears close to their heads, and their tails close to their backs, and wherever he could clutch their eyelids, he cut them to the very bone, and he disfigured the horses and rendered them useless.

And they came with these tidings unto Matholwch, saying that the horses were disfigured, and injured so that not one of them could ever be of any use again. "Verily, lord," said one, "it was an insult unto thee, and as such was it meant." "Of a truth, it is a marvel to me, that if they desire to insult me, they should have given me a maiden of such high rank and so much beloved of her kindred, as they have done." "Lord," said another, "thou seest that thus it is, and there is nothing for thee to do but to go to thy ships." And thereupon towards his ships he set out.

And tidings came to Bendigeid Vran that Matholwch was quitting the Court without asking leave, and messengers were sent to inquire of him wherefore he did so. And the messengers that went were Iddic the son of Anarawd, and Heveydd Hir. And these overtook him and asked of him what he designed to do, and wherefore he went forth. "Of a truth," said he, "if I had known I had not come hither. I have been altogether insulted, no one had ever worse treatment than I have had here. But one thing surprises me above all." "What is that?"

asked they. "That Branwen the daughter of Llyr, one of the three chief ladies of this island, and the daughter of the King of the Island of the Mighty, should have been given me as my bride, and that after that I should have been insulted; and I marvel that the insult was not done me before they had bestowed upon me a maiden so exalted as she." "Truly, lord, it was not the will of any that are of the Court," said they, "nor of any that are of the council, that thou shouldest have received this insult; and as thou hast been insulted, the dishonour is greater unto Bendigeid Vran than unto thee." "Verily," said he, "I think so. Nevertheless he cannot recall the insult." These men returned with that answer to the place where Bendigeid Vran was, and they told him what reply Matholwch had given them. "Truly," said he, "there are no means by which we may prevent his going away at enmity with us, that we will not take." "Well, lord," said they, "send after him another embassy." "I will do so," said he. "Arise, Manawyddan son of Llyr, and Heveydd Hir, and Unic Glew Ysgwyd, and go after him, and tell him that he shall have a sound horse for every one that has been injured. And beside that, as an atonement for the insult[372a], he shall have a staff of silver, as large and as tall as himself, and a plate of gold of the breadth of his face. And show unto him who it was that did this, and that it was done against my will; but that he who did it is my brother, by the mother's side, and therefore it would be hard for me to put him to death. And let him come and meet me," said he, "and we will make peace in any way he may desire."

The embassy went after Matholwch, and told him all these sayings in a friendly manner, and he listened thereunto. "Men," said he, "I will take counsel." So to the council he went. And in the council they considered that if they should refuse this, they were likely to have more shame rather than to obtain so great an atonement. They resolved therefore to accept it, and they returned to the Court in peace.

Then the pavilions and the tents were set in order after the fashion of a hall; and they went to meat, and as they had sat at the beginning of the feast, so sat they there. And Matholwch and Bendigeid Vran began to discourse; and behold it seemed to Bendigeid Vran, while they talked, that Matholwch was not so cheerful as he had been before. And he thought that the chieftain might be sad, because of the smallness of the atonement which he had, for the wrong that had been done him. "Oh, man," said Bendigeid Vran, "thou dost not discourse to-night so cheerfully as thou wast wont. And if it be because of the smallness of the atonement, thou shalt add thereunto whatsoever thou mayest choose, and to-morrow I will pay thee the horses." "Lord," said he, "Heaven reward thee." "And I will enhance the atonement," said Bendigeid Vran, "for I will give unto thee a cauldron, the property of which is, that if one of thy men be slain to-day, and be cast therein, to-morrow he will be as well as ever he was at the best, except that he will not regain his speech." And thereupon he gave him great thanks, and very joyful was he for that cause.

And the next morning they paid Matholwch the horses as long as the trained horses lasted. And then they journeyed into another commot, where they paid him with colts until the whole had been paid, and from thenceforth that commot was called Talebolion.

And a second night sat they together. "My lord," said Matholwch, "whence hadst thou the cauldron[374a] which thou hast given me?" "I had it of a man who had been in thy land," said he, "and I would not give it except to one from there." "Who was it?" asked he. "Llassar Llaesgyvnewid; he came here from Ireland with Kymideu Kymeinvoll, his wife, who escaped from the Iron House in Ireland, when it was made red hot around them, and fled hither. And it is a marvel to me that thou shouldst know nothing concerning the matter." "Something I do know," said he, "and as much as I know I will tell thee. One day I was hunting in Ireland, and I came to the mound at the head of the lake, which is called the Lake of the Cauldron. And I beheld a huge yellow-haired man coming from the lake with a cauldron upon his back. And he was a man of vast size, and of horrid aspect, and a woman followed after him. And if the man was tall, twice as large as he was the woman, and they came towards me and greeted me. 'Verily,' asked I, 'wherefore are you journeying?' 'Behold, this,' said he to me, 'is the cause that we journey. At the end of a month and a fortnight this woman will have a son; and the child that will be born at the end of the month and the fortnight will be a warrior fully armed.' So I took them with me and maintained them. And they were with me for a year. And that year I had them with me not grudgingly. But thenceforth was there murmuring, because that they were with me. For, from the beginning of the fourth month they had begun to make themselves hated and to be disorderly in the land; committing outrages, and molesting and harassing the nobles and ladies; and thenceforward my people rose up and besought me to part with them, and they bade me to choose between them and my dominions. And I applied to the council of my country to know what should be done concerning them; for of their own free will they would not go, neither could they be compelled against their will, through fighting. And [the people of the country] being in this strait, they caused a chamber to be made all of iron. Now when the chamber was ready, there came there every smith that was in Ireland, and every one who owned tongs and hammer. And they caused coals to be piled up as high as the top of the chamber. And they had the man, and the woman, and the children, served with plenty of meat and drink; but when it was known that they were drunk, they began to put fire to the coals about the chamber, and they blew it with bellows until the house was red hot all around them. Then was there a council held in the centre of the floor of the chamber. And the man tarried until the plates of iron were all of a white heat; and then, by reason of the great heat, the man dashed against the plates with his shoulder and struck them out, and his wife followed him; but except him and his wife none escaped thence. And then I suppose, lord," said Matholwch unto

Bendigeid Vran, "that he came over unto thee." "Doubtless he came here," said he, "and gave unto me the cauldron." "In what manner didst thou receive them?" "I dispersed them through every part of my dominions, and they have become numerous and are prospering everywhere, and they fortify the places where they are with men and arms, of the best that were ever seen."

That night they continued to discourse as much as they would, and had minstrelsy and carousing, and when it was more pleasant to them to sleep than to sit longer, they went to rest. And thus was the banquet carried on with joyousness; and when it was finished, Matholwch journeyed towards Ireland, and Branwen with him, and they went from Aber Menei with thirteen ships, and came to Ireland. And in Ireland was there great joy because of their coming. And not one great man or noble lady visited Branwen unto whom she gave not either a clasp, or a ring, or a royal jewel to keep, such as it was honourable to be seen departing with. And in these things she spent that year in much renown, and she passed her time pleasantly, enjoying honour and friendship. And in the meanwhile it chanced that she became pregnant, and in due time a son was born unto her, and the name that they gave him was Gwern the son of Matholwch and, they put the boy out to be foster-nursed, in a place where were the best men of Ireland.

And behold in the second year a tumult arose in Ireland, on account of the insult which Matholwch had received in Cambria, and the payment made him for his horses. And his foster-brothers, and such as were nearest unto him, blamed him openly for that matter. And he might have no peace by reason of the tumult until they should revenge upon him this disgrace. And the vengeance which they took was to drive away Branwen from the same chamber with him, and to make her cook for the Court; and they caused the butcher after he had cut up the meat to come to her and give her every day a blow on the ear, and such they made her punishment.

"Verily, lord," said his men to Matholwch, "forbid now the ships and the ferry boats and the coracles, that they go not into Cambria, and such as come over from Cambria hither, imprison them that they go not back for this thing to be known there." And he did so; and it was thus for not less than three years.

And Branwen reared a starling in the cover of the kneading trough, and she taught it to speak, and she taught the bird what manner of man her brother was. And she wrote a letter of her woes, and the despite with which she was treated, and she bound the letter to the root of the bird's wing, and sent it towards Britain. And the bird came to this island, and one day it found Bendigeid Vran at Caer Seiont in Arvon, conferring there, and it alighted upon his shoulder and ruffled its feathers, so that the letter was seen, and they knew that the bird had been reared in a domestic manner.

Then Bendigeid Vran took the letter and looked upon it. And when he had read the letter he grieved exceedingly at the tidings of Branwen's woes. And immediately he began sending messengers to summon the island together. And he caused sevenscore and four countries to come unto him, and he complained to them himself of the grief that his sister endured. So they took counsel. And in the council they resolved to go to Ireland, and to leave seven men as princes here, and Caradawc, the son of Bran[377a], as the chief of them, and their seven knights. In Edeyrnion were these men left. And for this reason were the seven knights placed in the town. Now the names of these seven men were, Caradawc the son of Bran, and Heveydd Hir, and Unic Glew Ysgwyd, and Iddic the son of Anarawc Gwalltgrwn, and Fodor the son of Ervyll, and Gwlch Minascwrn, and Llassar the son of Llaesar Llaesgygwyd, and Pendaran Dyved as a young page with them. And these abode as seven ministers to take charge of this island; and Caradawc the son of Bran was the chief amongst them.

Bendigeid Vran, with the host of which we spoke, sailed towards Ireland, and it was not far across the sea, and he came to shoal water. It was caused by two rivers; the Lli and the Archan were they called; and the nations covered the sea. Then he proceeded with what provisions he had on his own back, and approached the shore of Ireland.

Now the swineherds of Matholwch were upon the seashore, and they came to Matholwch. "Lord," said they, "greeting be unto thee." "Heaven protect you," said he, "have you any news?" "Lord," said they, "we have marvellous news, a wood have we seen upon the sea, in a place where we never yet saw a single tree." "This is indeed a marvel," said he; "saw you aught else?" "We saw, lord," said they, "a vast mountain beside the wood, which moved, and there was a lofty ridge on the top of the mountain, and a lake on each side of the ridge. And the wood, and the mountain, and all these things moved." "Verily," said he, "there is none who can know aught concerning this, unless it be Branwen."

Messengers then went unto Branwen. "Lady," said they, "what thinkest thou that this is?" "The men of the Island of the Mighty, who have come hither on hearing of my ill-treatment and my woes." "What is the forest that is seen upon the sea?" asked they. "The yards and the masts of ships," she answered. "Alas," said they, "what is the mountain that is seen by the side of the ships?" "Bendigeid Vran, my brother," she replied, "coming to shoal water; there is no ship that can contain him in it." "What is the lofty ridge with the lake on each side thereof?" "On looking towards this island he is wroth, and his two eyes, one on each side of his nose, are the two lakes beside the ridge."

The warriors and the chief men of Ireland were brought together in haste, and they took counsel. "Lord," said the nobles unto Matholwch, "there is no other counsel than to retreat over the Linon (a river which is in Ireland), and to keep the river between thee and him, and to break down the bridge that is across the river, for there is a loadstone at the bottom of the river that neither ship nor vessel can pass over." So they retreated across the river, and broke down the bridge.

Bendigeid Vran came to land, and the fleet with him by the bank of the river. "Lord," said his chieftains, "knowest thou the nature of this river, that nothing can go across it, and there is no bridge over it?" "What," said they, "is thy counsel concerning a bridge?" "There is none," said he, "except that he who will be chief, let him be a bridge. I will be so," said he. And then was that saying first uttered, and it is still used as a proverb. And when he had lain down across the river, hurdles were placed upon him, and the host passed over thereby.

And as he rose up, behold the messengers of Matholwch came to him, and saluted him, and gave him greeting in the name of Matholwch, his kinsman, and showed how that of his goodwill he had merited of him nothing but good. "For Matholwch has given the kingdom of Ireland to Gwern the son of Matholwch, thy nephew and thy sister's son. And this he places before thee, as a compensation for the wrong and despite that has been done unto Branwen. And Matholwch shall be maintained wheresoever thou wilt, either here or in the Island of the Mighty." Said Bendigeid Vran, "Shall not I myself have the kingdom? Then peradventure I may take counsel concerning your message. From this time until then no other answer will you get from me." "Verily," said they, "the best message that we receive for thee, we will convey it unto thee, and do thou await our message unto him." "I will wait," answered he, "and do you return quickly."

The messengers set forth and came to Matholwch. "Lord," said they, "prepare a better message for Bendigeid Vran. He would not listen at all to the message that we bore him." "My friends," said Matholwch, "what may be your counsel?" "Lord," said they, "there is no other counsel than this alone. He was never known to be within a house, make therefore a house that will contain him and the men of the Island of the Mighty on the one side, and thyself and thy host on the other; and give over thy kingdom to his will, and do him homage. So by reason of the honour thou doest him in making him a house, whereas he never before had a house to contain him, he will make peace with thee." So the messengers went back to Bendigeid Vran, bearing him this message.

And he took counsel, and in the council it was resolved that he should accept this, and this was all done by the advice of Branwen, and lest the country should be destroyed. And this peace was made, and the house was built both vast and strong. But the Irish planned a crafty device, and the craft was that they should put brackets on each side of the hundred pillars that were in the house, and should place a leathern bag on each bracket, and an armed man in every one of them. Then Evnissyen came in before the host of the Island of the Mighty, and scanned the house with fierce and savage looks, and descried the leathern bags which were around the pillars. "What is in this bag?" asked he of one of the Irish. "Meal, good soul," said he. And Evnissyen felt about it until he came to the man's head, and he squeezed the head until he felt his fingers meet together in the brain through the bone. And he left that one and put his hand upon another, and asked what was therein. "Meal," said the Irishman. So he did the like unto every one of them, until he had not left alive, of all the two hundred men, save one only; and when he came to him, he asked what was there. "Meal, good soul," said the Irishman. And he felt about until he felt the head, and he squeezed that head as he had done the others. And, albeit he found that the head of this one was armed, he left him not until he had killed him. And then he sang an Englyn:—

"There is in this bag a different sort of meal,
The ready combatant, when the assault is made
By his fellow-warriors, prepared for battle."

Thereupon came the hosts unto the house. The men of the Island of Ireland entered the house on the one side, and the men of the Island of the Mighty on the other. And as soon as they had sat down there was concord between them; and the sovereignty was conferred upon the boy. When the peace was concluded, Bendigeid Vran called the boy unto him, and from Bendigeid Vran the boy went unto Manawyddan, and he was beloved by all that beheld him. And from Manawyddan the boy was called by Nissyen the son of Eurosswydd, and the boy went unto him lovingly. "Wherefore," said Evnissyen, "comes not my nephew the son of my sister unto me? Though he were not king of Ireland, yet willingly would I fondle the boy." "Cheerfully let him go to thee," said Bendigeid Vran, and the boy went unto him cheerfully. "By my confession to Heaven," said Evnissyen in his heart, "unthought of by the household is the slaughter that I will this instant commit."

Then he arose and took up the boy by the feet, and before any one in the house could seize hold of him, he thrust the boy headlong into the blazing fire. And when Branwen saw her son burning in the fire, she strove to leap into the fire also, from the place where she sat between her two brothers. But Bendigeid Vran grasped her with one hand, and his shield with the other. Then they all hurried about the house, and never was there made so great a tumult by any host in one house as was made by them, as each man armed himself. Then said Morddwydtyllyon, "The gadflies of Morddwydtyllyon's Cow!" And while they all sought their arms, Bendigeid Vran supported Branwen between his shield and his shoulder.

Then the Irish kindled a fire under the cauldron of renovation, and they cast the dead bodies into the cauldron until it was full, and the next day they came forth fighting-men as good as before, except that they were not able to speak. Then when Evnissyen saw the dead bodies of the men of the Island of the Mighty nowhere resuscitated, he said in his heart, "Alas! woe is me, that I should have been the cause of bringing the men of the Island of the Mighty into so great a strait. Evil betide me if I find not a deliverance therefrom." And he cast

himself among the dead bodies of the Irish, and two unshod Irishmen came to
him, and, taking him to be one of the Irish, flung him into the cauldron. And
he stretched himself out in the cauldron, so that he rent the cauldron into four
pieces, and burst his own heart also.

In consequence of that the men of the Island of the Mighty obtained such
success as they had; but they were not victorious, for only seven men of them all
escaped, and Bendigeid Vran himself was wounded in the foot with a poisoned
dart. Now the seven men that escaped were Pryderi, Manawyddan, Gluneu
Eil Taran, Taliesin, Ynawc, Grudyen the son of Muryel, and Heilyn the son of
Gwynn Hen.

And Bendigeid Vran commanded them that they should cut off his head.
"And take you my head," said he, "and bear it even unto the White Mount[381a], in
London, and bury it there, with the face towards France. And a long time will
you be upon the road. In Harlech you will be feasting seven years, the birds of
Rhiannon singing unto you the while. And all that time the head will be to you
as pleasant company as it ever was when on my body. And at Gwales in Penvro
you will be fourscore years, and you may remain there, and the head with you
uncorrupted, until you open the door that looks towards Aber Henvelen, and
towards Cornwall. And after you have opened that door, there you may no
longer tarry, set forth then to London to bury the head, and go straight forward."

So they cut off his head, and these seven went forward therewith. And
Branwen was the eighth with them, and they came to land at Aber Alaw, in
Talebolyon, and they sat down to rest. And Branwen looked towards Ireland
and towards the Island of the Mighty, to see if she could descry them. "Alas," said
she, "woe is me that I was ever born; two islands have been destroyed because of
me!" Then she uttered a loud groan, and there broke her heart. And they made
her a four-sided grave, and buried her upon the banks of the Alaw.

Then the seven men journeyed forward towards Harlech, bearing the head
with them; and as they went, behold there met them a multitude of men and
of women. "Have you any tidings?" asked Manawyddan. "We have none," said
they, "save that Caswallawn382a the son of Beli has conquered the Island of
the Mighty, and is crowned king in London." "What has become," said they, "of
Caradawc the son of Bran, and the seven men who were left with him in this
island?" "Caswallawn came upon them, and slew six of the men, and Caradawc's
heart broke for grief thereof; for he could see the sword that slew the men, but
knew not who it was that wielded it. Caswallawn had flung upon him the Veil
of Illusion, so that no one could see him slay the men, but the sword only could
they see. And it liked him not to slay Caradawc, because he was his nephew, the
son of his cousin. And now he was the third whose heart had broke through
grief. Pendaran Dyved, who had remained as a young page with these men,
escaped into the wood," said they.

Then they went on to Harlech, and there stopped to rest, and they provided meat and liquor, and sat down to eat and to drink. And there came three birds, and began singing unto them a certain song, and all the songs they had ever heard were unpleasant compared thereto; and the birds seemed to them to be at a great distance from them over the sea, yet they appeared as distinct as if they were close by, and at this repast they continued seven years.

And at the close of the seventh year they went forth to Gwales in Penvro. And there they found a fair and regal spot overlooking the ocean; and a spacious hall was therein. And they went into the hall, and two of its doors were open, but the third door was closed, that which looked towards Cornwall. "See, yonder," said Manawyddan, "is the door that we may not open." And that night they regaled themselves and were joyful. And of all they had seen of food laid before them, and of all they had heard of, they remembered nothing; neither of that, nor of any sorrow whatsoever. And there they remained fourscore years, unconscious of having ever spent a time more joyous and mirthful. And they were not more weary than when first they came, neither did they, any of them, know the time they had been there. And it was not more irksome to them having the head with them, than if Bendigeid Vran had been with them himself. And because of these fourscore years, it was called "the Entertaining of the noble Head." The entertaining of Branwen and Matholwch was in the time that they went to Ireland.

One day said Heilyn the son of Gwynn, "Evil betide me, if I do not open the door to know if that is true which is said concerning it." So he opened the door and looked towards Cornwall and Aber Henvelen. And when they had looked, they were as conscious of all the evils they had ever sustained, and of all the friends and companions they had lost, and of all the misery that had befallen them, as if all had happened in that very spot; and especially of the fate of their lord. And because of their perturbation they could not rest, but journeyed forth with the head towards London. And they buried the head in the White Mount, and when it was buried, this was the third goodly concealment; and it was the third ill-fated disclosure when it was disinterred, inasmuch as no invasion from across the sea came to this island while the head was in that concealment.

And thus is the story related of those who journeyed over from Ireland.

In Ireland none were left alive, except five pregnant women in a cave in the Irish wilderness; and to these five women in the same night were born five sons, whom they nursed until they became grown-up youths. And they thought about wives, and they at the same time desired to possess them, and each took a wife of the mothers of their companions, and they governed the country and peopled it.

And these five divided it amongst them, and because of this partition are the five divisions of Ireland[384a] still so termed. And they examined the land where the battles had taken place, and they found gold and silver until they became wealthy.

And thus ends this portion of the Mabinogi, concerning the blow given to Branwen, which was the third unhappy blow of this island; and concerning the entertainment of Bran, when the hosts of sevenscore countries and ten went over to Ireland to revenge the blow given to Branwen; and concerning the seven years' banquet in Harlech, and the singing of the birds of Rhiannon, and the sojourning of the head for the space of fourscore years.

NOTES TO
BRANWEN THE DAUGHTER OF LLYR

369a — BENDIGEID VRAN

BRAN the son of Llyr Llediaith, and sovereign of Britain, derives, according to the Welsh authorities, his title of Bendigeid, or the Blessed, from the circumstance of his having introduced Christianity into this Island. They tell us that he was the father of the celebrated Caradawc (Caractacus), whose captivity he is said to have shared; and proceed to state that having embraced the Christian faith, during his seven years' detention in Rome, he returned to his native country, and caused the Gospel to be preached there.[1] The following Triad recites these events.

"The three blissful Rulers of the Island of Britain, Bran the Blessed, the son of Llyr Llediaith, who first brought the faith of Christ to the nation of the Cymry from Rome, where he was seven years a hostage for his son Caradawc, whom the Romans made prisoner through the craft, and deceit, and treachery of Aregwedd Fôeddawg [usually supposed to be Cartismandua]. The second was Lleurig ab Coel ab Cyllyn Sant, who was called Lleufer Mawr, [the great Light], and built the ancient church at Llandaff, which was the first in Britain, and who gave the privileges of land, and of kindred, and of social rights, and of society to such as were of the faith of Christ. The third was Cadwaladyr the Blessed, who gave refuge, with his lands, and with all his goods, to the believers who fled from the Saxons without faith, and from the aliens who would have slain them."—Tr. 35.

The benefit which Bran thus conferred upon his country procured for his family the distinction of being accounted one of the three Holy Tribes; the families of Cunedda Wledig and Brychan Brycheiniog were the other two.

All this, however, it may be observed, is much at variance with the particulars of Caradawc's captivity, and of his family, recorded by classical writers.

Bran is ranked with Prydain ab Aedd Mawr, and Dyvnwal Moelmud as one of the three Kings who gave stability to sovereignty by the excellence of their system of government.—Tr. 36.

Various ancient Welsh documents allude to the incidents recorded of Bran in the Mabinogi of Branwen. Thus in the curious poem entitled Kerdd am Veib Llyr ab Brychwel Powys, attributed to Taliesin, are the following lines,—

---

1 For an account of Bendigeid Vran, see Professor Rees's Welsh Saints p. 77.

I was with Bran in Ireland,
I saw when Morddwyd Tyllon was slain.[1]

And there is a Triad upon the story of his head being buried under the White Tower of London, with the face towards France, intended as a charm against foreign invasion. Arthur, it appears, proudly disinterred the head, preferring to hold the Island by his own strength alone, and this is recorded as one of the fatal disclosures of Britain.

"The three Closures and Disclosures of the Island; First the head of Bendigeid Vran ab Llyr, which Owain the son of Maxen Wledig buried under the White Tower in London, and while it was go placed no invasion could be made upon this Island; the second was the bones of Gwrthevyr the Blessed [Vortimer], which were buried in the chief harbour of the Island, and while they remained there hidden all invasions were ineffectual. The third was the dragons buried by Lludd ab Beli, in the city of Pharaon, in the rocks Of Snowdon. And the three closures were made under the blessing of God and his attributes, and evil befel from the time of their disclosure. Gwrtheyrn Gwrtheneu [Vortigern], disclosed the dragons to revenge the displeasure of the Cymry against him, and he invited the Saxons in the guise of men of defence to fight against the Gwyddyl Ffychti; and after this he disclosed the bones of Gwrthevyr the Blessed, through love of Ronwen [Rowena], the daughter of the Saxon Hengist. And Arthur disclosed the head of Bendigeid Vran ab Llyr, because he chose not to hold the Island except by his own strength. And after the three disclosures came the chief invasions upon the race of the Cymry."—Tr. 53.

The name of Bran is of frequent occurrence in the poems of Cynddelw, and other bards of the middle ages.

369b — HARLECH

MOST of the localities which occur in the Tale of Branwen are too well known to need any description; one or two, however, require a slight notice. Of Harlech, it may be remarked that it is also called Twr Bronwen, or Branwen's Tower. The name of Caer Collwyn was also bestowed upon it after Collwyn ab Tangno, chief of one of the fifteen Noble Tribes of North Wales. It possesses the ruins of a fine castle. Harlech stands on the sea coast, on the confines of Ardudwy, one of the six districts of Merionethshire, of which the portion called Dyffryn Ardudwy is a remnant of the Cantrev y Gwaelod, inundated in the time of Gwyddno Garanhir.

Edeyrnion, mentioned a little further on in the story, is also situated in Merionethshire.

---

1 Myv. Arch. I. p. 66.

Talebolion is a Commot in Anglesey.

Aberffraw, likewise in Anglesey, was the residence of the princes of Gwynedd from the time of Roderick the Great, in 843, to that of the last Llywelyn, in 1282.

369c — EUROSSWYDD

EUROSSWYDD is beyond doubt the Roman general Ostorius, the captor of Llyr Llediaith, and his family, including Bran and Caradawc (Caractacus).

He is mentioned as such in Triad L, already quoted.

369d — BELI THE SON. OF MANOGAN

BELI, surnamed the Great, was king over Britain forty years, and was succeeded in the sovereignty by his sons, Lludd and Caswallawn, better known as Cassivelaunus. In the Armes attributed to Taliesin, Beli is thus addressed,—

"Greatly do I honour thee
Victorious Beli,
Son of Manogan the king.
Do thou preserve the glory
Of the Honey Island[1] of Beli."

Myv. Arch. I. p. 73.

370a — BRANWEN

THE beautiful Branwen (or Bronwen, the "white-bosomed," as she is more frequently called), is one of the most popular heroines of Welsh romance. No less celebrated for her woes than for her charms, we find that her eventful story was a favourite theme with the bards and poets of her nation. Numerous instances might be adduced of the allusions to her, which their compositions contain; suffice it to refer to the words of Davydd ab Gwilym, who, in one of his odes addressed to Morvudd, compares her hue to that of Bronwen, the daughter of Llyr.

The indignities to which Branwen was subjected in Ireland are referred to in one of the Triads (49).

In 1813, a grave containing a funeral urn was discovered on the banks of the river Alaw, in Anglesey, in a spot called Ynys Bronwen. The appearance of the grave, and its remarkable locality, led to the inference that it might indeed be the

---

1 An ancient name for Britain.

"Bedd Petrual," the four-sided place of burial, in which, according to the text, her sorrowing companions deposited the remains of the unfortunate heroine of the Mabinogion. The following account of its discovery was communicated, in 1821, to the Cambro-Briton (and printed in that publication, II. p. 71), by Sir R. C. Hoare, on the authority of Richard Fenton, Esq., of Fishguard.

"An Account of the Discovery, in 1813, of an Urn, in which, there is every reason to suppose, the ashes of *Bronwen* (White Bosom), the daughter of Llyr, and aunt to the great Caractacus, were deposited.

A farmer, living on the banks of the Alaw, a river in the Isle of Anglesea, having occasion for stones, to make some addition to his farm-buildings, and having observed a stone or two peeping through the turf of a circular elevation on a flat not far from the river, was induced to examine it, where, after paring off the turf, he came to a considerable heap of stones, or *carnedd*, covered with earth, which he removed with some degree of caution, and got to a *cist* formed of coarse flags canted and covered over. On removing the lid, he found it contained an urn placed with its mouth downwards, full of ashes and half-calcined fragments of bone. The report of this discovery soon went abroad, and came to the ears of the parson of the parish, and another neighbouring clergyman, both fond of, and conversant in, Welsh antiquities, who were immediately reminded of a passage in one of the early Welsh romances, called the *Mabinogion* (or juvenile tales), the same that is quoted in Dr. Davies's Latin and Welsh Dictionary, as well as in Richards's, under the word *Petrual* (square).

'Bedd petrual a wnaed i Fronwen ferch Lyr ar lan Alaw, ac yno y claddwyd hi.'

A square grave was made for Bronwen, the daughter of Llyr, on the banks of the Alaw, and there she was buried.

Happening to be in Anglesea soon after this discovery, I could not resist the temptation of paying a visit to so memorable a spot, though separated from it by a distance of eighteen miles. I found it, in all local respects, exactly as described to me by the clergyman above mentioned, and as characterised by the cited passage from the romance. The *tumulus*, raised over the venerable deposit, was of considerable circuit, elegantly rounded, but low, about a dozen paces from the river Alaw.[1] The Urn was preserved entire, with an exception of a small bit out of its lip, was ill-baked, very rude and simple, having no other ornament than little pricked dots, in height from about a foot to fourteen inches, and nearly of the following shape. "When I saw the urn, the ashes and half-calcined bones were in it."

---

1 "This spot is still called *Ynys Bronwen*, or the Islet of Bronwen, which is a remarkable confirmation of the genuineness of this discovery."

Branwen appears to be the Brungwaine or Brangian of romance, though the character of the Welsh heroine, and the part she sustains, differ widely from those attributed to the confidante of Tristan and Yseult la Belle. In like manner Matholwch the Irishman also seems identical with Morholt the stern king of Ireland of the Trouvères.—See the Romances of Meliadus of Leonnoys, Tristan, &c.

370b — THE ISLAND OF THE MIGHTY

Ynys y Kedyrn, the Island of the Mighty, is one of the many names bestowed upon Britain by the Welsh. A Triad, in which several more of these ancient appellations are preserved, asserts that while yet uninhabited the Island was called Clas Merddin, but that after its colonization it bore the name of Vel Ynys, which was again changed in compliment to its conquest by Brut, into Ynys Prydain, or the Island of Brut. The same Triad states that some authorities attribute the more modern designation to its conquest by Prydain son of Aedd the Great.—Myv. Arch. II. p. 1.

372a — AN ATONEMENT FOR THE INSULT

THE compensation here offered to Matholwch, is strictly in accordance, except as regards the size of the silver rod, with what was required by the Laws of Hywel Dda, where the fine for insult to a king is fixed at a "hundred cows on account of every cantrev in the kingdom, and a silver rod with three knobs at the top, that shall reach from the ground to the king's face, when he sits in his chair and as thick as his ring-finger; and a golden bason, which shall hold fully as much as the king drinks, of the thickness of a husbandman's nail, who shall have followed husbandry for seven years, and a golden cover, as broad as the king's face, equally thick as the bason." In another MS. the payment, instead of being only partly in gold, is said to have been entirely in that metal; thus "a golden rod as long as himself, of the thickness of his little finger, and a golden tablet, as broad as his face, and as thick as a husbandman's nail."

374a — THE CAULDRON

THE powers exercised by this family through the influence of the cauldron, bear a strong resemblance to those possessed by the Tuatha de Danann, a race of necromancers, who once invaded Ireland. This tribe, whilst sojourning in Asia, were at war with the Syrians, and were enabled to triumph through the aid of magic, as they had the art of resuscitating such of their number as fell in fight by sending demons to animate their corpses, so that the Syrians found to their dismay that those whom they had slain met them in battle the next day as vigorous as ever. In this difficulty, they had recourse to the advice of their priests, who told them to drive a stake of mountain ash through the bodies of such as they slew, and that, if they had been animated by demons, they would instantly turn into worms. This counsel was followed, and the Tuatha de Danann were compelled to quit that country.

An ancient Irish poem contains a series of Triads respecting this race which remind us of some passages in the Mabinogi of Kilhwch and Olwen.

"Blackness, obscurity, and darkness were their three cup-bearers; strength, robustness, and vigour, their three horses; indignation, pursuit and swiftness, their three bounds, &c."—See Bunting.

377a — CARADAWC THE SON OF BRAN

THIS Prince, so well known under his Latinized name of Caractacus, is chiefly remarkable for his captivity in Rome, which, according to Welsh authorities, was shared by his father Bran, his grandfather Llyr Llediaith, and all his near kinsfolk. There are several Triads relating to this principal event of his life.[1] From one of these it seems that he was chosen by his countrymen as their general, or War-king, to repel the incursions of the Romans, and another corroborates this by styling him "One of the three Rulers of choice," having been elected by the voice of the country and the people, although he was not an elder. There is no doubt of his having stood high in the esteem of his nation; and we are told that "the men of Britain, from the prince to the slave, became his followers in their country's need against the progress of the foe and of destruction. And wheresoever he went in war, all the men of the Island went in his train, and none desired to remain at home."[2]

Caradawc is also extolled as one of those brave princes, who, by reason of their valour, could never be overcome save by treachery; and the treason by which he was cast into the hands of his enemies is very frequently alluded to. Avarwy ab Lludd ab Beli, and his daughter Aregwedd Foeddawg, were the traitors, and are mentioned in terms of disgust and execration. "One of the praiseworthy opposers," is another of the titles bestowed upon Caradawc, because he resisted the invasion of the Cæsarians.

---

1 Tr. 17, 23, 24, 34, 41, 55.

2 In this Triad (41) he is called one of the exalted servants, and is distinguished as the son of a Bard.

381a — WHITE MOUNT IN LONDON

UNDER the name of the Gwynvryn, or White Mount of the text, allusion is most probably intended to the Tower of London, in which the Welsh, who always regarded the capital as a city of their own foundation, appear to have felt a peculiar interest.

Llywarch ab Llewelyn (Prydydd y Moch), a poet of the twelfth and early part of the thirteenth century, speaks of it as "The White eminence of London, a place of splendid fame."—Myv. Arch. I. p. 280.

The keep of the metropolitan fortress of England has in turn been attributed to Celts, Romans, Saxons, and Normans; now, however, the "Towers of Julius" are assigned, upon irrefragable evidence, to the early Norman period.

382a — CASWALLAWN

CASWALLAWN the son of Beli, known more generally by the name of Cassivelaunus, bestowed on him by the Romans, is a celebrated character in Welsh history. He is recorded as one of the chiefs chosen to oppose the invasion of Caesar, and was styled one of the War-kings of Britain.—Tr. 24.

It is related that Caswallawn led an army of sixty-one thousand men against Julius Caesar. The charms of Flur, the daughter of Myguach Gorr, are said to have been the cause of this incursion, She had been carried off by Mwrchan, a Gaulish prince, in alliance with Caesar, to whom he intended to present his prize. The expedition which Caswallawn headed was successful; six thousand of the partisans of Caesar were slain, and Flur was recovered. Some of the circumstances of this exploit acquired for Caswallawn the designation of "One of the Three Gold-Shoemakers" (the other two being Manawyddan mab Llyr, and Llew Llaw Gyffes, as will be detailed hereafter), and the whole achievement occasioned him to be ranked among the three faithful lovers of Britain.

The army of Caswallawn did not return with their leader, whence it is called one of the three Emigrant hosts of Britain.[1]

Meinlas was the name of Caswallawn's horse.—Trioedd y Meirch ii.

384a — FIVE DIVISIONS OF IRELAND

BEFORE the invasion of the Anglo-Normans, in Henry II.'s time, Ireland was divided into a pentarchy composed of the kingdoms of Munster, Leinster, Connaught, Ulster, and Meath.

---

1 The above particulars with regard to Caswallawn are related in the Triads 14,102,124, and xl.

MANAWYDDAN THE SON OF LLYR

Here is the Third Portion of the Mabinogi

WHEN the seven men of whom we spoke above had buried the head of Bendigeid Vran, in the White Mount an London, with its face towards France; Manawyddan gazed upon the town of London, and upon his companions, and heaved a great sigh; and much grief and heaviness came upon him. "Alas, Almighty Heaven, woe is me," he exclaimed, "there is none save myself without a resting-place this night." "Lord," said Pryderi, "be not so sorrowful. Thy cousin is king of the Island of the Mighty, and though he should do thee wrong, thou hast never been a claimant of land or possessions. Thou art the third disinherited prince." "Yea," answered he, "but although this man is my cousin, it grieveth me to see any one in the place of my brother Bendigeid Vran, neither can I be happy in the same dwelling with him." "Wilt thou follow the counsel of another?" said Pryderi. "I stand in need of counsel," he answered, "and what may that counsel be?" "Seven Cantrevs remain unto me," said Pryderi, "wherein Rhiannon my mother dwells. I will bestow her upon thee and the seven Cantrevs with her, and though thou hadst no possessions but those Cantrevs only, thou couldst not have seven Cantrevs fairer than they. Kicva, the daughter of Gwynn Gloyw, is my wife, and since the inheritance of the Cantrevs belongs to me, do thou and Rhiannon enjoy them, and if thou ever desire any possessions thou wilt take these." "I do not, Chieftain," said he; "Heaven reward thee for thy friendship." "I would show thee the best friendship in the world if thou wouldst let me." "I will, my friend," said he, "and Heaven reward thee. I will go with thee to seek Rhiannon and to look at thy possessions." "Thou wilt do well," he answered. "And I believe that thou didst never hear a lady discourse better than she, and when she was in her prime none was ever fairer. Even now her aspect is not uncomely."

They set forth, and, however long the journey, they came at length to Dyved, and a feast was prepared for them against their coming to Narberth, which Rhiannon and Kicva had provided. Then began Manawyddan and Rhiannon to sit and to talk together, and from their discourse his mind and his thoughts became warmed towards her, and he thought in his heart he had never beheld any lady more fulfilled of grace and beauty than she. "Pryderi," said he, "I will that it be as thou didst say." "What saying was that?" asked Rhiannon. "Lady," said Pryderi, "I did offer thee as a wife to Manawyddan the son of Llyr." "By that will I gladly abide," said Rhiannon. "Right glad am I also," said Manawyddan;

"may Heaven reward him who hath shown unto me friendship so perfect as this."

And before the feast was over she became his bride. Said Pryderi, "Tarry ye here the rest of the feast, and I will go into Lloegyr to tender my homage unto Caswallawn the son of Beli." "Lord," said Rhiannon, "Caswallawn is in Kent, thou mayest therefore tarry at the feast, and wait until he shall be nearer." "We will wait," he answered. So they finished the feast. And they began to make the circuit of Dyved, and to hunt, and to take their pleasure. And as they went through the country, they had never seen lands more pleasant to live in, nor better hunting grounds, nor greater plenty of honey and fish. And such was the friendship between those four, that they would not be parted from each other by night nor by day.

And in the midst of all this he went to Caswallawn at Oxford, and tendered his homage; and honourable was his reception there, and highly was he praised for offering his homage.

And after his return, Pryderi and Manawyddan feasted and took their ease and pleasure. And they began a feast at Narberth, for it was the chief palace; and there originated all honour. And when they had ended the first meal that night, while those who served them ate, they arose and went forth, and proceeded all four to the Gorsedd of Narberth, and their retinue with them. And as they sat thus, behold, a peal of thunder, and with the violence of the thunderstorm, lo there came a fall of mist, so thick that not one of them could see the other. And after the mist it became light all around. And when they looked towards the place where they were wont to see cattle, and herds, and dwellings, they saw nothing now, neither house, nor beast, nor smoke, nor fire, nor man, nor dwelling; but the houses of the Court empty, and desert, and uninhabited, without either man or beast within them. And truly all their companions were lost to them, without their knowing aught of what had befallen them, save those four only.

"In the name of Heaven," cried Manawyddan, "where are they of the Court, and all my host beside these? Let us go and see." So they came into the hall, and there was no man; and they went on to the castle and to the sleeping-place, and they saw none; and in the mead-cellar and in the kitchen there was nought but desolation. So they four feasted, and hunted, and took their pleasure. Then they began to go through the land and all the possessions that they had, and they visited the houses and dwellings, and found nothing but wild beasts. And when they had consumed their feast and all their provisions, they fed upon the prey they killed in hunting, and the honey of the wild swarms. And thus they passed the first year pleasantly, and the second; but at the last they began to be weary.

"Verily," said Manawyddan, "we must not bide thus. Let us go into Lloegyr, and seek some craft whereby we may gain our support." So they went into Lloegyr, and came as far as Hereford. And they betook themselves to making saddles. And Manawyddan began to make housings, and he gilded and coloured them with blue enamel, in the manner that he had seen it done by Llasar Llaesgywydd. And he made the blue enamel as it was made by the other man. And therefore is it still called Calch Lasar [blue enamel], because Llasar Llaesgywydd had wrought it.

And as long as that workmanship could be had of Manawyddan, neither saddle nor housing was bought of a saddler throughout all Hereford; till at length every one of the saddlers perceived that they were losing much of their gain, and that no man bought of them, but him who could not get what he sought from Manawyddan. Then they assembled together, and agreed to slay him and his companions.

Now they received warning of this, and took counsel whether they should leave the city. "By Heaven," said Pryderi, "it is not my counsel that we should quit the town, but that we should slay these boors." "Not so," said Manawyddan, "for if we fight with them, we shall have evil fame, and shall be put in prison. It were better for us to go to another town to maintain ourselves." So they four went to another city.

"What craft shall we take?" said Pryderi. "We will make shields," said Manawyddan. "Do we know anything about that craft?" said Pryderi. "We will try," answered he. There they began to make shields, and fashioned them after the shape of the good shields they had seen; and they enamelled they, as them had done the saddles. And they prospered in that place, so that not a shield was asked for in the whole town, but such as was had of them. Rapid therefore was their work, and numberless were the shields they made. But at last they were marked by the craftsmen, who came together in haste, and their fellow-townsmen with them, and agreed that they should seek to slay them. But they received warning, and heard how the men had resolved on their destruction. "Pryderi," said Manawyddan, "these men desire to slay us." "Let us not endure this from these boors, but let us rather fall upon them and slay them." "Not so," he answered; "Caswallawn and his men will hear of it, and we shall be undone. Let us go to another town." So to another town they went.

"What craft shall we take?" said Manawyddan. "Whatsoever thou wilt that we know," said Pryderi. "Not so," he replied, "but let us take to making shoes, for there is not courage enough among cordwainers either to fight with us or to molest us." "I know nothing thereof," said Pryderi. "But I know," answered Manawyddan; "and I will teach thee to stitch. We will not attempt to dress the leather, but we will buy it ready dressed and will make the shoes from it."

So he began by buying the best cordwal that could be had in the town, and none other would he buy except the leather for the soles; and he associated himself with the best goldsmith in the town, and caused him to make clasps for the shoes, and to gild the clasps, and he marked how it was done until he learnt the method. And therefore was he called one of the three makers of Gold Shoes; and, when they could be had from him, not a shoe nor hose was bought of any of the cordwainers in the town. But when the cordwainers perceived that their gains were failing (for as Manawyddan shaped the work, so Pryderi stitched it), they came together and took counsel, and agreed that they would slay them.

"Pryderi," said Manawyddan, "these men are minded to slay us." "Wherefore should we bear this from the boorish thieves?" said Pryderi. "Rather let us slay them all." "Not so," said Manawyddan, "we will not slay them, neither will we remain in Lloegyr any longer. Let us set forth to Dyved and go to see it."

So they journeyed along until they came to Dyved, and they went forward to Narberth. And there they kindled fire and supported themselves by hunting. And thus they spent a month. And they gathered their dogs around them, and tarried there one year.

And one morning Pryderi and Manawyddan rose up to hunt, and they ranged their dogs and went forth from the palace. And some of the dogs ran before them and came to a small bush which was near at hand; but as soon as they were come to the bush, they hastily drew back and returned to the men, their hair bristling up greatly. "Let us go near to the bush," said Pryderi, "and see what is in it." And as they came near, behold, a wild boar of a pure white colour rose up from the bush. Then the dogs, being set on by the men, rushed towards him; but he left the bush and fell back a little way from the men, and made a stand against the dogs without retreating from them, until the men had come near. And when the men came up, he fell back a second time, and betook him to flight. Then they pursued the boar until they beheld a vast and lofty castle, all newly built, in a place where they had never before seen either stone or building. And the boar ran swiftly into the castle and the dogs after him. Now when the boar and the dogs had gone into the castle, they began to wonder at finding a castle in a place where they had never before seen any building whatsoever. And from the top of the Gorsedd they looked and listened for the dogs. But so long as they were there they heard not one of the dogs nor aught concerning them.

"Lord," said Pryderi, "I will go into the castle to get tidings of the dogs." "Truly," he replied, "thou wouldst be unwise to go into this castle, which thou hast never seen till now. If thou wouldst follow my counsel, thou wouldst not enter therein. Whosoever has cast a spell over this land has caused this castle to be here." "Of a truth," answered Pryderi, "I cannot thus give up my dogs." And for all the counsel that Manawyddan gave him, yet to the castle he went.

When he came within the castle, neither man nor beast, nor boar nor dogs, nor house nor dwelling saw he within it. But in the centre of the castle floor he beheld a fountain with marble work around it, and on the margin of the fountain a golden bowl upon a marble slab, and chains hanging from the air, to which he saw no end.

And he was greatly pleased with the beauty of the gold, and with the rich workmanship of the bowl, and he went up to the bowl and laid hold of it. And when he had taken hold of it his hands stuck to the bowl, and his feet to the slab on which the howl was placed, and all his joyousness forsook him, so that he could not utter a word. And thus he stood.

And Manawyddan waited for him till near the close of the day. And late in the evening, being certain that he should have no tidings of Pryderi or of the dogs, he went back to the palace. And as he entered, Rhiannon looked at him. "Where," said she, "are thy companion and thy dogs?" "Behold," he answered, "the adventure that has befallen me." And he related it all unto her. "An evil companion hast thou been," said Rhiannon, "and a good companion hast thou lost." And with that word she went out, and proceeded towards the castle according to the direction which he gave her. The gate of the castle she found open. She was nothing daunted, and she went in. And as she went in, she perceived Pryderi laying hold of the bowl, and she went towards him. "Oh, my lord," said she, "what dust thou do here?" And she took hold of the bowl with him; and as she did so her hands became fast to the bowl, and her feet to the slab, and she was not able to utter a word. And with that, as it became night, lo, there came thunder upon them, and a fall of mist, and thereupon the castle vanished, and they with it.

When Kicva the daughter of Gwynn Gloyw saw that there was no one in the palace but herself and Manawyddan, she sorrowed so that she cared not whether she lived or died. And Manawyddan saw this. "Thou art in the wrong," said he, "if through fear of me thou grievest thus. I call Heaven to witness that thou hast never seen friendship mere pure than that which I will bear thee, as long as Heaven will that thou shouldst be thus. I declare to thee that were I in the dawn of youth I would keep my faith unto Pryderi, and unto thee also will I keep it. Be there no fear upon thee, therefore," said he, "for Heaven is my witness that thou shalt meet with all the friendship thou canst wish, and that it is in my power to show thee, as long as it shall please Heaven to continue us in this grief and woe." "Heaven reward thee," she said, "and that is what I deemed of thee." And the damsel thereupon took courage and was glad.

"Truly, lady," said Manawyddan, "it is not fitting for us to stay here, we have lost our dogs, and we cannot get food. Let us go into Lloegyr; it is easiest for us to find support there." "Gladly, lord," said she, "we will do so." And they set forth together to Lloegyr.

"Lord," said she, "what craft wilt thou follow? Take up one that is seemly." "None other will I take," answered he, "save that of making shoes, as I did formerly." "Lord," said she, "such a craft becomes not a man so nobly born as thou." "By that however will I abide," said he.

So he began his craft, and he made all his work of the finest leather he could get in the town, and, as he had done at the other place, he caused gilded clasps to be made for the shoes. And except himself all the cordwainers in the town were idle, and without work. For as long as they could be had from him, neither shoes nor hose were bought elsewhere. And thus they tarried there a year, until the cordwainers became envious, and took counsel concerning him. And he had warning thereof, and it was told him how the cordwainers had agreed together to slay him.

"Lord," said Kicva, "wherefore should this be borne from these boors?" "Nay," said he, "we will go back unto Dyved." So towards Dyved they set forth.

Now Manawyddan, when he set out to return to Dyved, took with him a burden of wheat. And he proceeded towards Narberth, and there he dwelt. And never was he better pleased than when he saw Narberth again, and the lands where he had been wont to hunt with Pryderi and with Rhiannon. And he accustomed himself to fish, and to hunt the deer in their covert. And then he began to prepare some ground, and he sowed a croft, and a second, and a third. And no wheat in the world ever sprung up better. And the three crofts prospered with perfect growth, and no man ever saw fairer wheat than it.

And thus passed the seasons of the year until the harvest came. And he went to look at one of his crofts, and behold it was ripe. "I will reap this to-morrow," said he. And that night he went back to Narberth, and on the morrow in the grey dawn he went to reap the croft, and when he came there he found nothing but the bare straw. Every one of the ears of the wheat was cut from off the stalk, and all the ears carried entirely away, and nothing but the straw left. And at this he marvelled greatly.

Then he went to look at another croft, and behold that also was ripe. "Verily," said he, "this will I reap to-morrow. And on the morrow he came with the intent to reap it, and when he came there he found nothing but the bare straw. "Oh, gracious Heaven," he exclaimed, "I know that whosoever has begun my ruin is completing it, and has also destroyed the country with me."

Then he went to look at the third croft, and when he came there, finer wheat had there never been seen, and this also was ripe. "Evil betide me," said he, "if I watch not here to-night. Whoever carried off the other corn will come in like manner to take this. And I will know who it is." So he took his arms, and began to watch the croft. And he told Kicva all that had befallen. "Verily," said she, "what thinkest thou to do?" "I will watch the croft to-night," said he.

And he went to watch the croft. And at midnight, lo, there arose the loudest tumult in the world. And he looked, and behold the mightiest host of mice in the world, which could neither be numbered nor measured. And he knew not what it was until the mice had made their way into the croft, and each of them climbing up the straw and bending it down with its weight, had cut off one of the ears of wheat, and had carried it away, leaving there the stalk, and he saw not a single stalk there that had not a mouse to it. And they all took their way, carrying the ears with them.

In wrath and anger did he rush upon the mice, but he could no more come up with them than if they had been gnats, or birds in the air, except one only, which though it was but sluggish, went so fast that a man on foot could scarce overtake it. And after this one he went, and he caught it and put it in his glove, and tied up the opening of the glove with a string, and kept it with him, and returned to the palace. Then he came to the hall where Kicva was, and he lighted a fire, and hung the glove by the string upon a peg. "What hast thou there, lord?" said Kicva. "A thief," said he, "that I found robbing me." "What kind of thief may it be, lord, that thou couldst put into thy glove?" said she. "Behold I will tell thee," he answered. Then he showed her how his fields had been wasted and destroyed, and how the mice came to the last of the fields in his sight. "And one of them was less nimble than the rest, and is now in my glove; to-morrow I will hang it, and before Heaven, if I had them, I would hang them all." "My lord," said she, "this is marvellous; but yet it would be unseemly for a man of dignity like thee to be hanging such a reptile as this. And if thou doest right, thou wilt not meddle with the creature, but wilt let it go." "Woe betide me," said he, "if I would not hang them all could I catch them, and such as I have I will hang." "Verily, lord," said she, "there is no reason that I should succour this reptile, except to prevent discredit unto thee. Do therefore, lord, as thou wilt." "If I knew of any cause in the world wherefore thou shouldst succour it, I would take thy counsel concerning it," said Manawyddan, "but as I know of none, lady, I am minded to destroy it." "Do so willingly then," said she.

And then he went to the Gorsedd of Narberth, taking the mouse with him. And he set up two forks on the highest part of the Gorsedd. And while he was doing this, behold he saw a scholar coming towards him, in old and poor and tattered garments. And it was now seven years since he had seen in that place either man or beast, except those four persons who had remained together until two of them were lost.

"My lord," said the scholar, "good day to thee." "Heaven prosper thee, and my greeting be unto thee. And whence dost thou come, scholar?" asked he. "I come, lord, from singing in Lloegyr; and wherefore dost thou inquire?" "Because for the last seven years," answered he, "I have seen no man here save four secluded persons, and thyself this moment." "Truly, lord," said he, "I go through this land unto mine own. And what work art thou upon, lord?" "I am hanging a thief that I caught robbing me," said he. "What manner of thief is that?" asked the scholar. "I see a creature in thy hand like unto a mouse, and ill does it become a man of rank equal to thine to touch a reptile such as this. Let it go forth free." "I will not let it go free, by Heaven," said he; "I caught it robbing me, and the doom of a thief will I inflict upon it, and I will hang it." "Lord," said he, "rather than see a man of rank equal to thine at such a work as this, I would give thee a pound which I have received as alms, to let the reptile go forth free." "I will not let it go free," said he, "by Heaven, neither will I sell it." "As thou wilt, lord," he answered; "except that I would not see a man of rank equal to thine touching such a reptile, I care nought." And the scholar went his way.

And as he was placing the crossbeam upon the two forks, behold a priest came towards him upon a horse covered with trappings. "Good day to thee, lord," said he. "Heaven prosper thee," said Manawyddan; "thy blessing." "The blessing of Heaven be upon thee. And what, lord, art thou doing?" "I am hanging a thief that I caught robbing me," said he. "What manner of thief, lord?" asked he. "A creature," he answered, "in form of a mouse. It has been robbing me, and I am inflicting upon it the doom of a thief." "Lord," said he, "rather than see thee touch this reptile, I would purchase its freedom." "By my confession to Heaven, neither will I sell it nor set it free." "It is true, lord, that it is worth nothing to buy; but rather than see thee defile thyself by touching such a reptile as this, I will give thee three pounds to let it go." "I will not, by Heaven," said he, "take any price for at. As it ought, so shall it be hanged." "Willingly, lord, do thy good pleasure." And the priest went his way.

Then he noosed the string around the mouse's neck, and as he was about to draw it up, behold, he saw a bishop's retinue with his sumpter-horses, and his attendants. And the bishop himself came towards him. And he stayed his work. "Lord bishop," said he, "thy blessing." "Heaven's blessing be unto thee," said he; "what work art thou upon?" "Hanging a thief that I caught robbing me," said he. "Is not that a mouse that I see in thy hand?" "Yes," answered he. "And she has robbed me." "Aye," said he, "since I have come at the doom of this reptile, I will ransom it of thee. I will give thee seven pounds for it, and that rather than see a man of rank equal to thine destroying so vile a reptile as this. Let it loose and thou shalt have the money." "I declare to Heaven that I will not set it loose." "If thou wilt not loose it for this, I will give thee four-and-twenty pounds of ready money to set it free." "I will not set it free, by Heaven, for as much again," said he. "If thou wilt not set it free for this, I will give thee all the horses that thou seest in this plain, and the seven loads of baggage, and the seven horses that they are upon." "By Heaven, I will not," he replied. "Since for this thou wilt not, do so at what price soever thou wilt." "I will do so," said he. "I will that Rhiannon and Pryderi be free," said he. "That thou shalt have," he answered. "Not yet will I loose the mouse, by Heaven." "What then wouldst thou?" "That the charm and the illusion be removed from the seven Cantrevs of Dyved." "This shalt thou have also; set therefore the mouse free." "I will not set it free, by Heaven," said he. "I will know who the mouse may be." "She is my wife." "Even though she be, I will not set her free. Wherefore came she to me?" "To despoil thee," he answered. "I am Llwyd the son of Kilcoed, and I cast the charm over the seven Cantrevs of Dyved. And it was to avenge Gwawl the son of Clud, from the friendship I had towards him, that I cast the charm. And upon Pryderi did I revenge Gwawl the son of Clud, for the game of Badger in the Bag, that Pwyll Pen Annwvyn played upon him, which he did unadvisedly in the Court of Heveydd Hên. And when it was known that thou wast come to dwell in the land, my household came and besought me to transform them into mice, that they might destroy thy corn. And it was my own household that went the first night. And the second night also they went, and they destroyed thy two crofts. And the third night came unto me my wife and the ladies of the Court, and besought me to transform them. And I transformed them. Now she is pregnant. And had she not been pregnant thou wouldst not have been able to overtake her; but since this has taken place, and she has been caught, I will restore thee Pryderi and Rhiannon; and I will take the charm and illusion from off Dyved. I have now told thee who she is. Set her therefore free." "I will not set her free, by Heaven," said he. "What wilt thou more?" he asked. "I will that there be no more charm upon the seven Cantrevs of Dyved, and that none shall be put upon it henceforth." "This thou shalt have," said he. "Now set her free." "I will not, by my faith," he answered. "What wilt thou furthermore?" asked he. "Behold," said he, "this will I have; that vengeance be never taken for this, either upon Pryderi or Rhiannon, or upon me." "All this shalt thou have. And truly thou hast done wisely in asking this. Upon thy head would have lighted all this trouble." "Yea," said he, "for fear thereof was it, that I required this." "Set now my wife at liberty." "I will not, by Heaven," said he, "until I see Pryderi and Rhiannon with me free." "Behold, here they come," he answered.

And thereupon behold Pryderi and Rhiannon. And he rose up to meet them, and greeted them, and sat down beside them. "Ah, Chieftain, set now my wife at liberty," said the bishop. "Hast thou not received all thou didst ask?" "I will release her gladly," said he. And thereupon he set her free.

Then Llwyd struck her with a magic wand, and she was changed back into a young woman, the fairest ever seen.

"Look around upon thy land," said he, "and then thou wilt see it all tilled and peopled, as it was in its best state." And he rose up and looked forth. And when he looked he saw all the lands tilled, and full of herds and dwellings. "What bondage," he inquired, "has there been upon Pryderi and Rhiannon?" "Pryderi has had the knockers of the gate of my palace about his neck, and Rhiannon has had the collars of the asses, after they have been carrying hay, about her neck."

And such had been their bondage.

And by reason of this bondage is this story called the Mabinogi of Mynnweir and Mynord.

And thus ends this portion of the Mabinogi.

NOTE ON
MANAWYDDAN THE SON OF LLYR

THE Prince who figures as the hero of the present Mabinogi, is the subject of two Triads, in one of which his singular adventures are thus alluded to:—

"Three Makers of Golden Shoes, of the Isle of Britain: Caswallawn the son of Beli, when he went as far as Gascony to obtain Flur, the daughter of Mygnach Gorr, who had been carried thither to Cæsar the Emperor, by one called Mwrchan the Thief, king of that country and friend of Julius Cæsar, and Caswallawn brought her back to the Isle of Britain; Manawyddan the son of Llyr Llediaith, when he was as far as Dyved laying restrictions; Llew Llaw Gyffes, when be was along with Gwydion, the son of Don, seeking a name and arms from Arianrod, his mother."—Triad 124.

In the other, he is represented as one of the humble princes of the Island, because, having cultivated minstrelsy after the captivity of his brother Bran, he would not afterwards resume his rank, although be might have done so.—Tr. 38.

Manawyddan is mentioned in the Dialogue between Arthur, Kai, and Glewlwyd; and his name occurs in connexion with that of Pryderi in the Poem on the Sons of Llyr, "Kerdd meib Llyr,"[1] of Taliesin.

The other principal personages whose names appear in this Mabinogi, are here passed over in silence, having been already made the subjects of various preceding notes.

It may be useful to remind the reader that Lloegyr is the Welsh name for the eastern and greater part of the island; and corresponds in modern usage with the word England.

---

1 Myv. Arch. I. 67, 167.

MATH THE SON OF MATHONWY

This is the Fourth Portion of the Mabinogi

MATH the son of Mathonwy[413a] was lord over Gwynedd, and Pryderi the son of Pwyll was lord over the one-and-twenty Cantrevs of the South; and these were the seven Cantrevs of Dyved, and the seven Cantrevs of Morganwc, the four Cantrevs of Ceredigiawn, and the three of Ystrad Tywi.

At that time, Math the son of Mathonwy could not exist unless his feet were in the lap of a maiden, except only when he was prevented by the tumult of war. Now the maiden who was with him was Goewin, the daughter of Pebin[413b] of Dôl Pebin, in Arvon, and she was the fairest maiden of her time who was known there.

And Math dwelt always at Caer Dathyl[413c], in Arvon, and was not able to go the circuit of the land, but Gilvaethwy the son of Don, and Eneyd the son of Don, his nephews, the sons of his sisters, with his household, went the circuit of the land in his stead.

Now the maiden was with Math continually, and Gilvaethwy the son of Don set his affections upon her, and loved her so that he knew not what he should do because of her, and therefrom behold his hue, and his aspect, and his spirits changed for love of her, so that it was not easy to know him.

One day his brother Gwydion[414a] gazed steadfastly upon him. "Youth," said he, "what aileth thee?" "Why," replied he, "what seest thou in me?" "I see," said he, "that thou hast lost thy aspect and thy hue; what, therefore, aileth thee?" "My lord brother," he answered, "that which aileth me, it will not profit me that I should own to any." "What may it be, my soul?" said he. "Thou knowest," he said, "that Math the son of Mathonwy has this property, that if men whisper together, in a tone how low soever, if the wind meet it, it becomes known unto him." "Yes," said Gwydion, "hold now thy peace, I know thy intent, thou lovest Goewin."

When he found that his brother knew his intent, he gave the heaviest sigh in the world. "Be silent, my soul, and sigh not," he said. "It is not thereby that thou wilt succeed. I will cause," said he, "if it cannot be otherwise, the rising of Gwynedd, and Powys, and Deheubarth, to seek the maiden. Be thou of glad cheer therefore, and I will compass it."

So they went unto Math the son of Mathonwy. "Lord," said Gwydion, "I have heard that there have come to the South some beasts, such as were never known in this island before." "What are they called?" he asked. "Pigs, lord." "And what kind of animals are they?" "They are small animals, and their flesh is better than the flesh of oxen." "They are small, then?" "And they change their names. Swine are they now called." "Who owneth them?" "Pryderi the son of Pwyll; they were sent him from Annwvyn, by Arawn the king of Annwvyn, and still they keep that name, half hog, half pig." "Verily," asked he, "and by what means may they be obtained from him?" "I will go, lord, as one of twelve, in the guise of bards, to seek the swine." "But it may be that he will refuse you," said he. "My journey will not be evil, lord," said he; "I will not come back without the swine." "Gladly," said he, "go thou forward."

So he and Gilvaethwy went, and ten other men with them. And they came into Ceredigiawn, to the place that is now called Rhuddlan Teivi, where the palace of Pryderi was. In the guise of bards they came in, and they were received joyfully, and Gwydion was placed beside Pryderi that night.

"Of a truth," said Pryderi, "gladly would I have a tale from some of your men yonder." "Lord," said Gwydion, "we have a custom that the first night that we come to the Court of a great man, the chief of song recites. Gladly will I relate a tale." Now Gwydion was the best teller of tales in the world, and he diverted all the Court that night with pleasant discourse and with tales, so that he charmed every one in the Court, and it pleased Pryderi to talk with him.

And after this, "Lord," said he unto Pryderi, "were it more pleasing to thee, that another should discharge my errand unto thee, than that I should tell thee myself what it is?" "No," he answered, "ample speech hast thou." "Behold then, lord," said he, "my errand. It is to crave from thee the animals that were sent thee from Annwvyn." "Verily," he replied, "that were the easiest thing in the world to grant, were there not a covenant between me and my land concerning them. And the covenant is that they shall not go from me, until they have produced double their number in the land." "Lord," said he, "I can set thee free from those words, and this is the way I can do so; give me not the swine to-night, neither refuse them unto me, and to-morrow I will show thee an exchange for them."

And that night he and his fellows went unto their lodging, and they took counsel. "Ah, my men," said he, "we shall not have the swine for the asking." "Well," said they, "how may they be obtained?" "I will cause them to be obtained," said Gwydion.

Then he betook himself to his arts, and began to work a charm. And he caused twelve chargers to appear, and twelve black greyhounds, each of them white-breasted, and having upon them twelve collars and twelve leashes, such as no one that saw them could know to be other than gold. And upon the horses twelve saddles, and every part which should have been of iron was entirely of gold, and the bridles were of the same workmanship. And with the horses and the dogs he came to Pryderi.

"Good day unto thee, lord," said he. "Heaven prosper thee," said the other, "and greetings be unto thee." "Lord," said he, "behold here is a release for thee from the word which thou spakest last evening concerning the swine; that thou wouldst neither give nor sell them. Thou mayest exchange them for that which is better. And I will give these twelve horses, all caparisoned as they are, with their saddles and their bridles, and these twelve greyhounds, with their collars and their leashes as thou seest, and the twelve gilded shields that thou beholdest yonder." Now these he had formed of fungus. "Well," said he, "we will take counsel." And they consulted together, and determined to give the swine to Gwydion, and to take his horses and his dogs and his shields.

Then Gwydion and his men took their leave, and began to journey forth with the pigs. "Ah, my comrades," said Gwydion, "it is needful that we journey with speed. The illusion will not last but from the one hour to the same to-morrow."

And that night they journeyed as far as the upper part of Ceredigiawn, to the place which, from that cause, is called Mochdrev still. And the next day they took their course through Melenydd, and came that night to the town which is likewise for that reason called Mochdrev between Keri and Arwystli. And thence they journeyed forward; and that night they came as far as that Commot in Powys, which also upon account thereof is called Mochnant, and there tarried they that night. And they journeyed thence to the Cantrev of Rhos, and the place where they were that night is still called Mochdrev.

"My men," said Gwydion, "we must push forward to the fastnesses of Gwynedd with these animals, for there is a gathering of hosts in pursuit of us." So they journeyed on to the highest town of Arllechwedd, and there they made a sty for the swine, and therefore was the name of Creuwyryon given to that town. And after they had made the sty for the swine, they proceeded to Math the son of Mathonwy, at Caer Dathyl. And when they came there, the country was rising. "What news is there here?" asked Gwydion. "Pryderi is assembling one-and-twenty Cantrevs to pursue after you," answered they. "It is marvellous that you should have journeyed so slowly." "Where are the animals whereof you went in quest?" said Math. "They have had a sty made for them in the other Cantrev below," said Gwydion.

Thereupon, lo, they heard the trumpets and the host in the land, and they arrayed themselves and set forward and came to Penardd in Arvon.

And at night Gwydion the son of Don, and Gilvaethwy his brother, returned to Caer Dathyl; and Gilvaethwy took Math the son of Mathonwy's couch. And while he turned out the other damsels from the room discourteously, he made Goewin unwillingly remain.

And when they saw the day on the morrow, they went back unto the place where Math the son of Mathonwy was with his host; and when they came there, the warriors were taking counsel in what district they should await the coming of Pryderi, and the men of the South. So they went in to the council. And it was resolved to wait in the strongholds of Gwynedd, in Arvon. So within the two Maenors they took their stand, Maenor Penardd and Maenor Coed Alun. And there Pryderi attacked them, and there the combat took place. And great was the slaughter on both sides; but the men of the South were forced to flee. And they fled unto the place which is still called Nantcall. And thither did they follow them, and they made a vast slaughter of them there, so that they fled again as far as the place called Dol Pen Maen, and there they halted and sought to make peace.

And that he might have peace, Pryderi gave hostages, Gwrgi Gwastra gave he and three-and-twenty others, sons of nobles. And after this they journeyed in peace even unto Traeth Mawr; but as they went on together towards Melenryd, the men on foot could not be restrained from shooting. Pryderi dispatched unto Math an embassy to pray him to forbid his people, and to leave it between him and Gwydion the son of Don, for that he had caused all this. And the messengers came to Math. "Of a truth," said Math, "I call Heaven to witness, if it be pleasing unto Gwydion the son of Don, I will so leave it gladly. Never will I compel any to go to fight, but that we ourselves should do our utmost."

"Verily," said the messengers, "Pryderi saith that it were more fair that the man who did him this wrong should oppose his own body to his, and let his people remain unscathed." "I declare to Heaven, I will not ask the men of Gwynedd to fight because of me. If I am allowed to fight Pryderi myself, gladly will I oppose my body to his." And this answer they took back to Pryderi. "Truly," said Pryderi, "I shall require no one to demand my rights but myself."

Then these two came forth and armed themselves, and they fought. And by force of strength, and fierceness, and by the magic and charms of Gwydion, Pryderi was slain. And at Maen Tyriawc, above Melenryd, was he buried, and there is his grave.

And the men of the South set forth in sorrow towards their own land; nor is it a marvel that they should grieve, seeing that they had lost their lord, and many of their best warriors, and for the most part their horses and their arms.

The men of Gwynedd went back joyful and in triumph. "Lord," said Gwydion unto Math, "would it not be right for us to release the hostages of the men of the South, which they pledged unto us for peace? for we ought not to put them in prison." "Let them then be set free," saith Math. So that youth, and the other hostages that were with him, were set free to follow the men of the South.

Math himself went forward to Caer Dathyl. Gilvaethwy the son of Don, and they of the household that were with him, went to make the circuit of Gwynedd as they were wont, without coming to the Court. Math went into his chamber, and caused a place to be prepared for him whereon to recline, so that he might put his feet in the maiden's lap. "Lord," said Goewin, "seek now another to hold thy feet, for I am now a wife." "What meaneth this?" said he. "An attack, lord, was made unawares upon me; but I held not my peace, and there was no one in the Court who knew not of it. Now the attack was made by thy nephews, lord, the sons of thy sister, Gwydion the son of Don, and Gilvaethwy the son of Don; unto me they did wrong, and unto thee dishonour." "Verily," he exclaimed, "I will do to the utmost of my power concerning this matter. But first I will cause thee to have compensation, and then will I have amends made unto myself. As for thee, I will take thee to be my wife, and the possession of my dominions will I give unto thy hands."

And Gwydion and Gilvaethwy came not near the Court, but stayed in the confines of the land until it was forbidden to give them meat and drink. At first they came not near unto Math, but at the last they came. "Lord," said they, "good day to thee." "Well," said he, "is it to make me compensation that ye are come?" "Lord," they said, "we are at thy will." "By my will I would not have lost my warriors, and so many arms as I have done. You cannot compensate me my shame, setting aside the death of Pryderi. But since ye come hither to be at my will, I shall begin your punishment forthwith."

Then he took his magic wand, and struck Gilvaethwy, so that he became a deer, and he seized upon the other hastily lest he should escape from him. And he struck him with the same magic wand, and he became a deer also. "Since now ye are in bonds, I will that ye go forth together and be companions, and possess the nature of the animals whose form ye bear. And this day twelvemonth come hither unto me."

At the end of a year from that day, lo there was a loud noise under the chamber wall, and the barking of the dogs of the palace together with the noise. "Look," said he, "what is without." "Lord," said one, "I have looked; there are there two deer, and a fawn with them." Then he arose and went out. And when he came he beheld the three animals. And he lifted up his wand. "As ye were deer last year, be ye wild hogs each and either of you, for the year that is to come." And thereupon he struck them with the magic wand. "The young one will I take and cause to be baptized." Now the name that he gave him was Hydwn. "Go ye and be wild swine, each and either of you, and be ye of the nature of wild swine. And this day twelvemonth be ye here under the wall."

At the end of the year the barking of dogs was heard under the wall of the chamber. And the Court assembled, and thereupon he arose and went forth, and when he came forth he beheld three beasts. Now these were the beasts that he saw; two wild hogs of the woods, and a well-grown young one with them. And he was very large for his age. "Truly," said Math, "this one will I take and cause to be baptized." And he struck him with his magic wand, and he become a fine fair auburn-haired youth, and the name that he gave him was Hychdwn. "Now as for you, as ye were wild hogs last year, be ye wolves each and either of you for the year that is to come." Thereupon he struck them with his magic wand, and they became wolves. "And be ye of like nature with the animals whose semblance ye bear, and return here this day twelvemonth beneath this wall."

And at the same day at the end of the year, he heard a clamour and a barking of dogs under the wall of the chamber. And he rose and went forth. And when he came, behold, he saw two wolves, and a strong cub with them. "This one will

I take," said Math, "and I will cause him to be baptized; there is a name prepared for him, and that is Bleiddwn. Now these three, such are they:—

> The three sons of Gilvaethwy the false,
> The three faithful combatants,
> Bleiddwn, Hydwn, and Hychdwn the Tall."

Then he struck the two with his magic wand, and they resumed their own nature. "Oh men," said he, "for the wrong that ye did unto me sufficient has been your punishment and your dishonour. Prepare now precious ointment for these men, and wash their heads, and equip them." And this was done.

And after they were equipped, they came unto him. "Oh men," said he, "you have obtained peace, and you shall likewise have friendship. Give your counsel unto me, what maiden I shall seek." "Lord," said Gwydion the son of Don, "it is easy to give thee counsel; seek Arianrod[421a], the daughter of Don, thy niece, thy sister's daughter."

And they brought her unto him, and the maiden came in. "Ha, damsel," said he, "art thou the maiden?" "I know not, lord, other than that I am." Then he took up his magic wand, and bent it. "Step over this," said he, "and I shall know if thou art the maiden." Then stepped she over the magic wand, and there appeared forthwith a fine chubby yellow-haired boy. And at the crying out of the boy, she went towards the door. And thereupon some small form was seen; but before any one could get a second glimpse of it, Gwydion had taken it, and had flung a scarf of velvet around it and hidden it. Now the place where he hid it was the bottom of a chest at the foot of his bed.

"Verily," said Math the son of Mathonwy, concerning the fine yellow-haired boy, "I will cause this one to be baptized, and Dylan is the name I will give him."

So they had the boy baptized, and as they baptized him he plunged into the sea. And immediately when he was in the sea, he took its nature, and swam as well as the best fish that was therein. And for that reason was he called Dylan, the son of the Wave[421b]. Beneath him no wave ever broke. And the blow whereby he came to his death, was struck by his uncle Govannon. The third fatal blow was it called.

As Gwydion lay one morning on his bed awake, he heard a cry in the chest at his feet; and though it was not loud, it was such that he could hear it. Then he arose in haste, and opened the chest: and when he opened it, he beheld an infant boy stretching out his arms from the folds of the scarf, and casting it aside. And he took up the boy in his arms, and carried him to a place where he knew there was a woman that could nurse him. And he agreed with the woman that she should take charge of the boy. And that year he was nursed.

And at the end of the year he seemed by his size as though he were two years old. And the second year he was a big child, and able to go to the Court by himself. And when he came to the Court, Gwydion noticed him, and the boy became familiar with him, and loved him better than any one else. Then was the boy reared at the Court until he was four years old, when he was as big as though he had been eight.

And one day Gwydion walked forth, and the boy followed him, and he went to the Castle of Arianrod[422a], having the boy with him; and when he came into the Court, Arianrod arose to meet him, and greeted him and bade him welcome. "Heaven prosper thee," said he. "Who is the boy that followeth thee?" she asked. "This youth, he is thy son," he answered. "Alas," said she, "what has come unto thee that thou shouldst shame me thus? wherefore dost thou seek my dishonour, and retain it so long as this?" "Unless thou suffer dishonour greater than that of my bringing up such a boy as this, small will be thy disgrace." "What is the name of the boy?" said she. "Verily," he replied, "he has not yet a name." "Well," she said, "I lay this destiny upon him, that he shall never have a name until he receives one from me." "Heaven bears me witness," answered he, "that thou art a wicked woman. But the boy shall have a name how displeasing soever it may be unto thee. As for thee, that which afflicts thee is that thou art no longer called a damsel." And thereupon he went forth in wrath, and returned to Caer Dathyl and there he tarried that night.

And the next day he arose and took the boy with him, and went to walk on the seashore between that place and Aber Menei. And there he saw some sedges and seaweed, and he turned them into a boat. And out of dry sticks and sedges he made some Cordovan leather, and a great deal thereof, and he coloured it in such a manner that no one ever saw leather more beautiful than it. Then he made a sail to the boat, and he and the boy went in it to the port of the castle of Arianrod. And he began forming shoes and stitching them, until he was observed from the castle. And when he knew that they of the castle were observing him, he disguised his aspect, and put another semblance upon himself, and upon the boy, so that they might not be known. "What men are those in yonder boat?" said Arianrod. "They are cordwainers," answered they. "Go and see what kind of leather they have, and what kind of work they can do."

So they came unto them. And when they came he was colouring some Cordovan leather, and gilding it. And the messengers came and told her this. "Well," said she, "take the measure of my foot, and desire the cordwainer to make shoes for me." So he made the shoes for her, yet not according to the measure, but larger. The shoes then were brought unto her, and behold they were too large. "These are too large," said she, "but he shall receive their value. Let him also make some that are smaller than they." Then he made her others that were much smaller than her foot, and sent them unto her. "Tell him that these will not go on my feet," said she. And they told him this. "Verily," said he, "I will not make her any shoes, unless I see her foot." And this was told unto her. "Truly," she answered, "I will go unto him."

So she went down to the boat, and when she came there, he was shaping shoes and the boy stitching them. "Ah, lady," said he, "good day to thee." "Heaven prosper thee," said she. "I marvel that thou canst not manage to make shoes according to a measure." "I could not," he replied, "but now I shall be able."

Thereupon behold a wren stood upon the deck of the boat, and the boy shot at it, and hit it in the leg between the sinew and the bone. Then she smiled. "Verily," said she, "with a steady hand did the lion aim at it." "Heaven reward thee not, but now has he got a name. And a good enough name it is. Llew Llaw Gyffes[424a] be he called henceforth."

Then the work disappeared in seaweed and sedges, and he went on with it no further. And for that reason was he called the third Gold-shoemaker. "Of a truth," said she, "thou wilt not thrive the better for doing evil unto me." "I have done thee no evil yet," said he. Then he restored the boy to his own form. "Well," said she, "I will lay a destiny upon this boy, that he shall never have arms and armour until I invest him with them." "By Heaven," said he, "let thy malice be what it may, he shall have arms."

Then they went towards Dinas Dinllev[424b], and there he brought up Llew Llaw Gyffes, until he could manage any horse, and he was perfect in features, and strength, and stature. And then Gwydion saw that he languished through the want of horses and arms. And he called him unto him. "Ah, youth," said he, "we will go to-morrow on an errand together. Be therefore more cheerful than thou art." "That I will," said the youth.

Next morning, at the dawn of day, they arose. And they took way along the sea coast, up towards Bryn Aryen. And at the top of Cevn Clydno they equipped themselves with horses, and went towards the Castle of Arianrod. And they changed their form, and pricked towards the gate in the semblance of two youths, but the aspect of Gwydion was more staid than that of the other. "Porter," said he, "go thou in and say that there are here bards from Glamorgan." And the porter went in. "The welcome of Heaven be unto them, let them in," said Arianrod.

With great joy were they greeted. And the hall was arranged, and they went to meat. When meat was ended, Arianrod discoursed with Gwydion of tales and stories. Now Gwydion was an excellent teller of tales. And when it was time to leave off feasting, a chamber was prepared for them, and they went to rest.

In the early twilight Gwydion arose, and he called unto him his magic and his power. And by the time that the day dawned, there resounded through the land uproar, and trumpets and shouts. When it was now day, they heard a knocking at the door of the chamber, and therewith Arianrod asking that it might be opened. Up rose the youth and opened unto her, and she entered and a maiden with her. "Ah, good men," she said, "in evil plight are we." "Yes, truly," said Gwydion, "we have heard trumpets and shouts; what thinkest thou that they may mean?" "Verily," said she, "we cannot see the colour of the ocean by reason of all the ships, side by side. And they are making for the land with all the speed they can. And what can we do?" said she. "Lady," said Gwydion, "there is none other counsel than to close the castle upon us, and to defend it as best we may." "Truly," said she, "may Heaven reward you. And do you defend it. And here may you have plenty of arms."

And thereupon went she forth for the arms, and behold she returned, and two maidens, and suits of armour for two men, with her. "Lady," said he, "do you accoutre this stripling, and I will arm myself with the help of thy maidens. Lo, I hear the tumult of the men approaching." "I will do so, gladly." So she armed him fully, and that right cheerfully. "Hast thou finished arming the youth?" said he. "I have finished," she answered. "I likewise have finished," said Gwydion. "Let us now take off our arms, we have no need of them." "Wherefore?" said she. "Here is the army around the house." "Oh, lady, there is here no army." "Oh," cried she, "whence then was this tumult?" "The tumult was but to break thy prophecy and to obtain arms for thy son. And now has he got arms without any thanks unto thee." "By Heaven," said Arianrod, "thou art a wicked man. Many a youth might have lost his life through the uproar thou hast caused in this Cantrev to-day. Now will I lay a destiny upon this youth," she said, "that he shall never have a wife of the race that now inhabits this earth." "Verily," said he, "thou wast ever a malicious woman, and no one ought to support thee. A wife shall he have notwithstanding."

They went thereupon unto Math the son of Mathonwy, and complained unto him most bitterly of Arianrod. Gwydion showed him also how he had procured arms for the youth. "Well," said Math, "we will seek, I and thou, by charms and illusion, to form a wife for him out of flowers. He has now come to man's stature, and he is the comeliest youth that was ever beheld." So they took the blossoms of the oak, and the blossoms of the broom, and the blossoms of the meadow-sweet, and produced from them a maiden, the fairest and most graceful that man ever saw. And they baptized her, and gave her the name of Blodeuwedd[426a].

After she had become his bride, and they had feasted, said Gwydion, "It is not easy for a man to maintain himself without possessions." "Of a truth," said Math, "I will give the young man the best Cantrev to hold." "Lord," said he, "what Cantrev is that?" "The Cantrev of Dinodig," he answered. Now it is called at this day Eivionydd and Ardudwy. And the place in the Cantrev where he dwelt, was a palace of his in a spot called Mur y Castell[426b], on the confines of Ardudwy. There dwelt he and reigned, and both he and his sway were beloved by all.

One day he went forth to Caer Dathyl, to visit Math the son of Mathonwy. And on the day that he set out for Caer Dathyl, Blodeuwedd walked in the Court. And she heard the sound of a horn. And after the sound of the horn, behold a tired stag went by, with dogs and huntsmen following it. And after the dogs and the huntsmen there came a crowd of men on foot. "Send a youth," said she, "to ask who yonder host may be." So a youth went, and inquired who they were.

"Gronw Pebyr is this, the lord of Penllyn," said they. And thus the youth told her.

Gronw Pebyr pursued the stag, and by the river Cynvael he overtook the stag and killed it. And what with flaying the stag and baiting his dogs, he was there until the night began to close in upon him. And as the day departed and the night drew near, he came to the gate of the Court. "Verily," said Blodeuwedd, "the Chieftain will speak ill of us if we let him at this hour depart to another land without inviting him in." "Yes, truly, lady," said they, "it will be most fitting to invite him."

Then went messengers to meet him and bid him in. And he accepted her bidding gladly, and came to the Court, and Blodeuwedd went to meet him, and greeted him, and bade him welcome. "Lady," said he, "Heaven repay thee thy kindness."

When they had disaccoutred themselves, they went to sit down. And Blodeuwedd looked upon him, and from the moment that she looked on him she became filled with his love. And he gazed on her, and the same thought came unto him as unto her, so that he could not conceal from her that he loved her, but he declared unto her that he did so. Thereupon she was very joyful. And all their discourse that night was concerning the affection and love which they felt one for the other, and which in no longer space than one evening had arisen. And that evening passed they in each other's company.

The next day he sought to depart. But she said, "I pray thee go not from me to-day." And that night he tarried also. And that night they consulted by what means they might always be together. "There is none other counsel," said he, "but that thou strive to learn from Llew Llaw Gyffes in what manner he will meet his death. And this must thou do under the semblance of solicitude concerning him."

The next day Gronw sought to depart. "Verily," said she, "I will counsel thee not to go from me to-day." "At thy instance will I not go," said he, "albeit, I must say, there is danger that the chief who owns the palace may return home." "To-morrow," answered she, "will I indeed permit thee to go forth."

The next day he sought to go, and she hindered him not. "Be mindful," said Gronw, "of what I have said unto thee, and converse with him fully, and that under the guise of the dalliance of love, and find out by what means he may come to his death."

That night Llew Llaw Gyffes returned to his home. And the day they spent in discourse, and minstrelsy, and feasting. And at night they went to rest, and he spoke to Blodeuwedd once, and he spoke to her a second time. But, for all this, he could not get from her one word. "What aileth thee?" said he, "art thou well?" "I was thinking," said she, "of that which thou didst never think of concerning me; for I was sorrowful as to thy death, lest thou shouldst go sooner than I." "Heaven reward thy care for me," said he, "but until Heaven take me I shall not easily be slain" "For the sake of Heaven, and for mine, show me how thou mightest be slain. My memory in guarding is better than thine." "I will tell thee gladly," said he. "Not easily can I be slain, except by a wound. And the spear wherewith I am struck must be a year in the forming. And nothing must be done towards it except during the sacrifice on Sundays." "Is this certain?" asked she. "It is in truth," he answered. "And I cannot be slain within a house, nor without. I cannot be slain on horseback nor on foot." "Verily," said she, "in what manner then canst thou be slain?" "I will tell thee," said he. "By making a bath for me by the side of a river, and by putting a roof over the cauldron, and thatching it well and tightly, and bringing a buck, and putting it beside the cauldron. Then if I place one foot on the buck's back, and the other on the edge of the cauldron, whosoever strikes me thus will cause my death." "Well," said she, "I thank Heaven that it will be easy to avoid this."

No sooner had she held this discourse than she sent to Gronw Pebyr. Gronw toiled at making the spear, and that day twelvemonth it was ready. And that very day he caused her to be informed thereof.

"Lord," said Blodeuwedd unto Llew, "I have been thinking how it is possible that what thou didst tell me formerly can be true; wilt thou show me in what manner thou couldst stand at once upon the edge of a cauldron and upon a buck, if I prepare the bath for thee?" "I will show thee," said he.

Then she sent unto Gronw, and bade him be in ambush on the hill which is now called Bryn Kyvergyr, on the bank of the river Cynvael. She caused also to be collected all the goats that were in the Cantrev, and had them brought to the other side of the river, opposite Bryn Kyvergyr.

And the next day she spoke thus. "Lord," said she, "I have caused the roof and the bath to be prepared, and lo! they are ready." "Well," said Llew, "we will go gladly to look at them."

The day after they came and looked at the bath. "Wilt thou go into the bath, lord?" said she. "Willingly will I go in," he answered. So into the bath he went, and he anointed himself. "Lord," said she, "behold the animals which thou didst speak of as being called bucks." "Well," said he, "cause one of them to be caught and brought here." And the buck was brought. Then Llew rose out of the bath, and put on his trowsers, and he placed one foot on the edge of the bath and the other on the buck's back.

Thereupon Gronw rose up from the hill which is called Bryn Kyvergyr, and he rested on one knee, and flung the poisoned dart and struck him on the side, so that the shaft started out, but the head of the dart remained in. Then he flew up in the form of an eagle and gave a fearful scream. And thenceforth was he no more seen.

As soon as he departed Gronw and Blodeuwedd went together unto the palace that night. And the next day Gronw arose and took possession of Ardudwy. And after he had overcome the land, he ruled over it, so that Ardudwy and Penllyn were both under his sway.

Then these tidings reached Math the son of Mathonwy. And heaviness and grief came upon Math, and much more upon Gwydion than upon him. "Lord," said Gwydion, "I shall never rest until I have tidings of my nephew." "Verily," said Math, "may Heaven be thy strength." Then Gwydion set forth and began to go forward. And he went through Gwynedd and Powys to the confines. And when he had done so, he went into Arvon, and came to the house of a vassal, in Maenawr Penardd. And he alighted at the house, and stayed there that night. The man of the house and his house-hold came in, and last of all came there the swineherd. Said the man of the house to the swineherd, "Well, youth, hath thy sow come in to-night?" "She hath," said he, "and is this instant returned to the pigs." "Where doth this sow go to?" said Gwydion. "Every day, when the sty is opened, she goeth forth and none can catch sight of her, neither is it known whither she goeth more than if she sank into the earth." "Wilt thou grant unto me," said Gwydion, "not to open the sty until I am beside the sty with thee?" "This will I do, right gladly," he answered.

That night they went to rest; and as soon as the swineherd saw the light of day, he awoke Gwydion. And Gwydion arose and dressed himself, and went with the swineherd, and stood beside the sty. Then the swineherd opened the sty. And as soon as he opened it, behold she leaped forth, and set off with great speed. And Gwydion followed her, and she went against the course of a river, and made for a brook, which is now called Nant y Llew. And there she halted and began feeding. And Gwydion came under the tree, and looked what it might be that the sow was feeding on. And he saw that she was eating putrid flesh and vermin. Then looked he up to the top of the tree, and as he looked he beheld on the top of the tree an eagle, and when the eagle shook itself, there fell vermin and putrid flesh from off it, and these the sow devoured. And it seemed to him that the eagle was Llew. And he sang an Englyn:—

> "Oak that grows between the two banks;
> Darkened is the sky and hill!
> Shall I not tell him by his wounds,
> That this is Llew?"

Upon this the eagle came down until he reached the centre of the tree. And Gwydion sang another Englyn:—

> "Oak that grows in upland ground,
> Is it not wetted by the rain? Has it not been drenched
> By nine score tempests?
> It bears in its branches Llew Llaw Gyffes!"

Then the eagle came down until he was on the lowest branch of the tree, and thereupon this Englyn did Gwydion sing:—

"Oak that grows beneath the steep;
Stately and majestic is its aspect!
Shall I not speak it?
That Llew will come to my lap?"

And the eagle came down upon Gwydion's knee. And Gwydion struck him with his magic wand, so that he returned to his own form. No one ever saw a more piteous sight, for he was nothing but skin and bone.

Then he went unto Caer Dathyl, and there were brought unto him good physicians that were in Gwynedd, and before the end of the year he was quite healed.

"Lord," said he unto Math the son of Mathonwy, "it is full time now that I have retribution of him by whom I have suffered all this woe." "Truly," said Math, "he will never be able to maintain himself in the possession of that which is thy right." "Well," said Llew, "the sooner I have my right, the better shall I be pleased."

Then they called together the whole of Gwynedd, and set forth to Ardudwy. And Gwydion went on before and proceeded to Mur y Castell. And when Blodeuwedd heard that he was coming, she took her maidens with her, and fled to the mountain. And they passed through the river Cynvael, and went towards a court that there was upon the mountain, and through fear they could not proceed except with their faces looking backwards, so that unawares they fell into the lake. And they were all drowned except Blodeuwedd herself, and her Gwydion overtook. And he said unto her, "I will not slay thee, but I will do unto thee worse than that. For I will turn thee into a bird; and because of the shame thou hast done unto Llew Llaw Gyffes, thou shalt never show thy face in the light of day henceforth; and that through fear of all the other birds. For it shall be their nature to attack thee, and to chase thee from wheresoever they may find thee. And thou shalt not lose thy name, but shalt be always called Blodeuwedd." Now Blodeuwedd is an owl in the language of this present time, and for this reason is the owl hateful unto all birds. And even now the owl is called Blodeuwedd.

Then Gronw Pebyr[432a] withdrew unto Penllyn, and he dispatched thence an embassy. And the messengers he sent asked Llew Llaw Gyffes if he would take land, or domain, or gold, or silver, for the injury he had received. "I will not, by my confession to Heaven," said he. "Behold this is the least that I will accept from him; that he come to the spot where I was when he wounded me with the dart, and that I stand where he did, and that with a dart I take my aim at him. And this is the very least that I will accept."

And this was told unto Gronw Pebyr. "Verily," said he, "is it needful for me to do thus? My faithful warriors, and my household, and my foster-brothers, is there not one among you who will stand the blow in my stead?" "There is not, verily," answered they. And because of their refusal to suffer one stroke for their lord, they are called the third disloyal tribe even unto this day. "Well," said he, "I will meet it."

Then they two went forth to the banks of the river Cynvael, and Gronw stood in the place where Llew Llaw Gyffes was when he struck him, and Llew in the place where Gronw was. Then said Gronw Pebyr unto Llew, "Since it was through the wiles of a woman that I did unto thee as I have done, I adjure thee by Heaven to let me place between me and the blow, the slab thou seest yonder on the river's bank." "Verily," said Llew, "I will not refuse thee this." "Ah," said he, "may Heaven reward thee." So Gronw took the slab and placed it between him and the blow.

Then Llew flung the dart at him, and it pierced the slab and went through Gronw likewise, so that it pierced through his back. And thus was Gronw Pebyr slain. And there is still the slab on the bank of the river Cynvael, in Ardudwy, having the hole through it. And therefore is it even now called Llech Gronw.

A second time did Llew Llaw Gyffes take possession of the land, and prosperously did he govern it. And, as the story relates, he was lord after this over Gwynedd. And thus ends this portion of the Mabinogi.

NOTES TO
MATH THE SON OF MATHONWY

413a — MATH THE SON OF MATHONWY

THE fame of Math ab Mathonwy's magic, in which he would seem to have excelled all the enchanters of Welsh fiction (except, perhaps, the mighty Merlin and his own pupil, Gwydion the son of Don), is preserved in two separate Triads (xxxi. and xxxii.), where, he is styled a man of illusion and phantasy, and where one of the chief enchantments of the Island is attributed to him. Another version of the latter has already been given.

The mystical arts of Math appear to have descended to him from his father, whose magic wand is celebrated by Taliesin, in the Kerdd Daronwy. It is there asserted that when this wand grows in the wood, more luxuriant fruit will be seen on the banks of the Spectre waters.[1]

Taliesin also frequently speaks of the powers of Math himself.—See the Cadd Goddeu, Marwnad Aeddon o Vôn, &c.[2]

The Tale of Math ab Mathonwy has been already printed, with a translation in the Cambrian Quarterly.

413b — GOEWIN, DAUGHTER OF PEBIN

THE singular occupation assigned to this damsel in the Tale, is by no means inconsistent with the ancient customs of Wales. By the laws of Howel Dda, we learn that there was an officer at the king's court, called "The Footholder," whose especial duty was such as that title implies. The following particulars are given concerning him.

> "The Footholder is to sit under the King's feet
> He is to eat from the same dish as the King.
> He shall light the candles before the King at his meal.
> He shall have a dish of meat and liquor, though he is not top join
>   in the feast.
> His land shall be free, and he shall receive a horse from the King and
>   shall have a share of the visitors' gift money."

1 Myv. Arch. I. p. 63.

2 Myv. Arch. I. p. 30, 70.

413c — CAER DATHYL

CAER DATHYL in Arvon (the present Caernarvonshire), where Math is said to have held his court, and whence Gwydion set out on his mischievous journey, has been already noticed. The remains of this fortress are now called Pen y Gaer. They are situated on the summit of a hill, about a mile distant from Llanbedr, in Caernarvonshire, midway between Llanrwst and Conway. It appears to have been well defended by deep moats, which yet surround it. Foundations of circular buildings may still be traced in its vicinity. From this place Gwydion's route was in a southerly direction, and he found Pryderi at a place called Rhuddlan Teivi (possibly Glan Teivy, about a mile and a half from Cardigan Bridge), where we are told that his palace then was. Returning with his prize, he passed by Mochdrev (or Swine's Town), in Cardiganshire, to Elenid, most likely an error of the transcriber's for Melenid, a mountain near Llanddewi Ystrad Enni, in Radnorshire, which gives its name to the whole Cantrev. Thence, by the Mochdrev, between Keri and Arwystli, in Montgomeryshire, we find him entering the Commot of Mochnant (Swine's Brook), which is partly in Montgomery, and partly in Denbighshire, and in which the town of Castell y Moch (Swine's Castle) would seem to point out another allusion to the singular companions of his hasty retreat. Gwydion stopped at a third Mochdrev, in Denbighshire, now a village between Conway and Abergele, in the ancient Cantrev of Rhos, and rejoined his prince at Caer Dathyl, after placing his booty, in safety in the strongholds of Arllechwedd, a name applied formerly to two commots (Upper and Lower) of Arvon, which are at this time cursorily called Uchav and Isav.

The places between which Math the son of Mathonwy took his stand, and awaited the approach of the injured Pryderi, may be recognised as Maenor Penardd, near to Conway, and Maenor Alun, now Coed Helen, near Caernarvon. Nant Call, to which the men of the South were compelled to retreat, is a brook crossing the Dolpenmaen and Caernarvon road, about nine miles from the latter town. The course of the two armies may be easily traced from Nant Call to the well-known locality of Dolpenmaen (in the ancient Cantrev of Dunodig, now the hundred of Eivionydd); thence across the Traeth Mawr to Melenryd, and at length along the picturesque valley of Ffestiniog to Maen Twrog, where the expedition terminated in the ignoble victory obtained by Math through the agency of enchantment, and in the death of the gallant son of Pwyll. We are here told that he was buried at Maen Twrawg; the Beddau Milwyr, however, as has already been mentioned, place the grave of Pryderi at Abergenoli, "where the wave beats against the shore."

414a — GWYDION THE SON OF DON

GWYDION, as already seen in Triad 85, was one of the three famous tribe-herdsmen of the Island, and tended the cattle of Gwynedd Uch Conwy. He was also a great astronomer, and as such was classed with Gwynn ab Nudd, and Idris.[1] The Milky-way is after him termed Caer Gwydion: similar honours indeed appear to have been paid to the whole family of Don. Himself gave his name to the constellation of Cassiopeia, in Welsh, Llys Don, the Court of Don; and Caer Arianrod, Corona Borealis, is so called after his daughter Arianrod, one of the heroines of the present Tale.

Gwydion was an enchanter, and, as has been already noticed, learnt his magical arts from Math himself. As such he is repeatedly alluded to in the poems of the Welsh, especially in those of Taliesin. The remarkable instances of his powers of incantation, as displayed in the present Tale, are thus related in the composition ascribed to that Bard, entitled Kadeir Kerridwen.

"Gwydion the son of Don, of toil severe,
Formed a woman out of flowers,
And brought the pigs from the South,
Though he had no pigstyes for them
The bold traveller out of plaited twigs
Formed a cavalcade,
And perfect saddles."[2]

In another place (Cad Goddeu) Taliesin says of him,—

Minstrels have sung,
Armies have admired,
The exalting of Britons,
Achieved by Gwydion."[3]

He appears in the double character of seer and poet, in the lines (already quoted) composed by him on the Cad Goddeu, or Battle of the Trees, in which his brother Amaethon fought against Arawn king of Annwn, about a white roebuck and a whelp, which he had carried off from the realms of darkness. The party who should guess the name of a particular person among his opponents in this fight, was to be victor, and Gwydion, by his divinations, accomplished

1 Tri. 89, sec. ii. p. 325.

2 Myv. Arch. I. p. 66.

3 Myv. Arch. I. p. 29.

the required condition on behalf of Amaethon, in consequence of which he prevailed.

Two of his other brothers, Govannon and Eunydd, are also celebrated by the Bards, and to the latter of them magic powers are especially assigned.—See Marwnad Aeddon o Vôn. Myv. Arch. I. p. 70.

The grave of Gwydion ab Don has not been left unrecorded; it was in Morva Dinllev, the scene of one of his adventures with Llew Llaw Gyffes.

421a — ARIANROD

THE "Silver circled " daughter of Don, was one of the three beauteous ladies of the Island.—Tr. 107.

It has already been noticed that the Welsh name the constellation of the Corona Borealis after her, Caer Arianrod.

Besides Dylan Eil Don and Llew Llaw Gyffes, we find that Gwenwynwyn and Gwanar were sons of Arianrod, by her alliance with Lliaws ab Nwyvre.—See Tr. 14.

421b — DYLAN THE SON OF THE WAVE

THIS passage would appear to point at a Triad on the subject of this "Trydydd anvad ergyd," but none is to be found among those printed in the Myvyrian Archaiology.

In the Llyvyr Taliesin, preserved in the Hengwrt Collection, there is a short composition attributed to Taliesin, entitled "Marwnad Dylan Ail Ton." It is printed in the Cambro-Briton, I. 150.

422a — THE CASTLE OF ARIANROD

THE Rev. P. B. Williams, in his "Tourist's Guide through Caernarvonshire," speaking of Clynnog in that county, says: "There is a tradition that an ancient British town, situated near this place, called Caer Arianrhod, was swallowed up by the sea, the ruins of which, it is said, are still visible during neap tides, and in fine weather."

424a — LLEW LLAW GYFFES

THE incident related in the tale of the journey of Llew Llaw Gyffes (the Lion with the steady hand), with Gwydion mab Don, in the disguise of a maker of gold-coloured shoes, to seek a name and arms from his mother Arianrod, forms the subject of a Triad which has already been quoted.

Llew Llaw Gyffes was one of the three crimson-stained ones of the Island, than whom, however, Arthur was more conspicuous, for where he had trod neither herb nor grass sprang up for the space of a year.—Tr. xxiv.

His grave is noticed in the Englynion y Beddau Milwyr Ynys Prydain, as being protected by the sea.[1]

Melyngan mangre, the horse of Llew Llaw Gyffes, was one of the chief war-horses of the island.[2]

424b — DINLLEV

DINAS DINLLE is situated on the sea-shore, about three miles southward from Caernarvon, in the parish of Llantwrawg, on the confines of a large tract of land, called Morva Dinlleu. The remains of the fortress consist of a large circular mount, well defended by earthen ramparts and deep fosses.

426a — BLODEUWEDD

THE story of Blodeuwedd, the fair Flower-aspect, has ever been popular with the poets. Taliesin's lines relating to her romantic origin have been already given in the note upon Gwydion ab Don, and Davydd ap Gwilym has a very pretty poem on the subject of her transformation into an owl, where, after some preliminary questions as to the cause of her singular and retired habits, the poet proceeds to inquire her history and her name. The bird replies that formerly by nobles at the banquet she was called Blodeuwedd, and she swears by St. David that she is a daughter of a lord of Mona, equal in dignity to Meirchion himself.

And she goes on to say that Gwydion, the son of Don, on the Conway, transformed her with his magic wand from her state of beauty to her present misery, because she once presumed to love Goronwy, the tall and comely, the son of Perf Goronhir, lord of Penllyn.

---

1 Myv. Arch. I. p. 80.

2 Tr. Meirch. ii. ix.

426b — MUR Y CASTELL

MUR Y CASTELL, on the confines of Ardudwy, also called Tomen y Mur, is about two miles south of the Cynvael or Ffestiniog River, and distant about three miles from the Llyn y Morwynion, or Lake of the Maidens, in which the unfortunate damsels of Blodeuwedd met their untimely fate.

432a — TRIBE OF GORONWY PEBYR

A TRIAD (xxxv.) recites the circumstance of the want of devotion evinced by his tribe, as detailed in the text.

"The three disloyal Tribes of the Isle of Britain.—The Tribe of Goronwy Pebyr of Penllyn, who refused to stand instead of their lord to receive the poisoned dart from Llew Llaw Gyffes, by Llech Goronwy, at Blaen Cynvael, in Ardudwy. And the Tribe of Gwrgi and Peredur, who deserted their lords in Caer Greu, where there was an appointment for battle next morning against Eda Glinmawr, and they were both slain. And the third, the Tribe of Alan Vyrgan who returned back by stealth from their lord, leaving him and his servants going to Camlan, where he was slain."

Penllyn, of which Gronw was lord, is a commot on the borders of Llyn Tegid, or Bala Lake.

THE DREAM OF MAXEN WLEDIG

MAXEN WLEDIG[443a] was emperor of Rome, and he was a comelier man, and a better and a wiser than any emperor that had been before him. And one day he held a council of kings, and he said to his friends, "I desire to go to-morrow to hunt." And the next day in the morning he set forth with his retinue, and came to the valley of the river that flowed towards Rome. And he hunted through the valley until mid-day. And with him also were two-and-thirty crowned kings, that were his vassals; not for the delight of hunting went the emperor with them, but to put himself on equal terms with those kings.

And the sun was high in the sky over their heads and the heat was great. And sleep came upon Maxen Wledig. And his attendants stood and set up their shields around him upon the shafts of their spears to protect him from the sun, and they placed a gold enamelled shield under his head; and so Maxen slept.

And he saw a dream. And this is the dream that he saw. He was journeying along the valley of the river towards its source; and he came to the highest mountain in the world. And he thought that the mountain was as high as the sky; and when he came over the mountain, it seemed to him that he went through the fairest and most level regions that man ever yet beheld, on the other side of the mountain. And he saw large and mighty rivers descending from the mountain to the sea, and towards the mouths of the rivers he proceeded. And as he journeyed thus, he came to the mouth of the largest river ever seen. And he beheld a great city at the entrance of the river, and a vast castle in the city, and he saw many high towers of various colours in the castle. And he saw a fleet at the mouth of the river, the largest ever seen. And he saw one ship among the fleet; larger was it by far, and fairer than all the others. Of such part of the ship as he could see above the water, one plank was gilded and the other silvered over. He saw a bridge of the bone of a whale from the ship to the land, and he thought that he went along the bridge, and came into the ship. And a sail was hoisted on the ship, and along the sea and the ocean was it borne. Then it seemed that he came to the fairest island in the whole world, and he traversed the island from sea to sea, even to the furthest shore of the island. Valleys he saw, and steeps, and rocks of wondrous height, and rugged precipices. Never yet saw he the like. And thence he beheld an island in the sea, facing this rugged land. And between him and this island was a country of which the plain was as large as the sea, the mountain as vast as the wood. And from the mountain he saw a river that flowed through the land and fell into the sea. And at the mouth of the river he beheld a castle, the fairest that man ever saw, and the gate of the castle was open, and he went into the castle. And in the castle he saw a fair hall, of which the roof seemed to be all gold, the walls of the hall seemed to be entirely of glittering precious gems, the doors all seemed to be of gold. Golden seats he saw in the hall, and silver tables. And on a seat opposite to him he beheld two auburn-haired youths playing at chess. He saw a silver board for the chess, and golden pieces thereon. The garments of the youths were of jet-black satin, and chaplets of ruddy gold bound their hair, whereon were sparkling jewels of great price, rubies, and gems, alternately with imperial stones. Buskins of new Cordovan leather on their feet, fastened by slides of red gold.

And beside a pillar in the hall he saw a hoary-headed man, in a chair of ivory, with the figures of two eagles of ruddy gold thereon. Bracelets of gold were upon his arms, and many rings were on his hands, and a golden torque about his neck; and his hair was bound with a golden diadem. He was of powerful aspect. A chessboard of gold was before him, and a rod of gold, and a steel file in his hand. And he was carving out chessmen.

And he saw a maiden sitting before him in a chair of ruddy gold. Not more easy than to gaze upon the sun when brightest, was it to look upon her by reason of her beauty. A vest of white silk was upon the maiden, with clasps of red gold at the breast; and a surcoat of gold tissue upon her, and a frontlet of red gold upon her head, and rubies and gems were in the frontlet, alternating with pearls and imperial stones. And a girdle of ruddy gold was around her. She was the fairest sight that man ever beheld.

The maiden arose from her chair before him, and he threw his arms about the neck of the maiden, and they two sat down together in the chair of gold: and the chair was not less roomy for them both, than for the maiden alone. And as he had his arms about the maiden's neck, and his cheek by her cheek, behold, through the chafing of the dogs at their leashing, and the clashing of the shields as they struck against each other, and the beating together of the shafts of the spears, and the neighing of the horses and their prancing, the emperor awoke.

And when he awoke, nor spirit nor existence was left him, because of the maiden whom he had seen in his sleep, for the love of the maiden pervaded his whole frame. Then his household spake unto him. "Lord," said they, "is it not past the time for thee to take thy food?" Thereupon the emperor mounted his palfrey, the saddest man that mortal ever saw, and went forth towards Rome.

And thus he was during the space of a week. When they of the household went to drink wine and mead out of golden vessels, he went not with any of them. When they went to listen to songs and tales, he went not with them there; neither could he be persuaded to do anything but sleep. And as often as he slept, he beheld in his dreams the maiden he loved best; but except when he slept he saw nothing of her, for he knew not where in the world she was.

One day the page of the chamber spake unto him; now, although he was page of the chamber, he was king of the Romans. "Lord," said he, "all the people revile thee." "Wherefore do they revile me?" asked the emperor. "Because they can get neither message nor answer from thee as men should have from their lord. This is the cause why thou art spoken evil of." "Youth," said the emperor, "do thou bring unto me the wise men of Rome, and I will tell them wherefore I am sorrowful."

Then the wise men of Rome were brought to the emperor, and he spake to them. "Sages of Rome," said he, "I have seen a dream. And in the dream I beheld a maiden, and because of the maiden is there neither life, nor spirit, nor existence within me." "Lord," they answered, "since thou judgest us worthy to counsel thee, we will give thee counsel. And this is our counsel; that thou send messengers for three years to the three parts of the world to seek for thy dream. And as thou knowest not what day or what night good news may come to thee, the hope thereof will support thee."

So the messengers journeyed for the space of a year, wandering about the world, and seeking tidings concerning his dream. But when they came back at the end of the year, they knew not one word more than they did the day they set forth. And then was the emperor exceeding sorrowful, for he thought that he should never have tidings of her whom best he loved.

Then spoke the king of the Romans unto the emperor. "Lord," said he, "go forth to hunt by the way thou didst seem to go, whether it were to the east, or to the west." So the emperor went forth to the hunt, and he came to the bank of the river. "Behold," said he, "this is where I was when I saw the dream, and I went towards the source of the river westward."

And thereupon thirteen messengers of the emperor's set forth, and before them they saw a high mountain, which seemed to them to touch the sky. Now this was the guise in which the messengers journeyed; one sleeve was on the cap of each of them in front, as a sign that they were messengers, in order that through what hostile land soever they might pass no harm might be done them. And when they were come over this mountain, they beheld vast plains, and large rivers flowing there through. "Behold," said they, "the land which our master saw."

And they went along the mouths of the rivers, until they came to the mighty river which they saw flowing to the sea, and the vast city, and the many-coloured high towers in the castle. They saw the largest fleet in the world, in the harbour of the river, and one ship that was larger than any of the others. "Behold again," said they, "the dream that our master saw." And in the great ship they crossed the sea, and came to the Island of Britain. And they traversed the island until they came to Snowdon. "Behold," said they, "the rugged land that our master saw." And they went forward until they saw Anglesey before them, and until they saw Arvon likewise. "Behold," said they, "the land our master saw in his sleep." And they saw Aber Sain, and a castle at the mouth of the river. The portal of the castle saw they open, and into the castle they went, and they saw a hall in the castle. Then said they, "Behold, the hall which he saw in his sleep." They went into the hall, and they beheld two youths playing at chess on the golden bench. And they beheld the hoary-headed man beside the pillar, in the ivory chair, carving chessmen. And they beheld the maiden sitting on a chair of ruddy gold.

The messengers bent down upon their knees. "Empress of Rome, all hail!" "Ha, gentles," said the maiden, "ye bear the seeming of honourable men, and the badge of envoys, what mockery is this ye do to me?" "We mock thee not, lady; but the Emperor of Rome hath seen thee in his sleep, and he has neither life nor spirit left because of thee. Thou shalt have of us therefore the choice, lady, whether thou wilt go with us and be made empress of Rome, or that the emperor come hither and take thee for his wife?" "Ha, lords," said the maiden, "I will not deny what ye say, neither will I believe it too well. If the emperor love me, let him come here to seek me."

And by day and night the messengers hied them back. And when their horses failed, they bought other fresh ones. And when they came to Rome, they saluted the emperor, and asked their boon, which was given to them according as they named it. "We will be thy guides, lord," said they, "over sea and over land, to the place where is the woman whom best thou lovest, for we know her name, and her kindred, and her race."

And immediately the emperor set forth with his army. And these men were his guides. Towards the Island of Britain they went over the sea and the deep. And he conquered the Island from Beli the son of Manogan, and his sons, and drove them to the sea, and went forward even unto Arvon. And the emperor knew the land when he saw it. And when he beheld the castle of Aber Sain, "Look yonder," said he, "there is the castle wherein I saw the damsel whom I best love." And he went forward into the castle and into the hall, and there he saw Kynan the son of Eudav, and Adeon the son of Eudav, playing at chess. And he saw Eudav the son of Caradawc, sitting on a chair of ivory carving chessmen. And the maiden whom he had beheld in his sleep, he saw sitting on a chair of gold. "Empress of Rome," said he, "all hail!" And the emperor threw his arms about her neck; and that night she became his bride.

And the next day in the morning, the damsel asked her maiden portion. And he told her to name what she would. And she asked to have the Island of Britain for her father, from the Channel to the Irish Sea, together with the three adjacent Islands, to hold under the empress of Rome; and to have three chief castles made for her, an whatever places she might choose in the Island of Britain. And she chose to have the highest castle made at Arvon. And they brought thither earth from Rome that it might be more healthful for the emperor to sleep, and sit, and walk upon. After that the two other castles were made for her, which were Caerlleon and Caermarthen.

And one day the emperor went to hunt at Caermarthen, and he came so far as the top of Brevi Vawr, and there the emperor pitched his tent. And that encamping place is called Cadeir Maxen, even to this day. And because that he built the castle with a myriad of men, he called it Caervyrddin. Then Helen bethought her to make high roads from one castle to another throughout the Island of Britain. And the roads were made. And for this cause are they called the roads of Helen Luyddawc, that she was sprung from a native of this island, and the men of the Island of Britain would not have made these great roads for any save for her.

Seven years did the emperor tarry in this Island. Now, at that time, the men of Rome had a custom, that whatsoever emperor should remain in other lands more than seven years should remain to his own overthrow, and should never return to Rome again.

So they made a new emperor. And this one wrote a letter of threat to Maxen. There was nought in the letter but only this. "If thou comest, and if thou ever comest to Rome." And even unto Caerlleon came this letter to Maxen, and these tidings. Then sent he a letter to the man who styled himself emperor in Rome. There was nought in that letter also but only this. "If I come to Rome, and if I come."

And thereupon Maxen set forth towards Rome with his army, and vanquished France and Burgundy, and every land on the way, and sat down before the city of Rome.

A year was the emperor before the city, and he was no nearer taking it than the first day. And after him there came the brothers of Helen Luyddawc from the Island of Britain, and a small host with them, and better warriors were in that small host than twice as many Romans. And the emperor was told that a host was seen, halting close to his army and encamping, and no man ever saw a fairer or better appointed host for its size, nor more handsome standards.

And Helen went to see the hosts, and she knew the standards of her brothers. Then came Kynan the son of Eudav, and Adeon the son of Eudav, to meet the emperor. And the emperor was glad because of them, and embraced them.

Then they looked at the Romans as they attacked the city. Said Kynan to his brother, "We will try to attack the city more expertly than this." So they measured by night the height of the wall, and they sent their carpenters to the wood, and a ladder was made for every four men of their number. Now when these were ready, every day at mid-day the emperors went to meat, and they ceased to fight on both sides till all had finished eating. And in the morning the men of Britain took their food and they drank until they were invigorated. And while the two emperors were at meat, the Britons came to the city, and placed their ladders against it, and forthwith they came in through the city.

The new emperor had no time to arm himself when they fell upon him, and slew him, and many others with him. And three nights and three days were they subduing the men that were in the city and taking the castle. And others of them kept the city, lest any of the host of Maxen should come therein, until they had subjected all to their will.

Then spake Maxen to Helen Luyddawc. "I marvel, lady," said he, "that thy brothers have not conquered this city for me." "Lord, emperor," she answered, "the wisest youths in the world are my brothers. Go thou thither and ask the city of them, and if it be in their possession thou shalt have it gladly." So the emperor and Helen went and demanded the city. And they told the emperor that none had taken the city, and that none could give it him, but the men of the Island of Britain. Then the gates of the city of Rome were opened, and the emperor sat on the throne, and all the men of Rome submitted them selves unto him.

The emperor then said unto Kynan and Adeon, "Lords," said he, "I have now had possession of the whole of my empire. This host give I unto you to vanquish whatever region ye may desire in the world."

So they set forth and conquered lands, and castles, and cities. And they slew all the men, but the women they kept alive. And thus they continued until the young men that had come with them were grown grey-headed, from the length of time they were upon this conquest.

Then spoke Kynan unto Adeon his brother, "Whether wilt thou rather," said he, "tarry in this land, or go back into the land whence thou didst come forth?" Now he chose to go back to his own land, and many with him. But Kynan tarried there with the other part and dwelt there.

And they took counsel and cut out the tongues of the women, lest they should corrupt their speech. And because of the silence of the women from their own speech, the men of Armorica are called Britons. From that time there came frequently, and still comes, that language from the Island of Britain.

And this dream is called the Dream of Maxen Wledig, emperor of Rome. And here it ends.

NOTE TO MAXEN WLEDIG

443a

Maximus, the Maxen of the present Tale, was invested by his army with the Imperial purple in the year 383. He was of low birth, and Spanish origin. He served much in Britain, in which Island he commanded at the time of his elevation, and whence he proceeded with his army into Gaul, to support his claim against the lawful emperor Gratian.

It is said that he rendered part of Britain desolate by transporting the inhabitants into Gaul, where they are supposed to have formed the Breton immigration. He was put to death in the neighbourhood of Aquileia, after having been defeated by Theodosius and Valentinian the Younger, in 388.—Gibbon, chap. xxvii.

Maximus is the subject of many Welsh legends. Part of his history will be recognized as forming the basis of the exaggerated fictions of the text.

As regards the other personages who figure in the present Tale, we find that the two most conspicuous, Kynan (or Kynan Meriadawc, as he is usually called), and his sister Helen Luyddawg, or Helen of mighty hosts, were the children of Eudav. A Triad is preserved, which goes at some length into the account of the expedition they undertook for the purpose of supporting the claim of Maximus to the Imperial throne. They raised an army of sixty thousand men in Britain, and proceeded with it across the sea to Armorica, A.D. 383. The desolation caused by this abstraction of its inhabitants from the Island is said to have been the remote cause of the Saxon invasion.—Tr. 14.

The history of Kynan is also preserved in a Legendary Life.

The Brut Gruffydd ab Arthur gives a different account of the personages and events alluded to in this Mabinogi, but does not advert to the dream, though it mentions St. Ursula and the eleven thousand virgins, who were sent from Britain as wives for the emigrated hosts of Kynan Meriadawc, in Armorica. According to Gruffydd, Helen Luyddawg was the only child of King Coel (the founder of Colchester), and was bestowed in marriage, with the dominions she inherited, upon the Roman Constans. Their son, the celebrated Constantine, was called from his kingdom of Britain to the Imperial throne, in place of Maximus the Cruel; after his departure, Eudav earl of Cornwall, rose up and wrested the government of the Island from the hands of those princes to whom Constantine had consigned it, and, in spite of the Roman forces sent against him under Trahayarn, Helen's uncle, established himself on the throne.

Eudav's reign extended to the time of the emperors Gratian and Valentinian.

His heir was an only daughter, whose name does not appear, but whom, by advice of his nobles, he married to the Roman senator, Maxen Wledig, who boasted British descent, being the son of Helen's uncle Llewelyn. Maxen's marriage, and his succession to the sovereign power, were long and strenuously opposed by Eudav's nephew, Kynan Meriadawc, who himself aspired to the crown.

But peace having at length been concluded between them, Kynan accompanied Maxen in an expedition which he undertook on the continent, and was rewarded for his assistance with the kingdom of Llydaw, or Armorica, in which Maxen left him to establish himself, whilst he proceeded to contend for the nobler prize. But having killed Valentinian, and driven Gratian from the empire, Maxen himself was soon after slain at Rome; whereupon the vast hosts that had accompanied him from Britain dispersed, the chief part of them seeking refuge in Armorica with Kynan Meriadawc.—Myv. Arch. II. p. 205-225.

The same story is related by Nennius, who calls the emperor Maximianus.

"The seventh emperor was Maximianus. He withdrew from Britain with all its military force, slew Gratianus the king of the Romans, and obtained the sovereignty of all Europe. Unwilling to send back his warlike companions to their wives, families, and possessions in Britain, he conferred upon them numerous districts from the lake on the summit of Mons Iovis, to the city called Cant Guic, and to the western Tumulus, that is Cruc Occident. These are the Armoric Britons, and they remain there to the present day. In consequence of their absence, Britain being overcome by foreign nations, the lawful heirs were cast out, till God interposed with his assistance."

The lake here mentioned is thought to be that near the hospice of the great St. Bernard, and Cant Gwic is probably Cantavic, in Picardy. It is more difficult to identify Cruc Occident, the western Tumulus, but the author of the Hanes Cymru supposes it to be Mont St. Michel, near Quiberon, in Brittany.

Some copies of Nennius contain an account of the lingual disablement of the women, similar to that in the text; and add, that from this cause they were called Letewiccion [Lledfydion], that is Semitacentes. This is evidently an attempt to account for the name of Letavia [Llydaw], as applied to Armorica.

Gildas, in his work "De Excidio Britanniæ," also mentions the revolt of Maximus, and its disastrous consequences:—

"Afterwards Britain, being robbed of all its armed soldiery, and military forces, was abandoned to cruel rulers, being deprived of an immense number of youths who accompanied the above-named tyrant [Maximus], and never returned home; and being totally ignorant of the art of war, groaned in stupefaction for many years, under the oppression of two foreign nations," &c. &c.

This author, however, has not any allusion to the Armorican settlement.

The roads attributed in the text to Helen Luyddawc, are evidently the Roman Roads, which intersected our Island. Their remains in several places in the Principality, bear, to this day, the name of Sarn Helen, which some, however, consider to be a corruption Of Sarn y Lleng, the Road of the Legion.

The Welsh text of this Mabinogi, Breuddwyd Maxen Wledig, was printed in 1806, in a Welsh collection entitled the Greal, p. 289, but no translation of it has hitherto appeared.

HERE IS THE STORY
OF LLUDD AND LLEVELYS

BELI the Great, the son of Manogan, had three sons, Lludd, and Caswallawn, and Nynyaw; and according to the story he had a fourth son called Llevelys. And after the death of Beli, the kingdom of the Island of Britain fell into the hands of Lludd his eldest son; and Lludd ruled prosperously, and rebuilt the walls of London, and encompassed it about with numberless towers. And after that he bade the citizens build houses therein, such as no houses in the kingdoms could equal. And moreover he was a mighty warrior, and generous and liberal in giving meat and drink to all that sought them. And though he had many castles and cities this one loved he more than any. And he dwelt therein most part of the year, and therefore was it called Caer Lludd, and at last Caer London. And after the stranger-race came there, it was called London, or Lwndrys.

Lludd loved Llevelys best of all his brothers, because he was a wise and discreet man. Having heard that the king of France had died, leaving no heir except a daughter, and that he had left all his possessions in her hands, he came to Lludd his brother, to beseech his counsel and aid. And that not so much for his own welfare, as to seek to add to the glory and honour and dignity of his kindred, if he might go to France to woo the maiden for his wife. And forthwith his brother conferred with him, and this counsel was pleasing unto him.

So he prepared ships and filled them with armed knights, and set forth towards France. And as soon as they had landed, they sent messengers to show the nobles of France the cause of the embassy. And by the joint counsel of the nobles of France and of the princes, the maiden was given to Llevelys, and the crown of the kingdom with her. And thenceforth he ruled the land discreetly, and wisely, and happily, as long as his life lasted.

After a space of time had passed, three plagues fell on the Island of Britain, such as none in the islands had ever seen the like of. The first was a certain race that came, and was called the Coranians; and so great was their knowledge, that there was no discourse upon the face of the Island, however low it might be spoken, but what, if the wind met it, it was known to them. And through this they could not be injured.[1]

The second plague was a shriek which came on every May-eve, over every hearth in the Island of Britain. And this went through people's hearts, and so scared them, that the men lost their hue and their strength, and the women

---

1 The version in the Greal adds, "And their coin was fairy money;" literally, dwarf's money: that is, money, which, when received, appeared to be good coin, but which, if kept, turned into pieces of fungus, &c.

their children, and the young men and the maidens lost their senses, and all the animals and trees and the earth and the waters, were left barren.

The third plague was, that however much of provisions and food might be prepared in the king's courts, were there even so much as a year's provision of meat and drink, none of it could ever be found, except what was consumed in the first night. And two of these plagues, no one ever knew their cause, therefore was there better hope of being freed from the first than from the second and third.

And thereupon King Lludd felt great sorrow and care, because that he knew not how he might be freed from these plagues. And he called to him all the nobles of his kingdom, and asked counsel of them what they should do against these afflictions. And by the common counsel of the nobles, Lludd the son of Beli went to Llevelys his brother, king of France, for he was a man great of counsel and wisdom, to seek his advice.

And they made ready a fleet, and that in secret and in silence, lest that race should know the cause of their errand, or any besides the king and his counsellors. And when they were made ready, they went into their ships, Lludd and those whom he chose with him. And they began to cleave the seas towards France.

And when these tidings came to Llevelys, seeing that he knew not the cause of his brother's ships, he came on the other side to meet him, and with him was a fleet vast of size. And when Lludd saw this, he left all the ships out upon the sea except one only; and in that one he came to meet his brother, and he likewise with a single ship came to meet him. And when they were come together, each put his arms about the other's neck, and they welcomed each other with brotherly love.

After that Lludd had shown his brother the cause of his errand, Llevelys said that he himself knew the cause of the coming to those lands. And they took counsel together to discourse on the matter otherwise than thus, in order that the wind might not catch their words, nor the Coranians know what they might say. Then Llevelys caused a long horn to be made of brass, and through this horn they discoursed. But whatsoever words they spoke through this horn, one to the other, neither of them could hear any other but harsh and hostile words. And when Llevelys saw this, and that there was a demon thwarting them and disturbing through this horn, he caused wine to be put therein to wash it. And through the virtue of the wine the demon was driven out of the horn. And when their discourse was unobstructed, Llevelys told his brother that he would give him some insects whereof he should keep some to breed, lest by chance the like affliction might come a second time. And other of these insects he should take and bruise in water. And he assured him that it would have power to destroy the race of the Coranians. That is to say, that when he came home to his kingdom he should call together all the people both of his own race and of the race of the Coranians for a conference, as though with the intent of making peace between them; and that when they were all together, he should take this charmed water, and cast it over all alike. And he assured him that the water would poison the race of the Coranians, but that it would not slay or harm those of his own race.

"And the second plague," said he, "that is in thy dominion, behold it is a dragon. And another dragon of a foreign race is fighting with it, and striving to overcome it. And therefore does your dragon make a fearful outcry. And on this wise mayest thou come to know this. After thou hast returned home, cause the Island to be measured in its length and breadth, and in the place where thou dost find the exact central point, there cause a pit to be dug, and cause a cauldron full of the best mead that can be made to be put in the pit, with a covering of satin over the face of the cauldron. And then, in thine own person do thou remain there watching, and thou wilt see the dragon fighting in the form of terrific animals. And at length they will take the form of dragons in the air. And last of all, after wearying themselves with fierce and furious fighting, they will fall in the form of two pigs upon the covering, and they will sink in, and the covering with them, and they will draw it down to the very bottom of the cauldron. And they will drink up the whole of the mead; and after that they will sleep. Thereupon do thou immediately fold the covering around them, and bury them in a kistvaen, in the strongest place thou hast in thy dominions, and hide them in the earth. And as long as they shall bide in that strong place no plague shall come to the Island of Britain from elsewhere.

"The cause of the third plague," said he, "is a mighty man of magic, who take thy meat and thy drink and thy store. And he through illusions and charms causes every one to sleep. Therefore it is needful for thee in thy own person to watch thy food and thy provisions. And lest he should overcome thee with sleep, be there a cauldron of cold water by thy side, and when thou art oppressed with sleep, plunge into the cauldron."

Then Lludd returned back unto his land. And immediately he summoned to him the whole of his own race and of the Coranians. And as Llevelys had taught him, he bruised the insects in water, the which he cast over them all together, and forthwith it destroyed the whole tribe of the Coranians, without hurt to any of the Britons.

And some time after this, Lludd caused the Island to be measured in its length and in its breadth. And in Oxford he found the central point, and in that place he caused the earth to be dug, and in that pit a cauldron to be set, full of the best mead that could be made, and a covering of satin over the face of it. And he himself watched that night. And while he was there, he beheld the dragons fighting. And when they were weary they fell, and came down upon the top of the satin, and drew it with them to the bottom of the cauldron. And when they had drunk the mead they slept. And in their sleep, Lludd folded the covering around them, and in the securest place he had in Snowdon, he hid them in a kistvaen. Now after that this spot was called Dinas Emreis, but before that,

Dinas Ffaraon. And thus the fierce outcry ceased in his dominions.

And when this was ended, King Lludd caused an exceeding great banquet to be prepared. And when it was ready, he placed a vessel of cold water by his side, and he in his own proper person watched it. And as he abode thus clad with arms, about the third watch of the night, lo, he heard many surpassing fascinations and various songs. And drowsiness urged him to sleep. Upon this, lest he should be hindered from his purpose and be overcome by sleep, he went often into the water. And at last, behold, a man of vast size, clad in strong, heavy armour, came in, bearing a hamper. And, as he was wont, he put all the food and provisions of meat and drink into the hamper, and proceeded to go with it forth. And nothing was ever more wonderful to Lludd, than that the hamper should hold so much.

And thereupon King Lludd went after him and spoke unto him thus. "Stop, stop," said he, "though thou hast done many insults and much spoil erewhile, thou shalt not do so any more, unless thy skill in arms and thy prowess be greater than mine."

Then he instantly put down the hamper on the floor, and awaited him. And a fierce encounter was between them, so that the glittering fire flew out from their arms. And at the last Lludd grappled with him, and fate bestowed the victory on Lludd. And he threw the plague to the earth. And after he had overcome him by strength and might, he besought his mercy. "How can I grant thee mercy," said the king, "after all the many injuries and wrongs that thou hast done me?" "All the losses that ever I have caused thee," said he, "I will make thee atonement for, equal to what I have taken. And I will never do the like from this time forth. But thy faithful vassal will I be." And the king accepted this from him.

And thus Lludd freed the Island of Britain from the three plagues. And from thenceforth until the end of his life, in prosperous peace did Lludd the son of Beli rule the Island of Britain. And this Tale is called the Story of Lludd and Llevelys. And thus it ends.

NOTE ON LLUDD AND LLEVELYS

LLUDD is the celebrated King Lud, brother to Cæsar's opponent Cassibelaunus. The Brut and Geoffrey of Monmouth record his fortifying and decorating the City of London nearly in the same terms as the Mabinogi, stating that it was from him called Caerlud, afterwards corrupted into Caer London, then into London, and lastly by the foreigners into Londres. They also state that King Lud was buried near the gate, still called from his name, in the British language, Porthlud, and in the Saxon, Ludesgate.

Amongst the poems attributed to Taliesin, is one called "Ymarwar Lludd," "The Conciliation of Lludd," in which the meeting with Llevelys is mentioned; but the poem is very obscure in consequence of the allusions not being understood. Llewelyn the Bard also, in an ode to Llewelyn ab Iorwerth, refers to this occurrence, but in so cursory a manner, as not to throw any further light upon the subject.

The Coranians who occupy so conspicuous a place in the present Tale, form the subject of a Triad (Tr. vii.). They are by some supposed to be the Coritani.

The imprisonment of the Dragons in Dinas Emrys in Snowdon, is one of the most curious legends of romantic fiction. Their combats, five centuries later, led to the discovery of the enchanter Merlin, with which opens the great drama of Arthurian Romance. This story being related by Geoffrey of Monmouth, has by many been considered as the fabrication of that writer; but it must be noticed that it is also found in Nennius, who wrote in the eighth century, and of whose works, some copies as old as the tenth, are still extant. The substance of the tale as told by Nennius is as follows:—

Vortigern being forced to retire from his kingdom, in consequence of his various delinquencies, took refuge in Snowdon; and finding Dinas Emrys an eligible spot, commenced building a tower there. But, to his great dismay, he found that whatever he that whatever he built in the daytime, always fell down in the succeeding night. Having consulted his magicians upon the cause of this mystery, they told him that unless he could find a child without a father, and sprinkle the tower with his blood, it would never stand. Upon this Vortigern despatched messengers in every direction to search for the required victim, and at length they lit upon Merlin, whom they brought to Vortigern, that he might be slain. But the boy exposed the ignorance and imposture of the magicians, and caused the ground to be dug at the foundation of the building, where they found two sleeping dragons, one white and the other red. These dragons awaking from their sleep commenced a furious conflict. The white one at first had the advantage of the red, but at last the red dragon prevailed, and expelled his opponent. Merlin then informed them that the red was the British dragon, and the white one that of the invading Saxons. Then it was, according to Geoffrey and the Brut, that Merlin uttered the celebrated prophecy concerning the fate of Britain. Vortigern departing thence to seek some other place of refuge, bestowed that citadel upon the wonderful child, who declared his name to be Merlin Ambrosius, and after whom the spot was called Dinas Emrys.

Whatever date or origin may be assigned to this legend, it is well known that the red dragon has long been the national standard of the Welsh. Henry VII. bore it at Bosworth, and afterwards established the heraldic office of Rouge Dragon in honour of the occasion.

Dinas Emrys, the site of all these marvels, is a natural mound, or rather a small insulated hill in one of the valleys of Snowdon, between Beddgelert and Capel Curig. Giraldus Cambrensis speaks of it in connection with the story here referred to. He says, "At the head of the Snowdon Mountains, not far from the source of the Conway, which flows from this region towards the north, stands Dinas Emrys; that is, the promontory of Ambrosius, where Merlin, sitting on a rock, prophesied to Vortigern."

Lludd and Llevelys is found in the Myvyrian Archaiology, Vol. II., in the Brut Gruffydd ab Arthur, and the Brut Tysilio; and is printed in a separate form in the Greal, apparently from a different MS. An English translation of the Myvyrian copy has been given by the Rev. Peter Roberts, in "The Chronicle of the Kings of Britain."

TALIESIN

[471a] IN times past there lived in Penllyn a man of gentle lineage, named Tegid Voel, and his dwelling was in the midst of the lake Tegid, and his wife was called Caridwen. And there was born to him of his wife a son named Morvran ab Tegid, and also a daughter named Creirwy, the fairest maiden in the world was she; and they had a brother, the most ill-favoured man in the world, Avagddu. Now Caridwen[471b] his mother thought that he was not likely to be admitted among men of noble birth, by reason of his ugliness, unless he had some exalted merits or knowledge. For it was in the beginning of Arthur's time and of the Round Table.

So she resolved, according to the arts of the books of the Fferyllt, to boil a cauldron of Inspiration and Science for her son, that his reception might be honourable because of his knowledge of the mysteries of the future state of the world.

Then she began to boil the cauldron, which from the beginning of its boiling might not cease to boil for a year and a day, until three blessed drops were obtained of the grace of Inspiration.

And she put Gwion Bach the son of Gwreang of Llanfair in Caereinion, in Powys, to stir the cauldron, and a blind man named Morda to kindle the fire beneath it, and she charged them that they should not suffer it to cease boiling for the space of a year and a day. And she herself, according to the books of the astronomers, and in planetary hours, gathered every day of all charm-bearing herbs. And one day, towards the end of the year, as Caridwen was culling plants and making incantations, it chanced that three drops of the charmed liquor flew out of the cauldron and fell upon the finger of Gwion Bach. And by reason of their great heat he put his finger to his mouth, and the instant he put those marvel-working drops into his mouth, he foresaw everything that was to come, and perceived that his chief care must be to guard against the wiles of Caridwen, for vast was her skill. And in very great fear he fled towards his own land. And the cauldron burst in two, because all the liquor within it except the three charm-bearing drops was poisonous, so that the horses of Gwyddno Garanhir[472a] were poisoned by the water of the stream into which the liquor of the cauldron ran, and the confluence of that stream was called the Poison of the Horses of Gwyddno from that time forth.

Thereupon came in Caridwen and saw all the toil of the whole year lost. And she seized a billet of wood and struck the blind Morda on the head until one of his eyes fell out upon his cheek. And he said, "Wrongfully hast thou disfigured me, for I am innocent. Thy loss was not because of me." "Thou speakest truth," said Caridwen, "it was Gwion Bach who robbed me."

And she went forth after him, running. And he saw her, and changed himself into a hare and fled. But she changed herself into a greyhound and turned him. And he ran towards a river, and became a fish. And she in the form of an otter-bitch chased him under the water, until he was fain to turn himself into a bird of the air. She, as a hawk, followed him and gave him no rest in the sky. And just as she was about to stoop upon him, and he was in fear of death, he espied a heap of winnowed wheat on the floor of a barn, and he dropped among the wheat, and turned himself into one of the grains. Then she transformed herself into a high-crested black hen, and went to the wheat and scratched it with her feet, and found him out and swallowed him. And, as the story says, she bore him nine months, and when she was delivered of him, she could not find it in her heart to kill him, by reason of his beauty. So she wrapped him in a leathern bag, and cast him into the sea to the mercy of God, on the twenty-ninth day of April.

And at that time the weir of Gwyddno was on the strand between Dyvi and Aberystwyth, near to his own castle, and the value of an hundred pounds was taken in that weir every May eve. And in those days Gwyddno had an only son named Elphin, the most hapless of youths, and the most needy. And it grieved his father sore, for he thought that he was born in an evil hour. And by the advice of his council, his father had granted him the drawing of the weir that year, to see if good luck would ever befall him, and to give him something wherewith to begin the world.

And the next day when Elphin went to look, there was nothing in the weir. But as he turned back he perceived the leathern bag upon a pole of the weir. Then said one of the weir-ward unto Elphin, "Thou wast never unlucky until to-night, and now thou hast destroyed the virtues of the weir, which always yielded the value of an hundred pounds every May eve, and to-night there is nothing but this leathern skin within it." "How now," said Elphin, "there may be therein the value of an hundred pounds." Well, they took up the leathern bag, and he who opened it saw the forehead of the boy, and said to Elphin, "Behold a radiant brow!"[1] "Taliesin be he called," said Elphin. And he lifted the boy in his arms, and lamenting his mischance, he placed him sorrowfully behind him. And he made his horse amble gently, that before had been trotting, and he carried him as softly as if he had been sitting in the easiest chair in the world. And presently the boy made a Consolation and praise to Elphin, and foretold honour to Elphin; and the Consolation was as you may see:—

> "Fair Elphin, cease to lament!
> Let no one be dissatisfied with his own,
> To despair will bring no advantage.
> No man sees what supports him;

---

1 Taliesin.

The prayer of Cynllo will not be in vain;
God will not violate his promise.
Never in Gwyddno's weir
Was there such good luck as this night.
Fair Elphin, dry thy cheeks!
Being too sad will not avail.
Although thou thinkest thou hast no gain,
Too much grief will bring thee no good;
Nor doubt the miracles of the Almighty:
Although I am but little, I am highly gifted.
From seas, and from mountains,
And from the depths of rivers,
God brings wealth to the fortunate man.
Elphin of lively qualities,
Thy resolution is unmanly;
Thou must not be over sorrowful:
Better to trust in God than to forbode ill.
Weak and small as I am,
On the foaming beach of the ocean,
In the day of trouble I shall be
Of more service to thee than three hundred salmon.
Elphin of notable qualities,
Be not displeased at thy misfortune;
Although reclined thus weak in my bag,
There lies a virtue in my tongue.
While I continue thy protector
Thou hast not much to fear;
Remembering the names of the Trinity,
None shall be able to harm thee."

And this was the first poem that Taliesin ever sang, being to console Elphin in his grief for that the produce of the weir was lost, and, what was worse, that all the world would consider that it was through his fault and ill-luck. And then Gwyddno Garanhir[1] asked him what he was, whether man or spirit. Whereupon he sang this tale, and said:—

"First, I have been formed a comely person,
In the court of Caridwen I have done penance;
Though little I was seen, placidly received,
I was great on the floor of the place to where I was led;

---

1 The mention of Gwyddno Garanhir, instead of Elphin ab Gwyddno in this place is evidently an error of some transcriber of the MS.

I have been a prized defence, the sweet muse the cause,
And by law without speech I have been liberated
By a smiling black old hag, when irritated
Dreadful her claim when pursued:
I have fled with vigour, I have fled as a frog,
I have fled in the semblance of a crow, scarcely finding rest;
I have fled vehemently, I have fled as a chain,
I have fled as a roe into an entangled thicket;
I have fled as a wolf cub, I have fled as a wolf in a wilderness,
I have fled as a thrush of portending language;
I have fled as a fox, used to concurrent bounds of quirks;
I have fled as a martin, which did not avail;
I have fled as a squirrel, that vainly hides,
I have fled as a stag's antler, of ruddy course,
I have fled as iron in a glowing fire,
I have fled as a spear-head, of woe to such as has a wish for it;
I have fled as a fierce hull bitterly fighting,
I have fled as a bristly boar seen in a ravine,
I have fled as a white grain of pure wheat,
On the skirt of a hempen sheet entangled,
That seemed of the size of a mare's foal,
That is filling like a ship on the waters;
Into a dark leathern bag I was thrown,
And on a boundless sea I was sent adrift;
Which was to me an omen of being tenderly nursed,
And the Lord God then set me at liberty."

Then came Elphin to the house or court of Gwyddno his father, and Taliesin with him. And Gwyddno asked him if he had had a good haul at the weir, and he told him that he had got that which was better than fish. "What was that?" said Gwyddno. "A Bard," answered Elphin. Then said Gwyddno, "Alas, what will he profit thee?" And Taliesin himself replied and said, "He will profit him more than the weir ever profited thee." Asked Gwyddno, "Art thou able to speak, and thou so little?" And Taliesin answered him, "I am better able to speak than thou to question me." "Let me hear what thou canst say," quoth Gwyddno. Then Taliesin sang:—

"In water there is a quality endowed with a blessing;
On God it is most just to meditate aright;
To God it is proper to supplicate with seriousness,
Since no obstacle can there be to obtain a reward from him.
Three times have I been born, I know by meditation;

It were miserable for a person not to come and obtain
All the sciences of the world, collected together in my breast,
For I know what has been, what in future will occur.
I will supplicate my Lord that I get refuge in him,
A regard I may obtain in his grace;
The Son of Mary is my trust, great in him is my delight,
For in him is the world continually upholden.
God has been to instruct me and to raise my expectation,
The true Creator of heaven, who affords me protection;
It is rightly intended that the saints should daily pray,
For God, the renovator, will bring them to him."

* * * * *

And forthwith Elphin gave his haul to his wife, and she nursed him tenderly and lovingly. Thenceforward Elphin increased in riches more and more day after day, and in love and favour with the king, and there abode Taliesin until he was thirteen years old, when Elphin son of Gwyddno went by a Christmas invitation to his uncle, Maelgwn Gwynedd[476a], who some time after this held open court at Christmastide in the castle of Dyganwy, for all the number of his lords of both degrees, both spiritual and temporal, with a vast and thronged host of knights and squires. And amongst them there arose a discourse and discussion. And thus was it said.

"Is there in the whole world a king so great as Maelgwn, or one on whom Heaven has bestowed so many spiritual gifts as upon him? First, form, and beauty, and meekness, and strength, besides all the powers of the soul!" And together with these they said that Heaven had given one gift that exceeded all the others, which was the beauty, and comeliness, and grace, and wisdom, and modesty of his queen; whose virtues surpassed those of all the ladies and noble maidens throughout the whole kingdom. And with this they put questions one to another amongst themselves: Who had braver men? Who had fairer or swifter horses or greyhounds? Who had more skilful or wiser bards—than Maelgwn?

Now at that time the bards were in great favour with the exalted of the kingdom; and then none performed the office of those who are now called heralds, unless they were learned men, not only expert in the service of kings and princes, but studious and well versed in the lineage, and arms, and exploits of princes and kings, and in discussions concerning foreign kingdoms, and the ancient things of this kingdom, and chiefly in the annals of the first nobles; and also were prepared always with their answers in various languages, Latin, French, Welsh, and English. And together with this they were great chroniclers, and recorders, and skilful in framing verses, and ready in making englyns in every one of those languages. Now of these there were at that feast within the palace of Maelgwn as many as four-and-twenty, and chief of them all was one named Heinin Vardd[477a].

When they had all made an end of thus praising the king and his gifts, it befell that Elphin spoke in this wise. "Of a truth none but a king may vie with a king; but were he not a king, I would say that my wife was as virtuous as any lady in the kingdom, and also that I have a bard who is more skilful than all the king's bards." In a short space some of his fellows showed the king all the boastings of Elphin; and the king ordered him to be thrown into a strong prison, until he might know the truth as to the virtues of his wife, and the wisdom of his bard.

Now when Elphin had been put in a tower of the castle, with a thick chain about his feet (it is said that it was a silver chain, because he was of royal blood), the king, as the story relates, sent his son Rhun to inquire into the demeanour of Elphin's wife. Now Rhun was the most graceless man in the world, and there was neither wife nor maiden with whom he had held converse, but was evil spoken of. While Rhun went in haste towards Elphin's dwelling, being fully minded to bring disgrace upon his wife, Taliesin told his mistress how that the king had placed his master in durance in prison, and how that Rhun was coming in haste to strive to bring disgrace upon her. Wherefore he caused his mistress to array one of the maids of her kitchen in her apparel; which the noble lady gladly did; and she loaded her hands with the best rings that she and her husband possessed.

In this guise Taliesin caused his mistress to put the maiden to sit at the board in her room at supper, and he made her to seem as her mistress, and the mistress to seem as the maid. And when they were in due time seated at their supper in the manner that has been said, Rhun suddenly arrived at Elphin's dwelling, and was received with joy, for all the servants knew him plainly; and they brought him in haste to the room of their mistress, in the semblance of whom the maid rose up from supper and welcomed him gladly. And afterwards she sat down to supper again the second time, and Rhun with her. Then Rhun began jesting with the maid, who still kept the semblance of her mistress. And verily this story shows that the maiden became so intoxicated, that she fell asleep; and the story relates that it was a powder that Rhun put into the drink, that made her sleep so soundly that she never felt it when he cut from off her hand her little finger, whereupon was the signet ring of Elphin, which he had sent to his wife as a token, a short time before. And Rhun returned to the king with the finger and the ring as a proof, to show that he had cut it from off her hand, without her awaking from her sleep of intemperance.

The king rejoiced greatly at these tidings, and he sent for his councillors, to whom he told the whole story from the beginning. And he caused Elphin to be brought out of his prison, and he chided him because of his boast. And he spake unto Elphin on this wise. "Elphin, be it known to thee beyond a doubt that it is but folly for a man to trust in the virtues of his wife further than he can see her; and that thou mayest be certain of thy wife's vileness, behold her finger, with thy signet ring upon it, which was cut from her hand last night, while she slept the sleep of intoxication." Then thus spake Elphin. "With thy leave, mighty king, I cannot deny my ring, for it is known of many; but verily I assert strongly that the finger around which it is, was never attached to the hand of my wife, for in truth and certainty there are three notable things pertaining to it, none of which ever belonged to any of my wife's fingers. The first of the three is, that it is certain, by your grace's leave, that wheresoever my wife is at this present hour, whether sitting, or standing, or lying down, this ring would never remain upon her thumb, whereas you can plainly see that it was hard to draw it over the joint of the little finger of the hand whence this was cut; the second thing is, that my wife has never let pass one Saturday since I have known her without paring her nails before going to bed, and you can see fully that the nail of this little finger has not been pared for a month. The third is, truly, that the hand whence this finger came was kneading rye dough within three days before the finger was cut therefrom, and I can assure your goodness that my wife has never kneaded rye dough since my wife she has been."

Then the king was mightily wroth with Elphin for so stoutly withstanding him, respecting the goodness of his wife, wherefore he ordered him to his prison a second time, saying that he should not be loosed thence until he had proved the truth of his boast, as well concerning the wisdom of his bard as the virtues of his wife.

In the meantime his wife and Taliesin remained joyful at Elphin's dwelling. And Taliesin showed his mistress how that Elphin was in prison because of them, but he bade her be glad, for that he would go to Maelgwn's court to free his master. Then she asked him in what manner he would set him free. And he answered her:—

"A journey will I perform,
And to the gate I will come;
The hall I will enter,
And my song I will sing;
My speech I will pronounce
To silence royal bards,
In presence of their chief,
I will greet to deride,
Upon them I will break
And Elphin I will free.
Should contention arise,
In presence of the prince,
With summons to the bards,
For the sweet flowing song,
And wizards' posing lore

And wisdom of Druids,
In the court of the sons of the distributor
Some are who did appear
Intent on wily schemes,
By craft and tricking means,
In pangs of affliction
To wrong the innocent,
Let the fools be silent,
As erst in Badon's fight,—
With Arthur of liberal ones
The head, with long red blades;
Through feats of testy men,
And a chief with his foes.
Woe be to them, the fools,
When revenge comes on them.
I Taliesin, chief of bards,
With a sapient Druid's words,
Will set kind Elphin free
From haughty tyrant's bonds.
To their fell and chilling cry,
By the act of a surprising steed,
From the far distant North,
There soon shall be an end.
Let neither grace nor health
Be to Maelgwn Gwynedd,
For this force and this wrong;
And be extremes of ills
And an avenged end
To Rhun and all his race:
Short be his course of life,
Be all his lands laid waste;
And long exile be assigned
To Maelgwn Gwynedd!"

After this he took leave of his mistress, and came at last to the Court of Maelgwn, who was going to sit in his hall and dine in his royal state, as it was the custom in those days for kings and princes to do at every chief feast. And as soon as Taliesin entered the hall, he placed himself in a quiet corner, near the place where the bards and the minstrels were wont to come in doing their service and duty to the king, as is the custom at the high festivals when the bounty is proclaimed. And so, when the bards and the heralds came to cry largess, and to proclaim the power of the king and his strength, at the moment that they passed by the corner wherein he was crouching, Taliesin pouted out his lips after them, and played "Blerwm, blerwm," with his finger upon his lips. Neither took they much notice of him as they went by, but proceeded forward till they came before the king, unto whom they made their obeisance with their bodies, as they were wont, without speaking a single word, but pouting out their lips, and making mouths at the king, playing "Blerwm, blerwm," upon their lips with their fingers, as they had seen the boy do elsewhere. This sight caused the king to wonder and to deem within himself that they were drunk with many liquors. Wherefore he commanded one of his lords, who served at the board, to go to them and desire them to collect their wits, and to consider where they stood, and what it was fitting for them to do. And this lord did so gladly. But they ceased not from their folly any more than before. Whereupon he sent to them a second time, and a third, desiring them to go forth from the hall. At the last the king ordered one of his squires to give a blow to the chief of them named Heinin Vardd; and the squire took a broom and struck him on the head, so that he fell back in his seat. Then he arose and went on his knees, and besought leave of the king's grace to show that this their fault was not through want of knowledge, neither through drunkenness, but by the influence of some spirit that was in the hall. And after this Heinin spoke on this wise. "Oh, honourable king, be it known to your grace, that not from the strength of drink, or of too much liquor, are we dumb, without power of speech like drunken men, but through the influence of a spirit that sits in the corner yonder in the form of a child." Forthwith the king commanded the squire to fetch him; and he went to the nook where Taliesin sat, and brought him before the king, who asked him what he was, and whence he came. And he answered the king in verse.

"Primary chief bard am I to Elphin,
And my original country is the region of the summer stars;
Idno and Heinin called me Merddin,
At length every king will call me Taliesin.

I was with my Lord in the highest sphere,
On the fall of Lucifer into the depth of hell
I have borne a banner before Alexander;
I know the names of the stars from north to south;
I have been on the galaxy at the throne of the Distributor;
I was in Canaan when Absalom was slain;
I conveyed the Divine Spirit to the level of the vale of Hebron;
I was in the court of Don before the birth of Gwdion.
I was instructor to Eli and Enoc;
I have been winged by the genius of the splendid crosier;
I have been loquacious prior to being gifted with speech;

I was at the place of the crucifixion of the merciful Son of God;
I have been three periods in the prison of Arianrod;
I have been the chief director of the work of the tower of Nimrod;
I am a wonder whose origin is not known.

I have been in Asia with Noah in the ark,
I have seen the destruction of Sodom and Gomorra;
I have been in India when Roma was built,
I am now come here to the remnant of Troia.

I have been with my Lord in the manger of the ass:
I strengthened Moses through the water of Jordan;
I have been in the firmament with Mary Magdalene;
I have obtained the muse from the cauldron of Caridwen;
I have been bard of the harp to Lleon of Lochlin.
I have been on the White Hill, in the court of Cynvelyn,
For a day and a year in stocks and fetters,
I have suffered hunger for the Son of the Virgin,
I have been fostered in the land of the Deity,
I have been teacher to all intelligences,
I am able to instruct the whole universe.
I shall be until the day of doom on the face of the earth;
And it is not known whether my body is flesh or fish.

Then I was for nine months
In the womb of the hag Caridwen;
I was originally little Gwion,
And at length I am Taliesin."

And when the king and his nobles had heard the song, they wondered much, for they had never heard the like from a boy so young as he. And when the king knew that he was the bard of Elphin, he bade Heinin, his first and wisest bard, to answer Taliesin and to strive with him. But when he came, he could do no other but play "blerwm" on his lips; and when he sent for the others of the four-and-twenty bards they all did likewise, and could do no other. And Maelgwn asked the boy Taliesin what was his errand, and he answered him in song.

"Puny bards, I am trying
To secure the prize, if I can;
By a gentle prophetic strain
I am endeavouring to retrieve
The loss I may have suffered;

Complete the attempt I hope,
Since Elphin endures trouble
In the fortress of Teganwy,
On him may there not be laid
Too many chains and fetters;
The Chair of the fortress of Teganwy
Will I again seek;
Strengthened by my muse I am powerful;
Mighty on my part is what I seek,
For three hundred songs and more
Are combined in the spell I sing.
There ought not to stand where I am
Neither stone, neither ring;
And there ought not to be about me
Any bard who may not know
That Elphin the son of Gwyddno
Is in the land of Artro,
Secured by thirteen locks,
For praising his instructor;
And then I Taliesin,
Chief of the bards of the west,
Shall loosen Elphin
Out of a golden fetter."

* * * * *

"If you be primary bards
To the master of sciences,
Declare ye mysteries
That relate to the inhabitants of the world;
There is a noxious creature,
From the rampart of Satanas,
Which has overcome all
Between the deep and the shallow;
Equally wide are his jaws
As the mountains of the Alps;
Him death will not subdue,
Nor hand or blades;
There is the load of nine hundred wagons
In the hair of his two paws;
There is in his head an eye
Green as the limpid sheet of icicle;
Three springs arise

In the nape of his neck;
Sea-roughs thereon
Swim through it;
There was the dissolution of the oxen
Of Deivrdonwy the water-gifted.
The names of the three springs
From the midst of the ocean;
One generated brine
Which is from the Corina,
To replenish the flood
Over seas disappearing;
The second, without injury
It will fall on us,
When there is rain abroad,
Through the whelming sky;
The third will appear
Through the mountain veins,
Like a flinty banquet,
The work of the King of kings,
You are blundering bards,
In too much solicitude;
You cannot celebrate
The kingdom of the Britons;
And I am Taliesin,
Chief of the bards of the west,
Who will loosen Elphin
Out of the golden fetter."

* * * * *

"Be silent, then, ye unlucky rhyming bards,
For you cannot judge between truth and falsehood.
If you be primary bards formed by heaven,
Tell your king what his fate will be.
It is I who am a diviner and a leading bard,
And know every passage in the country of your king;
I shall liberate Elphin from the belly of the stony tower;
And will tell your king what will befall him.
A most strange creature will come from the sea marsh of Rhianedd
As a punishment of iniquity on Maelgwn Gwynedd;
His hair, his teeth, and his eyes being as gold,
And this will bring destruction upon Maelgwn Gwynedd."

* * * * *

"Discover thou what is
The strong creature from before the flood,
Without flesh, without bone,
Without vein, without blood,
Without head, without feet;
It will neither be older nor younger
Than at the beginning;
For fear of a denial,
There are no rude wants
With creatures.
Great God! how the sea whitens
When first it comes!
Great are its gusts
When it comes from the south;
Great are its evaporations
When it strikes on coasts.
It is in the field, it is in the wood,
Without hand, and without foot,
Without signs of old age,
Though it be co-æval
With the five ages or periods;
And older still,
Though they be numberless years.
It is also so wide
As the surface of the earth;
And it was not born,
Nor was it seen.
It will cause consternation
Wherever God willeth.
On sea, and on land,
It neither sees, nor is seen.
Its course is devious,
And will not come when desired;
On land and on sea,
It is indispensable.
It is without an equal,
It is four-sided;
It is not confined,
It is incomparable;
It comes from four quarters;
It will not be advised,

It will not be without advice.
It commences its journey
Above the marble rock,
It is sonorous, it is dumb,
It is mild,
It is strong, it is bold,
When it glances over the land,
It is silent, it is vocal,
It is clamorous,
It is the most noisy
On the face of the earth.
It is good, it is bad,
It is extremely injurious.
It is concealed,
Because sight cannot perceive it.
It is noxious, it is beneficial;
It is yonder, it is here;
It will discompose,
But will not repair the injury;
It will not suffer for its doings,
Seeing it is blameless.
It is wet, it is dry,
It frequently comes,
Proceeding from the heat of the sun,
And the coldness of the moon.
The moon is less beneficial,
Inasmuch as her heat is less.
One Being has prepared it,
Out of all creatures,
By a tremendous blast,
To wreak vengeance
On Maelgwn Gwynedd."

And while he was thus singing his verse near the door, there arose a mighty storm of wind, so that the king and all his nobles thought that the castle would fall on their heads. And the king caused them to fetch Elphin in haste from his dungeon, and placed him before Taliesin. And it is said, that immediately he sang a verse, so that the chains opened from about his feet.

"I adore the Supreme, Lord of all animation,—
Him that supports the heavens, Ruler of every extreme,
Him that made the water good for all,

Him who has bestowed each gift, and blesses it;—
May abundance of mead be given Maelgwn of Anglesey, who supplies us,
From his foaming meadhorns, with the choicest pure liquor.
Since bees collect, and do not enjoy,
We have sparkling distilled mead, which is universally praised.
The multitude of creatures which the earth nourishes
God made for man, with a view to enrich him;—
Some are violent, some are mute, he enjoys them,
Some are wild, some are tame; the Lord makes them;—
Part of their produce becomes clothing;
For food and beverage till doom will they continue.
I entreat the Supreme, Sovereign of the region of peace,
To liberate Elphin from banishment,
The man who gave me wine, and ale, and mead,
With large princely steeds, of beautiful appearance;
May he yet give me; and at the end,
May God of his good will grant me, in honour,
A succession of numberless ages, in the retreat of tranquillity.
Elphin, knight of mead, late be thy dissolution!"

And afterwards he sang the ode which is called "The Excellence of the Bards."

"What was the first man
Made by the God of heaven;
What the fairest flattering speech
That was prepared by Ieuav;
What meat, what drink,
What roof his shelter;
What the first impression
Of his primary thinking;
What became his clothing;
Who carried on a disguise,
Owing to the wilds of the country,
In the beginning?
Wherefore should a stone be hard;
Why should a thorn be sharp-pointed?
Who is hard like a flint;
Who is salt like brine;
Who sweet like honey;
Who rides on the gale;

Why ridged should be the nose;
Why should a wheel be round;
Why should the tongue be gifted with speech
Rather than another member?
If thy bards, Heinin, be competent,
Let them reply to me, Taliesin."

And after that he sang the address which is called "The Reproof of the Bards."

"If thou art a bard completely imbued
With genius not to be controlled,
Be thou not untractable
Within the court of thy king;
Until thy rigmarole shall be known,
Be thou silent, Heinin,
As to the name of thy verse,
And the name of thy vaunting;
And as to the name of thy grandsire
Prior to his being baptized.
And the name of the sphere,
And the name of the element,
And the name of thy language,
And the name of thy region.
Avaunt, ye bards above,
Avaunt, ye bards below!
My beloved is below,
In the fetter of Arianrod
It is certain you know not
How to understand the song I utter,
Nor clearly how to discriminate
Between the truth and what is false;
Puny bards, crows of the district,
Why do you not take to flight?
A bard that will not silence me,
Silence may he not obtain,
Till he goes to be covered
Under gravel and pebbles;
Such as shall listen to me,
May God listen to him."

Then sang he the piece called "The Spite of the Bards."

"Minstrels persevere in their false custom,
Immoral ditties are their delight;
Vain and tasteless praise they recite;
Falsehood at all times do they utter;
The innocent persons they ridicule;
Married women they destroy,
Innocent virgins of Mary they corrupt;
As they pass their lives away in vanity,
Poor innocent persons they ridicule;
At night they get drunk, they sleep the day;
In idleness without work they feed themselves;
The Church they hate, and the tavern they frequent;
With thieves and perjured fellows they associate;
At courts they inquire after feasts;
Every senseless word they bring forward;
Every deadly sin they praise;
Every vile course of life they lead;
Through every village, town, and country they stroll;
Concerning the gripe of death they think not;
Neither lodging nor charity do they give;
Indulging in victuals to excess.
Psalms or prayers they do not use,
Tithes or offerings to God they do not pay,
On holidays or Sundays they do not worship;
Vigils or festivals they do not heed.
The birds do fly, the fish do swim,
The bees collect honey, worms do crawl,
Every thing travails to obtain its food,
Except minstrels and lazy useless thieves.

I deride neither song nor minstrelsy,
For they are given by God to lighten thought;
But him who abuses them,
For blaspheming Jesus and his service."

Taliesin having set his master free from prison, and having protected the innocence of his wife, and silenced the Bards, so that not one of them dared to say a word, now brought Elphin's wife before them, and showed that she had not one finger wanting. Right glad was Elphin, right glad was Taliesin.

Then he bade Elphin wager the king, that he had a horse both better and swifter than the king's horses. And this Elphin did, and the day, and the time, and the place were fixed, and the place was that which at this day is called

Morva Rhiannedd: and thither the king went with all his people, and four-and-twenty of the swiftest horses he possessed. And after a long process the course was marked, and the horses were placed for running. Then came Taliesin with four-and-twenty twigs of holly, which he had burnt black, and he caused the youth who was to ride his master's horse to place them in his belt, and he gave him orders to let all the king's horses get before him, and as he should overtake one horse after the other, to take one of the twigs and strike the horse with it over the crupper, and then let that twig fall; and after that to take another twig, and do in like manner to every one of the horses, as he should overtake them, enjoining the horseman strictly to watch when his own horse should stumble, and to throw down his cap on the spot. All these things did the youth fulfil, giving a blow to every one of the king's horses, and throwing down his cap on the spot where his horse stumbled. And to this spot Taliesin brought his master after his horse had won the race. And he caused Elphin to put workmen to dig a hole there; and when they had dug the ground deep enough, they found a large cauldron full of gold. And then said Taliesin, "Elphin, behold a payment and reward unto thee, for having taken me out of the weir, and for having reared me from that time until now." And on this spot stands a pool of water, which is to this time called Pwllbair.

After all this, the king caused Taliesin to be brought before him, and he asked him to recite concerning the creation of man from the beginning; and thereupon he made the poem which is now called "One of the Four Pillars of Song."

"The Almighty made,
Down the Hebron vale,
With his plastic hands,
   Adam's fair form:

And five hundred years,
Void of any help,
There he remained and lay
   Without a soul.

He again did form,
In calm paradise,
From a left-side rib,
   Bliss-throbbing Eve.

Seven hours they were
The orchard keeping,
Till Satan brought strife,
   With wiles from hell.

Thence were they driven,
Cold and shivering,
To gain their living,
   Into this world.

To bring forth with pain
Their sons and daughters,
To have possession
   Of Asia's land.

Twice five, ten and eight,
She was self-bearing,
The mixed burden
   Of man-woman.

And once, not hidden,
She brought forth Abel,
And Cain the forlorn,
   The homicide.

To him and his mate
Was given a spade,
To break up the soil,
   Thus to get bread.

The wheat pure and white,
Summer tilth to sow,
Every man to feed,
   Till great yule feast.

An angelic hand
From the high Father,
Brought seed for growing
   That Eve might sow;

But she then did hide
Of the gift a tenth,
And all did not sow
   Of what was dug.

Black rye then was found,
And not pure wheat grain,
To show the mischief
  Thus of thieving.

For this thievish act,
It is requisite,
That all men should pay
  Tithe unto God.

Of the ruddy wine,
Planted on sunny days,
And on new-moon nights;
  And the white wine.

The wheat rich in grain
And red flowing wine
Christ's pure body make,
  Son of Alpha.

The wafer is flesh,
The wine is spilt blood,
The Trinity's words
  Sanctify them.

The concealed books
From Emmanuel's hand
Were brought by Raphael
  As Adam's gift,

When in his old age,
To his chin immersed
In Jordan's water,
  Keeping a fast,

Moses did obtain
In Jordan's water,
The aid of the three
  Most special rods.

Solomon did obtain
In Babel's tower,
All the sciences
    In Asia land.

So did I obtain,
In my bardic books,
All the sciences
    Of Europe and Africa.

Their course, their bearing,
Their permitted way,
And their fate I know,
    Unto the end.

Oh! what misery,
Through extreme of woe,
Prophecy will show
    On Troia's race!

A coiling serpent
Proud and merciless,
On her golden wings,
    From Germany.

She will overrun
England and Scotland,
From Lychlyn sea-shore
    To the Severn.

Then will the Brython
Be as prisoners,
By strangers swayed,
    From Saxony.

Their Lord they will praise,
Their speech they will keep,
Their land they will lose,
    Except wild Walia.

Till some change shall come,
After long penance,
When equally rife
    The two crimes come.

Britons then shall have
Their land and their crown,
And the stranger swarm
    Shall disappear.

All the angel's words,
As to peace and war,
Will be fulfilled
    To Britain's race."

He further told the king various prophecies of things that should be in the world, in songs, as follows.

* * * * *

NOTES TO TALIESIN

471a — TALIESIN

TALIESIN, literally, the "Radiant Brow," was a Welsh Bard of the sixth century. His name, regarded by his countrymen with the reverence due to the "Prince of Song," is known to the Saxon chiefly through the brief but spirited invocation of Gray.

The text records the fiction of which Taliesin is the hero. Of his real history little is known, excepting what may be gleaned from his works, and from the following notices given in the volume of Iolo MSS. recently published by the Welsh MSS. Society. The first of these latter is taken from Anthony Powel of Llwydarth's MS.

"Taliesin, Chief of the Bards, the son of Saint Henwg of Caerlleon upon Usk, was invited to the court of Urien Rheged, at Aberllychwr. He, with Elffin, the son of Urien, being once fishing at sea in a skin coracle, an Irish pirate ship seized him and his coracle, and bore him away towards Ireland; but while the pirates were at the height of their drunken mirth, Taliesin pushed his coracle to the sea, and got into it himself, with a shield in his hand which he found in the ship, and with which he rowed the coracle until it verged the land; but, the waves breaking then in wild foam, he lost his hold on the shield, so that he had no alternative but to be driven at the mercy of the sea, in which state he continued for a short time, when the coracle stuck to the point of a pole in the weir of Gwyddno, Lord of Ceredigion, in Aberdyvi; and in that position he was found, at the ebb, by Gwyddno's fishermen, by whom he was interrogated; and when it was ascertained that he was a bard, and the tutor of Elffin, the son of Urien Rheged, the son of Cynvarch:—'I, too, have a son named Elffin,' said Gwyddno, 'be thou a bard and teacher to him, also, and I will give thee lands in free tenure.' The terms were accepted, and for several successive years he spent his time between the courts of Urien Rheged and Gwyddno, called Gwyddno Garanhir, Lord of the Lowland Cantred; but after the territory of Gwyddno had become overwhelmed by the sea, Taliesin was invited by the Emperor Arthur to his court at Caerlleon upon Usk, where he became highly celebrated for poetic genius and useful, meritorious sciences. After Arthur's death he retired to the estate given to him by Gwyddno, taking Elffin, the son of that prince, under his protection. It was from this account that Thomas, the son of Einion Offeiriad, descended from Gruffydd Gwyr, formed his romance of Taliesin, the son of Cariadwen—Elffin, the son of Goddnou—Rhun, the son of Maelgwn Gwynedd, and the operations of the Cauldron of Ceridwen."

Next follows the Pedigree of Taliesin, Chief of the Bards, from Thomas Hopkin of Coychurch's MS.:—

"Taliesin, Chief of the Bards of the West, the son of Saint Henwg, of Caerlleon upon Usk, the son of Fflwch, the son of Cynin, the son of Cynvarch, the son of Saint Clydawc, of Ewyas, the son of Gwynnar, the son of Caid, the son of Cadren, the son of Cynan, the son of Cyllin, the son of Caradog, the son of Bran, the Son of Llyr Llediaith, King Paramount of all the Kings of Britain, and King, in lineal descent, of the country between the rivers Wye and Towy. Taliesin became Chief Bard of the West, from having been appointed to preside over the chair of the Round Table, at Caerlleon upon Usk."

A manuscript once in the Havod Uchtryd collection gives the following particulars:—

"Taliesin, Chief of the Bards of the West, the son of Henwg the Bard, of the College of Saint Cadocus, the son of Fflwch Lawdrwm, of Caerlleon upon Usk, in Glamorgan, the son of Cynvar, the son of Saint Clydog, the son of Gwynnar, the son of Cadrain, the son of Cynan, the son of Caradog, the son of Bran the Blessed, the son of Llyr Llediaith.

Taliesin, Chief of the Bards, erected the church of Llanhenwg, at Caerlleon upon Usk, which he dedicated to the memory of his father, called Saint Henwg, who went to Rome on a mission to Constantine the Blessed, requesting that he would send Saints Germanus and Lupus to Britain, to strengthen the faith and renew baptism there.

Taliesin, the son of Henwg, was taken by the wild Irish, who unjustly occupied Gower; but while on board ship, on his way to Ireland, he saw a skin coracle, quite empty, on the surface of the sea, and it came closely to the side of the ship; whereupon Taliesin, taking a skin-covered spar in his hand, leaped into it, and rowed towards land, until he stuck on a pole in the weir of Gwyddno Garanhir; when a young chieftain, named Elphin, seeing him so entangled, delivered him from his peril. This Elphin was taken for the son of Gwyddno, although in reality he was the son of Elivri, his daughter, but by whom was then quite unknown; it was, however, afterwards discovered that Urien Rheged, King of Gower and Aberllychwr, was his father, who introduced him to the court of Arthur, at Caerlleon upon Usk, where his feats, learning, and endowments were found to be so superior that he was created a golden-tongued Knight of the Round Table. After the death of Arthur, Taliesin became Chief Bard to Urien Rheged, at Aberllychwr in Rheged."

Another extract, given in the above volume, is from a manuscript by Llywelyn Sion, of Llangewydd:—

"Talhaiarn, the father of Tangwn, presided in the chair of Urien Rheged, at Caer-Gwyroswydd, after the expulsion of the Irish from Gower, Carnwyllion, Cantrev-Bychan, and the Cantred of Iscennen. The said chair was established at Caer-Gwyroswydd, or Ystum Llwynarth, where Urien Rheged was accustomed to hold his national and royal court.

After the death of Talhaiarn, Taliesin, Chief of the Bards, presided in three chairs, namely: the chair of Caerlleon upon Usk, the chair of Rheged, at Bangor Teivy, under the patronage of Cedig ab Ceredig, ab Cuneddav Wledig; but he afterwards was invited to the territory of Gwyddnyw, the son of Gwydion, in Arllechwedd, Arvon, where he had lands conferred on him, and where he resided until the time of Maelgwn Gwynedd, when he was dispossessed of that property, for which he pronounced his curse on Maelgwn, and all his possessions; whereupon the Vad Velen came to Rhos, and whoever witnessed it became doomed to certain death. Maelgwn saw the Vad Velen through the keyhole, in Rhos church, and died in consequence. Taliesin, in his old age, returned to Caer-Gwyroswydd, to Riwallon, the son of Urien; after which he visited Cedig, the son of Ceredig, the son of Cunnedav Wledig, where he died, and was buried with high honours, such as should always be shown to a man who ranked among the principal wise men of the Cymric nation; and Taliesin, Chief of the Bards, was the highest of the most exalted class, either in literature, wisdom, the science of vocal song, or any other attainment, whether sacred or profane. Thus terminates the information respecting the chief bards of the chair of Caerlleon upon Usk, called now the chair of Glamorgan."

It is probable that Taliesin was educated, or completed his education, at the school of the celebrated Cattwg, at Llanveithin, in Glamorgan. In after life he became the bard of Urien Rheged, to whom and to his son Owain, his principal poems are addressed. In the opinion of the most judicious critics these poems are undoubtedly genuine. They certainly contain passages of exquisite beauty, and are far superior to many of the other compositions attributed to him, of which some rest on very questionable authority, and some are evidently Middle Age productions. Indeed, the last of the poems translated in the text bears in some MSS. the name of Ionas Athraw o Fynyw.

The name of Taliesin is thus commemorated in the Triads:—

"The three Baptismal Bards of the Isle of Britain:—Merddin Emrys, Taliesin, Chief of Bards, and Merddin, son of Madoc Morvryn."—Tr. 125.

This Triad is more fully explained in an extract from MS. Triads of the Round Table, given in the Iolo MSS., p. 468.

"The Nine Impulsive Stocks of the Baptismal Bards of Britain.—The three primitive baptismal bards of the Cambro-Britons: Madog, the son of Morvryn, of Caerlleon upon Usk; Taliesin, the son of Saint Henwg, of Caerlleon upon Usk; and Merddin Emrys, of Maesaleg, in Glywysyg; after whom came Saint Talhaiarn, the father of Tangwyn, Merddin, the son of Madog Morvryn, and Meugant Hên, of Caerlleon upon Usk; who were succeeded by Balchnoe, the bard of Teilo, at Llandaff; Saint Cattwg; and Cynddylan, the bard. These nine were called the Impulsive Stocks of the baptismal bards of Britain; Taliesin being their chair-president; for which reason he was designated Taliesin, Chief Bard of the West. They are likewise called the nine superinstitutionists of the baptismal chair; and no institution is deemed permanent unless renewed triennially, till the end of thrice three, or nine years. The institution was also called the Chair of the Round Table, under the superior privileges of which Gildas, the prophet, and Saint Cattwg the Wise, of Lancarvan, were bards; and also Llywarch Hên, the son of Elidr Lydanwyn, Ystudvach, the bard, and Ystyphan, the bard of Teilo."

There are evidently in the foregoing notices some authentic historical facts, as well as legendary traditions of the age of chivalry, which it would require an able critic to separate from each other.

Tradition has handed down a Cairn near Aberystwyth as the grave of Taliesin, the locality of which agrees with the foregoing account.

At one of the meetings of the Cambrian Archæological Association this Cairn was visited. It contains a Cistvaen, eight feet long by two feet six wide, and about three feet deep, composed of rude slabs of stone. One of the top stones, which lies near it, measures five feet nine by three feet nine. The Cairn was opened some fifty or sixty years ago, and the Cistvaen then contained some earth of a different colour to that of the adjoining soil.

The various poems recited in the Tale of Taliesin appear to have been composed at different periods, and it is not improbable that the above-mentioned Thomas ab Einion Offeiriad collected the poems attributed to Taliesin, which were in existence before his time, and added others to form the Mabinogi, which from expressions, and the very numerous transformations stated in the poetry, but not given in the prose, must have been much more complete than in its present state.

That the story of Taliesin was current in the Middle Ages is well known. If proof were wanting the lines of Llywarch Prydydd Moch, in allusion to the liberation of Elphin, might be adduced. They occur in an ode to Llywelyn ap, Iorwerth, composed probably not later than 1220.

"I will address my Lord with the greatly greeting muse, with the dowry of Keridwen, the Ruler of Bardism, in the manner of Taliesin, when he liberated Elphin, when he overshaded the Bardic mystery with the banners of the Bards."—Davies's Myth. of the Druids.

From several poems being, addressed to Hopkin ap Thomas ab Einiawn, by Davydd y Coed, Iorwerth Llwyd, and others who flourished about the years 1300 to 1350, it may be inferred that Hopkin's father, the above Thomas ab Einiawn, was contemporary with Llywarch Prydydd y Koch, and therefore not the author but merely the compiler of the already well-known story of Caridwen, Taliesin, and Elphin.

No perfect copy of the Mabinogi of Taliesin being accessible, it has been necessary to print it in the present series from two fragments. The former of the two is contained in a MS. in the Library of the Welsh School, in London. It is written in a modern round hand and bears the title "Y Prif-feirdd Cymreig, sef

Canau &c. a gasglwyd ganwyf fi, William Morris o Gaergybi ym Môn, 1758."
The MS. is of quarto size.

The second fragment is from a MS. in the library of the late Iolo Morganwg, and was kindly communicated by his son, the late Mr. Taliesin Williams (Ab Iolo).

It should be mentioned that the Mabinogi of Taliesin has already been published, although not in so complete a form as the present version, with a translation, by the late Dr. Owen Paghe, in the fifth volume of the Cambrian Quarterly; and, with two exceptions (the poems beginning "Discover thou what is," and "I adore the Supreme, Lord of all animation"), the translations of the poems now published are extracted from that work, the necessary alterations being made where the text differed materially. The first portion of it is also to be found (untranslated) in the Myvyrian Archaiology, vol. I. page 17, and part of it is inserted in Jones's Welsh Bards.

The Transmigrations of Taliesin will remind the general reader of the adventures of the second Royal Calender in the Arabian Nights.

471b — CARIDWEN

CARIDWEN is generally considered to be the Goddess of Nature of Welsh mythology. The principal circumstances of her fabulous history are those detailed in the Mabinogi of Taliesin. Upon them are founded most of the allusions to her contained in the poems of the bards, with whom the cauldron of Caridwen, of Inspiration, or the Awen, is a subject of frequent reference. As regards her singular family we have but little information and few details. Several notices, however, occur in Welsh writings of her fair daughter Creirwy. Of these it may be sufficient to instance the Triad which celebrates her with Arianrod and Gwenn, verch Cywryd ab Crydon, as one of the three beauteous ladies of the island.[1] One of the two Triads extant on the subject of Morvran has been already cited. It alludes to the extreme ugliness assigned him in the text, to which, nevertheless, he was indebted for the preservation of his life in the battle of Camlan; the other ranks him with Gilbert mab Cadgyffro and Gwgan Gleddyvrudd, as one of the three stayers of slaughter.[2] No further particulars of him are preserved.

---

1 Triad 107.

2 Triad xxix.

472a — GWYDDNO GARANHIR

GWYDDNO GARANHIR was Sovereign of Cantref y Gwaelod, a territory bordering on the sea, and protected from its ravages by a high embankment. One evening there was revelry at the Court, and Seithenin,[1] the son of Seithyn Saidi, King of Dyved, upon whom it devolved to look after the embankment,[2] and see that all was safe, became inebriated and neglected his charge. The consequence was that the sea broke in through the bank in the course of the night. Gwyddno and his Court escaped with difficulty from the impending ruin, and the Cantrev y Gwaelod was submerged and irretrievably lost. By this calamity sixteen fortified cities, the largest and finest that were in Wales, excepting only Caerlleon upon Usk, were entirely destroyed, and Cardigan Bay occupies the spot, where the fertile plains of the Cantrev had been the habitation and support of a flourishing population. Such as escaped the inundation fled to Ardudwy, and the country of Arvon, and the mountains of Eryri (Snowdon), and other places not previously inhabited. By none was this misfortune more severely felt than by Gwyddno Garanhir, to whom the reverse of circumstances it occasioned was so great that, from being an opulent monarch, he was all at once reduced to the necessity of maintaining himself and his only son, the unfortunate Elphin, by the produce of the fishing weir mentioned in the text.

This disastrous event is commemorated in a proverb still repeated in the Principality.—

"The sigh of Gwyddno Garanhir
When the wave rolled over his land."

There is also preserved in the Myvyrian Archaiology (I. 165), a short poem upon the subject attributed to Gwyddno Garanhir, in which there are some exceedingly poetic and striking passages. The bereft monarch calls upon the author of his distress to view the calamitous effects of his intemperance, pronounces maledictions upon his head, and describes the outcry of the perishing inhabitants of that unhappy region. The piece bears a strong

---

1 Seithinyn the Drunkard's mischance in letting the sea overflow the Cantrev y Gwaelod, is related in Triad xli.

2 Traces of three ancient stone embankments are said to be still visible in the district where this inundation took place. They are called Sarn Cynvelyn, Sarn y Bwch, and Sarn Padrig. "The latter is particularly conspicuous, being left dry at low water to the extent of about nine miles, and the sailors of the neighbouring ports describe its whole length to be twenty-one miles, beginning near Harlech, and running in a south-west direction." (Cambro-Briton, 1. 362.) The Hanes Cymru contains some interesting remarks on this subject.

resemblance to some of the Works of Llywarch Hên, and is probably as old as
the sixth century.

> "Stand forth Seithenin and behold the dwelling of heroes,—the plain of
>   Gwyddno the ocean covers!
> Accursed be the sea guard, who after his carousal let loose the destroying
>   fountain of the raging deep.
> Accursed be the watcher, who after his drunken revelry, loosed the
>   fountain of the desolating sea.
> A cry from the sea arises above the ramparts; even to heaven does it
>   ascend,—after the fierce excess comes the long cessation!
> A cry from the sea ascends above the ramparts; even to heaven does the
>   supplication come!-after the excess there ensues restraint!
> A cry from the sea awakens me this night!-
> A cry from the sea arises above the winds!
> A cry from the sea impels me from my place of rest this night
> After excess comes the far extending death!"

Another composition, attributed to him, is to be found in the same valuable
collection. It is in the colloquial form, between himself and the king of Faerie,
Gwyn ap Nudd.

The magic basket of Gwyddno has a place amongst the Thirteen Precious
Things of Britain.

476a — MAELGWN GWYNEDD

THIS king succeeded his father Caswallon Lawhir in the sovereignty of
Gwynedd, about the year 517. He is the subject of a most violent invective by
Gildas, who accuses him of being a most cruel and profligate character; which
is rather confirmed by its being recorded that he was rebuked by St. Padarn,
for certain injuries committed by him in Ceredigion; and that he oppressed
Tydecho, one of the Armorican Saints, who had settled in his dominion; but
in consequence of some miracles said to have been performed by that Saint,
be was compelled to make ample amends. He afterwards founded a College at
Caergybi, and a Priory at Penmon, and also endowed Bangor, and erected it into
a Bishopric. His reign was more powerful than most of those we read of in those
unsettled ages; about the year 546 he was elected to the nominal sovereignty of
the Britons, and, according to the Brut, he added six *islands*, Ireland, Iceland,
Gothland, Orkney, Llychlyn (Norway), and Denmark to the British possessions.
He died of the Vad Velen, or Yellow Pestilence, usually called the Yellow Plague
of Rhos, which was said to have been caused by the number of unburied bodies

of the slain that remained on that spot, and whoever went within the reach of the effluvia fell dead immediately.

To avoid the effects of this pestilence it is said that Maelgwn retired from his castle of Dyganwy, to the church of Llaurhos, where he hoped to remain, shut up in the sanctuary, safe from all danger; but being impelled by curiosity, he looked out through the keyhole of the door, and thereby caught the infection, thus fulfilling the prediction uttered by Taliesin,—

> "A most strange creature will come,
> From the sea marsh of Rhianedd,
> As a punishment of iniquity,
> On Maelgwn Gwynedd;
> His hair and his teeth,
> And his eyes being as gold;
> And this will bring destruction
> On Maelgwn Gwynedd."

A traditionary remembrance of this circumstance is preserved in the adage "Hun Maelgwn Gwynedd yn Eglwys Llanrhos," or as it is given in the "Annales Cambriæ," published by the Record Commission, "Hir hun Maelgwn en llis Ros," The long sleep of Maelgwn in the court of Rhos.

This plague lasted from the year 557 to 562, and its ravages were fearful in the extreme. A Triad records it as one of the three direful maladies, and it is even employed as an image of horror in the compositions of the Bards.

477a — HEININ VARDD

IT would appear that Heinin was Bard to the College of Llanveithin, at Llancarvan, in Glamorganshire, and that he flourished between A.D. 520 and 560. In the "Chwedlau'r Doethion," or "Sayings of Wise Men," preserved in a Welsh MS. called "Llyfr Tre Brynn," and published in the collection of Iolo MSS. by the Welsh MSS. Society, the following saying is attributed to him.—

> Hast thou heard the saying of Heinin,
> The Bard of the college of Llanveithin?[1]
> The brave is never cruel!"

---

1 Qu. ? "Bangor"—Iolo Morganwg.

ESSAYS

THE FOUR
BRANCHES OF THE MABINOGI

An Essay by Ivor B. John

"THE very first thing that strikes one, in reading the Mabinogion, is how evidently the mediaeval storyteller is pillaging an antiquity of which he does not fully possess the secret: he is like a peasant building his hut on the site of Halicarnassus or Ephesus; he builds, but what he builds is full of materials of which he knows not the history, or knows by a glimmering tradition merely: stones 'not of this building,' but of an older architecture, greater, cunninger, more majestical. In the medieval stories of no Latin or Teutonic people does this strike one as in those of the Welsh."

These words of Matthew Arnold express with marvellous insight the impression left upon the reader by the medieval Welsh tales of which the origin and nature are discussed in the present study, and define with accuracy their interest and import for the student. The lover of literature will always turn to them for their intrinsic beauty; for the student they have the further charm of mystery, of possible survival from a past of which well-nigh all other remains have perished.

In the year 1849 Lady Charlotte Guest published the text and translation of a number of Welsh romances, all drawn from the fourteenth century manuscript known as the Red Book of Hergest, save the romance of Taliessin, of which the only known MS. dates back to the seventeenth century. Four of these tales, entitled respectively Pwyll Prince of Dyfed: Branwen daughter of Llyr, Manawyddan son of Llyr and Math son of Mathonwy, form a series. At the head of the tale of Pwyll we find the words: *Llyma dechreu Mabinogi*, "Here is the beginning of the Mabinogi," and Branwen, Manawyddan, and Math are called respectively the second, third, and fourth branches of the Mabinogi. From the singular *Mabinogi* was formed a plural *Mabinogion*, which was used by Lady Guest to designate the entire collection published by her. But strictly speaking the term *Mabinogion*—or, to be quite precise, *The Four Branches of the Mabinogi*—only applies to the four tales cited above, and it is with these four that the present study is alone concerned.

The most casual reader of Lady Guest's collection cannot fail to notice that the Mabinogion proper (we retain the convenient term) differ greatly in important respects from the other romances published by her. A word must be said about these. Two of them, *The Dream of Maxen Wledig* and the *"Contention"* (?) *of Lludd and Llevelys* have obvious affinity with the legendary history worked up by Geoffrey of Monmouth; *Kulhwch and Olwen, The Dream of Rhonabwy, The Lady of the Fountain, Geraint* (Tennyson's *Enid*), *Peredur,* introduce Arthur and other personages of the Arthurian cycle, but a distinction must be made: the first two have no affinity with any of the Arthurian romances handed down to us in French or German, whereas the last three have a close connection (the exact nature of which is a matter of dispute) with the Arthurian romances of the greatest twelfth-century French poet, Chrétien de Troyes, known respectively as *Yvain, Erec,* and *Le Conte du Graal.* Finally, the story of *Taliessin* has features and traits markedly akin to those of the Mabinogion proper, although it is formally connected through the personage of its hero with the Arthur cycle.

The earliest writers who brought this literature to the knowledge of the now Welsh world assumed that *Mabinogi* meant a youth, and that, as Stephens says in his Literature of the Cymry, the tales were "written to while away the time of young chieftains," that they were nothing but a collection of mediaeval Welsh nursery or fairy tales. In reality, as Prof. Rhys has shown, the term *Mabinog* belongs to the Welsh bardic system, and denotes a kind of literary apprentice, a scholar receiving instruction from a qualified bard. *Mabinogi* meant the subject matter of a *Mabinog's* course, the literary stock-in-trade which he had to acquire. This correct appreciation of the force of the term not only enables us to perceive that the Mabinogion must, at the outset at least, have had another object beyond recreation; it also enables us to equate the Welsh collection with another famous mediaeval work, the *Edda Snorra Sturlusonar.* Snorri systematised and summarised the northern mythology in narrative form with the express object of aiding the Skald or Icelandic poet to master one of the main elements of his craft. Again, just as the Skalds used this mythology as a source of what they deemed poetic ornament, introducing allusions, periphrases, variations upon a mythic theme, the merit of which seems to have been measured by their obscure, artificial and contorted character, so Welsh bards in a number of poems which have come down to us make allusions to the personages and incidents of the Mabinogion, allusions of so wilfully obscure a character that if we bad not the tales themselves we should be entirely at a loss to know what the bards were driving at. The fairy-tale, nursery-tale character of the Edda, as of the Mabinogion, is due to both bodies of literature belonging to the same early mythic stratum of belief and fancy as the nursery tale; but whereas the latter is now deliberately restricted to that class of readers, children, who, psychologically, still belong in part to that early stratum, the former were intended to be and were taken seriously by grown-up men.

The foregoing remarks will show the lines upon which we propose to discuss the Mabinogion. They will be regarded as remains of a literature fashioned by a special literary caste, the bards, one of whose definite duties it was to preserve the mythic and heroic traditions of the race.

On seeking to date the tales we find that orthographical peculiarities in the manuscript point to an archetype or archetypes not later than the end of the twelfth century, and the tenth-eleventh century is the date generally adopted by scholars for the fixing of the Four Branches of the Mabinogi in the form in which we are acquainted with them. The chief reason for this opinion is as follows: After the Norman conquest of England the Arthur legend acquired immense popularity, and in the second half of the twelfth century over-ran the literature of all Europe; Wales shared in this movement, and most of the special Welsh Arthurian literature shows affinities with the continental forms. Now the tales with which we are dealing know absolutely nothing of this later Arthur story, and must have been composed before it attained the important position it holds in Welsh literature of the twelfth century.

This date, however, is only of importance in helping us to fix a *terminus ad quem*, for while some tales contain elements which may date from the eleventh century, others go back to the beginning not of recorded history, but of the history of the Aryan race.

The Four Branches of the Mabinogi take the form of prose narratives forming a more or less coherent whole, and are concerned with persons who, generally speaking, are treated as human beings, but who, at the same time, are credited with supernatural powers. In this lies their resemblance to folk and nursery-tales: this is the peculiarity which has made many speak of the *"naivete"* of these tales. If by "naivete" is meant the fact that the supernatural is treated as the most natural thing in the world, and that the turning points of the tales are magical quite as a matter of course, then they *are "naive"*: otherwise these productions of a complex bardic system can lay no more claim to *"naivete "* than the rhapsodies known as the poems of Taliessin.

We have then to ask what is the source of this supernatural element? The characters are treated as human beings, and are often identified with historical or quasi-historical personages. If we accept the tales as originally told of human beings, we must suppose that the supernatural elements were added entirely from the imagination of the writers of the tales. The other alternative is to take the personages of the tales for supernatural beings who came to be treated by the legend mongers as human beings, but who, at the same time, retained their superhuman powers, upon which the incidents, and thus the very existence, of the tale depended.

In other words, we seek to know whether we are dealing with primitive mythology or with deliberate fiction. Analogy at once points out that we are dealing with the very lowest stratum of human thought, with primitive mythology, and the supernatural element in the Mabinogi is only to be understood if we regard it as a manifestation of this mythology.

The process which has taken place in the transmission of the Mabinogi down the ages has been one in which tales originally concerning gods (how these tales were formed at the outset does not now immediately concern us) became shorn of the idea that they really did concern gods, and were told as if of human beings possessing supernatural attributes. In fine, the Four Branches of the Mabinogi are nothing more nor less than degraded and adulterated mythological tales. The fact that the Mabinogi formed the literary equipment of the apprentice bard implies the existence and importance of story-telling in bardic circles; and there certainly existed an enormous number of stories, legends, and tales, of which the Four Branches of the Mabinogi—chosen for some reason unknown to us (or, indeed, the choice may have been perfectly arbitrary) as the ones to be repeated by the apprentice of some school of bards—can only have formed a very small part. We have overwhelming proof of this. Firstly, in the Four Branches themselves; secondly, in other mediaeval Welsh tales; thirdly, in the early Welsh poetry, chiefly that of the so-called Book of Taliessin; fourthly, in what we may call the "catalogue-poem" of the Graves of the Warriors; and fifthly, in the mediaeval prose literature known as the Triads.

It would take too long to enumerate all the plainindications of the existence of other similar tales which are to be found in the Four Branches. This line of research has been exhaustively followed up by Professor Anwyl in his articles in the *Zeitschrift für celtische Philologie*.

The early Welsh poetry—that, for instance, collected by Skene in the "Four Ancient Books of Wales"—contains numerous allusions to characters mentioned in the Four Branches. These characters are referred to along with others in such a manner as to warrant us in believing that they are all of the same type. There are also allusions to incidents in the Four Branches along with allusions to incidents the nature of which is unknown, but which must be similar. All these references are of such a nature—being, as already noted, utterly unintelligible but for our knowledge of the tales- as to preclude any idea of the tales being subsequent to the poems. They are, therefore, either references to the tales as we now actually have them, or to their prototypes. Little has been done in the way of satisfactorily dating these poems, but of those that have been dated by M. Loth, several contain references of the above-mentioned type. These poems range in date from the ninth to the twelfth century, and so, if we accept M. Loth's dating, we may postulate the existence of a mass of legends of the type of the Four Branches at least as early as the ninth century.

Taking next the case of the Triads and the Verses of the Graves, we find that many of the Triads and the whole collection of Verses may be looked upon from one point of view as mere catalogues of tales; for, unless, in the case of the Verses, each of the warriors mentioned was of note, or, in other words, had some tale told of his prowess, his memory would not have been thus preserved. The same is true of the Triads. In the case of heroes, places and events mentioned, there must have existed a tale which justified that mention.

In other Welsh mediaeval tales we have similar evidence of a huge wealth of Welsh stories. "Kulhwch and Olwen," for instance, which is an attempt to rejuvenate old material, coupled with a desire on the writer's part to air his own compendious knowledge of Welsh legend, contains enormous catalogues of personages, with their attributes, whom it would have been folly to name, were there not some object, in the way of recalling their story, in thus naming them.

In short, the evidence is overwhelming for the existence of a huge mass of legend of this type in Wales, and so we come back in another way to the point from which we started—namely, the fact that the Four Branches as they stand are a selection or a compilation of certain of these stories.

We have called these tales degraded from a mythological point of view. In fact, so far have they lost their original characteristics under the influence of oral tradition proceeding through long years amongst a people becoming more civilised, and under the influence of Christianity, that, if the Four Branches of the Mabinogi stood alone, it would be exceedingly difficult, if not impossible, to arrive at the original meaning of the legends. The fact already mentioned, of the crediting of personages otherwise human with superhuman attributes would be almost the only clue to the mythological "stratum" in the tales.

But, as we have said, the Four Branches do not stand quite alone; even in Welsh literature we have analogues and aids. Firstly, in the other mediaeval tales we find, scattered up and down, a little help, for they too contain some of the original mythological *données*. We have also the early poems, but in this case, unfortunately, the help we get is far less than we have a reason to expect, owing to their obscure nature. We have again the Bruts (Chronicles), which aid us chiefly in picking out the historical and quasi-historical adulterations. We have also the mass of legendary literature dating from the twelfth to the fifteenth centuries known as the Triads, and, finally, we have the legend of Taliessin, which, although late in the form in which we now have it (sixteenth-seventeenth century), is of equally early origin with the Four Branches, and is their closest analogue in Welsh literature. Going further afield, the abundant early Irish literature furnishes the greatest amount of help, and it is chiefly by comparison with it that the riddle of the Mabinogi may be read. Its greater extent renders the work of mythological identification easier; the Welsh characters corresponding to the Irish are thus also recognised as mythological.

Comparison with Irish literature reveals striking similarities between many Irish and Welsh tales, similarities which may be divided into two groups. Firstly, there are resemblances between the fundamental *données* of the tales, indicating as they do still closer resemblances between Welsh and Irish cycles of tales in their earlier stages. The Mabinogi have evidently been pieced together very like a mosaic, and it is palpably evident that, in the form in which we now have them, they are only a collection of more or less cleverly-joined fragments of earlier tales. Where, therefore, we find that many of these fragments exhibit a close connection with Irish legend, we are justified in supposing that the earlier forms of the Welsh tales bore a very great resemblance to those of Ireland. This is best seen on equating the characters. The children of Dôn, whom we meet in the story of Math, are undoubtedly equivalent to the Tuatha de Danann (the tribes of the Goddess Danu). These Irish beings are Irish gods, and the children of Dôn are possessed of such magic attributes as stamp them as gods of Welsh legend. Govannon, son of Dôn, the Welsh smith, can be none other than the smith Goibniu (genitive Goibnenn, the form nearest to the Welsh), of the Tuatha. Manawyddan mab Llyr is evidently the Manannan mac Lir of Ireland, the lord of the Otherworld, though not recognisable as such in the Mabinogi.

Owing to the degraded nature of the Welsh tales, and to their composite mosaic character, the relative importance of the personages has been disturbed, and we ought to be quite prepared to find that personages playing very shadowy parts in the tales are really of great importance from the original point of view. This is true, for instance, of a character called Beli. He plays no distinct part in the Four Branches. He is but mentioned. He seems to be the husband of Don, though this does not appear from the tales, and he is probably to be equated with the Irish Bile, the father of Mile, the eponymous hero of the Milesians. Bile's realm was Spain, which, in the strongly euhemerised mediaeval texts where alone this section of Irish mythic history is preserved to us, corresponds with the Otherworld or Hades.

Secondly, we have similarities between names and incidents in the tales which are not fundamental, but a great deal more superficial: cases where, undoubtedly, the Welsh have been borrowing from the Irish; in other words, we have cases of direct influence of the Irish upon the Welsh story-tellers. In Branwen, for instance, the Llinon is evidently the Shannon, while in other tales of the Mabinogion we have forms like Esgeir Oervel for Sescenn Uairbheoil, Garselit for Gearr-Selut, whilst in Kulhwch and Olwen we have Cnychwr mab Ness for Conchobar mac Nessa.

How are these resemblances to be accounted for?

Two differing theories have been suggested. It is known that at the beginning of recorded history there existed a large number of Goidels (Irish Celts, though an incorrect expression for that period, explains whom we mean by Goidels) in West Wales, and the differences in the two theories depend upon the different manner of accounting for the presence of these Goidels.

One theory believes that the Goidels formed the first wave of Celtic immigration or conquest from the Continent. They were followed by the Brythons, that branch of the Celts to which the Gauls and Welsh belong, who drove their predecessors westward until, when recorded history begins, very few of the first Goidelic inhabitants survived in West Wales. The conquest of the western part of North Wales by the North British Cunedda and his sons in the fourth century of our era, the first historical fact that emerges from the gloom and uncertainty of early tradition, would then appear to be the final crushing out of Goidelic resistance, after which the remaining Goidels would live peaceably with their conquerors and gradually amalgamate with them, adopting their language. The resemblance of Welsh to Irish legend is accounted for by those who hold this theory on the supposition that these Goidels transmitted their tales to the Welsh, and that the latter, developing them along their own lines, differentiated them somewhat from their originals. This is, in outline, the theory held by Professor Rhys.

Professor Kuno Meyer, on the other hand, holds that there is no jot of evidence, historical, philological, or traditional, to justify the idea that a Goidei ever set foot in Britain except as a conqueror from Ireland. The Goidels found in Wales he treats as piratical invaders from Ireland in the second-fifth centuries. Relying upon the evidence of names, he says that the Irish tales were borrowed by the Welsh not earlier than the ninth century, and that they were handed over by oral tradition.

On reviewing these two theories we find that the first accounts in a fascinating manner, analogous to that of other conquests from the Continent, for the coming of the Goidels and Brythons. The second theory does not touch this point.

Professor Meyer is able to bring forward much tangible evidence in support of his theory, while that of Professor Rhys, rests more upon conjecture.

Glancing back at our division of the similarities to be found in the tales we find that Professor Meyer's theory deals only with the second group, that of the more superficial resemblances. In the tale of the heated house in Branwen, which Professor Meyer equates with the Irish *Mesce Ulad,* we have an evident and natural interpolation. Professor Meyer's theory does not, really explain the vast amount of correspondence between the fundamental *données* of the tales which form our first class of similarities.

An argument against the late borrowing of Irish legend by Welsh bards, which has hitherto been entirely overlooked may be drawn from an examination of the relations of the borrowed incidents to the whole mass of Irish literature. Let us assume that the Welshmen did borrow in the ninth, tenth, and eleventh centuries: surely they would have borrowed those legends which were most popular with the Irish story-tellers. In that case we should find numerous adaptations of the great Ulster heroic cycle, whereas, save for a passing notice of Conchobar in Kulhwch, and one poem known as "*Marwnad Conroi mab Dairi,*" having for its theme the enmity between Cuchulainn and Curoi, Welsh literature ignores the Ulster cycle entirely. On the other hand it presents a mass of analogues with the mythological cycle, that in which the Tuatha de Danann are the protagonists. Now, from the tenth century on, at least, the Irish had begun to euhemerise this cycle, and to present its characters as pre-Christian kings and warriors. Only one long example of a romantic treatment of the mythological cycle has survived in Irish, although a considerable number of story-skeletons have been preserved owing to their inclusion in biographical and topographical works compiled by Irish antiquaries of the tenth and eleventh centuries. On the other hand we possess some fifty to sixty tales of the heroic cycle dating, in their present form, from this very period. These facts seem effectually to negative the proposition that Welsh mythic romance borrowed its substance and subject matter from Ireland in the tenth-eleventh centuries. That style, mode of narration, colouring, and subsidiary incident may have been affected is quite another matter.

Both theories agree in believing that since there was a Goidelic population in Wales, since the Mabinogi appear to belong to the Goidelic regions of Wales, and since there is a great similarity between the Welsh and Irish tales, therefore the Mabinogi must be Goidelic in origin. Approaching the question from the more purely Welsh side we find ourselves met by many difficulties in the way of accepting this view. The tales are avowedly mythological: why should the Goidels only have had a mythology? Or, if the Brythons are allowed to have had a mythology at all, why should the Goidelic mythology alone have survived? Again, are we to suppose that the whole jealous bardic system of Wales existed for the sole purpose of retailing exotic Irish legends? We have already proved that a vast amount of legend similar to that of the Four Branches existed at one time. Was that, too, Goidelic in origin? If not, why should only a Goidelic literature have survived?

Is it possible then to formulate a theory that will offer fewer difficulties?

It is plain that Goidels and Brythons are closely related branches of the Celtic stock; and of course the Celtic stock is itself but a branch of the Indo-European or Aryan family. Comparative Mythology and Folklore Study have demonstrated community of myth and legend between the most widely separated branches of the Aryan family, and this community is best explained by postulating the existence of primary Aryan myth-roots which the different branches of the Aryan race differentiated along their own lines. Applying this to the Celtic stock we find that the scission between Goidel and Brython is comparatively late in history and comparatively small when compared with those scissions that lie between the main branches of the Aryan family. There ought therefore to be no difficulty in supposing that the deeper community of legend, that indicated by our first class of similarities, depends upon the existence of an early Celtic mythology which Goidel and Brython shared in common.

The more superficial resemblances which we placed in our second group may possibly be but late borrowings, as Professor Meyer has argued with great force. Considering the close relation of Goidel to Brython it would be surprising if they had not borrowed from one another at all.

We shall therefore treat the Four Branches of the Mabinogi as the degraded Brythonic development of early Celtic myth-roots, owing their deeper resemblances to Irish tales to original community of myth, and their more superficial resemblances to late influence from Irish sources.

The form of these tales is, as we have already stated, that of prose narrative. In three places do we find verses embedded in the prose. These verses, however, are not like the verses found in Irish prose tales, either a kind of lyric outburst or a recapitulation of the incidents told in prose, but are more of the runic or riddling nature of the fragments of doggerel to be found in certain nursery tales. Skene's idea that the tales are founded upon the poems of "Taliessin," &c., in the same way as the great French prose romances of the thirteenth-fifteenth century are prose redactions of the poems of Chrétien de Troyes and his imitators, is absurd, for the poems contain references only, often most obscure, to already existing tales, and in themselves make not the slightest attempt to tell any connected story.

Nor have we any reason for believing that the tales are founded upon poems which are now lost to us, for there is not a particle of evidence with which to oppose Professor Zimmer's conclusion that the Celts threw their narratives into prose while the Teutons preferred to cast theirs in poetic form.

We shall now approach the tales more closely, pointing out the features of note as we go along.

PWYLL, PRINCE OF DYFED

Pwyll, prince of Dyfed, goes a-hunting in Glyn Cuch. Separated from his men, be meets a pack of wondrous hounds following a stag, which they pull down before him in a little clearing in the wood. After admiring for a while the beauty of the dogs, whose coats are a shining white, and whose ears are a brilliant red, he drives them off, and calls on his own pack to the quarry. A grey rider on a grey steed rides up and rebukes Pwyll for this discourteous deed. Pwyll offers to make amends, and the offer is at once accepted. Pwyll and the grey stranger, who is Arawn, King of Annwn (Hades), are to exchange appearances, kingdoms, and duties. Pwyll is to fight a duel with Hafgan, the enemy of Arawn, a rival king in Annwn. Pwyll will overcome his opponent at the first onset, and he is on no account to strike Hafgan a second blow, for a second blow has the power of reviving the vanquished king, instead of putting an end to him. In a year's time Pwyll and Arawn are to meet again in Glyn Cuch to exchange shapes once more, and they separate to carry out the bargain.

Pwyll is taken for Arawn at the latter's court, sleeps innocently with Arawn's queen, and on the appointed day mortally wounds Hafgan, unites Annwn under his own headship, and returns to the trysting-place to meet Arawn. They take once more their own proper shapes, and return to their own courts. Arawn at once discovers from his wife how true a friend he had in Pwyll, while Pwyll finds that Dyfed had never been so well ruled as during his year of absence. The two kings thereupon exchange valuable presents to re-affirm their friendship; and

Pwyll, because he governed so well in Annwn, and because he united Annwn under one headship in one day, is ever afterwards known as Pwyll Pen Annwn (Pwyll, Head of Hades), laying aside his former title of Pwyll, Prince of Dyfed.

Although in its relationship to the other parts of the tale of Pwyll, this first part appears suspiciously like an explanation, aetiological or sophisticated in nature, of the origin of the appellation Head of Hades, there is no mistaking the mythological element to be found therein. The grey rider on a grey horse is avowedly a King in Hades, one of the darker powers, the possessor of the famous Cwn Annwn (the Dogs of Hades), whose memory has hardly yet died out of the folklore of remoter Wales. His friendship with Pwyll prepares the way for his friendship with the apparent culture-hero of South Wales, Pryderi, the son of Pwyll: a friendship which is implied in the tale of Math mab Mathonwy.

It seems as if the explanation why Pwyll was called Pen Annwn is weak and insufficient, and when we ask why such an explanation was rendered necessary at all we are driven to the conclusion that there must have been two Pwylls— one a historical or quasi-historical Prince of Dyfed, and the other a Pwyll who had always been considered as Pen Annwn, *i.e.*, a mythological character who had always been King of Hades. The writer of our story had evidently identified and confused the two characters.

As an instance of the degradation of the tale from a mythological point of view we may notice that Annwn, the Celtic Otherworld, which in the Irish tales is generally treated as across the sea or within a hill, is here looked upon as a mundane region—an ordinary province seemingly bordering upon Dyfed.

In the next part of the story, Pwyll, during a great feast at Arberth (the modern Narberth), walks out and seats himself upon a mound called Gorsedd Arberth, This mound has a magic "privilege": every one of high birth seating himself upon it is either soundly beaten or sees a marvel. A strange lady riding slowly towards them upon a white steed appears to Pwyll and his companions. He sends one of his men to meet her but she passes by, and cannot be overtaken on foot. She is pursued on horseback, but, without any apparent hastening, she defies pursuit. Next day she appears to them again at the same time and place, and a squire mounted on the fastest horse procurable follows her in vain. On the third day Pwyll himself gives chase, and on his praying her to stop, she graciously does so, Pwyll is fascinated by her beauty, while she, on her part admits that she has come to seek him for a husband. She is Rhiannon, the daughter of Heveidd Hên, and is sought in marriage by an unwelcome suitor, Gwawl fab Clud. She gives Pwyll a rendezvous a year hence at her father's court, where the marriage feast will be prepared.

At the appointed time the feast is about to commence when a stranger appears and asks a boon. Pwyll promises to grant it, and the stranger (who is none other than Gwawl fab Clud) demands Rhiannon and the feast. Rhiannon, however, claims the feast for the retainers, and, telling Pwyll to grant the boon, shows him how to get the better of the unwelcome visitor. Rhiannon is to be given to Gwawl in a year's time, but on the day of the marriage Pwyll is to conceal a body of his men near the festal hall, and disguising himself in rags, is to enter and ask a boon of Gwawl. This boon is to be the filling of a magic bag, the gift of Rhiannon herself, with provisions; and this bag, no matter how much he put into it, will never get any fuller. On being questioned, Pwyll is to say that it will not be properly filled until a noble step in and press down its contents with his feet, saying, "Enough has been put in." Pwyll is to fasten the bag around Gwawl, whom Rhiannon engages to make enter the bag, and calling in his ambushed men is to dictate his own terms. Gwawl is satisfied with Pwyll's apparent compliance, and departs to his own country. Pwyll also returns to Dyfed.

At the end of the year the marriage feast is prepared for Gwawl. Rhiannon's cunning scheme works out perfectly: Gwawl is caught in the bag and beaten by Pwyll's men, and finally allowed to go on promising to seek no vengeance in the future. Pwyll and his bride return to Arberth with the blessing of Heveidd Hên, and they rule prosperously for two years.

This forms the second section of the tale, and we have here the legend which tells of the meeting of Pwyll with his wife Rhiannon. Seated on a wondrous mount Pwyll is sought by a supernatural bride. This looks exceedingly like the wooing of a mortal by a fairy bride; for we notice that in this part of the tale Pwyll is treated as a mere mortal credited with no supernatural powers or privileges, while the magic powers of Rhiannon show up in sharp contrast.

Rhiannon is a difficult character to identify mythologically. Professor Rhys was at first inclined to regard her as an embodiment of the dawn or dusk, but later connected her with the moon. She is the daughter of Heveidd Hên, and the appellation Hên, the Ancient, generally seems to refer in these stories to a dim mythological character appreciated as such to a certain extent by a writer who is evidently looking back upon the old order of things.

Since Gwawl fab Clud is an enemy of Pwyll's, and since Pwyll is one of the darker powers, Gwawl should be classed among the solar heroes. This section of the tale may therefore be interpreted as a representation of the struggle between the powers of light and darkness for the possession of the moon-bride.

At the end of two years Pwyll is still without an heir, and the nobles of the country utter their discontent, and ask Pwyll to take another wife. He demands, and is granted, a year's delay, and before the end of that time a son is born, who is, however, spirited away while the six women watchers are asleep. They discover the loss before Rhiannon awakes, and killing a puppy, they lay its bones near her, and swear to the unhappy mother that she herself has slain her child. The rumour spreads, and Pwyll is asked to separate from his wife. This he indignantly refuses to do, and Rhiannon, as penance, has to sit at the outer gate of the court, tell her story to every comer, and offer to carry him into the court. Seldom does any one consent to be carried.

At this time Teyrnon Twrf Vliant, "the best man in the world," is lord of Gwent-is-Coed. Every night of the Calends of May a beautiful mare of his gives birth to a foal which immediately disappears. At the time of our story Teyrnon resolves to watch at the fateful hour, fully armed. A frightful noise is heard; a great claw is thrust in through the window and seizes the new-born foal. Teyrnon cuts the claw through at the joint, and rushes out; in the darkness there is nothing to be seen, and he only hears a terrible noise. Returning, he finds at the door a man-child wrapped in a fair mantle. He takes the child to his wife, and they rear him up under the name of Gwri Gwallt Euryn (Gwri of the Golden Hair). He grows apace—wondrously for his age—and at four years wants to drive the horses to water. He is given the horse born the night he was found.

Teyrnon and his wife now hear of the doings and happenings at the court of Pwyll; Teyrnon recognises in Gwri the lineaments of Pwyll, and, out of pity for Rhiannon, the couple agree to send Gwri to the court. Next day Teyrnon sets forth with his foster-son to the court, and, after seeing Rhiannon doing her penance, and of course refusing to be carried, both are heartily welcomed at the court. Teyrnon makes known his object, and the child is at once recognised as the offspring of Pwyll. Pendaran Dyfed, to whom the child is afterwards given to rear, renames him Pryderi (Anxiety), from the first words uttered by Rhiannon on learning the truth. Teyrnon and his wife are promised great recompense, and the tale comes to a rapid close with a mention of the death of Pwyll, the consequent accession of Pryderi to the headship of Dyfed, and his marriage to Kicva.

It is only in this section that we come to the real kernel of the tale of Pwyll, namely the birth of Pryderi. Working backwards we can now surmise how the tale was put together. Firstly, we have the birth of Pryderi: then naturally follows the account of the meeting of his parents, and thirdly we have the explanation of his father's strange sobriquet, Pen Annwn. Not only is Pryderi the central character of the tale of Pwyll, but it is only through Pryderi that we connect together the Four Branches of the Mabinogi. This does not necessarily mean that the writers of the tales had any idea of securing the unity of the Four Branches in this manner.

From a mythological point of view Gwri Gwallt Euryn must be treated apart from Pryderi. His rapid growth and his golden hair are the characteristics of a solar hero, whilst Pryderi, friendly as he is with the powers of darkness, cannot be treated in the same way. There is probably here a fusion of different tales concerning opposed mythological characters whose opposition was not noticed or understood by the compiler of the tales. This seems likely because there is no explanation given why Pryderi should have been found at the door of Teyrnon's palace. It may very well be, as Professor Anwyl suggests, that one version of the tale made Teyrnon the father of Pryderi. The names Teyrnon and Rhiannon when reduced to their earlier Celtic equivalents, *Tigernonos* and *Rigantona (i.e.,* King and Queen) form a pair, a circumstance which warrants Professor Anwyl's suggestion. It does not seem safe to follow these hypotheses too far when based upon slender evidence, as they are apt to lead to contradictions. "Doctors disagree" about Pryderi for instance: for Mr. Nutt suggests that Manawyddan was once credited with being the father of Pryderi. Arguing from Irish analogues to the tale there is substantial ground for the supposition, and in the giving of Rhiannon to Manawyddan to wife in the third tale of the series, we find, according to Mr. Nutt, a trace of the original version of the story.

BRANWEN DAUGHTER OF LLYR

The tale of Branwen in itself does not follow directly from Pwyll, but is connected with that tale by the third in the series, Manawyddan. It is true that we do meet again with Pryderi, but he is barely mentioned, and when we attempt to Branwen we are met by evident confusion, as may be seen at once on examining the references to Pendaran Dyfed in both tales.

Bran the Blessed, son of Llyr, is seated one day with his brother Manawyddan, his half-brothers Nissyen the peacemaker and Evnissyen the mischief-maker, on a rock above the sea at Harlech. Thirteen vessels draw near, one of which advancing, makes signs of peace, and in due time Matholwch, King of Ireland, is welcomed on shore as a suitor for the hand of Bran's sister, Branwen. The Irish King is at once accepted, and the marriage feast is held in tents at Aberffraw—in tents because no house large enough for Bran had ever been built. Next day Evnissyen, because his consent to his half-sister's marriage has not been asked, cuts off the lips, ears, tails and eyebrows of Matholwch's horses. Matholwch, surprised and outraged, takes to his ships, but returns on being assured that Bran knew nothing of the insult, and is willing to make ample amends in horses and gold. Bran, seeing that at the feast Matholwch still appears melancholy, supplements his other gifts by that of a magic cauldron which has the power of regenerating by the morrow any dead warrior thrown into it. Matholwch seems pleased. Next evening they fall to talking about the cauldron. Bran informs Matholwch that it was brought from Ireland by Llasar Llaesgyfnewid and his wife Kymideu Kymeinvoll when they escaped from the white-hot iron house in Ireland. Matholwch knows the rest of the history-how one day he was sitting by a lake when an enormous man came up, along with a woman twice as big as he, and bearing a cauldron on his back; how the woman was soon to give birth to a fully-armed warrior; how these people (and their descendants evidently, although the tale does not state exactly how they multiplied) became a plague in the country: how they were imprisoned in an iron house which was made white hot: how the man and woman alone escaped, and evidently came to Britain, where, adds Bran, they have multiplied and become exceeding fine warriors.

This tale introduces us to new characters. We now meet the family of Llyr, whose fortunes, along with those of the family of Dôn and the family of Pwyll, make up, looked at from this point of view, the Four Branches of the Mabinogi.

Bendigeid Vran owes his appellation, not as a sophisticated Triad informs us, to the fact that he was one of the early Christianisers of the island, but in all probability to his being worshipped at some remote period. He was, seemingly, the tutelary deity of bardism and minstrelsy, and it is only in this light that we can succeed in making anything of the curious passage in the next section of the tale where he carries his musicians across to Ireland on his back.

The tale of the cauldron told during the feasting, which Professor Meyer equates with an incident in the *Mesce Ulad,* a tale of the Ulster heroic cycle, would very naturally be slipped in by the compiler knowingly as an Irish tale, told by an Irish visitor. It has no vital connection with the real tale of Branwen.

Magic cauldrons play a great part in Celtic literature. The Tuatha De Danaan, possessed one: the poems in the Book of Taliessin, and the prose legend of Taliessin speak of them. One of the Spoils of Annwn, obtained by the Culture-hero seems to have been a magic cauldron, and poetry and inspiration seem to have their origin in a cauldron. Perhaps, as Professor Rhys suggests, this last idea is a relic of the days when the Aryan medicine-man intoxicated himself or worked himself into a state of ecstacy or trance by means of a sacred brewage.

Matholwch takes Branwen to Ireland, and all goes well for a year. Suddenly the question of Evnissyen's outrage is revived, and Branwen is driven from the King's side to the kitchen, where she is struck every morning by the butcher. This goes on for three years unknown to any one in Britain, for all communication has been stopped by Matholwch's orders. Meanwhile Branwen rears a starling, who carries a letter to Bran. Leaving Britain to seven governors, Bran sets out for Ireland; his men are in ships, but he wades across himself, carrying his musicians on his back. (This passage is very obscure, and has probably suffered at the hands of a scribe.) To Matholwch's swineherds the fleet and the head of Bran appear like a wood and a mountain advancing: Branwen, however, knows and explains what they are. Matholwch and his men retreat across the Llinon (Shannon), which the Britons cross upon Bran's extended body. The Irish submit, but Bran seems unwilling to come to terms until he is won over by the Irish building for him a house big enough for him to enter, a thing never done before. This house is to be a trap, for men are concealed in bags all round the pillars of the building. Evnissyen, however, finds this out, and deliberately kills, one by one, all the hidden warriors. Peace is concluded in this hall, when suddenly Evnissyen throws Branwen's child into the blazing fire. Tumult and massacre ensue. The Irish make use of the magic cauldron of regeneration until Evnissyen, concealing himself among the Irish dead, is thrown in and bursts it, breaking his own heart in the effort. Seven Britons alone escape, along with Bran, who is wounded by a poisoned lance. He orders the seven to cut off his head and to take it to be buried in the White Hill in London, with the face towards France. On the journey, he tells them, they will be seven years feasting at Harlech, while the birds of Rhiannon will sing to them: at Gwales, in Pembroke they will rest eighty years, until one of them opens a door looking upon Cornwall. "With Branwen and the head the seven set out for Britain. On landing in Anglesey, Branwen, thinking upon the misery she has brought to two countries, falls dead of a broken heart. The bearers of the head find that the seven governors have been killed, and they proceed with their journey. Everything turns out as Bran has foretold, and the head is buried in the White Hill at London.

The tale ends with an obvious appendix explaining how Ireland was repeopled by the offspring of five pregnant women who were the sole remaining inhabitants of Ireland on Branwen's departure.

In this part of the tale Bran alters his mythological character. As a wonderful head, Professor Rhys compares him with the Janus of the Roman Pantheon, and with the Gallo-Roman Cernunnos. These comparisons are suggestive, but in the last degree hypothetical.

The tale of Branwen as a whole is exceedingly interesting in presenting, as Mr. Nutt points out, remarkable analogies with the Teutonic tales of the Nibelung and Gudrun cycles. It differs in character from the three other tales of the series, for it seems to paint for us pictures of deliberate cruelty—that of the casting of the child into flames, that of Evnissyen's cruelty to the horses, and his cold-blooded way of killing the bagged Irish—which have no parallels in the other tales. Bloodshed there certainly is in Math, but it seems there to be mentioned with regret, while in Branwen, we seem to catch some of the ferocity and fierce lust of blood peculiar to the Teutonic saga.

When Evnissyen fell upon Matholwch's horses, "he cut off their lips at the teeth and their ears close to their heads, and their tails close to their backs: and where he could not lay hold of the eyebrows (here the exact meaning is not clear), he cut them to the bone: and so he disfigured the horses and rendered them useless."

When the two hundred Irish warriors were concealed in bags hanging on the pillars of the festal hall, Evnissyen entered "and scanned the house with fierce and savage looks, and descried the leathern bags which were around the pillars." "What is in the bag?" asked he of one of the Irish. "Meal, good soul," said he. And Evnissyen felt about it until he came to the man's head, and he squeezed the head until he felt his fingers meet together in the brain through the bones. And he left that one and put his hand upon another, and asked what was therein? "Meal," said the Irishman. So he did the like unto every one of them until he had not left alive of all the two hundred save one only; and when he came to him, he asked what was there? "Meal, good soul," said the Irishman. And he felt about until he felt the head, and he squeezed that head as he had done the others. And albeit he found that the head of this one was armed, he left him not until he had killed him. And then he sang an *Englyn:*

> There is in this bag a different sort of meal,
> The ready combatant, when the assault is made
> By his fellow warriors, prepared for battle.

When peace was being concluded in the hall, and Gwern the son of Branwen and Matholwch was being fondled by all, "Wherefore," said Evnissyen, "comes not my nephew the son of my sister unto me? Though he were not king of Ireland, yet willingly would I fondle the boy." "Cheerfully let him go to thee," said Bendigeid Vran: and the boy went unto him cheerfully. "By my confesssion to Heaven," said Evnissyen, "unthought of by the household is the slaughter that I will this instant commit." Then he arose and took up the boy by the feet, and before any one could seize hold of him, he thrust the boy into the blazing fire. And when Branwen saw her son burning in the fire, she strove to leap into the fire also from the place where she sat between her two brothers. But Bendigeid Vran grasped her with one hand, and his shield with the other. Then they all hurried about the house, and never was there made so great a tumult by any host in one house as was made by them, as each man armed himself."

By dint of careful comparison with the various versions of the Teutonic legend, Mr. Nutt has succeeded in proving that the affinities of Branwen are with the more Northern forms, and when seeking to explain how a Welsh tale could be influenced by Northern Teutonic tales, we at once remember the fact, that both coasts of the Irish Sea were under the sway of the Danes and "Northmen" in the ninth and tenth centuries. Whether we accept the theory of the late Irish or of the more purely Welsh origin of the tales, the Danish influence could creep in equally well from Ireland or from Wales. It seems more natural, however, and is more in accordance with the hypothesis given above to take it as coming direct to the Welsh; for the Danes allied themselves with the Welsh against the Saxons, and appear to have formed considerable permanent settlements around the Welsh coasts. In the peninsula of Gower, for instance, an astonishingly large number of the place-names are of Danish origin.

The Danes therefore may well have told their sagas to the Welsh, and thus the Danish influence crept into the tale of Branwen.

Of course, it is not intended for an instant to say that the tale of Branwen is of Danish origin. Branwen, like the three other tales, is a conglomeration of various elements, the form into which they were finally thrown being alone influenced by the tales of the Northmen. The final incident shows that the tale in its extant form was not put together before the late eleventh century, as the Irish legend which it repeats is an antiquarian invention probably not older than the early part of that century.

MANAWYDDAN, SON OF LLYR

The next tale, Manawyddan, is a direct continuation of Branwen.

After burying the head of Bran, Manawyddan, one of the seven, turns to Pryderi, also one of the seven, and bewails the fact that he is now landless. Pryderi, however, gives Manawyddan his mother Rhiannon to wife, together with a portion of Dyfed, and for a while the four—Pryderi and Kicva and Manawyddan and Rhiannon—live very happily.

One evening they seat themselves upon Gorsedd Arberth. A thunderclap is heard, a thick mist arises which passes away to reveal the erstwhile smiling country utterly deserted and bare. They make the best of matters and live comfortably enough for two years, when provisions begin to run short. They now make for Lloegr, supporting themselves by making, first saddles, then shields, and then shoes, each time being driven away by the envy of the other makers of these articles. They eventually return to Arberth, and live for a month upon game. One morning the hunting dogs of Pryderi and Manawyddan follow a boar into a strange castle. In spite of the warning of Manawyddan Pryderi enters it too. There he sees a fountain, to which is chained a golden goblet. Seizing the goblet, his hands cling to it, while his feet are held to the marble slab on which he stands. Manawyddan returns to Arberth alone, and is reproached by Rhiannon, who seeks the castle, and suffers the same fate as Pryderi. A clap of thunder is heard, the castle and all within it disappear.

Kicva and Manawyddan are now left alone. Manawyddan swears to take no advantage of their position, and they set out to become shoemakers once more in Lloegr. Driven back to Dyfed by the jealousy of the other shoemakers, Manawyddan sows some wheat, which, when ripe, is carried away mysteriously. Watching the last of it, he finds that an army of mice, of which he captures one, are responsible for the theft. In spite of the entreaties of Kicva, he resolves to hang this mouse on Gorsedd Arberth, and while in the act of doing so a clerk rides up and endeavours to dissuade him in every way, even offering him much money for the animal. Manawyddan is not to be turned from his purpose, and a priest who rides up later has no better success than the clerk. Finally, with a bishop, Manawyddan makes a bargain. He will release the mouse if the bishop will bring back Pryderi and Rhiannon, explain his interest in the mouse, restore everything to its former condition, and swear to seek no vengeance in the future. This is done. The mouse is the wife of the bishop, who is himself Llwyd Kil Coed, a friend of Gwal fab Clud, and the enchantment of Dyfed and the rape of Pryderi and Rhiannon are in revenge for the treatment of Gwawl by the father of Pryderi as told in the tale of Pwyll.

The tale ends with a phrase indicating the existence of a variant version, where greater prominence is evidently given to the doings of Pryderi and Rhiannon during the time of the enchantment.

In the tale of Manawyddan we have on the largest scale that peculiar element of magic which so charmed the world later in the Arthurian romances of France. Here we have a whole province depopulated and laid waste for years by enchantment, and the event is written of quite soberly, and treated as quite a matter of course, as, indeed, are all the other magical incidents of the tales.

Mythologically, Llwyd Kil Coed, although his name means the Grey One, appears as a friend of Gwawl fab Clud, a solar hero, as we have seen; Llwyd, therefore, is to be called a solar hero. Pryderi, the darker divinity, and Rhiannon, the moon-goddess, fall into his power. Manawyddan—the Manannan mac Lir of Ireland, Lord of the Otherworld—is here shorn of all his magic attributes, and although he sets Pryderi and Rhiannon free, he seems to do so only by human foresight and cunning, and not by magic spells.

MATH, SON OF MATHONWY

The tale of Math introduces us to the cycle of legends centring round the children of Dôn—the cycle which seems to have been either the greatest in extent or that which was most popular, for we find more references in the poetry to the characters of the story of Math than to those of any other of the Four Branches.

The plainest and most obvious reference to incidents in the Mabinogion occurs in connection with this tale. It is to be found in poem xvi. of the so-called Book of Taliessin. We give Mr. Skene's translation of it, and it will serve as a fair example of the style of the "Taliessin" poems.

> The most skilful man ever heard of
> Gwydyon ab Don, of toiling spirits,
> Enchanted a woman from blossoms,
> And brought pigs from the south.
> Since he had no sheltering cots,
> Rapid curves and plaited chains,
> He made the forms of horses
> From the springing
> Plants, and illustrious saddles.
>
> When are judged the chairs
> Excelling them will be mine;
> My chair, my cauldron and my laws
> And my pervading eloquence meet for the chair.
> I am called skilful in the court of Don
> I and Euronwy and Euron.
> I saw a fierce conflict in Nant Ffrangcon

On a Sunday at the time of dawn
Between the bird of wrath and Gwydyou,
Thursday certainly, they went to Mona
To obtain whirlings and sorcerers.
Arianrod, of laudable aspect, dawn of serenity,
The greatest disgrace evidently on the side of the Brython.

It is easy to recognise the references to the incidents in Math, and it is equally easy to understand, even from the above instance, which is comparatively simple, why these poems, in the sections which are not explained by the tales, are called obscure.

Math, Head of Gwynedd, could only rest with his feet in a virgin's lap, and the virgin who performed this task was Goewin, the most beautiful girl of her time. Gilvaethwy, son of Dôn, confesses his love (under difficulties for Math can bear every whisper that the wind reaches) for Goewin to his brother Gwydion, and the latter promises, in default of other means, to raise the South in order to get Math off to war and so enable Gilvaethwy to work his will. Gwydion then sets off for South Wales with the ostensible object of obtaining from Pryderi some new animals which the latter had evidently obtained from Annwn. These animals are pigs. Disguising themselves as bards, Gwydion and his companions are well received at Pryderi's court, but are not successful in obtaining the desired animals as a boon. Finally they receive them in exchange for dogs and horses marvellously equipped, which Gwydion manufactures by enchantment. The tale now traces Gwydion's return journey northward, through all the places whose names are connected with pigs. The enchanted horses and dogs only keep their shape for a little while, and the army of Pryderi is soon in Gwynedd. Math marches out to meet the Southerners, and Gilvaethwy immediately takes the opportunity of having his will of Goewin. A terrible battle ensues in favour of the men of Gwynedd: a truce is agreed upon, but is broken by the victors, and finally a duel is arranged between Gwydion and Pryderi, in which the latter is slain chiefly through Gwydion's magic power. The people of the South seek their homes in sorrow.

On his return to his court Math discovers the treachery of Gilvaethwy and Gwydion. As a recompense to Goewin, Math takes her to wife, while he metes out a dreadful punishment to Gilvaethwy and Gwydion. For one year he transforms them into a couple of deer: for a second into a couple of pigs: for a third into a couple of wolves, and in each of these wild states they have issue, creatures turned into human beings later by the magic wand of Math. At the end of the third year the two brothers are allowed to return to their proper shapes.

Math now seeks another virgin foot-holder, and Arianrhod, daughter of Dôn, is suggested. Math, by aid of his magic powers, discovers that she is no virgin and fleeing from the proof, she gives birth to two male children. One is

Dylan Eil Ton (Dylan son of the Wave), who makes at once for the sea, and who is slain at some unknown time, by his uncle Govannon. The other, concealed and nurtured by Gwydion, grows remarkably fast, and is taken by him to Arianrhod's castle. On being told who the child is, Arianrhod says he will never be named except by her. Gwydion, calling his magic powers again to his aid, obtains a ship and material for shoemaking, and seeks, disguised, along with the boy, the castle of Arianrhod. Dissatisfied with the intentionally ill-fitting shoes sent her by Gwydion, she comes herself to the ship, and seeing the boy strike a bird cleverly she says, "With a sure hand the lion hit the bird." Gwydion immediately declares that the boy has been named the Lion of the sure Hand (Llew Llaw Gyffes), and the enchanted articles suddenly vanish. Arianrhod now declares that the boy shall never be given arms, except by her. Gwydion again gets the better of Arianrhod by entering her castle disguised along with Llew and causing an enchanted hostile fleet to appear. In fear of attack Arianrhod and her maids arm Llew and Gwydion, whereupon the latter informs Arianrhod of what she has done, and the enchanted fleet disappears. This time the incensed Alianrhod declares that Llew shall never have a wife except of her bestowing. But Math and Gwydion fashion him a bride from flowers, and she is called Blodeuwedd. Math gives the couple broad lands in Gwynedd.

One day, during Llew's absence, Gronw Pefr, Lord of Penllyn, seeks hospitality of Blodeuwedd, and the pair conceive and enjoy a guilty love. Gronw induces Blodeuwedd to worm out of Llew the secret of the only way in which he can be killed. She finds that only a javelin, fashioned in a year's time, and worked upon solely during Sunday mass, can serve to wound him: besides, this javelin can only harm him when standing at the side of a bath on a river bank with one foot on the back of a buck and the other on the side of the bath, Gronw prepares the javelin, and when it is ready Blodeuwedd persuades her spouse to show her exactly how the fatal blow would have to be dealt. Gronw, hidden behind a rock, casts the javelin at the right moment, and Llew, uttering a great cry, flies away in the guise of a bird. Gronw then enters into possession of Llew's lands.

Math and Gwydion are sorely grieved when the news of this reaches them, and Gwydion sets out to seek for Llew. Hearing of a sow in Arvon that every morning goes on a mysterious journey, Gwydion one day follows her, and is led to a place (called by a wrong derivation Nant-y-Llew) where an eagle sits dropping carrion from a tree. Gwydion sings some verses to the bird, which descends on his knee, and at a touch from his magic wand becomes a wasted Llew. In a year's time Llew has completely recovered, and marches out to take vengeance upon Gronw and his untrue wife. The latter flies before him, along with her maidens, who are all drowned in Llyn y Morwynion, and is finally turned by Gwydion, as a punishment for her sins, into an owl. To this day the owl is called Blodeuwedd. Gronw seeks to offer recompense to Llew, but the latter will hear of nothing except that Gronw shall allow a blow to be dealt him in the same way as he dealt the blow to Llew. After seeking in vain to find a substitute Gronw submits, but begs to be allowed to interpose a flat stone between him and the blow. In spite of the stone Llew's javelin is driven home: Gronw is killed, and to this day the pierced stone remains, and is known as Llech Gronw. Llew recovers his domains and governs happily, finally becoming Lord of Gwynedd.

The tale of Math, although not containing "magic" on quite so grand a scale as Manawyddan, is yet more deeply saturated with it, for almost every incident in the tale turns upon magic. This is only to be expected at the court of Math, where the two greatest magicians known to Welsh legend, Math himself and Gwydion, are to be found.

Math, son of Mathonwy, is the greatest of all the mythological characters to be found in the Mabinogi. He is called by Professor Rhys the Celtic Zeus. His characteristics in the tale are justice and magnanimity. He is referred to in the poems, and given the epithet Hên, an epithet which we have noticed in the case of Heveidd as being applied to characters of the old mythology dimly perceived as such by the compilers of the tales.

Gwydion may be treated as a culture-hero introducing into his country valuable animals for the first time. Pigs appear, from various indications, to have been of great importance to the Welsh, and Gwydion is represented as gaining them by craft from Pryderi, who himself had obtained them from Annwn, whence all things of value to man are supposed ultimately to come.

We have already mentioned the identification of the children of Dôn with the Tuatha De Danaan. Llew Llaw Gyffes, a grandson of Dôn, is identified with the Irish Lug Laim-fada, Gyffes apparently meaning something more like "long" than "sure." The proper form of his name is not Llew, but Lleu. Lleu probably meant light, and is apparently the same root as we have in the Welsh words, Goleu and Lleufer, meaning light, and Lleuad, the moon. Lleu is an appropriate designation for the sun-god. His disappearance, caused by Gronw Pefr, is the temporary victory of the powers of darkness: his being brought back by Gwydion is no uncommon feat for the Culture-hero, whom, in this case, we have seen patronising the sun-god all through.

In commenting upon these tales mythological origin and significance have been assumed for them, and they have been interpreted in the terms of that struggle between light and darkness, which, however exaggerated an importance may have been given to it, undoubtedly supplies the motive for a large portion of our mythologies. It should, however, be noted that in Ireland the Tuatha de Danaan, whom we have equated with the races of Dôn and Llyr, appear rather as powers of life and increase generally than specifically as powers of light. In any case, too, it should be clearly understood that the Welsh tales, if mythological, are, as we have pointed out, "degraded" mythology. Myths originally independent seem to have become fused, and in the process to have altered their primitive character and import. Nor is it implied that the bardic story-telling class had any belief in the stories as mythology, however tenaciously they, with the conservatism of the literary class in primitive communities, clung to the traditional framework and incidents. All idea of a bardic esoteric doctrine involving pre-Christian mythic philosophy must be utterly discarded. The bardic class in Wales, as in Ireland, was in so far pre-Christian, as, like the rest of their countrymen, Christianity had only affected them superficially. Their attachment to the old legends, though often undoubtedly frowned upon by the clerical class, is the natural attachment to old tribal tradition of the men who were, by training and calling, the appointed guardians and proclaimers of that tradition. Outside their professional interests, which in Wales, as in Ireland, never seem to have led to any serious conflict with the clergy, the bards were as good, or as bad Christians as their fellows.

But even if all mythological significance refused to the Mabinogion they have, apart from their intrinsic charm, an immense interest for the student of romantic literature. As we have seen, they almost certainly belong, in the present form, to a period antedating the year 1100. Now, they contain many story-themes, incidents, and scenes which figure in the great fairy-tale store common to all Europe, to a large part of Asia and to a portion of Africa. In especial they present most marked points of contact with such portions of that fairy-tale store as have been recovered from the Gaelic-speaking peasants of Ireland and Scotland. It has been asserted, with a vigour generally in precise proportion with the assertor's ignorance of early Celtic literature, that the fairy tales collected orally in modern Gaeldom are comparatively late importations from the Continent, which in its turn received them comparatively late from the East. One valuable feature of early Welsh, as of early Irish literature is the exhibition of what may be called fairy-tale themes bound up with the earliest traditions of the race, and recorded at a date preceding the great contact of West with East in the late eleventh-thirteenth centuries, to which the introduction of so many romantic themes into Europe has been ascribed.

Finally, a word must be said as to the literary merit of these tales. They are admirable examples of story-telling; the main thread of incident is presented clearly and vigorously; there is no lack of picturesque description; the personages, when we consider their fairy-tale nature, are well differentiated and characterised; the whole atmosphere of illusion glamour, and fantasy is admirably rendered. It would be hard to overmatch in its way the closing incident of Manawyddan, no matter what literature we turn to. This excellence of prose narrative is extremely remarkable in view of the date, eleventh century, or at latest early twelfth century, to which we must assign the redaction of these tales in their extant form. There are no examples of either French, German, or English prose narrative of the period which we can adduce by way of comparison. Irish and Scandinavian literature alone offer parallels, and in the case of Scandinavia we cannot be sure how much of pretwelfth century form is retained in what has come down to us. The mythological tales of Snorri's Edda, for instance—the most perfect examples of their style of story-telling in the whole range of literature—how far are their surpassing merits to be attributed to the Scandinavian story-tellers of the tenth and eleventh centuries? Or are they due to the literary genius of the thirteenth century Snorri? If we compare the two literatures as presumably of the same age, the comparison is by no means to the disadvantage of the Welsh. If the Mabinogion have not the realistic virility, the sober picturesqueness, the weight and import of the best examples of Scandinavian story-telling, they have an indefinable charm, a delicate precision of outline and colour, a special glamour of their own to which the others cannot pretend.

Comparison with Irish literature is even more interesting. The Irish tales are certainly older alike in component elements and in redaction, and they have most certainly exercised a marked influence upon the Welsh ones. But Ireland has left us no examples of story-telling as perfect in their way as those of Wales. The conventions are far more rigid, far more strenuously adhered to and insisted upon. Thus the Irish tales have more of the accidental, the modishness of the time. In the one case we have stories, the full appeal of which can only be felt by men familiar with a very elaborate and artificial set of conventions; in others the universal story-loving instinct has scarcely any conventional obstacles of presentment to overcome. It may be noted that besides the strongly conventionalised form of narrative in which most of the Irish heroico-mythic sagas have come down to us, Ireland can also show a number of historic tales as straightforward and natural as the Welsh Mabinogion, with a vein of vigorous realism almost as marked as that of the Scandinavian saga tellers. But the official representatives of Irish literature, the court story-tellers, preferred the artificial conventionalised forms of narrative. This fact supplies another argument against the theory which would make the Mabinogion a mere imitative offshoot of Irish literature. If so, they could not have escaped the peculiarities of style and presentment which distinguish Irish story-telling as practised by its chief official representatives in the tenth, eleventh, and twelfth centuries.

Thus we may regard the Mabinogion as fragments of the old mythic world of our British forefathers; we may consider them simply as links in that chain of Celtic romance which stretches uninterruptedly from the court *file* or *ollamh* of sixthcentury Ireland to the living peasant narrator of Connemara or Argyllshire; or we may read them as delightful examples of fairy-tale telling. Whatever view we take of them, the more we know of them, the greater the interest they arouse, the more enduring the charm they exercise.

An Essay from
'The Mabinogion' by Ivor B. John, printed in *Popular Studies in Mythology Romance and Folklore*, No. 11, 1901, by David Nutt

FOLKLORE AND
MYTH IN THE MABINOGION

An Essay by W. J. Gruffydd

1

For the purpose of this lecture, 'folklore' does not mean folk-culture in its various manifestations as you can see it exhibited and exemplified at St. Fagans and in the famous museums of Scandinavia, but the traditional beliefs and legends of the folk as distinct from the more respectable beliefs and legends which are accepted as facts, and which are called Theology and History respectively. The basis, however, of the greater part of folklore, in the sense in which I use it, is the theology and history of the past handed down from generation to generation and losing, in the passage of time, most of the indications of their original significance. Indeed the line between theology and history on the one hand and folklore beliefs and legends on the other may sometimes be very thin. For example, the existence of a personal Devil is a respectable and orthodox theological tenet, but that has not prevented his very unorthodox entrance into the folklore of the modern nations. Did he not, for instance, build the famous bridge over the river Mynach in Cardiganshire? And King Alfred may very well have burnt the good wife's cakes; if he did, then that story is sober history, but sober history or not, it has now become a folk-legend in England.

You will notice that the title contains the two words, 'Folklore' and 'Myth.' I have used both words because I do not wish at the outset to prejudge the issue whether almost all folklore is ultimately derived from myth, that is, from a primitive belief about the gods, or is of a more lowly origin and to be explained in terms of mass psychology or, as I think more likely, from a mixture of both. Further I must explain that I use the term 'primitive' comparatively. That is to say, 'primitive beliefs,' as far as this lecture is concerned, are only primitive because they belong to a kind of culture which existed before our era, and not necessarily because they are derived from a rude, undeveloped, and inferior state of society. Our knowledge of social conditions in Britain before the Roman Conquest is necessarily limited in spite of the magnificent work done by archaeologists among whom the staff of this museum has a very distinguished place. In short, when I use the term 'primitive,' I have in mind priority in time and custom and not an assessment of human values.

A further point. I have confined myself to one section only of folklore as I have defined it, namely the legends and beliefs about the *Tylwyth Teg*, the Welsh Fairies. There are other folklore details in the Mabinogion on which I cannot touch in this lecture, such as the onomastic stories (stories designed to explain a name); survivals of primitive society as seen in the avoidance of such terms as 'marriage,' 'husband,' and the abnegation of Christian baptism; old games such as the 'Badger in the Bag'; beliefs about *dihenydd*, 'fate'; the swearing of a *tynged*, 'destiny' upon a person, and even one survival of belief which might be related to the development of the *Tylwyth Teg*, namely the existence of an old race of giants as in *Branwen* and in the legends of Ireland. I hope to be able to deal with all these matters elsewhere.

2

If you consult any standard book on Welsh folklore such as Wirt Sikes's *British Goblins* or Sir John Rhŷs's *Celtic Folklore* or Professor Gwynn Jones's *Welsh Folklore* or Hugh Evans's *Tylwyth Teg*, you will find that the place of honour is occupied by stories about the Welsh variety of Fairies who are called in Welsh *Y Tylwyth Teg*, 'the Fair People.' And rightly, because with the exception of a few ghost stories which follow a well-defined formula, and some traditional beliefs and customs mostly connected with death, the bulk of Welsh folklore is concerned with *Y Tylwyth Teg*. Further, the fairy stories of Wales have a character of their own which distinguishes them from those of the rest of Britain and even to a certain extent from the more or less cognate tales of Ireland and Gaelic Scotland.

Now the name *Tylwyth Teg* is curious, so curious indeed that it is surprising that no one, to my knowledge, has questioned its authenticity,—that is, whether it is an old Welsh name to designate the other-world people of folklore, like the Irish *sídhe* which is found in the earliest literature, or whether it is of comparatively late origin. That the name *Tylwyth Teg* cannot be the original designation of the other-world beings known in England as 'fairies' can easily be seen on consideration of its etymological history. It does not occur in our older literature and there is no suggestion of it in the Mabinogion and the other Romances associated with them in the manuscripts. In short, tales of the *Tylwyth Teg*, under that specific name, belong to the comparatively modern folklore of Wales, though, as I hope to prove in this lecture, the material from which they were formed is ancient and abundantly exemplified in the Mabinogion. It should be noted that the name *Tylwyth Teg* is not the designation of the Fairies in every part of Wales; in South Wales the usual name is *Bendith y Mamau*, 'The Blessing of the Mothers.' Rhŷs and others have suggested that the *Mamau* represent the old Celtic *Matronae* and *Matres* of whose universal worship we have abundant archaeological and historical evidence. The Mother of the Immemorial Prisoner in *Culhwch* is Modron, which represents exactly the old Celtic *mātrŏna* whose altars still survive. As to *Bendith* 'blessing,' I can only suggest that it is used to propitiate the fairies just as the Greeks spoke of the Furies as *Eumenides*, 'the

Gracious Ones.' If this is correct then *Bendith y Mamau* is a propitiatory term for *Melltith y Mamau*, 'The Curse of the Matres.'

Let us now consider the name *Tylwyth Teg*. I have been unable to find any instance of it before that which occurs in *Cywydd y Niwl*, attributed to Dafydd ap Gwilym. Here the poet describes himself as lost in the mist which he calls

Hir barthlwyth y Tylwyth Teg

—'A vast accumulation on the forecourt of the *Tylwyth Teg*'. He has lost his way on the moorland, and the description is therefore particularly apt since the *Tylwyth Teg* are traditionally associated with the troubles of forlorn and benighted travellers. The *cywydd*, as I have said, belongs to the Dafydd ap Gwilym period, or at least to the first quarter of the fifteenth century. Why then, it may be asked, is Welsh literature before 1400 both prose and verse, silent about the *Tylwyth Teg*? It is because *their name shows that they were not, so to speak, constituted as a people until after the development of the Arthurian tales of France and their later introduction into the literature of England*; until, in fact a cycle of romance had been created which was based on 'the matter of Britain' and which was necessarily later than the original legendary material of Wales which is incorporated in the Mabinogion.

The name *Tylwyth Teg* betrays its late origin. The first part *tylwyth* roughly corresponds to the English 'household' or 'family' and *teg* means 'fair'; the whole phrase can be translated 'The Fair Folk' or, possibly, 'The Fair Household.' Now it is obvious that *teg* is to be explained in one of three ways. Either (1) it is a translation of the English *fairy*, or (2) the English *fairy* is a translation of the Welsh *teg*, or (3) the name was given independently in Welsh and English to designate the 'fair' people. Fortunately, we need not hesitate between the three explanations, because the derivation of English *fairy* shows that the Welsh *teg* must be a mistranslation of it, due to a complete misunderstanding of its meaning. *Fairy* has nothing whatever to do with *fair*, 'beautiful' or 'blonde,' which is from the Old English *faeger*. The first known instance of *fairy* in English is in the form *feiri* and is dated 1310. *Feiri* is derived from Old French *faerie*, (Mod. French *féerie*) which is the collective form of *fée*, (Mod. French *fée*). *Fae* is from the Latin *fata*, 'the Fates'; the same word is found in the Italian *fata Morgana* 'the fée Morgain,' the name of a mirage. It will be seen therefore that *fairy* has no connection with *fair*, 'teg'; the similarity is purely accidental. The fact that Welsh *teg* shows a misapprehension of the meaning of 'fairy' due to the accident of similarity proves that the English name is the original, and that the Welsh is modelled upon it. There are of course plenty of instances in every language of this kind of mistranslation; I need only remind you of that well-worn cliché 'psychological moment' which is due to a confusion between the neuter word *moment* 'momentum' in the original German phrase and the masculine *moment* 'moment of time.' So that the word *teg* in *Tylwyth Teg*, being due to a misunderstanding of the English, shows that its use in this particular context is late and derivative.

But that does not mean that the history, so to speak, of the *Tylwyth Teg* is either late or derivative. It means that this other-world people of Wales appears in a new dress cut according to the fashion in vogue in England. It means that the original legends and beliefs concerning the other-world folk have been grouped together in the popular mind to form the history of one unified people under a new name. Or I should rather say, perhaps, that whereas they were before nameless, they have now become identified with the English Fairy Folk. We shall see that this identification has obscured the high lineage of the *Tylwyth Teg*.

3

The stories current in Wales about the *Tylwyth Teg* fall into three well-defined classes which owe their origin to three different sources; in other words the *Tylwyth Teg* like many more politically important nations is composed of at least three different 'racial' elements. The first two may be regarded as forming together the main body of the *Tylwyth Teg*, and the third element is perhaps an alien immigration in later times. The first element is derived from mythology, whether at one remove or more it is unnecessary here to decide; the second element is derived from history, not indeed recorded history, but the imaginatively distorted recollection of the folk. Shelley speaks of Time as 'like a many-coloured dome of glass staining the white radiance of eternity'; his great phrase may be justly applied to humbler things. Time also stains with its own colours the white radiance of historical facts.

The three elements are:

1. The Welsh *Annwfn* (the Other-world of gods and heroes). I cannot give here a precise definition of what *Annwfn* meant to our ancestors. Sometimes it is regarded as the Land of the Dead, something like the Greek Hades, presided over by the 'dark' divinities; sometimes it is the Land of Youth and Promise, *Tir na nÓg*, the home of bliss and harmony; sometimes it is a mysterious border country, menacing the land of the living, the actual world. As we shall see, a great part of the Four Branches is concerned with the affairs of *Annwfn* and its lords.

2. The second element is the folk recollection of an aboriginal people living in inaccessible parts of the countryside, having no contact with the dominant race, and living in fear and suspicion of them.

3. The third element which seems distinct from the first two, may for the sake of convenience be called by a name borrowed from our Cornish brothers,— the Pixies. Whether these are part of the Welsh folk tradition or have been

introduced later through England from Teutonic folklore I am unable to decide. They comprise the mischievous, puckish and irresponsible portion of the fairy population of Wales. Whatever their origin and at whatever period they joined the men of *Annwfn* and the men of the moorland solitudes they are definitely authenticated in Welsh folklore.

I have placed these three classes in the order of their importance and in the probable order of their entry into folklore, but it will be convenient to deal first with the second and third classes.

4

One of the most widely-spread of all the fairy tales is that of the Lady of the Lake; the typical form of this *märchen* is the Legend of Llyn y Fan Fach in Carmarthenshire which purports to explain how a famous mediaeval family of physicians living at Myddfai obtained their knowledge of healing from an ancestor who had, some time in the twelfth century, married a fée, the Lady of the Lake of Y Fan Fach. This type of legend is widely spread all over Wales, and though all the features are not contained in any one version, they may be gathered from a comparison of all the versions. It would take more time than I have at my disposal if I were to attempt to make a full recension of these various versions; many of the details are what might be called local variations and derive their interest and importance, not from the original tradition of the Lady of the Lake, but from the light they throw on the social and cultural conditions of those who have handed it down to posterity. The following account, however, will be found to contain most of those features which are obviously essential to the story.

A young countryman happened to be one day near a lake in a wild and uninhabited part near his home. He saw a woman, the most beautiful that mortal eyes had ever beheld, sitting on a bank on the lake-side. He offered her the bread and cheese which he brought with him and tried to touch her, but she kept away from him, and taunted him with the quality of his bread:

Cras dy fara,
Nid hawdd fy nala.

'You with the baked bread, you will not easily catch me,' and then disappeared in the lake. Next day he came again, this time bringing unbaked bread, but with no better result. The lady still evaded him and said:

Llaith dy fara,
Ti ni fynna'.

'You with the moist bread, I will not have you.'

His mother seeing that there was a spell connected with the bread, gave him some soft-baked bread (perhaps unleavened) for his third attempt. This time when he went to the lake he beheld a herd of beautiful cows, white with spots of red, walking along its surface, followed by the maiden. He offered her the soft-baked bread and she allowed him to approach her. After much coyness and argument she consented to marry him on condition that he would never touch her with iron. (In some versions, on condition that she did not receive from him *Tri ergyd diachos*, 'three blows without cause.' I regard this as an obvious contamination from a triadic tradition such as *Trydedd anfad palfawd*, 'the three evil slaps,' which is quoted in *Mabinogi Branwen*). The next time her father appeared with her, and told him that he would consent to their marriage on condition that he could pick her out from among her five sisters. The sisters were so similar that he was unable to point to the one he loved, but she helped him by putting forward her toe whereas the others kept their feet together. When she finally came to him she brought with her the herd of marvellous cows, sheep, and goats which she counted by fives. They lived happily and had many children. The cows gave three times as much milk as those of their neighbours. She objected, however, to have the green sward in front of the house ploughed. After they were married he did not see her people again except when they came to market, a small queer looking folk with sallow complexions, but they said never a word, and used to point at what they wanted. After many years she went one day to the paddock to catch a horse. She was so unskilful that her husband came to help her, but the horse was by this time frightened and in trying to stop him the husband threw the bridle with the iron attached. He missed the horse and the bit struck his wife. 'You have now struck me with iron' she cried, and disappeared in the lake, calling her cattle to follow her.

Rhŷs, in his great work, *Celtic Folklore*, has listed the characteristics of the *Tylwyth Teg* as contained in the different versions. I quote his words (p. 660):

'the sallowness of their skin and the smallness of their stature, their dwelling underground, their dislike of iron and the comparative poverty of their homes in the matter of useful articles of furniture, their deeprooted objection of the green sward being broken up by the plough, the success of the fairy wife in attending to the domestic animals and the dairy, the limited range generally of the fairies' ability to count; and lastly one may perhaps mention their using a language of their own which would imply a time when the little people understood no other, and explain why they should be represented doing their marketing without uttering a syllable to anybody.'

Rhŷs's list may contain one misconception,—namely 'their dwelling underground.' This detail has crept in, I believe, from the first element in fairy lore which we shall consider later; the essential feature of the type of legend which I have summarized above is that the Fairy Folk dwell in a lake. He has also omitted two important characteristics—the apparent similarity of the members of the Fairy Folk—that is why the countryman in the story was unable to distinguish the woman he wanted from her sisters,—and their unacquaintance with horses and their ways.

Rhŷs has, without going very deeply into archaeological details, declared his belief that these characteristics of the Welsh Fairy Folk have an ethnological significance. I make no apology for accepting his explanation which has also been put forward by other scholars. Some later researchers however, have cold-shouldered this theory, but I think that their attitude is due to ignoring the fact that the fairy folklore of Wales is of mixed origin, that incongruous elements are combined in its composition, and that primitive inhabitants of more than one period may have contributed to its totality. It often happens that when a cliché of scholarship becomes discredited, a perfectly sound explanation which has become fortuitously attached to it suffers the same fate. It happened in this case: romantic writers used to enlarge on the 'Iberian' element in the Welsh nation,—Sir Owen Edwards in his *Wales* went so far as to publish a picture of the poet Islwyn as a typical 'Iberian,' and to suggest a fanciful contrast between the dreamy and artistic 'Iberian' and the practical hard-headed Celt. All this has gone, and with it, quite illogically, the ethnological explanation of this particular type of fairy folklore. But to reject it is to throw out the baby with the bath-water.

It is probable that, when the iron-using Celtic invaders became the dominant race, the previous inhabitants, perhaps for a very long time, lived a separate and secluded life of their own in some kind of lake dwelling or in isolated and inaccessible parts. Their manner of life and their language were different from that of the newer Celtic settlers; they may have had no ovens as the Celts had so that their bread was different; perhaps it was unleavened. They were small and had a sallow skin; it may be they had a 'Mongolian' type of countenance, so that the Celts could not distinguish one from the other just as we today find it difficult to distinguish the Chinese. They were mostly a pastoral people and horses were unknown to them. They had a different system of counting from the Celts, (who perhaps later, when the barriers between the two peoples were removed, partly adopted their system in the numbers from 15 to 19). Finally iron was something terrible, because it was new and *was the specific symbol of the invading race.*

In short, this type of legend preserves a folk-recollection of the aboriginal inhabitants and their impact on the Celtic settlers, and it is to be noted that, whereas in stories belonging to the first and third elements in my classification, the strange folk are called *Tylwyth Teg*, there are many versions of the Lady of the Lake type where the name is not mentioned, for instance in the long and detailed *versio princeps* of the Legend of Llyn y Fan Fach given by Rees of Tonn in the introduction to his *Physicians of Myddfai*. In other words, the *Tylwyth Teg* have not yet completely absorbed the strange folk of the Lake legends.

5

The third element is the Pixies, though of course that name does not occur in Welsh. In all North-European folklore there is a tradition of irresponsible and mischievous beings, sometimes benevolent but rather oftener malevolent, making stealthy raids on the well-ordered existence of normal people. In Wales the extent of their activities is somewhat restricted, compared for instance with that of the pixies of Cornwall and the goblins of Teutonic countries and the only really significant contribution which they seem to have made to the lore of the *Tylwyth Teg* is, first, their gifts of money and services in the dairy, (which probably betrays contamination by the second element), and secondly their mischief-making in displacing articles of furniture and so on, and in changing the property of the Welsh family by substituting their own, especially by taking away new-born babies and leaving children of their own in their place. How old this element is in Welsh folklore it is difficult to tell; it is possible that a belief in mischievous imp-like spirits is natural to all communities living in the country—Fairies in all lands wisely avoid the towns—but the part that the Pixies play in Welsh folklore is comparatively small, and the stories about them have neither the romance of the Lake legends of the second element nor the nostalgic mystery of the fairy Elysium of the first.

6

Now what traces are to be found in the Mabinogion and Romances of the second and third elements of our classification? It is outside my province to consider the French versions of original British themes, *Arglwyddes y Ffynnawn*, *Geraint*, *Peredur* and those over which the magic of Merlin, that high priest of *féerie*, holds sway, but in the rest of the collection (The Four Branches, *Culhwch*, *Macsen*, *Lludd a Llefelys* and *Rhonabwy*) it is possible to discern traces of the folklore attached to the Lake legends and to the Pixies. One striking feature common to the Mabinogion and the Fairy stories is the coyness of the fairy women and their half-reluctant 'leading on' of the men who have fallen in love with them. Pwyll fails to catch up with Rhiannon who clearly seeks him out but avoids him day after day until he speaks to her. 'She had something to say to some persons here,' says Pwyll, 'if her *contrariness* allowed her to say it.' Here we have the supernatural powers of the Queen of *Annwfn*, a feature of the first element, reduced to the more lowly shyness of the Lady of the Lake and the teasing puckishness of the Pixies.

There are other traces both of the Lake legend and of the Pixie fairies in

Branwen, but I make the suggestion here tentatively, because in order to establish their presence with certainty, it would be necessary to consider all the immense complex of contamination by contemporary folk tales which has made the *Branwen in Ireland* episode so puzzling. This portion of *Mabinogi Branwen*, which describes Branwen's degradation by being banished to the kitchen is, of course, a variant of *The Queen Falsely Accused*, the theme which was so popular in Europe in the middle ages and which is exemplified in the history of Constance in Chaucer's *Man of Law's Tale* and, of course, elsewhere in the *Mabinogion*, in the account of Rhiannon falsely accused and punished. It will be remembered that this was Branwen's punishment: 'They (the king's court) drove Branwen from the same chamber as the king, and compelled her to bake in the court, and bade the butcher, after he had been cutting flesh, to go to her and strike a blow on her every day.' Why the butcher?

Now *Branwen* abounds in instances of one of the latest *cyfarwyddiaid*, through whose hands the story passed, forgetting to record the one fact that can make sense of the episode which they describe, and here is such an instance. It is consequent of his having previously omitted another detail necessary to make the story coherent, namely the false charge against Branwen for which she was thus punished. The charge was, I suggest, that she was one of the *Tylwyth Teg*—or whatever name the Welsh fées bore at that time. She was a foreigner, a native of the mysterious *Ynys y Cedyrn*, just as Rhiannon was a woman of *Annwfn*. Consequently she was to be *struck by the iron of the butcher's knife*, in order to drive her back to her own people, or at least to test her whether she was a fairy or not.

I said that the charge made against her personally is not specified. What is specified is that her husband's people in Ireland allowed a previous episode to rankle in their minds, when Branwen's brother Efnysyen, out of sheer love of mischief, had mutilated her husband's horses by cutting off their ears and tails, and ripping the flesh off their mouths. Now this irresponsible action, which has no motive in the Mabinogi as it stands, is precisely the kind of thing that the pixie portion of the fairy population are constantly doing, and proved beyond doubt to the people of Ireland that Branwen was a fée, because she was Efnysyen's sister, or as we would say in Wales today, was one of the *Tylwyth Teg*.

But that is not all, for the most important indication of the belief in Branwen's fairy connexion is contained in another part of the Mabinogi, where the action as described is equally unmotivated. After Branwen has been delivered by her own people, the warriors of the Island of the Giants (*Ynys y Cedyrn*), from her unmerited punishment, a peace conference is held. Everything goes well till suddenly the puckish brother Efnysyen, seeing Gwern, Branwen's son, going willingly to his other uncles says:

'Why does not my nephew come to me? Though he were not king over Ireland yet would I gladly make friends with the child.' 'Let him go to you and welcome' said Bendigeidfran. The child went to him gladly. 'I declare to God' said he (Efnysyen) in his mind, 'that the household little expects the slaughter that I am going to cause now.' And he arose, and seized the child by his feet and straightway before anyone in the house could lay a hand on him, he plunged the child head first into the blaze. And when Branwen saw her child burnt (*yn boeth*) in the fire, she made to leap into the fire . . . but Bendigeidfran held her.

Then there was general fighting in which all but seven of the men of *Ynys y Cedyrn* and Branwen herself were slain.

This was the 'slaughter' which Efnysyen had in mind.

Of course, in this the final version of the *Mabinogi*, Efnysyen's action explains why the two peoples, now at peace, renew the fighting but, as I hope to prove elsewhere, the story of Branwen, especially in this section, is hopelessly tangled. In the original and well-authenticated form of the tradition, the fighting took place in a raid on *Annwfn* to capture the treasure of Pwyll, the Head of *Annwfn*, namely the magic Cauldron of Resurrection, and no other motive for the fighting was necessary. In any case, the result of an action need not (as all mankind is tragically aware) be consequent on the motive. It is probable that in an older version it was Branwen herself who held the child in the flames; the curious detail of seizing him by the feet suggests holding him *for a time* in the blaze rather than throwing him into the fire, which could be much more effectively done by taking hold of him bodily. As usual in the Mabinogion when two conflicting versions have to be harmonized, the *cyfarwydd*, knowing that tradition said that the act was Branwen's or even perhaps that Branwen had jumped with the child into the fire, covered himself against criticism by saying that Branwen *attempted* to leap into the blaze after him.

Now this episode is a confused version of the procedure for testing a Fairy Child or, in communities where the Fairies are definitely identified with Evil Spirits, a child of the Devil. There were two main tests—you either threw the child into water, and if he swam, then he was a changeling, a fairy child, or you held him in the fire and if he was burnt, then he was not a fairy; if he did not burn then he certainly was a fairy. Branwen had been charged with being a fairy, though the test of striking her with iron had apparently not been successful in driving her away, but the charge was still maintained and with special vigour against her son Gwern who was by this time in the royal succession. In order finally to refute the charge, Branwen herself held Gwern in the flames, where everyone saw that he was *poeth*, 'burnt,' and so Branwen was vindicated. I suggest that the mysterious words which follow in the Mabinogi and which have puzzled all commentators, *Gwern gwngwch uiwch uordwyt tyllyon*, are a confused jumble of a sentence in the test or of a gloss which originally explained why Gwern was one of the *Morddwyd tyllion*, 'men with holes in their thighs.' These holes were the result of his having been held in the fire.

7

While discussing the traces of the second and third elements in *Branwen*, I wish to remind you of another episode which, in itself a supremely interesting piece of folklore, may throw some light on the difficult question of folk-recollection in the traditions about an older race such as we saw inherent in the Lake legends. Into the already confused tangle of *Branwen* a long story has been inserted in the form of a conversation between Bendigeidfran and Matholwch, King of Ireland, explaining the circumstances in which Bendigeidfran obtained the miraculous *Pair Dadeni*, the 'Cauldron of Resurrection' which he has just presented to Matholwch. According to my reconstruction of the probable growth of the *Branwen* complex, the original myth on which this episode is based was an account of an attack on *Annwfn* by the Hero, under whatever name he went, and the carrying away of *Preiddeu Annwfn*, 'the Spoils of Annwfn,' the King's Magic Cauldron, but this myth, originally the basis of the main element in *Branwen*, has in the final form of the Mabinogi been reduced to a mere shadow. It is probable that it had no previous connexion with the story of the Iron House to which it is here attached.

Bendigeidfran informed Matholwch that he had received the Cauldron from a man who, with his wife, had escaped 'from the iron house in Ireland when it was made red-hot over their heads.' Matholwch then took up the story and related how he was hunting on the top of a *gorsedd*, 'mound' *near a lake*. He saw a large man of terribly hideous aspect with an even larger wife coming from the lake. 'In a fortnight and a month', says the stranger, 'this woman will give birth to a child fully armed.' Matholwch took them under his protection but within four months 'they made themselves hated and no one would countenance them, because they insulted and worried respectable men and women and were rapacious and truculent.' Matholwch could not get rid of them so he made an *iron* house for them. He plied them with food and drink and heaped charcoal all about the house. All the smiths in Ireland had been summoned, 'all the owners of tongs and hammer,' but *this was not to build the house*, since it was already erected. When they were drunk, they kindled the fire and worked the bellows, and so the heat of the iron house drove out the troublesome folk. By this time they had many descendants with them, but only two escaped, the husband and the wife. These two went to Bendigeidfran's realm where they greatly increased in numbers.

This episode is also found in an old Irish tale called *Mesca Ulad*, 'The Drunkenness of Ulster.' The victims in the Irish tale are Conchobar, King of Ulster, and his men, who are placed in the iron house by the King and Queen of Connacht. I hope to deal with the development of this story elsewhere; let it suffice to say here, that in this instance at least, the Welsh version is more primitive than the Irish. The main points to be noticed are: 1. The strangers meet Matholwch on a *gorsedd*, a *sídhe*, invariably associated with visitants from another world. 2. The large man comes up from a lake. 3. He and his wife are clearly of a different race from the respectable Irish. 4. In the true pixie tradition, they cause mischief wherever they go. 5. There is no reason given in the Mabinogi why they should be placed in an *iron* house in order to burn them. The elaborate preparations of heaping charcoal up to the eaves of the house and summoning all the smiths in Ireland and having bellows to blow the fire would be unnecessary if they were simply locked up in an ordinary house built of wood like all the royal habitations of Ireland. Then the smiths of Ireland, 'all the owners of tongs and hammer' are summoned *after* the iron house has been built! The essential feature is the iron, and the smiths were summoned not to build the house, but *because they wielded iron tools*, a detail carefully preserved in the narrative. This is well in the tradition of stories about the primitive inhabitants; iron has a devastating effect on the fairy folk.

I suggest therefore that this episode in *Branwen* had originally nothing to do with the Cauldron of Resurrection but was attracted to it during the evolution of the Mabinogi, and that it contains a very specialised form of the Lady of the Lake type of story. This time the Lady is not a beautiful maiden but, like her husband, and as in many other accounts of the *Tylwyth Teg*, a hideous monstrosity. It may be suggested that we have here in this episode a confused mixture of the two most important fairy tests, Iron and Fire.

8

To return to our third element, the Pixies. They appear in *Lludd and Llefelys*, a complicated *märchen* which has been inserted in some of the Welsh versions of Geoffrey of Monmouth's *Historia Regum Britanniae*, but which is also preserved as a separate unit. In this story three 'plagues' harass the Island of Britain; we are not concerned with the second and third, but the first is described as follows: 'A race of men came called *Coraniaid*, and so great was their knowledge that there was not a word (*ymadrodd*) over the whole island however low it was spoken, if the wind met it, that they did not know. And for that reason they could not be harmed.' Lludd consulted his brother Llefelys, king of France, (the name *Llevelys* is clearly based on a scribal misreading of *Leueeis*, the Norman-French form of *Louis*), who made a long horn (of brass in one version) through which they spoke to one another, but their words were perverted and made to mean the opposite, so Llefelys perceived that the Devil was hampering them. He cured that trouble by pouring wine into the horn, and then gave his brother some *pryfed*, vermin, (or insects or even dragons) to be pounded in water and the mixture sprinkled on the *Coraniaid* and his own subjects in a joint conference of the two peoples. He thus destroyed the whole nation (*ciwdawd*) of the *Coraniaid* without harming his own.

This account seems to be a mixture of the second and third elements. The

Coraniaid are a mischievous folk, possessing supernatural powers, but they are also a separate race living in the territory of normal men and interfering with their activities. In short, they are the same race as the unpleasant people who were exterminated in the iron house in Ireland. In two respects only does their history differ from theirs, they have supernatural powers and it is not said that iron is used against them, unless indeed the 'long horn' was made of iron; it is to be noticed that brass or bronze is not specified in some versions. Their ability to hear whatever the 'wind met,' that is whatever was in the air, is paralleled in many Welsh accounts of the Fairies,—that of Edmund Jones of Tranch, for instance, who says that 'the fairies knew whatever was spoken in the air without the houses, not so much what was spoken in the houses.' An early instance of this faculty is found in the Mabinogi of *Math fab Mathonwy*, where Math is described as knowing 'whatever whispering there be between men, however small it be, if the wind meets it.' That is to say, this attribute of the magician Math was derived from a 'pixie' belief already existent.

An important feature of the *Coraniaid* legend, is the fact that their name has survived into the first years of the nineteenth century to designate a savage and primitive race. In a hymn attributed to Anne Griffiths (1780-1805), but almost certainly by Edward Jones, Maes-y-plwm (1761-1836) are these lines:

> Caiff Hottentots, *Goraniaid* dua' eu lliw,
> Farbaraidd lu, eu dwyn i deulu Duw.

'Hottentots, *Coraniaid* of darkest hue, a savage host, shall be brought into God's family.'

9

We now come to the first element in my classification, the Welsh *Annwfn*, the other-world of gods and heroes, the most prominent and important feature in the Four Branches of the Mabinogi. How *Annwfn* itself was evolved in the imagination of our forefathers I have neither the occasion nor the ability to explain, but it will be necessary to give here some of the main facts about the inhabitants of this mysterious land and their interposition in the lives of ordinary men and women.

The *Annwfn* of the Mabinogion has two aspects, and it seems that the stories in the form in which we have them preserved in the complex of the Four Branches, are ultimately derived from two distinct sources. The first is mythological, in the strict sense of the word; that is to say, the great figures of *Annwfn* were once definitely gods and goddesses with a mythology which can be easily reconstructed from their legendary history and from a comparison with classical and other mythologies. The second source is harder to define, and I hesitate to apply the name 'myth' to the beliefs which are attached to it, and which are embodied in legends about the Happy Other-world, the Land of Youth, *Tír na nÓg*, the Land of Promise. There are two crucial questions—how did these two traditions of *Annwfn* come together, and in particular, had they come together in early times to form a unified mythology of *Annwfn* or were they only joined together when a belief in a world of féerie was evolved?

The great figures of *Annwfn* appear in the *Mabinogion* in the second stage of their evolution; that is to say, when they have ceased to be gods but have not yet become normally human; whatever of their god-like attributes they retain are indistinct. They trail around them clouds of their old divinity, but they are clouds without much form or substance. In general it may be said that what distinguishes them from the ordinary human beings of Dyfed and Gwynedd (where most of the action takes place) is that they move and have their being in an atmosphere of *hud*, 'enchantment.' That enchantment is of two kinds; it may be the possession of a mysterious power, as for instance, when Rhiannon's horse cannot be overtaken by the swiftest horse in Pwyll's stables though, to the onlooker, it only seems to move at a deliberate trot; or again it may be a malevolent magic which enables its possessor to shift his shape and to play tricks on his enemy. Gwydion, for example, can assume any form he wishes and enable others to do the same. He can even make a woman out of flowers, and in the final scene of the Four Branches he encompasses the death of Pryderi 'by magic and enchantment.'

It will be necessary, at this point, to indicate very briefly what the plot or basic form of the Mabinogion was, as I have reconstructed it elsewhere. The King of Dyfed was to marry a fairy visitant, Rhiannon, from the Other-world in circumstances somewhat similar to those of the countryman and the Lady of the Lake. The fée had fled from her own country of *Annwfn* because she did not wish to marry a man of *Annwfn*, Gwawl fab Clud. This started a feud between the Kingdom of *Annwfn* and the Kingdom of Dyfed. Gwawl turns up in disguise at the wedding and obtains possession of the bride, but Rhiannon had a superior magic and not only extricated herself from the result of the king's rash promise but subjects Gwawl to ridicule and insult. (*The first portion of the second part of* Pwyll).

The King of Dyfed and Rhiannon are married, but the Head of *Annwfn* still pursues his quest for Rhiannon. By a trick of shape-shifting he assumes the form of the king and so is enabled to beget a child on Rhiannon who will be Pryderi, the Hero of the Four Branches. (*First part of* Pwyll).

The feud between *Annwfn* and Dyfed continues. When Rhiannon gives birth to Pryderi, the Head of *Annwfn* whom we may call Gwawl again intervenes. He steals the child from Rhiannon's bed and substitutes a foal born on the same night. The child is missing for a long time but he is at last recognised and restored to the queen. (*Second portion of the second part of* Pwyll). This concludes the original First Branch but whether the abduction of the child was, in the first form of the Mabinogion, identical with his abduction as a young Man in *Manawydan* it is difficult to decide. If it was, then the original First Branch ended with the *Conception of Pryderi*.

Pryderi is now ruler over Dyfed, and the feud continues. Pryderi himself takes a hand in the struggle and he makes a raid upon *Annwfn* in a ship, since *Annwfn* is here conceived as being over the water. As a result of the raid only seven of his men survive but they bring with them back to Dyfed the famous Cauldron of Resurrection which, by resurrecting the slain of *Annwfn* had enabled the Head of *Annwfn* to destroy the men of Dyfed. (*Portions of* Branwen). The feud continues, Pryderi is captured and carried away to *Annwfn*. His mother and (originally) his father searched for him all over the land, and while he is away, a great desolation falls upon Dyfed; it becomes the fabled Waste Land. At last his mother Rhiannon descends into *Annwfn* and rescues him and when he is restored, fertility returns to Dyfed. This is pure myth, in the strict sense of the term, and is, of course, found in almost exactly the same form in the Greek myth of Demeter and her daughter Persephone. Thus ends the Third Branch. (Manawydan *and the second portion of the second part of* Pwyll).

The feud continues and *Annwfn* has the last word. What the exact form was of the plot by which Gwawl enticed Pryderi to his death, it is difficult to know. Whether Pryderi had stolen the Head of *Annwfn*'s swine or his father had brought them up from *Annwfn* when he and the Head of *Annwfn* changed forms, I cannot decide, but the essence of the plot was that Gwawl gave Pryderi twelve horses with fine accoutrements, all created by magic, in exchange for the swine, and departed. But the magic only lasted for a day, and Pryderi followed Gwawl to avenge the insult. In the battle that followed, Gwawl by means of his magic obtained the victory, and slew Pryderi. Thus the Saga of Pryderi, in four branches, came to an end. (*Math fab Mathonwy*).

The above is the barest outline of what I maintain to be the original plot of the Four Branches. A vast accumulation of the legends and folklore of Wales was squeezed—with consummate art it must be allowed—into this frame-work, so that we have the Mabinogion in their present astounding complexity. All the legends and all the folklore do not belong to the same period of development—some, such as the Rape of Pryderi in *Manawydan* still retain an easily recognisable form of the basic myth which was aeons old when the Mabinogion were related by the *cyfarwydd*. Others again have lost their original form and most of their meaning, such as the legend of Rhiannon, 'the great queen' who ruled over *Annwfn* with her husband Teyrnon, 'the great king.' Her myth during the passage of the centuries had become involved with that of the Great Mother, Modron, and her son Mabon, 'the great child,' and with another form of her own myth of *Epona* which, as Anwyl has suggested, represented her as a Horse-Goddess. Only confused traces of that myth are now found in the *Mabinogion*—her penance of acting as mare and carrying on her back the visitors to her husband's court, which presupposes a story in which she was accused of giving birth to the foal which her enemies had substituted for her child. Her legend became nonsense when, instead of this original accusation, the charge of having killed her child was substituted from the popular *Constance* legend.

Many other folk legends which had no part in the first form of the Four Branches are by this time inextricably mixed with the original theme. Some of them do not contain other-world features, as for instance, the *Eustace* legend of the long-suffering Christian Gentleman into the mould of which the Manawydan story is cast, and probably some of the onomastic stories, but others are accounts of magic and shape-shifting, as for instance the *Unfaithful Wife*, who in an earlier version of *Math*, transforms her husband into an animal. We have here a compound contamination, by which first the *Unfaithful Wife* has been intruded into the old Celtic legend of *Blodeuwedd and her lover* and then the resulting complex fitted into the myth of Lleu Llawgyffes, the god *Lugus* of the inscriptions.

Thus, in what I might call the *War-with-Annwfn* basis of the Four Branches, we have two main elements,—the legends of *Annwfn* themselves, some of which have been debased into mere stories about magic, and more recent folklore additions some of which also are concerned with magic. Whether all this latter element had originally a basis in myth, that is, in other-world belief we cannot at present discuss, but it is evident that here we have a considerable portion of the back-ground of the Fairy traditions of Wales. One question only is relevant and I am content for the time being to leave it as a question—had the belief in the Land of Faery, in other words belief about the *Tylwyth Teg* as such, had a period of independent life long enough to react on the final structure of the Four Branches? I can only say that I have been unable to discover even the faintest sign of the influence of faery, either as Welsh *Tylwyth Teg* or as the féerie of romance, on the Four Branches. Not only is the *Tylwyth Teg* not mentioned under any name, but there is no trace of that vast territory of magic over which Myrddin and his sister Gwenddydd preside and which is so prominent in French and Continental Romance. Which is only another way of saying that the Arthurian Legend with its Land of Féerie had not been evolved when the Mabinogion assumed their more or less final form in the tenth or eleventh century.

One detail, however, establishes a traditional connexion between the Fairies and the folk of *Annwfn*. When, in the Mabinogion, a man meets a stranger from *Annwfn*, he is seated on a *gorsedd*, a 'mound'; this corresponds to the *sídhe*, 'mound,' of the Irish tales, the home of the Fairy folk, which has come into English in the word *banshee*, from *bean sídhe*, 'a woman of the fairy mound.' Pwyll, when he meets Arawn, is on the *gorsedd* of Pen-llwyn upon Bwya, probably an old caer known today as Clegyrfwya; he meets Rhiannon on the *gorsedd* of Arberth (Narberth). Matholwch is seated on a *gorsedd* when he sees the strange folk of the Cauldron come up from the lake, and I suspect that the *Llech* of Harlech, on which Brân is seated when he sees the ships coming from Ireland and where his followers feasted for seven years, was also a *gorsedd*.

10

We come finally to the one feature of Fairyland which has always intrigued the Welsh mind more than any other and which is known all over the western world; it is the basis of Washington Irving's well-known story of *Rip van Winkle*. It is here that the old traditions of *Annwfn* intrude themselves most prominently into modern life, and when the *Tylwyth Teg* is mentioned in Wales it is to this particular story that one's mind naturally turns. Let me first of all give a résumé of this popular legend as it is related in every part of Wales though most of the records seem to have come from North Wales.

A young man was coming home late at night over an unfrequented country path. As he approached a secluded hollow in the moorland he heard music, the most enchanting he had ever heard. When he came to the hollow, he saw a company of the most beautiful women and men that eye had ever beheld dancing in the moonlight. As they whirled in a circle past him, he felt an overwhelming desire to join them; the more he fought against it, the nearer to the dancers he was driven by some inward urge. At last, under the compelling charm of the music, his feet began to move to the rhythm of the dance and before he knew what he was doing he was among the dancers who gradually led him away into their abode. This was a magnificent palace full of such luxuries as he had never dreamt of, and on a board in the hall was a sumptuous feast to which he was invited. Dimly he remembered an old warning, that no one who ate of the fairies' food could find his way back to the upper world. However he feasted with his hosts and listened to their charming conversation and marvellous music, forgetting all his troubles and worries. He was told by his companions that he must on no account drink of the water of a magnificent fountain in the middle of the courtyard. However, the temptation was too great; he drank and immediately the palace and all its men and women disappeared, and he found himself alone on the bare moorland. When he went home, he found that the neighbourhood of his home was completely changed; no one in the village knew him, but an old woman had heard her great-grand-father say that his great-grandfather's brother had disappeared one night and had not been heard of since. He had been away for hundreds of years.

Now compare that story with that portion of *Mabinogi Branwen* which is called *Ysbyddawd Ben*. Here is a résumé of it:

'Cut off my head,' said Brân 'and bury it in London. And ye shall be a long while on the way—in Harlech at a banquet (*cinyaw*) seven years and the birds of Rhiannon singing to you. In Gwales in Pembroke ye will be four score years. And until ye open the door towards Aberhenfelen in the direction of Cornwall ye may tarry there, and the head be still with you uncorrupted. And from the time ye open that door, ye may not tarry there . . .' And they went to Harlech, and began to sit and satisfy themselves with food and drink. And as soon as they began to eat and drink, there came three birds and sang to them a song and of all the songs they had heard, every one was worthless (*difwyn*) compared with it. The birds were far out over the sea, but as easily seen as if they were there with them. The banquet lasted seven years.

From Harlech they went to Gwales. There they had a fair royal place above the sea, in a large hall with two doors. That night they feasted abundantly and merrily. And for all the sorrow they had witnessed and that they had suffered, no memory had they of that or of any woe in the world. They were there eighty years and they had never known a merrier or more pleasant time. They had no more unease than when they first came there nor did they find by looking at each other that they were any older than when they came. They had no more unease in the company of Bran's head than when he had been there with them.

But one of them opened the door towards Cornwall and at once they remembered all the losses they had ever had, and all the kindred and companions they had lost as if it had only then happened . . . And from that moment they could not rest but started on their journey to London, bearing Bran's head.

It is unnecessary to point out that in this passage we have a slightly garbled description of the Happy Other-world which is a feature of one kind of Irish story, notably the *Voyage of Bran*. It is curious that, apart from a famous passage in the *Book of Taliesin*, the ancient literature of Wales has few reminiscences of this distinctive Celtic belief of a land of music and joy and forgetfulness of all sorrow which is variously called by the Irish the Land of Youth, the Land of Promise, the Land of the Living, and the Island of Women. It presupposes an aspect of *Annwfn* very different from that kingdom of menace as we saw it portrayed in the history of Pryderi, yet Rhiannon has her birds singing in this paradise and the description of the splendours of *Annwfn* in the first portion of *Pwyll* is more applicable to *Annwfn* as an Elysium than as the prison of *Mabinogi Manawydan*. It is probable that the *Annwfn* of the Mabinogion is an incomplete conflation of the two aspects, but in the folklore of the *Tylwyth Teg* the country of the Fairies is pre-eminently a land of forgetfulness. The points in common between the two summaries I have given above, the Rip van Winkle type of legend and *Ysbyddawd Ben*, are: 1. It is a land of music. 2. It is a land of feasting. 3. Time does not exist there; its inhabitants grow no older. 4. There is a definite taboo connected with life there, something that, if done, will destroy the enchantment.

There has been much speculation on the anthropological significance of this

Celtic Elysium, as any reader of Nutt's *Voyage of Brân*, for instance, knows. I am not concerned with that side of the question, which is highly speculative. But no one, I think, will deny that at least half the lore of the *Tylwyth Teg* owes its origin to this ancient belief.

A Lecture Delivered at
The National Museum of Wales on 27th October 1950

MABINOGION

An Essay by Josef Baudiš

It has long been recognised that the Mabinogion is a storehouse of old motives, but very little has been done in the way of tracing these particular motives to the methods adopted by the Welsh story-tellers in their arrangement of them. This paper is intended as a contribution to this inquiry.

PLAN OF THE INQUIRY

Part I: The First Branch of the Mabinogion

A. Pwyll and Arawn: Three motives: (*a*) Exchange of external appearance.—Norse parallels.—Explanation of the belief.—(*b*) Chaste cohabitation.—Parallels in Norse and the Twin Brothers Tale.—(*c*) Killing of Havgan.

B. The Other World: Pwyll's journey belongs to the Other World expeditions. Irish parallels.—Mr. M'Culloch's theory about the Celtic Elysium.— Are we to presuppose two different ideas: that of Elysium and that of the Land of the Dead? Irish *síde* and ancestral cult. *Síde* denotes Irish supernatural beings. *Túatha Dé Danann* belonged originally only to the side of the Connaught cycle. Abodes of side convey both ideas: that of Elysium and that of the Country of the Dead. In Welsh we find these two different aspects of the Other World, and similarly in other folklore. We confine ourselves to the Other World. The double aspect of the Other World is to be explained through the development of primitive belief. Connection of the insular Celtic belief with the Gaulish religion. The King of Other World is represented as Death the Hunter. Pwyll's relation to the Other World.

C. The Rest of the First Branch. Motives: Pwyll and Gwawl is an independent Mährchen.—Rhiannon.—Parallels to this story.—Kidnapping of Pryderi belongs to the Mysterious Hand motives.—Plight of Rhiannon and the Abandoned Wife story (and Female Taboo Breaker).—Traces of Supernatural Birth (two categories of such Birth stories).—Irish Birth stories.—How the fusion of all these motives came to pass?—Abandoned Wife motive was introduced to account either for some aspect of Rhiannon's character or it was to explain Pryderi's name, which was explained as derived from *pryder*. Etymology of the name. Pryderi's relation to Annwfn and to the Gaulish tradition about the origin of the Gaulish nation.

D. Gwri Wallt Euryn and Mabon vap Modron. Gwri is probably not identical with Mabon, because the history of Gwri (Pryderi) and that of Mabon are not identical.—If everything told about Pryderi relates to Gwri, how came Pryderi into the Mabinogion at all?—The similarities of different tales are to be explained in the way that in Wales there existed similar tales about different persons.

E. The Origins of the Mabinogi Tales. Mr. W. J. Gruffydd's theory. We have no proofs that the first branch of the Mabinogion is of the same origin as the Irish saga of Mongán. The history of Llew Llawgyffes is not identical with the Irish *Aided Conrói.* —Possibility of foreign influences.—There are striking similarities between the Welsh story and the Egyptian tale.—The Irish story of Étáin and a Jataka story.

Part I: The First Branch of the Mabinogi

A. Pwyll and Arawn

(*a*) The first motive, the mutual exchange of external appearance, forms a leading motive in the northern version of the Nibelungen-cycle (Norse *Niflung*). First, it occurs in the introduction to the whole cycle, and then later when Sigfrid (Sigurðr) wins Brunhild (Sigrdrífa) for Gunther (Gunnar). The idea of mutual exchange of the body is based on the conception of the body being similar to removable clothes (Icel. *hamr*, "skin"; cf *hamramr* or eigieinhamr, "able to exchange one's form"); a witch or magician can change the appearance of another man by putting the *hamr* on him, and it is the task of the hero to destroy this magical *hamr*. The swanmaidens cannot resume their bird-shape if their *hamr* is stolen from them. This belief is based on primitive conceptions of life. To primitive man there is no difference between an animal and a human being; their external form is only a casual accident: "the bear whom the savage meets in the woods is too cunning to appear and to battle with him as a man, but he could if he chose" (Hartland, *The Science of Fairy Tales*, 26). Our motive is only a logical consequence of this ancient savage belief: if shape-shifting is possible, why cannot two human beings also exchange their shape one with another? This motive is also very closely connected with the True Wife motive: the wife is changed into an animal and the sorceress or her daughter takes her place. In most of these stories the impostress maintains her position by disguise; in some stories the *quid pro quo* can be explained by the social conditions of the indigenous culture (cf M'Culloch, *Childhood of Fiction*, pp. 24 ff.), but some at least must belong to our group, so e.g. the Bushman story, "The Wife of the Dawn's Heart Star" (Bleek & Lloyd, *Bushman Folklore*, pp. 89 ff.), where a hyena takes the place of *Kó-ginuịń-tára*, the wife of Jupiter star. But is this belief commensurate with the belief that the soul retains the characteristics of the body (man's double)? To this we can answer that it is not necessary that those ideas should coincide ; we find many such discrepancies which may be due to different culture-strata. As regards the different conceptions concerning the soul and body, we have the best example in the old Egyptian creed. However it may be, the shape-shifting theory does not presuppose that the person is totally transformed; Norse belief makes the integral part of the original personality, the eyes, to persist, while all the rest is changed.[1] It is difficult to say whether there was anything similar in Welsh. At any rate we have no traces of it. It is, of course, not necessary to assume any historical continuity between the Welsh and Teutonic motives. It is, however, remarkable that in both Teutonic and Welsh we find this motive combined with that of *chaste co-habitation*.

(b) This last motive we find very often in the story of the Twin brothers (*vide* Hartland, *The Legend of Perseus*, i. pp. 24 ff.). The first brother, who has won the hand of a princess, is turned to stone; his twin brother, learning of his brother's peril, comes to his court, plays his *rôle* (at night he sometimes puts his sword between himself and his sister-in-law), and finally disenchants the petrified hero. This story is known as a modern folk motive through the whole of Europe. But here the resemblance between the two brothers accounts for the situation.

(c) As to the third motive, we often find that a magician or spirit can be killed only in some particular way, *i.e.* there are certain *taboos* limiting his life-powers. In the theme we are studying the taboo is that the hero shall not give his adversary a second stroke.[2] In modern Irish stories we find another motive: the giant's head after it has been hewn off creeps to the body again, and the hero prevents its reunion with the body; for if the head should be joined to the body, not even the fairy doctors could sever it from the body again.

B. Other World

This first part of the first Branch had originally to account for Pwyll's connection with Annwvn. This association of Pwyll with Annwvn is mentioned also in the fourth Branch of Mabinogi (Math vab Mathonwy), where Pwyll gets pigs as a present from the Other World (B.B. fo. 752, W.B. 191: *Moch y gelwir weithon. "Pwy bieivynt wy?" Pryderi vab Pwyll, yd anvonet idaw o Annwn, y gau Arawn vrenhin Annwvn*).

Pwyll's voyage to Annwvn belongs to the category of Other-World voyages (Ir. *eachtra*). These voyages are often of a friendly character, but sometimes they

---

1 The Irish lay stress on the preservation of the human voice: "Agus do ghabh aithreachas ann sin Aoife, agus adubhairt: 'Ó nach féadaim aon chabhair eile do thabhairt orraibh feasda biaidh bhur n-úrlabhra féin agaibh . . . agus biaidh bhúr dtreoir agus bhúr n-oirbheart agaibh.'" *Oidhe Chloinne Lir*, § 20.

2 Miss Weston wrongly compares with this motive Peredur's sword (*Percival*, I. 147).

take the form of a conquest of the Other World. Help given by mortals to the King of the Other World is a frequent motive;[1] in the Irish saga literature that of Cúchulainn (in Serglige Conculaind) is the most typical. Cúchulainn helps *Labraid Luath lám ar claideb*, the King of Mag Mell, against his enemies, who belong also to the inhabitants of the Other World. In modern Irish folk-tales we find a similar motive: a mortal man is requested by the *sídheógai* to help them in their match against other *sídheógai*, or he is to assist them in kidnapping the King of France's daughter.

From these later parallels we may argue that there was a belief that a human being is able to vanquish the fairy people, etc., and this doctrine may be the real reason why Arawn requests Pwyll to fight for him against Havgan.

Now, there might be another question: are the Irish *sídheógai* identical with the inhabitants of Annwvn, and what is Annwvn? There are scholars who accept two Other Worlds, *i.e.* "the Land of the Dead" and Elysium. Mr. M'Culloch (*The Religion of Anc. Celts*, p. 370) is of the opinion that "the origin of the Celtic Elysium belief may be found in several myths of a golden age long ago in some distant Elysian region, where men had lived with the gods. Into that region brave mortals might still penetrate. . . . Possibly the Celtic myth of man's early intercourse with the gods in a lost region took two forms. In one it was a joyful subterranean region whither the Celt hoped to go after death. In the other it was not recoverable, nor was it a land of the dead. The Celtic Elysium belief . . . is always of this second kind. We surmise, however, that the land of the dead was a joyous underworld ruled over by a god of fertility and of the dead, and from that region men had originally come forth. The later association of gods with the *síd* was a continuation of this belief, but now the *síd* are certainly not a land of the dead, but Elysium pure and simple. There must therefore have been at an early period a tendency to distinguish between the happy region of the dead and the distant Elysium, if the two were ever really connected."

This theory, however, does not account for all the tales which refer to the Other World, because there are stories where the inhabitants of the Other World are by no means friendly to the intruders into their domains. Again, it has to be proved whether the Irish *síde* do not owe their origin to ancestor-worship; and finally, the above-quoted theory presupposes that the old Celtic cultus was in olden times so developed and uniform that there was no room for contradictory ideas as regards the posthumous existence of man and more general conceptions of the universe.

Now, ancestor-worship has not been taken enough into account in the study of Celtic mythology, and yet we must take into consideration the fact that some of the fairy hills (*síd*) are really old burying places, *e.g.* the Brugh of Boyne is the abode of Oengus (*Mac ind-Óc*). According to Maelmuire Othna, the nobles

---

1 Cf. A. C. L. Brown, *Harvard University Studies and Notes in Literature and Philology*, viii. 41.

of the Túatha Dé Danann were buried in a Brugh (so Dagda with his three sons and Ollam and Ogma). According to Acallam na Senórach, three sons of Lugaid Menn came to the Brugh of Boyne and fasted; Bodb Derg (Dagda's son) came out of the Brugh and said: "It was revealed to the *Túatha Dé Danann* that ye would come to fast here to-night for lands and great fortune." They went into the Brugh, and remained there for three days. Another old burial place, Cruachan, is the abode of the *Síde* of Connaught. This proves that the *síde* are really connected with the old burial places. Now these *síde* are identical—as we have already seen—with the chiefs of the Túatha Dé Danann. We find the same in the old Irish sages; so Lug mac Ethlenn says to Cúchulinn (*Táin bó Cúailnge*, ed. Strachan, ll. 1805–6): *Is messe do athair a ssídib*. The composer of Fiacc's Hymn uses the word *síde* to denote the pagan gods (v. 41): *For tuaith h-Érenn bai temel tuatha adortais síde*. One might, however, suppose that this identification of *síde* is later, and that originally the *Túatha Dé Danann* were a race of gods. But what we know about the *Túatha De Danann* conveys a rather different idea; they were superhuman beings whose power was due to their knowledge of magic, and they differ very little from powerful magicians. It is, at least for me, a question whether the insular Celts had any idea of gods in the same sense as the Greeks and Romans. Neither does the name of *Túatha Dé Danann* suggest that the bearers of this name were real gods.[1] According to the Lebor Gabála, the *Túatha Dé Danann* preceded the Milesians, who deprived them of the possession of the land. Now, some Irish tribes only are of true Milesian origin, others derive their origin from the *Túatha Dé Danann*, and others again from the *Fir Bolg*. We find in Irish genealogies occasional names of the *Túatha Dé Danann*. We might explain these facts simply as arising out of the euhemeristic tendencies of the Irish genealogists, according to which the Christian historians endeavoured to change the old Irish nature gods into old kings; but such a tendency must have been supported somehow by the old tradition, for instance by the occurrence of the *Túatha Dé Danann* in the old pedigrees, or by a tradition according to which the old gods lived on the earth. Such traditions are by no means rare in the mythical history of nations. And, further, we must not forget that there were different strata of population in ancient Ireland, as *e.g.* Fir Bolg, Ulstermen, Picts and Milesians, and so it would be most natural to regard the *Túatha Dé Danann* as such a tribe, especially since some races derived their origin from them.

The name *Túatha Dé Danann* probably belonged only to some of these *síde*, and was extended by the Lebor Gabála to all such beings. It was the same case as with the Fir Bolg: the territory of Bolg is proved by L.U. 56 /T.B.C. l. 87 to have been somewhere near Roscommon, as L.L. 56a has instead of *Bolga*: *Badbgna*.

---

1 Cf. *Cath Maige Tuired Cunga*, § 20. "Imthusa Tuaithe De Danann (*N.B.* singular number), roforbredur co clos a scela fa (th)irib in talman. Robi dia drai[d]echta acu fen Eochaid Ollathir .i. in Dagda mor, uair ba daigdia é. Robadur ta(isig) trena talchara acu 7 fir caineladnacha gacha ceirde."

This *Bolga* (acc. plur.) was thus a name of local character, and Lebor Gabála has changed it to the name of a whole race. Now the cycle in which *Túatha Dé Danann* play a really important *rôle* is the cycle represented by Cath Maighe Tuireadh and similar stories, and even this Cath Maighe Tuiread is localised in Connaught, and the memory of this battle survives there to our own day. (I have heard it as *cath na bpunnann*) Take now the Ulster saga. What have the *Túatha Dé Danann* to do there? There were obviously no traditions of such a character. Here the supernatural characters appear only as *síde*. The same holds true for the *Érnai* cycle (Conaire Mór). Here the *síde* have a prominent role, and their supernatural character is here quite clear, but there is no sign that there ever existed in the Érnai district a saga about *Túatha Dé Danann*, a divine race, conquerors of the Fomorians and predecessors of the Milesians, and so it appears that *síde* is an original old Irish name for supernatural beings. The name Túatha Dé Danann was known only in some parts of Ireland (Connaught), and Lebor Gabála, employing this name for its purposes, made it known through the whole of Ireland. And so we see that our attention must be turned only to the *síde*.

We understand now quite well why the composer of Fiacc's Mymn wrote

> *tuatha adortais síde.*

Most of them were *dei terreni*, but this does not exclude (at least in some degree) ancestral character. In later times they are equivalent to fairies, and these are, *e.g.* in Slavonic, to a great extent "souls" of deceased maidens. This parallel would also account (at least partly) for the Irish *Tír na mban*. One might object to this explanation that *síd* is always a fairyland, a pleasant place, where there is no sorrow, and it is a privilege of some people only to come there. But this fairyland seems by no means to be always such a desirable country. In modern folklore the kidnappings of human beings by fairies are considered as something rather unpleasant. The Old Irish *Echtra Nerai* does not represent the inhabitants of Cruachan-Sid as very benevolent to the Connaught people. The same we might gather from the story of Etáin.

We must not forget, further, that for primitive man there was no precise break between death and life. The dead lived in the tomb (or in the Other World) the same life as he lived in this world, and it was not believed impossible that the dead could revive again.

After all, we must not forget that this same fairyland is sometimes the object of expeditions which resemble closely expeditions to Hades. So, for example, the expedition to the Isle of Falga, where the Irish people get the wonderful cauldron. We find a similar expedition mentioned in a Welsh poem (Skene, ii. 181, Book of Taliesin, 256), where this cauldron is called *peir pen annwvyn*, and we learn that Arthur made a disastrous expedition to this region (*A phan aetham ni gan Arthur . . . namyn seith ny dyrreith o Gaer Vedwit).* The *Caer Sidi* mentioned in the same poem is a horrible prison of Gweir, who sits there before spoils of Hades (*rac preideu annwvyn*), and yet the same place appears in another poem like paradise (Skene, ii. 155, B. of Tal. 16):

> *Ys kyweir vyg kadeir yg Kaer Sidi,*
> *Nys plawd neb heint a heneint a vo yndi.*
> *Ys gwyr Manawyt a Phryderi.*
> *Teir oryan y am tan a gan recdi.*
> *Ac am y banneu frydyeu gweilgi.*
> *Ar ffynnhawn ffrwythlawn yssydd o duchti.*
> *Ys chwegach nor gwin gwyn y llyn yndi.*

All these facts prove only that Annwvn and fairyland have two aspects: one of a beautiful blessed country and the other of a dangerous region. This other aspect is not infrequent in folklore; Teutonic and Slavonic folklore knows many stories dealing with expeditions to that country; the Old Babylonian has a story about Izdubar's expedition to Hades (*Archiv für Religions-wissenschaft*, xii. 275 f.), and the Kichés of Central America believed that Hun-Ahpu and Xbalanque came to the realms of Xibalba (Underworld) [Popol Vuh, bk. ii.].

And so, I think, it is safest to speak only about the Other World (or Other Worlds) and fairies.

It is obvious, however, that beside the old belief there might have been also other motives which might have influenced the conception of the Other World and of fairies; I mean especially ethnical motives: an alien race and a distant country might have been regarded as an Other World; the predatory expeditions of some successful chieftains against an alien country may have enriched this motive. So it is possible that the poem from B. of Tal. 25b (Skene, ii. 181) relates partially to some prehistoric expedition (cf Skene, i. 228). The same ethnical traces some scholars see in modern fairy-lore (cf Rhŷs, *Celtic Folklore*, but see also Hartland's *Science of Fairy Tales*, pp. 349 ff.). Similar traces of peoples who dwelt in some subterranean locality are suggested by Popol Vuh.

We see that the conception of the Other World is a complex one, that it results from various motives, and I do not suppose that we have any right to presuppose that in the earliest times this conception was much simpler. The Insular Celts, as they came to the British Isles, had already absorbed many foreign elements, and assimilating the older population of the British Isles they underwent further modifications; we can hardly expect that the different stages of culture through which they had to pass should not have left traces in Insular Celtic religious conceptions, coexisting with others which were quite contradictory to these. In many religions we find different strata and different or contradictory ideas one beside the other, the best example of this being found in the old Egyptian religion. One might, however, object that the analogy of Egyptian religion does not prove anything for the old Celtic, and I must agree with this ; but there are certain facts in folklore survivals which prove that in Britain two contradictory ideas existed. Sir Laurence Gomme has proved that there existed two different attitudes towards the deceased, one of which was based on fear of the dead, and another reflecting love towards the deceased (*Ethnology in Folklore*, pp. 109 ff. and especially 125 ff.). I will not argue that these different survivals presuppose different races. I think it possible that these new influences may be of other kinds beyond the racial admixture: this question is, however, the old *crux* of archaeology, being identical with the question: "Does a new culture presuppose a new race?" There is, however, another difficulty in Sir Laurence Gomme's deductions. He thinks the Indo-European creed was a clearly developed system; but there are so many difficulties in the reconstruction of this old creed, seeing that we know nearly as little about Indo-European beliefs as we know about the creed of the pre-Celtic inhabitants, that we come to the conclusion there is little definitely proved about either. Hence there remains nothing but to remember the often-quoted words (Caesar, *De bello Gallico*, vi. i8. i): *Galli se omnes ab Dite patre prognatos praedicant, idque ab Druidibus proditum dicunt. . .*, which would again point in favour of ancestral elements in Celtic religion. From this "Other World" some bold or chosen mortal can get precious gifts or immense booty. That this "Other World" is not represented always in the same manner is a known fact (*vide* M'Culloch, *Rel. of Anc. Celts*, pp. 362 ff.). In our case it has an actual existence in Britain, but there are in Welsh also other conceptions of this region, *e.g.* as a distant island (see Skene, ii. 153).[1]

Finally, it must be remembered that Arawn had some wonderful dogs, "and of all the hounds that he (*i.e.* Pwyll) had seen in the world he had never seen any that were like unto these. For their hair was of a brilliant shining white, and their ears were red; and as the whiteness of their bodies shone, so did the redness of their ears glisten" (R.B. fo. 710/11, W.B. fo. 171 a–b: *Ac or a welsei ef o helgwn y byt, ny welsei cwn un lliw ac wynt. Sef lliw oed arnunt: claerwynn llathreit ac cu clusteu yn gochyon. Ac val y llathrei wynnet y cwn y llathrei cochet y clusteu*). These hounds are the *cwn Annwn* of the Modern Welsh folklore (*vide* Miss Marie Trevelyan, *Folk-lore and Folk-stories of Wales*, pp. 47–54), which are regarded as an omen of death, a fact which speaks in favour of our conception of Annwvn. It may, of course, be objected that this modern belief may be a later development of the folk-belief, but we must acknowledge, on the other side, that the idea of *Death as Hunter* (cf. our hunting scene in Mabinogi) is a very old and very common one; and so it is quite clear that the King of *Annwvn* is represented as a king of the country of Death. But this region was not always

---

1 There is often a *taboo* not to eat any of the food of the Other World: whoso partakes of it cannot return to this world (Hartland, *Science of Fairy Tales*, pp. 37 *sqq.*), but in the Pwyll story we do not find any trace of such a taboo.

described as a beautiful and desirable country (*e.g.* Procopius, *De bello Gothico*, iv. 20. 24), but as the belief was never homogeneous, death appeared sometimes as a horrible demon and sometimes as a good man (so *e.g.* in the tales, *Death as a Godfather*).[1]

Pwyll is probably an ancestor of some *Dyved* (Demetae) tribe, but he is at the same time in a very close connection with the Under World, so we find in old Welsh poems (Skene, ii. 181; Book of Taliesin, 25 b):

Bu kyweir Karchar Gweir yg Kaer Sidi
Trwy ebostol Pwyll a Phryderi;

and (Skene, ii. 155):

Ys kyweir vyg Kadeir yg Kaer Sidi
* * * * *
Ys gwyr Manawyt a Phryderi,

which makes it probable that Pwyll is a supernatural being, *penn Annvyn*, chief of the Under World, and the tale is told to account for this title and to explain how *Pwyll penndevic Dyvet* was at the same time *penn Annwvn*.

[The name Pwyll means "sense" (Irish *cíall*). Such a name as an ancestor-name is not unique. The indigenous Bohemian kings derived their origin from a mythic ancestor (ploughman), *Přemysl*, which means a "thoughtful one."]

C. The Second Part of this Branch

The second part of this branch of the Mabinogi deals with *Pwyll* and *Rhiannon*, and it contains again three leading motives.

(α) Pwyll and Gwawl;
(β) Rhiannon punished for her supposed killing of her own child; and
(γ) "Stolen child."

(α) The first motive was originally an independent *Mährchen*; that the application of this *Mährchen* to *Pwyll* and *Gwawl* was pretty current is proved by the repeated mention of enmities between *Pwyll's* son *Pryderi* and *Llwyd vab Cil Coet*, who endeavours to avenge his friend Gwawl on *Pryderi* and *Rhiannon*; even the *gware broch yg cot* (R.B. 750, W.B. 170 a) is mentioned.

The name of Rhiannon is identical with the name of the Old Celtic *Rigantona*

---

1 Brown, *Harvard Studies*, viii. 48/7, suggests that Arawn is here used instead oi *Manawyddan* (Ir. *Manannán*); about this suggestion *vide infra*.

(name of goddess), but I do not know whether we are right in supposing that our Rhiannon is an ancient goddess; what we know of her from Mabinogi allows only one conclusion ; it is that she is a lady of great magical knowledge, and in this point she does not differ from Gwydyon, about whom the Old Welsh poem says (R.B.; Skene, ii. 302):

> *Neu Leu a Gwydyon*
> *a vuant gelvydyon.*
> *neu a wdant lyfyryon.*

> "Or Lleu and Gwydyon
> were they creators (or skilful producers),
> or did they know books?"

This suggests that these mythical personages were merely great magicians, or that even if they possessed a divine power, this power resulted merely from their knowledge of magic.

As to the tale itself, Miss Lucy Paton (*Studies in the Fairy Mythology of Arthurian Romance*, p. 225 n. 5) comcompares the entrapping of Gwawl with an incident from Parcival's career: a knight asked Parcival to rescue him from a tomb, which done, the ungrateful knight imprisoned Parcival himself in the tomb. This incident is, however, to be compared rather with a trick of the Irish *Naked Hangman* (*vide Ériu*, vii. 201). The magic bag, however, is well known from other stories, *e.g.* that of The Three Gifts. One of those gifts is a magical bag, and the hero imprisoned therein is a devil or Death. The imprisoned devil gets a sound hammering (cf. *gware broch*).

Prof. A. C. L. Brown (*Harvard Studies*, viii. 49) thinks that the original idea of this tale is similar to that of Iwain, "the idea of representing the fée as guarded by a suitor or husband who must be overthrown before she can be approached might naturally be developed." I am *a priori* disinclined to presuppose such very wide formulas for cycles containing such divergent motives. This method ignores, further, the fact that our stories are mostly compilations of different tales, and finally it must not be forgotten that two stories with some similar or identical motives do not necessarily presuppose the same original story.

The formula how Gwawl deceived Pwyll reminds us of Étáin's story: Mider won a game against Eochaid and named Eochaid's wife as the stake, and Eochaid was to give him Étáin.

As for the tabooed hill (Gorsedd), *vide* MacInnes, *Folk and Hero Tales*, p. 456 (note to p. 97).

(β) and (γ) It will be better to take the (γ) motive first. Pryderi is stolen by a mysterious hand. This motive is very frequent in Irish and Scotch Gaelic, and has two distinct variants:

(a) Either the child is saved by a werwolf (cf. *Scottish Celtic Review*, i. (Tuairsgeul mòr), note by A. Nutt, p. 140; Kittredge, *Harvard University Studies in Phil. and Lit.* viii. 227).

(b) Or the rescuer is a hero (Finn in MacInnes, p. 62 f.; J. M'Dougall, *Folk and Hero Tales*, pp. 12 ff.; *vide* Kittredge, *op. cit.* 223).

[Cr. A.S. Beowulf, but his name suggests a person with werwolf attributes. Cf. Kittredge, *l.c.* 227.]

(α) The motive of the kidnapped infant is sometimes entangled in the *Amor and Psyche* (Beauty and the Beast) Cycle (Mod. Ir. in C.Z. i. 176 ff.; Gaelic, M'Dougall, *Folk Tales and Fairy Lore*, p. 2 ff.). Soon after the Beast's wife has borne a child a mysterious hand steals the infant. Sometimes the incident of dropping or tearing away the hand does not occur. [A Scotch story seems to identify the Mysterious Hand with the Beauty's Husband (cf. also Kittredge, *op. cit.* 241, n. 4).]

(β) There is, however, another kidnapping motive; the tale where it occurs is pretty common in the whole of Europe. A maiden breaks the taboo not to enter a (tabooed) room; in consequence of her disobedience she is banished (and usually deprived of speech); a prince finds her and marries her, but whenever the young princess gives birth to a child, the being (whom she has offended by breaking the taboo) comes and steals the child away. The mother is accused of cannibalism and sentenced to death.

Sometimes the thief of the children throws the suspicion of cannibalism directly on the mother by smearing her mouth with blood. A similar incident is found in the *Abandoned Wife* (Genofefa) Cycle, where the wife is blackmailed by the mother-in-law or by her jealous sisters (see Kittredge *l.c.* 241 f.).

Now we find in the Mabinogi story a real *Mysterious Hand* motive, but we find also incidents which apparently belong to the other above-mentioned cycles, viz. (1) measures are taken to throw on Rhiannon a suspicion of cannibalism, (2) the mother is punished.

It is to be noticed that in tales where the Mysterious Hand steals the infant the mother is not suspected of any heinous crime. In cases where it is entangled in the Amor and Psyche motive the wife has to suffer from the jealousy of the other woman, and so we might think that it was also here a jealousy or hatred which brought Rhiannon into this evil plight. But, unfortunately, we have no proofs of it; it is just here that our story differs from those mentioned under (β). The attendants accuse Rhiannon of cannibalism merely to avoid the punishment for their carelessness; and so we can only say that two different cycles have been combined. It seems that there have been mixed up both cycles mentioned under (β); the fact that the child was stolen in the Taboo-Breaker Cycle may have contributed to overlapping in this direction. There is, however, one incident which points to the Abandoned Wife Cycle, viz. the lord's demand of Pwyll to put away his wife because of the heinous crime which she has committed

(R.B. 723, W.B. fo. 178 a-b, *Ar gwyrda a docthant y gyt y wneuthur cennadeu at Pwyll y erchi idaw yscar ae wreic am gyflavan mor anwedus a rywnaethoed*). Pwyll declined this request; now just such repudiation was the fate of the Abandoned Wife,[1] and so we are probably right in supposing that this cycle also has influenced our tale.

As for Rhiannon's punishment,[2] she has to sit at the outer gate of the court and to tell her story to every comer and to offer to carry him to the court, *i.e.* she is degraded to a mule. We find another such incident in her life: when she was imprisoned in the enchanted castle (Branch: Manawydan vab Llyr), she had the collars of the asses, after they have been carrying hay, about her neck (R.B. 751, W.B. fo, 191 a, *A Rhiannon a vydei a mynweireu yr essynn wedy bydyn(t) yn kywein gweir am y mynwgyl hitheu*); that is again a degradation to a mule. These two incidents relating to the same fact are probably two different ways of explaining some aspect of Rhiannon's character, about which we cannot say anything more.[3]

There are, however, two situations belonging to another quite different cycle, viz. (α) Pwyll's men were complaining of Rhiannon's barrenness. Pwyll asked a respite of one year, and at the end of this time Rhiannon was delivered of a son. (β) Gwri Wallt Euryn (=Pryderi) was given the horse born on the night the child was found.

According to the first passage we should expect that Rhiannon was barren, and that this barrenness was in some way removed. Stories of removed barrenness are very frequent in fairy lore. Sometimes the childless parents get a remedy from a mysterious being, but they are to give up the firstborn (son), who, after having been given to the demon, breaks the shrine-taboo (*vide* M'Culloch, *Childhood of Fiction*, 410–415). One might therefore suppose that Rhiannon was barren, and that the being who gave her the remedy was identical with the owner of the Mysterious Hand, but this combination does not, after all, appear quite probable, because there is a fact which speaks strongly against this point of view, *i.e.* the *Hand* takes every born (not only the firstborn) creature. Or is this a dim relic of some form of old belief?

---

1   Cf. Kittredge, *Harvard University Studies and Notes*, viii. p. 242 ff.

2   But cf. the Abandoned Wife's punishment in Dolopathos (Oesterley, 75):
    "Ipsam vero, *nulla sibi pro se respondendi aut negandi crimen facultate concessa*, vivam in medio palatii sni infodi usque ad mamillas iubet, precipiens omnibus militibus, servientibus, scurris et parasitis ut pransuri aut cenaturi manus super uxoris caput abluerent abstergerentque capillis, nullusque ei alius ad reficiendum daretur cibus quam qui canibus parabatur. *Mansit autem sub hac iniuria septem continnos annos.*"

3   Was it, perhaps, to explain some such name as the Gaulish *Epona*?

The second incident is frequent in the Supernatural Birth stories: the wife is given a meal, of which also some house animals partake; the wife then has a child, the bitch has a puppy, and the mare a foal; the wonderchild and the animals are a continuation (or rebirth) of the being incarnated in the meal (and so the animals become his brothers).[1]

In Ireland Supernatural Birth stories are very frequent; usually a girl swallows a small animal, which is then reborn as the respective hero or heroine (Conchobar, Conall Cernach, Cúchulainn, Étáin). In the story about Cúchulainn's conception we find, however, the version that in a certain mysterious house a child was born on the same night as two foals. Dechtire adopted the boy, and the foals were given to him (I.T. 1. 138 *dobert som na lúrchuiriu do macslabri don macc*). The boy died, however, very soon, but he was reborn to Dechtire as Cúchulainn, the incarnation of Lug (I.T. 1. 139). This rebirth of the foster-son is only a doublet of the first event, and we are right in assuming that the *Compert Conculaind* in L.U. is a contamination of two similar stories. According to one story Cúchulainn had a horse, or two horses, which were of the same origin as himself (I think that these horses are identical with Cúchulainn's horses, which are really represented as supernatural beings); according to another story there was no mention of the horses, and so there were tales "how Cúchulainn got his horses." These supernatural birth stories, as represented in Irish, seem sometimes to make a compromise, according to which the child has a nominal human father (whose name the child bears), but the real father is the higher being whose incarnation the child is. These ideas of conception presuppose a very primitive civilisation, such as we find to-day among the Arunta people of central Australia, according to whose ideas the conception is due to an ancestral spirit entering into the woman; when the child is born he is a reincarnation of that ancestral spirit.

Both the last-mentioned motives, especially the last, occur in Mabinogi in a very strange context, and we do not see the reason why they have been introduced. One might, of course, suppose that there was a story of a taboo-breaking woman, and that this story sometimes continued the story of removed barrenness, the taboo-breaking woman being bereft of her child. There was here a possibility of confusion with tales having the Mysterious Hand as the leading motive. This confusion would in our case result in the following way: The Mysterious Hand remained as the leading motive, but there were introduced important motives from other cycles: the smearing of Rhiannon's face with blood and the accusation of cannibalism (her proposed punishment, cf. Abandoned Wife) and the introduction (cf. Removed Barrenness) contributed only some inorganic details. But are we justified in such a theory? We have, no doubt, good reasons to believe that there were in Wales cycles of the Mysterious Hand, Abandoned Wife, etc., but we have no proof that the motive of the female

---

1   *Vide* E. S. Hartland, *The Legend of Perseus*, pp. 24 ff.

taboo-breaker was introduced by the motive of removed barrenness.

Now, there is another possibility, *i.e.* that at least some of these stories were applied to Rhiannon, and that the compiler of Mabinogi knew different stories about one and the same event (in one case the birth of Pryderi), and that he aimed at reconciling the different versions by combining one with another. It seems to me highly probable that the story of the imputed cannibalism was introduced to explain why Rhiannon was once degraded to a mule or donkey. Is it impossible that there existed still another tale about Pryderi's birth? It would presuppose that either Pwyll was not the real father of Pryderi, the latter being a reincarnation of some "divinity" (or rather some equivalent of Ir. *síde*), or that this divinity was Pwyll himself (and that Pryderi had another human father, and the name of this mortal father in later times gave way to that of the "divine" father, both personalities having been confused). Or, finally, there may have been different tales about Pryderi's birth and different tales about Pwyll, according to which the whole character of the various persons was differently represented. Now it is possible that Pryderi himself was in older tales represented as an incarnation of some spirit, for this would account for the fact that Pryderi is in Old Welsh poems brought in close relation with Annwvn. To explain such an incarnation a story of removed barrenness or rather some such incident as that found in *Compert Conculaind* might have been invented. Beside such a story there existed another pedigree explaining Pryderi's birth in some more natural way, and this tradition naturally prevailed in later times. I give here this possibility as a presumption which seems to me a most probable one, but I am quite well aware that it is only a suggestion; if I am, however, not right it must be at least acknowledged that two motives relating to Removed Barrenness and Supernatural Birth have been introduced into Rhiannon's story.

Pryderi's name is in Mabinogi explained as derived from *pryder* "angor," and the motive of the Abandoned (Calumniated) Wife may have been possibly introduced to explain why such a name was given to Pwyll's son. This cannot be, however, an original form of the story, because all such etiological stories presuppose the name. The original meaning of the name does not seem to me to be that of "angor"; anyhow, it is a derivative from the root **qrt*. . . which appears in Ir. *cruth*, Cy. *pryd*, "form, aspect," and in the Old Welsh name of Britain, *Prydain*, and the Ir. name of the Picts, *Cruithne*. Now the name of the British heros eponymos[1] *Prydain* is obviously invented to explain the name of the

---

1 R. B. Mabinogion, p. 309: *Kyntaf enw a vu ar yr ynys honn, kynn noe chael nae chyvanhedu Clas Myrdin a gwedy y chael a ae chyvanhedu y Vel Ynys a gwedy y goresgynn o Brydein vab Aed Mawr, y dodet arnei Ynys Prydein (cf. Iolo MSS., p. 1-2, llyma 'r enwau a fu ar yr ynys hon: cyn no'i chyfaneddu, sef Clâs Merddin, a chwedi dyfod o rai Cymry iddi y gelwid hi 'r Fel ynys . . . a phan wybu Aedd Mawr (lege Prydain) am hynny a theged gwlawd ydoedd, efe a roddes wŷr a moddion i oresgyn y Fel ynys a hynny a wnaeth efe a'i galw yn ol ei enw ei hun Prydain.*

country. But this personage is unknown in old sagas, and so it seems possible that *Pryderi* is the original heros eponymos of the race which gave the name to the island.

On the other hand, according to old poems, Pryderi is in close relation to the Underworld (*e.g.* Skene, ii. 155, 181), and this fact would again agree with Caesar's words: *Galli se omnes a Dite patre prognatos praedicant*. It seems to me that the Gauls derived their origin from the Otherworld (the person of the Otherworld's king differed probably in various districts), but we cannot conclude that the Celtic *"Dispater"* or any other divinity was a god in the Roman or classical sense.

D. Gwri Wallt Euryn and Mabon vap Modron

Pryderi's original name was Gwri Wallt Euryn; now Mr. W. J. Gruffydd (R.C. xxxiii. pp. 452 ff.) has attempted to prove that Gwri is identical with Mabon vap Modron (but Gwri and Pryderi were—according to his theory— two different persons), and later (*The Trajisactions of the Honourable Society of Cymmrodorion*, Session 1912–13, pp. 65 ff.) he would see in the first branch of Mabinogion a transformation of a Gaelic story identical with that of Mongán.

We will discuss the first theory first: Pryderi, according to Mr. Gruffydd, has sometimes taken the *rôle* of Gwri; now Mr. Gruffydd argues that Pryderi's imprisonment (in Mab. Manawyddan) is identical with that of Mabon. This imprisonment was, however, quite another matter, because Pryderi (or, as Mr. Gruffydd thinks, Gwri) was imprisoned in his later years and Mabon was stolen as an infant, and since that time nobody heard anything of him (cf. W.B. fol. 281 c, *Mabon mab Modroji a ducpwyt yn teirnossic y wrth y vam, ny wys py tu y mae na pheth yw ae byw ae marw*), and so we must suppose that he was imprisoned during some centuries; further, he was imprisoned in a horrible prison (he says, R.B. fol. 836: *Oia wr, yssit le idaw y gwynaw y neb yssyd yma . . . ac ny charcharwyt neb kyndosted yn llwrw carchar a mi na charchar Llud Llaw Ereint neu garchar Greit mab Eri*). The themes of stealing the child (*i.e.* The Mysterious Hand, etc.) and the imprisonment motive arise (thus, as we find them in Mabinogi) out of two independent motives, and they occur in two different stories. According to the investigations of Sir E. Anwyl they are of different local origin. The imprisonment motive, as it occurs in the third branch of the Mabinogi, goes back to the following formula: the hero is brought to a magical castle, he touches a thing which he ought not to, and he is imprisoned. This motive occurs very often in *the Quest of the Water of Life* or *the Magic Bird*. We know from the folk-tales that it is forbidden to take anything from the land of the fairies (unless, of course, the land is conquered). From the Irish stories we know of magical castles where people are imprisoned by merely sitting down there, as in *Bruidhen Chaorthainn*. And so we must conclude that Pryderi's imprisonment belongs to this motive.[1] But this cannot be proved of Mabon. It might be, however, probable of Gweir, because we read in the Book of Taliessin (Skene, ii. 181):

> Bu kyweir karchar Gweir yg Kaer Sidi
> Trwy ebostol Pwyll a Phryderi
> * * * * *
>
> Yr gadwyn tromlas kywirwas ae ketwi
> A rac preideu Annwvyn tost yt geni.

Here Pryderi seems to be the Lord of Annwn, and Gweir was probably captured while trying to get some of the Underworld jewels, as he is represented bound in heavy chains before the spoils of the Underworld. This Caer Sidi has already been identified by the late Sir E. Anwyl (Z.C. ii. 130) with the magic castle where Pryderi was imprisoned, but I do not suppose that we must necessarily identify these two places, because there were different local Otherworlds;[2] it seems, however, to me most certain that Gweir's imprisonment was something of the same kind as Pryderi's. Can we now presuppose something of the same kind about Mabon? I think not: we know of him that he was stolen from his mother, and after this time nothing was known of him till he was found in a horrible prison. This prison was in *Caer Loyw* (R.B. 836), and this tale might be consequently (but not necessarily) localised in Caer Loyw. Now, according to Sir E. Anwyl (C.Z. iii. 127) Gwri Wallt Euryn was a local hero of Gloucester, and so one could only suppose that both tales (that of Mabon and that of Gwri) have risen in the same locality; but if we accept the identity of Gwri and Mabon, we have to presume that the story told about Pryderi was originally told about Gwri,[3] and we must accept then that both the birth and the imprisonment story

---

1 The *Mabinogi Manawydan vab Llyr* is a contamination of three different cycles:
  Cycle I. has the following motives:
      (1) Devastation of Dyved and Mystic Fog,
      (2) Watching the Field (*the first two fail and are probably imprisoned (?);
      the third succeeds and rescues the first two).
  Cycle II. (1) Hunting; Mystic Fog and coming to the Magic Castle,
      (2) tabooed objects which are not to be touched, resulting in imprisonment
      of the taboo-breaker.
    Cycle III. Manawyddan as an excellent craftsman in Lloegr.

2 See also Sir E. Anwyl, *Celtic Religion*, p. 62.

3 In favour of this point of view we draw attention to the fact that Pryderi is not likely to be a prisoner in an Otherworld, being in old poems represented as its king.

related originally to Gwri Wallt Euryn, and what would remain then for Pryderi? Nothing at all. And yet Mr. Gruffydd postulates that Pryderi was originally a son of an immortal being who took possession of him [third night]. But in this case the kidnapping of the infant would be quite otherwise represented than the rape of Mabon (and of course that of Pryderi). These theories are simply contradictory, and consequently one of them at least is wrong, and, anticipating the later arguments, I may say that the identification with Mongan's story is not only improbable, but it is, from the point of view of method, hopelessly wild. But to return to the first part of this theory: the greater part is hypothetical; neither do we know how Pryderi comes into this story if all about him refers to Gwri Wallt Euryn. Further, Mr, Grufifydd has not taken account of the results of Sir E. Anwyl's work, where he has proved that in the Mabinogi different local traditions have been contaminated. Owing to this compilatory character of the Mabinogi, we must be very careful in identifying different persons, and, what is more, in reconstructing their original story, because there is always the possibility that one motive belonged originally to one person and the other to another. Now Sir E. Anwyl has made it probable that, in some parts of Dyved, Pwyll was considered as father to Pryderi, but in the districts near Gwent, Teyrnon (O. Gaulish *Tigernonos) passed for his father, and that Gwri Wallt Euryn belongs to the Gloucester tradition; this proves clearly enough that there have been fused together traditions of different local origin. May we now say that these persons were of similar character, and that they were therefore confused? This is, of course, possible, but we can hardly presuppose that the original stories of these persons were the same. We have shown that in the Mabinogi of Pwyll heterogeneous cycles of motives have been confused. Now it remains to be decided when these motives came to be applied to the persons in question. Without further proof we cannot argue that all the respective motives were already associated in pagan times, for example, with Pryderi or Rhiannon. The motives reflect only the old pagan belief in charms, in the Otherworld, and in supernatural beings who stole living creatures, but that is all. Some of these stories may be very old, in so far as they agree with the old poems, though even these may not represent the remotest antiquity.

E. The Origins of the Mabinogi Tales

There is, however, still another problem as to whether these motives are native or whether they are not due to a foreign influence. This would naturally be an Irish influence. Mr. Grufifydd endeavours to prove that Pryderi's birth-story is identical with the Irish story of Mongán, and he is inclined to regard the Mabinogi as of Gaelic origin. If what he tries to prove were true, then his theory would be very well founded, but I am afraid it is not true.

Mongán's story is as follows: Manannán agrees to fight for the King Fiachna on the condition that he shall be allowed to sleep in his (Fiachna's) shape with the King's wife. This done, he actually does fight for him. Manannán's son is Mongán, and Manannán carries him off when he is three days old. There are here similar motives:

(i) Exchange of shapes.
(ii) Fighting in the other's stead.
(iii) The carrying off of the child.

But these motives are either not quite identical or they are differently arranged, and, moreover, it is of great importance that we have in Irish much closer parallels to single motives in the Mabinogi than those which Mr. Gruffydd uses. To get an archetype identical with the Irish story of Mongán, Mr. Gruffydd postulates that in the original story Pwyll was a supernatural being and Arawn a human one; he thinks that only an "Immortal" can help the "Mortal," and he finds support for this suggestion in the account of the combat at the ford (R.B. 713, W.B. fo, 172 c), where Pwyll is alluded to as "the man who was in Arawn's place" (*y gwr a oed yn lle Arawn*). Mr. Gruffydd argues that this passage speaks about Pwyll as a mysterious stranger. But these words do not convey any other idea than that it was not Arawn himself. Now, there are really instances which prove that a man can give help to an "Immortal":

(*a*) Cuchulinn is asked to help the *síde*.
    The people of the *fiana* often help the *síde*.
    The fairies require the help of a man in playing ball against other fairies.
(*b*) Human heroes being able to destroy the *síde*,[1] a human being is
    consequently able to give aid to the Otherworld.
(*c*) [The man can help the gods or fairies in other ways. Gods really need
    the offerings of the people, and so do also the fairies who are, according
    to Irish folk-lore, entitled to spilled milk. The fairies are grateful when a
    hero aids their child (so, for example, in South Slav. Prince Marco and
    a Fairy).

And, finally, the limits between the Human and the Superhuman are never strictly defined to the primitive imagination. Superhuman beings are only superior to men through their higher knowledge of magic, and if any mortal can acquire this knowledge he can rise to the same rank as the "immortals." A man can be immortal so long as he has the water of life, or so long as his soul is hidden (*vide* the Egyptian tale of Anpu and Bata, Flinders Petrie, *Egyptian*

---

1 So the Connacht people destroyed the *síd* of *Cruachan* (see *Echtra Nerai*). In British folklore we have some similar instances, as *Child Roland*.

Tales, ii. 36 ff.). The gods are jealous of their superior knowledge, so *e.g.* Toth felt very much offended when Ahura had got his magical book (Flinders Petrie, *ibid.* 89 ff.). Jehovah was afraid that man would be as one of the gods if he partook of the fatal fruits.] All these instances show that Mr. Gruffydd's presumption is not proved at all.

The motive of Pwyll's chaste intercourse is naturally, according to Mr. Gruffydd's theory, a later alteration, due to the later *redactors* who were shocked that Pwyll should have a real intercourse with Arawn's wife. But why did not the redactors suppress all the "very shocking" scenes of the fourth Branch of the Mabinogi, where Gwydyon and Gilwaethwy pay very scandalous attention to Goewin, and where Arianrod is represented like an adventuress in a French love-story? I do not think that the *redactors* were so scrupulous as Mr. Gruffydd would have us believe. Of course, Arawn did expect that Pryderi would be less abstinent than he was, but this feature is not isolated in folklore. We know that Siegfrid was also not supposed to pay merely platonic attentions to Brunhild, and for this calumny he had to pay dearly. In the Twin Brothers' story the same motive occurs. There can, of course, be no doubt that there had existed another shape-shifting motive in which the man (or woman) takes another shape to get access to the object of his admiration. So Arthur's father, Uther Penn Dragon (through Merlin's aid) came in the Duke of Din-dagwl's shape to the Duchess of Din-dagwl.[1] The story of Mongán belongs, of course, to the same group. It is, however, of importance that Mongán belongs to the Christian era, and so we must presuppose that some older tradition was applied to him. (We have many instances of the exchange of one person for another, so *e.g.* a story told in north Ireland (Donegal) about Cúchulainn is told in the south about Fionn mac Cumhail.) It is further to be noticed that Alexander the Great's birth story also has many motives similar to those of the Irish tale, so *e.g.* both Olympias and Philip are told that a supernatural being wishes to enter into union with Olympias, and Philip, on another day, is satisfied to hear from the expounder of dreams that the child to whom his wife Olympias is about to give birth is the son of the god Ammon. The fact that such a story existed, both in Wales and Ireland, does not, however, prove that the Mabinogi of Pwyll must be originally of the same kind; against this point of view we must put the fact that we have more than one instance of this other motive, and so we must acknowledge that the first part of the Mabinogi of Pwyll, as it is, represents a *Mährchen* for itself.

It may, however, be objected that I myself have presupposed a Supernatural Birth story for the second part, but I said only that some supernatural birth story has affected this second part of the first branch of the Mabinogi; whether this supernatural birth was really analogous to the Mongán story we cannot

---

1 Cf. further: Signy, Wolsung's daughter, wishing to have a son of entire Wolsung's blood, exchanged her shape with some magician, and slept in her shape with her own brother, Sigmund (Volsunga saga).

tell. We cannot, of course, exclude the possibility that Pryderi himself may have had, according to some local tradition, a supernatural origin, but we cannot tell of what kind it was; the motives which point to Pryderi's supernatural birth occur always in stories different from the Mongán type (*e.g.* the wife takes some magical remedy, or she swallows the incarnation of some supernatural being).

Mr. Gruffydd finally identifies the kidnapping of the young Pryderi with the carrying off of Mongán by Manannán. But in the Welsh story the child is taken by a being which used to take also other beings besides children, and so the only way would be to presuppose that the Mysterious Hand motive was developed from the motive in which the supernatural father takes his son with him. Such a motive we find in some combinations of the Mysterious Hand with Amor and Psyche motives (*vide supra*), but this motive does not seem to be there in its right place. And so there is only the one way to explain the origin of the Mysterious Hand. The being stealing the children and young beasts is apparently of the same character and nature as other beings which demand the child from their parents for themselves—these beings play the prominent *rôle* in the Child's Sacrifice-Motives; now, some of these motives are closely connected with that of *Removed Barrenness*, so, *e.g.* in the *Aitareya Brahmana*: Harischandra prays to Varuna for a son, promising to offer the child as a sacrifice to the god, and after the child's birth he seeks to evade the promise. This seems to point to a primitive custom of sacrificing a first-born child in cases where barrenness had been removed. We know, besides, that the Irish sacrificed the firstlings of every issue, and the chief scions of every clan were offered to Cromm Cruach (R.C. xvi. 35); the church preached against the slaying of the yoke oxen and milk-cows and burning of the first-born progeny; the same custom is reflected also in the story that the Fomori required a third of children, corn and milk (Lebor Gabála). It is consequently possible that the Mysterious Hand motive may have developed out of such an old belief, the Mysterious Hand belonging—as we can gather from the Modern Gaelic stories—to a giant (Scotch Gael, *famhair*) who took the *rôle* of the old Fomorian. In favour of this explanation we may mention the fact that in the first branch of the Mabinogi there are really traces of the Removed Barrenness Cycle, which so often occurs in association with the Child's sacrifice. [Therefore, I cannot quite agree with Prof. Kittredge's suggestion that in the Mabinogi originally three children were stolen, the first two incidents having been suppressed in order to render the Calumniated Woman continuation feasible. This suggestion is unnecessary, because the Calumniated Woman is also sometimes bereft of three children, as is also the case in the female Taboo-breaker motive.] There is, however, the *Grendel* motive to be considered: here the monster does not steal any children, and yet he appears in the same way. We have then to accept that it was probably assumed that the first-born son, in a case of removed barrenness, was forfeited to some horrible monster closely related to the cannibals of the folk-tales (where the main objects of cannibal attacks are especially the children). In such tales the cannibals are sometimes supernatural beings, and possibly their character may have risen—at least partly—from the human sacrifices, and so we must not be surprised if we find that not only the first-born but every child is stolen by a giant. I make this suggestion, however, only as a possibility.

The fact that Mongán, when three nights old, was taken by his father Manannan to fairyland might reflect a similar idea: the child considered as a god's son belongs to the god (in the Removed Barrenness motive the child was also believed to be god's gift); this would, however, imply a slightly different motive, *i.e.* a *Supernatural Birth*, of which we have found some traces in the first branch of the Mabinogi; in such supernatural birth stories the child remains with the human parents, but if we admit that the child is sometimes really taken from them (not given to fosterage), we have to account for the change of such a Mongán story into one of the Mabinogi type. In the Mongán tale we have no traces of such savage ideas (as human sacrifice), and it is most improbable that in the archetype of this tale there ever was anything of this kind; how shall we, then, explain the fact that the supposed Welsh deterioration of the Irish tale has preserved the older, more savage, feature, *i.e.* the monster stealing the children? or shall we ascribe it to the "monkish redactor" who guessed our modern theories? I hardly think so.

The same difficulties appear in Mr. Gruffydd's association (*ibid.* pp. 20 ff.) of the tale of Llew Llawgyffes (R.B. 763 ff.; W.B. fo. 195d ff.) with Ir. *Aided Conroí*, which presupposes a common origin for these two tales. If these words were to mean that this common origin goes back to a very remote period, there would be little difficulty, but Mr. Grufifydd thinks that the Irish story is the original one, and he argues that the identities of both stories prove the Gaelic origin of the Mabinogion. But unfortunately there are not only similarities in both tales, there are also great divergences.

The main divergence is that the Irish tale had originally an *External Soul* motive (Ériu, vii. pp. 200 ff.), of which the Welsh story has no unmistakable traces; here the hero (Llew) is invulnerable except with a certain weapon and in a certain position. This magic weapon might be perhaps a remnant of an external soul motive: in Irish story Cúrói's sword is a necessary instrument for destroying Cúrói's soul, because it is his own sword. It would be only natural then if the slaying power of the sword were explained, not as a possession of the hero who is to be killed, but as a supernatural quality of the sword itself, and so it is possible that in this way the story-teller came to evolve the idea of a magical weapon. There is, however, still another motive which does not occur in the External Soul theme: the hero can be slain only under certain conditions; otherwise he is deathless: Llew cannot be killed either within a house or without; he cannot be slain on horseback or on foot (R.B. 705, W.B. fo. 196 d: *Ny ellir vy llad i y mywn ty . . . ny ellir allan, ny ellir vy llad ar varch ny ellir ar vyn troed*).

The words are a formula intended to mean: he cannot be killed at all and a situation is invented which satisfies this formula. This motive that somebody is cunning enough to avoid difficulties comprised in some regulation intended to be incapable of being performed is common enough. A lord gives an order to his peasant subject that his (*i.e.* the peasant's) daughter shall come to him neither riding nor going (on foot); the daughter comes walking on one foot and the other leg on the back of a goat. (It is very significant that Llew has to put one foot upon a buck.)

Another example of this motive we find in the Mahābhārata (18. 43. 2434): Indra made friends with Namuci, and promised not to slay him with wet nor dry, in the day nor in the night. One day Indra beheld a fog, and cut off the head of Namuci with foam of water. We see that in such stories only the negative form is given; the method of evading the formula is to be found by the opponent, and so I suppose that originally Llew himself said only the negative part of the formula: the situation in which he could be slain was invented either by his wife Blodeuwedd or by Gronw Pebyr. [The reason why Llew says the positive part of the formula as well may be confusion with the Separate Soul Cycle, where the giant himself says how he can be slain.]

The fabrication of the magical spear may reflect some traces of an old belief in the childhood of mankind that every new and better weapon was a magical one; metal weapons were of course regarded with great awe, and their fabrication was naturally considered as a magical performance; a trace of this creed is found in the belief that blacksmiths are cunning people who can perform magical things,[1] so we find in St. Patrick's prayer, vv. 48, 54:

> *Tocuiriur etrum . . . inna huli nert so*
> * * * * *
> *fri brichtu ban ocus gobann ocus druad.*
>
> "I summon all these powers between me [and these] . . .
> against the spells of women, blacksmiths and druids."

In modern Japan the fabrication of a sword is a religious performance.

The other main difference from the *Aided Conroí* is the fact that Llew was not yet killed: he was only transformed into an eagle (R.B. 766, V.V.B. 197 ab: *Ac ar gwenwyn wayw y vwrw ay vedru yn y ystlys yny neita y paladyr o honaw a thrigyaw y penn yndaw. Ac yna bwrw ehetvan o honaw ynteu yn rith eryr a dodi garymleis anhygar. Ac ny chahat y welet hynny allau*). There are two possibilities: either Gronw has made some mistake or Llew was really killed. Now Mabinogion does not mention any mistake, and so we should expect that Llew was really killed;

---

1   *E.g.* Vulcan's maidens; a smith makes a living stag, etc. (*Vide* M'Dougall, *Folk-Tales*, 16 ff.).

if we find that he was transformed, this agrees with primitive ideas according to which death and life are not so strictly separated one from another as in our modern ideas: the dead man is not really dead; he could live again. This old belief is reflected in many motives, one group of which is the most important for us, *i.e.* the dead takes the form of an animal or a plant (M'Culloch, *The Childhood of Fiction*, pp. 108 ff.); this group is connected with the old belief that the dead man assumes the shape of his clan totem. In our case the question is still simpler, as Llew is transformed into an eagle, and the soul has, according to the wide-spread belief, a bird's shape. The rest is only a logical consequence of this belief: if the dead continues living in another shape, there must exist some means to restore his original shape and he can live again. Usually the relatives and friends of the dead know what to do, and this of course is known also to Gwydyon, who in this episode plays the *rôle* of the relative, for he strikes Llew with his magic wand to restore his form (R.B. 768, *Ac yna y trewis Gwydyon a hutlath ynteu yny vyd yn y rith e hunan*). This results from Gwydyon's general magic nature (cf. Skene, ii 302, *Neu Leu a Gwydyon a vuant gelvydyon | neu a wdant lyvyryon?* "Or Llew and Gwydyon were they creators (artists), or did they know books?") So in a Basuto tale: a girl is devoured but her heart escapes as a bird, and when the wings are pulled off the girl assumes again her own shape. We might define this belief as follows: the dead gets only another *hamr* (skin), and it is his rescuer's task to get this *hamr* off.

It is worth while considering the tales in which this motive occurs; it is either the dead mother who takes the shape uf some animal (Cinderella motive) or a slain person seeks his revenge on his murderers (jealous sisters or cruel stepmother), or, finally, a woman is transformed by another woman who seeks to take her place. This motive is rarely connected with the motive of the *Treacherous Wife*, and yet we have a very old instance of this combination, viz. the Egyptian story of *Anpu and Bata* (Flinders Petrie, *Egyptian Tales*, ii. pp. 49 ff.): Bata took his heart (*i.e.* soul) out of his body and hid it in the flowers of an acacia tree. He told his brother Anpu that his (Rata's) death would be revealed to him by a "life token," and if this happened Anpu must come and search for his soul. They now took leave of each other, and Bata lived in the valley of the acacia. Once he met the Nine Gods, "and Ra Harakti said to Khnumu: 'Behold, frame thou a woman for Bata that he may not remain alive alone.' And Khnumu made for him a mate to dwell with him. She was more beautiful in her limbs than any woman who is in this land. The essence of every god was in her. The seven Hathors came to see her: they said with one mouth, 'She will die a sharp death.'" Bata lived happily with his wife, and told her of the secret of his life. A lock of her hair was carried down the river and taken to the Pharaoh, who bade to be made a search for its owner.[1] When found, she became Pharaoh's wife,

---

[1] Cf. Isolda's hair is brought to King Marc, and he desires to marry the owner of this hair.

and desired the acacia tree to be cut down. This done, Bata died, but his brother found his heart and restored it to the dead, and Bata "became as he had been." After this Bata transformed himself into an Apis bull, which his unfaithful wife caused to be killed. Two drops of the blood fell on either side of the door, and from them grew up two persea trees; she ordered them to be cut down, but a splinter flew into her mouth, and Bata was in due time reborn as Pharaoh's son, and as he became the king his mother (*i.e.* Bata's treacherous wife) was brought before him, "and he judged with her before him, and they agreed with him" (*i.e.* probably she met "a sharp death "). Professor Flinders Petrie remarks of this story:[1] "The sudden death of Bata so soon as the depository of his soul was destroyed is a usual feature in such tales about souls. But it is only in the Indian tale quoted by Mr. Frazer that there is any revival of the dead, and in no case is there any transformation like that of Bata." Now in our Welsh tale we have an instance of such a transformation, and the main frame of the story agrees more with the Egyptian version than with the Irish: in both versions the wife is made for the hero. (In the Irish version we have nothing of this kind, but the wife is kidnapped by Cúroi, and has therefore good reasons to hate him; her rescuer Cúchulainn is at first beaten.) In both tales the husband is transformed into an animal and takes his revenge personally on the faithless wife. (In the Irish, Cúroi's soul being totally destroyed, there is no possibility of his revival.)

Professor Flinders Petrie calls this tale a "patch-work," and it really seems as if there were two different *motives* mixed together, *i.e.* the "Separable Soul" and the "Shapeshifting of the Dead." If, now, in the Welsh story the "Separable Soul" motive had once a more important *rôle* than we find in the present version, it would be an extraordinary coincidence with the Egyptian tale; if there was no such motive it is the less similar to the Irish tale, and so the theory of the Goidelic origin of this tale proves to be quite improbable. I will not deny the Gaelic influence; but this does not yet imply that most of the Mabinogi stories are of Gaelic origin. The influence of Gaelic on Welsh is surely sometimes overrated, and philological researches prove that the influence of Brythonic on Gaelic was much greater than *vice versâ*, and we find in Irish a great number of Brythonic loanwords (see Pedersen, Vergleichende Grammatik der keltischen Sprachen, § 24).[2] In prehistoric times there were probably some Brythonic races

---

1 M'Culloch (*The Rel. of Anc. Celts*, 108) has already observed the identity of Llew's tale with the Egyptian. But he did not compare both stories; according to his opinion there is no "Separable Soul" motive (but see his *Childhood of Fiction*, p. 142 f.).

2 It is very important for our purpose that Cúchulainn's first name, *Setanta*, seems to be of Brythonic origin (cf. Brit. *Setantioi*; old *Setantios* would give in Ir. **Seθaide*, spelt **Sethaite*). If this name is of Brythonic origin it must have come to Ireland after the time of lenition and assimilation

in Ireland, and in later Christian times there was a great influx of Welsh students into Ireland, and so we must never forget that British folklore and traditions might also have influenced the Irish.

There is, however, a possibility of quite foreign influences, and this is far more important. We can never totally exclude the possibility of some Mediterranean culture elements influencing the insular culture. Archaeology proves only that Celtic art had absorbed some Mediterranean ornaments, etc., but we know that there was a commercial contact between the Mediterranean and the isles, and by this way some motives might have come to Britain already in prehistoric times. I think that the above discussed Llew story might have had such an origin. I will not argue that the Irish story is of foreign origin, but in Welsh the curious combination of motives, which is so similar to the Egyptian, puzzles me. But this part of the Bata story is, according to Professor Flinders Petrie (*l.c.*) of Asiatic and not of Egyptian origin.

It might be also of some interest to compare the Irish story of Etain's kidnapping and the Pāli Jātaka, No. 327. The Irish story has preserved much better the original features: King Eochaid Airem lost a game (in chess) against the fairy King Mider, and Mider was entitled to name the stake, and he demanded Eochaid's wife Étáin, whom later he carried off It is important that he eloped as a bird. In the Jātaka the King of Garudas (bird-demons) used to come to the King of Benares and play dice with him; he fell in love with the queen, whom he carried off. The king's poet, hidden in the Garuda-King's feathers, was carried to the palace of the queen. In the Irish story it is one of Eochaid's druids who finds Étáin.

Now in the Pāli tale the dice-playing is not explained; the Irish gives a good explanation for it; but, as regards the origin of this motive, I should rather think that it is not Irish; it is further very significant that also the first life of Étáin "has some unique features, as it alone among Western *Mährchen* saga variants of the 'True Bride' describes the malicious woman as the wife of Mider. In other words, the story implies polygamy, rarely found in European Folk Tales" (M'Culloch, *The Religion of Ancient Celts*, p. 83, note 2). Our Jātaka story is referred to in another part of the Jātakas as an example of woman's infidelity; Étáin is not directly described in the same way, but her conduct towards Ailill Anglonnach cannot be regarded by any means as a pattern of wifely chastity.

I am far from considering that these facts are a real proof of Oriental origin for the Étáin story, but they are remarkable enough to be worth considering in connection with this possibility.

First published in
Folk-Lore, Volume 27, March, 1916

INFLUENCE OF WELSH
TRADITION ON THE LITERATURE OF FRANCE

An Essay by Albert Schulz

In recapitulating the results at which we have so far arrived, we should say that the immediate influence of the Welsh traditions upon the literature of France was effected by their passage through that country, where they became imbued with the spirit of French chivalry, and formed a perfectly new style, of which the tendency was to represent the true life and spirit of chivalry. But there is also another equally important element, which passed into France with these traditions, and like them became diffused over Europe; this is the ancient popular belief of the Welsh and the Bretons,—the ancient Celtic mythology it may be called,—the wonderful and interesting World of Celtic Tales. For, the beneficent fairies who educated Lancelot du Lac, the giants conquered by Owain, Tristan, and Peredur, the enchanted fountains, the miraculous trees, the dragons and serpents, the magic rings, the sorcerer Merlin, the Fay Morgana sister of Arthur, these aerial spirits which once more resumed their power under Shakspeare, do not come from the North nor from the East—they are Celtic—and all these powers and beings which are still religiously preserved in the poetic memory of the people of Brittany and of Wales, who have always been so remarkable for their attachment to their ancient literature, are of a nature totally different from those which have passed from Asia to the West. In the German and Scandinavian religion, belief takes an animated nature, which shows itself even after the introduction of Christianity. In them nature and genius are not yet separated, and, in this primitive union, nature appears poetic from the mountains and rivers down to animated life. The miraculous beings of the East form still more a world apart, and foreign to man; magic does not exist as an elementary spirit in nature, these superhuman beings represent less the powers of nature than human passions; trees and flowers do not in themselves possess an intellectual life, but they shade the dwelling of the God, or serve to express these mysteries to man; they are symbols, but they are not beings; we see throughout less of internal life than of exterior marvels.

Supposing that, after the twelfth century, this style had entered by Spain from the East into the ideas of the people and the chivalric poems, and that these elements had given a certain tinge mingled with these ancient fabulous beings, and with the belief of the Celts, still we must decidedly deny that all is of oriental origin. This cannot be conceded, except in so far as that the Celts, like all other nations in Europe, had their primitive home in Asia, and might have brought with them certain remembrances, of which they partook equally with their brethren of the East.

A belief in superhuman and demoniacal beings, in hidden powers of nature and means to possess oneself of them, is common to every person, and penetrates harmlessly more or less into every religion, if it be not perverted by repulsive superstition. Jacob Grimm, in his unappreciable work on German Mythology, has shewn in what manner this imaginative World, of which we speak, and which is here called the *Fabulous Kingdom of Tales*, had its first origin, and a well founded and reasonable meaning in ancient paganism; how, at first, notwithstanding the bloody baptism by the sword of Charlemagne, Christianity insensibly bordered on pagan ideas, how places sacred to the pagans were chosen for Christian chapels, how they gradually made the pagan divinities subordinate to the one true God of Christianity, degrading them to powerless demons and diabolical beings, or to goblins and gnomes, and how, at last, the ancient belief in these beings was discarded by more enlightened minds, and dismissed to the nursery, to people the fresh and infantile imagination with those changeable and etherial beings which we meet with in these tales. We do not doubt that we could demonstrate a similar progress of the ancient belief from the altar of nature to the nursery, amongst the Cymry and Bretons, and that we should find amongst these people described to us, as possessing such lively imagination, and delighting always in fantastic speculations and curious philosophisms, many more documents than among the Germans, where the sources are very scarce, and are often derived from the Scandinavians; although such a research would present another peculiar difficulty, viz. that the Celts very early experienced a Roman, German, and Scandinavian influence, which produced a picture much more varied and complicated than in Germany, and we feel assured that the ancient pagan belief was transformed among the Celts much earlier in the Childrens' Tales, because Christianity penetrated much sooner into Wales and Armorica than into Germany and Scandinavia.

But we must not here enter more largely into the history of this civilization, we must confine ourselves to unravelling these stories only as far as they are mixed with the traditions of Arthur; for it is those traditions that have occasioned the circulation of these tales throughout Europe. We find that this species of poetry is, at first, exclusively displayed in the most ancient continental poems, of which the subject is the achievements and adventures of Arthur's Knights. These poems correspond so entirely with those Welsh stories called Mabinogion, that we have only to resolve the question whether the Mabinogion are the origin of the French romances, or vice versa, that is to say, feeble imitations of those eminently poetic creations of the period when chivalry was at its height.

The word Mabinogion is translated Tales for Children, or by Tales in general; and Lady Charlotte Guest, in a very pleasing letter, has dedicated her translation of the Mabinogion to her own children, but we doubt whether this title would have been employed in the twelfth century in the same sense. Tradition and fables are always supposed to contain faith and doubt. A tale is a dream of truth, with the full conciousness that it is but a dream. The relater knows that he repeats an imaginative poem. The manners of nations are reflected in the lives of individuals, and as, in mature age, man can only return to the fancies and pleasures of childhood and youth as to a dream, so, in like manner, a people cannot look upon their past history and historical traditions as fables, until they have long since passed that period, and have advanced to a much higher degree of civilization. In the poems of the most ancient bards, we find Owain, Peredur, Geraint, and others, mentioned as warriors, fighting with Arthur against the Saxons; these persons belong to history equally with Arthur. In the Mabinogion their historical character is annihilated with that of Arthur, who here appears in the same light as in the French romances, a spectator of the exploits of his companions; his court is the rendezvous of his heroes, whose adventures no longer appear as patriotic expeditions. So long as the people faithfully believed in the truth of the traditions of Arthur and his heroes, these Mabinogion could not have been composed. But we are aware of the tendency of tradition to amplification. This tendency does not show itself capriciously, but follows the general laws of nature, and only operates when the mind and body are satisfied. It consequently appears in this case, that tradition could not proceed to separate and enlarge on the histories of persons who had hitherto only acted a secondary part, until the glory of Arthur had attained its height, and the people began to find a monotony in the constantly repeated history of one person, and sought to replace it by fresh subjects. The bards and minstrels would then endeavour to revive their feelings with respect to this ancient personage by the addition of new facts, over which they diffused a higher interest, by interweaving them with ancient and celebrated occurrences. We have already seen, from the testimony of Nennius, the manner in which, as early as the ninth century, the original. Arthur and his histories are amplified. In the Welsh Archaiology p. 167, 175, &c. we find dialogues between Arthur, Kai, and Glewlwyd, between Arthur and Gwenhwyvar, between the latter and Eliwlod, and between Tristan and Gwalchmai, which the learned Turner places in the tenth and eleventh centuries; they prove that these historical heroes, like their chief, often received a fabulous glory, but we do not find any trace of those elements of chivalry which we shall hereafter describe more minutely. While traditions were thus added to, the Celtic fables and tales would also require a greater extension, as well as a poetical worship, for a stationary condition cannot be imagined where a real existence is demonstrated; it is only in Wales, or perhaps in Brittany also that authentic proofs could be produced, of where and at what time they were combined with ancient historical remembrances. In the Mabinogion in general, the opposition still exists,—Christianity and Paganism are completely opposed to each other. The giants and black men, those savage, sanguinary and inhuman

beings who so often appear, belong to Paganism, while the heroes of the tale
are always good Christians, but the dogmatic tincture of Christianity is always
wanting in these stories, and if their antiquity and purely Welsh origins, were
not even still more evident from the intimate connexion with the localities,
manners, and customs of the country, we should say that one of the strongest
proofs of it existed in our inability any where to discover in them the hand of
a priest or even of a monk. Courage and strength form the basis of chivalry;
faith, honour and love, only serve to give it a higher vocation or consecration.
Strength and courage are also the characteristic traits of the heroes of the
Mabinogion, but *Faith* remains at the bottom, even more than in our own
Niebelungelied; it never forms the motive of actions; Honour is not yet very
sensitive or refined, it is only introduced into the Mabinogion to prove strength
and courage; and with regard to *Love* the women appear more exacting than
the men, who constantly say that there is no lady whom they love more than
such a one, or such a one, but do not always prove it by their actions. In the
Mabinogion we can, therefore, only discover the first slight traces of the dawn of
Chivalry. These Heroes are called Marchawg, which Lady C. Guest, in speaking
of Owain, translates, and, no doubt justly, *Knight*. But they are knights before
whom the Seraphim of the Crusades had not yet carried the cross,—Knights
whose hearts had not yet been softened by the soft gales of Provence and Spain,
although they were more prepared to receive them than the bards of the sixth
century, who knew nothing of this species of adoration. In the ninth century the
bards had probably exhausted in the histories of the deeds of Arthur, the interest
which this avidity for achievements and physical strength had excited, but they
gained a variety by recalling this ancient world of fable; there they found giants
and dragons to combat, demoniacal powers to contend with, fairies to amuse
them; in short, a world made expressly for these indefatigable and invincible
warriors. In this consisted the interest that procured for these tales, which must,
of necessity, have existed in the eleventh century, that extraordinary reception
from the French and the Normans, who were their untiring auditors. This
reception would, on the other side, animate Wales and Brittany to improve still
further in this fertile branch of poetry. William the Conqueror profited by this
thirst for exploits in order to subdue England; the Church for the expeditions
against Toledo and the Saracens, and for the Crusades in the East; and it did
not cease so long as chivalry existed, and bodily strength retained its full
value. The dignity of knighthood was not hereditary, but purely individual; it
was the reward of merit, and its value depended on the person who bore it.
Bodily strength and the sword procured glory; which was the greater, if the hero
withstood the attack alone and without succour. The heroes of the Mabinogion
are knights-errant, who all seek adventures separately, and it was this, which
above all, engaged the attention of the listening knight, who, placing himself in
the situation of the hero, ruminated over the wonders of the tale as if he himself

had witnessed them.

The Peredur of the Red Book of Hergest is the most certain proof we have of a higher antiquity than 1150, and of the pure tradition of the Cymry without any French admixture, for it is perfectly free from any trace of the Graal which was so soon after interwoven with the traditions of Arthur. There is not a single French or English poem existing in which Perceval could be introduced in connexion with the Graal; and the latter became so generally known together with his hero, and created so great an interest, that we consider it psychologically impossible that a poet should have undertaken to separate the Graal and Percival. On the contrary, history teaches us that of all kinds of literature poetry has the strongest tendency to possess itself of new elements and to wander from its original source. Peredur is an invaluable document as regards the fiction of the Graal; but the same Mabinogi likewise proves that it is a recent compilation, and that the Tale existed long before it was committed to writing; for it refers in several places to anterior histories. "And Peredur was entertained by the Empress fourteen years, *as the story relates*" and "And the story relates nothing further of Gwalchmai respecting this adventure."

Thus it is not a fiction, it is not a fable, but it is a tradition perpetuated by writing. But nevertheless, it is a Mabinogi, i.e. according to Owen's Welsh Dictionary, *Juvenile Instruction*. We would propose this explanation; the Red Book of Hergest was a guide for the instruction of young bards, it was a means, whereby the huge and unformed mass of objects could be retained in the memory; but to give life, spirit, and ornament, to these drily related tales was reserved for the oral instruction of the master; if he had a tale written with the same spirit and imagination with which the Bard (*the cantor historicus*) recited it aloud, we should have a very different work before us to those which are in no way distinguished by beauty of composition, and which we may compare to mere skeletons—as helps only to the memory, and books for the use of youth, and which, *in that form* do not appear to us much more ancient than the manuscript in which they are found. Even if the poetry of the Welsh had arrived at its period of decay in the twelfth century, such works would not have been reckoned as belonging to *the* Art. On the other hand, Wales was not so raised above the civilization of the rest of Britain and the continent, that it should *then* present these tales, which excited an enthusiastic interest in the most distinguished men of the age as *Stories for Children*! We must draw attention to the circumstance that in the different compilations of the same story, as Iwain, Tristan, and Lancelot, and Erec, both in France and England, we see the most remarkable variations, together with certain adventures which are to be found in all, rendering it impossible to reduce them all to one common source. As they were perfectly new to the French, we cannot imagine that the French themselves should have invented these variations on their first introduction. But this difficulty is easily explained, if we seek for the common origin in the oral Tradition which was differently modified in the mouth of each Welsh Bard or Tale-teller. The outline which chance presented to the French clerk, always eager for novelty and reading, to reduce it to writing, was put into French verse in different ways by different persons, and thus these romances were formed.

First published in
'Fable—The Mabinogion', *An Essay on the Influence of Welsh Tradition upon the Literature of Germany, France and Scandinavia*, 1841

THE MABINOGION

An Essay Thomas Stephens

We should however form but an imperfect estimate of the literature of Wales, if we confined our notice to the bards alone. The Kymry had in the middle ages two literatures, essentially distinct from each other; which though springing from the soil had different features. The bardic literature, taken singly, forms but a faint reflection of the national character, as it is described by contemporaneous writers, and observers of Cambrian manners. The bards, properly so called, were a despotic and exclusive order, and had created an artificial taste, from which standard no one was allowed to depart. This had therefore the defect of narrowness; the poetry was the literature of the few, and found no great favour among the body of the people. Giraldus tells us the Kymry were a free, merry, and witty people, and passionately fond of music; but the latter characteristic only is found in their poetry. It was therefore in the nature of events, that the bulk of the people should have found some intellectual recreation more consonant with their character. There had been for hundreds of years traditions floating among them; and therefore when the general awakening, of which we have already spoken, took place, it was a natural desire that these should be connected, arranged, and written. This was the origin of the *Mabinogion*— tales written to wile away the time of young chieftains, to be repeated at the fire side, and ultimately to react very powerfully upon the national literature, and character.

It is utterly inconsistent with our knowledge of human history, to suppose that the national mind of Wales could have been for any lengthened period inactive; we may therefore conclude that the long and barren period, which intervenes between the death of Cadwaladr, and the arrival of Gruffydd ab Kynan, could not have been wholly unproductive. The bards were engaged in recording the actions of their countrymen, which becoming more and more known, became more and more glorious. Plain facts were embellished into glorious fictions, brave warriors became great heroes; and Arthur, an insignificant chieftain in the sixth century, grew into a valorous warrior in the eighth, and by the twelfth had become emperor of the whole civilized world. This growth of traditions is plainly evident in the works of Nennius, Geoffrey, and Alanus de Insulis; and as has been well remarked, there is as much difference between Gildas and Nennius, as there is between Nennius and Geoffrey. Fable had grown in the intervals. There is an evident growth of fable among the Kymry themselves, between the ages of Gildas and Nennius; and this becomes more apparent if we admit Mr. Price's happy conjecture, that Nennius translated his work, or at least a part of it, from Cambrian originals. We have in his work many of the elements of the greater romance. His work mentions Arthur as a "magnanimous hero;" and unless the passage be interpolated, he alludes to a visit paid by that "emperor," to Jerusalem. In the Mabinogi of Kilhwch and Olwen, the combing of another's hair implies relationship; Arthur combed the hair of Kilhwch with "a golden comb", and a "scissors the loops whereof were of silver;" and the boar Trwyth is hunted for nothing else than the comb, scissors, and razor which were between its ears. Now we find this same statement in the history of Nennius, where St. Germanus being charged with the paternity of a boy, takes the child and says, "I will be a father to you my son; nor will I dismiss you till a razor, scissors, and comb are given to me, and it is allowed you to give them to your carnal father." A very large portion of the romantic incidents in Geoffrey were most probably found in the home traditions; and the Dream of Rhonabwy, the Mabinogi of Kilhwch and Olwen, and the tale of Gwgan the poet, show that the Kymry were in the habit of writing tales, and that they knew well how to do so; for the second of these is very ingeniously constructed. We may therefore safely conclude, that the Mabinogion could have been produced here; and there is sufficient evidence to show that the Kymry did so produce them. Lady Charlotte Guest, in her preface, speaking of the Red Book of Hergest, says,—

It comprises, among other things, a collection of Mabinogion; some, like the present story, (The Lady of the Fountain) having the character of chivalric romances, and others bearing the impress of far higher antiquity, both as regards the manners they depict, and the language in which they are composed. So greatly do these Mabinogion differ in character, that they may be considered as forming two distinct classes, one of which generally celebrates heroes of the Arthurian cyclus, while the other refers to personages and events of an earlier period.

Those of the second class appear to be the earliest in point of time; they make no mention of Arthur at all, and treat of personages who lived much earlier; these are the Mabinogion of Pwyll Prince of Dyved, Branwen the daughter of Llyr, Manawyddan the son of Llyr, Math the son of Mathonwy, The Dream of Maxen Wledig, The Tale of Lludd and Llevelis, and the Mabinogi of Taliesin. The second class, Kilhwch and Olwen, The Dream of Rhonabwy, Owain and the Lion, Geraint ab Erbin, Peredur ab Efrawc, and the Story of St. Greal, are Arthurian Romances of a later date.

In the Arthurian group, there are however marked distinctions. The Hengwrt romance of St. Greal fixes the palace of that hero at Camelot, Cornwall. The Dream of Rhonabwy, with Kilhwch and Olwen, agree in placing it at Gelliwig in Cornwall; and the stories of Owain, Geraint, and Peredur mention Caerlleon. The second two also differ from the latter three, in several other respects. Arthur in the former is surrounded by an immense number of knights, while in the latter the number of his attendants is not so great, the prominence being given to individual and not collective achievements; and the confusion of the first gives place to order and regularity in the latter. In Kilhwch, and Rhonabwy, Arthur hunts the Twrch Trwyth with his knights, and is preparing to fight personally against Ossa Gyllellvawr; but in Owain and the others he is the emperor reposing on his laurels. In the former the knights act collectively; but in the latter, the knight errantry of the riper romance is fully developed. These facts warrant us in concluding that Kilhwch and Rhonabwy are the earliest of the Arthurian group. They seem to have emanated from sources purely Kymric, and bear out Geoffrey's assertion, that prior to the appearance of his history, the exploits of Arthur *were very commonly related in a pleasing manner*; the others appear to be later. This conclusion is also supported by the bardic writings; the earlier bards attach no importance to Caerlleon, but the latter do; and Bleddyn Vardd towards the close of the thirteenth century calls it "that best of places Caerlleon.

It is not easy to fix a date for these tales; perhaps they are not in their present form older than the twelfth century; but they were evidently in circulation years, if not centuries before. In the Ystori of Peredur, it is said, "And Peredur was entertained by the empress fourteen years, *as the story relates*;" and again, "The story relates nothing further of Gwalchmai respecting this adventure." At the end of the Dream of Rhonabwy, it is said, "And this is the reason that no one knows the dream without a book, neither bard, nor gifted seer; because of the various colours that were upon the horses, and the many wondrous colours of the arms, and of the panoply, and of the precious scarfs, and of the virtue-bearing stones." In that remark we have a sufficient proof that these stories were being frequently related without reference to written memorials; and Lewis Glyn Cothi's designation of a class of bards as story-tellers (ystorïawyr,) makes the probability certain. While so related, they, in accordance with the known laws of the development of fable, ascended from a brief to an expanded, from a simple to a complex and artistic form. A case of this nature occurs in connexion with Owain ab Urien. At the end of the thirteenth century it existed as it appears in Rhonabwy, for Bleddyn Vardd alludes to nothing more romantic than "Owen and his ravens;" but at the commencement of the fifteenth century, in Gruffydd Llwyd's ode to Owain Glyndwr, we find Owain described as the knight errant of "The lady of the Fountain." But though these stories grew with time, there were limits to their development imposed by the character of the national mind; and though the operation may be delicate, it is still possible to define what is of foreign, and what of native addition. In the earlier tales of Kymric origin, the machinery is invariably supernatural. The Mabinogion of Pwyll, Branwen, Math, and Manawyddan, are evidences of this; the marvellous and moving power, is seldom, indeed we may say never, personal courage, but invariably magic; and the same fact appears in the verse as well as prose legends. Nothing could be more remote from the Kymric conception than knight errantry; the spirit of adventure has no place even in our national character; and wherever that appears in our literature, we shall not greatly err in assigning to it a foreign origin. It only occurs in the stories of Owain, Geraint, and Peredur, and is, I think, clearly post-Norman. The existence of an earlier class of tales of a purely Cambrian origin, demonstrates satisfactorily that tale-telling was a natural attribute of the Kymry, and is a sufficient proof, were there not an abundance of others, to show that our Mabinogion are of Kymric origin; yet the source of some of the elements of the Arthurian group is more doubtful: the knight errantry is clearly Norman; but whence came Arthur?

Arthur is confessedly a Kymric hero; but a question having been raised as to whether he receives his romantic character from the Kymry of Wales, or those of Brittany, it is our duty to throw upon the point all the light we possess. His name is mentioned by Nennius, but as the passage occurs at various places in the different manuscript copies of that historian, there is reason, if not to doubt its genuineness, to consider it as an addition by his editor Mark the Hermit. I have thought that the discrepancy between the dates assigned to this history, might be explained in a similar way; but of that let riper scholars judge. Yet, though the name assumes a heroic garb in this historian, it did not take hold of the popular mind: there is no trace of the hero in the early poetry of Wales. has been so frequently shown that the earlier bards make no distinction between Arthur, and the other warriors of his day, that it is not necessary for me to travel over ground already trod by Turner, and Schulz; but the same fact is observable in the writings of later bards. Arthur is very reluctantly admitted, and even as late as the twelfth century, the bards showed much greater partiality to Cadwaladr. Indeed, strange as the assertion may appear, there is reason to believe that they discountenanced the Arthurian stories. Kynddelw mentions the battle of Badon twice, but we seldom find the name of Arthur introduced in his poems with any great degree of prominence; and until the force of public opinion forced them to give way, the bards continued to set their faces against him. They persisted in confining him to Cornwall, long after the rest of the world had turned their eyes to Caerlleon; and Kynddelw, twenty-nine years at least after Geoffrey's history had become well known, hints at the former glories of Gelliwig. Llywarch ab Llywelyn when from home compares Rhys Gryg to Arthur; but when at home he does not compare a much greater man, his patron Llywelyn ab Iorwerth, to that hero and although the bards were well acquainted with the story, the name of Arthur is not freely used for at least half a century after that time, and even then, he is simply the most renowned of warriors. There is therefore a strong presumption, that the heroic character did not originate, where being planted it found so much difficulty to grow. This anomalous position of the Kymry of the Principality, leads infallibly to one of two conclusions. Either they did really consider the Arthurian stories to be fabulous, or deeming them true, they were too apathetic to embrace them. The latter inference is utterly inadmissible; we have therefore no alternative but to fall back upon the other, and to conclude that at that time Wales was so raised above the civilization of the rest of Britain and the Continent, that it presented the Mabinogion and Romances as Tales for children, and Fabulous Stories. Professor Schulz asserts that this was not the case; but when we consider that he terms the age of Meilir, Gwalchmai, Kynddelw, Hywel ab Owain, Llywarch ab Llywelyn, and Davydd Benvras, as "a period of decay in Welsh poetry," we need not wonder that his speculations on the Mabinogion are not quite correct. These tales were certainly so considered by the bards; but there is a slight modification required in the Cambrian account. The term Mabinogion is applied indifferently to all the tales; but that is not strictly proper. Originally they appear to have been thus classified:

MABINOGION, OR JUVENILE TALES

Mabinogi Pwyll Pendevig Dyved	Pwyll Prince of Dyved
Mabinogi Branwen Verch Llyr	Branwen the daughter of Llyr
Mabinogi Math ab Mathonwy	Math the son of Mathonwy
Mabinogi Manawyddan ab Llyr	Manawyddan the son of Llyr
Mabinogi Taliesin	The Mabinogi of Taliesin

BREUDDWYDION, OR DREAMS

Breuddwyd Macsen Wledig	The Dream of the Emperor Maximus
Breuddwyd Rhonabwy	The Dream of Rhonabwy
Kyvranc Lludd a Llevelis	The Quarrel of Lludd and Llevelis

YSTORÏAU, OR STORIES

Ystori Bown o Hamtwn	The Story of Bevis Hampton
Ystori Dared	The Story of Dared
Ystori Saint Greal	The Story of St. Greal
Ystori Gwald Ievan Vendigaid	The Story of the Land of John the Blessed
Ystori Idrian Amherawdyr	The Story of the Emperor Hadrian
Ystori Kilhwch ac Olwen	The Story of Kilhwch and Olwen
Ystori Owen ab Urien,	The Story of Owen the Son of Urien,
neu Chwedyl Iarlles y Ffynnon	or the Tale of the Lady of the Fountain
Ystori Peredur vab Evrog	The Story of Peredur the Son of Evrawc
Ystori I draethu mal yd aeth	A Story relating how Mary went to Heaven
Mair I'r nev	
Ystori Geraint vab Erbin	The Story of Geraint the Son of Erbin

This classification is taken from Llwyd's *Archæologia Britannica*, (pp. 255-265.) He there professes to give the titles of the various MSS.; and as we know that the relaters of the larger tales were called Story-tellers, the names are probably strictly accurate. It hence results that Schulz is partially correct in his conjecture as to the actual facts; but the conclusion deduced therefrom is as unwarranted as before; for *Ystorïau*, and *Ystorïawr*, indicate with quite as much clearness as *Mabinogion*, the limited extent of the bardic credulity. Nothing can be more apparent to the student of Cambrian literature, than that the bards were among the last persons in Europe to admit the credibility of the Arthurian tales. We must therefore seek the first traces of the Arthur of Romance, among the Kymry of Armorica.

The people of Armorica, and of ancient Gaul generally, are supposed to have been the same people as the colonists of Britain; and this would seem to be the reason why during times of distress the Britons fled there for refuge. Besides this connexion there were others of which history takes note. In the triads we are told of "three combined expeditions that went from the Isle of Britain."—

The first went with Ur the son of Erin, and became Greeks.

The second combined expedition was conducted by Caswallon, son of Beli, the son of Manogan, and Gwenwynwyn and Gwanar, the sons of Lliaws, sons of Nwyvre, with Arianrod the daughter of Beli, their mother. Their origin was from the border declivity of Galedin and Essyllwg (Siluria), and of the combined tribes of the Bylwenny; and their number was three score and one thousand. They went after the Kaisarians over the sea to the land of the Geli Lydaw (Gauls of Letavia,) that were descended from the original stock of the Kymry. And none of them, or of their progeny, returned to this Island, but remained among the Romans in the country of the Gwasgwynion (Gascony) where they are at this time. And it was in revenge for this expedition that the Romans first came to this Island.

The third combined expedition, was conducted out of the Island by Elen the armipotent, and Kynan her brother, lord of Meiriadoc, into Armorica, where they obtained land and dominion, and royalty from Macsen Wledig (the Emperor Maximus,) for supporting him against the Romans. These people were originally from the land of Meiriadog, and from the lands of Seisyllwg (in Carmarthenshire) and from the land of Gwyr (Gower,) and Gorwennydd (in Glamorganshire,) and none of them returned, but they settled in Armorica and Ystre Gyvaelawg (Neustria and Valais,)[1] by forming a commonwealth there. By reason of this combined expedition the nation of the Kymry was so weakened and deficient in armed men, that they fell under the oppression of the Irish Picts; and therefore Gwrtheyrn Gwrthenau (Vortigern) was compelled to procure the Saxons to expel that oppression. And the Saxons, observing the weakness of the Kymry, formed an oppression of treachery, by combining with

---

1 According to the happy conjecture of the Rev. T. Price.

the Irish Picts, and with traitors, and then took from the Kymry their land, and also their privileges and their crown.[1]

The truth of the third part of the Triad, is proved by the occurrence of the same story in Gildas, Nennius, and Geoffrey; and these facts afford a strong presumptive proof of the correctness of the others. The oppressions of the Picts, led many more to leave this Island; and after the Anglo-Saxons had entered A.D. 513, fresh bodies fled to Armorica, and settled in the country of Vannes and Quimper[2], then called Lectavia, Littau, or Llydaw. If Geoffrey may be trusted, there was a close connexion between the Britons and Armoricans in the time of Arthur; and from the *Liber Landavensis*, we learn that the bishops Samson and Teilo went to and fro between the two countries. Again, there must be some authority for Geoffrey's assertion, that at the close of the reign of Careticus, a great fleet of Britons went over to Brittany; and there is most probably some truth in the statement, that there was a considerable emigration at the death of Cadwaladr.

The Kymry who left their native land on these occasions carried with them the histories of their ancestors; and as many, perhaps, intended to return at more favourable junctures—for the Kymro never forgets his native land—they would naturally magnify their own actions and those of their forefathers, and foster grand hopes of national restoration. Many of these were the Kymry of Cornwall, which, next to Wales, formed their last resting point; and these would very naturally exalt the actions of their countryman Arthur. It is also to be observed, that the dialect of the Bretons bears a closer resemblance to that of Cornwall, than to the language of the Principality. These seem to be the only conditions under which Arthur could have been singled out for distinction, from men whom the Cambrian bards praise quite as highly. How the conception was generated will best be explained by a partisan of the Breton hypothesis, the writer of a very able critique on the Essays of the learned Abbé de la Rue who expresses himself thus:[3]

If it be allowed that a mass of floating tradition was carried by the South British exiles, when in the sixth century they passed over to Armorica, that these traditions were fondly cherished among them, because they told of the former glory of that land to which they could never return, that the imagination of their descendants invested them with a halo of poetic beauty, because these fond recollections were their only heritage, we shall discover not merely the reason why every British tradition up to the sixth century was preserved among

---

1   *Myv. Arch.* Vol. II, p. 60. and Mr. J. H. Parry in the *Cambro-Briton*, Vol. p. 87.

2   Continental authorities quoted in Schulz's valuable *Essay on Welsh Traditions*, p. 23.

3   *Athenæum* for 1835, p. 842.

them, but a reason, too, why Arthur, merely one of the many brave warriors, in the enumeration of the Welsh Bards, is the all powerful monarch and hero of the Breton lay. Arthur, although known in Wales as the monarch of the Silures, and the valiant opponent of Cerdic, was but one of the many kings, and warriors, who fought, though in vain, against the Saxon; but to the Breton exiles he was their *own* king, who had led them to battle, and whose death was the cause of their flight. Thus the tales of Caerlleon and Camelot gathered splendour from each Breton bard, for they were visionary recollections of another land; but the Welsh bard saw Caerlleon in ruins, and Camelot in the power of the Saxons, and he left them unsung. The "Woody Isle of Avalon," too, that brightest spot in the realms of romance, was to the Welsh bard but "one of the perpetual choirs of Britain," and he well knew that tonsured priests alone wonned there; but the Breton, separated for centuries from his fatherland, showered upon this Island to which his forefathers saw their monarch borne, every imagined beauty, and peopled it with Morgan le Fay, and her attendant damsels, watching in hushed silence the tranced slumber of Arthur.

These remarks appear to be, in the main, just; but there is no sufficient warrant for making Arthur the king of the Silures; and the location of that hero at Caerlleon appears to be due to Geoffrey of Monmouth. The chief argument is not however greatly affected thereby; and there are other reasons in favour of that conclusion. Alanus de Insulis relates, towards the end of the twelfth century, that the Breton people would have stoned any one, who dared to deny the fact that Arthur lived[1]. His words are most significant:

"What place is there within the bounds of the empire of Christianity, to which has not extended the winged praise of the Arthur of the Britons? Who is there I ask who does not speak of the Brittanic Arthur, who is but little less known to the people of Asia than to the Britons, as we are informed by our pilgrims who return from the countries of the east. The Easterns speak of him, as also do the Westerns, though the breadth of the whole earth lies between them. Egypt speaks of his name, and the Bosphorus is not silent; Rome the Queen of the cities sings his deeds, and his wars are not unknown to her former competitor Carthage. His exploits are praised in Antioch, Armenia, and Palestine. He will be celebrated in the mouths of the people, and his acts shall be food to those who relate them?"

These remarks cannot be applied to the state of opinion in Wales; and therefore may we derive from this extract a cogent argument in favour of the Breton theory. Honourable mention of the chivalry of Llydaw, is made in the poem attributed to Golyddan, Geoffrey refers the origin of portions of his history to that country, and the romancists unanimously point out Brittany as the source of their legends; and therefore was there much point in the question of M. de la Rue, how could there be this uniformity of testimony, if there were

---

1 Schulz's *Essay*, page 32.

no truth in the allegations? The most striking argument in favour of the same conclusion, has however yet to be adduced. We have said that Rhys ab Tewdwr, (A.D. 1077,) is reported to have brought from Brittany the bardic system of the Round Table to Wales, "where," it is naively admitted, "it had become forgotten."[1] A bard named Iorwerth Vynglwyd, living about 1450, alludes to the bardic Roll of Rhys ab Tewdwr, in the words:[2]

> The regulations are faultless
> Of Rhys the son of Tewdwr, a good man who lived formerly,
> And the much respected Roll of Arthur,
> Which is also good and spirited.

Caradoc in speaking of Rhys says, "Great was the fame he had obtained for wisdom, and knowledge of the principles of government,"[3] though he makes no allusion to the Roll of Arthur; but as we find him, in giving an account of a bardic festival held by Cadwgan ab Bleddyn, Rhys' successor, stating that it was conducted according to the rules observed at the feasts of king Arthur[4], we may conclude that the above statement is historically true. From these numerous and various facts, the conclusion is both legitimate and irresistible, that the romantic Arthur is a creation of the Armorican Kymry.

There were several ways in which such a creation may have been, and probably was brought to this country, in which it only at first found favour among the clergy. Alain the Second of Brittany, reigned about 690; his sons Ivor and Ynyr, became princes of Wales in 683;[5] Ivor reigned twenty-eight years with much glory;[6] in commemoration of successes over the Saxons, he in 712[7] built the abbey of Glastonbury (Ynys Afallen;) and soon after went to Rome. These

---

1 *Iolo MSS.* page 630.

2 Defodau difai ydynt
   Rhys vab Tewdwr, da'r gwr gynt
   A Rhol Arthur o bur barch
   Da hefyd a dihafarch.—*Iolo MSS.* p. 391.

3 *Myv. Arch.* ii. p. 538.

4 *Myv. Arch.* ii. p. 521.

5 Caradoc, *Myv. Arch.* ii. p. 470.

6 *Ibid.* p. 471.

7 Brut Ieuan Brechva. *Myv. Arch.* ii. p. 471.

princes brought with them two powerful fleets, and recovered Cornwall, Devon, and Somersetshire. Mathuidoc, Count of Poher, with many nobles and Breton families, are said to have in their turn sought refuge in Britain, at the beginning of the tenth century, from the devastation of Rollo and the Normans[1]. There was probably an intercourse kept up between the two countries, such as we see in the case of Rhys ab Tewdwr, who resided in Brittany for eighty four years; and therefore we need experience no difficulty in accounting for the transmission of their traditions to this country. Yet it is strange, that the Bretons should have no romantic remains; the Tales published in French by the Comte de Villemarque, are translations from Lady Charlotte Guest's English version of the Romances of the Kymry of the Principality.

Several of the Kymric romances seem to have been lost; that of Creirwy and Garwy is frequently mentioned by the bards, yet we have it not; Cambrian ladies are frequently compared to Eliwri, but we know no more of her, than that she was the daughter of Urien Rheged[2]; and Kymric warriors are repeatedly compared to a now unknown Elivri. The bards were also acquainted with the most celebrated romances of other nations; and frequently allude to Tristan, Roland, Charlemagne, Sir Fulke, and Alexander.[3]

Of the Authors of the Kymric Mabinogion and other Stories, but little is known. Indeed it may reasonably be doubted whether the earlier portion ever had recognised authors; most probably the tales were orally transmitted for centuries before they were reduced to writing; and as they increased by being repeated it would be difficult to discover their paternity. No date can be well assigned to the tale of Kilhwch and Olwen; it was well known in 1169, as appears from Kynddelw's Elegy to Owain Gwynedd; an allusion is made to the hunting of the boar Trwyth in The Incantation of Kynvelyn, attributed to Aneurin; Lady Charlotte Guest, in her most interesting note[4], shows that this event is mentioned in a MS. which Mr. Stevenson, the Editor of Nennius, pronounces to be as old as the tenth century; and whatever may be the age of the tale of Kilhwch and Olwen, one of its chief incidents is impressed the coins of Cunobelinus. The Dream of Rhonabwy, is of necessity posterior to the time of Madawc ab Meredydd, prince of Powys, whose name is mentioned at the commencement,

---

1 Schulz's *Essay*, p. 25. 5 Iolo MSS. p. 458.

2 *Iolo MSS*. p. 458

3 The romance of Alexander, composed in France in 1210, was known in Wales soon after (Sismondi, i.191), as it appears to be referred to in a poem attributed to both Kynddelw and Prydydd y Moch (*Myv. Arch*. I, 247, 306, circa 1220) Tristran is mentioned in the *Myv. Arch*. i. 364, 424.

4 *Mabinogion* Vol. II. p. 359.

and who died in 1159. That tale was probably written in Powys, as Owain, Geraint, and Peredur were the products of Glamorgan, and the remainder of Dyved. Gruffydd ab Adda ab Davydd, a poet who flourished about A.D. 1340 to A.D. 1370, was the author of a chivalric tale of much interest; several of his pieces are preserved; he was killed at Dolgellau, and buried at the same place. Ievan Vawr ap y Diwlith was another writer of tales in his day. The following notice of him occurs in the *Iolo MSS.*:

The bards of Tir Iarll having gone to the Dewless Hillock, on one of St. John's Midsummer festivals, to hold there a chair of vocal song, found a new born child, half alive, on it. Rhys the son of Rhiccert ab Einion ab Collwyn, took it home with him, and placed it under the care of a foster-mother. The child lived, was put to school, and brought up to a learned profession. He imbibed knowledge with all the avidity that a child would suck its mother's milk; and early in life he took the lead of all preceptors in Wales. He wrote several books, one of which was called the 'Preservation of the Welsh language, the Art of Vocal Song, and all that appertained to them, according to the rights and usages of the Welsh Nation, and judicial decisions of wise men;' others were called 'The Greals,' 'The Mabinogion,' 'The nine tropes, and twenty four embellishments of diction,' 'The book of Fables,' and many more. He also composed a work for the preservation of the moral maxims and laws of the Welsh nation. He received the name of John, the son of the Dewless, because he was found, as already mentioned, on the Dewless Hillock, on St. John's midsummer festival; and because he was a large man, he was called Big John, the son of the Dewless. He lived and died at Llangynwyd, where he was buried with the family of Llwydarth. It was currently reported, that, in all probability, he was the son of Rhys ab Rhiccert, by a lady of high rank; and when it was so asserted in his presence, he merely held his tongue, allowing that belief to continue.[1]

Mr. Edward Williams states that Ievan lived between 1160 and 1180;[2] this date was a necessary consequence of his being the son of Rhys ab Rhiccert, whom the same antiquarian had previously placed about 1140; but as we shall presently show that Rhys lived two hundred years later, we must, assuming the paternity to be correct, conclude that Ievan lived nearer 1380[3]. The authorship of the Mabinogi of Taliesin is attributed to two persons. In the *Iolo MSS.*, at

---

1 *Iolo MSS.* p. 479, on the authority of the memoranda of Mr. John Bradford, extracted from Anthony Powel's MS., then (circ. A.D. 1760) at Goettref Hen, near Bridgend.

2 *Iolo MSS.* p. 88.

3 The minute fidelity of local colouring in the description of Cardiff renders it not improbable that the author of the Mabinogi of Geraint ab Erbin was our friend Ievan.

the close of an epitome of the history of Taliesin and Elphin, from the book of Anthony Powel, occur these words:

"It was from this account that Thomas, the son of Einion Offeiriad, descended from Gruffydd Gwyr, formed his romance of Taliesin, the son of Cerridwen; Elphin, the son of Gwyddno; Rhun the son of Maelgwn Gwynedd; and the operations of the Cauldron of Cerridwen."[1]

This Thomas ab Einion must have lived about 1260, as a work on grammar, written by his father, was copied between 1254 and 1280, by Edeyrn Davod Aur; and as, in addition to that fact, Gwilym Ddu, about 1320, terms Taliesin "Gwion Bach," as if that romantic name was well known, we may safely conclude that this Mabinogi probably belongs to the beginning of the reign of Llywelyn ab Gruffydd. The second person who is the supposed composer, is Hopkin Thomas Phylip, also of Glamorgan; Dr. Pughe supposes that he wrote the connecting prose passages, but that the poetical passages, were what he professes his book to be, collected from other works. In one place[2] Dr. Pughe says this person lived about 1370; but if we take another and more probable date given by the same author, and place him from 1590 to 1630[3], the two accounts may be reconciled, Thomas ab Einion being the author, and Hopkin Thomas Phylip the copyist.[4] These are all the facts that I have been able to glean, concerning the authors or rather compilers of the Mabinogion; and now it only remains to speak of the noble lady who has translated, and edited the English version of these antique tales.

The Mabinogion combine dignity of expression with a fine easy flow of language, and are remarkable for their quaintness and simplicity. They contain many passages of exquisite beauty, and a poetical colouring, enriching the whole, prevails throughout: such being their character, they demanded in a translator, qualities which are not of frequent occurrence. A knowledge of two languages is far from being the only quality required; for the spirit of the original should be as fully as possible transferred, in addition to the literal meaning. I have in many parts compared the translation of the Mabinogion with the original; and have uniformly found reason to think, that our ancient tales have been exceedingly fortunate in being translated by Lady Charlotte Guest. Her version correctly

---

1   *Iolo MSS.* p. 459.

2   *Cambrian and Caledonian Quarterly*, Vol. V. p. 381.

3   *Cambrian Biography*, p. 178.

4   They were two distinct persons: 1. Hopkin ab Thomas ab Einion, of Ynys Dawy, or Gower, lived circa 1350 (cf. *Myv. Arch*, i. 514, &c.) 2. Hopkin ab Thomas ab Phylip, of Gelli Fid, Glynegwr, circa 1596 – 1630 (*Myv. Arch*, iii.) Poems to the former appear in the *Myv. Arch*. (1870)

mirrors forth the spirit of these antique stories, and is as much distinguished for elegance as fidelity. Her ladyship's good taste, led her fully to appreciate the charm contained in the simplicity of the original; and she has been eminently successful in producing a version at once simple, animated, and accurate. It is not necessary to enter into an analysis of compositions, which, thanks to the munificence of that noble lady, must now be well known; and therefore it will suffice to cite one or two extracts, in illustration of both the ability of the translator, and the character of the Mabinogion. The following describes the heroine, Olwen:

So a message was sent, and she came.

The maiden was clothed in a robe of flame-coloured silk, and about her neck was a collar of ruddy gold, on which were precious emeralds and rubies. More yellow was her head than the flower of the broom, and her skin was whiter than the foam of the wave, and fairer were her hands and her fingers than the blossoms of the wood anemone amidst the spray of the meadow fountain. The eye of the trained hawk, the glance of the three-mewed falcon was not brighter than hers. Her bosom was more snowy than the breast of the white swan, her cheek was redder than the reddest roses. Whoso beheld her was filled with her love. Four white trefoils sprang up wherever she trod.[1]

We will add to this beautiful portrait, the description of her lover, prince Kilhwch, setting forth on his journey towards the court of Arthur:

And the youth pricked forth upon a steed with head dappled gray, of four winters old, firm of limb, with shell-formed hoofs, having a bridle of linked gold on his head, and upon him a saddle of costly gold. And in the youth's hand were two spears of silver, sharp, well tempered, headed with steel, three ells in length, of an edge to wound the wind, and cause blood to flow, and swifter than the fall of the dewdrop from the blade of reed grass upon the earth, when the dew of June is at the heaviest. A gold-hilted sword was upon his thigh, the blade of which was of gold, bearing a cross of inlaid gold of the hue of the lightning of heaven; his war-horn was of ivory. Before him were two brindled white breasted greyhounds, having strong collars of rubies about their necks, reaching from the shoulder to the ear. And the one that was on the left side bounded across to the right side, and the one on the right to the left, and like two sea swallows sported around him. And his courser cast up four sods with his four hoofs, like four swallows in the air, about his head, now above, now below. About him was a four cornered cloth of purple, and an apple of gold was at each corner, and every one of the apples was of the value of an hundred kine.

And there was precious gold of the value of three hundred kine upon his shoes, and upon his stirrups, from the knee to the tip of his toe. And the blade of grass bent not beneath him, so light was his courser's tread as he journeyed

---

1 *Mabinogion*, Vol. II. p. 276.

towards the gate of Arthur's Palace.[1]

The notes contain a mass of very interesting information, and I have derived from them much valuable assistance, They bring the past vividly to mind; very clearly elucidate the text; and are only defective in being too brief.

It is now generally admitted that romance originated from these traditions of the Armorican Kymry, which had a most important influence upon the literature of other European nations, by the publication of the *Historia Britonum*. All the names of the heroes in the Arthurian Cycle of Romances are of Kymric origin, so that no doubt can be entertained of their paternity. But in Wales the romance was never developed to the extent it assumed among other nations. Among them romances presented features which were not in the Mabinogion; and this arose from the following circumstances: The Normans infused into them an adventurous spirit, and the monks, or Catholic clergy chastened and refined their tone. We will offer a few remarks in elucidation of both these positions.

M. Sismondi is of opinion that the Normans were the inventors of the Romance literature, though he admits that the names of the Arthurian cycle belonging to a different race, present a difficulty not easily overcome; and he bases his opinion upon the fact that "of all the people of ancient Europe, the Normans showed themselves during the period which preceded the rise of the romance literature, to be the most adventurous and intrepid."[2] But the learned historian has overlooked an important fact. It is with nations as with men; there are some who can invent, but cannot improve; and there are some who can improve what they could not invent. To the first class belong the Kymry; to the second the Normans. The path had been already discovered, the frame work had been already formed, and it only remained to carry out what had been previously designed. The Kymry failed to do this; but it was done; the *Mabinogi* was pushed up into a romance; and a brief review of their character, will show that the Norman Trouveres were the persons who carried this into effect. They were on the spot, and happened to possess the very qualities necessary to bring about the changes we witness. Their faculties were illustrative; not creative. Behold their character, drawn by an able hand:

Above all men, the Norman was an imitator, and therefore an improver; and it was precisely because he was the least rigid, most supple, plastic, and accommodating of mortals-that he became the civilizer, and ruler wherever he was thrown. In France he became French, in England English, in Italy Italian, in Novgorod Russian; in Norway only, where he remained Norwegian, he failed to accomplish his elevated mission. Wherever his neighbours invented or possessed anything worthy of admiration, the sharp, inquisitive Norman poked his aquiline nose. Did Sicily invent a better kind of helmet, instantly the Norman

---

1 *Mabinogion*, Vol. II. p. 253.

2 Sismondi's *Hist. of Literature*, Vol. I. p. 198.

clapped it on his head. Did the Moor, *or the Breton breathe sentiment into a ballad, the Norman lay forthwith adopted the humanizing music.* From a Frank castle or a Lombard church, to a law by Canute, or a witan under Athelstan, the Norman was always a practical plagiarist. Wherever what we now call the march of intellect advanced, there was the sharp eager face of the Norman in the van. All that he retained, in his more genial settlement, of his ancestral attributes, were the characters of a seaman. He was essentially commercial; he liked adventure, and he liked gain; he was also a creature social and gregarious. He always intermarried with the people among whom he settled, borrowed its language, adopted its customs, reconciled himself to its laws; and confirmed the aristocracy of conquest, by representing, while elevating, the character of the people with whom he closely identified himself. This remarkable race exercised an astonishing influence for good, especially in their noblest settlement, England. No one who has not paid some attention to our Saxon poetry, with its most artificial structure, its meretricious alliterations, its tedious unanimated tone, relieved it is true by some descriptions, and an ethical allegorical spirit (as in the songs of the Phoenix,) can be aware how thoroughly it differs from the genius of our existing muse-and how much immediately from the Anglo Norman, and his kinsman, the Anglo-Dane, (and the Welsh and Bretons,) though perhaps remotely from the Saracen, we derive of sentiment, vivacity, character passion, simple construction, easy humour, and true pathos ;-all in short, that now especially distinguish the poetic and popular literature of England. But for the Norman and the Dane, we think it probable that we might have writers like Thomson, Young, and Wordsworth, but we feel a strong conviction that we should have wanted a Chaucer, Spenser, and Shakespeare. No one who has not made himself familiar with the wretched decrepitude of the Saxon church, its prostrate superstition and gross ignorance, at the age preceding the conquest, can appreciate the impetus given to learning by the Norman Ecclesiastics; and no one who has not studied the half disorganized empire of disconnected provinces and rebellious earldoms under the confessor, with laws of succession both to throne and to lordship, most irrregular, can comprehend all the advantages derived from the introduction of an hereditary aristocracy, singularly independent and high-spirited, quickly infusing its blood, and its character into the native population-leaguing its own interests with those of the whole subject community-and headed by a line of monarchs who, whatever their vices and crimes, had at least the power to defend the land from all other invaders, and the wisdom to encourage the trade and the commerce which have ultimately secured to England at once its fame and its freedom.[1]

Cambrian history furnishes numerous proofs of this strongly assimilative character of the Normans. Between them and the Kymry there were frequent intermarriages. On the one hand we find Nest the daughter of Rhys ab Tewdwr

---

1 *The Examiner*, April 1, 1848.

married to Gerald de Windsor, Nest the daughter of Trahaearn ab Caradoc to Bernard de Newmarch, Nest the daughter of Iestyn ab Gwrgant to Robert Fitzhamon, Marred, or Margaret daughter of Llywelyn ap Iorwerth to John de Breos, and another of that prince's daughters to Reynold de Bruce. While on the other hand, David ab Owain Gwynedd married a sister to Henry II., Llywelyn ap Iorwerth, Joan the sister of king John, and Llywelyn ap Gruffydd, Eleanor de Montford. Gruffydd the eldest son of the lord Rhys, took to wife, Mallt, or Matilda, a daughter of William de Breos, and his brother Rhys Gryg married a daughter of the Earl of Clare. We therefore, from a knowledge of these facts, soon perceive that the Normans must have exercised an extensive and very important influence upon our literature, as well as been influenced by it in return.[1]

The above finely drawn sketch of the Norman character shows us both what they were, and what they were not; and we thence learn that M. de Sismondi's conjecture contains a truth, though it is not the truth. The Normans did not invent the romance literature; but they greatly improved, and extended what they found already invented in Brittany and Wales. At first the Norman Trouveres confined themselves to embellishing the Keltic traditions; but they soon dragged in the kings of France with Charlemagne at their head; and ultimately enlisted in their service the classic names of ancient Greece.

The influence of the religious element, is next to be developed. At, and preceding the period of which this section treats, the church had become powerful in Wales, as well as over the rest of the civilized world. It exercised a very considerable influence over the moral and intellectual order in modern Europe, and upon public ideas, sentiments, and manners, as is shown by the essentially theological character of the works developed at this time. Papal theology possessed and directed the human understanding, and gave its impress to all opinions; philosophical, political, and historical questions, were all considered under a theological point of view.[2] In the twelfth and thirteenth centuries the order had increased; monks and friars were abundant; and there was no department of intellectual activity, in which they did not bear part. We have in the case of Geoffrey, a monk embellishing old traditions; and adding fabulous genealogies, and imaginary agents,—the products of his own brain. And coupling this with the fact, that Layamon, the author of the Brut known by his name, was a priest, we easily arrive at the conclusion, that the monks had not left romances to be exclusively produced by laymen. We have one striking proof of this in the Awdl Vraith, which is evidently an ecclesiastical production, of the romance era : This might have been inferred, from the tone of

---

1   The influence of the Normans in the erection of abbeys, cathedrals, and castles is well delineated in Berington, pp. 166, 216, &c.

2   Guizot's *Lectures on Civilization*—The Church.

the composition, its allusion to the consecrated wafer, its Latinized diction, and the fable of Trojan descent. This last fable, is evidently of monkish origin. There is also a very striking difference between the same facts when treated of by the bards and the priests; the poets speak of Arthur as a warrior only, while the monks, from Nennius downwards, continually endeavour to clothe him in an air of sanctity. Nennius, who states him to have borne the image of the Virgin on his shield, appears to have drawn upon an ecclesiast's imagination, rather than upon authentic history; and knowing this with many similar facts, can we doubt that Arthur, the religious hero, the greater part of whose memorials were found in convents, is partly at least, a being of monastic creation? If, after the consideration of all these facts, there should remain any doubt upon the subject, it would be dispelled by the fact, that Edward I prohibited the monks from being rhymers and raconteurs,—a sufficient proof that they frequently appeared as such. This fact would go far to explain the enmity which subsisted between the priests and the bards. Lewis Glyn Cothi openly assails them; but when the writer of the Avallenau spoke of them as "Myneich geuawg, gwydawg, gwydus," he thought it prudent to place the words in the mouth of Merddin. This enmity appears to have sprung from their being rival candidates for popular suffrages; it was in fact jealousy, and is therefore of itself a proof of the position here laid down. It being now manifest that the monks cultivated romantic literature, we shall proceed to estimate the influence they exercised upon it.

There is an erroneous opinion prevalent, that religious ascendency is inimical to, and incompatible with, mental development:

Opinions formed less from a knowledge of actual facts, and ascertained influences of religion upon civilized society, than from an infidel antipathy to religion itself, would deserve but little attention, were they not widely spread, and their upholders numerous. Religion, of all principles the most fruitful, multiform, and unconfined, does not express itself in a few unchanging modes of writing; it not only becomes the vehicle for knowledge, but it clothes it in the most attractive, noble, and dignified forms; it has the variety and bold contrasts of nature, which at the feet of rugged mountains scoops out the freshest, sweetest valleys, and embosoms in the wild troubled ocean, Islands, whose vernal airs, loveliness, and teeming fruitfulness, almost breathe the joys of Paradise.[1]

We have now to develop the influence of this principle upon our romantic literature.

The Catholic Church was now in its glory, and at the height of its power; and now, as at all times, was most studious to conform itself to the improvements

1 Channing's *Works*, Vol. I. p. 109.

of society[1]; it mingled with all things without excluding any[2]; and in Wales, as in other European countries at the period we now treat of, theological modes of thought, feeling, and expression are every where displayed. The Mabinogi of Taliesin is replete with theological expressions; and its conception proves that the tendency of theology was to mental expansion. Indeed, the very word shows that romance must have found more favour with the priests, than among the poets. The Bardic maxim, *Y Gwir yn erbyn y byd*, (Truth against the world) was essentially unfavourable to fictitious literature. The Bards were authors already, and possessed of much repute; they might therefore be naturally expected to look with contempt, and distrust upon any literature less authentic, studied, and laboured than their own. The very name Mabinogion (Juvenile Tales,) and Ystorïau (Stories,) are indicative of this contemptuous feeling; bardism they insinuated was the occupation of superior minds. The bards were the salt of the earth, the talented men of the country. They were men themselves, and provided mental food, for the adult intellect; but the romances were Mabinogion and Ystorïau, *tales for young men, and stories*. Even the writers of them were spoken of in the same derisive language, as the reader might have seen in Lewis Glyn Cothi's classification of the bards, as Bardd, Teuluwr, and *Ystoriawr*, (story-teller). But I am not disposed to form so low an estimate of these stories; for if I were compelled to decide between the Bards and the Ystorïwyr, the choice would most unhesitatingly be in favour of the Mabinogion. The bardic poems are more valuable as contemporary records, they are more strictly accurate, and in one word, are more "useful;" but the tales show most of the thought, and feeling of the times, and are at this day more readable, and interesting. Artificial systems, which impose upon the mind, the decrees of individuals, and associations, which prescribe rules for taste, and criticism, and which claim for themselves every imaginable perfection, cannot reflect the spirit of the times, must be at variance with the dictates of nature, and tend to sink man below, rather than to elevate him above mediocrity. Such was bardism; which, dissociated from, and in opposition to natural promptings, degenerated for the most part into a tame representation of the more tangible, and transient thoughts of the day; and measured intellectual capacities by rule and compass: it wanted life, elasticity, and truthfulness. From all our bardic remains we learn but three facts—that the Kymry loved war, mead, and music; but we learn from the Mabinogi, that they had great regard for chastity, that women were held in high estimation among them, that their chieftains were fond of literary associates, and devoted their time and talents to improve, instruct, and civilize their subjects. The laws of Howel show how the court was conducted; Giraldus

---

1   Robertson's *Scotland*, book II.

2   Guizot: "Dans le monde moderne, l'esprit religieux s'est mêlé a tout, mais sans rien exclure."

describes the more obvious popular habits; and the Mabinogion supply many traits of natural manners, not noticed in either. The latter are more really poetic, the life is more life-like, and the warriors more heroic, than the portraitures of the bards; the bardic heroes are at the best but exaggerations of warriors, while those of romance are really sublime creations. Of the fine and high-toned sentiments which breathe through the Mabinogion, we have no traces in the works of the bards, and no counter-parts in the civilization of the period; they must therefore have emanated from the clergy. Abstracting a warrior from the province of history, making him feel the impulses, and speak the language of a more civilized age, revealed in studies of the classics, and enriching him with all that cultivated minds deemed to be good, great, and gorgeous, was an idea which could only have found favour among ecclesiastics. It never appears to have entered the minds of the bards; the tumult of conflict, the excitement of warlike life, and the contemplation of actual every day scenes, were all that could interest those matter of fact personages; and they never attempted to analyze their own minds and feelings, to endow a sublime creation with the ardent promptings of their own nature, and to represent as actual existences beings which the ambitious minds of able men had alone considered possible to exist, and hoped themselves to be. Pictures of immutable truth, and of the deep-workings of the soul, were things too pure and sublime, ever to have subsisted in a literary atmosphere contaminated by the arbitrary rules and conventional regulations of the bards, and could only have been developed where the vivacity of the people had been heightened by the contemplation of Divine attributes, and their feelings chastened by God's goodness and loving mercy. Here all the pent up and cherished feelings of the nation found vent; and the fact that Arthur was reported to have worn the image of the Virgin Mary upon his shield, affords us proof that religion possessed great influence over men's minds, that the monks gave a religious colouring to popular traditions, and, that, setting aside the question of the accuracy of the statement, it is obvious that the assertion was consonant with the spirit of the time.

The influence of the church was two fold—immediate and mediate. Its immediate influence is shown in its positive teachings; its mediate in the movements it originated. The church was the great civilizing element of the twelfth and thirteenth centuries; it ameliorated the social condition of the people, and was greatly instrumental in bringing about the abolition of slavery in Europe; it laboured for the suppression of many barbarous practices; and framed a penal code upon principles elevated, and enlightened, and strikingly coincident with those enunciated by Jeremy Bentham, and his followers, Mill, Molesworth, Bowring, Grote, and others who are accounted, the profoundest thinkers of the present day. It looked upon continual wars as being inconsistent with the spirit of Christianity, and in all these various ways, it rendered productive the intellectual movement which at this time prevailed among most

European nations. The system of doctrine and precepts, under which it imparted the movement, was very superior to anything that the ancient world had known; and contained within itself tendencies to both exertion and advancement.[1] As regard the romance, the clerical influence is very apparent in the tales of the Greal, which, according to Schulz, date their origin from Provence.[2] The romance of St. Greal, which was written in verse, by Chrestien de Troyes, in the twelfth century, is a mixture of Breton chivalry and sacred history. The cup out of which the Messiah is said to have drunk during his crucifixion, or which contained his blood, was known to the romance writers under the name of St. Greal,[3] and this fact indicating a Christian tendency in the romancists, shows the statement made by Tegid[4], of the Greal being connected with druidic and anti-Christian tenets, to be altogether erroneous. The "Greal" of Chrestien de Troyes, may be found, according to the translator of Sismondi, in the Royal Library, Paris, No. 7523. His account of it is as follows:

It is a very large MSS. Volume, in 4to, written in double columns, and containing nearly the whole history of the Knights of the Round Table.

Now it is very evident from the description given by Llwyd of "Ystori Saint Greal," and by Guto'r Glyn in these lines,

> Am un llyvr y mae'n llevain,
> A gar mwy nag aur a main;
> Y Greal teg i'r wlad hon—
> Llyvr o enwog varchogion;
> Llyvr o *grefft yr holl Vord Gron,*

that the Greal, so much desired, was substantially the same as this very MS. which, as its contents show, was a Christian document—being in fact nothing more than the adventures of the knights of the round table, in search of the Greal or blessed cup, which, it was stated, was carried to England, and ultimately possessed by Launcelot, Peredur, and the other knights. There is a further account of this cup given in the notes to *Colyn Dolphyn*, by the late lamented Ab Iolo. In 1450, this Cambrian MS. was in the possession of a Glamorgan chieftain.[5] About 1500, we find the loan of a Greal asked of Lewis ab Davydd,

---

1 Guizot's *Lectures on Civilization—The Church.*

2 Schulz on *Welsh Traditions*, p. 48.

3 Sismondi's *History of South European Literature*, Vol. I. p. 197. (Bohn's Edition)

4 Lewis Glyn Cothi, p. 259, note.

5 *Iolo MSS.* page 704.

the abbot of Neath;[1] and in 1707 Llwyd states that there were copies in both the Mostyn and the Hengwrt libraries. His description of one MS. is as follows:

"Ystoriæ Saint Greal: Historia Gregorianæ. M & Vaugh. *Membr. nitid. Charact. Varias fabulas exhibet de Arthuro Rege,* & militibus suis, &c. *Init.* Megys ydoedd Arthur yn y Llys a eluid kamalot, nos Sadurn, Sylguyn oed yr Arglwydh Iesu Grist, pedair blynedh ar dheg a deugaint, a pheduar kant. *Fin.* Ag velli y tervyna Historiæ St. Greal. *Const.* p. 560 *in 4to. Consule Lexicon* Davisianum *sub voce* Greal.[2]

The Stories of Saint Greal: Gregorian Histories. M(ostyn) & Vaugh (an of Hengwrt.) Vellum, neat character. Various fabulous tales of king Arthur and his knights, &c,. beginning, "As Arthur was in his court called Camelot, on the night of Whit Saturday, in the year of our Lord Jesus Christ, four hundred and fifty four." Ending: "So ends the History of Saint Greal." It contains 560 pages 4to. Consult Davies's Lexicon under the word *Greal.*

The Editor of Lewis Glyn Cothi's Works, states that the MSS. copies of the Greal are lost; but it is gratifying to find that such is not the case. In the catalogue of the MSS. in the Gloddaith collection, published by Mr. Aneurin Owen, occurs the following notice:

5. Sang Royal ae cavas, ac ae duc y nev: nyt amgen Galaath vab Lawnselot de Lac, Peredur vab Evrauc, Iarll Bwrt vab Brenin Bwrt. Y copi cyntav a ysgrivenodd Mastir Philyp Davydd o unic lyvyr y urddedig ewythyr, Trahaearn ab Ieuan ap Meuric, ae ysgrivenodd Siancyn vab John, vab Siencyn, vab Ieuan Vychan, vab Ieuan, vab Einion, vab Rhys, vab Madoc, vab Llywelyn, vab Cadwgan, vab Elystan Glodrydd. Vellum Folio.[3]

Sang Royal, who had it, and who took it to heaven; being none other than Galaad the son of Launcelot du Lac, Peredur the son of Evrawc, Earl Bort, the son of King Bort. The first copy written by Master Philyp David from the sole book of his knighted uncle, Trahaearn ab Ievan ap Meiric, which was written by Siancyn the son of John, the son of Siencyn, the son of Ievan Vychan, the son of Ievan, the son of Einion, the son of Rhys, the son of Madoc, the son of Llewelyn, the son of Cadwgan, the son of Athelstan Glodrydd. Vellum, folio.

The Gloddaith MS. is probably the Mostyn MS. mentioned by E. Lhwyd.

The next notice is in the catalogue of the Hengwrt library, given in the same work:

49. Y Greal; the Exploits of Arthur and his Warriors; written in the sixth year

1 *Ibid.* page 706.

2 Llwyd's *Arch. Brit.* p. 265.

3 *Transactions of the Cymmrodorion,* iv. p. 402.

of Henry I. in a beautiful hand. Vellum, Quarto, five inches thick.[1]

The latter is evidently the MS. noticed by Llwyd; and possibly may be the identical MS. of Trahaearn ab Ievan ap Meuric. It is a most interesting document; and if the date A.D. 1106 be correct, it must be the first of the Arthurian cyclus; and it is hoped that Lady Charlotte Guest will not allow her work to remain incomplete, while this important MS. remains unpublished.[2] We shall then know more of the work; have additional light thrown upon the question of the origin of the romances; and probably be able to place Siancyn ab John, the descendant of Athelstan Glodrydd, at the head of our list of the authors of Cambrian Stories.

The mediate influence of the church was manifested through such movements as the Crusades. These form an historical problem of much interest; and Gibbon alone of all our historians, doubts their having had a most important influence upon European civilization. Since he wrote, the historians of the continent have studied the subject; and we now learn from the elaborate treatises of Heeren, and Villiers, Michaud, and Guizot, that they created quite a revolution in the thoughts and feelings of the time. It is impossible to believe that Europe should have been convulsed to its centre, that millions of its best, bravest, and most intelligent inhabitants should have poured themselves out upon the deserts of Arabia, and that the minds of whole nations could have been put upon the stretch, without the acquisition of much additional knowledge, the generation of novel sentiments, and the elaboration of grander and juster ideas of manners, history, politics, literature, and geography. Their effect is very concisely stated by M. Guizot, in the following words:

Here was the first and main result of the Crusades, a great step towards the enfranchisement of the mind, and a considerable advance towards more extended and unprejudiced ideas. Commenced in the name, and under the influence of religious principles, the Crusades took from religious ideas, I will not say their legitimate share of influence, but the exclusive and despotic possession of the human mind. The same fact happened to those travelling populations who have been called Crusaders, as usually happens to travellers; their minds were opened and elevated by the mere circumstance of witnessing a multitude of different things, and by becoming acquainted with manners distinct from their own. Besides, they came into relations with two civilizations,

---

1   *Ibid.* iv. p. 407.

2   See an interesting account of the early history of the Saint Greal in the *Athenaeum*, April 9, 1870, p. 481; consult also Tennyson's poem "Holy Grail." [The *Greal* is now (1875) passing through the press under the editorship of the Rev. Canon Williams, author *of Enwogion Cymru, Lexicon Cornu-Britannicum,* &c. The MS. Is of the early part of the fifteenth century, but the work was originally written about the year 1200. For "Henry I."—Ed.]

not only different, but more advanced, namely the Greek society on the one hand, and Mussulman on the other. There can be no doubt but that the Greek society, although its civilization was emasculated, corrupted, and expiring, had on the Crusaders the operation of a society in a more advanced state, more polished and enlightened than theirs. The Mussulman society, offered to them a spectacle of the same nature.

Now we cannot believe that these new feelings should have left no traces in literature-in fact, we see the effect of the Crusades in both the chronicles and romances. In their journeys towards the holy land, the Cambrian knights mixed on terms of intimacy and equality with those of other countries, and effected of course an interchange of literatures, as plainly appears from the frequent mention in Kymric literature of Orlando, Charlemagne, sir Fulke, and Guy of Warwick. Petrarch and Boccaccio had meanwhile revived a taste for classic literature; and we see the influence of the church in disseminating a knowledge of the "great of old" in the mention by the bards of Hector, Achilles, Priam, Alexander, and Caesar.

Having thus analyzed the agents at work in the production of the romance literature, the reader will be the better able to appreciate the following remarks, on the scope and tendency of the Mabinogion. Here we see depth of passion breathing in rapid transitions, and fiery tones; imagery, brilliant, glaring, and redundant to a fault; a sublime spirit of pure and uncreeded devotion—enlivening not darkening, elevating not depressing, and serving to show life, not as shaded by secluded ascetics, but irradiated by celestial light, with happy and perhaps unconscious allusions to contemporary transactions, national customs, and every day habits. These show that a daring and frank, a refined and generous, and a religious though lively people had freely, almost recklessly, poured out their souls into their romantic literature, and have had their peculiar habits of thought, passion, and sentiment faithfully portrayed by their Ystorïwyr. Pictures of external life, of the hidden workings of the passions, and of scenery, are drawn with a glow, animation, and truth, equal to the best efforts of Crabbe, "nature's sternest painter, but her best." The same force of expression, and unaffected, yet refined morality; the same generosity towards friends, and haughty defiance of Saxon foes, is visible in both its poetry, and history; but this sublimity of conception, is shown to the greatest advantage in the Mabinogion. From its early Chivalry, which furnished the first example for similar institutions, and awoke in other nations a similar feeling; from the restless aspiration after ideal greatness which became afterwards infused into the chivalry of Europe; from these, and the Kymry its founders, romance derives its origin. No modern people seem previously to have been able to surmount the cold reality of fact, nowhere does mind appear to have so readily renounced control, and ascended on daring pinions to such lofty heights. In no other country, among no other people, does mind appear to have been so early employed in contemplating as actual realities, things which found no parallels in actual instances, no companions in ordinary life, and which possess no tangibility, save as the embodiment of man's most cherished hopes, and highest wishes. Here man is raised far above himself, clothed with every attribute of power which men wish to possess, performing feats requiring superhuman strength, and slaying Saxon enemies in such numbers as harassed Kymry alone could desire. Life is decked out in the grandest colours; the most extraordinary acts are performed; the most simple, yet dignified sentiments are uttered; the most exquisite sensibilities are shown by the genius of romance, and its sublime creations. Its Arthurs, Tristrams, and Peredurs, revel in the most gorgeous scenes; they live in an atmosphere of their own; and though these beautiful pictures of imaginary perfection, are sometimes obscured by mystic allusions; the desire for happiness, the craving after ideal perfection, the irrepressible instinct to paint the future in the most illusory colours, soar transcendently over all.

This undoubtedly had its origin in the sanguine temperament of the Kymry; and other nations have derived their plots, actors, and acts from Kymric models. The round table is a fiction, though as we have seen as old as A.D. 1170, the age of Cadwgan ap Bleddyn ap Kynvyn; but Wales had always possessed a chivalric order, who have been praised by contemporary bards, and have been themselves rhymers. The cavalry of Bretagne, introduced the romances of the Kymry into France and Germany: thence they spread among the civilized nations of Europe. Great principles, wherever they flash, have in an eminent degree this universality, and diffusiveness. They find a response in every bosom, they touch the finest chords of the soul, and at whatever door they knock are readily admitted. Mahometanism spread over the Eastern world with a rapidity not astonishing only when compared with the wonderful dissemination of Christianity over the Western; second only to these was the progress of the Kymric romance. Like an electric current, it made its presence known by a series of brilliant flashes; with every clime it claimed affinity, and from every nation the brotherhood was acknowledged. Hence our English neighbours have derived the most brilliant gems in their early literature. Had the Kymric romance not made itself known to them, would Spenser have given birth to the *Faery Queen*? That fine piece of imagery was produced at a time when chivalry, as an institution, had become extinct,—when the feelings in which it originated, had in a measure subsided,—when they glowed with less intensity, and had been chastened by improved taste,—when, in fact, it could not have been produced without the previous preparation of public opinion, by the vivid and energetic description of heroic feats, which Kymric tradition had linked with the names of Arthur, and his companions. English history furnished no such brilliant achievements, no such ardent feelings; and one of England's sweetest poets was necessitated to borrow from a people whom his countrymen now affect to despise, the conception of his characters, and the description of the scenes amid which they existed, with the influence which such a being as Arthur was thought to have exercised upon surrounding people, in raising up a race of warriors only less noble than himself. The Kymry have therefore much reason to be proud of their Mabinogion.

Romances were during these and succeeding centuries objects of lively curiosity; and in an age when large libraries abound, the astonishing exertions made to obtain copies through loan or purchase will scarcely be credible. Of the stories of the Greal, it appears as if there was at that time but one copy known to exist throughout Wales; for the bard Guto'r Glyn was sent all the way from Denbighshire, in North Wales, to the extreme bounds of Glamorgan to borrow it. It was then in the possession of Tryhaearn ap Ievan ap Meyric ap Howel Gam, of Gwaenllwg, Glamorganshire; and the bard addresses a poem to the chieftain, in which he describes the book he wished to borrow, for David, Abbot of Valle Crucis Abbey. At that time it was customary to send the bards on important messages; and whenever an important favour was asked, the request was uniformly couched in verse. In the fifteenth century, this fashion became very common, and we owe to the custom some scores of very admirable compositions. The poem composed on this occasion, is very interesting; as, in addition to indicating the prevalent practice, it describes the book; throws light on the nature of the Greal, and shows the intense interest which the stories had at last excited, in even very intelligent minds; since a dignitary of the church was so exceedingly curious as he is here described, to peruse the adventures of the Arthurian knights. It is a picture of the time, and runs thus:

"The ages of three men be to thee Tryhaearn,
Patron of the bards in giving judgment,
Son of Ieuan, the chief of Penrhôs,
The son of Meuric, the object of my address.
The second from Howel Gam,
And the third of the race of Adam.[1]
A royal race of the kingly stock
Of Kynvyn and Bleddyn and Blaidd,
Is thy lineage, from the Usk to the vale of Neath;
The kindred is of South and North Wales.
Noble is thy blood, Tryhaearn;
May thy end in this world be the day of judgment.
Strong as the yoked ox, thy fame has
Traversed the Gwents and Southern lands.
The eye of Gwaunllwg art thou entirely,
The hand and the book of others also;

---

1 Howel's father.

The offerings of science hast thou
Truly distributed, as Arthur did.
The hand of Nudd to Caerlleon wast thou,
And its people assemble where thou art.
The mouth of the learning of the bards of Glamorgan;
The mouth of the literature of the land of Gwaenllwg.
The mouth of all the excellencies of Gwynedd,
From Edeyrnion to the land of Neath.
And the skilful tongue of our language;
The father who cherishes it, art thou that knowest it.
Let us go to the court, there shall we find thee,
At Haverford, like in a high fair.
Eight hundred thousand extol thee,
From Aberffraw to the Vale of Pembroke.
Well art thou styled the wise countenance
Of all the sciences of Dyved,
From the fair harbour where boils the wave
Of Daugleddau[1] to Caledonia;
One of the heroes of Earl Herbert of Narberth,
Art thou, and his lance and his might,
Possessing a name above that
In the dwelling of thy own eight territories;[2]
The name of teacher and director of every learning,
In a measure like unto the name of Moses.
The Abbot of Valle Crucis will make our land
Altogether one entire feast;
At his own charge shall wine and meat be free,
For the entertainment of you and Davydd,[3]
In the same manner as thou in the Dwyallt,
Excepting his vestments and his tonsure.
Like as all Cambrians assemble in thy house,
From all the Gwents, so shall it be with him.
He by his order is distinguished,
You by the sciences of the world.
All Gwynedd shall assemble here,
Like as the eight districts of Gwent at thy fair mansion.
The sciences and endowments of knowledge

---

1 Milford Haven.

2 Gwent.

3 The Abbot of Valle Crucis.

Assuredly does Davydd love,
For one book he does call out,
That he loves more than gold and gems,
And implores you to send
The goodly Greal to this land.
The book of the blood-the book of the heroes,
Where they fell in the court of Arthur;
The book of the renowned knights,
The book of the fair order of the Round Table.
A book still in the Briton's hand,
Which the race of Horsa cannot read.
The loan of this does Davydd, Principal of the Choir,
Request from the bountiful Ivor,
The kingly book, which should the venerable chief obtain,
He would be content to live without other food.
The holy monks also do desire to have
The sacred Greal in yonder land of Yale.
Nevertheless it will not tarry there;
From the land of Yale it will return again,
Your old blind Guto, he and his chattels,
Will be your surety for its return,
And gracious Providence, as from the dwelling of St David,
Will doubtless grant thee thy reward.[1]

In the Kymric lines quoted, p. 437, the book is differently described; for instead of "a book of the fair order of the Round Table," it is more pointedly termed,

Llyfr o grefft yr holl vort gronn,
A book of the doings of the whole Round Table.

The curiosity of the abbot is well described by the blind old bard; and it would appear to have been real; for Black Ievan of the Billhook, another bard, describes the anticipated gratitude of a different aspirant for the perusal of "the truthful grey book," in terms quite as forcible. Addressing Lewis ab Davydd Ddu, the abbot of Glyn Neath, he says:

"Let this book therefore be courteously sent
To us from the court of Neath by the worthy Lewis,
Who is exemplary in rebuking the ungodly,
And of true propriety in prayer to God.
And if I shall obtain from Davydd's son

---

1 *Iolo Mauuscripts*, p. 706.

The book of the Greal without delay,
And readily against Lent,
Its proud leaves will be worth its weight (in gold.)
We will observe the supreme law of St. Gregory,
We shall have Matins in the Choir,
And after Vesper manifold will be
The uttering of praise to Mary.[1]

The literature of the Kymry; being a critical essay on the history of the language and literature of Wales during the twelfth and two succeeding centuries, containing numerous specimens of ancient Welsh poetry in the original and accompanied with English translations, 1876.

An essay from
*The Literature of the Kymry; Being a Critical Essay
on the History of the Language and Literature of Wales
During the Twelfth and Two Succeeding Centuries...*, 1876

---

1   *Ibid.* p. 708. [The work mentioned in this poem was, apparently, not the Greal, but a *Gradual*, or antiphonary.—Ed.]